Ancient Cities

Ancient Cities surveys the cities of the Ancient Near East, Egypt, and the Greek and Roman worlds from an archaeological perspective, in their cultural and historical contexts. It brings to life the physical world of ancient city dwellers by concentrating on evidence recovered by archaeological excavations from the Mediterranean basin and south-west Asia. Its focus is on the physical appearance of cities – their urban form – and the architecture and geography that created it. Attention is also paid to non-urban features such as religious sanctuaries and burial grounds, places and institutions that were a familiar part of the city dweller's experience. Objects or artifacts, which represented the essential furnishings for everyday life, are also discussed and include pottery, sculpture, wall paintings, mosaics, and coins. *Ancient Cities* is unusual in presenting this wide range of Old World cultures in such comprehensive detail, giving equal weight to the Preclassical and Classical periods and in showing the links between these ancient cultures.

User-friendly features include:

- Use of clear and accessible language, assuming no previous background knowledge
- Lavish illustrations with nearly 300 line drawings, maps and photos
- Historical summaries, further reading arranged by topic, plus a consolidated bibliography and comprehensive index.

Ancient Cities will be essential reading for university students in archaeology, ancient history, and classical studies and will also appeal to students of ancient civilizations at high-school level.

Charles Gates is Assistant Professor of Archaeology and History of Art at Bilkent University in Ankara, Turkey. His research focuses on Minoan, Mycenaean, and Greek art, and archaeology. Since 1993 he has excavated in the Bronze and Iron Age settlements at Kinet Höyük (Turkey).

Ancient Cities

The archaeology of urban life in the Ancient Near East and Egypt, Greece, and Rome

Charles Gates

Routledge
Taylor & Francis Group

LONDON AND NEW YORK

First published 2003
by Routledge
2 Park Square, Milton Park, Abingdon, Oxon, OX14 4RN

Simultaneously published in the USA and Canada
by Routledge
270 Madison Ave, New York, NY 10016

Reprinted 2004 (three Times), 2006 (twice), 2007 (three times)

Routledge is an imprint of the Taylor & Francis Group, an informa business

© 2003 Charles Gates

Designed and typeset in Garamond and Univers by Keystroke,
Jacaranda Lodge, Wolverhampton

Printed and bound in Great Britain by
TJ International Ltd, Padstow, Cornwall

British Library Cataloguing in Publication Data
A catalogue record for this book is available from the British
Library

Library of Congress Cataloging in Publication Data
A catalog record for this book has been requested

ISBN 10: 0–415–01895–1 (hbk)
ISBN 10: 0–415–12182–5 (pbk)
ISBN 13: 978–0–415–01895–1 (hbk)
ISBN 13: 978–0–415–12182–8 (pbk)

Contents

Illustrations

Preface

> . . . the city is one of the most remarkable, one of the most enduring of human artifacts and human institutions. Its fascination is inevitable: its study is both duty and homage.
>
> (Kostof 1991: 40)

This book introduces the cities and civilizations of the Ancient Near East, Egypt, Greece, and Rome through the eyes of archaeology. Urban centers are the focus throughout: architecture and other material remains, historical and socio-economic contexts, and the experiences of the people who lived in them. The book traces cities from their origins in the Near East of the ninth–sixth millennia BC to the end of pagan antiquity in the early fourth century AD. The region treated is vast, ranging from the Indus Valley in modern Pakistan in the east to England in the west – the territory controlled by the Achaemenid Persians and conquered by Alexander the Great combined with that held by the Romans at the height of their empire. The parade of cultures is colorful and complex: Sumerians and Babylonians, Assyrians and Egyptians, Minoans and Etruscans, Greeks and Romans. Different as they can be, one from the other, these cultures nevertheless are linked together in a long chain of interconnections. The Romans looked to Greece for artistic and intellectual inspiration, for example, just as the Greeks would have inhabited a very different world without the stimulation and challenge of Near Eastern and Egyptian accomplishments. These disparate cultures form an Old World unity, and merit study together. Urbanism was not exclusive to south-west Asia and the Mediterranean basin, of course; but the independent urban traditions of East Asia, the Americas, and Saharan and sub-Saharan Africa lie outside the scope of this book.

The book has two sources of inspiration. The immediate stimulus for undertaking this project was the need for a textbook to accompany "Ancient Cities," a popular introduction to the ancient cultures of the Mediterranean basin and the Near East introduced by Emeline Hill Richardson and developed by fellow archaeologists in the Department of Classics at the University of North Carolina-Chapel Hill. The course never claimed impartiality: with its home in Classics, the syllabus has understandably given more weight to Greek and Roman cities than to the Ancient Near Eastern and Egyptian ones. Further, because of my own experiences and interests, I emphasize eastern Mediterranean sites over western Mediterranean and western European examples; this bias is clearest in Chapter 23. Apart from this last-mentioned gap, the selection of places and monuments presented here reflects, with reasonable faithfulness, the consensus that evolved among those who have offered "Ancient Cities" at UNC-Chapel Hill – of whom I, during the 1980s, was one.

The second source is more distant and indirect. When completing my undergraduate major in Archaeology at Yale University some thirty years ago, I elected to undergo a final oral examination in Hellenic city planning. In the presence of distinguished specialists in Mayan, Caribbean, Chinese, Egyptian, and Near Eastern as well as Classical archaeology, I displayed my imperfect knowledge of the ancient Greek urban experience. This book in a certain way has offered the opportunity to redo the oral exam, and with its completion I feel I have truly earned my undergraduate diploma.

A book like this could not be completed without the assistance of many people. Neslihan Yılmaz has drawn the bulk of the illustrations. To her my debt is enormous; I am most grateful. I also wish to thank Bilkent University for awarding me in 2001 a Faculty Research Development Grant, which relaunched the production of illustrations after several years of stagnation. Thanks also to Bülent Bozkurt, the Dean of the Faculty of Humanities and Letters, and İlknur Özgen, long-time Chair of the Department of Archaeology and History of Art, for support for this project over the course of many years.

The Greek and Roman sections of the book were revised largely during a sabbatical leave taken from Bilkent University in 1997–8, spent at the University of Cambridge. I owe thanks to Chris Scarre and Anthony Snodgrass for welcoming me as a Visiting Fellow at the McDonald Institute for Archaeological Research and Visiting Scholar at the Faculty of Classics, home bases that allowed for a profitable and enjoyable year.

I would like to express my gratitude to those who have helped by reading chapters, answering specific queries, procuring illustrations, or simply discussing the aims of "Ancient Cities": Julian Bennett, Mary T. Boatwright, J. V. Canby, Ben Claasz Coockson, Toni Cross, Benjamin Foster, Karen Foster, Caroline Gates, Irene Gates, Matthew Glendinning, Nancy de Grummond, Ann Gunter, Salima Ikram, Janet Jones, Norbert Karg, Dominique Kassab Tezgör, J. Mark Kenoyer, Gerhard Koeppel, Richard Liebhart, Jerzy Linderski, Steven Lumsden, Joann McDaniel, Erin Maloney, Gregory Possehl, Nicholas Rauh, Margaret Reid, Gay Robins, Jeremy Rutter, G. Kenneth Sams, Gil Stein, Cheryl Ward, Patricia Wattenmaker, Laurette Wharton, and Irene Winter. I am especially indebted to Mary Voigt for reading and commenting on a preliminary draft of Part One and to Jennifer Tobin for doing the same for Parts Two and Three; and to several anonymous readers for their criticisms and suggestions. Finally, I thank Richard Stoneman and his colleagues Catherine Bousfield and Coco Stevenson for exemplary patience and courtesy over many years; and Marie-Henriette Gates for her knowledge, sound advice, and encouragement generously offered at every step along the way.

Introduction

Goals, the approach, defining the city, determining dates, and some practical information

> City forms, their actual function, and the ideas and values that people attach to them make up a single phenomenon.
>
> (K. Lynch, quoted by Kostof 1991: 40)

This book surveys the cities of the Ancient Near East, Egypt, and the Greek and Roman worlds, with a focus on their physical appearance, on urban form, and on their cultural and historical contexts. Architecture is key: the buildings that marked ancient cities, streets, squares, and other spaces in between; the arrangement of these elements in a city plan; and their functions in ancient societies. Our aim is to see how buildings and objects made by people long gone help us understand the urban environments created and lived in by our distant ancestors in the Mediterranean basin and the Near East. Geographical conditions are also important; they are highlighted throughout. In addition, through most of the centuries treated here written records give invaluable information about people and their activities and concerns. The written sources are constantly called upon to illuminate ancient life. Archaeology as presented in this book is thus a discipline nourished by many specialties: art and architectural history, urbanism, anthropology, geography, history, philology and literary studies; Ancient Near Eastern studies; Biblical studies; Egyptology; and Greek and Roman studies.

Our period is long, from 8500 BC to the fourth century AD. One great interest of a survey of this sort is the possibility to observe changes in the same region over a great length of time. Inspiration for any student of the Mediterranean world comes from the great French geographer and historian Fernand Braudel (1902–85). Although his most famous work, *The Mediterranean and the Mediterranean World in the Age of Philip II*, focuses on the Mediterranean in a later period, the sixteenth century, he offers a framework for understanding environmental and human factors applicable to ancient as well as medieval and modern conditions. My hope is that readers will savor the *longue durée*, as Braudel termed the long chronological perspective, appreciating the unfolding of human actions in this rich cultural zone.

THE CITY DEFINED

Since the subject of the book is the city, we would do well to define the term. The city is an inhabited place, as the dictionary says, but of what sort? The word "inhabited" suggests that demographic considerations will be of prime importance in the concept of the city. The words "city" and indeed "civilization" come from the Latin *civis* (citizen) and *civitas* (community, state, city; citizenship) via Old French *cité* (capital city). The Latin word for city, *urbs*, has given us "urban" and "urbanism." The Romans distinguished between population centers of different scales, between city, town (*oppidum*), and village (*vicus*), and so do we. The absolute population of a city need not be big, but the city is larger than a town, a village, and a hamlet (to rank the English words for settlements in descending order, according to size). In demographic terms, a city exists as such only by virtue of its contrast to towns and other smaller settlements. These definitions are relative, however, and can vary according to the position of the observer. For the resident of a village, any larger settlement might seem worthy of the title of city.

In addition, a city (or town, etc.) as a place of habitation is defined in opposition to the countryside. Yet, although opposed in definition, city and countryside are in fact mutually dependent. The resources of the countryside (land, raw materials, agricultural products) support the city, while the city administers and protects the countryside.

That a city is a place attracting a concentration of people indicates the city has something to offer. The lures are often economic, with sources of livelihood based on a natural resource (such as copper, on Cyprus) or a geographical situation advantageous for commerce (a harbor, for example, or a natural crossroads) or an ecological base fostering agricultural prosperity. Attractions might be military (thanks to a defensible location) or ideological (choices made by the ruler: he has picked the place as a capital, or his family may come from there; or the place witnessed a sacred event or shelters a sacred object, either of which gives the place sanctity and draws pilgrims). These economic and ideological factors can change or disappear with time. A harbor might fill with silt, the area becoming malarial (as at Roman Paestum), thereby killing off both trade and agriculture. Military and defense requirements might change, and new ruling families might base themselves elsewhere.

The city thus becomes characterized by the functions that it serves. Such functions may include a ceremonial or ritual role, in which the city may be understood as the center of the universe, or reflecting cosmic or divine truths. The city might also serve as an administrative center or as a commercial center, or some combination of the above three. Whatever they may be, such functions reflect the city's dominant role in a society. Indeed, for L. Mumford (1938: 3), the city is "a point of maximum concentration for the power and culture of a community."

The social organization of the urban population indeed has much to say about the nature of a city. Cities, at the top of the hierarchy of settlements, are a product of socially stratified societies. The city happens when the group living in a community is larger than an extended family unit, a band, or a tribe, and is organized into something more diversified than a military, political, or religious unit (such as a fort, a national capital, or a monastery). Further, city dwellers cannot possibly know each other; they are too numerous for that. The concept of "city" thus implies social distinctions among its populace. Just as the urban-rural contrast denotes difference, so too within the city we find contrasts between rulers (elite groups) and the ruled, between richer and poorer. Differences in work, with specializations of occupation, some more prestigious than others, also contribute to the social hierarchy. In addition, inhabitants might be marked by ethnic and religious differences. Hence L. Wirth's 1938 definition of a city: "a relatively large, dense, and permanent settlement of socially heterogeneous individuals." These social distinctions can affect the appearance and layout of a city, with monumental temples and palaces erected in certain areas, but with commercial and industrial establishments and lower-class residential neighborhoods grouped elsewhere.

A related definition of the city would be *socio-economic*: the city is a unit that supports itself economically, and extends its economic and political influence over an area broader than its immediate territory. A detailed definition of this sort was offered in 1950 by the Australian prehistorian V. Gordon Childe in an investigation of the origins of cities in the Ancient Near East. For Childe, the earliest true cities were marked by ten criteria or conditions:

1   concentrations of a relatively large number of people in a restricted area
2   developed social stratification
3   although most citizens were farmers, some pursued non-agricultural occupations: craft specialists, priests, traders, administrators, etc.
4   the production of an economic surplus and its appropriation by a central authority, such as a king or a deity
5   writing, to record economic activity and the myths, events, and other ideological issues that served to justify the discrepancies between the privileged and lower classes
6   exact and predictive sciences, to forecast the weather for agricultural production
7   monumental public architecture, which could include such structures as temples, palaces, fortifications, and tombs
8   figural art
9   foreign trade
10   residence-based group membership, in which people of all professions and classes could share in a sense of community.

These criteria, when applied to south-west Asia, place the origin of cities in the fourth millennium BC, when writing was developed. But several of these characteristics appeared earlier, in the Neolithic period, as attested at various villages and towns largely explored after Childe's article of 1950. We shall investigate these issues in the next chapters, Chapters 1 and 2, when we examine the early cities of the Levant, Anatolia, and Mesopotamia.

The concept of the city thus contains demographic, geographic, social, economic, and ideological aspects. Cities are rich, full, many-faceted; reducing the city to a single, all-purpose definition seems neither possible nor even desirable. Let us use the considerations presented above as a point of departure. As we analyze the variations on the theme of the city created by different cultures in different periods, we shall be able to deepen our understanding of the urban experience in our featured region, the Mediterranean basin and the Near East.

SOURCES OF INFORMATION

Information about ancient cities comes from various sources.

(1) Buildings in continuous use from antiquity to the present, such as the Pantheon, a temple built in Rome in 118–25, later converted into a church; and the continuation into modern times of ancient urban layouts, as in the street systems of such cities as Aosta (northern Italy), originally founded as a Roman military colony, Augusta Praetoria, in the later first century BC.

(2) Standing monuments no longer in use, but with their ancient functions documented in literary sources, such as the pyramids of Egypt.

(3) Archaeological surveys and excavations. They reveal the material remains of ancient cities: city plans, architecture, art, small finds (such as pottery, metal tools, stone objects). Careful recording of find spots can illuminate how these objects were used by ancient people. Offerings found in undisturbed burials can be especially helpful, for tombs are closed contexts that connect objects perhaps of different styles and sources. Material remains give evidence for plans and types

of spaces, for the religious and political character of a culture, for contacts with other cities and cultures. Patterns perceived among material objects and their material contexts can lead to new understandings of their role in ancient life, clarifying relationships that eluded or did not interest ancient writers.

(4) Ancient written sources about cities and their monuments, their inhabitants and their activities. Pausanias's account of his travels in Greece in the second century AD gives invaluable descriptions of sites and monuments, for example. Also surviving in written form are a huge mass of legends, information sometimes complemented or even authenticated by archaeological findings (as at Troy), but sometimes not (Atlantis).

Types of written materials include tablets, inscriptions, manuscripts (often the surviving copies date from post-antique times), and small items such as coins and seals. Texts can give details which other material objects cannot, such as names (of persons, cities, states, buildings, objects, topographical features), dates or periods of time, events and actions, usage and behavior, and ancient people's interpretation of a culture, including its symbolic and religious elements. Although ancient written materials can clarify or complement material remains, they can also be irrelevant or unreliable. Caution is often needed.

(5) Ethnography, the systematic recording of the lifestyles of the living cultures of modern times, can offer a rich spectrum of explanations for the functions and meanings of material objects used in antiquity. *Ethnoarchaeology* is ethnographic field work applied specifically toward illuminating the behavior of ancient peoples who created objects preserved in the archaeological record.

DETERMINING DATES

The narrative of ancient cities presented in this book is arranged roughly in chronological order, from earliest (Neolithic) to latest (late Roman empire). Dates are routinely supplied; they offer a framework for learning and appreciating the evolution of cultures. Dates are the glue that link events one to another. It is the larger chain, or mosaic, of dates, the when, combined with information on *what* happened and *where* that allows us to trace the unfolding of human achievements and, eventually, to understand *how* and *why* these developments took place. But dates for ancient events are often difficult to determine with accuracy. The frequent appearance in this book of the abbreviation "ca." meaning circa, or approximately, indicates how imprecise our knowledge can be. The problems of dating, puzzles with which all archaeologists wrestle, are introduced at various points in the text; some introductory remarks are also offered here.

There are two different types of dates: the *relative* and the *absolute*. A relative dating simply places one occurrence earlier or later than another. For example, this pot was made earlier than that bronze dagger. An absolute date assigns a precise calendar date: the pot was made in 4000 BC, the bronze blade in 2300 BC. The conventional framework for absolute dates used in western civilization is the Julio-Gregorian calendar, based on a solar year of 365¼ days, decreed by Julius Caesar in 46 BC, later corrected under Pope Gregory XIII in 1582. The system of recording dates as either before or after the birth year of Jesus (but without a Year Zero) was established in the sixth century AD by the monk Dionysius Exiguus, who proposed the birth of Jesus as the measuring point for dates and calculated this event to have happened 753 years after the foundation of the city of Rome. Hence the dating conventions of BC and AD, "Before Christ" and "Anno Domini" ("In the Year of the Lord" = "After Christ") and, today, their non-Christian equivalents, BCE ("Before the Common Era") and CE ("Common Era"); and with it, the enshrining of 753 BC as the traditional foundation date of Rome.

Relative dating of archaeological materials is determined primarily through *seriation* and the interpretation of *stratigraphy* (see below). Absolute dating is calculated by means of such scientific techniques as radiocarbon measurements and dendrochronology (analyzing and matching the patterns formed by the annual growth rings of trees), and, in historical periods, through information provided by written documents, especially the recording of astronomical observations whose dates can be converted to our Julio-Gregorian calendar.

Seriation

Seriation means the arranging of items in an order, or series. In archaeology, seriation indicates the ordering of human-made artifacts in a sequence of assumed date of manufacture, from earliest to latest. *Style* is the key to the arrangement; style is the combination of visual, compositional, and technological features that characterize an artifact. Objects are grouped on the basis of shared stylistic features, such as details of shape, decorations, and materials and techniques used, and on the frequency of their occurrence. Because such features change over time, a sequence of stylistic development can be proposed for any particular artifact type. Pottery, a standard artifact made in the regions and periods treated in this book, is commonly analyzed in this way. A classic early formulation of pottery seriation was developed in the 1890s by the British archaeologist W. M. Flinders Petrie studying Egyptian Predynastic ceramics in order to help date tombs. Ideally, the validity of any sequence will be confirmed by evidence from stratigraphical excavations (see below) or from independent historical evidence. Sometimes, however, as in the case of the kouroi, the life-size nude male sculptures produced by the Greeks from the late seventh to the early fifth centuries BC, the seriated sequence established by twentieth-century art historians follows assumed laws of stylistic development (a progression from abstraction to naturalism) that are not easy to verify in excavations and that may in fact be incorrect.

Stratigraphy, and the formation of tells

The concept of stratigraphy is basic in archaeological analysis. Stratigraphy can be clearly explained by a look at the formation of *tells*, the hill-like remains of multi-period habitations that are a characteristic feature of the Near Eastern landscape.

The Near East is dotted with hills, some smaller, some larger, many of which are not natural rises but rather the accumulated remains of ancient settlements. Sometimes the ancient sites are still occupied by modern villages, if the surrounding fields remain productive, but sometimes the ruins lie isolated in wasteland. Such artificial hills are called tells, tepes, or höyüks (hüyüks), after the Arabic, Persian, and Turkish words for them.

The tells of the Near East owe their striking appearance to a favored building material, air-dried mud brick. In many parts of the Near East, in Sumer (southern Iraq), for example, stone and wood are scarce. Houses and temples were thus built of bricks. Laborers mixed soil rich in clay with a temper such as straw (to prevent cracking), formed bricks in a mold, and then set them out in the sun to dry. The bricks would harden sufficiently for building purposes. Baking them in a kiln was considered too costly, a needless expenditure of fuel. Roofs consisted of reeds or small branches laid across a few larger branches, the whole sealed with a layer of clay; normally this surface could support people. An application of whitewash (lime plaster) protected the outer walls from wind and rain. Inside, floors were usually beaten earth, but occasionally coated with plaster.

Sooner or later the house would have to be replaced. It may have been collapsing from old age, its walls weakened by moisture seeping in through capillary action or by roots, or by roots infested with insects or even snakes. Perhaps new owners had different intentions for the land on which it stood. Had the house been built of stone, that stone would have served to make the new house. But sun-dried mud bricks are just dirt. The elements erode the bricks or reduce them to dust. Since there were no bulldozers to push the debris away, the new builders simply leveled the area, packing the rubble into the spaces between the surviving wall stubs, and began the new building on top of the remains of that old house. Now the ground level had risen a foot or two. And so it continued, generation upon generation, the surface of the tell gradually rising higher and higher.

For archaeologists, defining the levels of occupation, or strata, is of paramount importance. The abandoned building – or the layer of ash, or the huge garbage pit cut deep into the mound – contains not only decayed mud brick or discarded soil but the remains of human actions as well. Fragments of the pot which the child knocked over and broke, the lamb bones the dog was given after the family finished dinner, the gold coins that grandmother buried in the corner just before the invaders sacked the city: all these objects are grouped together within the remains of a single stratum. They can be contrasted, then, with the objects found in earlier and later strata. Indeed, as noted above, the styles of artifacts change through time, thus providing another useful distinction to help us date what we discover. Eventually, by matching, say, our pot fragment with one found at another site – that one too from a well-defined level – we can link the sequence of strata at our site with the sequence at that other site.

This study of the strata of occupation is known as stratigraphy. If we can determine which strata come earlier or later than others, we are able to place them, and the objects found in them, in a relative sequence. I say "if" because the situation I have described is the ideal. In reality, strata can be difficult to identify: irregular in shape, or of soil type barely distinguishable from other deposits, or cut deep into earlier levels (building foundations or garbage pits, for example). Stratigraphy thus becomes an interpretive art, a skill for which some, but not all, archaeologists have a gift.

Absolute dates: radiocarbon determinations

Thanks to the invention of calendrical systems and writing in Egypt and Mesopotamia and the keeping of historical records, absolute dates can, with varying degrees of reliability, be assigned to occupation levels beginning in the late fourth and especially the third millennium BC (see below). For earlier, pre-literate periods, the attribution of absolute dates remained a matter of guesswork until the development of the carbon 14 dating method just after the Second World War by Willard Libby of the University of Chicago. Researchers have continued to refine the calibrations of dates, notably through testing of dendrochronological samples from such long-lived trees as the bristlecone pines of the south-west United States.

All organic material contains a small amount of carbon 14, the radioactive isotope of carbon, in a fixed ratio to the amount of non-radioactive carbon (atomic weight: 12). But the radioactive carbon 14 is unstable. From the moment the organic item dies, little by little the radiocarbon 14 disintegrates into nitrogen and a low-energy radiation. Over the course of 5,730 years, half the original amount disappears. After an additional 5,730 years, the remaining carbon 14 is once again reduced by half. The regular carbon 12, meanwhile, has remained constant. So the ratio between the quantity of carbon 14 and carbon 12 is continually changing, but at a predictable rate. Libby and his colleagues monitored the time span of the changing ratio, and promoted its application for the dating of materials from archaeological excavations. The archaeologist sends a sample of a find with high organic content, for example burnt wood or seeds (the burning helps preserve the item), to a laboratory equipped to measure its carbon 14 content. After comparing that content to the list of known ratios, an absolute date can be assigned. Radiocarbon date determinations can extend back 50,000 years, although earlier than 35,000 BC the precision of measurements decreases because of the increasingly minute amounts of carbon 14 remaining in a sample.

The method is not foolproof. A margin of error always accompanies any radiocarbon determination: for example, "3540 BC, plus or minus 80 years." The plus or minus indicates the standard deviation: that is, there is a 66 per cent probability that the date falls somewhere between 3460 and 3620 BC. If you double the deviation (to plus or minus 160 years, using our example), then the probability increases to 95 per cent.

Furthermore, samples can be contaminated (say by modern ants who have set up house-keeping in an ancient deposit and carry in food and other items from outside) or difficult to interpret (what if beams from a 500-year-old tree were used in a new house or burned as firewood?). And scientists themselves have continued to debate such aspects as the actual length of the half-life of carbon 14 and whether or not carbon 14 always disintegrated at the same rate. Despite these difficulties, the radiocarbon method of dating remains invaluable for determining chronology in prehistoric and even early historic times.

Absolute dates: historical records in Egypt and Mesopotamia

Writing, the systematic use of signs that correspond to elements of a language, was invented separately in different places and times around the world. In the Near East and eastern Mediterranean, the first writing systems were Sumerian cuneiform and Egyptian hieroglyphs, developed in fairly quick succession in the later fourth millennium BC. Recording systems already existed, however, from the notched bones of the Upper Paleolithic (15,000–10,000 BC) to the clay tokens of the Neolithic. But history proper, based on written records and with events whose dates can be correlated with the Julio-Gregorian calendar, begins around 3100 BC in Egypt and in the mid third millennium BC in southern Mesopotamia.

The organization of Egyptian history according to dynasties, or ruling families, is the work of Manetho, a Greek-speaking scribe who lived in Alexandria during the early Hellenistic period, late fourth to early third centuries BC. His writings have not survived independently, but are preserved in edited form in the texts of such late Roman authors as Julius Africanus and Eusebius; his information has been supplemented by surviving Egyptian king lists of the sort he would have consulted. Manetho chronicled 30 dynasties that spanned some 2,500 years, listing the kings in each with the length of their reigns. Despite inaccuracies, his work remains the invaluable framework for the study of Egyptian history.

The absolute chronology of this historical framework depends upon ancient sightings of the star Sirius (Sothis, for the Greeks, the "Dog Star"). Especially important are the observations recorded in the seventh year of the reign of the Twelfth-Dynasty pharaoh Senwosret III; in the ninth year of the Eighteenth-Dynasty ruler Amenhotep I; and in Roman imperial times, in AD 139. The first sighting is generally calculated as 1872 BC, the second as 1541 BC. The accuracy of the ancient reports is not, however, completely certain. Moreover, the place where the observation was made was not specified; a northern location such as Memphis or Heliopolis is assumed, but if the astronomers were watching in the south, at Thebes or even at Elephantine on the southern border of Egypt proper, the dates would be slightly different. Such uncertainties give a flexibility of forty-two years for the start of the Twelfth Dynasty, 1979 BC (high) or 1937 BC (low), and a play of twenty-one years for the start of the Eighteenth Dynasty, 1550 BC (high) or 1539 BC (low).

Other difficulties in establishing an accurate absolute chronology include occasional conflicting reports in ancient documents concerning the length of individual reigns and the numbers and lengths of possible coregencies. Despite these problems, the absolute chronology can be extended back to ca. 3100 BC, the beginning of dynastic history, thanks to such king lists as the Turin Canon of Kings, a papyrus document written in the Nineteenth Dynasty now in the collection of the Egyptian Museum in Turin, Italy. From the later Eighteenth Dynasty on, Egyptian chronology is agreed upon; during the first millennium BC, frequent correlations with Assyrian, Babylonian, and Hebrew sources produce accurate time determinations.

Mesopotamian chronology is more complex than the Egyptian, because of the many states in the region, each with different methods of recording the passing of time. From 910 to 668 BC the chronology is secure, thanks to the Babylonian Chronicles, with their daily astronomical observations, and to the Neo-Assyrian Eponym Lists, lists of kings and high officials whose names were used as labels for individual years. Before 910 BC, the lists have unbridgeable gaps. As a result, different reference points are needed to establish the absolute chronology for earlier periods.

The backbone of historical reconstructions for third millennium BC Sumer is the Sumerian King List, a chronicle compiled ca. 2100 BC listing the kings of various cities from the previous 500 years and the lengths of their reigns. But problems remain. Because the clay tablets can be fragmentary and their contents contradictory, matching the sequence from one city with that of another is difficult. Further, while the relative sequence of dynasties and kings seems credible, the attribution of absolute dates to the events and periods is not reliable. And information about the earliest periods contains a heavy dose of myth and cannot be taken literally. The eight kings of the earliest era were said to have ruled for thousands of years each. This epoch ends with a great flood, an event that recalls the story near the beginning of the Hebrew Bible. Archaeological exploration has revealed traces of flooding at various sites, but the remains date to different periods, suggesting localized rather than general flooding. After the flood the list of kings begins to inspire more confidence. The list picks up with King Etana of Kish, and moves eventually to Gilgamesh, the fifth king of the First Dynasty of Uruk and subject of the best known of Mesopotamian narratives, the *Epic of Gilgamesh*. This period may correlate with the Early Dynastic (ED) II period. The picture provided by the King List and other texts becomes clearer still in the ED III period, by now the middle of the third millennium BC.

The absolute chronology of the first half of the second millennium BC depends on an astronomical observation. At the time of a new moon in the sixth year of the reign of the Babylonian king Ammi-saduqa, the planet Venus was spotted on the horizon just before dawn. Such a combination occurs once every sixty-four or fifty-six years, an event not quite rare enough to provide an absolute date with complete certainty. Ammi-saduqa ascended the throne ninety-four years after the death of the important king Hammurabi; Babylon itself was destroyed thirty-one years after Ammi-saduqa's death by the Hittites under Murshili I. This sighting leads to not one but four possibilities for the absolute chronology of Babylonian history at this time: for the start of the reign of Hammurabi 1848 BC, 1792 BC, 1728 BC, or 1696 BC; and for the fall of Babylon 1651 BC, 1595 BC, 1531 BC, or 1499 BC. The chronological systems based on these dates are known as high, middle, low, and ultra-low. Not even the radiocarbon dating method can settle the dispute, because the margin of error in the determinations is too great. Although each system has its ardent champions, we shall follow the low chronology, the system preferred at present by the majority of specialists on Near Eastern chronology.

With the first millennium BC we are much more secure. Our own Julio-Gregorian calendar was developed by the Romans of the late Republic. Like the Mesopotamian and Egyptian calendrical systems of the time, many of the various dating systems used by the Greek city-states and Hellenistic kingdoms can be linked to this calendar. With this, the framework for absolute chronology is firm.

TERMINOLOGY

Information about dating, relative and absolute, is used to help establish a relative framework of cultural developments to which period titles are given: the Hellenistic period, the late Roman Empire, the Bronze Age, the Iron Age, and so on. These names are artificial, but they are helpful markers for student and specialist alike.

The terms Paleolithic, Mesolithic, and Neolithic periods (= Old, Middle, and New Stone Ages), Bronze Age, and Iron Age were developed in the nineteenth century to describe different stages in the technology practiced by humans. An additional term, Chalcolithic, or "copper stone" (that is, both metal and stone tools were used together), was later coined to denote a transitional stage between the Neolithic and the Bronze Age. These stages were reached at varying times in different parts of the world. The prime material used for making tools determined the names. A progression from simpler to more sophisticated technology was assumed. Continuing research, however, has revealed these definitions as too simplistic, for they hide other important factors of human development. For example, the Neolithic period – where our story begins, in Chapter 1 – is now defined by the introduction of food production (agriculture and animal husbandry) and pottery making, with simple metallurgy (working of copper and malachite) appearing, too. The picture is even more complicated because traditional subsistence methods, such as pastoralism, continued to be practiced. Regional variations, with the presence and absence of such features, can blur the definition. These period titles are thus more usefully seen as umbrella designations convenient to indicate a certain time span within which various combinations of technological and cultural features occurred.

Finally, as we shall see in the chapters ahead, different regions have their own specialist terminology for denoting cultural developments and chronological distinctions. In Mesopotamia, the "Bronze Age" is defined by terms rooted in history: the Protoliterate or Uruk, Early Dynastic, and Akkadian periods, and the like. Similarly, Bronze Age Egypt is divided according to historical dynasties (as mentioned above), grouped within the larger units of the Old, Middle, and New Kingdoms. With patience and attention, the beginner should be able to absorb in short order these cumbersome structures of terminology.

PRACTICAL INFORMATION

Metric vs. American/imperial weights and measures

Metric measurements are used throughout. The abbreviations used, with their American or Imperial equivalents, are:

Distances
cm = centimeter. One centimeter = 0.39 inch. One inch = 2.54 cm
m = meter. One meter (100 centimeters) = 3.28 feet = 1.09 yards. One yard = 0.91 m

km = kilometer. One kilometer (1,000 meters) = 0.62 mile. One mile = 1.61 km

Area

ha = hectare. One hectare = 10,000 m² = 2.47 acres. One acre = 0.41 ha. One square mile = 259 ha

Weight

kg = kilogram. One kilogram = 2.20 pounds. One pound = 0.45 kg

Spelling ancient names

The names of persons and places of the cultures treated in this book can often be spelled in several ways, because different languages have interpreted foreign names in their own way. English has anglicized the most familiar, such as Athens (for Athenai). Ancient peoples did likewise, with the Greeks, for example, hellenizing Egyptian names, and the Romans latinizing Greek names. An additional difficulty is posed by Egyptian and cuneiform scripts, whose often uncertain pronunciation can provoke debates among scholars; transliterations in English are still being changed.

I aim to use names as given in the language of the culture to which that person or language belonged. If the person or place was Greek, I shall use the Greek version of the name. But complications often arise. If a place is both Greek and Roman, the Latin version will be preferred. If an English version is well known, such as Athens, that will be used. The goal is to avoid confusion, even at the occasional expense of consistency.

PART ONE

NEAR EASTERN, EGYPTIAN, AND
AEGEAN CITIES: NEOLITHIC,
BRONZE AGE, AND IRON AGE

CHAPTER 1

Neolithic towns and villages in the Near East

Upper Paleolithic and Mesolithic periods: ca. 35,000–8550 BC

Neolithic period in the Near East: ca. 8550–5000 BC

Halaf and Ubaid periods: ca. 5000–3500 BC

Urbanism is a recent phenomenon in the long history of humankind. If we subscribe to Childe's ten-point definition of a city (see Introduction), then cities proper, with all ten criteria present, began in the fourth millennium BC in south-western Asia. These cities did not spring from nowhere, however, but developed from the experiences of towns and villages established in ecologically favored locations throughout western Asia during the previous 5,000 years. With the final receding of the glaciers around 10,000 BC, a warmer, moister climate was established that proved favorable for a radical change in human social and economic development. This new era, known as the Neolithic period, is the time when men and women first organized themselves in fixed settlements and brought the reproduction and exploitation of plants and animals under their control. Many of Childe's ten characteristics of a city first appeared in towns and villages of this long period.

The true city, then, had a long gestation. After considering first the physical world of the Ancient Near East and then the nature of Neolithic food production and its consequences for human habitation, this chapter will present three sites that illustrate the development of towns during this important era: *Jericho* (in Palestine), *Çayönü*, and *Çatalhöyük* (both in Turkey).

GEOGRAPHY, CLIMATE, AND THE NEOLITHIC REVOLUTION

The Ancient Near East includes cultures stretching from Turkey to Pakistan (Figure 1.1). This large region contains a variety of topographic and climatic zones: alluvial lowlands, uplands, mountains, and desert. In the heart of the Near East lies Mesopotamia, the land between the two great rivers, the Tigris and the Euphrates. This area corresponds with modern Iraq, north-east Syria, and south-east Turkey. The Euphrates, the longer of the two rivers, makes its leisurely way down from the mountains of eastern Turkey across Syria and southwards through Iraq. The Tigris also originates in Turkey, but follows a swifter path to the south. The two rivers meet in southern Iraq and flow together to the Persian Gulf in a marshy waterway known as the Shatt al-Arab.

The southern half of Iraq is flat, its climate hot and dry. Farmers depend on irrigation from the rivers, not on rainfall. This is the area in which Sumerian civilization flourished in the fourth and third millennia BC.

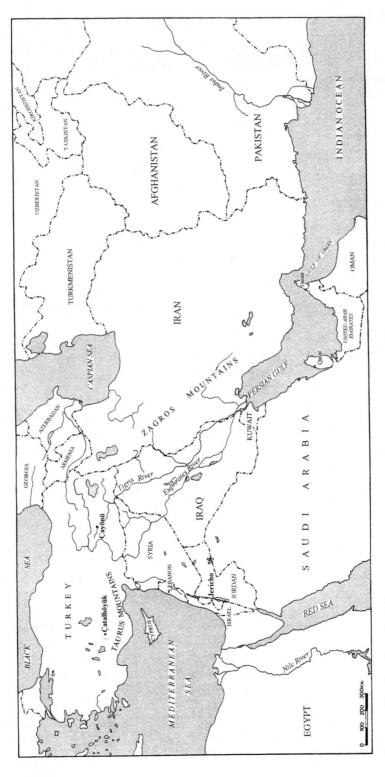

Figure 1.1 The Near East: Neolithic towns

The Taurus Mountains run east–west, crossing southern and eastern Turkey, northern Syria, and northern Iraq, and link with the Zagros Mountains of western Iran. Beyond the mountains lie great plateaus: the Anatolian to the north of the Taurus, and the Iranian to the east of the Zagros. The remote mountain regions provide the snow that feeds the great rivers of the Near East. The difficult terrain has discouraged social and economic unification, although trade and movement of peoples can be active. The mountain people have always been autonomous and independent, and throughout antiquity, just as today, have often annoyed or terrorized the established cultures of the lowlands. The hostile environment of the desert has nurtured similarly free-spirited peoples.

Between mountains and lowlands lie the uplands, or foothills. This zone, which forms a great arc from eastern and northern Iraq westwards across northern Syria and then southwards toward the southern Levant (Lebanon, Israel, Palestine, and Jordan) is often called the Fertile Crescent (Figure 1.2). Although not part of the traditional Fertile Crescent, the Anatolian plateau of central and eastern Turkey shares the same features and thus merits its place on our map. Despite dry summers, precipitation (rain and, in places, snow) during the cooler months of the year is sufficient to sustain agriculture. This region had rich natural resources; most important for early people were gazelle, acorns, and wild grasses. Also among the species present, but not necessarily so significant for food foragers, were the ancestors of plants and animals that would be domesticated during the Neolithic period. Wheat, barley, and other grains grew wild, and wild sheep, goats, cattle, and pigs roamed freely.

In this region, with food sources close at hand, early men and women could sustain themselves with relative ease. They subsisted by hunting wild animals and gathering edible plants. They lived in small groups, and moved with the seasons to track animals or collect ripened fruit and vegetables. Natural shelters, such as caves, often served them as seasonal dwelling places. These hunters and gatherers crafted tools made from flakes of flint or pieces of bones; their European contemporaries even painted fantastic scenes of such crucial events as the hunt or modeled figurines of plump nurturing mothers. This situation lasted through the fourth glaciation. This long period is variously known as the late Pleistocene (the geological term) or the Upper Paleolithic and the succeeding Mesolithic (the cultural terms).

But these Paleolithic and Mesolithic men and women did not know the art of pottery or metalworking, they couldn't read or write, and they had little control over their food sources. These skills – agriculture (including cultivation and animal husbandry), pottery making, and metallurgy – plus recording systems utilizing clay tokens (but not yet actual writing) were developed during the Neolithic period in the Near East. So important was the transformation that Childe termed this the "Neolithic Revolution." The word "revolution" may be misleading, however. Although indeed drastic, these changes did not take place overnight. They developed over long periods, at varying rhythms in different regions, often blending or coexisting with earlier modes of subsistence and seasonal movements.

Anyone can spot the existence of pottery or metal objects. In contrast, the search for specimens of domestic vs. wild plants and animals from this period of transition demands special skills and training. Archaeologists working at such early sites collect animal bones and plant remains, with the smaller specimens obtained by passing excavated dirt through a fine-meshed screen. Plant remains can also be collected by means of *flotation*: a sample of excavated earth is poured into water; seeds and other plant remains will then float to the surface, from which they can easily be removed. Since the forms of the domesticated versions of seeds and bones have changed distinctly if slightly from their wild ancestors, the specialist can assess how far the process of controlling certain plant and animal species had advanced at a particular place and time.

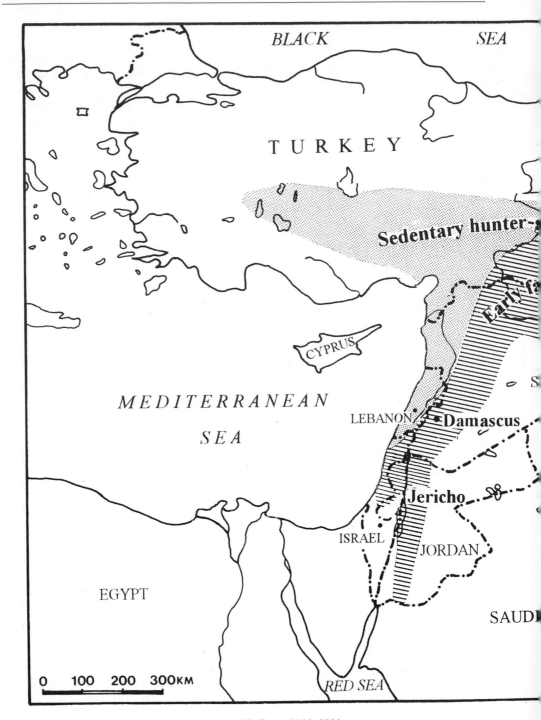

Figure 1.2 The Fertile Crescent in the earlier PPNB, ca. 7500–6500 BC

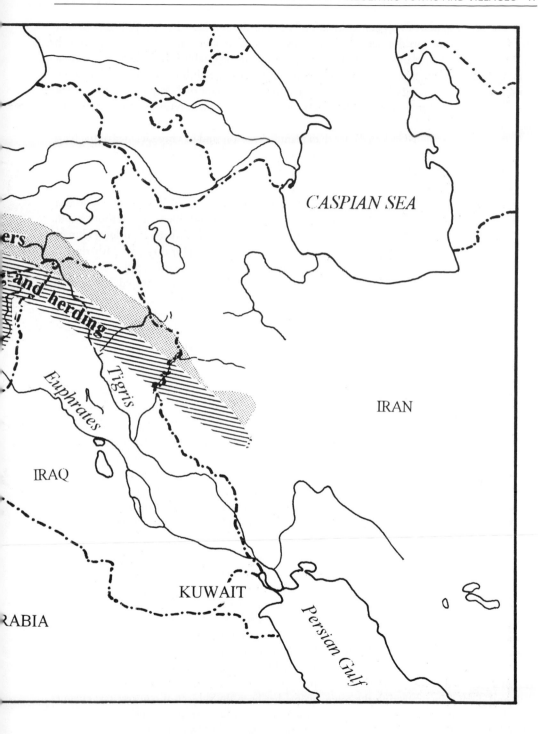

CASPIAN SEA

ers

and herding

Euphrates

Tigris

IRAN

IRAQ

KUWAIT

RABIA

Persian Gulf

At present, it appears that plant cultivation began in the southern Levant, probably in that part of the Levantine corridor between Damascus and Jericho. Here, in well-watered areas with a range of edible wild plants and animals, people had already established settlements (even as simple as seasonal encampments) during the late ninth to early eighth millennia BC. The onset of a drier climate, reducing the fertility of wild plants, may have spurred people to cultivate their own plants as a supplement to dwindling wild supplies. A subsequent return to a wetter climate ensured the survival and growth of these experiments in farming.

Animal domestication developed later than plant cultivation, and in a broader area of the Near East, the Levantine corridor plus the highlands of Anatolia and the Zagros (Iran). Settled farmers kept herds of, first, goats and sheep, beginning in the late eighth millennium BC. Cattle and pigs would be widely domesticated later, from the later seventh millennium BC.

With the control of food sources developed in the Neolithic Revolution, people no longer needed to move around in order to take advantage of seasonal and fluctuating resources, but could remain in one place. Farmers could sow crops as they wished (subject to local climate and soil conditions, of course), and maintain herds of animals. Hunting and gathering of wild animals and plants would continue, but now for the purpose of supplementing the diet. This sort of agricultural economy was the basis for permanent, year-round settlements. Out of small village clusters would emerge towns and eventually cities. Just as the existence of sedentary settlements, however simple, was a prerequisite for plant cultivation, so in turn would the practice of agriculture (plant cultivation and animal husbandry) give rise to concepts of land use and ownership that would influence the nature of the settlements, and subsequent urbanism.

JERICHO

Jericho, in the Jordan River Valley in Palestine, inhabited from ca. 9000 BC to the present day, offers important evidence for the earliest permanent settlements in the Near East. Explored during the 1930–36 excavations of British archaeologist John Garstang and more extensively in 1952–58 by his compatriot Kathleen Kenyon, the first settlements at Jericho surprise us still with a variety of features of town layout unexpected (and still unparalleled) at such an early date.

Two early levels from the mound at Jericho are of particular interest for us: the Pre-Pottery Neolithic ("PPN") A and B phases, ca. 8500–6000 BC. They lie on top of the earliest known settlements at Jericho, seasonal occupations attributed to so-called "Natufian" Mesolithic and Proto-Neolithic (= earliest Neolithic) hunters and gatherers. A key attraction for all these early inhabitants was the spring, a reliable source of water.

Spread over an area of ca. 4ha, the PPNA settlement has yielded both houses and a fortification wall (Figure 1.3). The houses are round, and made of sun-dried mud bricks with a distinctive rounded top ("hog backed," or "plano-convex"). The town was protected on the west side, at least, by an impressive stone wall 3.6m high with an internal circular tower of undressed stones measuring 9m in diameter at its base and preserved 8m in height, and a rock-cut ditch in front. Internal stairs led to the top of the tower, perhaps the site of cultic activities. Exactly what the wall and ditch were protecting the town against has been the subject of controversy; enemies both human and natural (such as seasonal flash floods) have been proposed. The mere existence of this complex fortification system implies a society organized in a way quite different from that of earlier hunters and gatherers. Conflicts with people outside were serious enough to warrant a major fortification wall, and nature need not dominate but could be subdued. The actual

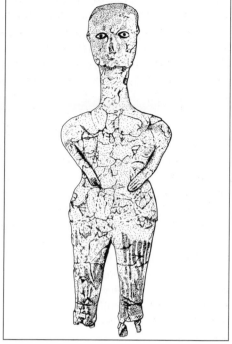

Figure 1.3 Tower with staircase, PPNA, Jericho

Figure 1.4 Anthropomorphic figurine, PPNB, Ain Ghazal. Archaeological Museum, Amman

construction of the wall demanded a concerted, sustained effort on the part of the inhabitants. It was a remarkable architectural and social achievement.

The presence of obsidian objects in the town indicates trade contacts with far-off lands. A volcanic glass prized as a material for sharp blades in this era before metalworking, obsidian occurs in only a few scattered and, for the inhabitants of Jericho, distant sources. Finding it here demonstrates that even at this early period materials could be transported long distances, in this case from the volcanic mountains of central and eastern Anatolia.

Jericho in the subsequent PPNB phase featured new architectural forms, possible indicators of social changes. House builders abandoned the round house in favor of the rectangular plan, with rectangular rooms arranged around a central courtyard. Construction used a different form of air-dried mud brick: "cigar-shaped" bricks with finger impressions across the top to key in the mud mortar. House decoration now included walls often painted red or pink, floors plastered with gypsum, and the occasional reed mat, attested by impressions surviving on the floors.

The PPNB has also yielded evidence for religious practices. One particularly large room (6 × 6m) may represent a shrine. A dramatic find from beneath a house floor was a series of ten human skulls with faces carefully recreated from added plaster and, for the eyes, pieces of shell. Related are two anthropomorphic figurines made of lime plaster on a wicker core, with painted decoration and shell for eyes. These two are now supplemented by 32 examples found at Ain Ghazal, near modern Amman; they measure 0.35–1.00m in height, thus monumental in relation to the smaller images of earlier times (Figure 1.4). These objects must have had some cultic purpose, the former perhaps relating to the veneration of ancestors, the latter perhaps representing deities. Ancestor worship has been an important practice in those farming societies in which the extended family is the major social grouping, for a long chain of ancestors lends authority to a family's claim to its land and helps justify and stabilize the family unit.

In terms of the economy, the PPNB period marked a growing agricultural prosperity. The success of plant cultivation in PPNA led to the spread of domesticated plants elsewhere in the Near East during PPNB. In addition, animal husbandry began at this time. Wild game would have dwindled in the immediate vicinity of settlements, so the domesticated herd animals were relied on for food. In addition to this primary product, meat, the so-called "secondary products" of these animals (such as milk, hair, skin, transport, and their use for traction, that is, pulling plows and vehicles) now became valuable. Consequences of this agricultural prosperity included agricultural surpluses, an increase in human population, specialization of occupation (not everyone had to be a farmer), and an increasing complexity in social organization. No wonder, then, that Bar-Yosef and Meadow have called the PPNB "the brewing period for the emergence of major civilizations" (1995: 92).

Following the end of the PPNB town at Jericho, a gap in occupation lasted some 1,500 years. This collapse of the social "proto-urban" system was general throughout the southern Levant, with a few exceptions in Transjordan. The reasons for this change are not clear. Eventually Jericho was resettled, but by a pastoralist community smaller than the earlier PPNB town. The newcomers counted pottery making among their skills. But Jericho was no longer at the forefront of innovation. Already in the seventh millennium BC, at the same time as the PPNB phase at Jericho, the art of pottery had emerged in Iran, northern Iraq, and Anatolia.

ÇAYÖNÜ

Excavations at Çayönü allow us to trace the development of early towns ca. 8250–5000 BC, from the PPNA and PPNB phases, as seen at Jericho, to the next stage, the Pottery Neolithic. Particularly striking are the varieties of architectural expression that occur over this long span of time, and the early appearance of such technologies as metallurgy. Unlike Jericho, Çayönü never had a fortification wall. What we do see are houses and public buildings of varied plans and materials, and open spaces, arranged in differing ways. Çayönü gives us a broad range of the possibilities of town plans in the Neolithic period.

The site of Çayönü is located 60km north of Diyarbakır in south-eastern Turkey, on a tributary of the Tigris River that flows by the foothills of the Taurus Mountains (Figure 1.5). Excavations were conducted here from 1964 to 1991 by the Universities of Istanbul, Chicago (the Oriental Institute), Karlsruhe, and Rome, under the direction of, first, Halet Çambel and Robert Braidwood, and later, Mehmet Özdoğan. Although Çayönü is far from being the largest of Near Eastern Neolithic sites, it does boast the largest area of Neolithic settlement as yet exposed by archaeological excavation: 8,000m².

The PPN (PPNA and PPNB together = Phase I) consisted of six subphases, each named after its characteristic architectural type (Figure 1.6). Subphases 2, 5, and 6 are the most striking. In *Subphase 1*, the Round Building subphase, the village contained round or oval houses made of wattle-and-daub, a rough lattice of twigs and branches covered with a mix of mud, straw or grass, and perhaps dung. Floors were sunk below ground level. *Subphase 2*, the Grill Plan subphase, featured rectangular houses with foundations of parallel stone walls, a pattern that resembles a grill. Flooring, laid on top of these foundations, consisted of twigs and branches covered with lime and clay. The superstructure continued to be made of wattle-and-daub. In

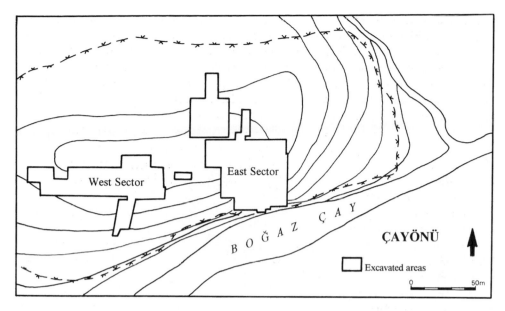

Figure 1.5 Overall site plan, Çayönü

plan, houses had three parts, a living area (on the foundations described above), an enclosed courtyard, and a small storage area. Houses resembled each other in size, plan, and orientation, and were arranged in a checkerboard pattern. These regular features suggest the existence of a well-defined architectural code obeyed by all.

In *Subphase 3*, the Channeled Building subphase, the house foundations were largely filled in, leaving only drainage channels. The village grew larger in area, but with houses scattered at greater intervals. A cult area was established on the eastern edge of the settlement, a neatly kept open space called the "Plaza" by the excavators. In this subphase, two rows of large standing stones were set onto the clay floor.

Subphase 4, the Cobble-paved Building subphase, saw houses protected from groundwater by cobble fill instead of drainage channels. The Plaza continued as before.

In *Subphase 5*, the Cell Building subphase, houses were much larger than before. As in all the subphases, earlier buildings were deliberately abandoned and filled in, with the new type erected on top as a concerted renewal project. The division of the stone foundations into cell-like compartments, perhaps used as storage rooms, characterizes the architecture. The superstructures were made of mud brick, not wattle-and-daub. House plans and sizes varied, sometimes including large courtyards. The Plaza was now encircled by the largest houses of the settlement, a testimony to the importance of the space. Furthermore, the finds within the houses varied. Such differences of house plans and contents, contrasting with the uniformity of Subphase 2, suggest social distinctions in operation: Childe's second criterion of the city, "developed social stratification."

Subphases 1–5 featured four striking communal buildings. The latter three have been identified as cult centers, because of their distinctive architectural features and contents. Their exact placement in the architectural subphases is not certain, because they were erected on their own terraces cut into the edge of the site and co-existed through various rebuildings. Nonetheless, the order of construction seems to be as follows. The earliest was a large round structure. The

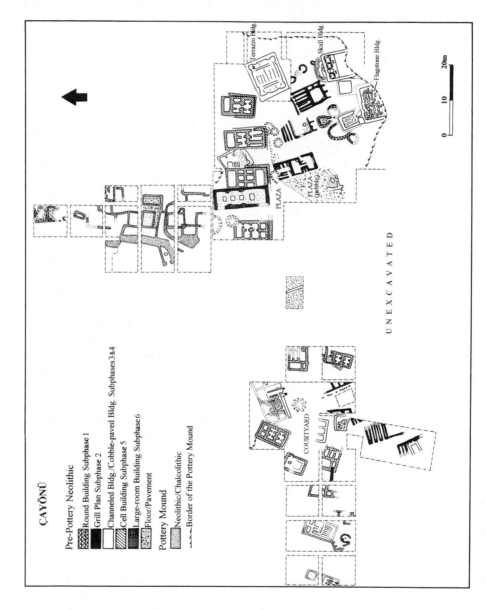

Figure 1.6 Plans, Neolithic and Chalcolithic levels, Çayönü

next, the large "Flagstone Building," contained a floor of polished limestone slabs 2m long; large stones were set upright on the floor. The third is the "Skull Building," rebuilt at least six times, but always containing human skeletons or fragments. Seventy human skulls were found when the building was first excavated; the bones represent the remains of over 450 individuals. This building must have been a charnel house for secondary burials. Perhaps it served as well as a focus for the commemoration of the dead, a variant of the ancestor worship postulated for Jericho.

The fourth and last has been called the "Terrazzo Building." Its large single room featured a well-prepared floor, a very hard layer 40cm thick of polished cobbles and pinkish lime, this last made by burning limestone. Linear patterns were created by white stones set into the floor. Such "terrazzo" floors have been found elsewhere, but after this period the technique was forgotten until the Iron Age some 5,000 years later.

In *Subphase 6*, the Large-room Building subphase, the character of the village changed dramatically. The settlement became smaller. Communal buildings were absent, and the Plaza was used as a refuse dump. Houses consisted of one or two large rooms only. Clearly some major social change happened at Çayönü; further evidence for change has come from the economic data, as noted below.

The *Pottery Neolithic (Phase II)*, ca. 6000–5000 BC, is defined by the sudden appearance of pottery, a technique assumed to be imported from outside because no beginning, experimental stages have been identified. The settlement continues from before, without dramatic break, but now the neat arrangement of buildings originally established during the Grill Plan subphase (Subphase 2) is replaced by the clustering of irregularly shaped houses along narrow streets. Communal buildings continue to be absent.

As for the economy of Neolithic Çayönü, the excavations have documented the evolution of a village economy from food collection into food production over this continuously inhabited period of 3,000 years. During Subphases 1–5, the villagers depended on the collecting of wild plants and the hunting of wild animals. The cultivation of pulses, lentils, and vetch, followed by the addition of Einkorn wheat, offered supplements to the diet. Only in the later PPNB, in Subphase 5, did this pattern change. Domesticated sheep and goat then appeared in great numbers, becoming a dietary staple. The hunting of wild animals diminished considerably.

Çayönü has yielded striking evidence for early metallurgy. Native copper and malachite, found nearby, were worked in Subphase 2, with an intensification in metallurgy in Subphases 3 and 4; subsequently, metalworking declined. The ore was hammered unheated to create such tools as pins, hooks, and drills – a simple start to a technology that would later prove so important. The finds at Çayönü represent the earliest known use of metal in the Near East.

Other crafts were practiced as well, such as bead making and weaving. A cloth impression made of domestic linen gives the earliest evidence in the Near East for the craft of weaving. The presence of obsidian and sea shells, used for tools and decoration, indicates long-distance trade.

Not known is whether or not the artisans of Çayönü practiced their crafts full-time. If they did, they fulfill Childe's third criterion for the city, "occupations other than farming." Other factors on Childe's list present at Çayönü may include social stratification (as noted above) and monumental public architecture. But other elements of his definition are absent. What the excavations of Çayönü have revealed to us is the gradual appearance during the Neolithic period of certain features of social life that will eventually coalesce into the fully developed city of the later fourth and third millennia BC.

ÇATALHÖYÜK

Trends of the Neolithic period discussed above – developments in town planning, architecture, agriculture (including animal husbandry), technology, and religion – come together dramatically at Çatalhöyük (western Turkey, near Konya), in twelve well-preserved building levels dated ca. 6500–5500 BC. The site lies in the Konya plain, in a favorable environmental setting. Geomorphological study has revealed that in Neolithic times the town stood near a river, a lake, and marshes, with hills not far off. The site consists of two adjacent mounds, east and west. The eastern mound contains the Neolithic remains that interest us here, whereas the western mound has later occupation, Early Chalcolithic. The eastern mound measures over 13ha, unusually large for this period. Only 0.4ha was excavated in the early 1960s by James Mellaart of the British Institute of Archaeology at Ankara, but current investigations, begun in 1993 under the direction of Ian Hodder, University of Cambridge, are expanding our knowledge.

The appearance of the town recalls the Native American pueblos of the south-west United States and is otherwise unattested in the Ancient Near East (Figure 1.7). Houses were made of mud brick, often with a framework of wooden pillars and beams. The flat roofs consisted of clay on top of a network of wood. The houses clustered together, their walls touching those of their neighbors. Although small courtyards connected by streets lined the edges of the excavated area, within the cluster courts existed but streets did not. People entered houses from the flat rooftops, descending to the floor by means of a ladder. Since the town lay on sloping ground, the height of the roofs varied. Could this honeycomb arrangement have been intended as a system of defense? Was it used throughout the site, or just in this neighborhood? Some of these questions may be answered by the new excavations.

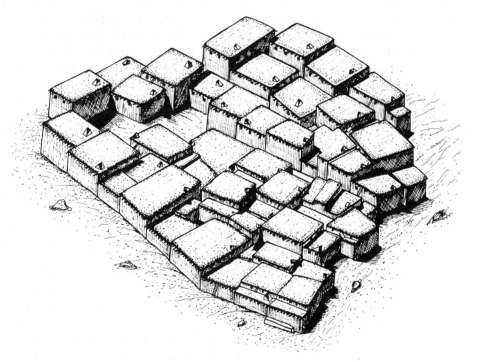

Figure 1.7 Houses (reconstruction), Çatalhöyük

The rather small interior of a typical house consisted of a main room with an adjacent storeroom, together making up a maximum 30m^2 of floor space. It is hypothesized that small windows high up in the walls provided light and, together with the usual hole in the roof, allowed smoke from the hearth and ovens to escape. Each house contained at least two low platforms, with a raised bench at one end of the main platform. The built-in "furniture" must have led to a division of the room for different purposes, for work or for leisure. In addition, the bones of the dead were buried beneath these platforms, perhaps after the bodies had been exposed outside the settlement, the flesh removed by vultures. As at Jericho, the presence of ancestors beneath the floors of a house may have been a way for early agriculturalists to mark eternal possession of the land, to legitimize their occupation. Such intramural burials contrast sharply with the later Classical practice of scrupulously keeping cemeteries outside the city walls: for the Greeks and the Romans, the dead menaced and polluted the land of the living and had to be kept at a distance.

Organic remains were unexpectedly well preserved, thanks to the high water table. The water table has dropped dramatically since Mellaart's excavations, because of developments in the local farming industry; archaeological preservation may be adversely affected. Plants grown at Çatalhöyük included cereals (such as barley and wheat), nuts (pistachios and almonds), and legumes (peas and bitter vetch). The largely vegetarian diet was supplemented by beef, sheep, and goat. Analysis of the cattle bones has revealed that cattle were domesticated, among the earliest examples yet known from West Asia. Wild animals hunted include red deer, boar, wild cattle, and sheep (although traces of woollen textiles show the presence of domesticated sheep, wool being a product of domesticated animals).

The residents of Çatalhöyük included accomplished craftsmen. Beautiful pressure-flaked obsidian spearheads and arrowheads and flint daggers attest to the skill of the makers of chipped stone tools. The finding of lead pendants and copper slag indicates knowledge of metallurgy. Pottery, always handmade without recourse to a potter's wheel, occurs from the earliest levels, but finds of wooden bowls, cups, and boxes remind us that containers of normally perishable materials (skins and basketry as well as wood) played an equally important role in daily life. Fragments of woollen and perhaps flaxen textiles, like the wooden items preserved by burning, are unusually early examples. Patterns used in weaving may be depicted in the wall paintings here.

Çatalhöyük participated in an extensive trade network, with obsidian a key commodity. Much obsidian was found here, not surprising with sources in central Anatolia, near the volcanoes Karaca Dağ and Hasan Dağ. Items from farther distances include Mediterranean sea shells, valued especially as beads, and turquoise from the Sinai.

Evidence for religious practices is abundant. Over forty houses scattered through the many building levels have been identified as shrines. While their plans do not differ from those of regular houses, their decoration does. Craftsmen appointed these particular rooms with wall paintings, relief sculpture, free-standing figures, and the actual horns of bulls and caprines and jaws of foxes (Figure 1.8).

The wall paintings are of exceptional interest for their depictions of life in a Neolithic town. Some walls have up to 100 layers of plaster, any of which might bear paintings – quite a challenge for the conservators. The technique of painting consisted of natural pigments mixed with fat and applied on a background of white plaster. Subjects included the textile patterns already mentioned; vultures attacking headless humans; cattle and deer hunts; and wild bulls relentlessly pursued by humans. One wall painting shows a stylized depiction of a town beneath an erupting volcano (Figure 1.9). Certain paintings were three-dimensional, reliefs built up from plaster.

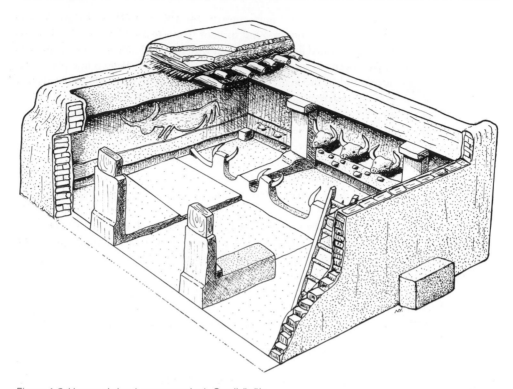

Figure 1.8 House shrine (reconstruction), Çatalhöyük

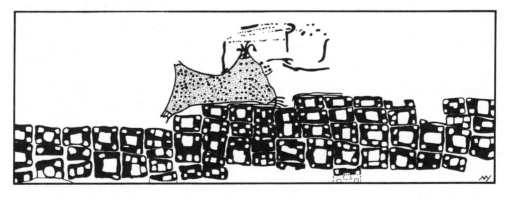

Figure 1.9 Erupting volcano and town, wall painting, Çatalhöyük. Museum of Anatolian Civilizations, Ankara

They depict bull or ram heads (often with real horns incorporated into the relief), occasionally leopards, and a woman in childbirth.

Free-standing figures similarly emphasize the magical power of animals and the desire for fertility. The figurine of a massive woman (a goddess?) expresses these beliefs to great effect (Figure 1.10). Seated between two leopards (or panthers), the woman is in the process of giving birth. For ancient men and women her obesity must have denoted abundant, dependable food

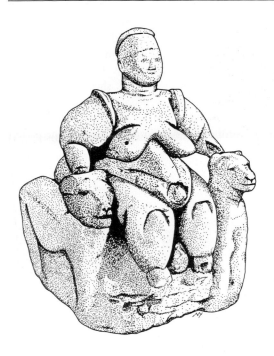

sources. Her prosperity, her fecundity, and her mastery over wild animals made her a symbol of much that Neolithic people wished to attain.

To reconstruct the religious practices of the inhabitants of Çatalhöyük, we must rely on analogy with practices attested for later literate cultures and for those recorded by modern ethnography. The striking images provided by the paintings and sculpture of Çatalhöyük tempt us to be concrete in our interpretations. But we should be cautious. We must keep reminding ourselves that the beliefs of people who lived 7,500 years ago still lie largely in shadow.

Figure 1.10 Seated fat woman (goddess?), terracotta figurine, Çatalhöyük. Museum of Anatolian Civilizations, Ankara

THE DEVELOPMENT OF CHIEFDOMS AND STATES

Çatalhöyük has seemed so remarkable in part because, when it was initially excavated, its cultural context was largely unknown, with little research available to evaluate contemporary settlements in the area. Subsequent projects in central and south-eastern Turkey (such as Çayönü), Syria, Iraq, and Iran have been filling in the picture. Nonetheless, Çatalhöyük, with its exceptional preservation, gives us in a still distinctive way an idea of what other Neolithic towns and villages may have looked like.

With the abandonment of Çatalhöyük in the mid sixth millennium BC, the striking innovations of central Anatolia came to a halt. Villages continued in the region, but for important developments our focus shifts eastward to Mesopotamia. The next 2,000 years, the Halaf and Ubaid periods, witnessed the gradual evolution of the Neolithic communities into chiefdoms and states, both centralized political systems, culminating in the great urban civilization of the Sumerians. A chiefdom is a political system in which a single ruler, a chief, almost always a man, exercises authority over two or more local groups, with power distributed downwards through a ranked hierarchy of subordinates. The state is a more formal system, with power invested in a centralized government, a combination of economic, military, legal, and ideological institutions. The state is able to regulate its affairs in an impersonal way, and can use force, can mete out punishments in order to support its decisions. Social stratification is a characteristic feature of the state, as indeed it is of the chiefdom.

Although the precise nature of the development of Near Eastern society during the Halaf and Ubaid periods is controversial, the broad outlines seem clear. Social organization was varied. In some towns an egalitarian society was the norm, with no groups holding special privileges, but elsewhere economic and social hierarchies emerged, whereby some members of the community enjoyed more status, privileges, and possessions than others. Eventually hierarchy would prevail. Management of food sources seems to have been responsible for this, with excess production, which can be stored and sold or traded, providing accumulated wealth and power for some. Religion may have offered an ideological justification for such inequality. These periods were marked in addition by innovations in technology (wheelmade pottery, sheet metal), transportation (boats with sails), and agriculture (tree crops). Trade networks continued, as the broad distribution of Halaf and Ubaid pottery indicates, from Mediterranean Turkey to Iran. Little by little the technological, commercial, and social world of the Ancient Near East was preparing itself for the rise of full-fledged cities.

CHAPTER 2

Early Sumerian cities

The Sumerians (first period of domination):

Ubaid period: ca. 5000–3500 BC

Protoliterate (Uruk) period: ca. 3500–2900 BC

Early Dynastic period: ca. 2900–2350 BC

The first cities in the Near East-Mediterranean basin appeared in southern Mesopotamia, or Sumer, the creation of a people we call the Sumerians (Figure 2.1). We have seen that environmental changes in south-west Asia during the previous 5,000 years led to human control over food production; with this mastery came major social changes, including fixed settlements. The socio-economic development of these towns and villages is marked by the gradual appearance of the ten criteria proposed by Childe as a mark of the true city. All ten factors finally emerge in Sumer during the later fourth millennium BC.

This chapter will explore early Sumerian cities. We will want to ask why true cities originated in southern Mesopotamia, a small region that did not figure in the Fertile Crescent and the Anatolian-Zagros highlands, areas so important for the domestication of plants and animals. What factors led the Sumerians to develop writing, the tool that propelled their settlements into the rank of "city"? What characterized the Sumerian city, and how did it compare and contrast with the Neolithic towns presented in Chapter 1? As examples, we shall inspect in particular the city of *Uruk* and its northern colony at *Habuba Kabira*. Aspects of two additional cities will also be examined: the *Temple Oval*, an important religious complex at Khafajeh; and the *Royal Tombs of Ur*, a spectacular group of burials from the Early Dynastic III period, found intact. But first, before we turn to Uruk, some background information about the Sumerians is needed.

THE SUMERIANS AND THEIR ENVIRONMENT

The Sumerians, the inhabitants of southern Mesopotamia from the fourth into the early second millennium BC, are so called after the ancient Akkadian name for this region, "Shumer." Thanks to their writing, invented during the fourth millennium BC, far more is known about the Sumerians than about their anonymous predecessors of the Neolithic age. The survival of the clay tablets on which they wrote, together with the remains of their cities, allow us to trace with greater confidence the increasing complexity of society in the ancient Near East.

The Sumerians stand alone in human history. Their language has no known relatives, and their architecture and artifacts do not indicate ethnic ties with cultures of other regions. The continuity of the material remains at their cities suggests, however, that the Sumerians had

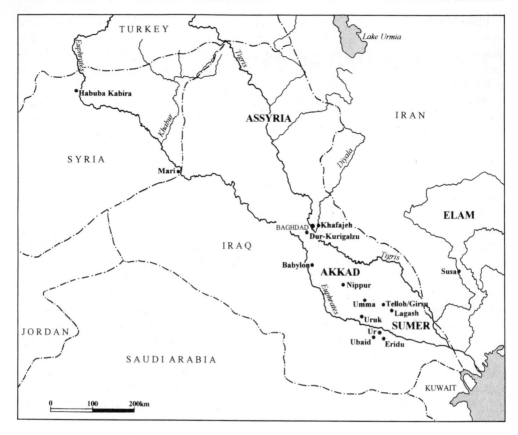

Figure 2.1 Mesopotamia: early Sumerian cities

already settled in southern Iraq in the later Neolithic period, at the end of the sixth millennium BC, well before they developed the art of writing. This era of the earliest known settlements in the region is called the Ubaid period, named after a site that has yielded a good sample of these early remains. Subsequent periods are the Protoliterate or Uruk period (when the city of Uruk was dominant); then the Early Dynastic period, divided into three parts (abbreviated as ED I, II, and III), during which the Sumerian city-states became increasingly prosperous.

Cities are a distinctive feature of the Sumerians. Indeed, the independent, self-governing city was their basic political unit. In this respect Sumer resembles ancient Greece, as we shall see. Geography seems not to be the determining factor in this political development, for the landscape of Sumer is flat, its terrain marked only by rivers and canals, whereas Greece is divided by mountains and valleys. Instead, religious reasons seem responsible. Each Sumerian city-state nominally belonged to a god or goddess. The temple was thus the focus of both ritual and economic activity. It also became the regional administrative center. Each town that grew around such a temple was entrusted, on behalf of the presiding deity, to the care of a mortal king (*lugal*, in Sumerian) or viceroy (*ensi*). Kingship first began in the city of Eridu, according to Sumerian myth. The institution was later copied and spread to other towns. The city-state, then, originated in remote, heroic times, the work of the gods; the divinely sanctioned city-state would be for the Sumerians the basic unit of political organization.

Rivalries between cities grew intense in the Early Dynastic period, thanks to territorial disputes in this region where agricultural land was precious. Warfare drove people from the countryside into the cities, now well protected with serious fortifications. No one city gained the upper hand. Instead, a certain balance prevailed, resulting in the reinforcement of the city-state as the basic political, religious, and social unit.

Why did cities arise in southern Mesopotamia? Sumer is some distance from the Fertile Crescent and adjacent highlands in which the domestication of plants and animals developed. Two factors, however, promised agricultural prosperity in Sumer: the alluvial soil deposited here by the Tigris and the Euphrates Rivers was extremely fertile, and the two great rivers themselves assured the supply of fresh water. When introduced in this region by the early settlers of the sixth millennium BC, the agricultural innovations from the Fertile Crescent took root and flourished.

The developing complexity of the economy and society that led to the rise of cities may be the result of a unique interplay of different environmental niches within southern Mesopotamia. The region contains not only fertile farmland but also marshes (with opportunities for fishing and hunting), steppeland (useful for grazing), and, further afield, mountains and sea (important for long-distance trade, reaching out to sources of raw materials such as wood, stone, and metals). These niches were mutually accessible, thanks to the relatively small size of the region, with the result that those people working in one sector would seek exchanges of products with the others.

Another factor in the rise of the Sumerian city-states was the need to organize an effective system of irrigation. Blisteringly hot in the summer, pleasantly cool in the winter, central and southern Mesopotamia has a dry climate. Irrigation is required for successful agriculture. Although the Euphrates and Tigris swell in the late spring with the water melted from the snow-covered mountains of Turkey and northern Iraq, an annual overflow of the silt-bearing rivers was not critical for farming – in contrast with Egypt. Late spring, the period of flooding, does not coordinate well with the two growing seasons of winter and summer crops. Consequently, a sophisticated system of canals was developed to bring water to the fields at the appropriate times, and to protect newly sown crops from being washed away.

The land drains poorly, however. Whereas the annual flooding of the Nile flushed away the noxious salts in Egyptian fields, in Mesopotamia the irrigation channels brought salts but did not remove them. Salt-tolerating barley became the chief grain. But these salts accumulated in the fields and gradually ruined the great fertility of the land. Even barley couldn't survive. The problem of salinization preoccupied the ancients, as documents as far back as the end of the third millennium BC testify. They had no remedy for it, and eventually it defeated them.

Today this flat, often marshy area is remote, worked only by herders and modest farmers. Only the many tells dotting the landscape remind us that this region was once home to a flourishing urban civilization.

URUK

The dominant city of early Sumer was Uruk (*Warka*, in Arabic). From its long and often distinguished history, we shall focus here on Uruk in the Protoliterate period (Levels IV and III), the important formative era of Sumerian urbanism.

Archaeological survey conducted notably by Robert Adams and Hans Nissen in the 1960s and 1970s has revealed that Uruk was far and away the largest settlement of the region in the Protoliterate period. The city was indeed immense. Although walls of its earliest settlements of the Ubaid and Protoliterate periods have not been discovered, the mud brick fortification of the ED I period measured nearly 10km in length and enclosed a vast area of 435ha (Figure 2.2). The site of the ancient city has been extensively explored since just before the First World War by teams from the German Oriental Society. Excavations have focused on the temples, the major public buildings of the city.

The prominence of monumental religious buildings in Sumerian cities is striking and marks an important difference from earlier Neolithic towns. In later periods, palaces, the dwellings of kings, occupy this central position, but in Sumer, from very early times, temples dominated. After all, as noted above, the god or goddess worshipped in a city's main temple was considered the true ruler of the city, the ruler of all. Other divinities would be celebrated in smaller temples scattered throughout the city. Not only at Uruk, but also at such towns as Eridu, considered by the Sumerians as the oldest in the world, and Nippur, the preeminent holy city, temples were constructed, remodeled, and reconstructed, the mound on which they were erected growing higher and higher from the debris of their ruins. In the flat landscape of southern Mesopotamia, these towering platforms must have seemed like mountains. Eventually the "mountain" became indispensable, so that, if the city could afford it, any new temple would be provided with its own imitation sacred mountain. These specially built stepped platforms, called *ziggurats*, are one of the key forms of Mesopotamian architecture (see Chapter 3 for the best-known example, the ziggurat of Ur-Nammu at Ur).

The temple quarter generally lay not in the center of a Sumerian town, but either off-center or at the edge. The sacred was thus carefully set apart from the secular. This peripheral location

Figure 2.2 Overall site plan, Uruk

might come as something of a surprise, considering the important role the temple played in the economic life of the city as the central clearing house for agricultural and other products. A Sumerian city would be further divided into different neighborhoods, residential, administrative (including palaces, if present), industrial (including craft workshops), and a cemetery. Different social classes mixed together; they were not segregated in their separate neighborhoods. Similarly, overlapping of tasks occurred. Craft workshops, for example, were scattered throughout the residential districts, and burials might take place beneath houses. There was therefore no standard placement of these functions in the overall city plan.

Neighborhoods were divided by such features as streets, walls, and water channels. Indeed, these last gave Sumerian cities a distinctive character. These canals were part of the larger regional system of watercourses. That they routinely flowed through cities as well as alongside them demonstrates their supreme importance in Sumerian geography. The canals, being navigable, gave rise to separate markets, commercial centers, and harbors, all reachable by boat.

The White Temple and the Eanna Precinct

Uruk contained two main temple areas, one dedicated – at least in later times – to the worship of the sky god, Anu (the *White Temple*), the other to Inanna, the goddess of fertility, love, and war (the *Eanna Precinct*). The White Temple of ca. 3000 BC is a fine example of a Sumerian "High Temple" (Figures 2.3 and 2.4). It sits alone on a terrace 13m high, the last rebuilding of a temple that goes back at least to the early/mid fourth millennium BC. Since worship of the god Anu characterized this sector of the city in historical times, it is assumed that Anu was already being venerated in the prehistoric White Temple.

The mud brick walls were covered on the outside with white plaster; hence the modern name of the building. In addition, the exterior walls are buttressed. Such buttresses created a pattern of indentions that became a characteristic Mesopotamian way of incorporating a three-dimensional decoration into brick architecture. Three long rectangles form the "tripartite"

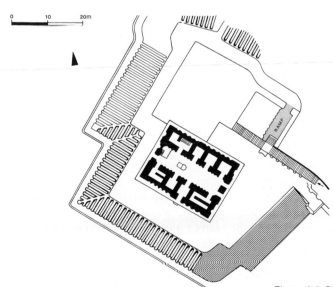

Figure 2.3 Plan, White Temple, Uruk

Figure 2.4 White Temple (reconstruction), Uruk

ground plan of the temple. The center portion, one large room, contained a stepped altar at one end and a central table for burnt offerings. The two flanking sections consisted of small rooms. Stairs led up to a flat roof.

The city of Uruk survived until the third century AD thanks to the prestige of its ancient shrines. It seems unlikely, however, that the White Temple was used until then. In contrast, in the second and first millennia BC, worship continued in the many shrines of the other principal sanctuary of the city, the Eanna Precinct, "the house of heaven" (Figure 2.5). The goddess Inanna reigned in this area. Outliving the Sumerians, this important deity was adopted under the name of Astarte or Ishtar by Akkadians and Babylonians and shares features with the Anatolian Kubaba (Cybele) and the Greek goddess Artemis.

Excavations have revealed the long history of the Eanna Precinct in the Protoliterate period, when an extensive series of temples and related religious buildings occupied this area. These structures are badly ruined, their plans not always sure. Figure 2.5 shows some of the buildings of two important Protoliterate levels, IVb (the earlier) and IVa (the later). The Mosaic Court, a large court and portico, served as a grand approach to the precinct in Level IVb. The architectural decoration here is remarkable: large cones of baked clay, their broad ends painted with shiny black, red, or white glaze, were set like fat nails into the surfaces of both columns and walls, creating a vast mosaic of geometric patterns in bright colors. Such cone-mosaics became a favorite decorative device for the builders of Protoliterate Sumer.

In contrast to Anu's area, none of the temples of the Eanna precinct stood high on artificial platforms. All are "ground-level" temples, although built, rebuilt, and replaced many times. While individual temples show symmetry in their layout, there is no such symmetry between component buildings of an architectural complex. Floor plans include not only the standard tripartite plan used in the White Temple, but also a T-shaped variant. In the Level IVa Temples C and D, good examples of this T-shaped plan, the central section flares into two transepts in an uncanny but entirely coincidental foreshadowing of the Early Christian basilica. Finds of

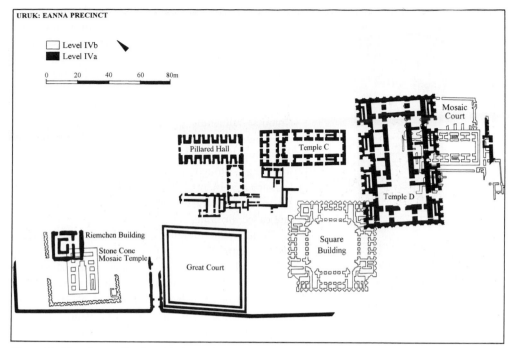

Figure 2.5 Plan, Eanna Precinct, Uruk

burnt timbers indicate that the central rooms were roofed, not open-air. There were no altars inside, but hearths sunk into the floors. The architectural prominence of one particular end of the temple suggests the cult statue was placed there.

Religious imagery at Uruk

The creation of figural art was one of Childe's criteria for the city. Pictorial art indeed becomes an important aspect of city life in the Near East and Mediterranean basin, a reflection of the changing ideologies of the peoples of the region. Throughout this book we shall be exploring pictorial imagery, keeping in mind how it enhanced the world of the ancient city dweller, from the Ancient Near East through the Roman Empire.

Religious imagery early takes on an important role in the pictorial art of Sumerian cities, with Protoliterate-period Uruk yielding key examples. The religious practices of the Sumerians, their gods and goddesses, mythology, and sacred architecture are of particular interest because they greatly influenced the character of religion and ritual in the ancient Near East until Christianity became the official faith of the Roman Empire in the fourth century AD. For knowledge of Sumerian religion in the Protoliterate period, before written documents yield fuller information, we depend on depictions in such works of art as the *Uruk Vase* and a sculpted head, both from Uruk, and cylinder seals with carved decoration.

The Uruk Vase is a tall (1.05m including the modern base), slender alabaster vessel with sculptured scenes of ritual activity, homage to the goddess Inanna (Figures 2.6 and 2.7). Found in the Eanna Precinct, the vase was made ca. 3000 BC. Similar ritual vessels are illustrated, always in pairs, in cult scenes on cylinder seals. The most important action takes place in the top

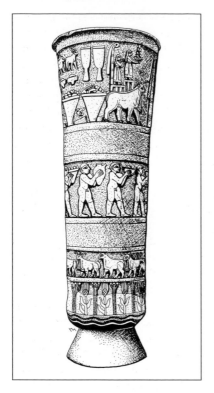

Figure 2.6 Uruk Vase, alabaster, from the Eanna Precinct, Uruk. Iraq Museum, Baghdad

register, where a priestess or perhaps Inanna herself receives gifts brought by priests, naked, in conformance with early Sumerian practice, as they approached the divinity. Behind them stands an intriguing figure, largely damaged, who presents a tasselled belt to the goddess. Attended by a clothed servant, this prominent person must be the ruler. The two standards behind Inanna, tall staffs of reeds with looped tops and streamers down the back side, represent the gateposts of her temple, a shorthand way of suggesting the entire building. Throughout Sumerian history these standards accompany Inanna, identifying her for the viewer. In archaeology and art history such identifying features are called *attributes*.

In the smaller middle zone of the vase, nude priests process with offerings of food and drink. The bottom register, divided into two smaller zones, shows the two realms which provide this wealth for the goddess: the world of animals (upper) and of plants (lower). Just below the plants an undulating band represents the ultimate source of the fertility of Uruk's lands: the Euphrates River.

Even if its narrative scenes of processions and offerings find countless echoes throughout the art of Near Eastern and Mediterranean antiquity, this vase is unique. Someone in ancient Uruk thought so, too, and went to the trouble of repairing with copper rivets the section of rim just above the head of the goddess.

The Uruk Vase signals two important conventions of Ancient Near Eastern and Mediterranean art. First, the carvings on the vase would have been painted, a habit perpetuated by Greek and Roman sculptors and architects. Second, the figures were shown in profile, the standard pose in relief sculpture and painting in the Ancient Near East, Egypt, and early Greece. Only in the later sixth century BC did Greek artists break from this tradition with their depictions of the human body in a great variety of movements.

Figure 2.7 Uppermost register, Uruk Vase

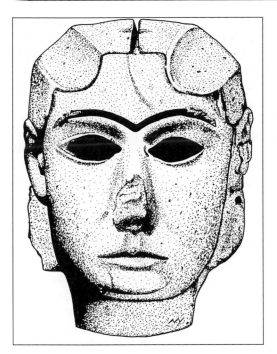

Figure 2.8 Head of a woman, limestone, from the Eanna Precinct, Uruk. Iraq Museum, Baghdad

A second object from Protoliterate Uruk that ranks among the most striking finds from ancient Mesopotamia is a limestone mask of a woman, 20cm high (Figure 2.8). This too was found in the Eanna precinct. Is this the face of a goddess or a priestess? Although the mask seems marvelous as is, we have to realize that it was carefully prepared to be adorned with inlays and attachments. The broad grooves on the top of the woman's head were surfaces that supported realistic hair or a headdress. Colored pastes or stones would have filled the eyes and eyebrows.

The mask was only one portion of a figure we can no longer reconstruct. Four holes in the flat back side of the mask permitted attachment to a flat surface. No traces survive of the accompanying body. We need not assume that limestone was used for the body; clay or wood, when painted and decorated, perhaps with precious metals, would have served perfectly well. Such figures created from a variety of materials are described in later texts from Mesopotamia; indeed, multi-media figures were produced by all subsequent cultures of Mediterranean and Near Eastern antiquity. In today's world they recall the construction of dolls more than anything else, or religious statuary that bears clothes.

Finally, religious imagery frequently decorates a category of objects which first appear in the Uruk period and which would become one of the hallmarks of the Ancient Near East: the *cylinder seal*. Although stamp seals were used from the sixth millennium BC, stone cylinders with designs carved on the curved surface became a far more popular way to indicate ownership or authority. Jars sealed with cloth, string, and clay; storage room locks sealed with clay; and documents on clay tablets were among the items marked with these distinctive pictures. The owner would roll out the seal, pushing the design onto wet clay; since the cylinders were

Figure 2.9 Rolling out a cylinder seal

usually pierced longitudinally for a string, the seal could then be attached to one's clothes or body (Figure 2.9). Fortunately for us, geometric designs did not satisfy the ancient Mesopotamians. They wanted to see gods, humans, and animals in action. As a result, these miniature scenes, enormously varied because of the need to individualize the designs, provide fascinating information about Ancient Near Eastern religious beliefs. Secular subjects, such as hunting or warfare, were not nearly so popular.

Not only the cylinder seals themselves but also the impressions left in clay have survived well in the archaeological record. Since the style of carving and the subject matter change markedly through time, seals are helpful indicators for dating. In addition, tracking their distribution has yielded valuable information about Mesopotamian economies, about the increasing circulation of goods between villages and cities, and the increased control of elite groups over these resources.

It is interesting to note that the use of cylinder seals corresponds closely with the lifespan of the distinctive Mesopotamian writing system, the cuneiform script. When cuneiform was replaced by alphabets in the first millennium BC, cylinder seals faded, replaced once more by stamp seals. Before we continue our look at early Sumerian cities, let us pause to examine this writing system, for it is one of the great achievements of Ancient Near Eastern civilization. Like the representational art just discussed, the development of writing is associated particularly with the city of Uruk.

THE DEVELOPMENT OF WRITING

The cuneiform script developed by the Sumerians in the late fourth to early third millennia BC as a tool for bureaucratic recording would become the principal writing system for the cultures of the Near East for some 3,000 years. It was adapted for use by languages from different families, Semitic (Akkadian and Ugaritic) and Indo-European (Elamite/Old Persian, Hittite, and Urartian). During the first millennium BC, this system gave way to the simpler Phoenician alphabet and its derivatives (which include the Latin alphabet used for English). The last datable tablets using cuneiform come from the first century AD. Only in the nineteenth century would knowledge of this script be recovered.

The name "cuneiform" ("wedge-shaped") refers to a narrow V-shaped wedge that was the basic element of signs used to represent single sounds, syllables, and entire words. In ancient Mesopotamia scribes wrote on clay tablets, the favored writing material, by pressing a reed stylus with a wedge-shaped point into the moist surface. The tablets would be left to dry. On rare occasions they would be baked hard, either deliberately in a kiln or accidentally in a fire. Baked tablets have survived extremely well; the naturally dried tablets are prone to damage. Excavations in Iraq and neighboring countries have yielded thousands of these tablets, although it should be said that archaeologists may dig for years before recovering tablets, and many sites have none at all. The tablets contain an enormous amount of information on economy, society, and history, and form the backbone of our knowledge of the Ancient Near East. Those who study these tablets (or indeed any inscription) call themselves *epigraphers* and add a further label that designates the cuneiform language in which they specialize, such as *sumerologists*; *hittitologists*; or *assyriologists* (for the Akkadian language), after the people whose ruined Iron Age cities were the first Mesopotamian sites explored by Europeans in the nineteenth century.

Cuneiform writing developed from a pictographic or "protocuneiform" system first used during the later Protoliterate period in order for temples to keep track of their accounts. Uruk seems key in the early development of writing, for the greatest number of such protocuneiform tablets have come from this city, from Level IV in the Eanna precinct. Most of these tablets are inventories, showing the picture of an animal, for example, accompanied by a number, with circles for tens and lines for ones. These tablets with lists seem to correlate with tokens used for counting discovered at many Mesopotamian sites. According to Denise Schmandt-Besserat, the clay tokens (spheres and cones) and the bullae (hollow balls) with numeral markings on their exteriors were reduced to the more manageable system of signs on a clay tablet. This streamlining of the procedure to record numbers lay at the heart of the Sumerian invention of writing. Schmandt-Besserat's theory is controversial, however. Some scholars believe that the proto-cuneiform script did not derive directly from earlier tokens and bullae, but instead was developed separately and rapidly as another tool useful for bureaucratic recording.

To say anything more complicated than "nine sheep" or "15 baskets of barley" necessitated modifications. Unlike the Chinese, who retained and expanded the original logographic character of their script (one sign per word), the Sumerians moved toward a syllabary. Some pictures continued to stand for entire words, but others began to represent sounds. More and more abstracted, the pictures finally became simply clusters of wedges. This transformation was completed in the Early Dynastic period, an age when the uses of writing spread dramatically. Further adaptations occurred when Sumerian cuneiform was utilized to transcribe the Akkadian language.

Akkadian was deciphered by the middle of the nineteenth century, but documents in Sumerian were still rare and poorly understood. Only with French excavations at Telloh (ancient Girsu), begun in 1877, and American excavations at Nippur, from 1889, did Sumerian tablets emerge in quantity. The language could then be studied in detail.

HABUBA KABIRA

Discoveries since the 1960s have confirmed that the Sumerians of the Protoliterate period extended their influence to the north, with settlements in northern Mesopotamia and the adjacent mountainous areas of Turkey and Iran, far beyond the Sumerian heartland in southern Iraq. The likely reason for this expansion was to secure access to raw materials lacking in Sumer itself. One of these towns, Habuba Kabira/Tell Qannas on the Euphrates River in north-west Syria, shares so much material culture in common with the cities of Sumer – ceramics, seals, and house types – that some scholars consider it an actual colony with resident Sumerians rather than a settlement of local people. Its town plan, more complete than any as yet known from Uruk or its neighbors in southern Mesopotamia, gives Habuba Kabira a special place in the early history of ancient Near Eastern cities.

Habuba Kabira and Tell Qannas are modern Arabic names that designate two sectors of a single site, excavated separately by German and Belgian archaeologists during the construction of a hydroelectric dam at Tabqa on the Euphrates (Figure 2.10). The city's ancient name is unknown. Tell Qannas, the higher area, contained the major temples of the city, in the manner already seen at Uruk. Habuba Kabira, extending to the north, represents the residential quarter. Only 15 percent of Habuba Kabira could be uncovered before the site was flooded beneath the lake that formed behind the dam.

The city lasted only some 150 years at the end of the fourth millennium BC. Spared the destructive remodeling of later builders, the ground plan of the town was well preserved only 30cm below the modern surface. The town extended over 1km along the Euphrates. An imposing wall some 3m thick with frequent squared, protruding towers and a smaller wall in front protected it on the land side, enclosing an area estimated at 17ha–18ha. Two gates gave access through the west wall, but the probable gate on the south had disappeared.

The town was built as a complete entity in a short time, another factor indicating it was a colony rather than a gradually expanding settlement. Laid out in a rough grid plan, the town had some paved streets, although most were unpaved, strewn with refuse and potsherds. It also had an impressive sewerage and water conduit system, usually with stone slabs lining the drains. Tiles

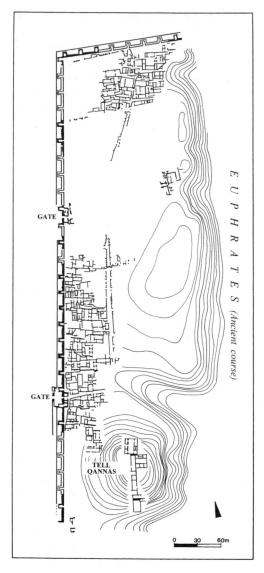

Figure 2.10 City plan, Habuba Kabira

and terracotta pipes linked the drainage of the town with the land outside the walls. A water channel in an unbuilt area south of Tell Qannas suggests the presence of a garden.

Houses were large. From a courtyard that contained irregularly shaped workrooms and the kitchen, one entered the house proper. Plans could be either (1) tripartite, recalling the ground plan of the White Temple at Uruk, with a large, high-ceilinged central room and two sets of smaller, lower-ceilinged side rooms, or (2) two-part, with small rooms off one side only of the main room. The main room often contained two hearths on the central axis, one at each end. Entrance into such houses was on the long side, that is, into one of the small side rooms.

It is curious that in a town with a certain number of amenities no particularly large houses have been identified which might have belonged to wealthy or powerful people or served administrative purposes. Also absent are open market areas. But Habuba Kabira is not unusual in this respect. One structure in the Eanna precinct at Uruk served as an assembly hall, it has been suggested, but palaces, as far as is known, began only in the Early Dynastic period. In all periods, government offices and shops probably occupied not separate buildings, but the rooms which lined temple complexes. Additional shops would be scattered throughout the town.

THE EARLY DYNASTIC PERIOD: HISTORICAL SUMMARY

The Early Dynastic period (abbreviated as ED, further divided into ED I, II, and III) which succeeds the Protoliterate marks the first historical era in Mesopotamia. However, the written evidence about the history of ED city-states is very sketchy until ca. 2500–2400 BC, when king lists become credible (see the Introduction) and objects inscribed with kings' names become prevalent. As a result, archaeological finds have continued to provide our fundamental knowledge of this period. The relative stratigraphy of the ED period was established in excavations in northeast Sumer, in the area along the Diyala River east of Baghdad. One of those sites, important for its temples, is Khafajeh, presented below.

Dominant among Sumerian cities through ED I, Uruk lost its preeminent position in ED II and especially ED III. In this period of increasing prosperity, many cities had now joined Uruk in firmly establishing their political and economic authority. But the period was hardly peaceful: warfare between city-states was unremitting. Never very distant one from another, the cities frequently quarreled over territory, with all-important water supplies often a bone of contention. Since so many texts come from Lagash, we hear much about the struggles between that city-state and its arch-rival, Umma. A depiction of this rivalry has survived in the fragmentary *Stele of the Vultures*, discovered by the French at Telloh (ancient Girsu, a town in the state of Lagash) and now on display in the Louvre Museum (Figures 2.11a and b). The reliefs celebrate the victory of Eannatum, ensi (ruler) of Lagash, over Umma. Eannatum, one of the powerful rulers of late ED Sumer, leads a group of helmeted, sword-wielding infantrymen, depicted tightly together as if in a box. Elsewhere he presides from his chariot over a mass of marching soldiers, carrying spears. On the reverse, the warrior-god Ningirsu, the patron deity of Eannatum, has trapped their enemies in a net. Anzu, the lion-headed eagle, watches over the capture. This collaborative triumph of king and god together becomes a staple of pictorial imagery in the official, royal art of the Ancient Near East, Egypt, and, later, the Roman empire.

The ED period and the first era of Sumerian supremacy came to an end with the victory of Sargon the Great, the Semitic ruler of Akkad, over Lugalzagesi, the powerful ensi of Uruk, and Sargon's subsequent conquest of the entire region (see Chapter 3).

To illustrate selected aspects of ED city life, we shall examine the Temple Oval at Khafajeh and evidence for temple decoration and religious practice from Ubaid and Tell Asmar, and an important cemetery at Ur, the so-called "Royal Tombs."

EARLY DYNASTIC RELIGIOUS LIFE: THE TEMPLE OVAL AT KHAFAJEH

Sumerian cities of the ED period were located on a watercourse and protected by fortification walls. As before, temples to the patron deity, his or her spouse, and their children occupied a prominent position in the town. Smaller shrines, popular as well as official, were scattered throughout the city, in residential quarters marked by cramped and winding streets. Construction of huge palaces began in the ED III period, reflecting the increasing power of the ruler. These palaces, of which good examples can be seen at Eridu, Ubaid, Kish, and, to the north-west, Mari, served both as residence of the king and as the administrative and bureaucratic center. But it is the religious buildings that continue to be so distinctive of Sumerian cities.

The co-existence of a "high temple" with "ground-level temples," which we have seen at Protoliterate Uruk, is a pattern that is maintained in the layout of a Sumerian city's religious buildings. One of the most striking of all ED "high temples" was the Temple Oval, uncovered at Khafajeh (ancient Tutub), north-east of Baghdad in the Diyala River basin (Figure 2.12). Since the identity of the god worshipped here is unknown, the modern name of the complex reflects its most distinctive trait, the unusual oval contour of its outer walls. In addition to this "high temple," the city of Khafajeh also contained a huge complex of "ground-level" temples, the main one of which was dedicated to the moon-god, Sin.

Although the Temple Oval was poorly preserved, with only a few brick courses of the ground plan surviving, three stages of construction and remodeling during ED II and III could be documented. Before the construction of the walls, the entire sacred area, approximately 100m across, was cleared to a depth of 4.6m and filled with clean sand. The excavator, Pinhas Delougaz

Figure 2.11a Obverse, Stele of the Vultures, ED III from Telloh (Girsu). Louvre Museum, Paris

of the Oriental Institute at the University of Chicago, estimated the quantity of sand at 64,000m³. After this ritual preparation, the area was bounded by an oval wall. Plano-convex bricks were used, bricks with a flat bottom and a curved top, a shape that enjoyed great popularity in ED Mesopotamia.

An inner oval enclosed a rectangular court lined with rooms used for workshops and for storage. Such non-religious concerns in the heart of the temple complex remind us of the multi-

Figure 2.11b Reverse, Stele of the Vultures

faceted concept of the temple as an economic and administrative as well as spiritual center. At the rear of this court the temple proper stood on a platform. Only the outline of the platform and a trace of the stairway leading up to it have survived. The temple plan is uncertain. It would not, however, have repeated the familiar tripartite plan with exterior indentations; that type had disappeared in early ED I. The reconstruction drawing presents a simple temple based on evidence from a nearby city, Tell Asmar.

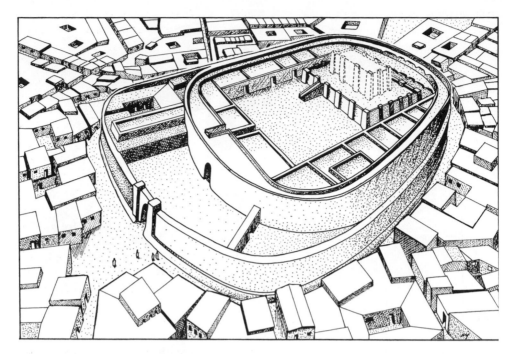

Figure 2.12 The Temple Oval (reconstruction), Khafajeh

The decoration of the Temple Oval has entirely disappeared, but some idea of the elaborate architecture ornament is supplied by a large bronze lintel discovered at another oval temple complex, dated to ED III (ca. 2550 BC), at Ubaid. The lintel, 1.07m high, consisting of copper sheeting over a wooden core, carries in high relief depictions of the ferocious lion-headed bird Anzu flanked by two stags with spiky antlers (Figure 2.13). Such monsters had a magical protective role in Mesopotamian antiquity. This lintel, it is conjectured, graced the top of the

Figure 2.13 Bronze lintel with Anzu and stags, from Ubaid. British Museum, London

main doorway into the temple to the mother goddess Nin-Khursag. Fragments of similar relief sculptures sheathed in copper may have decorated other walls of the temple, but, because the building itself has disappeared, the exact deployment of the decorations is not known.

The appearance of Sumerian worshippers at such temples survives in sculpture, for example in a group found at the Square Temple at Tell Asmar (capital of the ancient state of Eshnunna of which Khafajeh was a part) (Figure 2.14). They date to ED II, ca. 2700 BC. According to the inscriptions on similar examples of later (ED III) date, these statues are *votives*, that is, gifts offered by worshippers to the deities. The tallest of the statues are 0.75m, half life-size. They represent the worshippers themselves, not gods, all clasping their hands in front of their chest in the proper position for prayer. The large eye sockets and grooves for eyebrows, filled with bright white and black paste, shell and lapis lazuli, and the square shoulders and pointed elbows give them a distinctive appearance. The women dress in a simple garment that passes diagonally across the breast and is draped over one shoulder, whereas the men choose wool skirts with fringe on the bottom. Priests can be recognized by their clean-shaven heads and faces. Lay people also have distinctive hairstyles: women feature a braid encircling the head with a knot in the rear, while men wear their hair long and have squared beards. These squared beards which fall in tiers will remain a favorite fashion throughout Mesopotamian civilization (see the Neo-Assyrian reliefs of the first millennium BC). One wonders if the wave patterns of the beards resulted from special treatment, such as curling with hot irons or waxing.

Figure 2.14 Worshippers, stone figurines, from Tell Asmar. Iraq Museum, Baghdad; and Oriental Institute, University of Chicago

UR: THE ROYAL TOMBS

Ur is the most extensively explored of the great Sumerian cities, revealed notably by the excavations conducted in 1922–34 by the British archaeologist Sir Leonard Woolley on behalf of the University Museum of the University of Pennsylvania and the British Museum. Modern interest in this ancient city has been sparked not only by Woolley's discoveries but also by the site's identification with Ur of the Chaldees, the home of the Biblical patriarch Abraham.

Like so many cities of southern Mesopotamia, Ur was inhabited for several thousand years, from the fifth well into the first millennium BC. Here we shall examine the most famous part of the ED city, the Royal Tombs. In the next chapter our attention will focus on aspects of Ur in a later period, during the reign of the city's greatest ruler, Ur-Nammu: the city walls, the city center with its ziggurat, and the private houses (Figure 2.15).

The sixteen Royal Tombs of the ED III period were among the earliest burials in a centrally located cemetery containing some 2,000 interments ranging in date from ED III to Neo-Sumerian. The names of some of the persons buried here are known, written on objects found in the tombs: a queen or priestess Pu-abi (called Shubad by Woolley), and two kings of Ur, Akalamdug and Meskalamdug. The unknown may well include high-ranking administrators or religious figures.

The Royal Tombs, unique to Ur, are striking not only for the splendor of the grave offerings and for the tomb construction but also for the traces of the elaborate mortuary ritual that included human sacrifice. In each tomb, the important person, on occasion with companions, and a magnificent array of objects were placed in one or more burial chambers at the foot of a

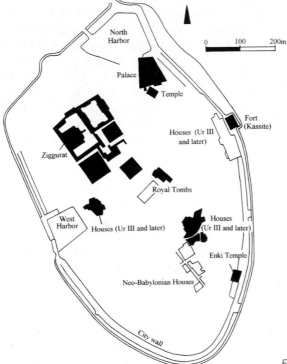

Figure 2.15 City plan, Ur

steep ramp. The participants in the funerary procession lay neatly arranged on the ramp: the remains of the draft animals in front of the wheeled vehicles they pulled and the skeletons of soldiers and female attendants. Although their clothes had disintegrated, adornments of precious metal survived. Tomb no. 1237, whose occupant remains anonymous, contained the largest number of bodies: seventy-four, including sixty-eight women still wearing their finest gold jewelry. Did these attendants meet death willingly, with resigned acceptance? What purpose did they believe they were serving? Such practices have been attested at no other city. Textual evidence offers no explanation.

Grave goods: a bull's headed lyre and the Royal Standard

Although Sumerian thieves had cleared out some of the graves, many funerary gifts remained *in situ*, such as jewelry, vessels of gold and silver, musical instruments, weapons, game boards. Shown here are two of the finds, a lyre decorated with a bull's head and inlay on the sound box and the so-called Royal Standard of Ur.

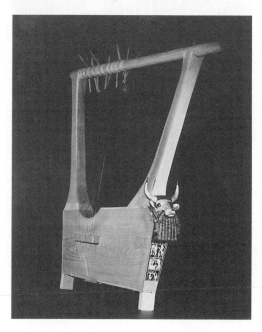

Figure 2.16 Lyre (reconstructed), from Ur
University Museum, University of Pennsylvania, Philadelphia

This lyre, the finest of several examples from the tombs, was discovered in the tomb of King Meskalamdug (Figure 2.16). Although the wooden parts had rotted away, the shape of the lyre was preserved in the ground. By pouring liquid plaster into the cavity, the excavators could accurately reassemble the form and the non-perishable decorations. Measuring 1.22m in height, the instrument consists of a wooden sounding box on the bottom and an upright section on either end, all inlaid with colored materials. A horizontal bar across the top would have held the strings running up from the sounding box, and tuning pegs. The golden head of a bearded bull decorated the front, perhaps an apotropaic image (to ward off evil). Such lyres were not just for show, for on one side of the Royal Standard of Ur a priest can be seen plucking happily on a virtually identical instrument.

The Royal Standard may itself have been an elaborate sounding box for a harp or lyre, or, as originally thought, a standard placed on a pole and carried before the king in ceremonial processions (Figure 2.17). The wooden core measures ca. 20cm × 45cm. After preparing the surface with bitumen, a tar used in antiquity as a sealant and glue, the artisan applied the mosaic, figures and borders of bits of shell against a blue background made of pieces of lapis lazuli. The Royal Standard is notable not only for the fine preservation of its inlay, one of the favorite crafts of the Sumerians, but also for its figural scenes, expressions of royal imagery. Each side has three registers; the scenes are read as a continuous story from the lowest register to the uppermost. The obverse, sometimes called "Peace," shows banqueting, and the transport of animals and agricultural products, whereas the

Figure 2.17 "Peace," the obverse of the "Royal Standard," inlaid panel, from Ur. British Museum, London

reverse, "War," depicts the king, his infantry, and his chariots, with enemies trampled. The ungainly four-wheeled chariots are pulled by onagers (wild asses), it is worth noting. The horse would not be introduced into Mesopotamia until the middle of the second millennium BC, an import from Central Asia.

Roofing techniques: arches and vaults

The roofing of the tomb chambers is of particular interest, because evidence for the roofs of Sumerian buildings is rare. Stout timbers, reed or palm frond matting, and a sealing of clay would have created a sturdy roof for a house, strong enough to hold the weight of a person. The same system could have been used for larger buildings, if interior columns divided the span of a room into manageable dimensions. In certain cases a more elaborate roofing of mud bricks was attempted. In the Royal Tombs of Ur, the chambers were vaulted or, rarely, domed with brick or limestone rubble, using the technique of *corbelling* (see below). Valuable evidence for vaulting techniques has come from excavations conducted in the 1960s at the second millennium BC site of Tell al Rimah, in north-west Iraq; well-preserved mud brick arches and vaults, some in the *pitched-brick* technique, are essential components of a large temple of the early second millennium BC.

The progression to the true arch and domical vault (= the dome) is one of the important architectural developments in the ancient Mediterranean and Near East and will be examined later in this book. The early techniques just mentioned, corbelling and pitched-brick, merit explanation. But first, the distinction between an *arch* and a *vault* needs to be appreciated: an arch is a two-dimensional span, covering a doorway or window, whereas a vault is three-dimensional, covering a room. The principles of arch construction can often be applied to vaults.

In a *corbelled arch*, on each of the two sides each successive block projects further inward until finally the two sides touch at the top (Figure 2.18d). If left by itself, the corbelled arch will eventually collapse: the weight pressing down toward the empty center of the arched space is not sufficiently counterbalanced by the weight of one brick on top of another. To solve this problem, a counterweight needs to be placed on the outside, to press the outer edges of the bricks downwards, to direct pressure toward the brick just below. If well incorporated into a sturdy wall, a corbelled arch could stand. In contrast, vaults made in the corbelling technique never stand alone, without counterweight, unless the space they cover is small (as in a small room of a house). Good-sized corbelled vaults are underground, with a packing of earth around and above the structure to provide the necessary counterpressure.

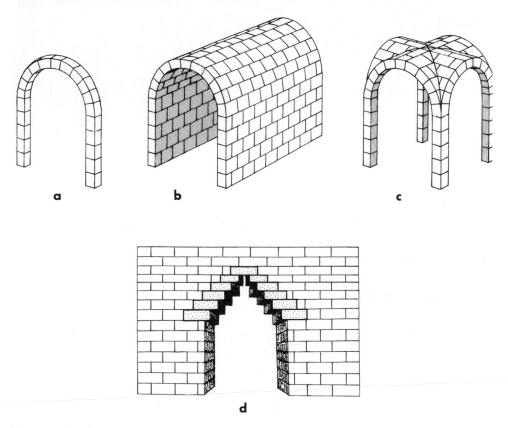

Figure 2.18 (a) true arch; (b) barrel vault; (c) groin vault; and (d) corbelled arch

In the *true arch* as distinct from the corbelled, stones are specially cut in wedge shapes to fit into one continuous curve (Figure 2.18a). The form and placement of the keystone, the wedge at the top of the arch, illustrates how the pressure from each stone is not directed exclusively downwards, but also to the side. The vertical struts that support the arch need to be reinforced in order not to buckle outwards, but the arch itself should not collapse. As with corbelling, the principles of true arch construction can be extended to three-dimensional forms, the vault (two are important in Mediterranean antiquity, the *barrel vault* and the *groin vault*: Figures 2.18b and 2.18c, respectively) and the *dome* (a hemispherical vault).

The *pitched-brick* technique of roofing falls somewhere between the above two methods (Figure 2.19a–2.19b). The bricks are not specially cut into wedge shapes, nor are they placed flat

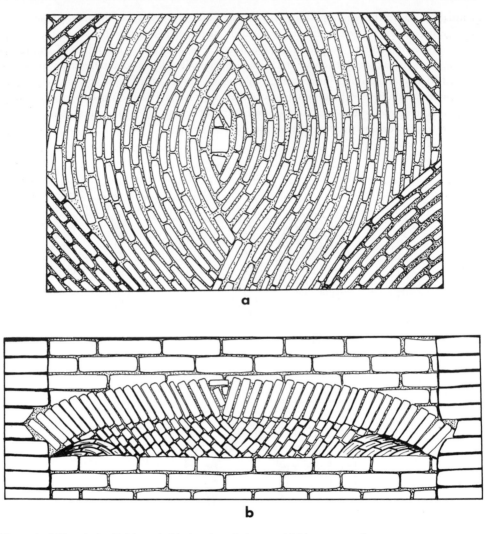

Figure 2.19 The pitched-brick vault: (a) view from below; and (b) in cross-section

one on top of the other. Instead, each successive brick is tilted slightly in order to form a curved line. The extra space at the top is filled with fragments. Although much more fragile than a true dome, such a structure can stand on its own.

SUMMARY

By 2350 BC, the city was already firmly established in southern Mesopotamia as the center of social, economic, and political life. Owned by the gods, administered for them by kings, Sumerian cities controlled their regional agriculture and water supplies, promoted industries, and participated in the long-distance trade that ensured provisions of raw materials unavailable locally. The cities themselves were fortified nuclei located on agricultural land and their life-giving watercourses. The temple of the tutelary deity dominated the city, even if located on the edge of the city plan. The temple was the city's original religious, economic, and administrative center. During the ED period the royal palace first appeared, the focus of the rising rival power of the earthly ruler. The town would be further divided into neighborhoods by canals, streets, and walls, but not according to any general pattern repeated from one Sumerian city to the next. Social and economic aspects of the early Sumerian city include – and here we can remind ourselves of Childe's list of ten criteria for the true city – a hierarchical society; a variety of non-agricultural occupations; the development of scientific observation, especially to assist agricultural practice; an expanded range of monumental architecture; figural art with extensive royal and religious imagery; and writing, by 2350 BC recording not only the economic data that inspired its initial development but also myth, ritual, and historical and contemporary events. If the Neolithic period gave rise to the embryonic city, in southern Mesopotamia in the fourth and third millennia BC the full-fledged city was born.

CHAPTER 3

Mesopotamian cities in the late third and second millennia BC

The Akkadians: ca. 2350–2150 BC

The Gutians: ca. 2150–2000 BC

The Sumerians (second period of domination):

   Neo-Sumerian period: ca. 2125–2000 BC

      Gudea of Lagash

      Ur III period (= Third Dynasty of Ur): ca. 2100–2000 BC

   Isin-Larsa period: ca. 2000–1760 BC

Old Babylonian period: ca. 2000–1530 BC

   First Dynasty of Babylon: ca. 1750–1530 BC

      Hammurabi of Babylon: ca. 1736–1694 BC

The Kassites: ca. 1530–1150 BC

In this chapter our examination of Mesopotamian cities reaches into the late third and second millennia BC. This is a period of important political change, when the traditional Sumerian concept of the city-state is challenged by state builders, even empire builders, resulting in the larger, more comprehensive political units of the Akkadians and the Third Dynasty of Ur. With these political changes come new emphases in architecture and royal imagery, always important elements of the ideology of cities and their rulers. Most attention will be given to the Sumerian city of Ur, already introduced in Chapter 2, and to Mari, famous for its monumental palace, a city created by one of the non-Sumerian Semitic peoples of central and northern Mesopotamia who would dominate the region for many centuries to come.

THE AKKADIANS

The first era of independent Sumerian city-states in southern Mesopotamia was shattered by Sargon, King of Akkad (reigned ca. 2370–2315 BC), who conquered the entire region ca. 2350 BC. This great king's likeness may survive in a life-size (30cm high) bronze head found out of context in a much later Neo-Assyrian temple at Nineveh in northern Iraq (Figure 3.1). With the elaborately braided hair tied in the back, the curled beard, and the placid smile, this head is elegant and serene. Only the damaged eyes and ears, perhaps intentional mutilations by the ruler's enemies to destroy the spirit present in the statue, mar the tranquility.

Figure 3.1 Bronze head, Akkadian period, from Nineveh. Iraq Museum, Baghdad

The Akkadian state is generally considered the first empire in south-west Asia. The heart of Sargon's kingdom was central Mesopotamia, in the region of Babylon and modern Baghdad. He established a new capital city, Agade (Akkad), thus breaking with traditional Sumerian seats of power. To the chagrin of archaeologists, Agade has not yet been identified, and so we have no Akkadian city to describe.

Sargon's activities, however, and those of his successors are amply reported in the cuneiform tablets. Once he had conquered the Sumerian cities, Sargon turned his attention to the east, to Elam (south-west Iran), and then northwards up the Tigris and westwards up the Euphrates into central Anatolia. If the ancient accounts are to be believed, he ventured even as far as the southern edge of the Arabian peninsula and into the Mediterranean to Cyprus and Crete. Only parts of this vast area could be firmly maintained under his authority. But these campaigns must have had the effect of stimulating commercial contacts between Akkad and distant suppliers of timber, metals, and other raw materials.

Sargon was a Semite, not a Sumerian. The language he spoke, Akkadian, written in a modified cuneiform script based on the Sumerian, would remain the lingua franca of the Near East for some 2,000 years until gradually it ceded its place to Aramaic. The evidence of names of people and places in the Sumerian tablets indicates that a substantial contingent of Semites lived in ED Sumer. The further north one went within Mesopotamia, the greater their numbers. Their origins are uncertain, as is true for the Sumerians themselves. Despite different speech, these peoples shared the same cultural patterns, the same religious beliefs. For example, Enheduanna, a daughter of Sargon, became a priestess of Nanna, the moon god of Sumerian Ur. The Akkadian rulers, however, contributed a new concept of kingship to ancient Mesopotamia, the elevation of the mortal rulers to the position of ultimate authority in the state, in place of the gods.

The Stele of Naram-Sin

The Stele of Naram-Sin is a parabola-shaped slab of pink sandstone, almost 2m tall, decorated on one side with relief sculpture that commemorates an Akkadian victory over the Lullubi, a people living in what is today western Iran (Figure 3.2). The victorious king, here celebrated by his dominant place in the relief, is Naram-Sin, the grandson of Sargon. During a later, twelfth-century BC Elamite invasion of Mesopotamia, the stele was seized as booty and taken to Susa, the Elamite capital – where the French archaeologist Jacques de Morgan uncovered it in the late nineteenth century.

Figure 3.2 Stele of Naram-Sin, from Susa. Louvre Museum, Paris

The martial theme is already familiar from earlier Near Eastern art, but the composition of the scene differs from Sumerian examples. Naram-Sin stands high on a steep forested hillside. He wears a horned helmet, the symbol of divinity, and carries a bow. A representative collection of defeated enemies lies wounded or dead at his feet. In the middle of the stele one victim plunges head first into the ravine. Below the king, his own soldiers stride up the hill, or turn to gaze upwards (those on the right side of the scene). The sun and the moon (the two rosette disks in the sky), divinities here, look down on Naram-Sin and on what may be a conical mountain – or perhaps a parabola-shaped commemorative stele.

The relief serves the same propaganda purpose as, for example, the earlier Stele of the Vultures: the exaltation of the king and his great victory. On the Stele of the Vultures (Figure 2.11), the identity of the king Eannatum among the warriors is never in doubt, for he is shown larger than life. But the god Ningirsu, larger still, very much takes part in the battle; victory is in fact won because of the favorable intervention of the god. The Stele of Naram-Sin builds on this ideological and visual foundation, but the pictorial expression of the ruler and indeed the very concept of kingship have moved in a new direction. No longer confined to the narrow horizontal bands of Sumerian art, the Akkadian ruler is displayed in a single grand image. Assisted by the diagonal lines of the hillside and the soldiers' faces turned upwards, the eye of the viewer focuses immediately on the king. Not only is he much larger than the other men, he is also virtually the sole figure in the entire upper half of the scene. Most important, as his horned helmet signifies, he has himself become a god. In confirmation of the image, texts tell us that Naram-Sin was addressed as a god during his lifetime, the first Mesopotamian ruler to be accorded this distinction. In this way, the king could claim a share of the prestige and possessions attributed to the deities.

Assertions of might and divinity did not suffice to protect Naram-Sin and his son Shar-kali-sharri. The Akkadian dynasty established by Sargon, now over-extended and weakened, was brought to an end by the Gutians, a mountain people from western Iran, neighbors of the Lullubi. A Sumerian poet writing several centuries later attributed the disaster to an act of sacrilege committed by Naram-Sin. According to this poet, Naram-Sin sacked the holy city of Nippur and defiled the Ekur, the sanctuary to the god Enlil. In revenge, Enlil sent the Gutians on a rampage. To spare the other cities of Sumer, eight major gods agreed that Agade must suffer the same fate it inflicted on Nippur:

> City, you who dared assault the Ekur, who [defied] Enlil,
> May your groves be heaped up like dust . . .
> May your canalboat towpaths grow nothing but weeds,
> Moreover, on your canalboat towpaths and landings,
> May no human being walk because of the wild goats, vermin (?), snakes, and
>   mountain scorpions,
> Agade, instead of your sweet-flowing water, may bitter water flow.
>
> (from "The Curse of Agade: the Ekur Avenged,"
> in Kramer 1963: 65)

And indeed, that seems to be exactly what happened to this proud city.

THE NEO-SUMERIAN REVIVAL: HISTORICAL SUMMARY

The Gutians, the conquerors of the Akkadians, controlled Mesopotamia for less than a century, leaving few traces in the material record. Gradually the Sumerian cities reasserted themselves, first Lagash, notably under the reign of Gudea, and later Uruk, leader of a widespread revolt against the Gutians ca. 2120 BC. Gutian domination was finally ended by Ur-Nammu, king of Ur. For the next century, Ur-Nammu and his four successors ruled over a united central and southern Mesopotamia. This great period in the history of Ur is known as the Ur III period, or the Third Dynasty of Ur. Although Sumerian was restored as the official administrative language, in other respects the Ur III kingdom took its inspiration from the state of Akkad. Administration was centralized, from taxation and weights and measures to religious and military matters. Moreover, Shulgi, the second of the Ur III kings, followed the precedent set by Naram-Sin and declared himself a god.

GUDEA OF LAGASH

Gudea, a Neo-Sumerian king of the city-state of Lagash, occupies a special position in Mesopotamian archaeology. Tablets discovered during the early French excavations at Telloh (ancient Girsu) document his reign exceptionally well. In addition, his image and that of his son, Ur-Ningirsu, have survived in an unusual series of diorite statues – unusual, because free-standing statues of rulers are rare in all periods in ancient Mesopotamia (Figure 3.3). The image of kingship they present differs markedly from that seen in the Stele of Naram-Sin. For Gudea, a king best serves his city not as a warrior but as a devoted servant of the gods.

At most half life-size, the statues reflect the predilection for small-scale figures already seen in the ED figurines of worshippers from Tell Asmar (Figure 2.14). It is fortunate that inscriptions on the statues themselves identify the figures as kings, because the features of face and dress alone do not indicate this. Not true portraits, these are standardized, idealized representations of a king in the position of worshipper. Although occasionally bare-headed and bald, Gudea usually wears a characteristic headdress, a cap with a broad woven brim. Whether sitting or standing, he always

clasps his hands reverently in front of his chest. In one unusual example, a drawing board with the plan of a temple rests on his knees. The god Ningirsu ordered Gudea, in a dream, to rebuild his temple; the pious king duly carried out the order, and had the statue made, with an explanatory text carved on it, to commemorate the deed.

The statues would have been given as gifts to temples. Unfortunately, the exact architectural context is unknown. While retrieving figures of hard black stone presented no difficulties to the explorers of Telloh in the last quarter of the nineteenth century, recovering the remains of mud brick temple walls from a matrix of dirt lay beyond their interest and capabilities.

Figure 3.3 Gudea, seated statue made of diorite, from Telloh (Girsu). Louvre Museum, Paris

UR IN THE UR III AND ISIN-LARSA PERIODS

The city of Ur reached its apogee in the late third and early second millennia BC, first as the seat of the kingdom of Ur-Nammu and his successors. After the demise of the Ur III kingdom, following an invasion of Elamites, the city rebounded during the succeeding Isin-Larsa period, enjoying economic prosperity and continuing as a prestigious religious center. In Chapter 2, we looked at the Royal Tombs from ED III. More extensive information about the appearance of the city comes from the later Ur III, Isin-Larsa, and Neo-Babylonian periods and will be examined here: the fortification walls, the religious center, and the residential neighborhoods (for the city plan, see Figure 2.15).

At its greatest extent during the Isin-Larsa period, the city measured ca. 60ha, with additional settlement outside its walls. Population of the city proper may have been approximately 12,000, using one standard benchmark of 200 persons per hectare, calculated according to an estimated number of houses per hectare, and of persons per house. But it should be kept in mind that ancient populations are extremely difficult to determine, and the figures proposed by modern specialists can vary significantly.

The extant city walls were built in the sixth century BC by Neo-Babylonian monarchs. The dating of the walls and indeed other construction is much helped by the ancient use of bricks stamped with the insignia of rulers. Because he did not find in the walls any bricks stamped with the name of Ur-Nammu, Woolley assumed that the Ur III fortifications were deliberately dismantled by the Elamite conquerors. However, the impressive Neo-Babylonian walls may well have resembled the Ur III fortifications in both location and appearance. Situated on a promontory between an arm of the Euphrates and a navigable canal, the city could be approached by land only from the south. Despite the protection of water on three sides, an imposing wall 27m thick was built all around. The lower part consisted of a steeply sloping mud brick rampart, or *glacis*. This section enclosed and capped the edge of the already existing mound. On this stood the upper section of baked brick, the wall proper. Defended by water and such massive walls, the city must have seemed impregnable. But as history has witnessed time and time again, fortifications and the weapons of war are only as strong as the men and women who use them.

The religious center of Ur

The religious center, devoted to the cult of Nanna, the moon god and patron deity of Ur, and his wife, Ningal, was a focus of Woolley's excavations; as a result, much is known about it (Figure 3.4). This *temenos*, or sacred area, lay in the north-west, the traditional site of the important buildings of a Sumerian city. The propitious north-west sector had the healthiest air, it was believed. Such an attitude may lie behind the frequent orientation of buildings throughout the site toward the cardinal points: one side would normally face the north-west and its soothing breezes.

Its corners oriented toward the cardinal points of the compass, the entire temenos measured some 400m × 200m. Buildings were preserved in foundations only, the upper parts having been destroyed during the Elamite invasion at the end of the Ur III period. The precinct contained temples, courtyards, and rooms to house the religious personnel and store offerings and cult paraphernalia, and an enormous ziggurat (see below). In ground plan, the area looks quite forbidding, with its many thick and reduplicated walls protecting courts and labyrinthine buildings such as the Giparu, a complex of shrines dedicated principally to Ningal and a residence for high priestesses.

Closely linked to the sacred compound and probably in greater need of the security provided by the walls was the royal center. The king held audience in the small rooms of the gateway into the compound for the ziggurat. His palace, the Ehursag, stood close by, just to the east, and immediately beyond that lay the Royal Cemetery. The tombs of the kings of the Third Dynasty were not as well hidden as the earlier ED Royal Tombs. They were looted in antiquity, and only their architecture has survived: the stairs down to vaulted tombs and the remains of mortuary chapels above – construction on a scale much grander than in the ED tombs.

The best-known building of the temenos is the ziggurat, the best-preserved example in Mesopotamia (Figure 3.5). Erected under Ur-Nammu and his son Shulgi, the ziggurat was restored by successive generations of kings in Mesopotamia for 1,500 years after its initial construction, and again in modern times by the Iraqi government.

A ziggurat is a tower built of successively smaller platforms one on top of the other, with a small shrine on the summit. The name may come from Akkadian words for "summit" or "mountain top" (*ziqquaratu*) and "to be high" (*ziqaru*). It serves as an artificial mountain in flat land, reaching up to heaven and the gods, an elaboration of the tall platform which had held up the Mesopotamian "high temple" ever since the fifth millennium BC.

The ziggurat at Ur consists of three platforms. The temple on top did not survive, so its appearance is conjectural. The lowest platform measures 61m × 45.7m × 15m. A majestic triple staircase leads up to it and then on to the upper two stages and the shrine on top. Sun-dried mud bricks and periodic layers of woven reeds make up the solid core of the structure. The exterior was faced with a thick (2.4m) layer of more durable baked bricks, set in bitumen. Drainage holes pierced the façade of the lowest platform, a detail that has intrigued observers. Noting finds of

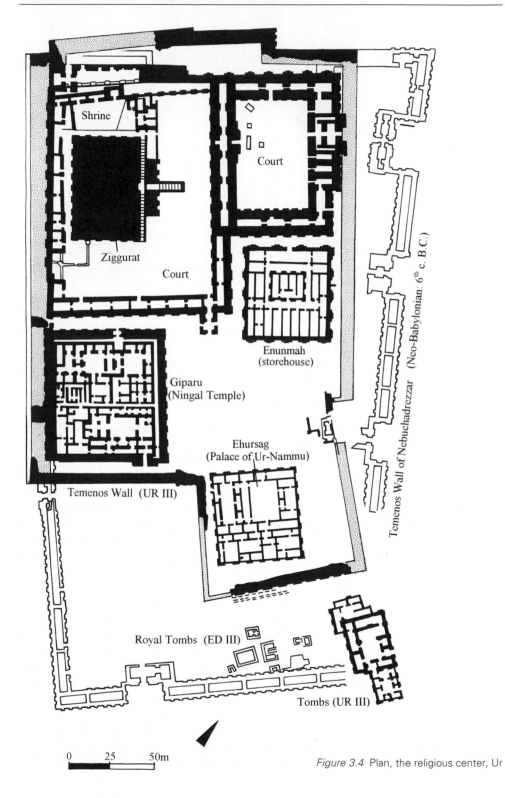

Figure 3.4 Plan, the religious center, Ur

Figure 3.5 Ziggurat of Ur-Nammu (reconstruction), Ur

Figure 3.6 Stele of Ur-Nammu, Ur. The University Museum, University of Pennsylvania, Philadelphia

carbonized tree-trunks, Woolley proposed that the tops of the terraces were planted with trees. The holes would have helped drain the specially watered garden. This appealing vision of the ziggurat as a forested mountain peak has not been confirmed elsewhere.

The Stele of Ur-Nammu

The building projects of Ur-Nammu in the temenos at Ur are honored in relief sculpture on the Stele of Ur-Nammu, a fragmentary stele discovered during Woolley's excavations (Figure 3.6). As did other Mesopotamian rulers, Ur-Nammu wished to record his piety in sculptural form. Like the art of Gudea, and in contrast with much other, the Stele stresses the king's adoration of the gods rather than his considerable military achievements. Not only does its message about kingship contrast with that of the Stele of Naram-Sin (Figure 3.2), the composition of the relief also differs from the earlier work, divided as it is into horizontal bands in traditional Sumerian fashion. In the best-preserved register, the king appears twice, in audience with two different divinities, a goddess (left) and a god (right). In each scene, the deity, seated on a platform, watches as the king pours a libation into a plant or small tree growing in a tall conical pot. Behind the king stands a woman, her hands upraised; also a goddess, she has the responsibility of presenting the king to the seated gods. Lower, damaged zones depict a good work of the king, the construction of a temple. Ur-Nammu carries builder's tools, assisted by a clean-shaven priest. Nanna, wearing the horned hat reserved for gods, accompanies them in procession to the building site.

Private houses

Woolley excavated several residential neighborhoods within the city. The best examples, found south-east of the temenos, date to the Isin-Larsa period, in the twentieth century BC. The plan with its curving streets and massing of houses contrasts with the regular layout of Protoliterate Habuba Kabira of some 1,200 years before. There was no attempt to place straight, wide streets at regular intervals. The paths granting access to pedestrians and pack animals never received much consideration from home owners or municipal authorities, and their courses must have weaved back and forth as the buildings that lined them were demolished and rebuilt. Further, trash would be randomly discarded into the streets. In the ancient city, as indeed in the Middle East today, the interior of the home, one's private space, was the focus of respect and attention, not the public streets outside. Even so, the need for some regulation of public streets was recognized, as this omen text indicates:

> If a house blocks the main street in its building, the owner of the house will die; if a house overshadows (overhangs) or obstructs the side of the main street, the heart of the dweller in that house will not be glad.
>
> (Frankfort 1950: 111)

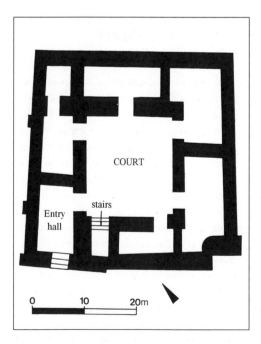

Figure 3.7 House plan, Isin-Larsa period, Ur

The grandest houses at Ur surpass their counterparts at Habuba Kabira. They consist of two storeys of rooms arranged around an open-air court (Figures 3.7 and 3.8). This design differs from house plans at Habuba Kabira, in which a single storey and set of rooms lay at the rear of a court. As typical in all periods, the walls as seen from the street are completely unadorned. What lies inside belongs strictly to the family and their friends. In addition, the dead were often buried in the house beneath the ground floor, a practice reminiscent of Neolithic Çatalhöyük. But burial practices could vary. Cities would often have separate areas for cemeteries.

Simpler house plans also exist. These evidently belonged to shops, distributed throughout the residential quarters with heavier concentrations in the southern part of the city. In addition to houses and shops, the city plan also contained small shrines, located at street crossings.

Figure 3.8 House interior (reconstruction), Ur

HAMMURABI OF BABYLON AND THE OLD BABYLONIAN PERIOD

The second period of Sumerian domination in southern Mesopotamia came to an end with the conquest of Hammurabi, king of Babylon, in the late eighteenth century BC. Indeed, Babylon, one of the great cities of the Ancient Near East, first emerged as a major political center at this time. Hammurabi's achievements were considerable. Not only did he bring north and south Mesopotamia under his control, duplicating the accomplishment of Sargon of Akkad, he also revamped the administrative system of the country. Noted particularly for codifying the traditional laws of Mesopotamia, he had his laws inscribed on a near-cylindrical basalt stele 2.1m high, the so-called Stele of Hammurabi (Figure 3.9). On the top of the stele is a single scene, a relief sculpture that shows Hammurabi in audience with the seated god Shamash, god of justice. The encounter of king with god resembles that shown on the Stele of Ur-Nammu. The imagery on the latter stele stresses the deference of the king to the deities, however, as Ur-Nammu pours a ritual libation before both god and goddess. In contrast, Hammurabi seems to be consulting directly with the god. It is almost, but not quite, a relationship of equals.

The era in Mesopotamian history that centers on Hammurabi and the dynasty to which he belonged is called the Old Babylonian period. With the ascendancy of the Semitic Babylonians, Sumerian disappeared as a spoken language, replaced by Akkadian. Sumerian did continue as a written language, however, esteemed as the vehicle of religious and literary values – one reminder of the enduring strength of Sumerian culture.

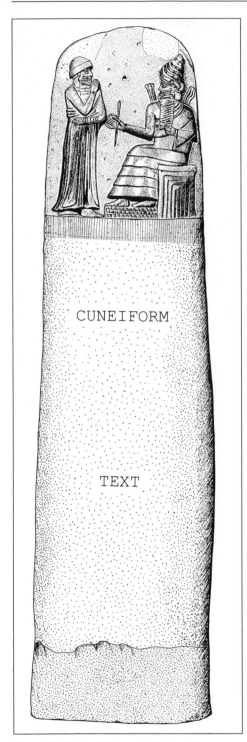

CUNEIFORM

TEXT

Figure 3.9 Stele of Hammurabi, from Susa. Louvre Museum, Paris

MARI: THE PALACE OF ZIMRI-LIM

The key example of an Old Babylonian city is not Hammurabi's capital at Babylon, where later constructions of the first millennium BC survive best (see Chapter 10), but Mari, halfway up the Euphrates in modern Syria just across the Iraqi frontier. The evidence provided by the Palace of Zimri-Lim, the principal building of eighteenth-century BC Mari, is well complemented by the important find of 20,000 clay tablets; together, architecture, art, and texts give us a full picture of the life of this city. Excavations conducted by French teams since 1933 have barely touched the town beyond the walls of the palace. Because the palace by itself seems like a town in miniature, this lack has not drawn much attention until recently.

Already important in the Early Dynastic period, Mari reached its height during the rule of Zimri-Lim, a regional potentate, ca. 1715–1700 BC. Zimri-Lim and the inhabitants of Mari were Semites. They wrote in the Akkadian language, but proper names and non-Akkadian words found in the Mari tablets place them in the North-west Semitic sphere together with such peoples as the Amorites. Mari grew rich thanks to its advantageous location on the trading routes from the west and the Mediterranean to both the Assyrian area to the north-east and Babylonia to the south-east. Taxes were imposed on all goods that passed through. The palace that Zimri-Lim inherited and remodeled so grandly was destroyed by Hammurabi of Babylon in ca. 1700 BC, but the substantial remains initially excavated in only five years under the direction of André Parrot allow a good look both at the architecture and at the workings of society and economy in the eighteenth century BC.

This palace illustrates an important shift in the government of ancient Mesopotamian cities. For the early Sumerians, everything belonged ultimately to the gods; human beings merely held the cities and the land and its fruits in trust for them. During the Protoliterate and

Early Dynastic periods, the major constructions in a city honored these divine beings. Eventually, however, the ruler assumed a more deeply entrenched authority. This process began in the ED period, but developed significantly under the Akkadian Empire and the states that followed. The affirmation of kingship associated especially with the Akkadians seems to result not from any deliberate invention but from the expansion of the political unit from the city-state to empire. Gods ruled in city-states, but empires were the creation of men. Such exalted treatment of kingship appealed to subsequent monarchs, needless to say, even when the territories they ruled hardly qualified as empires.

Changes in the role of the ruler were paralleled by new emphases in urban architecture. In the Ur III period, for example, palaces of the rulers crept closer to the temples, even in the heart of a classically Sumerian city such as Ur. By the time of Old Babylonian Mari, the prerogatives of the ruler were great. Kingship had become the umbrella that sheltered both the secular and the religious aspects of administration. Although royal palaces had been built as early as the ED period, including a substantial example at Mari itself, complexes that predate the eighteenth century BC are incompletely known. It is thanks to the accidents of archaeological discovery and exploration that the Palace of Zimri-Lim, thoroughly excavated and well published, has won its reputation as the prime example of the early Mesopotamian palace.

"Show me the palace of Zimri-Lim! I wish to see it." Thus wrote an eighteenth-century BC king of Ugarit on the Mediterranean coast to the king of Yamhad (modern Aleppo) in central Syria. The palace was indeed a wonderful architectural complex that combined spaces for religious ritual, public ceremony, the private life of the ruler, and a wide range of commercial activities. Today, its mud brick walls, preserved in the south-west to over 4m in height, are sadly disintegrating from unchecked exposure to rain, wind, and sun, but, even so, the visitor can understand its ancient renown. A complex of over 260 rooms in the surviving ground floor, the palace measured 200m × 120m, covering an area of ca. 3ha (Figure 3.10). The exterior walls,

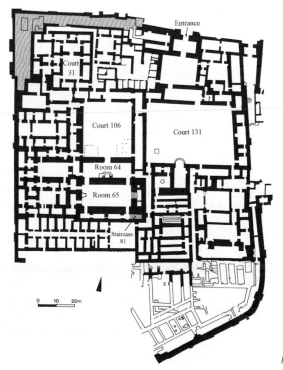

Figure 3.10 Plan, Palace of Zimri-Lim, Mari

mud bricks piled in places to an impressive thickness of 4m, were protected with a coat of clay plaster. The main entrance gate lay on the north, off a paved street. From this gate, an important visitor proceeded to two large courtyards at the heart of the palace (131 and 106 on the plan) and to two key rooms off court 106, an antechamber (64) and an audience hall, generally identified as the throne room (65).

Paintings decorated the south wall of court 106 on either side of the doorway leading into room 64. The investiture of the king was illustrated to the west of the door, and a sacrificial procession, now badly fragmented, to the east. An overhanging roof may have protected these important figural scenes. On the other three walls of the court, a red and blue geometric band ran 2m above the ground.

The Investiture Scene, the best known of the wall paintings from Mari, imparts a visual message appropriately placed here at the entrance to the throne room: the king has the blessing of the gods, and the result is agricultural plenty (Figure 3.11). The painting measures 1.75m × 2.50m. The key scene takes place in the center in a small rectangular panel, a spatial form that hearkens back to Sumerian art. In the presence of three other divinities, the goddess Ishtar, with one foot on the back of a lion, hands the insignia of power to the king. The insignia, a circle and a stick, resemble the items held out to Hammurabi by Shamash on the Stele of Hammurabi. The theme is thus familiar to us, but the elaboration offered here is new. In the secondary panel just below, two goddesses, identifiable as such by the horns on their headdresses, are holding vases from which emerge a plant (a sign of vegetal fertility) and streams of water adorned with fish, the representation of the Euphrates River, the source of life in this arid region. These two panels are framed by a fantastic landscape created by two tall papyrus-like trees and two date palms with

Figure 3.11 Investiture Scene, wall painting, Mari

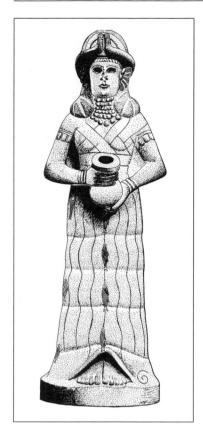

Figure 3.12 Goddess holding a
flowing vase, statue from Mari.
Aleppo Museum

monkeys climbing up to clusters of fruit. Three tiers of winged human-headed lions, a composite creature much loved in Mesopotamian mythology, also inhabit the garden, as do female divinities standing beyond the lions.

The goddesses who hold the vases take on three-dimensional form in a statue discovered in fragments both in Court 106 and in Room 64. Reassembled for display in the Aleppo Museum, the almost life-size (1.43m) goddess stands stiffly, her feet held together and revealed beneath the hem of her dress (Figure 3.12). Her eyes no longer contain the inlay, and her nose is broken off, but her pleasant smile and full face give this goddess of fertility an appeal still effective today. In addition, the craftsmen of Mari rigged this statue as a fountain. Water from a tank would have flowed through the channel carved inside her body and out the vase, just as the wall painting illustrates. The inhabitants of Mari took their water imagery seriously.

From Court 106 one entered the two long narrow rooms, 64 and 65. In Room 64, just opposite the doorway from the court, stood a brick podium with a limestone surface decorated to imitate marble. Since steps led up to it, it would seem a likely spot for a dais surmounted by a canopy, as Parrot proposed. The inner room, 65, was the throne room of the palace. A low base at the west end marks the location of the throne. At the opposite, east end of the room, a broad flight of steps led to another platform, generally restored as a shrine. The lavish use of the sealant bitumen on the steps and on the statue bases flanking the stairs suggests rituals utilizing much liquid, perhaps provided by goddesses with flowing vases.

The rooms around this core of courts and audience halls can be divided into four main sectors (Figure 3.13). The functions of these rooms is in dispute, however. The arguments illustrate the difficulties of interpreting archaeological remains. A room may contain material collapsed from an upper floor or merely random trash, or looters may have stripped it of its identifying contents. How can the archaeologist know which is the correct explanation of what he or she finds? At Mari, for example, Parrot located the king's private quarters in the north-west rooms grouped around Court 31. This area, which recalls the traditional Mesopotamian house with rooms arranged around a court, is furnished with such amenities as toilets and terracotta bathtubs. But Jean Margueron, Parrot's successor, assigns this sector to dignitaries, and prefers to see the king at home in an upper storey above the long, narrow storerooms south of Court 131 (the eastern end of the quadrant marked "King's Residence" on Figure 3.13). Those upper rooms collapsed and disappeared in antiquity, but the remains of Staircase 81 prove they did exist. Limiting his remarks to the surviving ground floor rooms, Parrot had conjectured little about possible upper storeys.

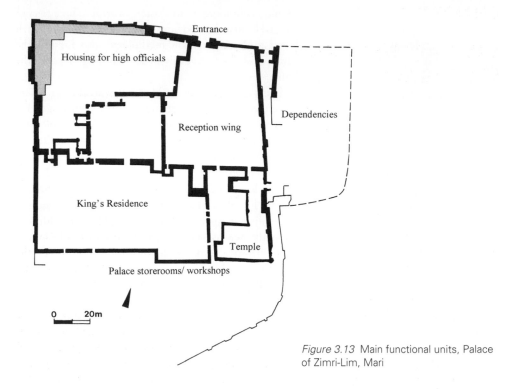

Figure 3.13 Main functional units, Palace of Zimri-Lim, Mari

THE KASSITES

After its destruction by the forces of Hammurabi, the city of Mari never recovered and habitation ceased. As for the empire of Hammurabi and his successors, it gradually eroded before threats on various fronts. In the south, peoples from the Arabian Gulf moved northwards, while the Kassites pressed in from the north-eastern mountains. The fatal blow was delivered by the Hittite king Murshili I, who captured and sacked Babylon ca. 1530 BC. Quickly returning to Anatolia, Murshili I never consolidated his victory in Mesopotamia. In the absence of the Hittites, the Kassites moved in and took control of central and southern Mesopotamia. They founded a new capital city at Dur Kurigalzu, some 30km west of modern Baghdad. Like the Akkadians, the Kassites soon absorbed the traditional Sumerian culture of the region they now ruled.

Our investigation of Ancient Near Eastern cities has concentrated on developments in southern and central Mesopotamia. To the north, meanwhile, the Assyrians prospered throughout the second millennium BC. In the Iron Age, in the ninth to seventh centuries BC, they would burst forth from their homeland and take their turn as masters of empire, creating monumental cities in the process. But that is a story for Chapter 10. Let us first turn our attention to other Bronze Age civilizations of south-west Asia and the Mediterranean basin, the contemporaries of the Sumerians, Akkadians, Old Babylonians, and Kassites.

CHAPTER 4

Cities of the Indus Valley Civilization

The Indus Valley Civilization

The Harappan, or Mature, phase: ca. 2600–1900 BC

The Indus Valley Civilization, also called Harappan after one of its major cities, is the second of the three great river-based civilizations of the third millennium BC in northern Africa and south-west Asia. Its cities, with their distinctive choices in architecture and town planning, provide an instructive counterpoint to those of regions further west, Mesopotamia and Egypt. In certain features, the Harappans seem particularly advanced.

The Indus Valley Civilization arose in the vast alluvial plain of two roughly parallel rivers, the Indus and the now dry Saraswati (or Ghaggar-Hakra), a region now situated in modern Pakistan and north-west India (Figure 4.1). Although the general similarity of the geographical setting and the sophistication of its architecture and city plans suggest a cultural development comparable to that experienced in Mesopotamia and Egypt, some major differences in the material record make it difficult to assess this hypothesis. First, the wealth of information available from Mesopotamian clay tablets and Egyptian papyri and stone inscriptions has no counterpart in the ancient Indus Valley. The Harappans did use writing, but their script has not been deciphered. Even if it were, the results would not yield much: inscriptions, mostly on seals or sealings, tend to be very short. Second, we know little about the social structure. This is due not simply to the lack of textual information, for non-textual evidence can have much to contribute about such matters. Here, the material remains give no clear picture of social distinctions. For example, lacking are elaborate tombs with rich grave gifts, burials of the sort that have brought the upper echelons of society so strikingly to our attention in lands further west. The rulers of these Harappan cities are as yet invisible to our modern eyes. Third and last, after the Indus Valley Civilization dissolved in the early second millennium BC, its traditions were not carried on, at least not directly, by succeeding peoples. Moreover, texts from later antiquity remain silent about the Harappans. As a result, this region did not have a continuity of cultural traditions comparable to what we see in Mesopotamia and Egypt.

Until recent decades, little was known about cultural developments in the Indus Valley before the Harappan period proper. Did the Harappan cities spring up quickly, or were they the result of a long period of gradual development? Such important questions could not be answered. Evidence from Mohenjo-Daro itself, for example, is meager, and more would in any case be difficult to obtain, the relevant deposits lying buried deep in the silt brought by the river. Excavations elsewhere, at such sites as Mehrgarh, are now documenting developments of the preceding 4,000 years, the Neolithic into the Bronze Age. The picture emerging is one of gradual development, of the sort we have traced in Anatolia, the Levant, and Mesopotamia, although with regional variation important.

Figure 4.1 The Indus Valley Civilization

ENVIRONMENT

The Indus River originates in Lake Mansarovar in south-west Tibet. The Indus still today makes its way westward through Kashmir, then south through Pakistan, through the Punjab and Sind to the Indian Ocean. Harappan sites have been found in a huge triangle, along 1,200km of coastline from south-west Pakistan to the Gulf of Khambat (Cambray) in India, and, heading inland, along the final 1,600km of the river and its tributaries. Geographical conditions vary throughout this area. The northern sector lies largely in the Punjab, a well-watered region, thanks to adequate rainfall and to its rivers. The best-known site here is Harappa. Rakhigarhi, a site of similarly large size but as yet unexcavated, lies at the eastern edge of the Punjab, 350km from Harappa, the north-eastern limit of the Indus Valley Civilization.

Directly south of the Punjab is Cholistan, a drier region. Its major Harappan site is Ganwariwala, an unexcavated city that lay alongside the Saraswati River. Further south still is Sind, a hot, rainless area whose geography and climate recall southern Iraq. Mohenjo-Daro, 570km south of Harappa, is the major site of this region, and indeed the most extensively excavated and best known of all Harappan sites. The last of the geographical regions is the coastal zone along the Arabian Sea, a largely inhospitable area, rocky and with limited fresh water supplies. Despite this hostile environment, the important Harappan city of Dholavira was established here, on a small island (the region has since filled with silt, however; Figure 4.1 shows the modern coastline).

The five sites mentioned above, the largest known Harappan sites, have been identified as the major regional centers. They are distributed at fairly regular intervals from north-east to south. Each would have controlled a large hinterland, with its agricultural production and natural resources. In addition, Dholavira must have profited from its maritime location. What we do not know is whether these five cities, surely preeminent in their respective regions, and indeed all cities and towns, were joined together in a single state, or whether, as in Sumer, the city-state was the basic unit of government.

Of these five major cities, three have been excavated: Mohenjo-Daro, Harappa, and Dholavira. We shall focus here on *Mohenjo-Daro*, with a brief look at *Lothal*, a smaller city in the extreme south-east of the Harappan region, to see how the layout and architectural features of a provincial town compare with those of a metropolis.

MOHENJO-DARO

Mohenjo-Daro is the largest known city of the Indus Valley Civilization, with an inhabited area now estimated, thanks to surface survey work, at over 250ha. The city proper, covering an area of ca. 80ha as explored through excavations, is a well-planned city located today some 5km from the Indus River. It is not known whether the river flowed closer to the town in Harappan times.

Mohenjo-Daro is also the most extensively explored Harappan city, thanks to excavations conducted first in 1921 by R. D. Banarji, then from 1922 to 1927 by Sir John Marshall, the first director of antiquities of British India, with E. J. H. Mackay continuing until 1931. Work has continued sporadically since the Second World War by British, American, and German teams. Struck by major floods in antiquity on at least three occasions, the city continues to face danger today. Through capillary action, the ancient brick buildings suck water from deep in the ground. The salts left behind after the water evaporates corrode the buildings. Effective protection against the rapid disintegration of Harappan architecture has yet to be found.

Although the city wall has not yet come to light, Marshall assumed Mohenjo-Daro was fortified, as has been attested at Harappa and at other, smaller sites. The wall would lie buried beneath the unexcavated alluvial deposits in the surrounding plain. The city plan consists of two main sectors, a higher part in the west, misleadingly called the "citadel" (Figure 4.2), and a lower, larger town to the east. The placement of important public buildings in the north-west, characteristic of the major Harappan sites, recalls Mesopotamian practice: one thinks of the ziggurat and temenos at Ur, sited in the north-west of that city. In contrast with Mesopotamia, however, the lower town was laid out on a rough grid plan, with straight streets crossing at right angles. The streets were oriented to the cardinal points of the compass, perhaps for religious reasons, such as to connect the city with the cosmos. In another major difference, baked brick

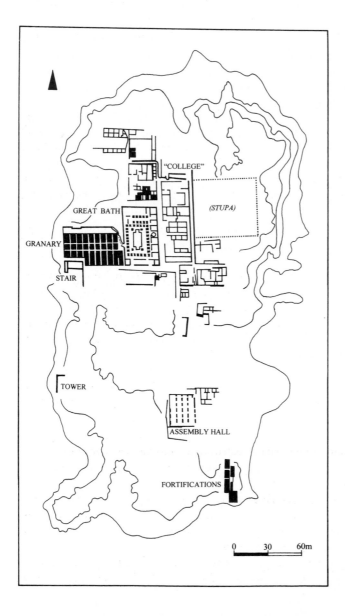

Figure 4.2 Plan, the Citadel, Mohenjo-Daro

was extensively used, with sun-dried mud bricks reserved for fill. Both baked and sun-dried bricks came in standard sizes, such as 7cm × 14cm × 28 cm. In bathrooms they might be sawn into smaller pieces, and for curved structures such as wells wedge-shaped bricks were used. This ratio of 1:2:4 for thickness to width to length was standard throughout the Harappan world. These proportions were not only used for bricks but appeared often in the design of rooms, houses, and public buildings. Similarly, stone weights, abundant at Mohenjo-Daro, conform to a uniform system of weights and measures.

Why baked bricks? It has been proposed that baked bricks were developed as protection against flooding. Whatever the reason for the initial development, baked brick became standard in another construction where its water-resistant qualities were key: lining the drains routinely installed in Harappan streets. Such networks of drains, from the latrines of private houses to side streets to large drains from the main streets, covered with bricks or dressed stone, were a common and distinctive feature of Harappan cities. Such systems of public hygiene far surpassed contemporary Mesopotamian or Egyptian efforts.

The "citadel"

The "citadel" must be a city center. Its physical setting is prominent, and it features large, imposing buildings, some most likely the sites of religious ritual or public ceremony. The citadel is built on an artificial platform, ca. 400m × 200m, made of sand and silt enclosed in a mud brick retaining wall 6m thick. It rises some 13m above the plain, and well above the rest of the city.

The exact functions of its fascinating, enigmatic buildings can only be guessed. Textual evidence is, as noted, silent. In addition, the excavators did not uncover inside these buildings objects that clearly revealed their functions. Today, excavators faced with such a situation would hope that answers might come from the modest remains, such as potsherds, animal bones, and plant remains, where their types, frequencies, and find spots have been carefully recorded, this evidence then scrutinized for instructive patterns. But this was not standard practice in the 1920s on sites with monumental architectural remains. Moreover, the plan of the "citadel" is incompletely known, because of erosion, and because of the preservation in a key position on the top of the mound of a second-century AD Buddhist stupa and monastery. Nonetheless, certain hypotheses can be advanced. Absent are any cult centers comparable to the temples that characterize Sumerian cities. Also lacking are buildings associated with secular rulers: palaces, for example, or royal tombs. What, then, was going on here?

The most striking building on the citadel is the so-called Great Bath (Figure 4.3). This complex contained in its core a large rectangular basin of baked brick, ca. 12m × 7m × 2.5m, with steps, originally timber treads set in bitumen, at both short ends. The floor of the bath was made of sawn bricks set on edge in gypsum mortar, with a layer of bitumen sealant between the inner and outer "brick skins." Water was supplied from a well in an adjacent room. An outlet from one corner of the bath led to a drain that evacuated water onto the west side of the mound.

This Great Bath lay in the open air, surrounded by a portico on all four sides. The entrance lay on the south, providing access into a long, narrow room. The entire eastern side beyond the portico consisted of small, cell-like rooms, while to the north lay an irregularly spaced set of larger rooms, including at the far north a group reached by a staircase. It is usually assumed that the Great Bath served some ritual purpose involving water, not merely hygiene or sheer pleasure, the main functions of later Roman bathing establishments.

Next to the Great Bath, on the west, was found the substructure of a building identified as a granary by Sir Mortimer Wheeler, thanks to his explorations in 1950. This substructure, whose

Figure 4.3 The Great Bath, Mohenjo-Daro

original core measured 46m × 23m before an enlargement was made on the south side, consisted of 27 solid blocks of baked bricks divided by a grid of narrow passageways, two east–west, eight (later nine) north–south. The building proper, set on these foundations, was made of wood. Traces of the sockets for holding wooden beams were discovered embedded into the brick podium. The passageways would have contributed to the aeration of the building and its contents. Wheeler's interpretation is controversial, however. The finds from the building neither support nor disprove his theory, for they were not carefully recorded at the time of the original excavations in the 1920s. All we can be certain of, then, is a large wooden building. According to Mark Kenoyer, this may well be a large hall. It does differ in design, however, from another candidate for such a function, the "Assembly Hall" located to the south (see below).

A similar building at Kalibangan in the Indian Punjab may shed light on the function of this building. Here, clear traces of ritual practice were found, evidence lacking in the "granary" of Mohenjo-Daro. In the south part of the citadel mound at Kalibangan, brick platforms were separated by narrow brick-paved passages. The surfaces of these platforms were damaged. On one platform a row of seven fire altars was discovered, as well as a rock-lined pit containing animal bones and antlers; a well head; and a drain. This area, entered by a broad flight of steps on the south, must have been a ritual center for animal sacrifice, ritual bathing, and a cult of the sacred fire. Similar fire pits have been found in a small brick-walled courtyard set apart in the lower town of Kalibangan. Because fire worship was associated with the later Indo-Aryans, some scholars have postulated their presence here, even at this early date.

Although it is tantalizing to imagine such functions for the "Granary," excavations have not yielded supporting evidence. The link between the two buildings may simply be in the common approach to monumental architecture, with solid brick foundations separated by channels – a structural basis that could be adapted for a variety of purposes.

Buildings to the north and east of the Great Bath at Mohenjo-Daro include one called the "College." Marshall attributed it to a high priest or group of priests, but there is no evidence to support such an interpretation. Its function remains unclear.

The last of the major buildings on the citadel lies in the south-east, apart from the above mentioned three. The "Assembly Hall," as it is called, originally measured 28m². Its interior was divided into equal aisles by three rows of five brick plinths, bases for wooden columns. The floor consisted of finely sawn brickwork, recalling the typical flooring of bathrooms. Large square rooms of this sort with columns or piers to hold up the roofing are found most notably in Egyptian and Achaemenid Persian architecture, and served public gatherings on the grand scale, either religious or secular. The name of the building, the Assembly Hall, was suggested by this analogy.

The lower town

The town proper lies to the east of the citadel. Streets running approximately north–south and east–west divided the large area into blocks of ca. 370m × 250m. Of perhaps 12 blocks, seven have been investigated by archaeologists. The citadel may, in fact, occupy one of the central blocks on the west side. Main streets could be as wide as 10m, while side streets were narrower, 1.5m–3.0m in width. Although unpaved, the streets were provided with covered drains of baked brick. Manholes, covered, located at periodic intervals provided access into the drains. Clay pipes and chutes allowed waste material from private houses to reach the drains in the street. What happened to the refuse when it reached the edge of the city is not known.

Private houses appear comfortable. They vary in size, from single-room houses to medium-sized (court and one dozen rooms) to big (several courts, several dozen rooms). As in Mesopotamia, the house focused on a central courtyard. Rooms surrounded it, usually arranged on two storeys. Baked brick was the standard building material for walls, an urban practice that contrasts with the mud brick typically used in towns and villages. House floors consisted either of beaten earth or brick, baked or sun-dried. Roofing materials have not survived, but we may guess they consisted of lighter timber, reeds, and clay, as elsewhere in the Near East. Cuttings, sometimes square, indicate the use of precisely cut wooden beams; such beams spanned distances as great as 4m. Although mud plaster was occasionally used to coat internal wall surfaces, the walls were never decorated with paintings.

Houses usually had their own well. Indeed, 600 wells have been found at Mohenjo-Daro. Houses were furnished also with bathrooms, generally on the ground floor. The flooring of bathrooms was lined with finely sawn bricks or, in some cases, a plaster of brick dust and lime. Smaller rooms constructed in the same technique were identified as toilets.

Throughout the city, other buildings surely sheltered a variety of functions: residential, religious, or commercial. Of particular interest are the following. First, some barrack-like groups of single-roomed tenements were found, possibly housing for the poor, or even for slaves. Second, House A1, a building in an area labelled HR, may indeed be a prominent house, or it might be a temple. It stands out, with its monumental entrance and double stairway leading to a raised platform on which was discovered a rare stone sculpture of a seated figure. Other buildings with thick walls or unusual plan have also been tentatively interpreted as temples, but the evidence is nowhere compelling. Third, shops existed throughout the lower town; potters' kilns, dyers' vats, metal works, shell-ornament makers, and a bead-maker's shop have been identified.

The architectural features seen in this major city appear throughout the vast region occupied by the Harappan civilization. The quality of the baked brick construction, the regular layout of city blocks in a rough grid plan, the extensive and well-built drainage system, and the large buildings on the "citadel" indicate a complex society fully as sophisticated as any seen in Mesopotamia and Egypt. In contrast, during the final stage of the Harappan period, Mohenjo-Daro experienced a marked deterioration in town planning and in the quality of construction.

LOTHAL

On the south-east edge of the Harappan world, in the Indian state of Gujarat, the ruins of Lothal were explored in the 1950s by S. R. Rao of the Archaeological Survey of India. Although much smaller than Mohenjo-Daro, this city displays many of the same key features of urban design and architecture. Size differences thus did not affect the basic template of the Harappan city.

Laid out on a grid plan and provided with a good system of drainage, the city originally occupied 12ha within a fortification wall (Figure 4.4). Later the town expanded beyond the wall, eventually doubling its area. Like other Harappan sites, Lothal too had its "citadel," 48.5m × 42.5m, built on an artificial platform of mud brick, ca. 4m high. But this citadel lay clearly within the town and, unusually, in the south-east sector. The citadel would have served for defense against floods, to secure storage for food, and as a showcase for the prestige of the rulers of the town. The notable building on the citadel is a mud brick structure with ventilating channels, here, Rao proposed, possibly the foundation for a warehouse.

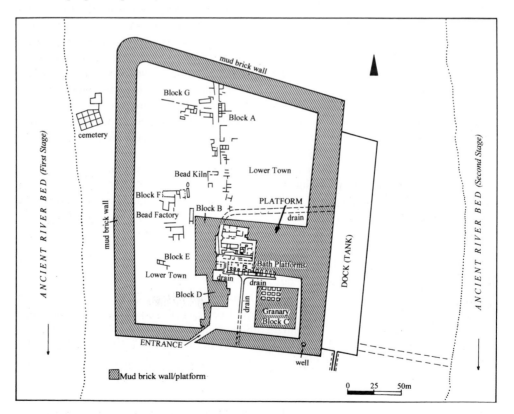

Figure 4.4 City plan, Lothal

In the town proper, the main street runs north–south. The principal streets are 4–6m wide, the lesser streets only 2–3m. Houses were built of baked brick, and were routinely provided with brick-lined drains. Workshops have been identified, among them a copper and goldsmith shop and a bead factory.

On the east side of the city mound, at the edge of the citadel, lies Lothal's most fascinating monument, a massive brick platform alongside a large rectangular enclosure, ca. 225m × 37m × 4.5m, lined with baked brick. The enclosure had a sluice gate at one of the short ends. Heavy pierced stones, perhaps ancient anchors, were found on its edge. The excavator considered this structure a dock for ships sailing up the river from the Indian Ocean. Lothal lies ca. 20km from the sea, near a tributary of the Sabarmati River. Channels or estuaries would have provided a connection with the river. If this is interpretation is correct, Lothal has given us an unusually early and sophisticated port installation from western Asia. A more recent analysis, however, has proposed this to be a vast storage tank for fresh water in this low-lying region where the modern water resources, at least, are saline. The issue is not yet settled.

AGRICULTURE, TECHNOLOGY, CRAFTS, AND ARTS

The well-being of Harappan cities depended on successful agriculture. In addition, urban life was enriched by a variety of crafts, no doubt the work of specialists. Agriculture prospered through the natural flooding of the river. Evidence is lacking for irrigation, since alluvial deposits have covered any traces of irrigation systems. Among the crops grown, wheat, barley, and millet were staple cereals. Rice may have been grown in the south-east sector on the Indian coast. Mohenjo-Daro and Lothal have yielded cotton cloth, rare evidence for early cultivation of this plant that would continue to be so important for textiles of the subcontinent. Animals raised featured two varieties of domesticated cattle, one humped (see Figure 4.5), the other humpless. Other animals exploited included water buffalo, donkeys, and elephants.

The best-known surviving craft is the stamp seal, usually made of steatite. About 2,000 examples have been discovered. Most are square with a perforated boss on the back for the

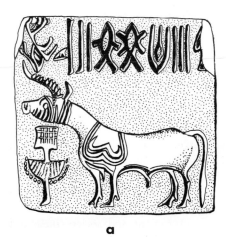
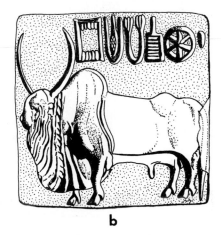

a   b

Figure 4.5 Stamp seals, with (a) unicorn, and (b) humped bull, both from Mohenjo-Daro. National Museum, Karachi (a); and Islamabad Museum (b)

attachment of a cord. Round stamp seals and cylinder seals are rare. After the piece of stone was cut with a saw, designs were carved with a small chisel and a drill. A coating of alkali was applied to the entire surface, then heated to produce a luster. Animals were the favored subject. The repertoire focused on animals of daily life, often shown posed in front of a standard, a manger, or an incense burner, but imaginary composite creatures sometimes appeared (Figure 4.5). Most seals were inscribed. At Lothal, several clay sealings with impressions of cord or matting on the rear were found among the ashes in the ventilation shafts of the brick platforms of the "granary" or "warehouse." This find spot suggests that these seals had a commercial function.

Such stamp seals as well as etched carnelian beads, bone inlays, and other small objects have been found at Mesopotamian towns dating from ED III through the Larsa period (2600–1750 BC). Indeed, Harappan traders set up a small colony at Tell Asmar, where their houses stand out because of the fine bathrooms, toilets, and drains. In contrast, Mesopotamian objects are exceedingly rare at Harappan sites. Imports from Mesopotamia and south-west Iran (Susa) must have consisted of raw materials or perishable products, foodstuffs and textiles, transported principally by entrepreneurs by boat through the Persian Gulf. Evidence for an overland route is meager.

Metallurgy was practiced, copper and bronze for tools, with gold used for jewelry. Pottery, a development of the Neolithic period, continued to be produced, now including examples painted with motifs both decorative and, it seems, religious. Textiles may have been a focus for Harappan creativity, although evidence for textile production is scanty. A well-documented craft of Harappan cities is bead-making, thanks to finds of workshops with materials, tools, and beads in different stages of completion. In addition to the above mentioned products, terracotta figurines of birds, animals, and humans are frequent. An elaborately dressed and adorned female, well represented among these figurines, might be a goddess. Sculpture in stone and metal was rare and tended to be small in scale. Most examples of stone sculpture were cult images destined for temples, it is thought. A bronze statuette of a dancing girl from Mohenjo-Daro must have filled some quite different purpose (Figure 4.6). About 11.5cm high and cast in the lost-wax method (see p. 233), she came not from a temple, but from a private house. Clad only in a necklace, an elegant hairdo, and a mass of bracelets, this woman delights us with her jaunty pose and cool, confident expression. This kind of image is unusual in the art of south-west Asia, in which stiff formality is much preferred.

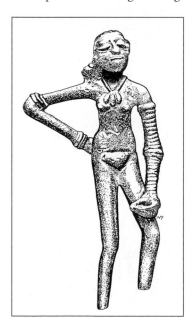

Figure 4.6 Dancing girl, bronze figurine, from Mohenjo-Daro. National Museum, New Delhi

Lacking in Harappan representational art are clearly identifiable images of rulers. Also absent are depictions of warfare. Both subjects are staples of Mesopotamian art, as we have seen. Among the many Bronze Age civilizations of the eastern Mediterranean, Egypt, and the Near East, only Minoan Crete (see Chapter 7) similarly excludes both rulers and warfare from its arts. One must wonder what elements of government and society these two otherwise very different cultures might have had in common that would result in such a distinctive approach to the subjects deemed appropriate for pictorial art.

THE END OF THE HARAPPAN CITIES

The Harappan Phase of the Indus Valley Civilization came to an end some time at the beginning of the second millennium BC. The unified urban civilization dissolved into local village-based cultures lacking the technological and architectural competence of their predecessors. The breakdown was gradual, the result of many factors. Some elements can be spotted. Environmental changes weakened the economy, such as flooding, deforestation, and overgrazing, and the drying up of the Saraswati River. Other factors elude us, such as possible political and religious changes. Early in the modern study of Harappan civilization, invasions had been proposed as an agent of change. Speakers of Indo-European languages, the writers of the Rig-Veda and the ancestors of most of the inhabitants of the northern half of India today were thought to have entered the subcontinent at this time. But traces of invasion are few on Harappan sites. A suitable group of skeletons scattered in the latest habitation of Mohenjo-Daro may show the eruption of violence, but this has yet to be matched at other sites. Outright invasion is thus rejected now as an explanation of the dissolution of the urban culture of the Harappans. Future excavations will surely continue to shed light on what must have been a complex series of events.

CHAPTER 5

Egypt of the pyramids

Predynastic: ca. 5000–3050 BC

Early Dynastic (Archaic): ca. 3050–2675 BC

    First and Second Dynasties

Old Kingdom: ca. 2675–2190 BC

    Third, Fourth, Fifth, and Sixth Dynasties

First Intermediate period: ca. 2190–2060 BC

    Seventh to Tenth Dynasties and earlier Eleventh Dynasty

The civilization of ancient Egypt, the third of the three great river-based cultures of West Asia and the east Mediterranean basin, stands in brilliant contrast to both Mesopotamia and the Indus Valley. The Egyptian remains seem so abundant, so well preserved, so awesome: pyramids, gold coffins, inscriptions meticulously chiselled in stone. In contrast, Mesopotamian remains can seem drab and fragmentary, the Harappan curiously limited. This state of affairs represents an accident of survival. The Egyptians lavished attention and material resources on religion and death. Temples and tombs were either built or carved from stone and, thanks to remote locations or the protective covering of sand, these stone structures have survived remarkably well.

    The impression such monuments give is that ancient Egypt was a civilization without cities. The reality was different. The Egyptians had cities, but archaeologists have generally ignored them because their remains are difficult to trace. For civic buildings, houses, and even palaces, sun-dried mud bricks were the preferred building material – much less resistant than the stone of the temples and tombs. Compounding the archaeological problem, towns were situated alongside the Nile and so have been buried deep under the mud left by the annual flooding of the river, and in some cases covered by habitation continuing to the present day. When excavators have not shied from the practical difficulties, their results not only confirm that the Egyptians had cities, but also make clear that cities played a key role in the perpetuation of Egyptian culture.

    Because of this distinctive case of material survival, this chapter and the next will concentrate less on the remains of cities than on other sorts of experiences an Egyptian city or town dweller would have encountered during his or her lifetime. Aspects of Egyptian life that we shall explore include the power of the ruler as conveyed through art and architecture; rituals and religious architecture; burial practices, tombs, and funerary monuments; warfare, weaponry, and fortresses; and geography, economy, and trade. But cities will not be ignored, with Kahun, Amarna, and greater Thebes examined in Chapter 6.

GEOGRAPHY

The borders of modern Egypt trace a large area, but most of it consists of desert. Only a small portion can sustain human life: the fertile strips alongside the Nile and a handful of oases in the western desert.

The Nile runs northward from two main sources, Lake Victoria in central Africa and Lake Tana in Ethiopia. The White Nile and the Blue Nile, as these two branches are called, join at Khartoum, the capital of the Sudan, and continue another ca. 3,000km until emptying into the Mediterranean Sea. At six places between Khartoum and Aswan the smooth course of the water is obstructed by granite rock formations known as "cataracts" that render navigation difficult. These cataracts are numbered from north to south, in reverse order to the direction of the river's flow. The First Cataract, located at Aswan some 950km south of the Mediterranean, marked the southern boundary of ancient Egypt.

For much of its course northward from Aswan, the Nile flows through a narrow channel formed first in granite (at Aswan), then sandstone (from Aswan to Edfu), and finally limestone (from Edfu to Cairo) (see Figure 5.1). Just north of Cairo, the Nile enters a flat coastal plain and, as it makes its way to the Mediterranean, fans out over an area shaped like an inverted triangle – the inverted form of the Greek letter "delta," as the ancient Greeks observed. The long, narrow stretch from Aswan to Cairo and the short, broad delta marked two distinct regions in ancient Egypt: Upper Egypt, the former (called "upper" because it lies upstream), and Lower Egypt, the delta. Unification of the two regions (in ca. 3050 BC) marked the beginning of Egyptian history, but during times of governmental crisis the two areas would typically split apart.

Because Egypt has little rainfall, the fertility of the land has depended on the Nile and especially, until the construction of the Aswan Dam (built in 1960–71) blocked the natural flow of the river, on its annual flood. Swelling from spring rains in central Africa and the Ethiopian highlands, the river becomes rich with silt washed from the hills. Gradually this surfeit of water and silt travels northward, reaching Egypt a few months later. Egypt saw the Nile at its lowest in May, but then the river would rise until mid-August when it spilled over its banks into the adjacent fields. For two months the land lay buried beneath the floodwaters. Then in October the river receded, flushing away noxious salts and leaving behind a new layer of rich, fertile soil. Farmers repaired their system of dikes and began the chores of planting. A 6m–9m rising of the river was reckoned beneficial. A higher or lower rising could seriously disrupt the agricultural system, causing famine in the worst instances. Small wonder that the Egyptians worshipped the flood as a god, Hapy – a man, but supplied with pendant breasts, attributes of fertility. The Aswan Dam now keeps the waters at predictable levels, but the nourishing silt no longer comes. Artificial fertilizers must be used, and damaging salts have built up in the soil.

EARLY HISTORY

Egyptian history proper, dynastic Egypt, begins with the unification of the country ca. 3050 BC. In chronological terms, this corresponds to the transition from the Neolithic to the Bronze Age. Following this event, Egypt was ruled for nearly 3,000 years by a sequence of thirty dynasties, or ruling families (see the Introduction). These dynasties have been grouped by historians into periods of strength and weakness. The three great periods of cultural achievement, marked by a strong central government, are known as the Archaic period and the Old Kingdom, the Middle Kingdom, and the New Kingdom. Each was followed by a period of weakness in which the

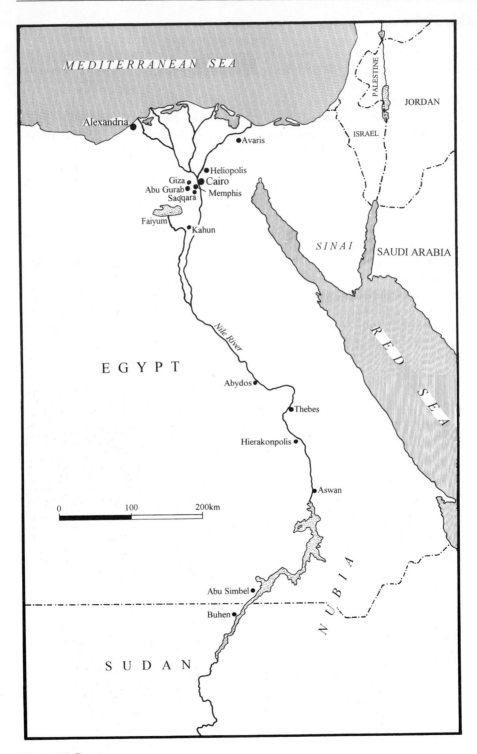

Figure 5.1 Egypt

central government disintegrated, with regional rulers wielding power: the First, Second, and Third Intermediate periods. The Late period, which followed the Third Intermediate period, comprises the final centuries of independent Egypt before the conquests of the Persians, Greeks, and Romans.

According to Manetho, the important ancient chronicler of Egyptian history, the unification of Upper and Lower Egypt ca. 3050 BC was accomplished by Menes. The name "Menes" is not attested on remains or documents of the period, however. Instead, those objects indicate a king Narmer as the great conqueror, but it may be that Menes and Narmer are in fact the same person. In any case, Manetho may have simplified events. Mounting evidence suggests that political and cultural unification did not occur suddenly, but developed over 100–200 years, with the south gradually imposing its control over the north. The recently coined term "Dynasty 0" is used by some to denote this period of transition.

The Narmer Palette

Striking evidence for Narmer and the unification of Egypt comes from the Narmer Palette (Figure 5.2). Slate palettes were flat slabs much used in Predynastic Egypt for the grinding of minerals for cosmetics. Although most were small, some, like the Narmer Palette (63cm high), were large ritual objects, elaborately decorated with relief carving. Found in 1898 during the excavations of J. E. Quibell in the Temple of Horus at Hierakonpolis, the Predynastic capital of Upper Egypt, the Narmer Palette was evidently a votive gift to the temple.

Figure 5.2 Narmer Palette: obverse, cross-section, and reverse. Slate palette, from Hierakonpolis. Egyptian Museum, Cairo

The scenes carved in relief on both sides of this palette represent a remarkable pictorial expression of contemporary events that is rare for its time. They illustrate the victory of Narmer: the conquest of northern Lower Egypt by southern Upper Egypt. Narmer is named in a glyph denoting the king on both sides of the palette, on the top between images of the sky goddess shown as a cow. On one side, the king dominates the scene. Wearing the conical white crown of Upper Egypt, his native region, and accompanied by his sandal bearer, the king grabs an enemy by the hair and prepares to strike him with his mace. The king is depicted with face and legs in profile, eye and torso frontal. This method of showing the human body would remain standard through the many centuries of Egyptian civilization even into the Roman period. To the right of the king, a falcon, representing the sky-god Horus, holds by a cord the curious figure of a man with papyrus leaves sprouting from his body. Horus, the alter ego of the pharaoh, has captured Lower Egypt, personified here by the papyrus man. In a smaller zone at the bottom of the palette, humiliatingly placed below the king's feet, two naked captives are shown as if floating, stripped of the dignity of clothing and the security of firm ground.

The other side is divided into three zones. In the uppermost, the pharaoh inspects the beheaded bodies of the defeated. The artist indicates his kingly status by showing him towering above his attendants. To complement the royal headgear on the other side, the king here wears the red crown of Lower Egypt, the land he has conquered. In the second zone, two long-necked monsters are secured by a rope in the hands of an attendant; the monsters may represent larger, cosmic forces of chaos, now subdued by the king. At the bottom, a bull, another symbol for the king, tramples a naked enemy. Beyond them lies a walled town, an example of the Lower Egyptian settlements captured by Narmer and his forces.

The glyphs for the king's name and the pictographic nature of some images on the palette remind us that writing began in Egypt in the century or two before Narmer's unification of Upper and Lower Egypt. Egyptian writing, in use for over 3,000 years, is one of the fascinating achievements of this culture.

EGYPTIAN WRITING

The language of the ancient Egyptians belongs to the Hamito-Semitic language family at home in south-west Asia and north Africa. The idea of writing arose in Egypt at approximately the same time as it did in Mesopotamia, and marks a certain stage in the development of the state reached in both regions. Although we can now understand Egyptian scripts, we do not know how words were pronounced.

The Egyptians wrote in three scripts. *Hieroglyphs*, or "holy writing," the picture signs, were used from ca. 3050 BC to 394 AD. They could be written in lines or columns from either left to right or right to left, and were reversible according to the direction in which they were read. The second script is *hieratic*, used from Dynasty I well into the Late period. Written from right to left only, hieratic was a cursive version of hieroglyphs, adapted in particular for writing with a reed brush in ink on papyrus (Egyptian paper, made from the fibrous interior of the papyrus reed) or on *ostraka* (potsherds or limestone flakes). The third script was *demotic*, a Late Egyptian cursive script used especially for secular documents. Eventually, in the late third century AD, the much-evolved Egyptian language was written in an adapted Greek alphabet. The language and this new script are called Coptic. Spoken into the sixteenth century AD, Coptic is still the liturgical language of the Christian Coptic church in Egypt.

The hieroglyphic script consists of approximately 700 signs. These signs can be phonograms (conveying sounds) representing one, two, or three consonants; ideograms (an image of the object or idea); and determinatives (showing the class to which a word belongs). Words often consisted of a combination of phonograms followed by an ideogram and a determinative. Although the system may seem awkward, as a monumental script used for visual effect it has had few rivals in the history of writing.

The decipherment of the hieroglyphic script was made possible by the Rosetta Stone, a bilingual inscription discovered in 1799 by French soldiers near the town of Rosetta (Rashid) in the Nile Delta. The inscription, a decree of the Hellenistic king Ptolemy V Epiphanes issued in 196 BC, is actually written in three scripts, two Egyptian (with different forms of the Egyptian language) – hieroglyphs (top) and demotic (middle) – and the third Greek (bottom). Comparison of the Greek with the Egyptian texts allowed rapid advances in the understanding of the Egyptian scripts. The comprehensive breakthrough, announced in 1822, was made by Jean-François Champollion. Champollion had mastered Coptic en route, believing (correctly) that it held a key to the long-forgotten ancient language.

BURIALS OF THE ARCHAIC PERIOD

The first two dynasties are often labeled the Early Dynastic or Archaic period. Although this period is poorly known, it seems that the main features of Egyptian civilization were established then: not only the conventions of drawing the human body and hieroglyphic writing, but also the organization of the state, religious and funerary beliefs, and art and architectural forms. Our assessment of these important developments depends heavily on the monumental tomb complexes that have survived so well. Written documents are short, and the towns, such as Memphis, the early capital, buried in Nile silt or under modern occupation, are difficult to investigate. Since the tomb complexes were erected in the desert beyond the zone of cultivation, they have been much more accessible to archaeologists. Abydos and Saqqara contain the key cemeteries of the period.

The dry climate of Egypt, because it preserves organic materials – including the human body – surely influenced Egyptian notions of the afterlife. The Egyptians believed that life continued after death with little change. The body was resurrected, and the deceased led the same sort of life he or she did before: the same family members, village, and socio-economic conditions. But this afterlife did not materialize automatically. Burial procedures and rites had to be performed correctly and, at least from the Fifth Dynasty on, Osiris, the god of the underworld, had to give his approval. The wrapping of the body, the selection of objects placed in the grave, and the decoration of the tomb were carefully done to ensure that the deceased reached the afterlife and flourished there. Thieves could disrupt this well-planned journey, however. In consequence, the long history of tomb design in ancient Egypt was the never-ending search for the perfect protection for the body and accompanying materials.

Embalmment and mummification

In Predynastic Egypt, a body buried in a simple pit would be well preserved by the hot, desiccating sand. As tomb structures became more complex, the body was placed in shafts or chambers well removed from that beneficial sand. Despite advances in tomb design, the body decomposed rapidly. Eventually the Egyptians became aware of the consequences and, to counter them, developed elaborate procedures of mummification, that is, embalmment and wrapping of the body. The term comes from the Arabic word "mumiya," meaning bitumen, a tar in which, it was mistakenly thought, the blackened, poorly embalmed bodies from the late periods had been dipped.

The earliest known evidence of classic or standard mummification is from the tomb at Giza of queen Hetep-heres, the mother of Khufu, the important king of the Fourth Dynasty. Although her body was not found, a *Canopic chest* containing four of her organs proved that the standard process of embalmment was already being performed. The most skillful mummifications come from the New Kingdom. Although classic techniques faded in the Hellenistic period, the practice continued, with different degrees of elaboration (depending on how much one could afford), into the early Christian period.

The organs were removed (except for the heart, the spiritual sentinel, which remained in the body in order to testify at the moment of Judgment), since they putrified first. Four key organs were given special treatment: the stomach, the intestines, the lungs, and the liver, but not, interestingly, the brain, which was apparently discarded. They were washed, packed and dried in natron (a naturally occurring salt), painted with resins, wrapped in separate bundles, and packed in four *Canopic jars*, and placed in the tomb. Each was protected by a special divinity.

The body was dried in natron. After a certain period, at least forty days, the natron was removed and the body was prepared for burial by packing with stuffing to restore its original shape. Finally it was tightly wrapped with linen strips to safeguard that shape, with amulets interspersed in the wrapping.

Mastaba tombs at Abydos and Saqqara

In Predynastic times, burials were simple, with bodies placed in flexed position in shallow rectangular pits. Simple grave gifts might be added, such as a few pots, figurines, tools, and ornaments. In the Archaic period, practices became more elaborate. The body was wrapped in

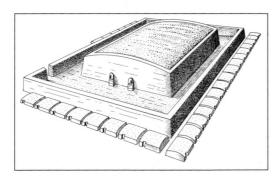

Figure 5.3 Mastaba tomb of queen Merneith (reconstruction), Abydos

linen and placed with grave goods in a pit sunk 3m–4m into the ground. This burial spot and any adjacent rooms were covered and protected first by a low mound of earth, and then by a *mastaba*, a low, flat, rectangular structure made of mud brick, a series of compartments covered by a single roof (Figures 5.3 and 5.4). The façades were decorated to resemble a house, with the grandest showing the same sort of indented façades believed to have been featured on the palace at Memphis, the capital city. Such indented façades were standard in the mud brick architecture of Mesopotamia and, together with the use of cylinder seals and the idea of writing, indicate the high level of Near Eastern contact in this formative period of Egyptian civilization.

Mastaba tombs beginning with that of king Aha (First Dynasty; Narmer's successor) at Abydos were surrounded by simple graves for servants and craftsmen buried with the tools of their particular trades (Figures 5.5 and 5.6). Thirty-four such tombs accompanied Aha's burial; they belonged to seemingly healthy young men, none older than twenty-five, plus a pair of lions. The men may have been dispatched to accompany their master in the afterlife; their presence

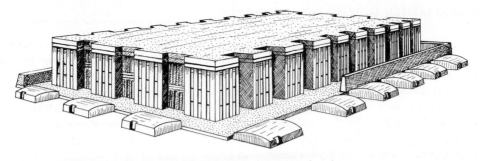

Figure 5.4 Mastaba tomb of queen Merneith (reconstruction), Saqqara

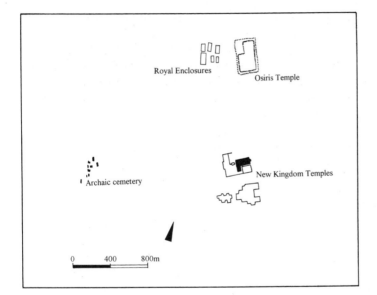

Royal Enclosures

Osiris Temple

Archaic cemetery

New Kingdom Temples

0   400   800m

Figure 5.5 Overall site plan, Abydos

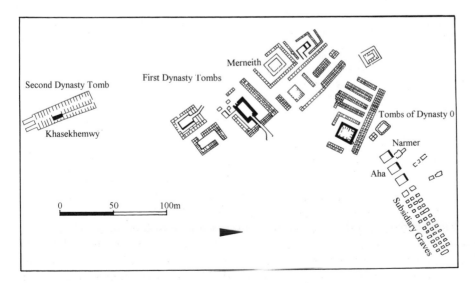

Second Dynasty Tomb

Khasekhemwy

First Dynasty Tombs

Merneith

Tombs of Dynasty 0

Narmer

Aha

Subsidiary Graves

0   50   100m

Figure 5.6 Plan, the Archaic cemetery, Abydos

recalls the array of sacrificed servants in the Royal Cemetery at Ur. This practice did not continue beyond the Archaic period. A good supply of servants was eventually assured by the placing in tombs of such stand-ins as figures painted or sculpted on tomb walls (beginning in the Fourth Dynasty); small-scale models of activities from daily life (farming; preparation of food and drink; etc.), from the First Intermediate period on; and *shabtis* (mummiform statuettes), starting in the Middle Kingdom. All these images were given life through the texts written on the walls and the magic of ritual.

The Archaic cemetery at Abydos contains an important feature absent at Saqqara: funerary enclosures. The enclosures may represent palace courtyards, impressive locations for ceremonial appearances of the kings (Figure 5.7). A few kilometers separate them from the tombs; they lie closer to the cultivation zone, more accessible for the living. Their walls have indented "palace-façade" decoration, like the mastabas. Inside they are largely empty space; but the best-preserved enclosure, the "Shunet ez-Zebib," that of the late Second Dynasty king Khasekhemwy, contained a small building in one corner; a low mound in the center; and, outside the eastern wall, twelve wooden boats (19–29m in length) buried in pits. The presence of the enclosures and the buried boats in the first two dynasties is significant, for both will reappear dramatically in the great tombs of the succeeding Third and Fourth Dynasties (see below).

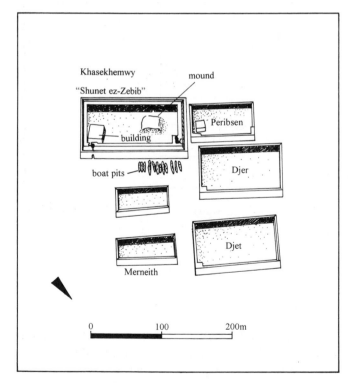

Figure 5.7 Royal funerary enclosures, Abydos

The identity of those buried in the Early Dynastic mastaba tombs at Abydos and Saqqara has been uncertain and much argued. Which belonged to the kings? The combination of mastaba tomb and funerary enclosure makes it probable that Abydos, not Saqqara, was the location for most First and several Second Dynasty royal burials. Also favoring Abydos is apparent continuity in burials of distinguished individuals from the later Predynastic Period, and the greater number of subsidiary graves of retainers. In this view the Saqqara mastabas would belong to high officials, or might represent northern cenotaphs of the rulers buried at Abydos. The question remains controversial, however, for the mastaba tombs at Saqqara were larger, grander than those at Abydos, even if without enclosures, and the capital city, Memphis, lay conveniently nearby.

SAQQARA: THE STEP PYRAMID

The cultural transition from the Archaic period to the Old Kingdom was smooth. The Old Kingdom consists of Dynasties III–VI, spanning nearly 500 years from ca. 2675 to 2190 BC. Saqqara, to the west of Memphis, became the prime burial site of the Old Kingdom. Other sites in the region were also used for cemeteries, but none had the lasting appeal of Saqqara. The grandest tomb at Saqqara, and one of the key buildings of all Egyptian architecture, is the Step Pyramid, built for the pharaoh Djoser (or Zoser) of the Third Dynasty, ca. 2650 BC (Figures 5.8 and 5.9).

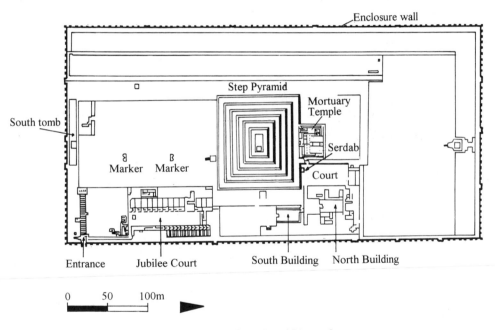

Figure 5.8 Plan, the Step Pyramid and Funerary Complex of Djoser, Saqqara

The Step Pyramid shows bold innovations in both form and building technique. Its form marks a transition for royal burials from the earlier mastaba tombs to the smooth-sided pyramids of the Fourth Dynasty and later. In construction technique, it is equally important. Instead of sun-dried mud bricks, stone is the building material. As far as we know, such use of stone has no precedent. Stone was used earlier for details, but never for an entire building. Because the Egyptians themselves so admired this complex, the name of the architect was remembered through the centuries: Imhotep. Later Egyptians revered Imhotep as the architect and wise counsellor of the pharaoh Djoser and as a physician. In the Late period he was deified; during the Greco-Roman era he was identified with the Greek god of healing, Asklepios.

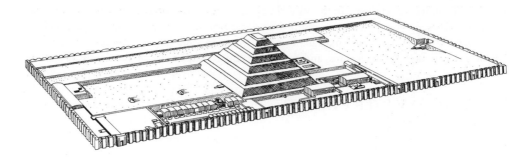

Figure 5.9 The Step Pyramid and Funerary Complex of Djoser (reconstruction), Saqqara

The funerary complex of Djoser developed the burial practices and tomb forms of the Archaic period on a grand scale. The large area of 15ha, a rectangle oriented north–south, was enclosed by a wall, 545m × 278m, made of small stones and decorated with "palace-façade" indentations familiar from mud brick architecture and from the funerary enclosures at Abydos. Like many elements of the complex, the wall has been restored in modern times. The walls have fourteen apparent entrances, but only one is real, the south-east entrance. Dummy doors carved in open position lead into a colonnade lined with twenty pairs of columns, each attached to the side wall and carved with convex fascicles to resemble thick bunches of reeds. The ceilings originally resembled palm logs. Such details throughout the complex make clear an important source for Imhotep's creation, for they are all translations into stone of traditional architecture in less durable materials: mud brick, wood, and reeds.

The colonnade eventually leads to a large court, bordered on the north by the Step Pyramid that overlies the king's burial, and on the south by a walled court that contains an underground cenotaph, or dummy tomb, a simpler version of the northern burial. Such duplication of features is one of the interesting aspects of the complex, perhaps reflecting the celebration of certain kingly rituals such as funerals in both Upper Egypt (at Abydos) and Lower Egypt (here at Saqqara), as homage to the two regions perhaps still imperfectly welded into a single state. Now, with two sets of buildings, the rites could be conveniently celebrated in this single location. The large court contained two B-shaped markers, evidently used for a ceremonial race run by the king during the important rite of rejuvenation, the *sed*-festival. The presence of sed-festival paraphernalia in this funerary complex indicates that these ceremonies would be performed in the afterlife as well. Related rituals also took place in the smaller Jubilee Court to the east, a long, narrow space lined by dummy shrines housing statues of the gods that represented the nomes, or provinces, of Upper and Lower Egypt.

North of the Jubilee Court lie two additional complexes of courts and buildings, possibly representing administration buildings for Upper and Lower Egypt. Architectural details include columns with fluting (vertical concave channeling), an early occurrence of a feature seen in later Egyptian and Greek architecture. Just inside the doorway of the South Building, graffiti, in hieratic script, record the visit of New Kingdom tourists from Thebes some 1,000 years later.

The Step Pyramid itself dominates the entire complex. First conceived as a mastaba on a square plan, the structure ended as a pyramid of six tall, unequal steps, rising to a height of 60m. The stages of construction have been clarified by the limestone casings, the fine stonework used as exterior surfaces for rubble cores, found at various points within the pyramid. The final

Figure 5.10 Djoser, seated statue, from Saqqara. Egyptian Museum, Cairo

version was originally encased in Tura limestone, the high-quality limestone from nearby quarries on the east bank of the Nile. The burial chamber, a granite-lined room measuring 2.96m × 1.65m × 1.65m, lay below the pyramid at the bottom of a shaft 28m deep, in the middle of a large complex of corridors and rooms perhaps intended as an underground version of the royal palace (Figure 5.13). Despite the depth of the burial and the protection of the labyrinthine corridors, the grave was robbed, probably in the First Intermediate period.

North of the pyramid the ruins of the mortuary temples overlie the entrance to the corridor leading to the burial chambers. In these temples rituals were performed for the king, to benefit his spirit in the next life. Pyramids were generally entered from the north, an auspicious direction because of the presence there of the circumpolar stars that the king would want to join, and because the rising of Sothis, the Dog Star, in the northern sky on 19–20 July signalled the imminent arrival of the annual Nile flood and the revitalization of farmlands.

The visitor with sharp eyes will note a tiny chamber about the size of a telephone booth tilting backward against the lowest of the six sloping steps on the north-east side of the pyramid. The front wall is pierced by two small holes at eye level; otherwise, there is no access. This chamber is the *serdab*. Inside was found a seated statue of Djoser (Figure 5.10), the original now replaced by a copy.

The statue had a precise religious function. It was intended as the residence of the *ka*, one of the various souls with which, according to ancient Egyptian belief, each mortal was born. The ka was a person's double, or "self," the life force animating the body; but, when the person died, the *ka* survived. It was free to move about, but needed a home base. The corpse of the deceased, preserved by careful wrapping and later by mummification, was best, but statues could serve perfectly well if they bore written identification and were properly activated by such rites as the Opening of the Mouth (see below). The two holes in the north wall of this serdab allowed contact between the living and the dead, and permitted the statue to enjoy such pleasures as the smell of incense that might seep in.

The statue of Djoser, 1.42m in height, of painted limestone, displays certain standard features of pose and costume that will continue for centuries. The king, identified by his name carved on the base, sits stiffly, his feet together, on a chair with a low back. He wears the cloak of the sed-festival, but the thin cloth reveals his body beneath. He also wears a royal wig and headdress, and a long false beard, another symbol of kingship. His downturned mouth and his mutilated eyes, once inlaid in separate materials, give him a grim look. Because the full mouth also occurs on depictions of Djoser in relief sculpture, the image we see here must to some degree reflect the actual appearance of this king.

TRANSITION TO THE TRUE PYRAMID

The purpose of the pyramid form is uncertain. Perhaps the pyramid represented the first land that emerged from the waters, or a staircase to heaven, following indications in the Pyramid Texts (ritual texts inscribed on the interior walls of pyramids beginning in the Fifth Dynasty), or a solar symbol – or indeed all the above. Whatever its meaning, the form developed smoothly from previous funerary architecture, from the mound heaped over early burials, to the mastaba that encased a mound, to Djoser's Step Pyramid, an elaboration enclosing a mastaba and rising from it. Other step pyramids are known from the Third Dynasty, but none has survived as well as Djoser's. The change to the true pyramid, that is, a pyramid with smooth sides, took place at the end of the Third and the beginning of the Fourth Dynasties. Built to shelter royal tombs throughout the Old Kingdom, pyramids continued into the Middle Kingdom, with the last major pyramids erected in the Thirteenth Dynasty at Mazghuna and Saqqara. But thieves always managed to penetrate the pyramids and rob the burials. Because they failed in their prime mission, the protection for the afterlife of the king's body and belongings, during the New Kingdom pyramids disappeared, replaced by tombs secretly cut out of the rock in remote locations on the west bank at Thebes. Yet despite the precautions, virtually all these tombs, too, were robbed. After the New Kingdom, the placement of royal burials changed again. Such tombs were now located not in remote desert valleys but in the precincts of urban temples.

GIZA: A FOURTH-DYNASTY FUNERARY COMPLEX

During the Fourth Dynasty, major royal tombs were constructed just north of Saqqara at Giza – still close to the ancient capital, Memphis. Because of its three monumental pyramids and the Great Sphinx, and its convenient location on the western outskirts of Cairo, Giza has long been a prime destination for tourists (Figure 5.11).

The great pyramids

Three of the six kings of the Fourth Dynasty were buried here, Khufu, Khafre, and Menkaure (ca. 2575–2500 BC). In addition to the great pyramids that mark their burials, Giza contains smaller pyramids for queens, temples devoted to the funerary cults, and a large number of mastaba tombs, set out in rows, belonging to high officials and their families (Figure 5.12). The size of the pyramids and the proximity of the mastaba tombs indicate the great prestige and power of the pharaohs in this period. With their walls decorated with scenes of daily life, carved in low-relief sculptures and painted bright colors, these tombs have given important information about Old Kingdom society. Also discovered at Giza are remains of the villages housing pyramid builders and those who later maintained the area and serviced the cult needs of the many shrines.

Since little is known of the history of these rulers, these grandiose funerary monuments have generated much speculation about the socio-economic conditions that promoted their construction. The building methods themselves are still debated. It has been proposed, for

Figure 5.11 The Great Sphinx and the Pyramids of Menkaure (left) and Khafre (right), Giza

example, that a step pyramid was erected first, with the steps later filled and the entire structure faced with good quality stone. Such hypotheses are difficult to test, however, for no one is about to disassemble these famous, well-preserved monuments to see how the inner blocks were laid.

Despite these difficulties, certain details of construction seem clear. After the rocky ground was levelled, a limestone platform was constructed, the base for the pyramid. When the pyramid was finished, it was enclosed by a low wall. The long sides were oriented to the cardinal points, with the main entrance on the north. The interior was made of local limestone, the visible exterior of high-quality limestone from Tura. Later pyramids might have cores of different materials, rubble or even mud brick.

The largest pyramid at Giza, that of Khufu, originally measured ca. 230m × 230m × 146.6m, but due to some loss of the outer casing blocks it now measures 227m × 227m × 137m. The four sides rise at an angle of 51.5 degrees. It has been estimated that some 2,300,000 blocks were used, at an average weight of 2.5 tons each, with some weighing as much as 15 tons. The construction probably continued throughout the entire 23 years of Khufu's reign, with most of the work undertaken in the late summer and fall during the season of the Nile flood when farmers were free to work on the building project. Shipped to harbors adjacent to the pyramid site, the blocks were then dragged into place up earth ramps built around the ever rising building. Herodotus, the ancient Greek historian writing 2,000 years after the construction of these pyramids, stated that the work force consisted of 100,000 men. Modern specialists find this figure improbably high; 4,000 men at a time seems more credible, with additional workers performing supporting tasks, such as maintaining equipment and providing food and water.

The second pyramid, that of Khafre, Khufu's son, is somewhat smaller, originally ca. 215m × 215m × 143.5m, but it stands on higher ground than Khufu's pyramid and its sides rise at a

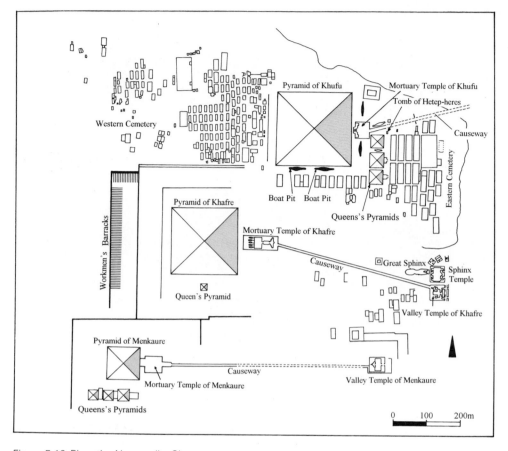

Figure 5.12 Plan, the Necropolis, Giza

slightly steeper angle. A good portion of the limestone casing survives near the top; this gives some idea of the original finish of the entire monument.

The third of the three main pyramids was erected for Khafre's brother, Menkaure. It is considerably smaller than the other two, originally 108m × 108m × 66.5m. Casing, in granite, was provided only for the lowest 16 courses.

The arrangement of chambers inside these pyramids is complex (Figure 5.13). Khufu's pyramid has three principal chambers, thought to be the result of changing plans, not an attempt to confuse would-be thieves. The first chamber was cut into the bedrock, below the lowest course of the pyramid, and was reached by a descending passage. A second, unfinished chamber, erroneously called the "Queen's Chamber," lies in the lower part of the pyramid proper, and is reached from a corridor that ascends from the entrance on the north side of the pyramid. The actual burial chamber is located higher up in the pyramid. It is larger (10.8m × 5.2m × 5.8m) and lined with red granite slabs. Access to this is gained by the Grand Gallery, a dramatic sloping corridor 47m long and 8.5m high, with a corbelled ceiling. The horizontal passage between the end of the Grand Gallery and the burial chamber was blocked by three granite plugs, dropped into place like portcullises, guided by slots in the side walls. These efforts to protect the burial were in vain. All three pyramids were robbed long ago, probably in the First Intermediate Period.

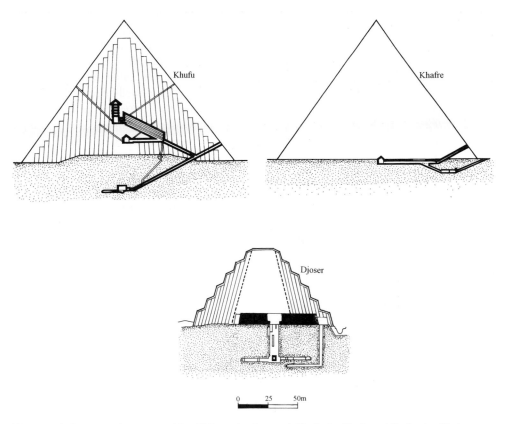

Figure 5.13 Cross-sections, pyramids of Djoser (at Saqqara), Khufu (at Giza), and Khafre (at Giza)

In Khufu's burial chamber the only surviving remnant of what must have been a lavish collection of grave goods was the lidless outer sarcophagus of red Aswan granite.

Along the east and south sides of the Pyramid of Khufu and to the north and south of the Mortuary Temple of Khafre are several long, deep lenticular (lens-shaped) pits. Most have been found empty, but one, on the south side of Khufu's pyramid, still contained in 1954 a cedar boat, 43m long, partly dismantled, with a second boat appearing in the 1980s – a monumentalization of the smaller boats discovered interred outside the funerary enclosure of Khasekhemwy at Abydos. Such boats may have been used in the funeral procession, with continuing service in the king's afterlife. This impressive discovery is now on display in a special museum near its find spot.

Temples at Giza: the Valley Temple of Khafre

Each royal pyramid was provided with two temples in which funerary rites were performed. Gone, it is important to note, are the funerary enclosure of previous dynasties and architectural facilities for the performance of the sed-festival. The two temples both lie on the east side of the pyramid. Indeed, the linear east–west arrangement of these pyramid-temple complexes relates to the course of the sun and to the new prominence of the sun god, Re. The furthest east, on the edge of the zone of cultivation, is known as the Valley Temple. A causeway, or raised stone-paved

Figure 5.14 Khafre, seated statue, from the Valley Temple of Khafre, Giza. Egyptian Museum, Cairo

road, linked the Valley Temple with the Mortuary Temple located at the east base of each pyramid. Final rites took place in this temple, as did periodic ceremonies thereafter, designed to maintain the king's well-being in the afterlife.

The best preserved are the temples of Khafre, accompanied by a unique monument, the Great Sphinx. The Valley Temple of Khafre measures ca. 45m², although the north wall projects out at a diagonal. It was built of large limestone blocks faced with massive ashlar blocks of red granite from Aswan. Its monolithic pillars were also of granite. Its walls, still standing 13m high, are battered, that is with a slightly sloping exterior face, a feature of this period. Inside the walls were undecorated, but elsewhere, such as in the mortuary temple at the base of Khufu's pyramid, scanty evidence suggests that low reliefs originally decorated the limestone facing.

The king's titles were carved in a band around each doorway, the only inscriptions in the building. The entrances led to high-ceilinged vestibules and then into a long antechamber. A deep pit in its floor contained a virtually complete statue of Khafre (Figure 5.14), found shattered but now reassembled in the Cairo Museum, and portions of others. These statues formed a set of 23, of diorite, schist, and alabaster, which stood in the main room of the temple, the T-shaped columned hall that lies to the west of the antechamber. Each statue perhaps symbolized one or, in three cases, two of the 26 parts of the king's body.

The statue of Khafre resembles that of Djoser (Figure 5.10), but there are significant differences. Khafre, a benign expression on his face, sits stiffly on a high-backed throne, but with both arms placed on his thighs, the right fist clenched, the left hand open, palm down. Like Djoser he wears the royal *nemes* headdress, now decorated with a *uraeus* or erect cobra, and the royal beard, but instead of the sed-festival cloak he wears a royal kilt with a precise pattern of folds.

This statue, by displaying additional emblems of the king's power, shows more clearly than the statue of Djoser how the king, the land, and the gods were intertwined. Two lions, symbols of strength, support his seat. On each side of the throne, enframed by the lion's body, is the motif that represents the union of the two regions of ancient Egypt: the hieroglyphic sign for "union" surrounded by the knotting of the two plants that symbolize Lower and Upper Egypt, the papyrus and the lily. Lastly and most dramatically, a falcon sits on the top of the throne, perched behind the king's head. This representation of Horus, the sky god, spreads his wings to either side of the king's head in a protective embrace – in addition, a symbol that the king is the earthly manifestation of Horus.

A different vision of royalty is given by a statue found in the Valley Temple of Menkaure (Figure 5.15). Menkaure stands with his wife Khamerernebty in the striding pose characteristic of Egyptian art. Both are about the same size, somewhat under life-size (the height of the statue: 1.38m). The king clenches his fists, while the queen has her arm around her husband. This family portrait shows an idealized youthful, healthy couple, a vision that subsequent Egyptians would often emulate in their funerary art. The statue, made of slate schist, was unfinished when placed in the temple, with only the heads and upper bodies completely polished. Traces of paint indicate that the entire statue was originally painted.

The exact purpose of the Valley Temple is not clear. There are several ceremonies connected with the preparation of a royal body for burial, known from texts, that possibly were carried out here. The body was "purified by washing," a ceremony which assured regeneration. Second, the body was embalmed, either actually or symbolically (if the actual embalmment was done elsewhere). And third, the "Opening of the Mouth" ceremony was performed, to give life to statues and other images of the king, so they could serve as homes for the king's spirit, his *ka*.

The Mortuary Temple of Khafre

According to traditional interpretation, after the rites in the Valley Temple were completed, the royal body was taken along the causeway, walled and covered to protect the purified body from contamination, to the Mortuary Temple, located at the east base of the pyramid. Final funeral rites were performed here. In addition, the temple offered access to the narrow terrace on which the pyramid stood, enclosed by a wall. But Dieter Arnold, supported by Mark Lehner, now questions this view on practical grounds: rooms, doorways, and corridors seem too small for the funeral procession to pass. Instead, the royal body would have been brought into the pyramid

Figure 5.15 Menkaure and Khamerernebty, statue from the Valley Temple of Menkaure, Giza by a more direct route. Arnold then speculates about the function of mortuary temples. In addition to their ritual purpose, whatever that was, these buildings may also have served as a symbolic royal residence, because their layout corresponds, albeit in a very loose way, to that of certain later palaces and mansions.

The Mortuary Temple of Khafre is poorly preserved. It measures 110m × 45m. Like the Valley Temple, it was made of a limestone core faced with granite. Its ground plan displays for the first time the five elements that will be standard in royal mortuary temples of the rest of the Old Kingdom: (1) entrance hall; (2) colonnaded court; (3) statue chamber, typically with five niches for five statues; (4) magazines, or storerooms; and (5) the sanctuary, a tiny room at the rear. The sanctuary contained a stele carved with a false door. Through this, the ka would emerge from the pyramid, and sample the offerings placed daily on the low altar in front of the false door.

The Great Sphinx

The colossal image of a sphinx, 73.2m long and 19.8m high, stands next to the Valley Temple of Khafre (Figure 5.11). It was carved out of the limestone bedrock during the Fourth Dynasty. In later periods, perhaps in the Eighteenth Dynasty and during the Roman Empire, parts were shored up with masonry. In addition to these restorations, remains of chapels and stelai have emerged during explorations of the nineteenth and twentieth centuries. For example, a small ruined temple of the Fourth Dynasty was discovered in front of the paws of the Sphinx.

The Great Sphinx is unique. Such statues do not normally form part of a pyramid complex. The term "sphinx," a Greek word, perhaps deriving from the Egyptian for "living image," *shesep ankh*, denotes a composite creature with a lion's body and a human head. Here, the head wears royal accoutrements: the nemes headdress with the uraeus on the forehead and a false beard (now gone). The face has been damaged, notably the nose, but may be a portrait of Khafre. It could also represent a guardian deity of this necropolis, since a lion was believed to stand watch at the gates of the underworld.

Sand accumulating around the Great Sphinx has had to be cleared periodically, in ancient as well as modern times. In his detailed account of Egypt, Herodotus did not mention the Sphinx; perhaps in his day, the fifth century BC, it was completely buried in sand. The most interesting clearing took place in the Eighteenth Dynasty, a story recounted on a gray granite stele discovered in 1816–17 in front of the Sphinx. Thutmose IV, while still a prince, was resting in its shade during a hunting expedition. In a dream, the Sphinx promised him the throne if he would clear the Sphinx of sand. Thutmose IV did so, and after he became king he built a temple here and set up the commemorative stele mentioned above.

THE SUN TEMPLE OF NIUSERRE AT ABU GURAB

The sun god Re rose to prominence in the Fourth Dynasty, a position he would continue to hold in the Middle and New Kingdoms. The cult of Re originated at Heliopolis on the east bank of the Nile (now in the northern suburbs of Cairo), but six of the kings of the Fifth Dynasty constructed special temples to Re on the west bank. The best preserved is that built by the pharaoh Niuserre at Abu Gurab, just north of Abu Sir, where he and most kings of his line built their pyramids. The temple may have been constructed during the period 2430–2400 BC, but as with much Egyptian chronology the dating is subject to controversy.

The Sun Temple of Niuserre contrasts with the funerary temples already discussed, and with the cult temples at Luxor and Karnak that will be examined in the next chapter. Worship of the sun god was typically done in the open air, not in the small dark rooms in which other gods were reverently housed.

The temple, constructed entirely of limestone, sits on an artificial mound, itself faced with limestone (Figure 5.16). From a pavilion lying to the east an enclosed causeway led to the temple. The temple consisted of an open-air court, 100.5m × 76.2m, oriented east–west in accordance with the path of the sun. The walls of the surrounding portico were decorated with painted reliefs depicting miscellaneous subjects, most not specifically illustrating the cult: the king at his sed-festival, the king trampling his enemies, various plants and animals, etc. Reliefs of the seasons may, however, relate to the life-giving force of the sun. In the west side of the open-air court stood the great solar symbol, a squat obelisk built of limestone blocks set on a rectangular podium. The court also included an area for the slaughtering of animals, the sacrificial offerings; an altar, exposed to the sun; and storerooms. Directly outside the temple, to the south, a solar boat was erected, out of brick, oddly enough.

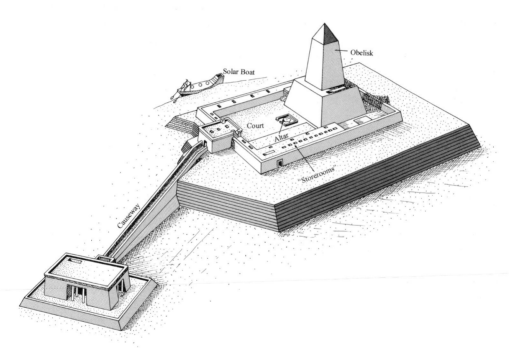

Figure 5.16 Sun Temple of Niuserre (reconstruction), from Abu Gurab

The word "obelisk" comes from Greek and means "little roasting-spit," but the function was purely Egyptian. These pillars represented the first place the sun landed on earth. The original obelisk was the *benben*, "the radiant one," a stone venerated at Heliopolis; it may have represented the first ray of light to touch the earth at the moment of creation. The obelisk that once stood at Abu Gurab imitated this prototype. Especially in the taller, elongated version current in the New Kingdom, the obelisk would become a distinctive element of ancient Egyptian architecture.

Although Re and obelisks continued in popularity, the Sun Temples as seen at Abu Gurab did not outlive the Fifth Dynasty. Of course, to construct such a temple in addition to a pyramid and its funerary temples must have been extremely expensive. Of greater significance may have been a shift in cult focus, with the increasing importance of the cult of Osiris, centered in Abydos.

THE FIRST INTERMEDIATE PERIOD

During the Fifth and Sixth Dynasties, the power of regional officials gradually increased at the expense of the central authority in Memphis. In what is known as the First Intermediate Period, political instability became acute as weak royal families, jockeying for power with provincial governors, ruled over truncated sections of the country. Conditions did not favor achievements in architecture and literature; these would reemerge only with the ascendancy of the city of Thebes in the Eleventh Dynasty and the eventual restoration of a strong centralized power by the king Mentuhotep II.

CHAPTER 6

Egyptian cities, temples, and tombs of the second millennium BC

Middle Kingdom: ca. 2060–1795 BC

    Eleventh (later) to Twelfth Dynasties

Second Intermediate period: ca. 1795–1550 BC

    Thirteenth to Seventeenth Dynasties

New Kingdom: ca. 1550–1070 BC

    Eighteenth Dynasty: ca. 1550–1295 BC

    Nineteenth Dynasty: ca. 1295–1186 BC

    Twentieth Dynasty: ca. 1186–1070 BC

Third Intermediate period: ca. 1070–715 BC

    Twenty-first to Twenty-fourth Dynasties

Late period: 760–332 BC

    Twenty-fifth to Thirtieth Dynasties and the second Persian occupation

Alexander the Great conquers Egypt: 332 BC

Although never dominant in the archaeological record of dynastic Egypt, cities do come into better focus during the second millennium BC, in contrast with earlier times. The best-known is *Akhetaten*, modern Tell el-Amarna, created as a new capital in the fourteenth century BC. We shall also examine *Kahun*, a Middle Kingdom town, and *Thebes*, the administrative center of Upper Egypt during the New Kingdom, at least for the monumental temples and tombs built in its environs. Finally, this chapter will introduce two sites from Nubia, the frontier region south of Aswan: first, *Buhen*, a fortress from the Middle Kingdom, and second, *Abu Simbel*, famous for its Temple of Ramses II.

THE MIDDLE KINGDOM

Although the Middle Kingdom lasted far less time than either the Old or the New Kingdom, it was an important period for ancient Egyptian civilization. In this era of renewed power of the ruler, the Egyptian language reached its finest flowering and literature flourished. So too did arts and crafts, notably sculpture and jewelry. Evidence for cities during this period is sporadic. The rulers of the Twelfth Dynasty shifted their capital from Thebes in the south to Lisht, near Memphis. Little is known of this city, largely buried deep under Nile silt. More important in the archaeological record are the "pyramid town" of Kahun and the forts erected on the Nubian frontier, of which Buhen is an excellent example.

Kahun

The neatly planned Middle Kingdom town of Kahun (modern name) was built near the entrance to the Faiyum (a large, fertile depression connected to the Nile, south-west of modern Cairo) in order to house the builders of the nearby pyramid of king Senusret II (ruled ca. 1880–1872 BC) and the priests, soldiers, officials, and other personnel who would maintain the monument and its cults. Lying on the edge of the desert away from farmlands and modern habitation, the town proved accessible to archaeologists; about half the town was excavated in the late nineteenth century by the British Egyptologist Sir William Flinders Petrie. Although the mud brick walls had disintegrated, house foundations were well preserved, allowing an appreciation of the town's layout.

The plan of this specially founded "pyramid town" is regular (Figure 6.1). Inside a nearly square area, 384m × 335m, straight streets cross at right angles, in an orthogonal grid. In the main north/north-east section, approximately 20 large houses were identified, measuring ca. 60m × 42m, each with a plain wall and door onto the street but sharing walls with its neighbors.

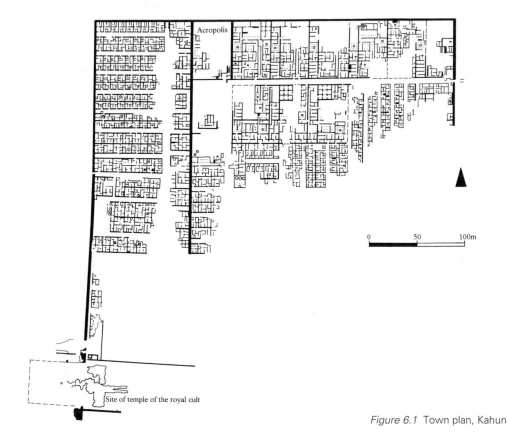

Figure 6.1 Town plan, Kahun

Inside, houses include reception and residential rooms, a garden with a shaded portico, and large granaries for food storage; details of their appearance and decoration are furnished by house models recovered from Middle Kingdom tombs. The smaller section of Kahun, separated from the larger by a wall, contained some 220 small houses, also arranged on straight streets. These house plans varied considerably, but unlike the large houses, they rarely included granaries. The social and economic structure of the town, understood from finds of papyrus documents as well as from the house remains, depended on top bureaucrats who inhabited the large houses, maintained retinues of clients and servants (who lived in the small houses), and controlled the distribution of food from their large granaries. The ruins of Kahun impart the impression of a well-regulated society – which all evidence indicates was indeed the central characteristic of Middle Kingdom Egypt.

Buhen

The fortress at Buhen, in Nubia (the region along the Nile from Aswan to Khartoum), is a good example of the strongholds the Egyptians of the Middle Kingdom erected on their southern frontier. Excavated by W. B. Emery and others during the salvage campaign that accompanied the construction of the High Dam at Aswan, the ruins were subsequently flooded by the lake that formed behind the dam.

The Egyptians had two frontier zones over which they kept watch: the north, opening both westwards toward Libya and eastwards toward south-west Asia, and the south, beyond the First Cataract, leading up the Nile into central Africa. At various points in Egyptian history, peoples from the outside attempted to enter Egypt through these corridors. Sometimes they succeeded. The Egyptians had another reason to patrol the southern border region. Central Africa was a source for precious metals and exotic raw materials, and the Egyptians did not want this trade disrupted.

The fort at Buhen was built early in the twentieth century BC, one of several forts along the Nile north of the Second Cataract. The plan consisted of an inner citadel, an open yard, and a massive outer fortification wall of mud brick, 5m thick, originally 8m–9m in height. The inner

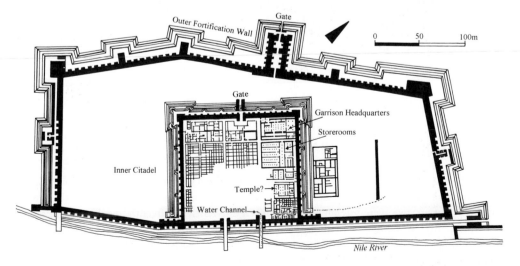

Figure 6.2 Plan, the Citadel, Buhen

citadel (150m × 138m), itself walled, featured buildings of mud brick, with stone and wood details neatly arranged in a grid plan, a regular layout that brings to mind Roman military camps of nearly 2,000 years later (Figure 6.2). Functions included garrison reception rooms, housing, storerooms, and a possible temple. Two gates opened onto the river, the northernmost protecting a stone-lined channel that could supply river water in times of siege. The outer fortifications contained one gateway only, a passageway lined with parallel walls and towers that opened toward the western desert. The wall itself consisted of, in cross-section from the exterior to the interior, a ditch, an outer parapet wall with arrow slits, a rampart or walkway, and the main wall, with crenellations on top (Figure 6.3). The indentations in the architecture recall the Mesopotamian-influenced design of the walls of tombs and towns in Early Dynastic Egypt, a method of decoration considered appropriate for mud brick regardless of the purpose, funerary, civil, or military.

Figure 6.3 Outer fortification wall (after excavation), Buhen

THE SECOND INTERMEDIATE PERIOD

With the breakdown of central authority at the end of the Twelfth Dynasty, control over Egypt devolved once again on regional rulers. Of the five dynasties that make up this period, three were native Egyptian, two were foreign. The two foreign dynasties, Fifteenth and Sixteenth, are of particular interest: people from south-west Asia who settled in the eastern Delta, eventually establishing a separate kingdom there, with their capital at Avaris (modern Tell el-Dab'a). They are known as the Hyksos, a Greek term deriving from an Egyptian phrase meaning "princes of foreign countries." To them are attributed the introduction into Egypt of the horse and chariot, the composite bow, and the vertical loom. The discovery in 1991 of Minoan-style wall paintings at Avaris indicates stronger links with the Aegean region than heretofore suspected.

Eventually the native rulers in Upper Egypt mustered the strength to challenge the Hyksos. Under the leadership of Amosis (Ahmose), the Egyptians defeated these immigrants and drove them from the country. Thus began the Eighteenth Dynasty and the New Kingdom, the greatest period in ancient Egyptian history.

THE NEW KINGDOM AND THEBES

Three dynasties, Eighteenth to Twentieth, make up the New Kingdom (ca. 1550–1070 BC). Most major monuments preserved from this period lie in the region of ancient Thebes, modern Luxor, the major city of Upper Egypt in ancient times. We shall also travel northwards to Tell el-Amarna for an instructive look at a New Kingdom city, and southwards to Abu Simbel, to inspect the grandiose temple built by Ramses II (see map, Figure 5.1).

The Eighteenth Dynasty established their capital in Upper Egypt at Thebes. Memphis continued as a regional capital of Lower Egypt, but little survives. Thebes has a long history of habitation, and indeed had been the royal center during the Eleventh Dynasty, but it gained particular prominence at this time and served as a capital for most of the New Kingdom. The ancient Egyptians called the city "Waset" or "No-Amun ("City of Amun"). The name "Thebes" was given by the ancient Greeks, for unknown reasons; there is no known connection with the famous Greek city of Thebes. For the Egyptians, Thebes was "The City," the prototype of all cities:

> Waset is the pattern of every city,
> Both the flood and the earth were in her from the beginning of time,
> The sands came to delimit her soil,
> To create her ground upon the mound when the earth came into being.
> Then mankind came into being within her;
> To found every city in her true name
> Since all are called "city" after the example of Waset.
>
> (Seton-Williams and Stocks 1993: 536)

The early rulers of the Eighteenth Dynasty re-established control over Egypt's frontiers and trade routes. In the north, campaigns were led into west Asia against the Hyksos in Palestine and the Mitanni in north-east Syria. More important was the south, where the Egyptians penetrated Nubia beyond the Third Cataract, refurbishing the Middle Kingdom forts and establishing new towns. An Egyptian trading mission to a more remote region, the land of Punt, usually identified with the east horn of Africa, is recorded on the first of the great surviving buildings of Eighteenth Dynasty Thebes, the mortuary temple of Queen Hatshepsut at Deir el-Bahri.

Deir el-Bahri: the mortuary temple of Hatshepsut

The town of Thebes straddled both banks of the Nile. The habitation quarters, poorly known today, must have been located on the east bank under the modern city of Luxor. Also on the east bank are the two major temple complexes, the temples to Amun and other gods at Karnak and at Luxor (see below). The west bank served different purposes. Some royal palaces were found on this bank beyond the zone of cultivation, but today the region is better known for its cities of the dead, the tombs and the temples devoted to funerary cults, and dwellings for those who worked making tombs (Figure 6.4).

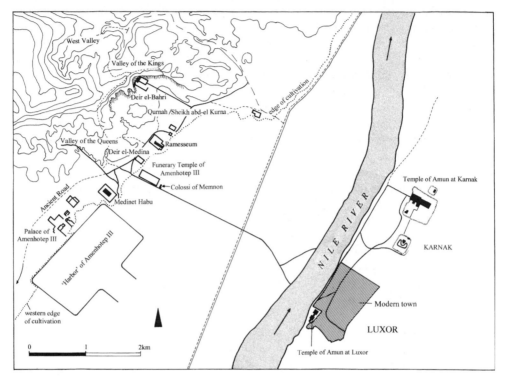

Figure 6.4 Regional plan, Thebes

Deir el-Bahri lies on the west bank, on the east side of massive limestone cliffs. To the west, on the other side of the cliffs, is found the Valley of the Kings, the desolate burial ground of most New Kingdom rulers. In this striking spot, adjacent to an important mortuary temple built by the pharaoh Mentuhotep II of Dynasty XI, Hatshepsut (reigned ca. 1479–1457 BC) had a magnificent temple erected for the perpetuation of her funerary cult. It marks a new trend, the formal separation of the mortuary temple from the actual burial place, hidden far from the temple. The ruined temple at Deir el-Bahri was largely buried in sand when members of Napoleon's expedition examined it in 1798. Serious restoration work began in the 1890s under the direction of the Swiss Egyptologist Edouard Naville for the Egypt Exploration Fund, and continues today by a Polish/Egyptian team.

Rarely did women rule in their own right in ancient Egypt. Indeed, Hatshepsut began as coregent with her young nephew, Thutmose III, but, quickly assuming full control and complete royal regalia, she dominated the government for some 20 years. Although her texts frequently used feminine grammatical gender, she had herself depicted as a man, the expected sex of pharaohs, with the usual ceremonial beard. Her eventual fate is a mystery. Her mummified body has never been found, and no one knows whether she died a natural death or was overthrown and killed. We do know that Thutmose III (reigned ca. 1479–1425 BC, including the period of

Hatshepsut's coregency) regained power, becoming one of the celebrated military leaders of New Kingdom Egypt. But bad blood remained between them, it has been proposed, for he did his best to eradicate all public mention of her by having her depictions and names hacked away or replaced by his own.

The temple is laid out on a series of three terraces (Figures 6.5 and 6.6). With its use of pillared façades, the layout resembles models seen in the Middle Kingdom, both in the adjacent temple of Mentuhotep II and in tombs of nobles elsewhere in Upper Egypt, and differs, as will be seen, from the plan typical of later cult temples. The relief sculptures that decorate the walls sheltering the colonnades promote the accomplishments of Hatshepsut, presenting a reign full of achievement despite the absence of the usual masculine exploits of war and hunting.

The lowest terrace consisted of a large walled area originally planted with trees. A double colonnade, 22 columns arranged in two rows, lies at the rear of this terrace, divided into two sections by the ramp that ascends to the second terrace. Painted reliefs on the rear wall of the

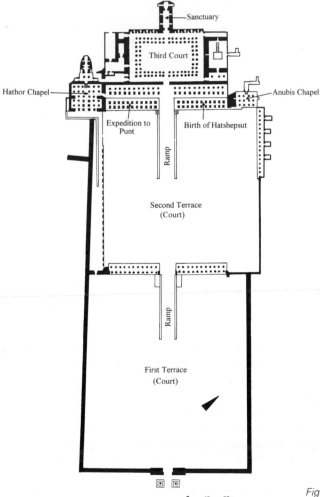

Figure 6.5 Plan, the Mortuary Temple of Hatshepsut, Deir el-Bahri

Figure 6.6 The Mortuary Temple of Hatshepsut, Deir el-Bahri

colonnade show the transport of the two obelisks Hatshepsut had made for the temple of Amun in Karnak. The second terrace, smaller than the first, is itself bordered on the rear by a colonnade (the Second Colonnade), again two sections of eleven columns arranged in two rows. The walls of the south half display in painted reliefs scenes from the expedition to Punt, a distant land that provided Egyptians with myrrh trees for the temple terraces, incense for religious ceremonies, wild animals, electrum, hides, and timber. This delightful and unparalleled ethnographic record illustrates scenes of the village of round huts on stilts where the Egyptians were received by the chief, his obese wife, possibly a victim of elephantiasis, and their children. In the north section of the Second Colonnade additional reliefs recount the divine birth of Hatshepsut. In order to substantiate her right to rule, she asserted that her true father was not the pharaoh Thutmose I, but the god Amun who entered the body of Thutmose I at the crucial moment of conception; the full story was depicted here.

The Second Colonnade is flanked by two chapels, one on the south to the goddess Hathor, and another, on the north, to the god Anubis. The portico of the Anubis Chapel and the colonnade that borders the north side of the second terrace just beyond the chapel are lined with a series of columns that with their faceted sides and capitals, like columns from subsidiary buildings in the Step Pyramid complex at Saqqara, recall later Greek columns. Later Greeks were indeed greatly influenced by Egyptian stone working traditions in architecture and sculpture, and models such as these would have made a lasting impression.

A second ramp leads to the Third or Upper Terrace, an open-air court surrounded on four sides by a portico. The sanctuary of the temple lies to the rear, cut into the limestone cliff, later enlarged in Ptolemaic (Hellenistic) times, a small dark room typical of the Egyptian holy of holies.

THE TEMPLE OF AMUN AT LUXOR

The main god of Thebes was Amun, worshipped as Amun-re, a fusion with the sun god, Re. He formed a triad with his wife Mut and their son Khonsu. He is generally shown as a man wearing a crown with two tall plumes and a disk, his characteristic headdress. The two major temples at Thebes, one at Luxor, the other at Karnak, were dedicated to the cult of Amun, although both complexes contained chapels to other deities. One might wonder what sort of relations these large, neighboring temples enjoyed. One important link between the temples is illustrated on the walls of the first hypostyle hall, or colonnade, in relief sculpture carved during the reign of Tutankhamun (ca. 1336–1327 BC). Each year, at the height of the Nile flood, the *Opet*, or Great New Year Festival, was celebrated. The sacred barge of Amun was brought upriver from Karnak to Luxor for a visit lasting some three weeks, the occasion for sacrifices, pomp, and entertainment. This relationship, at least, was friendly.

In plan, both temples differ significantly from the funerary temples excavated at Giza and at Deir el-Bahri. Little is known, however, of cult temples without funerary associations before the New Kingdom. The Temple of Amun at Luxor is easier to comprehend than the temple at Karnak, because it is the smaller of the two and because it was built in only two main stages (Figure 6.7). The main part was constructed over an earlier, smaller Middle Kingdom temple by Amenhotep III (ruled ca. 1391–1353 BC), a monarch who presided over an exceptionally prosperous Egypt. In the following century, the great Nineteenth Dynasty king Ramses II added a court and the entrance pylon onto the north. (A pylon is a gateway consisting of a wall, normally wedge-shaped in cross-section (that is, with walls that slope slightly outwards from top to bottom), with a passageway through the middle.)

The temple is oriented north–south, parallel to the Nile, unusual for Egyptian temples, which are normally oriented east–west, attuned to the rising and setting of the sun. Otherwise the temple follows tradition, containing the standard elements of a cult temple: an entrance pylon; open-air courtyards; colonnaded (*hypostyle*) halls; and a sanctuary surrounded by small cult rooms. These elements had symbolic meaning. The sanctuary or small holy of holies, the home of the god, where his or her statue was kept, was built on the highest ground, which symbolized the original earth that emerged from the watery chaos at the world's creation. A hypostyle hall,

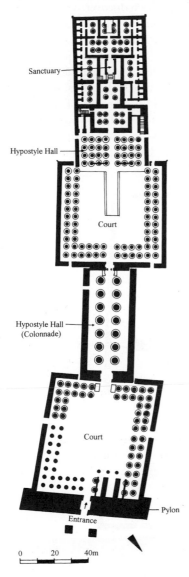

Figure 6.7 Plan, the Temple of Amun, Luxor

with floor, columns, and ceiling, represented the marshy ground of the earliest world, the reeds that grew there, and the sky above. The open-air court permitted worship of the sun; and the pylon represented the mountains of the distant horizon between which the sun rises and sets.

THE TEMPLE OF AMUN AT KARNAK

The Temple of Amun at Karnak follows the basic principles of temple layout seen at Luxor but on a much grander scale (Figure 6.8). This temple had its origins in the Middle Kingdom. Indeed, remains of the Middle Kingdom town of Thebes have been discovered in the precinct. But the temple seen today is largely the work of the New Kingdom, with important additions of the Late and Hellenistic periods (first millennium BC). Its plan is agglutinative. The sanctuary, the residence of the god's statue, was the key room of a temple. Once this was built, an endless succession of the other elements of a cult temple could be added: hypostyle halls, courts, and pylons. This is what happened at Karnak. It was not conceived as a unified plan; rather, a pharaoh would add a section to the existing complex, thereby increasing the size of the building. Hatshepsut was a contributor, as was Thutmose III; they were followed by many others. Some monarchs even disassembled existing shrines, reusing the blocks in new constructions, or had their names inscribed in the place of the original sponsors. The building history of the complex thus becomes difficult to unravel.

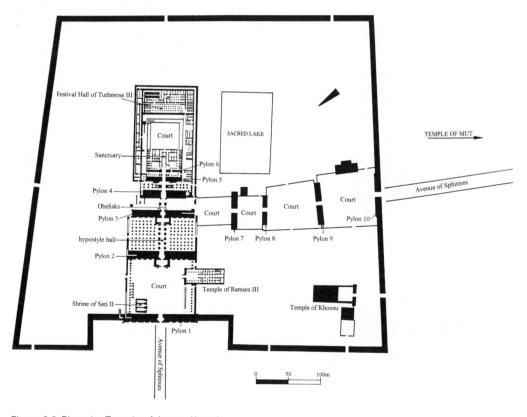

Figure 6.8 Plan, the Temple of Amun, Karnak

The ruins cover an area of 2ha, a large sacred precinct enclosed by a low wall that includes the Temple to Amun with its southern projection; the Sacred Lake; and various small temples. Today's visitor approaches the temple from the west along an avenue of sphinxes with ram's heads. The major section of the temple lies on this east–west axis. The avenue leads to the first of the six pylons on this axis, the massive barriers or cross-walls with doorways, sloping sides, and niches for flagpoles that mark the transitions between inner and outer spaces. The so-called First Pylon, the first entrance on the west, was the last to be built, begun perhaps during the Twenty-fifth Dynasty; it was never completed.

The first court contains two temples of the later New Kingdom, a small tripartite shrine built by Seti II to Amun, Mut, and Khonsu, and, on a north–south axis, a temple to the same triad built by Ramses III. This last is more than a chapel; it is a complete temple in itself, with court, hypostyle hall, and sanctuary.

The Second Pylon, contributed by Ramses II, included in its core a portion of the 60,000 small sandstone blocks that belonged originally to a temple to the Aten, the sun god worshipped as the sun disk, erected here at Karnak by the heretic pharaoh Akhenaten (other blocks were found also inside the Ninth and Tenth Pylons and underneath the main Hypostyle Hall). In reaction to Akhenaten's religious policies, Horemheb had this temple dismantled, but carefully, so the blocks could be reused. Beyond this pylon lies the great Hypostyle Hall, completed by Seti I and Ramses II, and reconstructed in the twentieth century by French archaeologists working for the Egyptian Department of Antiquities (Figure 6.9). This huge room, perhaps the most famous in all Egyptian architecture, measures 102m × 53m, with the twelve columns along the central passage rising 21m, the remaining 122 columns to the north and south rising 13m. The higher columns in the center permitted a clerestory arrangement, that is, a line of windows, which was the only source of illumination for this room. The resulting area is said to be large enough to contain the entire cathedral of Notre Dame of Paris and the column capitals broad enough that a hundred people could stand on each. But the columns are thick and tightly spaced, and it is difficult to sense the overall dimensions of the space.

Such buildings devoted to the cult of the state god served also as vehicles for the recording of royal achievements. This hypostyle hall is decorated on its columns and side walls, both inside and out. The exterior walls, for example, feature episodes from the military victories of Seti I and Ramses II. If the human audience for these images was restricted, the gods were always present. Royal successes accomplished with divine support merited such commemoration on a grand scale.

Figure 6.9 Central passageway, Hypostyle Hall, Temple of Amun, Karnak

The Third Pylon, built by Amenhotep III, the patron of the Temple of Amun at Luxor, marks the beginning of the earlier Eighteenth Dynasty section of the temple. Modern exploration has revealed that this pylon, originally covered with gold and silver, contained in its fill ten dismantled shrines and temples, notably the Jubilee Pavilion for the Twelfth Dynasty pharaoh Senusret I. Re-erected just north of the main entrance, this pavilion is the earliest building to be seen at Karnak today.

The Third Pylon is followed by the Central Court of the temple. Two pairs of obelisks originally stood here, gifts of Thutmose I, the mortal father of Hatshepsut, but only one survives *in situ*. By the New Kingdom, obelisks had become tall, slender poles, square in section with a pyramidal top, usually donated in pairs perhaps for symmetry, perhaps to represent the sun and the moon. They were carved from single blocks of granite, quarried near Aswan. The pink granite obelisk of Hatshepsut that still stands between Pylons 4 and 5 measures 27.5m in height and weighs an estimated 320 tons; it was originally sheathed in electrum. Quarrying, transporting, and erecting such massive pieces of stone, which took seven months for these obelisks, would be an amazing triumph of engineering even today.

A second set of courts and four pylons (pylons 7–10) extends southward from this court on a north–south axis. These too date to the Eighteenth Dynasty. Pylons 7 and 8 are attributed to Thutmose III and Hatshepsut, respectively, 9 and 10 to Horemheb. In the court just north of Pylon 7, an enormous pit was discovered in 1902 which contained over 2,000 stone statues and 17,000 bronze figures, apparently a ritual clearing late in the temple's history of the offerings left in what must have been a very cluttered temple complex. From Pylon 10 one can leave the precinct sacred to Amun and follow a sphinx-lined route southward to the Temple of Mut.

Let us instead return to the main east–west axis and the early Eighteenth Dynasty core of the temple. Pylons and courts become compressed here. Pylons 4 and 5, built by Thutmose I, enclose a small colonnade, originally roofed. Some of the drama of Eighteenth Dynasty history is attested in this small area. Hatshepsut had her pair of obelisks installed here, and removed part of the roof to do so. Their transport is depicted on the rear walls of the First Colonnade at Deir el-Bahri. Thutmose III not only replaced his aunt's name with his own but erected a wall around the obelisks (as high as the ceiling of the hall) to hide them instead of tearing them down.

Beyond Pylon 5 lies a second small colonnaded hall, also erected under Thutmose I, and then the last and smallest of the pylons, Pylon 6, an insertion of Thutmose III. Finally one reaches the Sanctuary for the divine boat, a typically small room, long, narrow, and dark. The statue of Amun lived here, and three times each day was washed by the high priest, dressed, perfumed, and presented with food and drink. The original boat shrine was built by Hatshepsut; its dismantled blocks have been recovered from inside Pylon 3. The present sanctuary, of pink granite, was a late remodeling of ca. 330 BC, a contribution of Philip Arrhidaeus, the half-brother of Alexander the Great. On the outside wall, south side, Philip is shown being crowned and taken in hand by the gods. Despite Philip's Greek origin, the style of these reliefs is purely Egyptian.

Behind the Sanctuary lies an open court and the Festival Hall of Thutmose III. Of the many small rooms that lie beyond the hall, one is of particular interest, the so-called "Botanical Room," with reliefs of exotic plants, birds, and animals brought to Egypt by Thutmose III from his campaigns in western Asia. To the south lies the Sacred Lake, 200m × 117m, fed by underground channels from the Nile. Priests purified themselves in its waters. The visitor who finds himself or herself here in the late afternoon is rewarded with a magnificent view of the ruined temple illuminated in deep golden sunlight.

AKHENATEN AND TELL EL-AMARNA

Amidst centuries of Theban preeminence, presided over by the supreme god Amun, one ruler of startling originality briefly challenged this status quo: Amenhotep IV (ruled ca. 1353–1337 BC). He became a passionate devotee of a single deity, the Aten, the life force depicted as a sun disk with radiating rays (Figure 6.10). In promoting this cult, he rejected Amun and other established gods with the exception of Re, identified as an aspect of the Aten. He changed his name to Akhenaten, meaning "He who is useful to the Sun-disk" or "Glorified spirit of the Sun-disk," and instituted a distinctive style for representing himself and his family in sculpture and painting, with exaggerated curves and elongations of the head and body. And in the fifth year of his reign he moved his capital from Thebes to the newly founded city of Akhetaten ("Horizon of the Sun-disk"), located halfway between Thebes and Memphis. Akhetaten is commonly known as Tell el-Amarna, or simply Amarna, modern names derived from two of the local villages, Et-Till and El-Amran.

The ruins of Amarna give us our best and fullest look at an ancient Egyptian city. The reasons are three. First, much of ancient Amarna lay just inland from the river's flood zone; its remains were thus accessible to archaeologists, not buried beneath meters and meters of Nile silt. Second, the city had an extremely short life. Constructed on previously uninhabited land, the new capital was occupied only during the final eleven years of Akhenaten's reign and a few years after. The site was then abandoned; apart from a small Roman fort, no building activity ever disrupted the remains. And third, we know much about the city thanks to extensive excavations conducted intermittently from the late nineteenth century until 1936, and again since 1977 by the Egypt Exploration Society under the direction of British archaeologist Barry Kemp.

Figure 6.10 Akhenaten and his family worshipping the Aten, relief sculpture, from the Royal Tomb, Amarna. Egyptian Museum, Cairo

With such a short life, Amarna should not be considered typical. Established cities such as Memphis must have been crowded, full of buildings arranged in haphazard city plans developed over centuries. Nonetheless, the results from Amarna are valuable for their insights into fourteenth-century BC Egyptian notions of what a planned city, and a royal capital, should look like.

Although the city proper lies on the east bank of the Nile, a larger area totalling some 18km² marked by fourteen boundary stelai extended across the river to the edge of the western desert. The city was not walled. It was divided into various sectors, loosely linked by a north–south "Royal Road" that paralleled the river (Figure 6.11). Temples, storehouses, police barracks, administrative buildings (including the "Records Office" that contained the invaluable "Amarna Letters," clay copies of correspondence with foreign states in west Asia), and a huge palace occupied the central zone, laid out on a grid of streets in an orthogonal plan. Secondary residential and commercial areas were spread out to the north and south in a line that stretched over 8km parallel to the river. On the edge of the north suburb, an accretion of slum dwellings had appeared by the end of the occupation of the town, crowding the more spacious housing. To the east, an arc of desert cliffs provided the location for rock-cut tombs. Of these many informative sectors we shall examine in more detail the Palace and the Great Temple, both in the Central City (Figure 6.12), and the houses, which provide good evidence for the daily life of the ancient Egyptians.

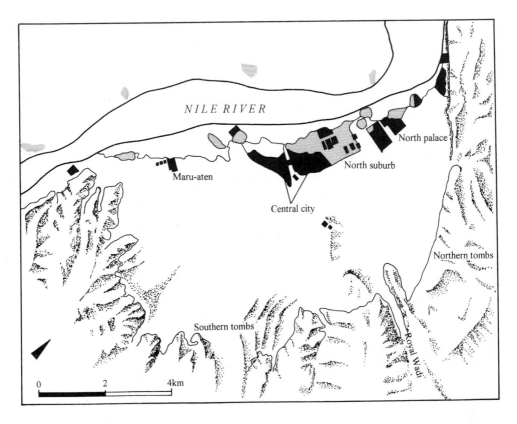

Figure 6.11 Overall plan, Amarna

The Palace

The Palace straddles the Royal Road slightly to the south of the Great Temple. Much of the complex lies beneath the zone of cultivation, and so has not been excavated and probably never will be. Far larger than any private dwelling, the Palace demonstrates the vast distance between the pharaoh and the rest of society. Its plan consisted of a succession of flat-roofed buildings, courts, and gardens, and larger pillared reception halls, some decorated with colossal statues of Akhenaten. The king's private quarters lay on the east side, the reception and administrative area on the west. A covered bridge across the Royal Road linked the two sides. From a large window in the bridge, the Window of Appearances, the pharaoh and his family could be greeted by their subjects. The Palace was built quickly, as were all buildings in this city, of mud brick, with wood or stone for columns and such details as doorsills. Limestone revetments were used for wall decoration. Some bore reliefs; some were plastered and then painted.

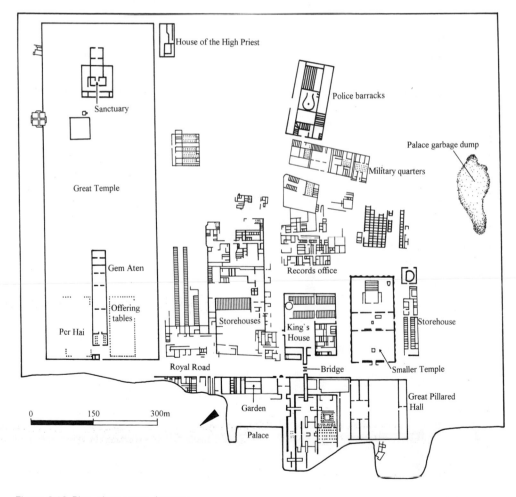

Figure 6.12 Plan, city center, Amarna

The Great Temple

The Great Temple occupied a large walled area, 760m × 290m. Our knowledge of the original appearance of this temple and the rituals performed there depends on pictures of ceremonies carved on the walls of tombs at Amarna. The main entrance lay on the west side, a small brick pylon on the Royal Road. The sacred enclosure contained several shrines. A long narrow building consisting of a hypostyle hall called the Per Hai, the "House of Rejoicing," led to the Gem Aten ("Aten has been found"), a series of six open-air courts, each one smaller than the preceding one. This building was surrounded by 365 offering tables on both the north and the south sides, tied to the days in the solar year. Offerings were not strictly vegetarian, as the discovery of a butcher's yard in the vicinity of the temple has made clear. Since much of the yard was open to the sky, and since Egypt gets very hot, especially during the summer, performing ceremonies outdoors must have been a strenuous task, the food offerings on the countless tables quick to spoil and smell.

The main temple lay in the east sector of the enclosure. In contrast with usual Egyptian practice, the main temple was not roofed but open-air, because the Aten, unlike other Egyptian gods, did not inhabit a statue in a dark room but manifested itself in the direct rays of the sun.

Houses

Amarna has given us fine examples of private free-standing houses of the well-to-do, in districts to the north (North suburb) and south of the Central City (Figures 6.13 and 6.14). Their features are fairly constant. Generally raised slightly on a low platform, the typical house had a small entrance room, followed by a larger two-storeyed loggia ("North Room" on Figure 6.13) whose roof was supported by wooden columns. A square hall lay in the center of the house, insulated against extremes of temperature by surrounding rooms. Its ceiling, held up by columns, rose above that of the adjacent rooms (with the exception of the loggia), allowing for high windows or clerestories immediately below the roof line. The room might contain a low brick platform where the owner and his wife would sit, a plastered stone washing place for water jars, and a shrine to the Aten and the royal family. Decoration was simple: plastered walls, perhaps with painted geometric designs. Off this main room lay smaller rooms, bedrooms, toilets and bathrooms, storage rooms and stairs up to the flat roof. Houses of the well-to-do were set in a walled yard. Such compounds would contain a well for water; a garden with trees, food plants, and flowers; storage for grain and other foodstuffs; servants' quarters;

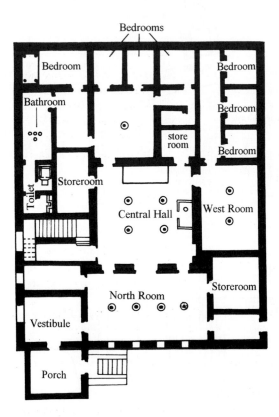

Figure 6.13 Plan, house, Amarna

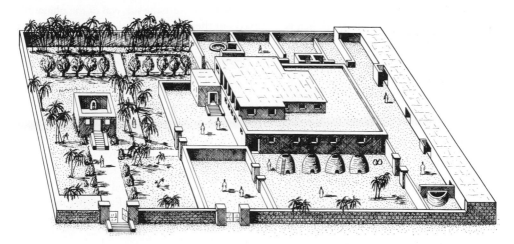

Figure 6.14 House (reconstruction), Amarna

kitchens (with circular clay ovens for baking bread, open fires for the rest); a shelter for animals; and frequently a chapel to the Aten. Sanitation remained primitive. There was no public drainage system at Amarna. Although bathrooms could be lined with stone, liquid wastes simply drained into the closest ground.

The end of Amarna

Upon Akhenaten's death, the dynastic succession entered a period of turbulence. As traditional interests reasserted themselves, Amarna was abandoned in favor of Thebes, and the Aten gave way to Amun. Eventually the state was salvaged by the general Horemheb and his vizier, later Ramses I, the first of the family that would rule as the Nineteenth Dynasty. But between Akhenaten and Horemheb briefly ruled a young king who would have been a mere footnote in the long list of Egyptian monarchs were it not for the almost miraculous survival of his tomb virtually intact into the twentieth century: Tutankhamun.

THE VALLEY OF THE KINGS

Akhenaten was buried at Amarna, his now empty tomb identified by archaeologists. Virtually all other New Kingdom monarchs were buried at Thebes, in a remote desert valley known as the Valley of the Kings. This valley is but one part of the extensive Theban necropolis that lies on the west bank of the Nile beyond the zone of cultivation.

The Valley of the Kings lies over the cliffs to the west of the Mortuary Temple of Hatshepsut at Deir el-Bahri. Beginning with Thutmose I, most kings of the Eighteenth to Twentieth Dynasties were buried here. Sixty-two tombs have been located, including some belonging to high officials. Many are decorated with wall paintings, but some are plain and some were never finished.

By the New Kingdom, the incidence of tomb robbery was high enough that kings were no longer interested in visible signs that marked their graves, such as pyramids. Mortuary temples, placed in the Nile Valley proper, would fulfill the desire for prestige as well as offering a setting for the necessary ritual. The tomb itself had to be hidden, to ensure the survival of the pharaoh's body and his possessions. The workmen who carved out these tombs and decorated them lived in a small, walled village, isolated from the rest of the Thebes in order to keep their projects secret. This village is today known as Deir el-Medina. Excavations of its houses, with finds such as *ostraka*, the stone bits on which people wrote and sketched, have yielded fascinating information about the daily life of these workmen.

The tombs were laid out according to one of two ground plans. In the first plan, followed in the first half of the Eighteenth Dynasty from Thutmose I to Amenhotep III, galleries arranged on a north–south axis descend along a gradual slope to a pit or well and an offering chamber beyond. But the burial chamber, often a large oval in shape (like the royal cartouche, the written form of the pharaonic name), lies to the west side, perpendicular to the main axis of the galleries (Figure 6.15a: Tomb of Thutmose III). Later tombs preferred a second plan, in which the galleries and burial chamber all lay along a single east–west axis (Figure 6.15b: Tomb of Ramses VI).

The Tomb of Tutankhamun

The elaborate precautions taken to conceal the royal burials rarely sufficed. Only one tomb in the Valley of the Kings was found substantially intact in modern times, the burial of the late Eighteenth Dynasty king, Tutankhamun (ruled ca. 1336–1327 BC), the young son-in-law, perhaps also the son, of Akhenaten. Robbed twice in antiquity, although little was taken, the resealed tomb was effectively hidden by the later construction of the adjacent tomb of Ramses VI, a king of the Twentieth Dynasty. The discovery of the tomb in November 1922 by the

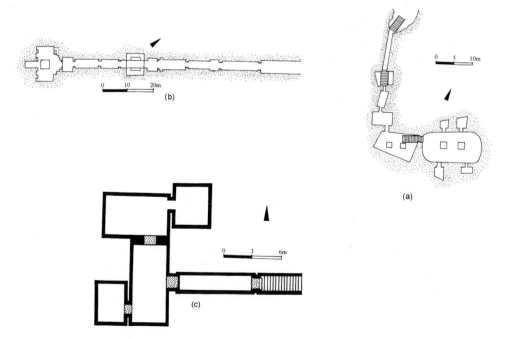

Figure 6.15 Ground plans of three tombs, Valley of the Kings, Thebes: (a) Tomb of Thutmose III; (b) Tomb of Ramses VI; and (c) Tomb of Tutankhamun

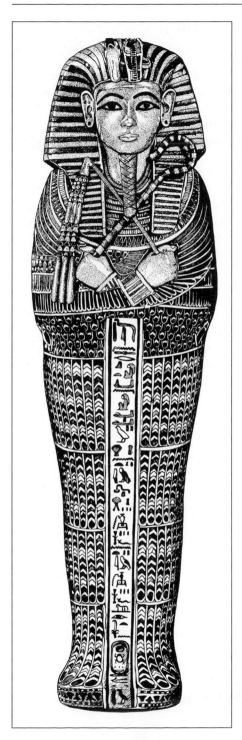

Figure 6.16 Coffin for the Organs, Tomb of Tutankhamun. Egyptian Museum, Cairo

British Egyptologist Howard Carter represented the culmination of years of painstaking examination of the already scrutinized valley. Ten more years were needed to record the grave goods and remove them from the chambers, and the scholarly publication of the objects continues to this very day, long after Carter's death in 1939.

The tomb of Tutankhamun differed from the standard type, but then it was originally destined not for royalty but for an official. Upon the early death of the king, it was hurriedly pressed into service. At the foot of a descending passage lie four small unfinished rooms (see Figure 6.15c), only one of which has wall paintings. A tremendous array of objects was packed into this small space. Included were statues of sentries, both human (in the image of the king) and of Anubis, the jackal-headed god; furniture, such as chairs and beds; hunting equipment, such as chariots, bows and arrows; personal effects, such as gaming boards; and food. Most of these are on display in the Egyptian Museum in Cairo.

The king was only sixteen or seventeen when he died. An examination of his skull suggests his death may have resulted from a blow to the head. He was buried inside an elaborate complex of shrines and coffins that took up most of the space in the burial chamber proper. Four shrines covered with gold leaf, one inside the other, contained a rectangular sarcophagus of yellow quartzite. Inside the sarcophagus were found three anthropomorphic coffins, also one inside the other. The innermost coffin was solid gold, weighing 110kg. Holes were left for the eyes, however, so that the mummy could look out. A mask of gold in the likeness of Tutankhamun, inlaid with glass and lapis lazuli, provided further protection for the king's head (Figure 6.16: this miniature coffin for the organs imitates the full-sized middle coffin). Tucked into the linen strips that wrapped the body was a magnificent collection of jewelry and amulets. As for the body itself, it has not fared so well; despite careful mummification, the copiously used embalming fluids proved corrosive rather than protective.

THE NINETEENTH DYNASTY: RAMSES II AND ABU SIMBEL

Although Ramses I ruled only two years, his descendants of the Nineteenth Dynasty continued for another century (ca.1295–1186 BC). His son, Seti I, and especially his grandson, Ramses II, presided over a particularly powerful period in Egyptian history.

Ramses II is especially well known. He reigned sixty-seven years (ca. 1279–1213 BC), with adminstrative centers at Thebes and at Per-Ramses in the Delta. He built some of the best surviving and largest of Egyptian monuments, famously clashed with the Hittites, and has been associated with the biblical story of the Hebrew exodus (this last is controversial). He avidly promoted his own glory through his building projects, supplemented with wall decorations and colossal statues of himself. We have already noted his additions to the Temples of Amun at Luxor and at Karnak. One more monument of his merits our attention: the remarkable temple at Abu Simbel, located in a remote spot near the southern frontier of modern Egypt.

This temple, and an accompanying smaller temple of his queen, Nefertari, were carved out of the sandstone cliffs that lined the Nile in Nubia. Like the fort at Buhen, these monuments lay in the region destined for flooding after the construction of the High Dam in Aswan. But these temples met a kinder fate than Buhen: an international team under the aegis of UNESCO cut the temples into blocks and reassembled them on dry land, some 210m inland and 65m higher.

Ostensibly honoring the gods, in actuality this shrine at Abu Simbel glorifies Ramses II – a monument to royal power exceptional even in a culture in which rulers rarely shrank from public display of their greatness. The façade of the larger temple overwhelms the visitor with its four colossal seated statues of Ramses II, each 20.1m high (Figure 6.17). Everyone else is smaller and

Figure 6.17 Exterior, Temple of Ramses II, Abu Simbel

subordinate: the wives and children who stand by his lower legs, the prisoners paraded beneath his chair in front of the entrance, even the god Re-Harakhte to whom Ramses II pays homage above the doorway. Inside, the temple consists of four rooms on axis, a larger hall, a smaller hall, a vestibule, and the sanctuary. Several side chambers, probably used as storerooms, lie off this axis. The large hall is dominated by two rows of columns carved with the standing likeness of the king as Osiris, the important god of the afterlife. The side walls show reliefs of the king's military triumphs, including the Battle of Qadesh fought in Syria against the Hittites. Scholars believe this battle was actually a stand-off, but Ramses II had no interest in being objective about the result. The sanctuary at the rear contains four seated statues, Ramses II and three major gods, Re-Harakhte, Amun, and the supreme god of Memphis, Ptah. The temple was aligned so that twice a year, in February and October, the sun's rays would reach the rear of the temple and shine on the three gods and the pharaoh. The first date may correspond to Ramses II's coronation day, or perhaps the date of his first jubilee, since the temple was built to celebrate this event.

AFTERMATH

The Egyptian kingdom prospered through the early twelfth century BC. Two kings, Merneptah of the later Nineteenth Dynasty, and Ramses III, the greatest ruler of the Twentieth Dynasty, fought off foreign challengers, the Libyans from the north-west, and the Sea Peoples, an enigmatic coalition of peoples from south-east Europe and western Asia who had already caused great destruction in the coastal cities of the eastern Mediterranean. In traditional fashion, the triumphs against the Sea Peoples are recorded in the relief sculptures on the walls of the massive mortuary temple of Ramses III at Medinet Habu, Thebes. Ramses III was succeeded by eight more kings of that name. None would match his greatness, and once again the Egyptian kingdom would feel the weakening of central authority. The New Kingdom was followed by the Third Intermediate period and the Late period, Dynasties Twenty-one to Thirty, the final dynasties of Manetho's list. Dynastic Egypt ended with a second brief occupation by Persians, themselves overcome in 332 BC by a greater conqueror, the Macedonian king Alexander the Great. Egypt then passed into the world of the Greeks and the Romans, first pagan, later Christian. After 3,000 years, pharaonic culture was slowly extinguished.

CHAPTER 7

Aegean Bronze Age towns and cities

Minoan Crete:

Old Palace (Protopalatial) period: ca. 1930–1700 BC (= Middle Minoan IB-II)

New Palace (Neopalatial) period: ca. 1700–1450 BC (= Middle Minoan III, Late Minoan IA and B)

ca. 1450 BC, most sites destroyed, with the major exceptions of Knossos and Khania

Late Minoan II: ca. 1450–1400 BC

Probable Mycenaean occupation at Knossos and Khania

Post-Palatial: ca. 1425–1050 BC (= Late Minoan IIIA, B, and C)

Major destructions at Knossos ca. 1375 BC and probably ca. 1200 BC

Thera (Santorini): Volcano erupts ca. 1520 BC

Mycenaean Greece:

Middle Helladic (late) and Late Helladic I: ca. 1650–1500 BC

Shaft Graves at Mycenae

Late Helladic II: ca. 1500–1400 BC

Late Helladic IIIA: ca. 1400–1340 BC

Late Helladic IIIB: ca. 1340–1185 BC

Treasury of Atreus at Mycenae; Citadels at Mycenae and Tiryns; Palace at Pylos

Late Helladic IIIC: ca. 1185–1050 BC

AEGEAN CIVILIZATIONS AND CITIES

In Mediterranean archaeology, the term "Aegean" refers to the Neolithic and Bronze Age cultures of the land that borders the Aegean Sea, and the Aegean islands, land now belonging to modern Greece and Turkey (Figure 7.1). These cultures first came to scholarly attention in the second half of the nineteenth century, especially with the discoveries of Heinrich Schliemann, a businessman interested in ancient history. Determined to discover historical truth behind the Greek legends of the Trojan War, Schliemann excavated some of the important towns participating in the drama, Troy, Mycenae, and Tiryns (see also Chapter 8). On Crete, large-scale excavation became possible by 1900 when the island was newly freed from the Ottoman Empire; within a decade the main characteristics of the distinctive Bronze Age culture of Crete were clear. This culture was dubbed "Minoan" by Arthur Evans, the excavator of Knossos, after Minos, the legendary king of the island. On mainland Greece, the Late Bronze Age culture that flourished in its southern and central sections is called "Mycenaean," after the city of Mycenae. A spectacular new chapter in Aegean prehistory was opened in 1967 with the first large-scale excavations at Akrotiri, a settlement on the Aegean island of Thera, well preserved under the volcanic debris from the eruption of the island that may have taken place around 1520 BC.

Figure 7.1 Aegean Bronze Age towns, second millennium BC

Although the names of many Bronze Age cities are well known, thanks to the literature of the later Greeks, the nature of Aegean urbanism is not well understood. With a few notable exceptions, excavations have focused on certain monumental elements of the city, such as palaces, villas, and citadels, or on tombs, their design and their contents. Moreover, the textual evidence is limited: the written documents surviving from the Bronze Age Aegean, when they can be clearly understood, record a limited range of subjects. However, if we consult Childe's definition of a city (see Introduction), it seems likely that the main settlements were indeed cities. All criteria from his list are clearly met, with the one possible exception of the practice of exact and predictive sciences, as yet unconfirmed. Our look at Minoan, Theran, and Mycenaean cities and towns will follow the lead of traditional research concerns. Nonetheless, we will want to keep in mind that future investigation has much to reveal about how these striking structures and finds relate to the overall settlements of which they form a part.

CRETE: KNOSSOS AND THE MINOANS

Crete is the largest island of modern Greece, about 200km long and, at its maximum, 58km wide. It sprawls at the southern end of the Aegean Sea, the last landfall between Greece and Africa. The Cretan landscape combines rugged mountains with pockets of fertile agricultural land, while its Mediterranean climate features rainy, chilly winters and long hot, dry summers.

Minoan history

In the absence of legible records – the "hieroglyphic" and Linear A scripts used by the Minoans are imperfectly understood – the history of the Minoans still has many mysteries. During the New Palace period, the high point of Minoan civilization, the Minoans seem to have controlled the southern Aegean, including the coastal regions of south-east Greece and south-west Anatolia (Turkey). The New Palace period ended ca. 1450 BC in a wave of destruction, the cause of which is uncertain. The Mycenaeans of mainland Greece either contributed to or profited from the collapse. They were on the ascendant, and apparently occupied Knossos and Khania (the important town in as yet little explored western Crete) at this time. They took control of the Minoan territories in the southern Aegean, and probably continued their occupation of Crete through the Late Bronze Age, imposing their own language (the earliest known form of Greek) and writing system (the Linear B script) as the medium of administration. The remains of this period, the fourteenth and thirteenth centuries BC, are poorly known, with the history of Knossos being particularly controversial.

Knossos: the Palace of Minos

The palace is the hallmark of Minoan architecture. Four large palace complexes are known from Bronze Age Crete: Knossos, Mallia, Phaistos, and Kato Zakro. Smaller structures, comparable in design and built of the same ashlar masonry technique, have been discovered at Galatas, Gournia, and Petras. Of these, Knossos is the largest and most important, and has yielded examples of most characteristic features of Minoan civilization. Indeed, so dominant was its position in Cretan culture from the Neolithic to the Bronze Age that archaeologist Jeffrey Soles has persuasively identified it as a cosmological center: a focus of cultural origins, a wellspring of human and divine energy and cultural creativity.

A sustained campaign of excavation began in 1900. Arthur Evans, then 50 years old, had the good fortune to live another 41. He was able to present his findings in a magisterial four-volume publication, *The Palace of Minos*. Not only did he expose the palace and several of the outlying buildings, he also restored portions of the architecture and numerous objects so the public could have a better understanding of the remains. These restorations, virtually impossible to dismantle, are now viewed by scholars as a handicap, for they make it difficult to imagine the evidence in its original state at the time of discovery – important for any reevaluation of its significance.

Although occupation began at Knossos during the Neolithic period and continued through the Bronze Age and indeed well beyond, the ruins one sees today are largely from the heyday of the palace in the New Palace period and the ensuing 75 years, ca. 1700–1375 BC. The terminology for the different phases of Minoan civilization can be confusing, because two systems are used, each serving a useful purpose. The original framework designed by Evans divided Minoan culture into three periods, Early, Middle, and Late Minoan, with further subdivisions (I, II, and III; A and B). Although it continues to serve well the study of pottery development, this system does not correlate with the major breaks in the architectural sequence. To highlight these events, a second system was devised: the Pre-Palatial (= Early Bronze Age), Protopalatial (= Old, or First, Palace), Neopalatial (= New, or Second, Palace), and Post-Palatial periods. The correspondences between the two systems are given in the introductory chart.

The palace occupies an area of 1.3ha on a low hilltop in a well-watered valley some 10km from the sea, not far from the modern city of Heraklion (Figure 7.2). The site is unfortified; indeed, the lack of fortification walls is a striking feature of Minoan towns and palaces during the New Palace period. Only Mallia has yielded a hint of a city wall, nothing more. This absence of fortifications suggests an age of political harmony throughout the island, perhaps under the leadership of Knossos.

The palace complex served many functions, such as royal residence (although we are not sure who ruled at Knossos), seat of administration, treasury, depot for agricultural and manufactured products, and cult center. In general, what survives is the basement floor, and many of the above functions are attested in the small basement rooms. The appearance and function of the now largely vanished upper storeys are uncertain. Nevertheless, some evidence survives to suggest the

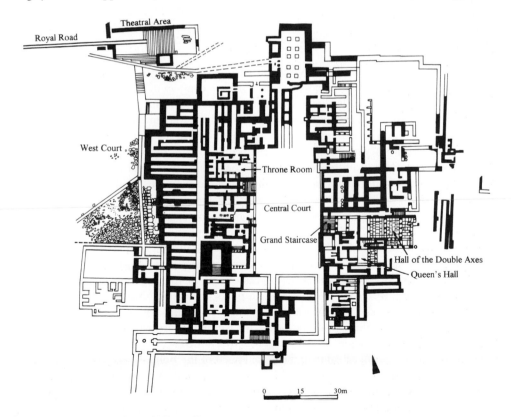

Figure 7.2 Plan, the Palace of Minos, Knossos

reconstruction of these sections. In the south-east, the "Residential Quarters," the Grand Staircase connected at least four superposed levels. Periodic indentations in the west façade of the palace, thickened ground floor walls, fallen debris (such as shattered wall paintings), and large columns bases found *in situ* on upper floors suggest that large public rooms lay upstairs, covering a cluster of basement rooms. So the original appearance of the palace, and the overall balance of larger and smaller rooms, would have been quite different from what one can visualize today.

The palace at Knossos is linked by its complicated plan with a striking legend of the later Greeks, that of King Minos, the Minotaur, and the labyrinth. According to the legend, Pasiphae, Minos's wife, was struck with a passion for a bull. She had Daedalus, the master craftsman, construct a model of a cow for her to climb inside. So skillful was the model that the bull was fooled. In due course Pasiphae gave birth to a monstrous creature, half man, half bull, called the Minotaur. The unfortunate Minotaur was banished to a specially built complex, again designed by Daedalus, a maze-like warren of rooms called the Labyrinth. There the monster consumed an annual tribute of fourteen Athenian youths, male and female, until at last he was slain by Theseus, with the assistance of Minos's daughter, the Princess Ariadne.

Although no evidence from the Bronze Age attests to the existence of Minos or his family, the remains of the "Palace of Minos," as Evans called it, do conjure up the legend of the labyrinth. The plan shows a profusion of small rooms, and at first glance makes little sense. But Minoan architecture has its own logic. Indeed, the general similarities between the palaces and other sites indicate that labyrinthine layout was not a specifically Knossian feature but a general trait, and these ground plans were deliberate. J. W. Graham, a specialist on Minoan architecture, even claimed that a Minoan foot measured 0.3036m, slightly smaller than the English foot, and proposed that the indented west blocks of the palace at Phaistos, at least, were laid out in even numbers of Minoan feet.

If we approach the palace at Knossos from the north-west, coming in along the paved Minoan street known today as the Royal Road, we reach first a low complex of two flights of shallow steps that meet at a right angle, one leading eastwards toward the north entrance to the palace, another leading south toward the flagstone-paved west court and the west entrance. Evans labeled these steps the Theatral Area, imagining ritual dances taking place in the small paved area at the base of the steps. Probably they served simply to direct people toward the two entrances of the palace. The palace entrances are both modest, especially considering the size of the palace. They lead into narrow corridors, not grand halls, providing access to the central court or to stairs to the upper floor. From the north entrance one passes through one side of a pillared hall which supported a dining room above. The discovery of many cooking pots just to the east suggests a kitchen in the area.

The rectangular Central Court is a standard feature in all Minoan palaces. At Knossos it measures ca. 50m × 25m, somewhat larger than the courts elsewhere. Oriented north–south, the axis of the court points toward the notched peak of Mount Juktas, the prominent landscape feature to the south. Minoans revered mountain peaks; they established shrines near summits and sometimes, as here, deliberately oriented their major buildings toward them. In addition to providing access to most sections of the palace, the Central Court may have been the location for bull sports. Several representations of a sport between men (or boys), women (or girls), and bulls survive from Minoan art, among them the Fresco of the Bull Leapers (also known as the Taureador Fresco), a wall painting from the Court of the Stone Spout in the north-east sector of the palace (Figure 7.3). The evidence such images present is somewhat confusing, but it seems the sport involved vaulting over a bull, either by grabbing its horns or by doing a handspring on its back. The risk of getting gored was great, as some depictions show. In what context these

Figure 7.3 Fresco of the Bull Leapers, partly restored, from Knossos. Herakleion Museum

Figure 7.4 Snake goddess, or priestess; faience figurine, head and left forearm restored, from Knossos. Herakleion Museum

sports were performed, whether religious or secular, we don't know.

The basement rooms along the west side of the Central Court were devoted to cult. The Throne Room, so-called by Evans on the basis of the armless stone chair with the back cut out in a flame pattern that was found against its north wall, was in reality a cult room. This small complex consisted of the chair; stone benches along the walls; wall paintings of griffins, imaginary creatures with a lion's body and an eagle's head that served as magical protective beings; and, adjacent to the main room, a so-called Lustral Basin, a gypsum-lined space sunk below the floor of the main room and accessible by two flights of steps. Another common feature in Minoan palaces and villas, Lustral Basins could be used as bathrooms (Minoans eventually took up bathing in clay tubs) or as places for ritual anointings or ablutions. To the south of the Throne Room, beyond the broad staircase that leads to the upper floor, lie a Triple Shrine façade and storerooms for cult objects, including two stone-lined pits sunk in the floor, the Temple Repositories. In these were discovered statuettes of women in typical Minoan multi-layered flounced skirts and tight short-sleeved jackets that exposed the breasts, with snakes wound around their arms (Figure 7.4). These figurines may represent the goddess who seems to stand at the head of the deities worshipped by the Minoans, or these women might be priestesses. The material is faience, a substance related to glass.

To the west of the cult rooms one finds a series of storerooms, narrow rooms that give onto a north–south corridor. The rooms contained *pithoi* (large clay jars) and boxes, lined variously with gypsum, plaster, or lead, sunk into the floor. The pithoi were used for the storage of olive oil, grain, and lentils, important crops in the subsistence-based (or agricultural) economy of the Minoans; the lined boxes could hold valuables as well as food products. Valuable information about the economy of Knossos during the later Post-Palatial period comes from the clay tablets inscribed in the Linear B script. But these tablets are associated with the Mycenaean occupation of the palace; how accurately they reflect earlier Minoan-controlled economic activity is unclear.

The north-east sector of the palace, badly ruined, was the center for craft workshops, such as the production of stone vases. The south-east sector contained the Residential Quarters. Thanks to Evans's reconstructions, these rooms can be well appreciated by visitors. The hill slopes down toward the east, as in fact it does toward the south and west, but on this side the builders of the palace took advantage of the slope and cut down two floors worth from the level of the Central Court. A Grand Staircase leads down, lined with red columns, oval in cross-section, that taper downwards, and round black column capitals (the red and black colors have been restored, based on the evidence of wall paintings). The main rooms on the lowest floor were named by Evans the Queen's Megaron and the Hall of the Double Axes. Both illustrate key features of Minoan domestic architecture.

The Queen's Hall, as it is better called to avoid confusion with the megara of Mycenaean palaces (see below), consists of a main room with a Lustral Basin, or bathroom, off it, on the west side. On the east side, one looks through first a row of piers, then beyond, through a row of two columns to a light well, a tiny open-air courtyard enclosed by high walls. The first row of piers contains niches in their sides, into which the wooden door flaps could be folded during the warm months when the circulation of air was desired, or opened across the spaces between the piers, to close the main room off from the outside air. This sort of divider that can be converted into a wall from a series of piers, either as a whole or in part, is called a pier-and-door partition. The light well provided air and light down to this low level. The Queen's Hall was decorated with wall paintings, mostly geometric patterns. A fresco of dolphins has been installed on the north wall, but this is not its original location. The fragments of the painting, found in the adjacent light well, had fallen from an upper room where they belonged to a decorated floor. The fresco illustrates the Minoan love of sea creatures as subjects for art (for another example of this theme, see Figure

Figure 7.5 Lentoid flask with octopus; Marine Style, LM IB; from Palaikastro. Herakleion Museum

7.5). Presumably the Queen's Hall served as a bedroom, but for whom, despite the regal name given in modern times, is completely unknown. A corridor leads westward to small rooms, stairways to upper floors, and a toilet, this last linked to the extensive system of stone-lined drains that ensured sanitation in this part of the palace.

The bigger Hall of the Double Axes has a somewhat different layout. It too has a main room, paved with gypsum flagstones, that looks out through pier-and-door partitions across a second room toward a light well. But here the main room is enclosed on three sides by pier-and-door partitions, and the second room is just as large as the first. In addition, in the direction opposite the light well, the main room gives onto a colonnade and a terrace, with a private and soothing view, we might imagine, to a garden or grove of trees, the stream below, and the ridge beyond. The Hall takes its name from the symbol carved on its walls. The double axe seems to have had mystical importance for the Minoans. Why there should be so many carved in this room, whether private apartment or public audience hall, is a mystery.

The other palaces known so far show similar features in function and plan. So, too, on a smaller scale, do the "villas" or mansions, found both in the Knossos area and in the countryside. But variations occur as well, especially in siting, dimensions, and decoration. For a comparison with Knossos, the palace at Mallia offers a good contrast (Figure 7.6).

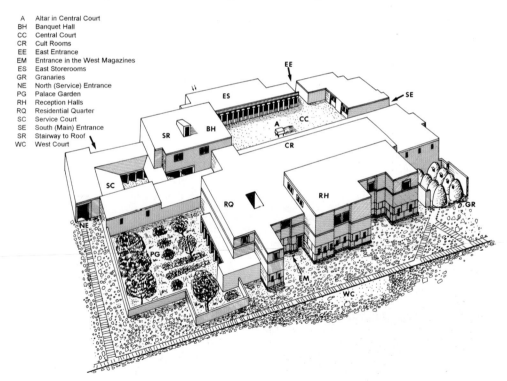

A	Altar in Central Court
BH	Banquet Hall
CC	Central Court
CR	Cult Rooms
EE	East Entrance
EM	Entrance in the West Magazines
ES	East Storerooms
GR	Granaries
NE	North (Service) Entrance
PG	Palace Garden
RH	Reception Halls
RQ	Residential Quarter
SC	Service Court
SE	South (Main) Entrance
SR	Stairway to Roof
WC	West Court

Figure 7.6 Palace of Mallia from the north-west (reconstruction)

Minoan towns: Knossos and Gournia

Although the palaces dominate any consideration of Minoan architecture, we must not forget that they were only the cores of larger towns. At Knossos, a region of 10km² (1,000ha) around the palace has been explored over many decades by the British School of Archaeology at Athens. In the course of excavations and surface surveys, buildings, tombs, roads, and other features of Neolithic, Bronze Age, and Classical antiquity have been recorded on the overall urban plan. The coastal settlement at Amnisos apparently served Knossos as its port. Sinclair Hood, an expert on this region, has estimated that the palace and city of Knossos during the New Palace period occupied 75ha, with 12,000 inhabitants. Greater Knossos, an area estimated at 20km², comprising the city and its immediate hinterland including the harbor, may have contained 15,000–20,000 persons. Colin Renfrew, another specialist, has estimated 4,000–5,000 in the palace, 50,000 in the entire territory controlled by Knossos.

The only Neopalatial Minoan town excavated in its entirety is Gournia. This small settlement on a hill by the sea in eastern Crete was excavated by the American Harriet Boyd Hawes in the first decade of the nineteenth century. Barred from the then men-only excavations, she decided to undertake her own project, and set off on donkey-back for eastern Crete with fellow archaeologist Edith Hall. Gournia has a palace-like building that sits at the summit of the hill and dominates the settlement. The slopes of the hill are covered with blocks of small houses divided by meandering paved streets (Figure 7.7). Houses were often two-storeyed, with rooms for animals and storage on the ground floor, and living quarters for the owners on the upper floor. A stairwell led up through the center of the house. Where it emerged on the flat roof, or onto a terrace covered with light materials (a thatch awning, for example), it was protected by a built cover. This and other features can be seen in a series of small faience plaques from Knossos known as the Town Mosaic, and in the remarkable clay model of a house discovered at Arkhanes (Figure 7.8).

Figure 7.7 Town plan, Gournia

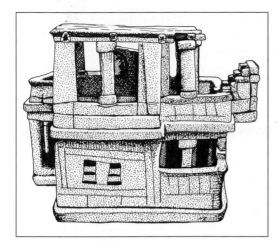

The plan of Gournia, a main building dominating a village of small houses, is but one type of town layout seen in Neopalatial Crete. Other configurations include a central palace surrounded by large houses, or villas (e.g. Knossos); house blocks aligned along cobbled streets, without a dominating palace or villas (Palaikastro); a cluster of villas (Tylissos); and solitary villas off in the countryside, the centers of agricultural estates (Vathypetro).

Figure 7.8 House model, terracotta; MM IIIA; from Arkhanes. Herakleion Museum

THERA: AKROTIRI

Thera, or Santorini (its medieval name), is a cluster of islets in the southern Aegean that once formed part of a single irregularly shaped volcanic island. When the volcano erupted in the mid second millennium BC, the center collapsed into the sea, leaving only the broken rim above water – the islands we see today (Figure 7.9). Volcanic activity since the Bronze Age has produced a new island in the center of the caldera, and from this fumes continue to spew forth.

In 1967, spectacular results from the new excavations at Akrotiri on the southern end of the main island of Thera focused attention on the Bronze Age explosion and its effect throughout the Aegean region. Spyridon Marinatos, the Greek excavator of Akrotiri, had long believed that the explosion of Thera caused or triggered the widespread destructions at the end of the New Palace period on Minoan Crete, ca. 1450 BC. This theory seemed to receive confirmation at Akrotiri: an entire town buried in volcanic pumice and ash. But the pottery found at Akrotiri is contemporary with an earlier phase on Crete, LM IA, and so the date of the explosion has now often been placed ca. 1520 BC. This date is, however, highly controversial. Arguments based on scientific evidence, such as ice-cores from Greenland and growth patterns in tree rings from Ireland, and on new interpretations of correlations of archaeological materials between the Aegean and the Levant and Egypt, have led some to champion an even earlier date, ca. 1628 BC. At least it is now clear that, whatever its effects on Crete, the eruption had no direct influence on the end of the New Palace period.

Only a small portion of Akrotiri had been uncovered by 1974 when the accidental death of Marinatos brought the excavations to a halt. Nevertheless, one gets a good impression of the ancient town. Houses are preserved up to the third storey. Sometimes they stand alone, but often they are grouped in clusters. Doorways, windows, stairs, sewage drains, and the walls of mud brick and irregular stones with wooden branches and beams added for reinforcement can be seen. Streets are not straight and even, but turn, widen, and narrow with irregularity. Sometimes small squares are formed (Figure 7.10). The architecture resembles that of Minoan Crete, but differs in detail, both in form and in construction techniques. The Therans liked pier-and-door partitions, for example, but rarely used light wells. The north façade of one building, Xeste 4, shows an interesting technique of stone masonry, one not seen on Crete: its ashlar courses get progressively smaller from top to bottom.

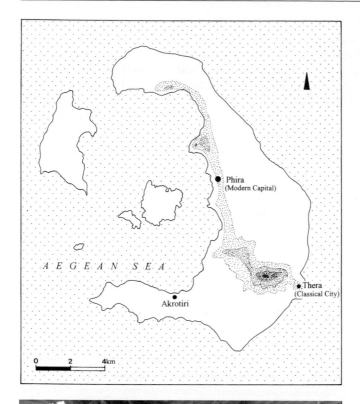

Figure 7.9 Thera (Santorini)

Figure 7.10 West House, Akrotiri, Thera

Although Akrotiri has been called a Bronze Age Pompeii, after the Roman town buried in the eruption of the volcano Vesuvius (see Chapter 21), it differs from Pompeii in one important respect. The inhabitants of Akrotiri were aware of impending disaster, perhaps through earth tremors or fumes, and so escaped, taking their precious belongings with them. Objects left in the houses included pottery and cooking equipment, as well as furniture such as beds, and stone tools and vases, but virtually no metal or other truly valuable luxury items. The many wall paintings, however, they could not remove. These frescoes were in general well preserved, indeed far better than any other from the Bronze Age Aegean, although they often survived only as plaster fragments heaped at the bases of the walls. Restoring and reassembling the pieces has been a painstaking task.

The most important of the paintings is a long strip 40cm high that shows a group of elegant boats making their way between two towns (Figure 7.11). This miniature wall painting comes from Room 5 on the upper floor of the West House, where it was part of a larger program of wall decorations showing people in five towns and a variety of landscapes. The precise subject is much debated: which towns, and which occasion? Lyvia Morgan, in a comprehensive analysis of the painting, favors a nautical procession, a festival celebrating the resumption of the navigation season in late spring, from a minor Theran town to the important center of Akrotiri itself.

Figure 7.11 Ship Fresco (detail); south wall, West House; Akrotiri, Thera

THE MYCENAEANS: MYCENAC AND PYLOS

The Mycenaeans held sway in central and southern Greece during the Late Helladic period (the term used to denote the Late Bronze Age on the Greek mainland), ca. 1650–1050 BC. Their culture jelled in two regions, in Messenia in south-west Greece, and in the home region of Mycenae, the Argolid, the area dominated in Classical Greek times by the city of Argos. From the fifteenth century BC on they expanded their holdings across the Aegean to the Anatolian shore, taking over the territories once controlled by the Minoans. They developed extensive contacts not only with the established civilizations of Egypt and the Levant but also with Europe and the lands of the western Mediterranean. At some point they fought the Trojans of north-west

Anatolia, if we accept that some kernel of truth lay behind the later Greek legends of the Trojan War. Economic conflicts may have sparked the war, perhaps a dispute over access to the rich lands of the Black Sea.

The Mycenaeans were speakers of the earliest known form of Greek. They wrote in the Linear B script, a syllabary derived from the Minoan Linear A. It is not known when the Greek language originated or where, whether inside Greece or brought from elsewhere, but its development has been connected with the movements of peoples speaking other Indo-European languages of which Hittite was another early example (see Chapter 8). The archaeological record shows major changes in material culture during the final phases of the Early Bronze Age, ca. 2300–2000 BC, but after that, a smooth development through the Middle Helladic into the Mycenaean period. We might postulate, as many have, major immigrations of people from Anatolia and south-east Europe into Greece toward the end of the Early Bronze Age, with a continuing trickle afterwards, and gradual fusion of the newcomers' language with those of the locals into what we know as Mycenaean Greek. But this is only a hypothesis. Movements of language groups cannot always be traced in distribution of pottery or other objects, and, conversely, a change in material culture need not indicate a change in ethnic group.

Mycenae

Mycenae, the city that has given its name to the culture, lies 15km from the sea at the north end of the Argive Plain. Its citadel sits on a prominent hilltop, itself in the protective crook of two larger hills. The site was first explored in 1876 by Heinrich Schliemann, the great pioneer of

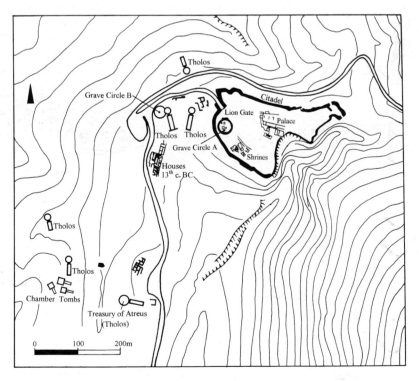

Figure 7.12 Overall site plan, Mycenae: the Late Bronze Age

Aegean prehistory, and has been excavated to the present day by a succession of Greek and British archaeologists (Figure 7.12). As an urban entity, Mycenae seems disconcertingly fragmented. Because of erosion and the building activities of post-Bronze-Age inhabitants, remains of the Late Bronze Age town have been erratically preserved. Its 600 years of history have to be assembled from bits and pieces – some of which are quite spectacular.

The Shaft Graves of Mycenae

The first dramatic evidence of the Mycenaeans comes from Mycenae itself: the Shaft Graves, with their fabulous gold treasure. The Shaft Graves occur in two clusters. The earliest group, dating to ca. 1650–1550 BC, lies outside the thirteenth-century BC citadel, near the modern parking lot. It was surrounded by a low circular wall. Because this cluster was the second to be discovered, in 1951–2, it is known as Grave Circle B.

The later group, ca. 1600–1500 BC, in part contemporaneous with the burials of Circle B, in part later, was discovered by Schliemann in 1876 and P. Stamatakis shortly thereafter just inside the entrance to the citadel. These graves were also surrounded by a circular wall. But this wall was built some 250 years later, part of the rebuilding of the citadel in the thirteenth century BC. Although this later group of Shaft Graves is conveniently known as Grave Circle A, there is no convincing evidence for the existence of a circular wall around them at the time the graves were dug.

A shaft grave is a stone-lined rectangular trench placed at the bottom of a shaft dug out of the bedrock or accumulated earth and lined with rubble walls. The deceased was placed on a floor of pebbles; objects were left in the tomb with the body; the trench was covered with a roof of thin stone slabs supported on wooden beams; and the remaining shaft was then filled with earth. After the funerary meal, the debris, bones, and crockery were thrown into the shaft. Earth was mounded over the top, and in many cases a stele, or thin stone slab, sometimes carved, was planted upright in the earth as a grave marker. When the tomb was reused, as was often the case, the shaft had to be cleared and the roof of the tomb removed. This proved cumbersome, and may explain why the shaft grave type fell out of use by the fifteenth century BC.

Circle B contained fourteen true shaft graves and one later tomb built of masonry. Twenty-four persons were buried here. In Circle A, six Shaft Graves were found, as well as remains of other miscellaneous burials. Nineteen persons were buried in the six shaft graves, eight men, nine women, and two children. The grave goods in these tombs were far more lavish than in the burials of Circle B. Now on display in the National Archaeological Museum in Athens, they include gold funeral masks (Figure 7.13); gold jewelry; bronze daggers inlaid with hunting scenes depicted in gold, silver, and niello, a black metallic

Figure 7.13 Gold funeral mask; Shaft Grave V, Grave Circle A; Mycenae. National Archaeological Museum, Athens

compound; a silver *rhyton*, or ceremonial drinking cup with a pointed bottom, with the siege of a fortress depicted on it in repoussé (the technique of making an image in relief by delicately hammering the metal sheet from the back); and vessels of pottery, stone, and precious metals. Minoan influence is strong. The Mycenaeans had not yet conquered Crete but, although just emerging from the rustic doldrums of the Middle Helladic period, they already recognized the Minoans as the providers of the finest in design and craftsmanship. Minoan style would continue to exert a great attraction for Mycenaean artists long after Minoan Crete had lost its political independence. Certain motifs, however, are specifically Mycenaean in taste, not Minoan: for example, the scenes of hunting and warfare mentioned above. The grave stele found over Shaft Grave V exemplifies this, with its crude but animated carving of a horse, chariot, charioteer, and servant, bordered by thick bands of spirals (Figure 7.14). Despite its feline tail, the creature shown does indeed seem to be a horse, and reminds us that the horse had only recently entered Greece, sometime in the Middle Bronze Age, long after its fellow domesticates, the sheep, goat, pig, and cow. The horse, an import from central or western Asia, may be an authentic sign of migrating Indo-Europeans.

Figure 7.14 Grave stele; Shaft Grave V, Grave Circle A; Mycenae. National Archaeological Museum, Athens

The Treasury of Atreus

By the fifteenth century BC, the burial form of choice for the top of Mycenaean society was no longer the shaft grave but the *tholos* tomb. As we shall see, tholoi (pl. of tholos) are elaborate structures. For ordinary citizens, the chamber tomb sufficed, a room cut out of the rock.

The Greek word "tholos" means simply a round building, and is applied to round structures serving a wide array of functions from all periods of Greek antiquity. In the Mycenaean world, tholoi are round beehive-shaped tombs built of fieldstones or, exceptionally, well-cut stone masonry, laid in the corbelling technique (see Figure 2.18), and then buried, so the earth will provide the necessary counterpressure for the corbelling.

Mycenaean tholoi are first attested in Messenia, but the largest and best known are at Mycenae itself. The best preserved of the nine tholoi at Mycenae is the so-called Treasury of Atreus, a misnomer bestowed already in Classical antiquity. Dating of tholoi is difficult because most of them were stripped of their contents in antiquity. On the basis of the masonry techniques and a deposit of datable pottery found under the threshold, this tomb is placed fairly late in the series, ca. 1300 BC. A *dromos*, or entrance way, 36m long and lined with fine masonry, leads up to the round tomb chamber (Figure 7.15). It is not known whether the dromos remained clear in antiquity, so one could see the great doors, or whether it too was hidden under earth.

Figure 7.15 Dromos and entryway, Treasury of Atreus, Mycenae

One passes through the grand doorway, originally closed with double doors of wood with bronze fittings, and flanked by half columns of green stone (lapis Lacedaemonius) that rose in two tiers. Red porphyry was used for a triglyph and half-rosette frieze in the upper storey. Two massive lintel blocks form the top of the doorway. The larger inner block measures over 8m long and weighs more than 100 tons. To relieve pressure, a triangular space above the lintels was left empty; masked by the frieze just mentioned, it was invisible from the exterior. This feature is called the "relieving triangle."

The interior is 14.5m in diameter at the base, 13.20m in height. Horizontal rows of nail holes suggest gilded bronze rosettes may have decorated the walls. The Treasury of Atreus is unusual in having a side chamber, hewn out of the bedrock. The burials would have been in pits in the floor, to judge from intact examples from other sites, in this case probably in the side chamber. Not a trace has survived. Interestingly, a virtually identical tomb, although less well-preserved, the so-called Treasury of Minyas, was discovered quite some distance away at Orchomenos in Boeotia (central Greece). It may well have been the work of the same architect.

The Citadel

Fortified citadels are characteristic of the Mycenaean centers, especially in the coastal regions of the eastern mainland of Greece. Strong walls protected the nucleus of the settlement. Like the Minoan palace, this core served a variety of activities, administrative, economic, and religious. Unlike the Minoan palace, these purposes were carried out in separate buildings. The most notable of the buildings is the palace, but the Mycenaean palace differs from its Minoan counterpart in several important respects.

The bulk of the populace lived outside the walls. No comprehensive town plan has been recovered from the Mycenaean world, nothing comparable to Gournia, say, on Minoan Crete. But surface surveys conducted in many areas of central and southern Greece have revealed abundant traces of Mycenaean presence. The Mycenaeans had an extensive system of roads; other civil engineering projects, such as the securing of water supplies, large-scale drainage, and dams, have also been located by archaeologists. The best-known project, the draining of the low-lying Copaic basin in Boeotia and protection of the land from encroachment by the sea with a series of dikes, still seems an astonishingly ambitious undertaking for the Bronze Age Aegean.

The citadel walls at Mycenae, 900m in perimeter, enclose an area of ca. 38,500m². The walls seen today were built in the LH IIIA and B periods. The main entrance is in the northwest (see Figure 7.12), the Lion Gate. This gate, erected in the thirteenth century BC, was made of four enormous blocks of local conglomerate, comprising the threshold, the two jambs, and the lintel. Round cuttings can be seen in the lintel and threshold blocks for the fitting of door posts onto which door leaves were attached, and in the jambs for a horizontal bar to insert behind the closed gates. Above the lintel is a relieving triangle covered in front with a striking relief sculpture of two lions in a heraldic pose, their forepaws resting on a pair of altars supporting a single column (Figure 7.16). The lions give their name to the gate. Their heads are missing, however. The possibility therefore exists that these animals were griffins, mythical protective beasts with the heads of eagles and the bodies of lions. Such griffins were earlier depicted by

Figure 7.16 The Lion Gate, Mycenae

the Minoans in the frescoes that flank the carved stone seat in the Throne Room at the Palace of Minos at Knossos. The Mycenaeans featured them as well, notably at the palace at Pylos.

The citadel walls contain different types of masonry, easily distinguished by the visitor today. These include coursed conglomerate ashlar, used at the Lion Gate; *Cyclopean masonry*, that is, huge blocks crudely fitted with tiny stones filling the interstices; and a rusticated limestone polygonal masonry, employed much later in Hellenistic times. Cyclopean masonry received its name from the later Greeks who believed that only giants such as the Cyclopes could wield such large stones. Cyclopean masonry is also seen at Hattusha, the Hittite capital – a puzzling coincidence, considering that links between the Mycenaeans and the Hittites are otherwise rare.

By the mid to late thirteenth century BC the fortified enclosure was completed, an enlargement of the earlier citadel. Also refurbished at this time was Grave Circle A, with a circular parapet constructed around the much earlier Shaft Graves. Notable among the buildings inside the citadel are a series of shrines discovered in the south-west sector of the citadel, including the Room with the Fresco and the House of the Idols, small dark rooms with, respectively, wall paintings and grotesque clay figurines of humanoids and coiled snakes. Such small rooms, all that Mycenaean sites have so far yielded in terms of temples, recall the shrines in Minoan palaces. Names of divinities revealed on Linear B tablets include gods familiar from the later Greek period, such as Zeus, Hera, and Poseidon.

The ground rises steeply from the Lion Gate. The highest ground within the walled citadel was occupied by the palace, as was typical. Owing to its lofty and exposed location, the palace at Mycenae has largely eroded away. The tourist standing amidst its fragmentary ruins must content himself or herself with the magnificent view over the Argive Plain. For a clearer understanding of the layout of a Mycenaean palace, one must travel across the Peloponnesus to extreme south-west Greece, to Pylos in Messenia.

Pylos: the Palace of Nestor

In 1939, the American archaeologist Carl Blegen discovered a Mycenaean palace at Ano Englianos, a hilltop overlooking the Bay of Navarino to the south, not far from the modern town of Pylos. Under the influence of Homer, Blegen attributed the palace to Nestor, the wise ruler of Pylos in the *Iliad* and the *Odyssey*. Although the place is named (PU-RO) in several of the many Linear B tablets found here, Nestor is not, so Blegen's leap of faith must be regarded with caution.

The palace we see today was built largely in the thirteenth century BC, in the LH IIIB period, and burned ca. 1200 BC. This palace did not have a fortification wall, most unusual for a Mycenaean center. Evidently it had no rivals in its immediate vicinity, unlike Mycenae. Its destruction would be the work of invaders from afar. Indeed, the palace served as the nerve center for a large area in south-west Messenia, a region whose history from the Bronze Age to the present is now being documented by an ambitious multi-disciplinary survey project, the Pylos Regional Archaeological Project (PRAP, for short).

The palace is small, only one-fourth the size of the palace at Knossos (Figure 7.17). Walls were built of rubble cores reinforced with a timber framework, and faced with pale limestone ashlar masonry. One enters through a modest gateway, flanked by two archive rooms on the left (find spot of ca. 1,000 Linear B tablets and fragments) and a possible tower on the right. After passing through a small court, one reaches the distinctive core of this and all Mycenaean palaces, the *megaron*. "Megaron" is the word used in Homer to denote the great hall. From Schliemann on, Classically minded archaeologists have attached this word to a variety of hall-like rooms. In

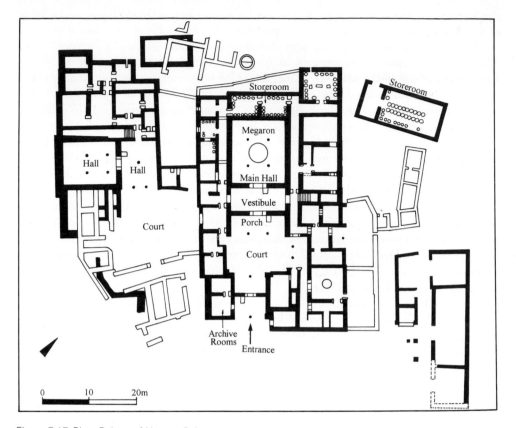

Figure 7.17 Plan, Palace of Nestor, Pylos

Mycenaean architecture the word has assumed a distinct meaning. The Mycenaean megaron is a unit of normally three rectangular spaces, arranged along a single axis: a porch, a vestibule, and a much larger main room. At Pylos, the main room would have been attractive, although dark and smoky. Dominating the room is a large, low circular platform: a hearth. The hearth rim was repeatedly coated with lime plaster and painted with spirals, its sides with flame patterns. The floor and walls of the room were plastered and decorated with frescoes. Four wooden columns, arranged around the hearth, held up the ceiling. The columns have long since vanished, but the small round holes into which they were inserted can still be seen, preserved by the plastered floor laid around them. Also gone is the roofing, of branches, twigs, and clay, but the broad clay pipes through which smoke from the fire on the hearth escaped have survived. What sort of windows might have existed, if any, is unknown. In the floor along the north wall is a cutting for a wooden chair, probably similar in design to the stone chair in the Throne Room at Knossos. Next to this is a curious and unexplained hollow in the plaster floor, two small basins connected by a curved groove.

The megaron is surrounded by rooms devoted to the important economic activities of the palace. As the Linear B tablets attest, the palace was the center for the collection and redistribution of the agricultural produce and manufactured products of the region. Storerooms for wine, olive oil, and grain have been identified, as have workshops for smiths, masons, and the manufacture of perfume. The palace has also yielded much pottery. In one room, 2,853 stemmed drinking cups were found, leading Blegen to joke that Nestor, an august figure in Homeric poems, was a dealer in kitchenware.

THE END OF MYCENAEAN CIVILIZATION

The Palace of Nestor was destroyed ca. 1200 BC. The people responsible are unknown, but the destruction fits in with a pattern of disasters that overwhelmed the established cultures of the eastern Mediterranean in the late thirteenth and twelfth centuries BC. At Mycenae and the neighboring fortress of Tiryns, impending danger is seen in the citadel architecture. At both sites, the inhabitants secured their supply of water by enclosing a spring within a new north-east extension of the walls (Mycenae) or digging an underground passageway from within the citadel to the spring just outside (Tiryns). Mycenae underwent a series of challenges during this period. Invaders were perhaps responsible, but local unrest may also have contributed, perhaps stimulated by climate changes and crop failures. Whatever the reasons, by the end of the twelfth century BC the sophisticated economic and social system based on the palaces and citadels and their dependent cities, with records written in Linear B, had collapsed. The Aegean basin reverted to a village-based economy, with little external trade and few luxuries. Self-sufficiency became the byword of the Greek Dark Ages.

CHAPTER 8

Anatolian Bronze Age cities

Troy and Hattusha

Troy:

    Troy I: ca. 2900–2400 BC

    Troy II: ca. 2400–2100 BC

    Troy III–V: ca. 2100–1800 BC

    Troy VI: ca. 1800–1300 BC

    Troy VIIa: ca. 1300–1260 BC

    Troy VIIb 1: ca. 1260–1190 BC

    Troy VIIb 2: ca. 1190–1100 BC

The Hittites:

    Old Hittite Kingdom: ca. 1575–1400 BC

    Middle Kingdom: ca. 1400–1350 BC

    Hittite Empire: ca. 1350–1200 BC

The term Anatolia, derived from the Greek word for "east," is commonly used to denote the Asian territory of modern Turkey in pre-Classical antiquity. Anatolia is divided into two geographical zones, the coast and the interior. The coastal zones have a moderate climate, with cool, rainy winters and hot, rainless summers, whereas the interior plateau, at an elevation of 1,000m, has a continental climate with snowy winters and dry summers. The geographical distinctions between the two areas have been accompanied by cultural differences even down to the modern day. Cities of the coast have looked across the seas for their livelihood, while the interior has depended on its conservative self-contained farming and craft traditions. The two best-known cities of Bronze Age Anatolia illustrate well the dichotomy between these two regions: Troy, in the coastal region of north-west Anatolia, and Hattusha, the capital of the Hittites, in the central plateau (Figure 8.1).

TROY

Troy is one of the most famous cities of Mediterranean antiquity. The war supposedly fought here between the Trojans and the Myceneans (or Achaeans, as Homer called them) occupied a

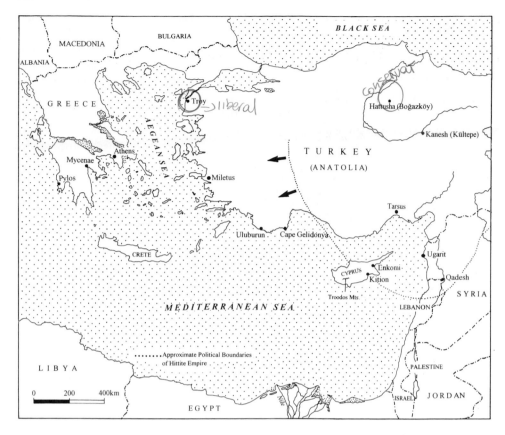

Figure 8.1 Anatolia and the eastern Mediterranean in the Late Bronze Age

preeminent place in the consciousness of the ancient Greeks, with the works of countless writers, sculptors, and painters bearing witness to the pull of this dramatic conflict. The archaeological evidence, however, presents a Troy rather different from that described in the literary sources. We should see this discrepancy not as a roadblock but as a fascinating intellectual problem: how should we interpret the complementary but often conflicting contributions that literary and archaeological evidence make to our understanding of antiquity?

If we follow the indications of the ancient Greeks, the war must have taken place during what we call the Late Bronze Age. No contemporary accounts of the war exist. Some modern scholars have even doubted whether this conflict took place at all, considering it instead a myth developed by later Greeks to flesh out their remote past. The question is difficult to answer. Most probably the story contained a kernel of truth, even if the actual events were much distorted in the telling. What that kernel might be has been much debated, and with it, the explanation of the archaeological site of Troy.

The site came to public attention in the mid nineteenth century with the excavations of Heinrich Schliemann. Schliemann (1822–90), the son of a German pastor, made a fortune in business in Russia and in the United States. But since childhood, or so he claimed, he cherished an obsessive interest in the *Iliad* and the *Odyssey*, the great epic poems of Homer. Against prevailing scholarly opinion, he believed the poems had a basis in reality, and he determined to prove it. In 1870, he obtained a permit from the Ottoman government and began excavations at the mound of Hisarlık in north-west Turkey, the site he equated with the Troy of Homer. Although controversy still surrounds the accuracy and honesty of his reports, it cannot be denied that in the course of his work at Troy, and at other sites mentioned in the Homeric poems, notably Mycenae and Tiryns, he completely altered the study of the pre-Classical Aegean world.

The site of Hisarlık was known in Classical times as Ilion, a name used in Homer as an alternate for Troy. Through the Roman period it was only a small town, but Greeks and Romans venerated it as the site of Homeric Troy. Alexander the Great and Julius Caesar both paid their respects here to the long-vanished heroes. After antiquity, the site was abandoned and by the nineteenth century had lost all association with the events recorded in Homer. Consequently, even for those who believed in the reality of the war, the plain in which Troy sits offered other appealing candidates for the site of the famous citadel.

Schliemann believed Hisarlık the best candidate. He was not, however, the first to dig at this site. That distinction belongs to Frank Calvert, an Englishman who served as the American consul in the nearby city of Çanakkale, and who first directed Schliemann's attention to Hisarlık. But Schliemann's campaigns, on a large scale hitherto unmatched and with precise intellectual aims, captured the attention of the educated world at large. Schliemann at first had no idea of the significance of his finds. But he was a pioneer, with precious little to guide him; before he began at Troy, the sequence and dating of cultures in the Aegean Bronze Age were poorly understood. Great advances were made in the following decades, but Schliemann's life drew to a close before he could fully assimilate these new findings. It would fall to Wilhelm Dörpfeld, the young architect Schliemann had taken on as an assistant, to clarify, in the 1890s, the sequence at Troy, with further modification in the 1930s by Carl Blegen and a team from the University of Cincinnati and, since 1988, by a joint project of the Universities of Tübingen and Cincinnati under the direction of Manfred Korfmann.

Troy is a _höyük_, that is, an artificial mound consisting of the remains of successive layers of human habitation, very much like other such mounds in the Aegean and Anatolia. Built at the end of a natural ridge that projects from east to west into the plain of the Scamander River, just south of the Dardanelles, the mound developed in the standard manner with, in general, each succeeding town built on top of the preceding one and enlarging its boundaries, spilling out beyond the confines of the earlier settlement (Figure 8.2). Today's visitor does not see this clearly, because the construction in the Greek period of a temple to Athena sheared off the top of the mound. Moreover, extensive modern excavations have also removed much. What one sees, then, is a series of concentric circles, the remains of the outer sections of each level.

Schliemann and Dörpfeld divided the many habitation levels into nine major periods; subsequent research has split these into numerous phases. These 'nine cities' of Troy range in date from the Early Bronze Age (Troy I) through the Greek (Troy VIII) and Roman (Troy IX) periods. Which level corresponds to the Troy of Priam and Homer is still a subject of debate (see below).

The current excavations, begun in 1988, have contributed important new information about the site. The previously excavated mound has been demonstrated to be only the small (2ha) fortified citadel of a larger town. Exploration south of the citadel has revealed the existence of an enclosed lower city of Troy VI and VII, 18ha in area, underlying the much later Roman town. The combination of citadel and lower city is familiar from such Aegean sites as Tiryns. Middle and Late Bronze Age Troy has now become a respectably sized town, comparable to other Aegean centers, and as such a credible opponent of Mycenae and its allies. But Troy also had Anatolian connections. The fortification wall is of Anatolian-Near Eastern type, with foundations consisting of stone-walled compartments filled with earth. Such "casemate" walls have been

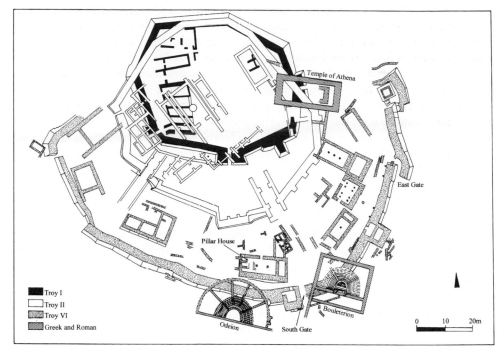

Figure 8.2 Plan, the Citadel, Troy: major buildings

discovered also at LBA Miletus, further south on the Aegean coast, and at Hattusha, the Hittite capital.

What was the nature of the site? It would seem that the walled citadel contained houses and meeting places for rulers and some of their subjects, and offered refuge in times of trouble. The Lower City of Troy VI and VII contained more extensive habitation. Beyond the walls would be farmhouses and such connected areas as cemeteries, but this is still poorly known. For a sample of the remains of Troy, let us look at three levels of particular interest: Troy II, with its fortifications and megarons; Troy VI, with its walls, gates, and representative houses; and Troy VII A, with its possible preparations for a siege.

Troy II

Troy II is the major level of the Early Bronze Age. The walls enclose a roughly circular area some 110m in diameter. Like those of the preceding Troy I, these walls were built of stone foundations with a sun-dried mud brick superstructure. The foundations alone survive, 2m high, made of small, unworked stones. Their exterior surface is battered, that is, sloping, a distinctive characteristic of the walls of Troy in all periods. Towers stood at intervals of 10m. Today, the visitor can admire in particular the south-west gate. A long steep ramp leads up to the gateway, laid out on a three-part plan, outer and inner gates with a central room in between. Such a plan allows for a better control of those coming in or out.

The main buildings inside Troy II are called megarons, after Homer – here, simple long rectangular structures, with a front porch and a larger rectangular room behind. In contrast with later Mycenaean megarons, the Troy II examples are free-standing, not embedded inside a larger palace complex. They stand parallel to each other, aligned on a north-east–south-west axis. The largest has been labeled Megaron II A. Although much of its western side was destroyed by Schliemann before he realized what he was digging through, its measurements can be reconstructed as roughly 30m × 10m. Its walls consisted of sun-dried bricks, reinforced by wooden beams, erected on foundation of large unworked stones. Remains of a circular clay platform, the ancestor of the hearth in the Mycenaean megaron, were discovered in the middle of the beaten clay floor. The building is sufficiently wide that a central row of columns must have supported the flat roof of clay and reeds laid on beams. Presumably the columns were of wood, but all traces have vanished. As the centuries progressed, smaller houses filled the open spaces in front of the large megarons, as if the need to shelter more people within the fortified space grew more pressing.

Troy VI and VIIa

Troy VI, the next major period of the citadel's history, encompassed a significantly greater area than its predecessors: again a rough circle, but now with a diameter of nearly 200m. Much has been destroyed, but we can appreciate the improved quality of the construction in certain surviving sections. The walls are particularly striking. The east wall, tower, and baffle gateway are the first features that greet the modern visitor. The walls are tall, their stone foundations surviving to a height of some 9m in places, fortified with massive towers 8m square. The stones are somewhat larger than in the Troy II walls, and they are now well cut and placed without mortar in fairly regular courses. As in earlier walls, the exterior face slopes outward. In addition, the wall face frequently juts out slightly in vertical offsets that serve to alter the direction of the wall, perhaps simply a handsome elaboration of a continuously curving wall. As usual, the superstructure would have been made of mud brick, now disappeared.

The baffle entry on the north-east provides good defense. The wall reaches out to the east, overlapping the continuation of the wall to the south. The entryway runs between the parallel stretches of wall, creating a corridor which soldiers could patrol from above on both sides. In contrast, the badly ruined South Gate, the main entrance to the citadel, has a simple plan: just an open passage 3.30m wide within the wall, with a tower eventually added at one side. A paved street ran uphill from the gate.

The center of Troy VI was destroyed by later Classical builders and by early excavations. Had there been a palace, it must have stood there, on that commanding spot. Some houses or buildings have survived on the fringes; a striking example is the so-called Pillar House. As in Troy II, these buildings are generally free-standing, brick walls (now gone) on stone foundations. Wooden beams were occasionally used as reinforcements. Different and very interesting is the slight trapezoidal shape of many of these houses. Apparently oriented toward a central point in the citadel, the side walls of the houses are not parallel but converge slightly toward the center of the mound. The other two sides of a house, perpendicular to the converging sides, are parallel. The purpose of such planning is unclear. Perhaps, as Dörpfeld suggested, builders intended to maintain the even width of paths leading into the citadel. But the surviving ground plan of Troy VI, not particularly regular, does not substantiate Dörpfeld's thesis.

Archaeology and the Trojan War

Such fragments of fortification walls and houses are the archaeological reality of the site of Troy. Onto them are projected visions of the literary Troy, the citadel attacked by the Achaeans in ancient Greek legend. It is easy to see that the fit is not neat. For over a century, attempts have been made to determine which habitation level at Hisarlık might have been Priam's city, sacked by the Achaeans. The controversy continues to this very day. For those who believe in the historicity of the Trojan War there are two options.

First, Troy VIIa. The inhabitants of VIIa rebuilt the walls of VI. Most significantly, this settlement shows signs of enduring a siege. Like VI, its houses are preserved only on the edges of the citadel. But those houses are packed together, sharing walls, and contained an extraordinary quantity of pithoi, or clay storage vessels, often sunk into the house floors. This settlement was destroyed by fire. Some, but not many, human skeletal remains were found in the debris. For Blegen, such evidence indicated a town facing an invasion. Its inhabitants retreated from the surrounding countryside into the fortified citadel, built shelters hastily, and laid up food supplies. In the end the town was captured and burned.

The date of the end of Troy VIIa seems to fit: ca. 1260 BC, according to Blegen, based on the datable Mycenaean pottery finds, a period when Mycenaean Greece (= the Achaean attackers) was at its most prosperous. But current opinion has veered back to the level favored by Dörpfeld: Troy VI. The destruction of Troy VI has been attributed to people or to earthquake; it is in fact not easy to distinguish the one agent from the other. Perhaps both worked together, as has been suggested: an earthquake crippled the city of Troy, allowing the besieging invaders easy access.

Blegen's datings have been challenged, too. Such revisions depend on a different interpretation of the decoration on a particular handful of sherds. Some have even placed the end of VI in the mid thirteenth, and the end of VIIa in the early twelfth century BC. According to this scenario, the besieged VIIa would have been destroyed during the vast movement of marauding peoples that disrupted the eastern Mediterranean during the late thirteenth and twelfth centuries BC.

The Trojans left no written documents. The Mycenaeans, although they did write, left no testimony about such a conflict; and the Hittite records do not report it, at least not directly. Tantalizing, therefore, are possible Hittite mentions of relevant places and participants. Are "Ahhiyawa," "Wilusa," and "Aleksandus" to be equated with Achaea, Ilios, and Alexandros (Paris, the son of Priam)? And if so, can the snippets of information help us understand the nature of the war, and when it took place? These matters are highly controversial. The Aegean world lay outside the direct control of the Hittites. Although the Trojans and the Hittites both inhabited the same land mass, Anatolia, the central plateau where the Hittites reigned supreme is physically and psychologically far removed from the coastal regions.

HATTUSHA AND THE HITTITES

Hattusha, the capital of the Hittite Empire in the Late Bronze Age, is of paramount importance for the ancient history of Anatolia. This ruined city is by far the major source for information about the Hittites. No other site in LBA Anatolia has yet matched the vast sweep of its ruins nor the richness of its archives of clay tablets written in the Hittite language. Without the excavations at Hattusha, our knowledge of the Hittites would be scanty indeed.

The Hittites are the earliest attested speakers of an Indo-European language. Indo-European is the name given by modern scholars to a large group of languages related in grammar and vocabulary, a family that stretches eastwards across Europe from Ireland, including most of the languages of modern Europe, to western Asia (Persian) and northern India (Urdu and Hindi).

This family is distinct from the Semitic (ancient Akkadian; modern Arabic and Hebrew) and Uralo-Altaic (Turkish) languages also represented in this region today. The Hittite language was first written in the early sixteenth century BC, in a cuneiform adapted from the Old Babylonian scripts used in northern Syria, and later in a hieroglyphic script as well. It thus predates the Greek of Linear B by some 200 years.

The Indo-European speakers, some believe, originated in the Caucasus or central Asia and migrated west and southwards at various times throughout antiquity. Over time and in different geographical locations, and mixing with local peoples speaking different languages, the original Proto-Indo-European language (which is only a hypothetical construct) developed in many different ways. The group that became the Hittites entered Anatolia sometime before 2000 BC, during the Early Bronze Age. They gained control of central Anatolia in the succeeding centuries, and continued as rulers until the destruction of their empire around 1200 BC. After that, in the Iron Age, a variant of the Hittites regrouped in small kingdoms in south-east Anatolia. One important center was Carchemish, now on the Turkish–Syrian border. These people are known as the Neo-Hittites or Syro-Hittites; they are one of the two groups of people called "Hittites" in the Hebrew Bible, the other being the "sons of Heth" living in Palestine. Neither is to be confused with the Hittites of the Late Bronze Age discussed in this chapter.

The LBA Hittites emerged after the collapse of the Assyrian Colonies, commercial outposts of northern Mesopotamians established in central Anatolia during the Middle Bronze Age, ca. 1850–1650 BC. The Assyrian Colonists had their most important *karum*, or center, at the city of Kanesh (the site of Kültepe, near Kayseri). They wrote on clay tablets in the Akkadian language, the earliest written documents from Anatolia, which provide much valuable information about economic and social matters.

Early rulers mentioned in the tablets of the Assyrian Colonists were Hittites. One of them, Anitta (early seventeenth century BC), is confirmed by a dagger, discovered at Kültepe, inscribed with the phrase, "the palace of Anitta the ruler." The palace was surely at Kanesh. Anitta did settle at Kanesh, and Kanesh became a symbolically important ancestral home for the Hittites; indeed, they called themselves "Neshites" after their name for Kanesh, "Nesha." The name "Hittite" comes from the place name of "Hatti," the land inhabited by pre-Hittite peoples of central Anatolia.

Among the conquests of Anitta was the city of Hattusha, then occupied by Assyrian Colonists and Hattic locals. Ironically, after he destroyed the town, Anitta cursed it so no one would settle there again. A few generations after Anitta, however, Hattusha was resettled under the ruler who adopted the name of Hattushili, which means "Man of Hattusha." From this new capital, Hattushili I expanded his territory toward the south-east, into modern Syria. His successor, Murshili I, pushed even further, sacking Babylon ca. 1530 BC and ending the Old Babylonian dynasty founded by Hammurabi. But Babylon proved too distant for the Hittites to hold permanently; their south-east frontier would remain in Syria.

A later king, Shuppiluliuma I (ruled ca. 1343–1318 BC), had unusual diplomatic dealings with the Egyptians, perennial rivals in the Levant. A letter preserved in the Hittite archives gives a touching glimpse into the chaos of post-Amarna Egypt, at the end of the Eighteenth Dynasty. Ankhesenamun, the widow of Tutankhamun, wrote to the Hittite king: "My husband has died. A son I have not. But to thee, they say, the sons are many. If thou wouldst give me one son of thine, he would become my husband. Never shall I pick out a servant of mine and make him my husband . . . I am afraid!" (Redford 1984: 217). After much negotiation, Shuppiluliuma did send one of his sons. But power in Egypt was already being wrested from the queen. The unfortunate Hittite prince was murdered, his potential bride never heard from again.

Although this disaster did not ignite a war, the Hittites came to blows with the Egyptians in 1275 BC at Qadesh, the result of their conflicting interests in Syria. The battle was a standoff, with the Hittites fending off the Egyptians and keeping control of their Syrian territories. Original copies of the peace treaty prepared some 16 years later have survived, a clay tablet written in Hittite, discovered at excavations at Hattusha, and the Egyptian version, carved on the walls of the temple of Amun at Karnak. But Ramses II was not content with merely a standoff, so in the relief sculptures at Abu Simbel he had the Battle of Qadesh proclaimed as a great victory.

Despite prosperity for much of the thirteenth century BC, the empire weakened swiftly at the end of the century. We don't know what happened, but the menace was real: the city was captured and destroyed ca. 1200 BC, a disaster that fits within the larger picture of the chaotic conditions prevailing throughout the eastern Mediterranean at the end of the Late Bronze Age.

Hattusha (Boğazköy)

Hattusha is located in central Anatolia, a three-hour drive to the east of Ankara. The site is often called Boğazköy, the older name of the modern village of Boğazkale that occupies the edge of the ancient city. Brought to public notice by Charles Texier after a visit in 1834, the ruins were explored sporadically during the rest of the nineteenth century by various people, and then systematically during the twentieth century by the German Oriental Society and the German Archaeological Institute, with excavations still continuing.

The topography of Boğazköy is dramatic and on a grand scale. The site, measuring 2.1km on the north–south axis, includes rocky pinnacles and deep, narrow valleys as well as level areas. In addition, the terrain slopes sharply, with the southern rim lying ca. 280m higher than the north edge (Figure 8.3).

During the thirteenth century BC, this vast walled area served as a royal and sacred enclosure, containing palaces and numerous temples. Archaeology has done much to expose the royal and the ceremonial aspects of Hattusha, with four sectors being of particular importance: the walls and gates, the Great Temple, the citadel, and the rock-cut sanctuary at nearby Yazılıkaya. The town proper lay outside to the north-west, near and under the modern village. Excavations in this zone have been few, and nothing can be seen today. Fortunately the Hittite tablets give a lively picture of the society, so we have some compensation.

Walls and gates

To fortify the site, the Hittites combined natural topographical features with walls. The walls have stone foundations, not solid, but consisting of linked cells or compartments, which were then filled with earth. This distinctive casemate plan offered the advantage of economizing on stone. The now vanished superstructures were of sun-dried mud brick.

Of the many gates into the city, the three on the south are particularly impressive. Two are similar, the King's Gate on the south-east, and the Lion Gate on the south-west. The third, the Sphinx Gate in the south center between the other two, is different.

The King's Gate and the Lion Gate are both named after reliefs sculpted on their doorways. But the positioning of the sculpture differs. The profile figure of most probably a god rather than a king stands on the inner entry, to the left of the doorway as one faces it, whereas the lions, and there are two of them, face frontward on either side of the outer entry of that gate (Figure 8.4). This difference in position may relate to the direction of a ceremonial procession that passed through these gates.

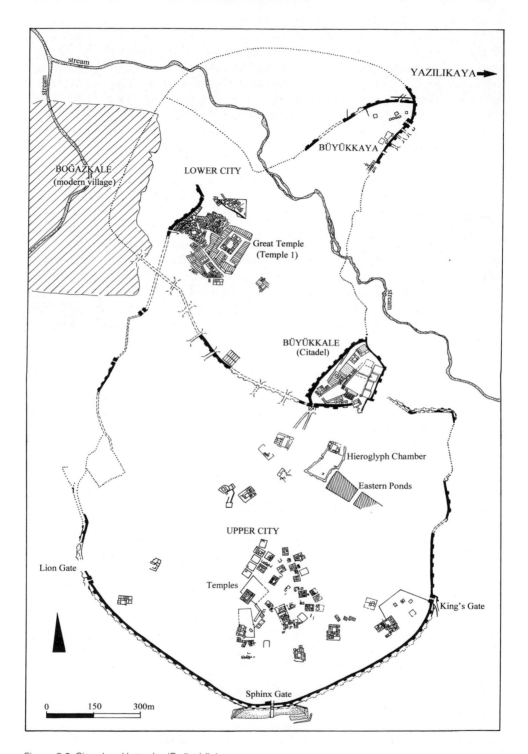

Figure 8.3 City plan, Hattusha (Boğazköy)

Figure 8.4 The Lion Gate, Hattusha

The gates themselves consist of a chamber within two monumental doorways. The massive stone frames of these portals were of distinctive parabolic shape. Alongside the outer doorways patches of Cyclopean masonry extend the feeling of monumentality. This technique recalls Mycenaean construction, as does the corbelled vaulting in the postern gate below the Sphinx Gate, but it is not clear whether this reflects direct contacts between the two cultures or is coincidental.

The Sphinx Gate stands at the highest point of the city, on its southern end. Its ground plan featuring the usual chamber with inner and outer doorways, the gate was protected on both the interior and the exterior by a pair of smiling sphinxes. Unlike the other two gates, however, this one stands on top of a vast glacis, a sloping earthwork covered with paving stones. Access is not direct, but comes via one of the steep flights of steps at either end of the glacis. These steps excluded any access by wheeled vehicles. In their elaboration, the gate and the glacis seem specially constructed for ceremony. The main, practical entrance into the city must have been below to the north, near the residential area.

The discovery of 31 temples in the upper (southern) sector confirms the ceremonial purpose of the three monumental gates. The Hittites seemed loath to discard the gods of the peoples they conquered, preferring instead to bring them into their own burgeoning pantheon. To service these cults, many temples were required. The grandest of the temples at Hattusha did not lie in this upper sector, however, but to the north, on lower ground.

The Great Temple

The Great Temple, the largest of the temples at Hattusha and the cult center for the lower town, is sometimes called Temple I because it was the first one discovered. It is preserved only in foundations, as is true for the other temples, but nonetheless its complexity can easily be appreciated. At its core is the temple proper, a rectangular building with a central court and surrounding rooms. Two large cult rooms lie to the north of the court. These rooms have windows in the north side, thus allowing much more light than was typical in the eastern Mediterranean region, where the deity usually lived in either indirect light obtained through clerestories (Mesopotamia) or total darkness (Egypt). The gods worshipped here are thought to be the two main Hittite gods, the storm or weather god and the sun goddess. Their statues have not survived, but they are depicted in the reliefs in the rock-cut sanctuary at Yazılıkaya (see below). Other rooms that surround the temple court must have been devoted to ritual, for the priests and for the rulers (who themselves served as priests and priestesses). The temple was built in the distinctive manner of Hattusha: a timber framework filled with mud bricks, plastered and painted, was erected on top of massive stone foundations. One can still see the foundation blocks, and in them the drill holes into which the dowels that secured the wooden framework were fitted, but timber and mudbrick are gone.

The temple proper was surrounded by a paved street, and beyond that by blocks of long narrow storerooms. Several passages gave access into the paved street, but the main gateway lay on the south-east side. The thickness of the stone foundations and the presence of several stairwells indicate that the storerooms had two, sometimes three floors, with rooms on upper floors perhaps spanning several of the long narrow foundation rooms. What was stored in the rooms is uncertain. Apart from an important find of tablets, some seal impressions, and pithoi (for storing liquids) sunk in the ground, little was left after the destruction of the city. But the extent of the storerooms shows clearly that this complex was a center for the receiving and distribution of goods – rather like a Minoan palace.

The Citadel: Büyükkale

Overlooking the Great Temple is the citadel, today best known by the Turkish name of Büyükkale. This hilltop is naturally fortified on the north and east by a gorge. On the west and south, walls were added. This fortress was the seat of government, the site of the ruler's palace, his residence and official quarters. It was also the location of the archives, and, along with Temple I, was the great source for the thousands of clay tablets that have told us so much about the Hittites. The area is divided into outer and inner sectors, each a series of buildings grouped around an open-air court. The king's private quarters lay on the inside. Today the visitor sees the stone foundations of the buildings of the thirteenth century BC. The site was occupied both earlier and later, but those remains have been recorded and either covered over or removed. The foundations show what appear to be long narrow rooms, or compartments without access. We must remember that we are looking at basements, as was the case with Minoan palaces. The rooms proper would have been on higher floors. The long traverses held the columns that in large halls, at least, supported the ceiling or upper floor.

Yazılıkaya

The most striking religious site of the Hittites is the sanctuary of Yazılıkaya, which lies 2km north-east of the city. The shrine was built during the thirteenth century BC, apparently for the performance of a New Year's festival in honor of the storm god. It consists of three open-air chambers formed by the natural rock. The area was originally concealed by a series of buildings erected in front, but today we can peer in, for these buildings survive only in stone foundation. In addition, the smallest of the three chambers has been sealed off (Figure 8.5).

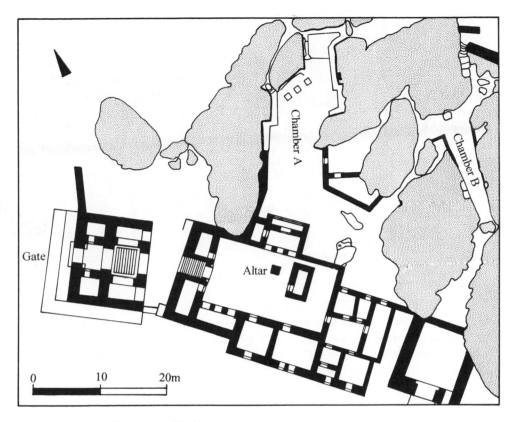

Figure 8.5 Plan, the Sanctuary at Yazılıkaya

The sanctuary is of particular interest for the reliefs carved on its walls. In the main chamber, two processions of gods, one primarily of males, one of females, head toward the rear of the chamber. Most of these gods are identified by inscriptions; they turn out to have Hurrian names, not Hittite, evidence for the strong cultural influence of the conquered Hurrians upon the Hittites. The main scene at the rear of the chamber shows the meeting of the two principal gods (Figure 8.6). Teshub, the great weather god of Hatti, stands on the left, on top of two mountain gods represented as two men bending over. He wears a tall horned cap, which indicates his divinity and his rank. Alongside him stands a small bull in running position; the bull's pointed hat indicates its divinity. Behind Teshub, on a twin-peaked platform, is the weather god of the city of Hattusha. Teshub faces his wife, the sun goddess of Arinna, labeled here by her Hurrian name, Hepat. She stands on a panther, which in turn is on pedestals perhaps representing mountains. She wears a long skirt and a tall flattened hat. Alongside her is another running bull with hat. These two bulls are Hurri and Shurri, who pull their chariots. To the right of Hepat are their children, first their son, Sharruma, standing on a panther on mountains, and then their two daughters, perched on a double-headed eagle. The children and indeed all the other gods shown in the entire procession are much smaller in scale than are Teshub and Hepat. The males are depicted in the traditional style of Ancient Near Eastern art, with profile heads and legs, but frontal torsos. Females, on the other hand, are mostly depicted in profile, because both arms are held outstretched.

Figure 8.6 Meeting of the Gods, relief sculpture, Yazılıkaya

On an isolated panel on the right side of the chamber, but facing the meeting of the main gods, a Hittite king dressed in a round cap and a long robe stands in profile on mountain peaks. This is Tudhaliya IV (ruled 1235–1215 BC), identified by the hieroglyph inscribed above his outstretched fist, perhaps the builder of this sanctuary, a king much interested in the proper practice of religion. Because the king is shown even larger than the main deities, it is possible that this panel was added later, perhaps even after his death when he would have been considered a god.

The relief sculptures do not form a neat, continuous band, but instead consist of panels which to our eyes seem arbitrarily placed. The reason for this arrangement is unclear. Other features in the room include rock-cut benches beneath certain panels and various depressions in which offerings could have been placed. The flooring originally consisted of stone slabs.

The main side chamber, entered through a narrow passage guarded by the carved figures of two demons, may have been a funeral chapel for Tudhaliya IV, although no burials were found here. This long narrow room contained a few niches cut out of the wall, possibly for crematory urns. Three reliefs physically unconnected with each other decorate the walls. The first is a complex image of a god rising out of a vertical dagger blade partly sunk into the ground, with a profile lion's head at each shoulder and with its lower torso covered by two inverted lions' bodies. The god is not labeled, but may be the god of the underworld, known in Mesopotamia as Nergal. The second relief repeats the scene of twelve male gods running in unison, shown also in the main chamber. They, too, are associated with death. Tudhaliya IV appears once again in the third relief, but this time in the protecting embrace of the much larger figure of Sharruma, his tutelary deity.

THE END OF THE BRONZE AGE IN ANATOLIA

The destructions of the late thirteenth and twelfth centuries BC hit coastal and interior Anatolia alike. Hattusha was attacked, the Hittite Empire destroyed. The region passed into a period about which little is known. By the eighth century BC, the mid Iron Age, when cultural developments become clearer, new peoples had established themselves in west Anatolia: Greeks along the Aegean coast, Lydians, Carians, and Lycians just inland. On the central plateau, the Hittite lands were now controlled by the Phrygians. New arrivals during this Dark Age, possibly migrants from south-east Europe, the Phrygians nonetheless picked up the thread of Anatolian tradition and occupied the cities and other settlements previously inhabited by Hittites, notably Hattusha and the town they would make their capital, Gordion.

CHAPTER 9

Cypriots, Canaanites, and Levantine trading cities of the Late Bronze Age

Cyprus: Late Bronze Age (= Late Cypriot): ca. 1650–1050 BC

  Late Cypriot I: ca. 1650–1475 BC

  Late Cypriot II: ca. 1475–1225 BC

  Late Cypriot III: ca. 1225–1050 BC

Ugarit: flourished fourteenth to thirteenth centuries BC; destroyed ca. 1190–1180 BC

Shipwrecks: Uluburun: late fourteenth century BC

  Cape Gelidonya: ca. 1220 BC

We have been surveying ancient cities of the eastern Mediterranean and Near East in their separate cultural contexts: the Ancient Near East, the Indus Valley, Egypt, Anatolia, and the Aegean. But these cultures did not each exist in a vacuum; indeed, as one might expect, they maintained extensive relationships with their neighbors. To highlight the interconnections in the eastern Mediterranean, let us examine cities that thrived for exactly this reason, from contacts between regions. A key area for such cultural intersections is the coastal region of the east Mediterranean (see Figure 8.1), with two examples from the Late Bronze Age offering a useful focus: *Enkomi*, on Cyprus, and *Ugarit*, on the Syrian coast opposite Enkomi. From this period comes as well the remarkable testimony of two shipwrecks found off the south-west Turkish coast at *Uluburun* and *Cape Gelidonya*. The scientific excavation of these wrecks has given a fascinating and important glimpse into the mechanisms of trade in the Late Bronze Age.

ENKOMI

The island of Cyprus lies in the north-east Mediterranean, cradled between Anatolia and the Levant. A stepping-stone between east and west, north and south, Cyprus has been prized by military and commercial strategists from antiquity to the present. In addition, rich copper resources provided the island with an important export commodity that supplemented the traditional agricultural base of its economy.

The city of Enkomi developed in the Late Bronze Age precisely because of these economic factors. Enkomi is located in eastern Cyprus, one of several new towns such as Kition and Hala Sultan Tekke that sprang up on the east and south coasts in the Late Bronze Age in order to profit from trade with the Levant and Egypt, now prosperous and politically stable in the empire of the New Kingdom. The ruins of Enkomi lie a few kilometers from the seacoast. Originally the city had a sheltered harbor, perhaps a navigable estuary, but erosion has filled it in and today the ruins lie high and dry, trapped in the plain. In the first millennium BC, habitation would shift to the seaside, to the city of Salamis.

The tombs of Enkomi have been known from the late nineteenth century. Identification and excavation of the city itself began with a single season of investigation in 1934 by French archaeologist Claude Schaeffer, who wished to supplement his findings at Ugarit/Ras Shamra on the Syrian coast (see below). Schaeffer later resumed work in 1946. Subsequent collaborators included Porphyrios Dikaios on behalf of the Cypriot Department of Antiquities. Excavations continued intermittently until 1974 when the Turkish invasion of Cyprus led to the partition of the island, with Enkomi falling into the Turkish-controlled northern zone.

Occupation at Enkomi began in the Middle Bronze Age, but the city flourished in the Late Bronze Age. Evidence comes from archaeology, first and foremost, but we do have some information from the texts of neighboring peoples. It is generally accepted that the kingdom of Asy or Alashiya, a copper-producing country mentioned in texts beginning in the eighteenth century BC from Alalakh (near Antakya, Turkey), Mari, Egypt, and Hattusha, is in fact Cyprus. The French excavators, at least, believed Enkomi to be the capital of Alashiya; moreover, a recently discovered text from Mari speaks of "the city of Alashiya." About Enkomi specifically and its rulers and inhabitants these texts give no information. From the Cypriots themselves we have only potential evidence, for the local Cypro-Minoan script, first attested at Enkomi ca. 1500 BC and used throughout the Late Bronze Age, has not yet been deciphered.

Enkomi grew rich as an important center for the trade in copper, the essential element in bronze, an alloy highly valued for the manufacture of tools and weapons. Cyprus had important sources of copper in the north-west part of the island, on the north and north-east slopes of the Troodos Mountains. Exploited from the Early Bronze Age into modern times, the mines are now exhausted. The ore was first collected and partially smelted before being brought to towns like Enkomi. After further processing, the copper was formed into ingots for shipment to Syria, Egypt, and other areas without adequate metal sources. How the internal copper trade was organized we do not know; possibly a single authority oversaw mining activities, or perhaps each city took care of its own interests.

Copper (and even tin) ingots were sometimes made in the distinctive "oxhide" form, flat, thin, and roughly rectangular, with the four corners pulled out (Figure 9.1). Measurements vary from 30cm–60cm × 20cm–45cm × 4cm–6cm. Weights range from 10kg to 37kg, with an average of 30kg. The distinctive shape, resembling an animal skin nailed in four corners for drying with its center shrunken during the process, earned these objects the picturesque name of "oxhide ingots." It was even proposed that these ingots represented a monetary value equivalent to that of an ox. The link with oxen has been disproved – the discovery of both four and two-handled copper ingots on the Uluburun shipwreck makes clear that the shape was designed for easy handling – but nevertheless the name has taken a firm place in the jargon of Mediterranean archaeology.

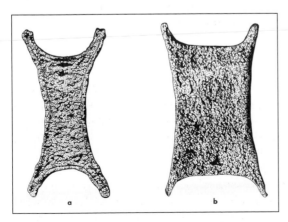

Figure 9.1 "Oxhide" ingots, of copper, ca. 1200 BC: (a) from Serra Ilixi, Sardinia; (b) from Enkomi

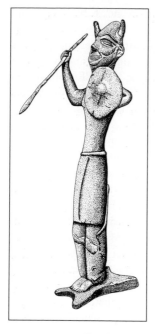

Figure 9.2 God standing on an ingot, bronze figurine, from Enkomi. Cyprus Museum, Nicosia

Ingots have appeared in Sardinia in the western Mediterranean, on Crete and in the Near East, with important depictions in Egyptian New Kingdom tomb paintings at Thebes. Scientific analyses of the lead isotopes and trace elements in the copper ingots have in many cases supported a Cypriot origin. The wide distribution of the ingots shows the importance of Cypriot copper resources to a very broad region. The most striking use of an oxhide ingot in Cypriot art may well be as a base for a solid bronze statuette found in an early twelfth-century BC sanctuary at Enkomi. A tall (35cm), willowy bearded god protected by a horned helmet and greaves (shin guards) brandishes a shield and a spear (Figure 9.2). Because he stands on an ingot, he has been identified as the "ingot god," the protector of the copper mines of the island. So important was he considered by the excavators that they named the Enkomi shrine after him: the Sanctuary of the Ingot God.

The turbulent changes that swept the eastern Mediterranean at the end of the Late Bronze Age did not spare Cyprus. Understanding exactly what happened has depended on the interpretation of pottery finds. Some pottery is imported from the Peloponnesus, according to the results of scientific analysis of the fabric, but there was also local production in the Mycenaean pictorial style, with large pots such as kraters and amphoras being favored. Such Aegean pottery types found at Enkomi, especially in tombs, have led to the conclusion that large numbers of Mycenaeans emigrated to Enkomi. In like manner, finds in eleventh-century BC contexts of Minoan types of goddess figurines with upraised arms and certain ceramics have suggested a wave of refugees from Crete arriving in Cyprus after 1100 BC. Such hypotheses that equate Aegean ceramics found on Cyprus with actual Mycenaean and Minoan settlers have been challenged in recent years. Just as in today's America the widespread use of objects from China (to take one example) does not stem from a massive emigration of Chinese but from more complex economic relationships, so too the reasons for Aegeanizing objects on Cyprus might be quite different from the traditional explanation. As we search for the truth, we need to keep many possibilities in mind.

Other foreigners who passed through were not as benign as the possible Mycenaean and Minoan emigrants. The Sea Peoples, a loose coalition of marauders who unsuccessfully fought the Egyptians in naval battles off the Nile Delta in the late thirteenth and early twelfth centuries BC, may well have put Enkomi to the torch on two occasions when the Late Bronze Age city suffered severe damage. This pattern of destruction is attested at other Cypriot cities, notably at Kition. Cypriot cities recovered and their prosperity continued during the twelfth century BC; eventually, however, the general economic decline in the eastern Mediterranean affected the island, for in the mid eleventh century BC Enkomi was abandoned.

Architectural remains

Architectural remains from the entire Late Bronze Age have survived at Enkomi, with the most impressive belonging to the end of the period. Among the earliest architectural traces is the fortress of Late Cypriot I. Several such fortresses were built throughout the island at this time, reflections of the political uncertainty and unrest at the end of the Middle Bronze Age. The fortress at Enkomi, placed at the north edge of the town, measured 34m × 12m and was distinctive for its very thick walls. Rooms were disposed on two storeys, with an internal stairway giving access to the upper storey and the roof.

Late Cypriot II remains include houses and tombs. Houses of LC II typically feature rooms built around three sides of a courtyard. Bathrooms are well supplied with cemented floors, clay bathtubs, and drains. Burials of LC I and LC II include tombs built of stone masonry, some of which resemble the built tombs of Ugarit, and three small tholoi. Elsewhere on Cyprus, the standard grave type in LC I–II is the rock-cut chamber tomb.

At the end of LC II, ca. 1225 BC and again ca. 1200 BC, Enkomi experienced severe destruction, but each time was rebuilt. In the late thirteenth century BC, the people of Enkomi enclosed their city with a fortification wall. Measuring ca. 400m north–south, 350m east–west, this wall consisted of a base of a parallel row of large blocks 1.5m high, the interstices filled with rubble. The superstructure would have been made of mud bricks. Rectangular towers projected at intervals. Inside the wall, the LC III town is strikingly laid out in a grid plan with a single main street, straight and oriented roughly north–south, and side streets off it at right angles (Figure 9.3). The architecture shows a variety of construction techniques and qualities, indicating an economic hierarchy in the local society. Along the main street stood well-built temples, public buildings, and houses, whereas further removed, along the side streets, one encounters modest houses made from inferior materials. Other discoveries included a workshop for copper-smelting (in the North Gate area, the earlier Fortress of LC I) and several tombs, including underground vaults of the Ugaritian type.

The most impressive house of LC III Enkomi is Building 18. Its purpose is uncertain, despite Schaeffer's claim that it may have been a palace for an Aegean chief. Building 18 occupies an entire city block, measuring 40m on its main south side. The south side also has four doorways, each 2m wide, and four windows. The walls were made of ashlar masonry, a construction technique that becomes prevalent in late LC II and LC III. In Bronze Age architecture, the term "ashlar masonry" refers to rectangular (or sometimes trapezoidal) blocks of varying sizes finished on the visible side. Such slabs often served as the outer facings of a rubble or earth-filled wall. Here in Building 18, large ashlar blocks, set on a rubble levelling and stone base, form the lowest course of the building (Figure 9.4). These blocks could be large, up to 3m (length) × 1.4m (height) × 0.7m (width). On top, set into cuttings, were two thinner blocks, placed parallel to each other, but with a space in between that was filled with rubble or earth. A horizontal slab was placed on top of this second course. This elegant construction was a mark of Enkomi's prosperity. By the end of LC III A, that prosperity was disappearing. Building 18 was then divided into smaller rooms by means of rubble walls, and in part served as a place for copper-smelting.

The most important religious building of LC III Enkomi is the Sanctuary of the Horned God, named for a solid bronze statue found in one of two cult rooms, an image (54.2cm high) of a god shown as a young man wearing a helmet with two horns. The sanctuary consisted of a large rectangular hall with ceiling supported by two square piers, and, off it to the east, the two cult rooms. The hall contained an altar and offering table, around which were found libation bowls and the skulls of several horned animals, such as oxen, deer, and goats. Other shrines discovered at Enkomi have hearths, offering tables, and sometimes piers as focuses of worship, this last perhaps reflecting the Minoan pillar cult.

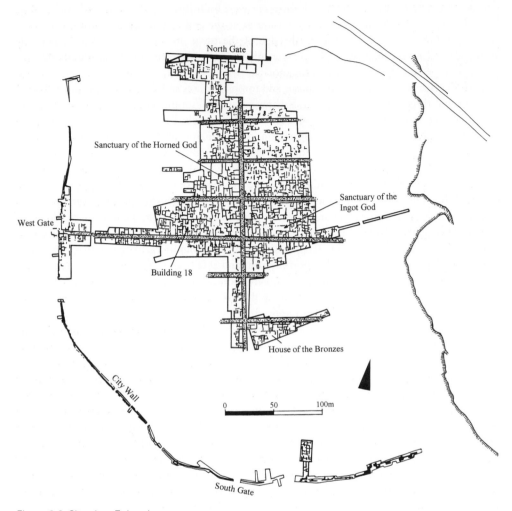

Figure 9.3 City plan, Enkomi

UGARIT (RAS SHAMRA)

Enkomi and the other cities of east and south Cyprus had close ties with the important Canaanite trading city of Ugarit, located just across the sea on the Syrian coast. The name of Ugarit appeared in tablets found at Mari, Amarna, and Hattusha/Boğazköy, but until well into the twentieth century the location of this city was unknown. After a farmer chanced upon a tomb chamber near the large tell of Ras Shamra, north of Lattakia, a French team led by Claude Schaeffer began excavations on the tell and in adjacent areas in 1929. By 1933, locally found cuneiform tablets made clear that Ras Shamra was to be equated with Ugarit, and the puzzle of Ugarit's location was solved. With few interruptions, excavations have continued ever since. Campaigns since 1978 are aiming at a comprehensive understanding of urbanism at Ugarit, whereas earlier seasons had concentrated, in more traditional fashion, on uncovering monumental buildings.

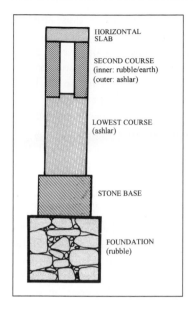

HORIZONTAL SLAB

SECOND COURSE
(inner: rubble/earth)
(outer: ashlar)

LOWEST COURSE
(ashlar)

STONE BASE

FOUNDATION
(rubble)

Figure 9.4 Cross-section of wall construction as practiced in Building 18, Enkomi

Settlement at Ugarit began in the Neolithic period, then continued through the Chalcolithic and Bronze Ages. Contacts with Egypt and Cyprus were established already in the Early Bronze Age, with Minoan Crete in the Middle Bronze Age. We know of a nameless Middle Bronze Age king of Ugarit, now famous for his curiosity about foreign wonders. He wrote to Hammurabi, a king of Yamhad (Aleppo), requesting to see the palace at Mari: "Show me the palace of Zimri-Lim! I wish to see it." His letter, written on a clay tablet, was preserved in the Mari archives.

During the Late Bronze Age, the city enjoyed its greatest prosperity. The people of Ugarit were Canaanites, a Semitic people of the Levantine coast. Much is known about local history, religion, and mythology because of important finds in fourteenth- to thirteenth-century BC levels of tablets in various languages, including Akkadian, Hittite, Hurrian, Cypro-Minoan, and the local Ugaritic language itself. This last was written in an alphabetic cuneiform script of some 30 signs, the oldest known alphabetic writing system anywhere in the world.

Despite pressure from their powerful neighbors, the Ugaritians maintained a certain degree of autonomy. Indeed, under the umbrella of first Egyptian, then Hittite overlordship, a local dynasty held sway through the fourteenth and thirteenth centuries BC. Whatever controls these great powers exercised, they clearly did not impede Ugarit's prosperity. The city's wealth derived from the local agricultural base, which provided for exports of grain, wine, and timber; from local industries such as metalworking, perfumes, and especially the manufacture of a highly esteemed purple dye from the murex, a local shellfish; and from the importing and transshipment of copper from Cyprus. Although the city itself lay in from the sea, Ugarit maintained a port on the nearby coast in an area known today as Minet el Beida, from the modern Syrian name for the small bay. Minet el Beida was not Ugarit's only port; recent excavations at nearby Ras Ibn Hani have revealed another active commercial center on the Ugaritian coast.

Like most cities, Ugarit endured fire and earthquake, but always managed to come back. In the early twelfth century BC, however, circumstances were different. The city was thoroughly destroyed ca. 1190–1180 BC by invading Sea Peoples, one event amidst the turmoil and catastrophe that afflicted the eastern Mediterranean basin at this time. This destruction ended the great era of local Ugaritic culture. Subsequent occupation would be only small in scale.

The site of Ras Shamra

Ras Shamra/Ugarit lies just inland in a coastal plain. Seasonal rivers bordered the city on both north and south; both streams were probably bridged in antiquity, part of the road system from north and south that gave access to the town. The southern stream, the Delbeh, served the city in an additional capacity. Traces of a stone dam blocking the southern stream were discovered in 1986, evidence for an additional component, along with wells, of the system of obtaining and keeping water. The dam has been dated to the Late Bronze Age because of certain construction techniques, notably the use of double swallow-tail clamps, that correspond with those attested in some tombs and the west postern gate, all datable to the Late Bronze Age.

The tell measures just over 22ha on top, with certain sections having eroded away since antiquity, and rises some 20m above the surrounding plain. Population has been estimated by M. Liverani at 6,000–8,000 people. Approximately one-fourth of the tell has so far been explored, although primarily only the top layer, the last major phase, the Late Bronze Age. Understanding the architecture and urban plan of Late Bronze Age Ugarit has been much helped because stone, not mud brick, was the main building material, thus allowing for good preservation. In addition, because there was little subsequent building in the area, Late Bronze Age building materials were not carried off and reused, but remained quietly in place.

The Royal Palace

Excavations have have revealed two major sectors (Figure 9.5). The first, in the north-west, is the area of the Royal Palace. On this west side was found a fortified gate, but this led only to the palace area, not to the city proper. The main entrance into the city, that used by farmers, merchants, and others, is thought to have been on the south, for the road crossing the southern stream. Further excavation is awaited to confirm this hypothesis. The second important sector is the acropolis, in the north-east. This area contains the main religious buildings of the city: two temples to the main city gods, Baal and his father, Dagan, and the House of the Chief Priest (also known as the Library). In areas outside the palace area and the acropolis, mixed functions are seen, with an intermingling of houses, cult buildings, shops, and industrial centers.

The Royal Palace dominates the large palace sector. A special fortification wall originally built in the fifteenth century BC protected the area, a wall with an outward slope of 45 degrees, covered in its lower portion by a glacis of packed stones. In addition, a cluster of towers by the entrance provided extra security. Aptly named the Fortress, thanks to its 5m-thick walls, this complex protected both the main gateway and also a postern gate, a stone-lined passageway built through the lower part of the defense system. Certain construction techniques such as corbelled vaulting show connections with Hittite and Mycenaean architecture.

The Royal Palace was built over the course of the fifteenth to thirteenth centuries BC in at least four major stages. In typical east Mediterranean/Near Eastern fashion, it consisted of rooms grouped around courtyards (Figure 9.6). But it was unusually large, covering 6,500m² by the time of the destruction of the city in the early twelfth century BC, and it had an international reputation for magnificence. On a tablet preserved in the Amarna archives of the fourteenth century BC, a prince of Byblos writing to the Egyptian pharoah, when describing the palace at Tyre, likens it to the palace at Ugarit about which he adds, "Considerable is that which is found between its walls."

The ground floor of the palace contained ninety rooms, five courts, four mini-courts, one tower by the entrance, and, in the rear, a large garden. The rooms on the ground floor served for public receptions and for administration, and included offices, archives, storerooms, guard rooms, and lodgings for the staff. Below ground, under two northern rooms, were the family tombs, three large stone-lined chambers with corbelled vaults. These were found emptied of objects. Twelve staircases led to the now vanished upper floor, which must have contained the private quarters of the royal family.

The plan of the ground floor is not symmetrical but flows freely, no doubt reflecting additions and alterations made at different times. The outline is irregular, with the north façade, which ran along a major street, varying in its line with intermittent indentations and projections. The main

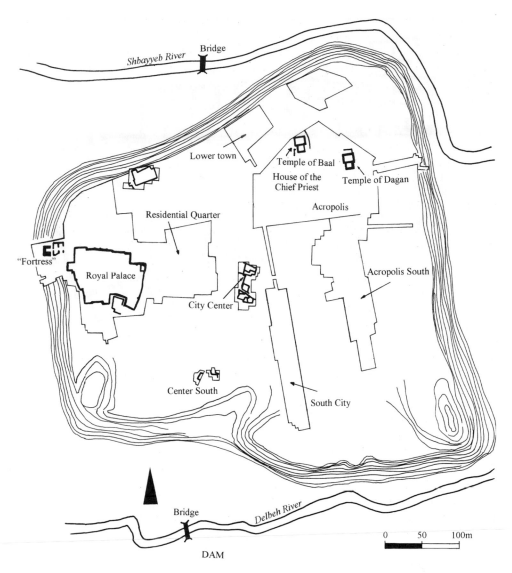

Figure 9.5 City plan, Ugarit

entrance to the palace lies asymmetrically placed in the north-west. Clearly marked, it consists of a paved porch with a ceiling supported by two wooden columns on stone bases, a stone bench on either side, and a tower on the south for security. Two smaller entrances were located in the north-east and south-west.

Construction quality was high. The palace was built of stone, using ashlar blocks preserved in places to 4m in height. Wooden crossbeams were used too, placed in slots in the stone masonry. A thick coating of undecorated plaster covered the walls.

The ruins have yielded an abundant harvest of objects, notably ivory carvings, stone stelai, and figurines, and the many tablets mentioned earlier. The tablets, found in important archives in several places in the palace, have much to say about the administrative functions of this center.

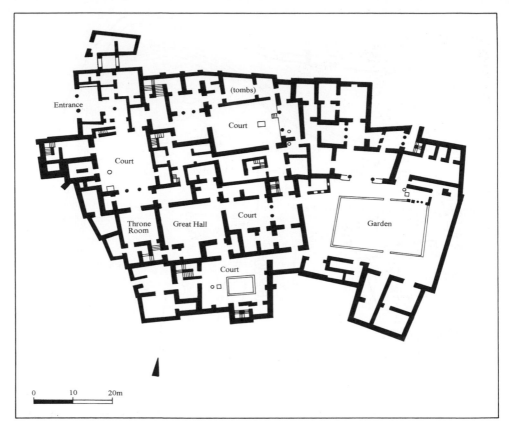

Figure 9.6 Plan, Royal Palace, Ugarit

Their contents include reports about outlying districts, judicial records (especially from the south central archives of the palace), and even the practice writing attempted by scribal students. The original excavation report recorded an oven, located in the south court, in which clay tablets were baked for permanent preservation. Tablets were found inside it, abandoned at the moment of the destruction of the city, thus constituting a special group of texts written on the last day of the LBA palace. Recent research has, however, cast doubt on this dramatic and colorful hypothesis. The existence of an oven is not certain, and moreover, the tablets from that spot belong to a larger group of tablets and other objects fallen from the upper storey and mixed with debris from the burning of the palace.

The city plan and private houses

The investigation of the urban plan, neighborhoods, and private houses has been an important interest of recent excavations at Ugarit. In contrast with Enkomi, the layout of Ugarit was highly irregular. Streets were never straight, and they varied in width from ca 2.50m to 0.90m for alleys. Public squares were rare. The irregular streets and alleys in turn determined the form of housing blocks, or *insulae*. The insulae were divided into houses that shared walls, but excavations have shown that the house was not the basic design unit, modified internally to fit changing needs or situations. Instead, it was the insula itself that could be redivided when needed into different

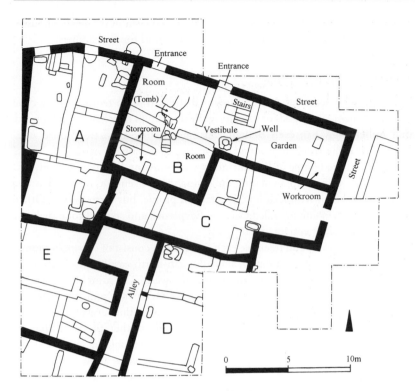

Figure 9.7 House plans from the city center, Ugarit

shaped houses, with shops, work areas, etc. Houses were thus of many different sizes and shapes (Figure 9.7).

Rooms were often arranged around a courtyard. A house generally had an upper storey for bedrooms, and a flat roof, itself used as an activity area. Better houses, such as House B on the plan, were supplied with an entrance vestibule, a well, a toilet and appropriate drainage, a small room on top over the stairwell, ovens for bread and stone troughs placed in the courtyard, and even a stone-built funeral chamber below ground, the family tomb. In the plan of houses shown in Figure 9.7, House C seems originally to have been part of House B. But with the population pressures of the late thirteenth century BC, these rooms were walled off to create a separate dwelling unit. Although the prime building material was stone, both neatly cut ashlar blocks and rubble, wood was extensively used, for courses in walls and as roof supports. Roofs were made of reeds covered with mud, compacted after rain or after renewal by a stone roof-roller, a tool with which almost every house at Ugarit was supplied. The irregular, often deep (even to 1.8m) building foundations dug into the sloping ground of the city may have been intended as protection against earthquake damage.

The above examples represent a standard neighborhood. But a high-rent district of high-quality houses has also been discovered just east of the palaces. As one might expect, living close to the palace conveyed prestige. The largest known is the House of Rap'anou, named after a man mentioned on some tablets found inside this house. Although Rap'anou is not specifically named as the owner, he is a good possibility. Rap'anou was an important court official and intellectual active during the reign of Amistamar II (ruled 1274–1240 BC), a biographical detail that gives a date for the house and its library. This house contained thirty-four rooms, spread over an area of 800m². Features very much resemble those seen in the palace and even in the smaller houses: courtyard, upper storey, a well-equipped bathroom, and underground tomb chambers.

The religious center on the Acropolis

The Acropolis in the north-east sector of the site contained the two main temples of the city, dedicated to Baal and his father Dagan, gods of vegetation. Both temples may have been founded early in the second millennium BC, even though existing remains are Late Bronze Age. Identifications for the cults come from stelai found in the area that show or name these gods. Objects found in and around the temple of Baal include a stele showing Baal striding forward, a (thunderbolt) club brandished in an upraised arm. Following the conventions of Near Eastern and Egyptian art, the god is shown with feet, legs, and face in profile, but torso frontal. Other objects include statues and stelai, sometimes dedicated by Egyptians, and sixteen stone anchors, offered, like the statues and stelai, as votives.

The plans of the temples are simple and resemble each other. Both consist of two main rooms, a *pronaos* (porch) and a *naos* (the sanctuary proper), aligned north-north-east–south-south-west. The Temple of Dagan is notable for its thick (4–5m) foundation walls. The ruins of the Temple of Baal (Figure 9.8) include portions of a wall that enclosed the precinct, a probable altar in a courtyard in front of the pronaos, monumental steps up to the higher ground level of the pronaos and naos, and another probable altar in the naos itself, accessible by separate steps. Marguerite Yon, current director of the Ugarit excavations, has suggested that these buildings situated high in the city may also have functioned as lighthouses.

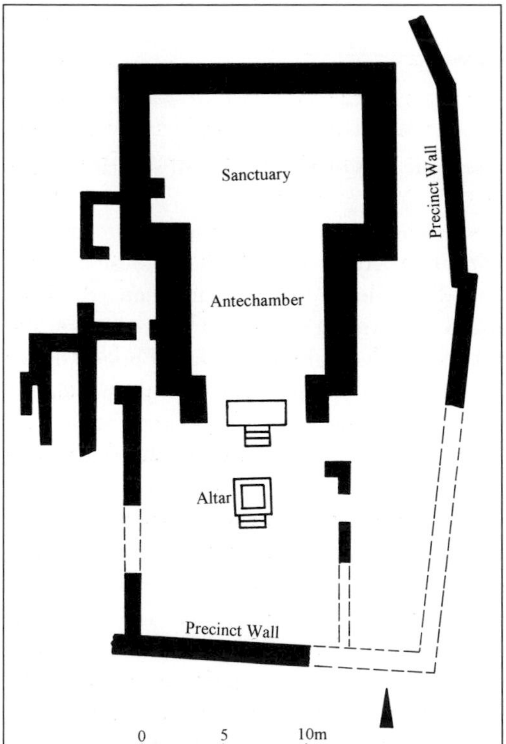

The third major building of the Acropolis was the House of the High Priest, found west of the Temple of Dagan. This large, two-storeyed house, well constructed for the most part, is of particular importance for the tablets found here, especially for texts of mythological poems. Some tablets show writing exercises, examples of the syllabary, and bilingual lexicons, indicating that the building was used as a center for the training of scribes. That it was also the residence of the city's chief priest is suggested by its location close to the main temples and especially by four small bronze adzes and one hoe inscribed with dedications to the Head of the Priests. These last objects formed part of a large deposit of 74 bronze weapons, tools, and one elegant tripod decorated with pendants in the shape of pomegranates discovered beneath the threshold of a doorway inside the house.

Figure 9.8 Plan, Temple of Baal, Ugarit

The port at Minet el Beida

Ugarit's port was 1.5km away, at Minet el Beida. Today, because of the action of alluvial fill, the bay is smaller than it was in the Bronze Age. Excavations on the south side of the bay have revealed remains of the town first settled in the late fifteenth and especially the fourteenth centuries BC. The town plan resembled that of the main city nearby, with irregular streets. Houses consisted of a courtyard with surrounding rooms, a well, an oven, sometimes an underground tomb. In addition to houses and shrines, the port town had warehouses for storing goods both imported and awaiting export, including one with 80 shipping jars still preserved inside.

The objects found here indicate that Ugaritians formed the main element in the population, but there was also a large contingent of foreigners, including Egyptians, Cypriots, Hittites, Hurrians, and people from the Aegean. Cypriot pottery both imported and locally made; ivory cosmetic boxes from Egypt; a terracotta plaque of the Egyptian goddess Hathor; Mycenaean pottery; bronze weapons and tools; cylinder seals; stone weights; a deposit of the murex shells that remained from the manufacture of purple dye; and inscribed tablets are among the remains that attest to the vitality of this vibrant, multi-cultural trading center struck down in the early twelfth century BC.

THE SHIPWRECKS AT CAPE GELIDONYA AND ULUBURUN

We have no examples of Ugaritian boats, although texts speak of both a navy and a commercial fleet. Two Late Bronze Age shipwrecks of undetermined nationality discovered off the south-west coast of Turkey may, however, give an idea of what such boats looked like. In addition, since these wrecked ships filled with a great range of objects were clearly on commercial voyages, they offer us valuable evidence for trading practices in the east Mediterranean that complements information retrieved from land sites and from texts.

The first wreck was discovered in the late 1950s by sponge divers off Cape Gelidonya, south-west of Antalya (see map, Figure 8.1). It was subsequently excavated in 1960 by George Bass, then of the University of Pennsylvania. This excavation was a pioneer project with Bass and colleagues, all archaeologists, doing the diving themselves. Previously, archaeologists had tried to direct underwater excavations from the surface by giving instructions to and interpreting reports from divers with no training in archaeology. With the excavation of the Cape Gelidonya wreck, nautical archaeology became a scientific field of its own, an important and technically demanding sub-field of archaeology.

The Cape Gelidonya wreck dates to ca. 1220 BC. The second shipwreck, found in 1982 in deep (40m–60m) waters at Uluburun, near Kaş, sank in the late fourteenth century BC. The hull of this ship was much better preserved than that of the Cape Gelidonya wreck. Both ships were built by the "shell-first" method. Instead of starting with a framework onto which planking is fastened, shipwrights built the hull first. They laid planks in place; joined the plank edges with tenons, locked into place with pegs; and lastly, added internal supports, the equivalent of the frame. A similar technique was used also by the Egyptians from the twenty-sixth century BC as well as by the Greeks and the Romans, and it is of great interest to see its practice here in the late fourteenth century BC. The modern system, "frame-first," is first attested in the Middle Ages, in the eleventh-century AD shipwreck found at Serçe Liman, west of Marmaris (south-west Turkey).

One or even both ships may well have been Canaanite, but the nationality of the ships has caused controversy, with some specialists championing a Mycenaean identity. Mycenaean pottery has traditionally been the artifact easiest to spot in foreign lands, whereas Levantine objects have rarely come to light in the Aegean. As a result, Aegean prehistorians in particular have favored a reconstruction of east Mediterranean trade dominated by Mycenaean shipping. Opponents consider this view a distortion created by the peculiarities of archaeological preservation. They believe that materials traded by Levantines for Mycenaean pottery and their contents might have been invisible in the archaeological record, notably raw materials that would be consumed (such as foodstuffs) or manufactured into objects.

The results from Cape Gelidonya and Uluburun have shown that the trade in raw materials was indeed important and that Canaanites and other Levantines in fact took part in maritime commerce. Seaborne trade was not a Mycenaean monopoly. The personal objects of the crew members on the Cape Gelidonya wreck were Near Eastern, such as Syrian and Egyptian weights, a Canaanite lamp, and a cylinder seal. The cargo proper consisted of metal: oxhide ingots from Cyprus, scrap bronze tools also from Cyprus, and tin ingots from an unknown source. The only Mycenaean objects were in fact two stirrup jars, a distinctive shape in Late Bronze Age Aegean pottery. It thus seems likely that the ship with its Canaanite captain and crew set sail from a Levantine or Cypriot port and was heading for the Aegean when it sank off Cape Gelidonya.

The shipwreck from Uluburun shows similar features, but the ship was larger than the Gelidonya wreck (approx. 17m vs. 10m), its cargo richer and much more varied. The date of the ship, late fourteenth century BC, is given by finds of Mycenaean pottery and a gold scarab inscribed with the name of the Egyptian queen Nefertiti, wife of Akhenaten. The cargo featured metal, with 10 tons of copper shipped as over 500 ingots, and one ton of tin ingots. Other raw materials included over 170 glass ingots of various colors, the earliest ever found; elephant ivory; hippopotamus teeth, which would be carved like elephant tusks; tortoise shells; African black wood logs; ostrich egg shells; and, stored in Canaanite amphoras, the remains of one ton of terebinth resin, a substance used especially by Egyptians, apparently for incense, and by Mycenaeans for perfume. Cypriot pottery was another major item in the cargo, with several pithoi filled with new Cypriot bowls and jars. Food items found include figs, olives, grapes, almonds, chickpeas, pomegranates, and spices such as coriander and sumac. Worked objects in this amazing inventory feature swords, both Canaanite and Mycenaean types; seals, from various places; jewelry and precious objects, such as silver bracelets, amber beads, and the gold scarab of Nefertiti already mentioned; and 24 stone anchors, of Near Eastern or Cypriot type. A tiny diptych and one side of a second were also recovered. These folding wooden books with an ivory hinge, with cavities on each leaf for wax which could be wiped smooth when a new message was to be written, are the earliest examples of this kind of writing medium.

The raw materials on board suggest that the ship began its voyage in the Levant and was heading westward, via Cyprus, like the ship later wrecked off Cape Gelidonya. The heterogeneous nature of the objects on the Uluburun wreck makes it difficult to pinpoint the nationality of the ship. Opinion is divided on the issue; perhaps it was Canaanite like the Cape Gelidonya wreck, but it could possibly have been a Mycenaean ship on its return voyage to the Aegean. Whatever the truth, both shipwrecks demonstrate clearly the international nature and complexity of the trade in raw and manufactured materials in the Late Bronze Age Mediterranean.

CHAPTER 10

Near Eastern cities in the Iron Age

The Iron Age in the Near East: tenth century BC – 330s BC

Mesopotamia: Neo-Assyrian Empire: ca. 1000–612 BC

                 Neo-Babylonian Empire: 612–539 BC

Anatolia: Phrygians (eleventh to fourth centuries BC)

           Urartians (ninth to seventh centuries BC)

The Levant: Phoenicians and Hebrews

   Phoenicians: flourished ca. 1000–700 BC

     Major cities: Tyre, Sidon, Byblos

   Hebrews: David: ruled ca. 1000–965 BC

           Solomon: ruled ca. 965–931 BC

              Jerusalem: First Temple

          Conquest of Nebuchadrezzar II: 586 BC

            Destruction of First Temple

            "Babylonian Captivity" to 539 BC

The Persians

   Medes: eighth century–550 BC (capital: Ecbatana, modern Hamadan)

   Achaemenids: 550–330 BC (capitals: Persepolis and Susa)

In this chapter, we follow the story of cities in the Near East during the Iron Age, with a focus on the urban centers of the most powerful states of the region, the Assyrians in northern Mesopotamia, the Babylonians in central Mesopotamia, and the Achaemenid Persians. In addition, a brief look will be taken at certain important centers in Anatolia and the Levant: Phrygian Gordion, Phoenician cities, and Hebrew Jerusalem. Our ending point will be the conquest of the region by Alexander the Great in the 330s BC, an event that marked a significant change of direction in the political and cultural history of the Ancient Near East (Figure 10.1).

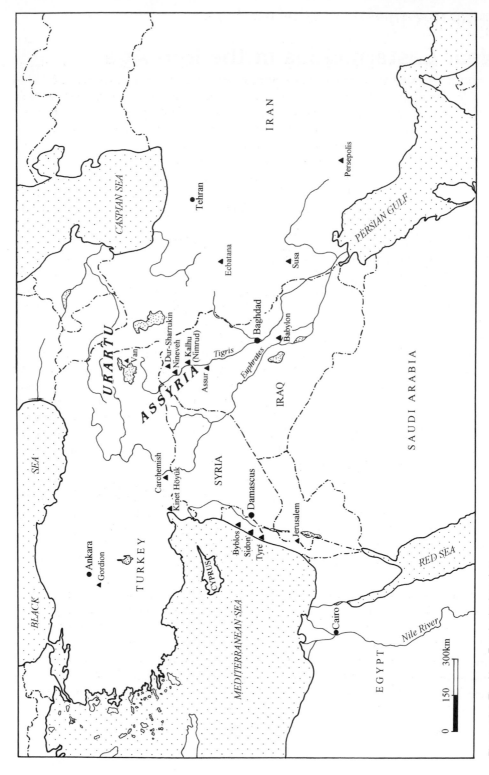

Figure 10.1 The Near East in the Iron Age

THE NEO-ASSYRIAN CITIES OF NORTHERN MESOPOTAMIA

The urban history of northern Mesopotamia or Assyria (= today's north Iraq and north-east Syria) to a large extent connects with that of the south, traced earlier in Chapters 2 and 3. The physical environments of north and south are in large part different, however, which certainly affected the development of cities. Although the arid countryside along the Euphrates River gave rise to cities dependent on river water, in a fashion seen in southern Mesopotamia, the area to the north and north-east, between the Euphrates and the Tigris, lies within the Fertile Crescent, a region in which rainfall is adequate to sustain agriculture without recourse to irrigation. Thanks to this rainfall, people settled throughout the landscape, not needing to cluster by the rivers. Settlements tended to be smaller as well, villages for the most part, since people could spread out and live closer to their fields and flocks without worrying that they might be occupying precious farmland.

Although not directly part of the Sumerian world, the north was quickly absorbed into the larger Mesopotamian cultural sphere. Cities developed especially in the third millennium BC, and prospered through the second millennium BC. We have noted in Chapter 8 how the important city of Assur established mercantile outposts at Kanesh and other Anatolian cities in the Middle Bronze Age (early second millennium BC). We shall pick up the story of these Assyrian cities in the early first millennium BC, with the well-documented sites of *Kalhu* (modern Nimrud), *Dur-Sharrukin* (modern Khorsabad), and *Nineveh*.

"Neo-Assyrian" is the adjective applied to the resurgent state of Assyria in northern Mesopotamia during the early Iron Age. The opening centuries of the first millennium BC witnessed a tremendous expansion of Assyrian power under a series of absolute monarchs intent on fashioning empires and maintaining open trade routes with the west. In the early ninth century BC, Assurnasirpal II (883–859 BC) set the precedent of relocating his capital. He left Assur, the traditional capital and home of the state's main god, also named Assur, in favor of the city of Kalhu. Then, in good Assyrian military tradition, he led his conquering army westward across the Euphrates to Aleppo and the Mediterranean coast.

Conquests of subsequent rulers enlarged Assyrian territory into north-west Iran, Anatolia, Egypt, and Babylonia (southern Mesopotamia). Powerful kings included Sargon II (ruled 721–705 BC), who founded his capital at a new site, Dur-Sharrukin; Sennacherib (704–681 BC); and Assurbanipal (668–631 BC), these last two both reigning from the older city of Nineveh. The Assyrian empire fell in the later seventh century BC, when the Medes of north-west Persia captured Kalhu and Assur in 614 BC and, with the help of the Babylonians and the Scythians, Nineveh in 612 BC.

The ancient cities of Kalhu, Dur-Sharrukin, and Nineveh are important in the history of archaeology. Pioneer excavations in the 1840s–1870s by Paul Emile Botta, Austin Henry Layard, and Hormuzd Rassam first brought the reality of the Ancient Near East into the consciousness of the general public. Here, we will inspect these sites to see how they illustrate essential features of Assyrian architectural planning and decoration, this last featuring a long-lasting royal interest in the power of pictorial imagery. The palace at Kalhu, with its remarkable finds, will be our first stop. We shall then examine the city plan at Khorsabad and, lastly, the city plan and stone relief sculptures from Nineveh.

KALHU (NIMRUD)

Kalhu, the capital of Assurnasirpal II located on the east bank of the Tigris River, was first explored by Layard and others from 1845 to 1854, by another British archaeologist, Max Mallowan, from 1949 to 1963, and in recent years by Iraqi archaeologists. The city demonstrates four features characteristic of northern Mesopotamian cities in the Iron Age. First, the city was laid out in a rough rectangle and enclosed by a mudbrick fortification wall. Here at Kalhu, the wall, 7.6km long, enclosed an area of 360ha. Second, palaces and temples together occupied a walled citadel, raised high on the mound containing the remains of an earlier, smaller town (Figure 10.2). Such citadels never lay in the center of a redesigned Neo-Assyrian city, but on the edge, alongside the city wall. At Kalhu, the walled citadel, 24ha in area, was located in the south-west corner alongside the river (today, it should be noted, the Tigris flows a certain distance to the west). Here stood the Northwest Palace of Assurnasirpal II, plus additional palaces constructed by later rulers. The presence here of temples and a ziggurat alongside the palaces is key; in contrast with Sumerian city centers, the religious has now become subordinate to the secular. A third characteristic is a second citadel, also placed along the city wall but at some distance from the main citadel. This second raised area featured military activities. At Kalhu, at the far south-east of the city, Assurnasirpal II's son Shalmaneser III (859–824 BC) added such a fortress with an arsenal, a palace, a parade ground with a dais for the king's throne, workshops, and storage rooms. This walled complex of 300m × 200m is known as Fort Shalmaneser. And fourth, the citadels are placed high above the rest of the city. Differences between city sectors were marked by differences in elevation, rather than by canals or large streets as was the custom in southern Mesopotamia.

The Northwest Palace of Assurnasirpal II

The formal opening in 879 BC of Assurnasirpal's Northwest Palace is recorded on a stele with 153 lines of text discovered in a recess off the throne room: 69,574 people were said to have partied for 10 days! Whatever the true number, most would have been inhabitants of the city below, not included among the ambassadors and other dignitaries invited to inspect the palace. Used as a king's residence only during the ninth century BC, the Northwest Palace subsequently served a variety of functions until the fall of the empire: housing for important officials, a center for the caravan trade, a treasury, and a granary.

The palace was built on the platform of 120 courses of bricks that elevated the citadel, the ancient mound, ca. 15m above the rest of the city. It is divided into two large sections, one public (north end), the other private (south), containing altogether dozens of rooms arranged around courtyards, a design that recalls the palace of Zimri-Lim at Mari. The main entrances, one central and two side, were on the north, from the large Outer Court. They led directly to the long narrow Throne Room, 47m × 10m. Lining each doorway were relief sculptures, a pair of colossal human-headed winged bulls, magical protective creatures called *lamassu* (Figure 10.3). The huge stone blocks, up to 5.5m², were hauled into place from quarries near Mosul, then carved.

The Throne Room and many rooms nearby were decorated with stone slabs, or *orthostats*, placed upright against the lowest section of the walls. Only a handful of the Neo-Assyrian palaces had such reliefs, so they must have been particularly expensive and significant. They were made of a local gypsum known as Mosul marble or alabaster. The slabs were set in place, and then carved. The purpose of the sculpted imagery was to illustrate the Assyrian concept of kingship. Sculptures of ferocious demons and monsters guarded the entrances against evil forces. Inside

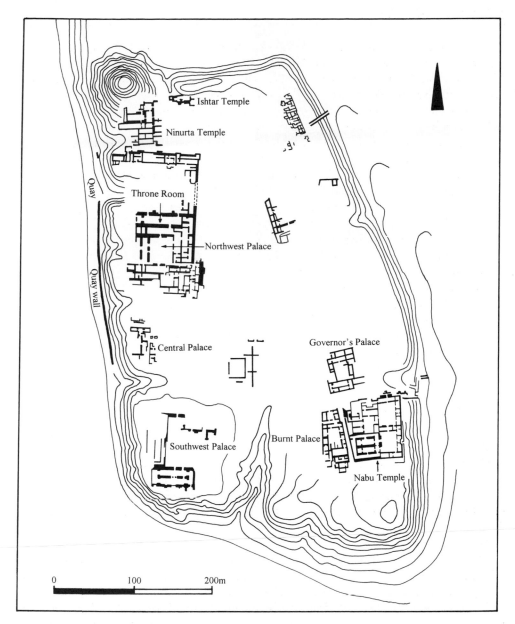

Figure 10.2 Plan, the Iron Age citadel, Kalhu

the rooms, the subject of the sculpted orthostats was the king: triumphant in battle and hunt, and making appropriate offerings and libations to secure the blessing of the god Assur. The battles scenes, recounted with scrupulous detail, reminded visiting subjects of the fate awaiting them should they withhold their annual tribute or consider revolt.

Offerings and libations are seen in the Throne Room, in relief panels behind the king's throne and also opposite the central door. The king, recognizable from his truncated conical hat, is

Figure 10.3 Lamassu, from Khorsabad.
Louvre Museum, Paris

Figure 10.4 Assurnasirpal supplicates the god Assur by a sacred tree, relief sculpture, from Kalhu.
British Museum, London

shown twice, standing beside a sacred tree (Figure 10.4). On the left, the king supplicates the god Assur, appearing above the tree as a man inside a winged disk. On the right, his prayer answered, the king is blessed by the god. Behind the figures of the king stand winged genies, guardian creatures who hold a pail and a cone, tools for fertilizing the stylized date palm tree or for sprinkling the king with their magical protection. Following the conventions of Near Eastern art, the figures are shown in profile.

Since the rooms were cool and dark, the reliefs were originally painted with bright colors so the subjects could be seen. The written message was important too; bands of cuneiform, recounting royal deeds, are carved right across the figures. These orthostats served no structural function, for the palaces were sturdily built of extremely thick mud brick walls, but these depictions of the important aspects of Assyrian kingship surely filled the viewer with appropriate awe and respect.

In addition to the reliefs, the Northwest Palace has yielded a beautiful series of ivory carvings, many originally attached to furniture as decorations. Further spectacular finds have come from excavations conducted in the palace in the late 1980s. Underneath the floor in the residential quarters Iraqi archaeologist Muzahim Mahmud Hussein uncovered three burial vaults of Assyrian royalty, including the wives of Ashurnasirpal II, Tiglath-pileser III (744–727 BC), and Sargon II, with hundreds of pieces of elaborate gold jewelry draped over the skeletons. When these discoveries are fully published, they will have much to tell us about burial practices and the jeweler's craft in Iron Age Assyria.

DUR-SHARRUKIN (KHORSABAD)

Sargon II (721–705 BC) founded his capital at a previously uninhabited location on the Khosr River, a tributary of the Tigris, 24km to the north of Nineveh. He named his new city Dur-Sharrukin, the "Fortress of Sargon," but today it is generally called Khorsabad, after the modern village nearby. Like Akhenaten's Amarna, this town was used only in the lifetime of its builder. After Sargon was killed in battle, his successors preferred Nineveh. Without royal patronage, Dur-Sharrukin did not survive.

The site has been well explored, from the early efforts of Botta and Victor Place to the expedition of the University of Chicago in the 1920s and 1930s, and the city plan is clear and instructive (Figure 10.5). Other finds have not fared well: much of the sculpture was sadly lost in 1855 when brigands in the lower Tigris region attacked and capsized boats transporting some 300 cases of finds to Basra and Europe.

The city occupied a square-shaped area of nearly 300ha. Its sturdy walls, 20m thick, were of mud brick on a stone foundation, and studded with towers. Seven gates, placed asymmetrically, gave access to the city. As at Kalhu and Nineveh, two sectors were set off from the town proper, protected by a separate set of walls, the Citadel, with the royal palace, in the north-west, and the Imperial Arsenal in the south.

The palace of Sargon II dominates the citadel (Figure 10.6). It sits elevated on a brick platform that rises to the height of the city walls, above the ground level of the rest of the citadel. Like the Northwest Palace at Kalhu, this palace was laid out with a public and a private section. The public rooms were grouped around an outer and an inner court. The Throne Room lay off the inner court, with access given by three doorways. Colossal lamassu guarded the entrance. The interior was decorated with relief sculpture behind the throne and wall paintings else-where; painting was a cheaper alternative to sculptured slabs. Behind the Throne Room a smaller

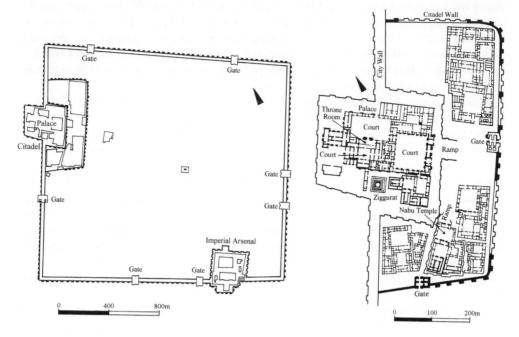

Figure 10.5 City plan, Dur-Sharrukin (Khorsabad)

Figure 10.6 Citadel plan, Dur-Sharrukin (Khorsabad)

court served as the focus of the private quarters of the ruler. Throughout the palace stairs gave access to the flat roof, held up by long beams of such wood as cedar, cypress, juniper, and maple.

Buildings on the citadel seem to have been placed together in haphazard fashion. The axis of the palace is not perpendicular to the city walls. This asymmetrical layout is seen also in the overall palace enclosure and the walls of the citadel. The Nabu Temple, composed of two courts and enclosed sanctuaries aligned on a separate brick terrace, connected to the palace platform by a bridge, is oriented on its own diagonal, and wedged into the southern part of the citadel. For a complex laid out in a single period this lack of concern for harmony in the placing of buildings is curious and distinctive.

Few architectural remains have been found in the interior of the city. The excavation team spent little effort here, to be sure, but it may well be that the city, in its short life, never attracted much of a population.

NINEVEH

The final capital of the Neo-Assyrians was Nineveh. Sennacherib (704–681 BC), who chose this old city for new duty, enlarged and refurbished it, and left a detailed account of his good works. He built a lavish palace, called the "Incomparable Palace," planted a wonderful park full of many varieties of herbs and fruit trees, created a reserve for birds and wild animals, and had stone aqueducts and water channels cut through over 80km of varying terrain to bring water to the city. But this nature-loving monarch did not shrink from kingly duty. He dealt harshly with unrest throughout the empire and struck a hard deal with the king of Judah in exchange for sparing Jerusalem. He even sacked and destroyed rebellious Babylon, despite the veneration long accorded its prestigious gods throughout Mesopotamia. "To quiet the heart of Ashur, my lord, that peoples should bow in submission before his exalted might, I removed the dust of Babylon for presents to the (most) distant peoples, and in that Temple of the New Year Festival (in Assur) I stored up (some) in a covered jar" (Roux 1980: 297).

This time such arrogance did not go unpunished. Sennacherib was murdered by his son or sons while praying in a temple, "smashed with statues of protective deities" (Roux 1980: 298). And some 75 years later the Babylonians would take their revenge.

Nineveh occupies a large area on the east bank of the Tigris across from Mosul, in modern times the largest city of northern Iraq, and has been much explored from the mid nineteenth century to the present (Figure 10.7). The walls of the seventh century BC measure almost 13km in length, enclosing a huge area of 750ha, the largest city yet known in the Ancient Near East. Only Babylon would eventually surpass it (see below). Fifteen gateways have been identified. The west sector, alongside the river, includes two prominent mounds, a pattern familiar from other Neo-Assyrian sites: the citadel and the arsenal. The former, here known as Kuyunjik, was investigated by such nineteenth-century pioneers as Botta, Layard, Place, and Rassam. Here stood the palaces of Sennacherib and the last of the great kings of Assyria, Assurbanirpal (668–627 BC).

The latter mound, called Nebi Yunus, lies 1km south of Kuyunjik; the two are separated by the Khosr River, a tributary of the Tigris that divides the ancient city into northern and southern halves. The Nebi Yunus mound has on it a Muslim shrine associated with Jonah, the prophet who preached to the Ninevites after he was liberated from the belly of a big fish. Excavations in and around this religious site have been restricted. Nonetheless, it has been clearly established that the nerve center of the Assyrian war machine was located here.

Apart from these two major mounds, excavations have been carried out in the north-west corner of the city, where the "old city mound" was not built upon by the king, but instead served as an upper-class district. Workshops for ceramics and copper were found nearby. The vast remaining sections of the city, the Lower Town, were little explored until a surface survey conducted in 1990. The Gulf War of 1991 put a stop to this. But with the city of Mosul expanding into the south part of the ancient city, the resumption of this important salvage work is urgently needed.

Both royal palaces on the Kuyunjik mound have yielded impressive sculptured slabs. Subjects conform to those used in the time of Assurnasirpal II, as seen at Kalhu, with the king's might illustrated by triumphs in lion hunts and military campaigns (Figure 10.8). Assurbanipal's first victory over the Elamites is celebrated in a startling relief from his palace at Nineveh (Figure 10.9). The king, reclining on a couch in a pleasant garden, and his queen, seated in a heavy chair, are fanned by attendants as they drink. To the far left a harpist plays. In the middle of this idyllic scene a head hangs from a tree, the head of Teumman, the Elamite king killed in the Battle of Til-Tuba. In this matter-of-fact way the fate of enemies and the sang-froid of monarchs were impressed upon those privileged to see the sculptural decorations of the royal palace.

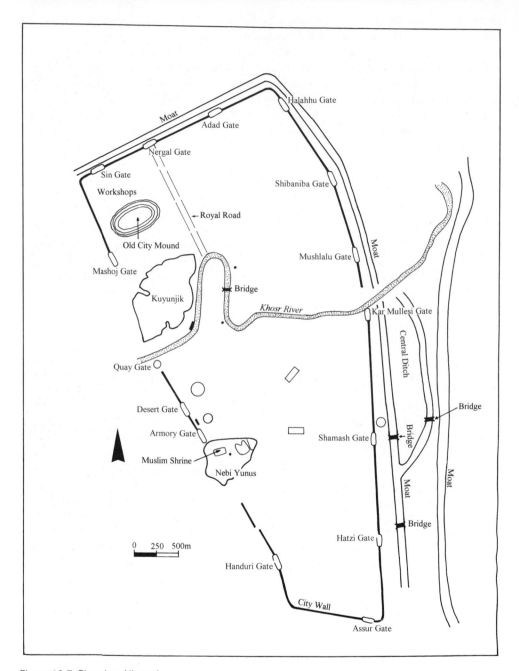

Figure 10.7 City plan, Nineveh

Figure 10.8 Capture of Ethiopians from an Egyptian city, relief sculpture, from Nineveh. British Museum, London

Figure 10.9 Assurbanipal and his queen, relief sculpture, from Nineveh. British Museum, London

ANATOLIA AND THE LEVANT: PHRYGIAN, URARTIAN, PHOENICIAN, AND HEBREW CITIES

In addition to the Assyrians, many other peoples created cities in the Near East during the Iron Age. The Phrygians, the Neo-Hittites, and the Urartians in Anatolia, the Phoenicians and the Hebrews in the Levant, and the Babylonians of southern Mesopotamia all had important urban centers.

The Phrygians, migrants into Anatolia from the Balkans in the early Iron Age, settled in central Anatolia and established their capital at *Gordion*, now a large höyük west of Ankara. Assyrian texts mention a king Mita of Mushki, defeated in battle by Sargon II in south-east Anatolia in the late eighth century BC. Mita is identified with Midas of Greek legend, the Phrygian king cursed with the golden touch. Excavations conducted at Gordion by the University of Pennsylvania have revealed impressive architecture from this period, the massive stone foundations of the city walls and a district of rectilinear buildings, simple in plan but well-built and luxuriously furnished, regularly placed side by side along a main street. The immediate predecessor of Midas, or Mita, may be the man buried in a log chamber underneath a huge tumulus, an earthen burial mound over 50m high located a few kilometres from the ancient city center. According to the Greek historian Herodotus, the Phrygian kingdom and Midas were destroyed in the early seventh century BC by the Kimmerians, nomadic invaders from the Caucasus. But Gordion would soon be rebuilt. Excavations have demonstrated that this destruction was just an interruption, not a decisive cultural break. Much later, in 333 BC, Alexander the Great, passing through during his campaign against the Persians, would undo the fabulously intricate Gordion knot with a slice of his sword, an act that foretold his future as world conqueror.

In North Syria, closer to home, the Assyrians encountered city-states such as *Carchemish*, capitals of the Neo-Hittite and Aramean kingdoms that were the Iron Age descendants of the Hittites. To the north lay the Kingdom of Urartu, centered in eastern Anatolia, north-west Iran, and the Caucasus. The Urartians spoke a language descended from Hurrian, and wrote it in cuneiform. They owed much of their prosperity to copper and iron mines, and indeed have left a distinctive repertoire of metal objects. The influence of Assyrian (Mesopotamian) art is great. In this mountainous area their urban centers such as the *Citadel of Van* are hilltop fortresses enclosing palaces and temples, from which the trade routes and the surrounding farms could be watched and protected.

During the Iron Age, the northern Levant, the coast of modern Lebanon and Syria, was the heartland of the Phoenicians, the descendants of earlier Canaanites. The Phoenicians were organized in independent city-states, ruled by kings. Favored locations for cities included offshore islands, easily fortified, of which the most famous was *Tyre*. Because of continuing habitation of these sites, the nature of the Iron Age Phoenician cities is poorly known. Some insights come from excavations of their many daughter cities, colonies founded throughout the Mediterranean to further their commercial interests, from Cyprus to western Sicily, North Africa, and the coast of Spain. The greatest of these was *Carthage*, near modern Tunis. Founded in the eighth century BC, Carthage would later challenge the emerging city of Rome for dominance in the central Mediterranean, only to be totally defeated in 146 BC. In addition, other cultures have borne witness to Phoenician achievements. The Greeks adopted their alphabet in the eighth century BC, and the Hebrew Bible attests to the skill of Phoenician craftsmen in the great building projects of Solomon and his successors.

The southern Levant, modern Israel and Jordan, was occupied by several peoples during the Iron Age, of whom the Philistines and the Hebrews are the best known. The Philistines, descendants of the Peleset, one of the components of the Sea Peoples who roamed the eastern Mediterranean at the end of the Bronze Age, settled in the coastal plain, whereas the Hebrews dominated the hilly interior. The Hebrew Bible traces the history of the region from, of course, the Hebrew point of view. *Jerusalem* was their great capital. Important Hebrew kings included David (ca. 1000–965 BC) and his son Solomon (ca. 965–931 BC). From David through the next 350 years, Jerusalem was the capital of the Hebrew kingdom of Judah.

Jerusalem and the Hebrew temples

The great Temple, home of the god Yahweh and the Ark of the Covenant, the divinely given laws, was built under Solomon on a hill (today called "Temple Mount" or, in Arabic, "Haram esh-Sharif") just to the north of the earliest settlement of Jerusalem (Figure 10.10). According to tradition, construction took seven years, and depended heavily on Phoenician artisans and Phoenician materials, such as cedar and cypress (or juniper) wood. This First Temple was destroyed by the Babylonians in 586 BC, but is thoroughly described in the Bible (I Kings 5–6). It was a small but lavish rectangular structure measuring 27m × 9m × 13.5m, with three main

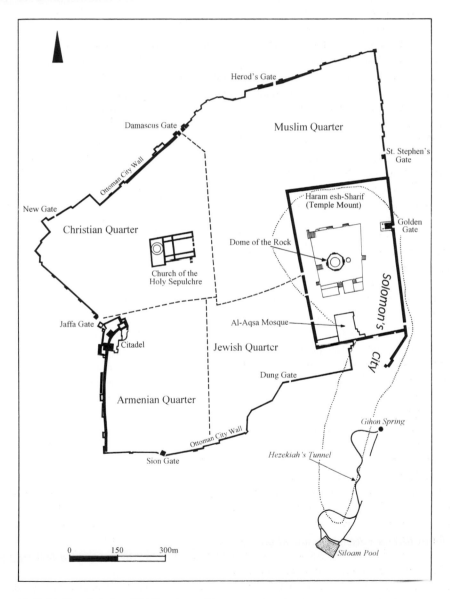

Figure 10.10 Multi-period plan, Old City, Jerusalem

parts, an entrance hall, a main room, and an inner sanctuary. The interior was floored with cypress then covered with gold, the walls paneled with cedar. The sanctuary was lined with gold, as was the outside of the Temple. Two cherubim, part animal, part human guardians of the sacred, were suspended in the air to protect the Ark of the Covenant with their outstretched wings. Decorations elsewhere in the Temple included carved cherubim, palm trees, and rosettes, all covered with gold leaf. Access to the Temple would have been restricted to priests and their attendants. The people at large worshipped and presented their sacrificial offerings outside.

The Assyrian threat to Jerusalem in the late eighth and early seventh centuries BC, when Judah lay on the direct route from Assyria to Egypt, occasioned new fortifications. A remarkable tunnel ca. 540m long still survives, Hezekiah's Tunnel, cut to bring water into the city from the Gihon Spring just outside the city walls during the unsuccessful siege of Sennacherib in 701 BC.

Jerusalem prospered in the seventh century BC, eventually freeing itself from Assyrian domination. Hebrew independence ended in 586 BC when the Babylonians captured and destroyed Jerusalem and carried off many of its inhabitants. A reprieve came in 539 BC, when Babylon itself fell to the Persian king, Cyrus the Great. The exiles returned home, and, with the permission of Cyrus, the Second Temple was begun. Jerusalem was established once again as the focus of Jewish culture. The Second Temple would be enlarged and refurbished by Herod the Great in the first century BC, but destroyed by the Romans in AD 70. The temple has never been rebuilt. The site is now occupied by important Muslim shrines, the Dome of the Rock and the al-Aqsa Mosque. One key remnant of the Second Temple has survived, however – the Western Wall of the temple platform. The Wailing Wall, as it is popularly known, is a major site of Jewish veneration.

BABYLON

Babylon, or "Gate of the Gods," is one of the most celebrated cities in the Ancient Near East. Like so many Mesopotamian cities, it has a long history. First inhabited in the later Early Dynastic period, Babylon came to prominence during the reign of Hammurabi in the eighteenth century BC. The period best documented by archaeological research and textual evidence comes later, however, in the mid Iron Age, when Babylon was the monumental capital of a kingdom that controlled central and southern Mesopotamia. The physical appearance of this seventh to sixth century BC city continues certain long-standing traditions of southern Mesopotamian urbanism, but also displays new features. The contrast with the slightly earlier Neo-Assyrian cities of northern Mesopotamia is especially striking.

Historical background

During the Iron Age, the kingdom of Babylon endured a turbulent relationship with the Assyrians to the north. The city was destroyed by Sennacherib in 689 BC, but much rebuilt by his son Esarhaddon (ruled 680–669 BC). When the Assyrians fell in 612 BC, the victorious Medes turned their attentions northward, thus leaving Babylon master of central and southern Mesopotamia. Under kings Nabopolassar and Nebuchadrezzar (the latter ruled 604–562 BC), the Neo-Babylonians restored their cities, with special emphasis on temples; they revitalized trade networks; and they fought the neighbor states who threatened their prosperity. The capital city, Babylon, was established as a political, cultural, intellectual, and religious center.

Succeeding rulers proved weak. The curious, fascinating intellectual Nabonidus, who ascended the throne in 556 BC, had the misfortune of being a contemporary of Cyrus the Great, the dynamic king of expanding Persia. By 539 BC the Persians, outflanking Babylonia to the north and east, controlled a vast territory from the Aegean Sea to Afghanistan. When the Persians attacked Babylon, the Babylonian forces led by Belshazzar, Nabonidus's son, disintegrated, and the Persians peacefully occupied the great city. Thus ended the last of the independent states of ancient Mesopotamia.

The city plan

The Neo-Babylonian city is known from ancient writers Babylonian and Greek, notably the historian Herodotus, and from modern exploration. Major excavations were conducted by the German archaeologist Robert Koldewey from 1899 to 1917. Because of the high water table, Koldewey could not reach the earlier levels of Hammurabi's town, so he had to concentrate on the Neo-Babylonian plan. Apart from the Ishtar Gate, the ancient buildings were not well preserved. Already by Seleucid (Hellenistic) times baked bricks were being removed for building projects elsewhere. Reconstructions have been undertaken in recent decades, however, as part of excavations conducted by the Iraqi Directorate-General of Antiquities.

Greater Babylon covered an area of 850ha, the largest city of ancient Mesopotamia, larger than Nineveh (750ha) and far larger than Ur (60ha). Even the inner city was huge: ca. 400ha. By using the figure of 200 persons per hectare, a standard benchmark for determining urban populations in central and southern Mesopotamia, we can estimate the population of the inner city at 80,000. The city comprised two fortified sections, one inside the other, with the Euphrates, flowing north–south through the city, an important element of this defensive system (Figure 10.11). The outermost fortifications were laid out as a huge triangle, of which one side was the Euphrates itself. The other two legs stretching to the east consisted of a triple line of walls and a moat. Inside this triangle lay a rectangular core, the inner city, separately fortified. One component of this was the city center, site of the major monuments of the city: the royal palace, the cult centers, and the old residential quarter (Figure 10.12).

The rectangular core of Babylon began as a fortified square on the east bank of the Euphrates River. The area was expanded to the west bank by Nebuchadrezzar, making a total area of ca. 1.6km × 2.4km. The fortification consisted of a double line of mud brick walls, the inner measuring 6.5m in thickness, the outer 3.7m. The unfilled space between them served as a roadway. A moat was cut in front of the exterior of the walls and linked to the Euphrates, with iron gratings protecting against intruders. Baked brick set in the sealant bitumen reinforced walls in contact with the water. Bridges gave access to the eight gates into the city.

The city was laid out in a grid, with straight streets oriented toward the river. Such a regular layout was unusual for a central or southern Mesopotamian city. The names of several streets are known, listed on tablets together with the neighborhoods, the many cult places, and other topographical features. The street names are striking. Some honor the gods to whose gates the streets lead: e.g. "Ishtar, intercessor for her men (people)." Other names promote morality: "Bow down, proud one!" or "Pray and he will hear you," or are simple: "Gemini Street" and "Narrow Street" (an alternate name for "Bow down, proud one!").

Private houses follow traditional Mesopotamian types: two or three storeys (according to ancient accounts) with a courtyard in the center. The exceptionally large size of these houses, and indeed of contemporary examples at Uruk and Ur, shows the prosperity of the region in the sixth century BC.

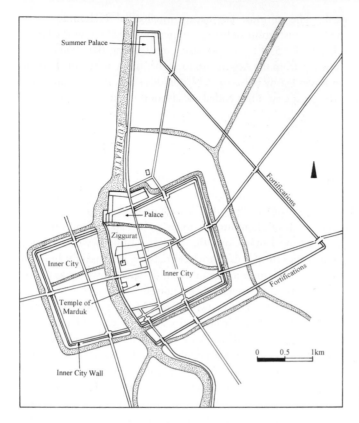

Figure 10.11 Overall city plan, Babylon

The city plan of Babylon differs from the typical Neo-Assyrian urban layout in restoring the main religious buildings to a place of eminence. The palaces are grandiose, to be sure. But it is the Temple of Marduk and the Ziggurat, not the palace, that occupy the center of the city. The palaces stand apart, at the edges of the Inner City. In another contrast with Neo-Assyrian practice, the religious center and the palace areas are not elevated, but are located on the same flat plane as the rest of the city.

The Processional Way and the Temple of Marduk

Access to the religious center was along a Processional Way that began outside the northern Ishtar Gate. Images of the gods were carried along this route during the New Year Festival of March or April. The street approached the gate between the high walls of the North Palace and the bastion opposite, decorated with glazed brick figures of lions, the symbol of Ishtar, goddess of love and war. The preservation of the Ishtar Gate is curious. Of Nebuchadrezzar's third and final version, which was decorated with glazed bricks, little survived above the paved street. However, the foundations of the gate descended 15m into the ground, buried in clean sand as befitted sacred buildings, and were decorated with plain (unglazed) brick reliefs depicting dragons and bulls, symbols of the gods Marduk and Adad respectively. It is these walls, cleared, that the visitor sees today, and that provide the basis for the reconstruction in the Pergamon Museum in Berlin (Figure 10.13). The original gate would perhaps have measured over 23m in height, and spanned both inner and outer fortification walls. As the Berlin reconstruction shows, the gate and adjacent

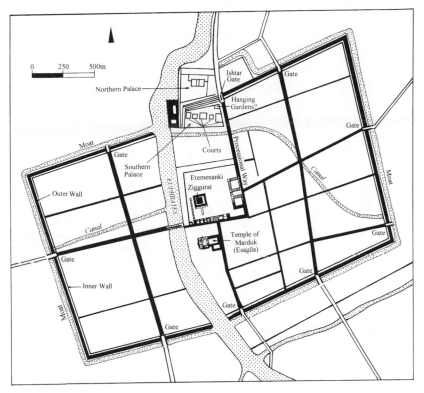

Figure 10.12 Plan, inner city, Babylon

walls were well protected with lions, bulls, and dragons (Figure 10.14) made with colored glazed bricks, sometimes flat, sometimes in relief, set against a bright blue background.

The Processional Way continued from the Ishtar Gate and the palace southwards over a large canal toward the Etemenanki, the compound that contained the ziggurat. This ziggurat would be the Tower of Babel of the Old Testament, but rebuilt many times. Unfortunately, this structure has survived only in its foundations, ca. 91m square, but it no doubt resembled ziggurats better preserved elsewhere. According to Herodotus's description (Book I.181–2), it was an eight-stepped tower with, on top, a temple consisting of a single room furnished with a large couch where the god Marduk would sleep and, next to the couch, a golden table. Guard duty was entrusted to a woman.

The street then turned to the west, heading for the Euphrates and the west bank. It passed between the Etemenanki and the Esagila (or E-sangil), "Temple that raises its Head," the temple to Marduk, the principal god of the city. Recovering the plan of the E-sangil posed problems for the German excavators, because it was buried beneath 21m of later habitation debris and, in keeping with the religious tradition of this spot, an Islamic shrine. The temple was located by a lucky hit when Koldewey's deep test pit struck a paved floor with identifying inscriptions. By tunnelling along its walls workmen recovered its dimensions: 86m × 78m, with two outer courts to the east. Interior details are few. According to Herodotus, the temple contained a seated statue of the god, a table, throne, and base, all of gold, but of these precious objects not a trace remained.

Figure 10.13 Ishtar Gate (reconstruction), Babylon

Figure 10.14 Dragon, panel of glazed bricks, Ishtar Gate, Babylon

The Southern Palace of Nebuchadrezzar

Nebuchadrezzar had three main palaces. The huge Southern Palace was constructed on a raised platform of baked brick. In plan it resembles the Assyrian type, with public and private rooms grouped around rectilinear courtyards, here five in number, aligned on an axis. The rectangular Throne Room, off the largest of the courts, is entered on its long side through three doorways. This palace, perhaps even this room, we might imagine as the site of both Belshazzar's feast, immortalized in the Old Testament Book of Daniel, and, 200 years later, the death of Alexander the Great.

The exterior wall of the Throne Room was decorated with panels of glazed bricks, with geometric patterns, trees, and animals. In contrast with the Assyrians, the Neo-Babylonians did not line rooms with stone orthostats or protect entrances with colossal guardian lamassu. Indeed, apart from the glazed bricks, the ruins of sixth-century BC Babylon have yielded little in the way of arts or crafts. Texts tell us, however, that the rooms were elegantly furnished with fine woods and trimmed with bronze or gold.

In the extreme north-east of the palace lies a puzzling self-contained cluster of 14 small vaulted storerooms surrounded by an unusually thick wall and containing a distinctive well of three adjacent shafts, seemingly designed for the hauling of water with buckets on a chain. These rooms may have been the foundations of the celebrated Hanging Gardens, a sort of lavish penthouse garden. Nebuchadrezzar built these gardens, according to the third-century BC historian Berossus, to satisfy his Median wife's longing for the forests of her northern homeland. This achievement so impressed the Greeks that they would include the Hanging Gardens among the Seven Wonders of the World.

Building the city: the workforce and the money to foot the bill

These many building projects required great manpower. This was supplied in large part by foreign labor, skilled and unskilled, brought to Babylon following victorious campaigns. The deportation of peoples was a common occurrence in the Ancient Near East, a method of reducing the possibility of rebellion. The Hebrews, exiled to Babylonia following the capture of Jerusalem in 586 BC, were not alone in their plight. But often, after a specific project was completed, such foreigners were allowed to live in better conditions, owning land and rising in social status.

Also needed for these projects was much money, but this was not so easily found. By the mid sixth century BC, the economy of Babylon was under strain, for the conquered territories were no longer contributing at previous levels. The resulting pressure on the populace may have been an important element favoring the invading Persians and Cyrus the Great.

THE ACHAEMENID PERSIANS AND PERSEPOLIS

With the conquest of Babylon by Cyrus the Great in 539 BC, the mastery of Mesopotamia passed to foreigners. And yet the Persians, on the eastern edge of Mesopotamia, were very much in its cultural sway. Cyrus II the Great (559–530 BC) hailed from Fars, the south-western Iranian province that gave its name to the state as a whole, Persia. Iran was dominated at this time by the Medes, centered in the west and north with their capital at Ecbatana, modern Hamadan. Cyrus's father, king of Fars, had married a Median princess. In 550 BC, Cyrus defeated Astyages, the Median king and his grandfather, thereby beginning an extraordinary career of conquest. His family, the Achaemenid dynasty, achieved mastery of the Near East from the Aegean Sea to Central Asia, from the Indus River to Egypt. The dynasty lasted until 330 BC, when it fell to Alexander the Great.

Like the Neo-Assyrian kings, the Achaemenid Persians founded new capitals to mark the advent of new monarchs. Pasargadae was the newly created capital of Cyrus the Great. Although a subsequent ruler, Darius I, would designate the ancient Elamite city of Susa in the Mesopotamian lowlands as his administrative capital, he also established a fortified palatial center at Persepolis in Fars, the homeland of the dynasty. It is this citadel, Persepolis, that remains the best known of Achaemenid cities.

Persepolis

Begun early in the reign of Darius I (ruled 521–486 BC) and completed some 100 years later, Persepolis served as a major center until sacked and burned by Alexander. Extensive excavations were carried out in the citadel during the 1930s by the Oriental Institute of Chicago under the direction of Ernst Herzfeld and Erich Schmidt. The lower town, home for ordinary people, has not yet been identified.

The citadel at Persepolis was destined to be a center for both government and ceremonials (Figure 10.15). The palace complex sits on a large platform ca. 455m × 305m. A mud brick wall once enclosed most of it, although a low parapet on the west allowed a view across the plain. Access was through an impressive stairway and a gatehouse, named "All Countries" by its builder, Xerxes (485–465 BC). Although the palace is divided into public and private sectors with occasional courtyards, the architecture follows traditions different from those seen in the Iron Age palaces of Mesopotamia discussed above. Instead of a single integrated whole, the complex

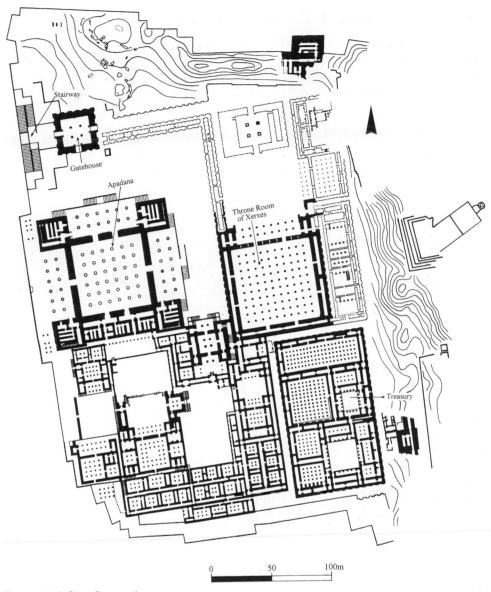

Figure 10.15 Plan, Persepolis

is made up of a cluster of separate buildings on loosely connected individual platforms. The use of square rooms, large and small, and abundant columns further characterizes the architecture. The largest of these structures is the Apadana, the great audience hall begun by Darius I, ca. 76m², with a restored height of ca. 20m. Elaborate stone capitals of lions, bulls, or human-headed bulls were used. Balancing the Apadana on the east is another enormous pillared hall, the Throne Room of Xerxes, also known as the Hall of 100 Columns.

The complex was extensively decorated with relief sculptures that show men from different parts of the far-flung empire bringing their tribute to the great king in dignified procession (Figure 10.16). The king himself appears in a relief from the Treasury, seated on his throne and

Figure 10.16 Apadana, Persepolis: platform viewed from the north-east

Figure 10.17 Darius receives homage, relief sculpture, from Persepolis

approached by a dignitary who presents his homage (Figure 10.17). Behind Darius stand Xerxes, the crown prince, and officials. The theme of these reliefs is the power and prestige of the Persian king. Although the idea of using reliefs to convey such a message may well have come from the Assyrians, the Persians present a different interpretation of royal achievement. Violent triumphs in battle and hunt are not shown. In further contrast with earlier Mesopotamian art, no god is present to affirm divine support. Instead, order and obedience characterize the success of this empire.

Although Greek sculptors from Ionia (western Anatolia) participated in the carving of these reliefs, the manner of presentation is traditional Near Eastern. In the relief illustrated here, Darius and Xerxes are shown in larger scale than the other men, a familiar technique for signaling high status used as early as the Narmer Palette at the beginning of dynastic Egypt. In addition, the profile view is standard, and the tribute bearers march in fairly flat relief with little individuality other than ethnic identifiers such as their costume.

Royal tombs

Other buildings in this citadel include private areas or palaces, and a treasury, but cult rooms are lacking. The Persians were Zoroastrians, worshipping the god Ahuramazda, represented as a winged sun disk. They held ceremonies at open-air fire altars. Fire altars are depicted in reliefs on the façades of four royal tombs carved out of the cliffs at Naqsh-i Rustam, 6km north-west of Persepolis. Four of Cyrus's successors were buried here. The tombs were robbed in antiquity, but the decorated façades have survived. The façades are carved in the shape of a cross, with the entrance to the tomb chamber in the center. The doorway is flanked by two pairs of columns with bull capitals; they support a couch-like platform held up by two rows of men. On this stands the king, worshipping at a fire altar, while Ahuramazda hovers overhead.

As for Cyrus the Great, he was buried in a free-standing building at Pasargadae, a simple single-roomed structure standing on its own stepped platform. The tomb was spared the ravages of the Macedonian army on the express orders of Alexander the Great, a man well-versed in history and full of respect for Cyrus. Miraculously it has survived to the present day.

PART TWO

GREEK CITIES

CHAPTER 11

Early Greek city-states of the Iron Age (eleventh to seventh centuries BC)

Cultural periods of ancient Greece

Sub-Mycenaean and Sub-Minoan: eleventh century BC

Protogeometric: ca. 1000–900 BC

Geometric: ca. 900–700 BC

Orientalizing (Early Archaic): ca. 725–600 BC

Archaic: ca. 600–479 BC (to the end of the Persian Wars)

Classical: ca. 479–323 BC (to the death of Alexander the Great)

Hellenistic: ca. 323–31 BC (to the Battle of Actium)

Although the Mycenaeans of the Late Bronze Age were Greek speakers, the cultural label "Greek" is habitually applied first in the Iron Age. In the next seven chapters, we shall examine the cities of the Greeks in the first millennium BC, the heyday of ancient Greek civilization before it was absorbed into the expanding Roman state. The nature of the Greek urban experience will be our focus, with attention paid to city plans and architecture; pottery, sculpture, and other objects that characterized the ancient Greek world; and the social, economical, and ideological contexts. This first chapter will explore the early development of cities, their cemeteries, and religious centers (sanctuaries), and such fruits of foreign contacts as the alphabet and coinage.

Although unified in their culture, the Greeks lived divided into a multitude of *city-states* and *ethnoi* until the later fourth century BC. No one city, no great warrior king rose out of the village-based society of the eleventh to ninth centuries to dominate the others. This political organization recalls that of Sumer, but contrasts with the kingdoms of the Near East in the second and first millennia BC and of Egypt. The city-state, or *polis* as the Greeks called it, became a characteristic unit of government during the eighth century BC in the eastern half of southern and central Greece and throughout the Aegean basin: areas, perhaps coincidentally, where Mycenaean culture had flourished. In contrast, the ethnos, often translated as "tribal state" or "nation," typically a loose association of villages spread over a large area, was found in the western and northern areas of the Greek peninsula. The great achievements of Greek culture are associated with the city-states, so we shall focus on them.

HISTORICAL BACKGROUND

The collapse of the Bronze Age cultures of Greece in the late thirteenth and twelfth centuries BC initiated a period of some 400 years often called the Greek Dark Ages. But the term "dark" conveys a primitivism, a cultural regression that prejudices a view of these centuries. "Iron Age Greece" is a more neutral term, and more useful too, in that it brings developments in Greece in line with the Near East and indeed the rest of Europe, areas where this term has long been used. Although the Iron Age could be ended in the later eighth century BC with the development of the Greek alphabet, we shall extend it an additional century, to the end of the seventh century BC. By this time certain major features of Greek culture were well in place: the city-state had emerged as a characteristic unit of government; the migrations of Greek speakers throughout the Aegean, Mediterranean, and Black Seas had defined the territory of ancient Greece; contacts with the venerable cultures of the Near East and Egypt were resumed; and, as mentioned, literacy had returned.

Migrations

In the absence of contemporary documents, we rely on the writings of later Greeks and on modern archaeologists for information about the earlier Iron Age. The first key events are two roughly contemporary waves of migrations within the Aegean basin. The first is the so-called Dorian Invasion, recorded by later Greek historians. Greece would be divided into regions speaking different dialects of the Greek language: Dorian, Ionic, Aeolic, and others. The Dorian dialect predominated in southern Greece: the Peloponnesus, the islands of the south Aegean, including Crete, and the south coast of Aegean Anatolia. The other main dialect, the Ionian, was spoken in Athens, on the islands of the central Aegean, and in Ionia, the central zone of Aegean Anatolia. Later Greeks believed that the Dorian dialect speakers had migrated southwards into Greece at the end of the Bronze Age, fighting en route to their new lands. Several writers tied the Dorian Invasion to the fall of Troy, another firm fact for the ancient Greeks; Thucydides, for example, dated the Dorian Invasion to ca. 1120 BC (as measured in our calendrical system), 80 years after the Achaean capture of Troy. Archaeology has provided little confirmation of this story, although excavators have searched for it with eagle eyes. But migrations are difficult to trace in the material record. Nomads do not always oblige us by scattering distinctive objects along their trail. On the other hand, the dialects could well have developed spontaneously in the different regions without notable inmixture of new people. In sum, the reality behind the Dorian Invasion remains elusive.

In contrast, the second round of early migrations can be observed in the archaeological record. During the eleventh century BC, Greeks from mainland Greece migrated eastwards across the Aegean to the shores of Anatolia. This coastal zone and the islands immediately offshore, known collectively as East Greece, were divided into three regions marked by different dialects: Aeolis, Ionia, and Doris, from north to south. The heartland of ancient Greece thus embraced all shores of the Aegean Sea. Today the region is divided between the modern countries of Greece and Turkey (Figure 11.1).

At a later time, especially from the mid eighth to the later sixth centuries BC, various Greek cities sent colonizing missions by sea to more distant shores. Motives for these journeys varied. Commercial interests, such as the search for minerals and other raw materials, would be important. Other factors provoking this flood of emigration from the Greek homeland included the rapid expansion of the population in the eighth century BC and the competition for land to

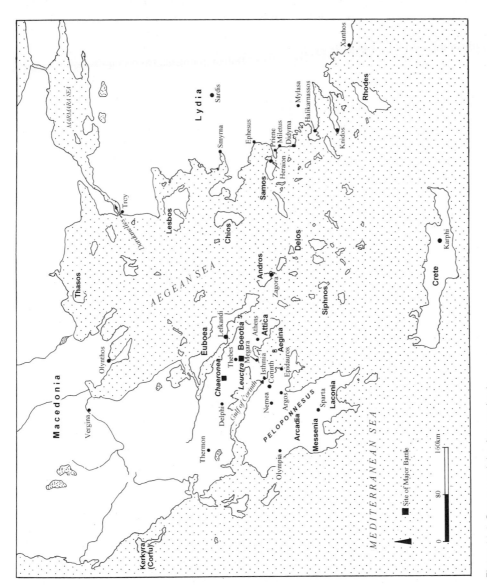

Figure 11.1 Greece and the Aegean basin

grow food, and the availability of an outlet for dissidents in the competition for political power among the aristocrats struggling to gain control of the governments of city-states. Usually the daughter cities would maintain strong sentimental ties to their founders, although in time they became autonomous in government and economy. Two destinations in particular attracted the Greeks, South Italy and Sicily in the west, and the Black Sea and its approaches in the north. Scattered colonies were founded elsewhere, in Libya, Egypt, the Levant, and on the south coast of Anatolia. The earliest settlers headed west, founding colonies first in the Bay of Naples: at Pithekoussai on the small island of Ischia, ca. 760 BC, then at Cumae on the adjacent main-land, and Naxos on Sicily (see Figure 18.1). The Italian peninsula from Naples south and the eastern two-thirds of the island of Sicily, together known as Magna Graecia (Latin term), or West Greece, would eventually become an integral part of the Greek world, containing several important cities. These colonies survived because the local peoples, based in the interior, did not challenge the coastal Greeks. Other parts of Italy were less hospitable, however, and the Greeks avoided them. The lands north of Naples belonged to the powerful Etruscans, and western Sicily had already been staked out by the Phoenicians, as had much of North Africa and Mediterranean Spain.

THE RISE OF THE POLIS

The reasons for the origins of the city-state are controversial. It is sometimes said that the mountainous landscape of the Greek peninsula gave rise to the city-state. Although favorable for such developments, this sort of geography need not be determinative: city-states dominated in flat Sumer, and kingdoms have often held sway over mountainous regions, indeed in Greece itself. Particular historical circumstances must also contribute. Villages may have coalesced into larger units as communications and economies improved. Towns may have developed their identities in conjunction with local cults, to promote and protect the favored gods and heroes. In this too, the parallel with Sumer is strong.

Some early towns developed as fortified centers in isolated places, if menaced by pirates or untrustworthy foreigners. Such is the case of Karphi, a village of Minoan refugees established high in the hills of Crete but occupied for a short time only, from ca. 1050 to 950 BC. Coastal sites too needed to be picked with care. Smyrna, founded during the migrations to Ionia, was built on a promontory jutting into a bay. Indeed, the early Greeks favored such peninsulas, because they could be easily defended. A good example of a long-lived settlement on such a land form is Kinet Höyük on the north-east Mediterranean coast near modern Dörtyol (Turkey), probably the city of Issos in the Classical period (see Figure 10.1). The Iron Age town, shown here in an imaginative reconstruction (Figure 11.2), was built directly on top of at least 2,000 years of continuous occupation.

Also valued were hilltops near the sea: again, defensible situations. Some important sites of the early Iron Age profit from this latter sort of location. *Lefkandi*, on the island of Euboea, occupied a prominent mound right by the sea, and *Zagora*, an eighth-century BC town on Andros, was built on a bluff rising high above the Aegean, an advantage in security that outweighed meager water supplies and ferocious winds. As dangers of marauders receded, those towns that were well situated to profit from trade or agriculture survived and prospered, whereas those built strictly for protection, such as Karphi and Zagora, were abandoned.

The polis consisted of an urban center and a varying amount of rural territory. Some were quite small, while others were huge. Syracuse, in Sicily, one of the largest, possessed 4,740km^2

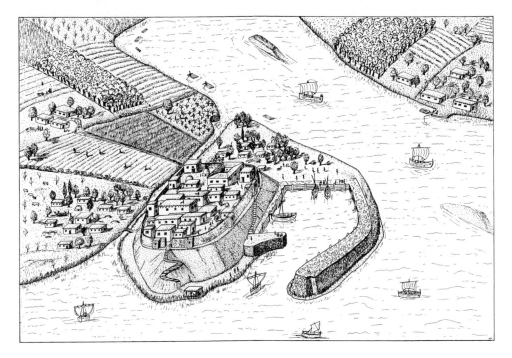

Figure 11.2 Kinet Höyük in the Iron Age (reconstruction)

of land, port city and hinterland, with a population of perhaps 250,000 in its heyday in the fifth and fourth centuries BC. Control of the government varied. In general, the early city-states were ruled by kings, according to later Greek tradition; we might think of them as chiefs, in anthropological terms. Gradually the power base widened. Kings gave way to aristocracies, a group of wealthy citizens, and, in some cities, aristocracies eventually yielded to the citizenry at large. Occasionally a tyrant, a man who seized power illegally, would intrude. Whatever good he might do, and the term "tyrant" originally had no quality of bad or good attached to it, his descendants usually lacked the father's gifts, roused animosities, and were overthrown.

Citizens lived in both city and countryside. Political rights, including the famed democracy of ancient Greece, were restricted to male citizens. Women were expected to manage the household and raise children. In addition to the citizens and their families, Greek cities contained large numbers of non-voting free persons (such as foreign emigrants), sometimes indentured servants and farmers (the Spartan helots), and slaves.

THE EARLY GREEK TOWN: ZAGORA

Zagora, an eighth-century BC town on the west coast of the island of Andros, exemplifies modest Greek settlements of the Iron Age. Zagora was small, occupying an area of 6.7ha (Figure 11.3). Its location on a bluff 150m above the Aegean demonstrates a concern for effective defense. Steep cliffs below protected the settlement on three sides; the land access was fortified by a stone wall ca. 140m long and 2m thick, penetrated by one gate. Water was not immediately available, but had to be carried from springs in the region, with rainwater perhaps collected as spill off the roofs.

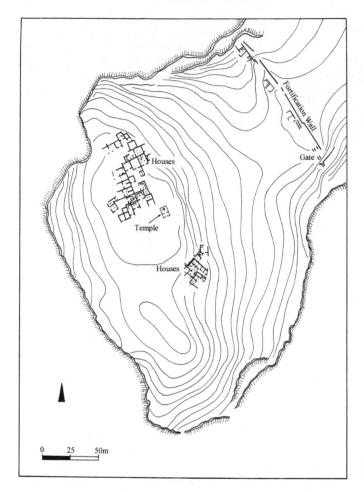

Figure 11.3 Town plan, Zagora

The town contained clusters of houses sharing walls, representing a population of possibly 1,000. Houses were single-storey with flat roofs of thin pieces of schist covered with clay, laid on wooden roof beams supported by wooden columns. In plan they were rectangular, with a large central room and often a court and secondary rooms for storage and shelter for animals. The local schist, a stone that separates into layers, was used as the prime building material, just as it has been into modern times on this island. Also used was gray marble, the main stone of the bluff itself. Elsewhere in the Greek world, as in early Smyrna, sun-dried mud bricks were commonly used, normally placed on stone foundations to prevent moisture from causing the walls to crumble at their base. Floors were of beaten earth, and clay would have served as a sealer for walls and roofs.

The Australian excavators of Zagora identifed a small temple in the center of the town. Although the cult site is probably earlier, the shrine was built in the mid sixth century BC, well after the town had been abandoned. The importance of the area as a sacred place was evidently kept alive by the descendants of the villagers.

The temple at Zagora stood by itself. Although only its lowest walls survive, the construction was clearly of high quality. The temple consisted of a porch and a main room (cella), with, it is thought, a flat roof. Its simple floor plan is typical of the shrines of Iron Age Greece. The original appearance of these normally poorly preserved shrines is reflected in two eighth to early seventh

century BC clay models, one from Perachora and another from the Argive Heraion, the sanctuary to the goddess Hera in the region of Argos (Figure 11.4). The model from Perachora has an apsidal (curved at one end) ground plan and a parabolic roof profile thought to represent thatch, whereas the later model, from the Argive Heraion, has a rectangular room and a pointed, or gabled, roof. Both are decorated on the exterior with geometric designs.

Figure 11.4 Temple model, clay, from the Argive Heraion. National Archaeological Museum, Athens

CEMETERIES AT LEFKANDI AND ATHENS

Only isolated graves have been found at Zagora. The likely location for the cemetery lies beneath cultivated terraces, difficult of access for archaeologists. For important cemeteries we must look elsewhere, notably to Lefkandi (on Euboea) and to Athens.

Lefkandi: the Heroon

A remarkable discovery made in the Toumba cemetery at Lefkandi in the early 1980s is the elaborate burial from the mid tenth century BC of a man, a woman, and four horses in two compartments in a shaft cut into the floor of a large building (Figure 11.5). The man (age 30–45) and the woman (age 25–30) were buried in a compartment lined with mud bricks and faced with clay plaster. The man was cremated, his ashes placed in an already old bronze *krater* (broad-mouthed bowl) of late thirteenth to early eleventh century BC Cypriot type with a rim decorated with animals and their hunters. Folded and packed inside was a shroud, one sheet of linen folded over and sewn up the side, surprisingly well-preserved for this period; placed beside the krater were an iron sword, a spearhead, and a whetstone. The woman was not cremated; her skeleton, with feet crossed and hands crossed at the stomach, was covered with gold jewelry. The skeletons of four horses were discovered in the adjacent compartment.

The building itself was exceptionally imposing, measuring ca. 9m × 50m, with unusual architectural features. Oriented on an east–west axis, it was divided into several sections, an east porch for the entry, an east room, a large central room beneath which the burials were made, a west corridor with a north and a south room off it, and an apsidal room on the west. Three parallel rows of posts held the roof, in the center and along the interior faces of the north and south walls. An additional series of at least 28 posts set 2m outside the building on the north and south sides indicate that the roof continued beyond, forming a sort of veranda, a forerunner of the covered colonnade of later Greek temples. As if the burials and impressive building alone did not indicate the special status of the deceased, the excavators found that the building had been partially dismantled and then filled and covered with a tumulus of earth, pebbles, and stones.

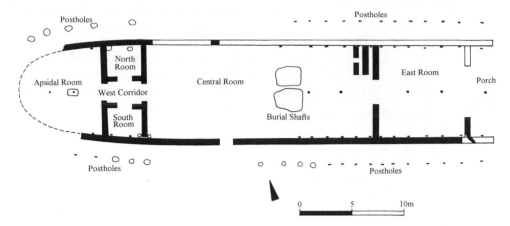

Figure 11.5 Plan, "Heroon," Lefkandi

Additional burials continued to be made until ca. 825 BC in an arc-shaped area around the east end of the revered building and tomb site. The excavators have labeled this monumental grave a *heroon*, that is, a tomb or shrine commemorating a hero, a man of larger-than-life qualities; who the venerated hero was we cannot say, in the absence of written records. But for their date early in the Iron Age; for the connections with the Near East, Egypt, and Cyprus revealed by the grave goods throughout the Toumba cemetery on an island whose role in early overseas ventures was clearly major; and for the striking architecture of the long building, the discoveries at Lefkandi are of great importance.

Athens: the Kerameikos cemetery and pottery in the Geometric style

The second of the two famous cemeteries of early Greece belongs to Athens and has been long under excavation: the Kerameikos cemetery just outside the Dipylon Gate on the north-west outskirts of the city. Since the ancient Greeks believed the dead to be ritually polluting, cemeteries were always placed outside the city limits, as here. In this, the main cemetery of Athens, burials have been discovered dating from Late Helladic IIIC to the Roman Empire. During the later eighth century BC, the wealthier cremation graves in the Dipylon sector were marked with enormous vases up to 1.75m in height, decorated in the distinctive Geometric style that gives its name to the entire period. The pots, either *amphoras* (a shape with narrow mouth and two vertical handles) or kraters, had perforated bases or bottoms to allow liquid offerings and rainwater to trickle into the earth below. The careful, elaborate decoration consists of countless horizontal zones filled with meanders, lozenges, and other motifs that frame broader bands in which funerary scenes are depicted (Figure 11.6), all painted in black glaze on the natural orange-red clay of Attica. Humans and animals are shown largely in silhouette, their bodies a cartoon-like combination of triangles, cylinders, circles, and lines. In the arrangement of the figures, clarity of understanding was the paramount goal. If horses stood side by side, the painter made sure the viewer could count how many there were. Each head, leg, and tail was painted separately. In the scene that shows the laying out of the body of the deceased, each element – the corpse, the bier and its legs, and the shroud – would be painted individually without overlapping other features. This emphasis on the conceptual rather than the optical

reality has a long tradition in the arts of the cultures surveyed in this book. Egyptian art comes to mind in particular. In Egyptian tombs, the precision of the rendering had a practical purpose: the complete outline guaranteed the completeness of the object in the Afterlife. But 200 years later, as we shall see, Greek pot painters would shatter this tradition.

Figure 11.6 The Dipylon Amphora. Geometric vase found in the Kerameikos cemetery, Athens. National Archaeological Museum, Athens

CORINTH: ORIENTALIZING POTTERY AND HOPLITE WARFARE

The city of Corinth, an active mercantile center during the later eighth and seventh centuries BC with many overseas connections, developed a type of pottery decoration quite different from that of Athens: the Orientalizing styles. First seen in Corinth ca. 725 BC, the "Protocorinthian" Orientalizing style was adopted by Athens some 25 years later ("Protoattic") and then spread to other regions of Greece in the early seventh century BC. The subject matter and style contrast sharply with the Geometric. Under the influence of Near Eastern art, animals became popular, especially wild animals such as lions, deer, and wild goats, and mythical or composite creatures such as the sphinx and the griffin. The style of drawing slowly breaks from the Geometric. The silhouette is enlivened with more and more internal details, expressed by lines incised through the black glaze to reveal the light clay below and by open spaces defined by outlines, sometimes treated with added colors, purple or white. The increased use of curving lines allows for a more naturalistic modeling of the subjects than in the angular Geometric style.

One of the remarkable vases produced at Corinth is the so-called Macmillan aryballos of ca. 650 BC, now in the British Museum (Figure 11.7). The *aryballos* was a common shape in Protocorinthian pottery, a tiny tear-shaped or round flask for perfumed oil, a major export of Corinth. Instead of the usual flattened spout, the Macmillan aryballos has a lion's head out of which the liquid was poured. The body of the small pot contains four zones of decoration: in the tallest and most important band, soldiers are fighting; below, horsemen race in a line; and in comic contrast, pygmies and dogs chase rabbits. Finally, the bottom is decorated with the flame pattern frequent in pre-Classical art. For a vase only 6.8cm high, the amount of pictorial imagery placed on it is astounding.

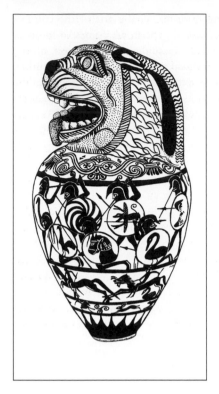

Figure 11.7 The Macmillan aryballos. Protocorinthian vase found in Thebes. British Museum, London

Hoplite warfare

The depiction of soldiers recalls critical changes in warfare that took place during the Iron Age, changes in both equipment and tactics. Despite their cultural ties, the Greek city-states often fanned their rivalries to the point of war. Indeed, the summer campaigns of armies of citizen infantrymen, or hoplites, became a characteristic feature of the landscape. The development of improved defensive armor in the late eighth century BC made this possible, torso-fitting bronze body armor with accompanying helmet and shin guards, or greaves. For attacking, the hoplite was equipped with a spear, held in the right hand, and a large round shield with grips for the left forearm and hand. Hoplites were deployed in a phalanx formation, that is, in lines of men standing close together, each brandishing his shield so as to give some protection to his comrade at his left. The soldier on the far right would not have this extra protection; hence the tendency of the entire line to shift toward the right. This armor, or panoply, was expensive, but increasing trade and colonization made metals more readily available and affordable for the landowning class. As a result of this development, more citizens gained control of the tools of power, a crucial step in the path from aristocracy to democracy.

THE GREEK SANCTUARY: THE HERAION ON SAMOS

The temple at Zagora has yielded few finds. This is not unusual. Temples were considered the homes of the gods. Mortals rarely disturbed them, but worshipped instead at altars placed well outside the temple. The altar and the temple were the main elements in a compound marked off, often by a low wall, as sacred. In Greek archaeology, this entire holy area is called the *sanctuary*, or *temenos*. Sanctuaries might lie within a city, as did the Acropolis at Athens, or they might well be located in the remote countryside. Whichever, their importance in the lives of the ancient Greeks, both city dwellers and country folk, was enormous. In reflection of this, we shall be exploring several famous sanctuaries in this chapter and the following.

One of the best-known examples from early Greece is the Samian Heraion, the sanctuary to the goddess Hera on Samos. Samos, an island that hugs the Anatolian mainland, was an important component of Ionia. The early and lasting fame of the Heraion ensured that. The sanctuary lies on the south coast of Samos, at the west end of a plain 6.5km from the town of Samos (modern Pithagorio), the capital of the island in Classical antiquity; town and sanctuary were in fact linked by a special road, the Sacred Way. Use of the site goes back to the Bronze Age, but its sacred character becomes certain in the Iron Age. According to legend, Hera was born here underneath a lygos tree, a type of willow. In addition a curiously shaped board, the earliest sacred object symbolizing the goddess, was found on the beach nearby, so it was in this area that the holy object was housed and Hera's cult promoted. The highlight of the religious year was the celebration of the sacred marriage of Hera and Zeus, the reigning couple among Greek divinities. In another festival, the cult image was bathed by the sea in a basin fed by the Imbrasos stream, dressed in a new robe sewn by the women of Samos, and tied with ropes to (or with foliage of) the sacred lygos tree, to restore her to virginity until her marriage day returned.

As always in Greek sanctuaries, the outdoor altar was the focus of worship. Seven early versions have been discovered here by German excavators, dating from the tenth to the late seventh centuries BC. The first temple to Hera, where she resided in the form of her cult image, was erected well after the earliest altar, perhaps in the early eighth century BC (Figure 11.8). The temple was oriented not toward the already existing altar that faced south-east, it is interesting to note, but directly east on an east–west axis, with its entrance on the east – an orientation that would become standard for Greek temples. The remarkably long narrow structure, ca. 33m × 6.5m, was built of mud brick walls on stone foundations. Three wooden columns *in antis* (aligned between the ends of a pair of walls) marked the entrance. Behind the middle column a single line of 12 or 13 additional columns on stone bases extended to the rear of the hall; these columns supported the cross beams of the roof. Ending just before a stone base on which the cult image was placed, this line of columns blocked the view of the cult image. In later temples, in contrast, the statue of the god or goddess would be placed unobstructed for optimal viewing. Here, in this early experimental temple, the main concern of the builders must have been simply to guarantee the goddess a solid roof over her head.

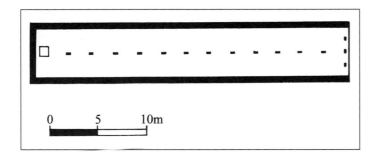

Figure 11.8 Early Temple of Hera, eighth century BC, Samian Heraion

In a remodelling of the temple, perhaps later in the eighth century, a peristyle was added around the exterior, that is, a covered colonnade. The exterior colonnade would become a hallmark of Greek temple architecture. But the arrangement of columns had not yet attained the regularity of later times. The front side now had seven columns, the central column aligned with the interior row, but the rear had only six, and the sides had 25.

In the early seventh century BC, the temple was rebuilt (Figure 11.9). This second temple was still long and narrow, but important changes had occurred. The central row of columns disappeared, so the view of the statue in the rear of the cella was unencumbered. Some support for the roof beams may have been provided by wooden posts on benches alongside the interior walls. The exterior colonnade now numbered six in front and back and 18 on the long sides. The front was emphasized with a second row of six columns.

In addition to the altar and the temple, the sanctuary in the seventh century BC consisted of a formal gateway, or *propylon*; a stone-lined basin for the bathing of the cult image; and, beside the Imbrasos, the stream flowing to the sea, a long *stoa*, which formed the south-west boundary of the temenos. The stoa, a colonnaded porch with a roof and a solid rear wall or, in elaborate

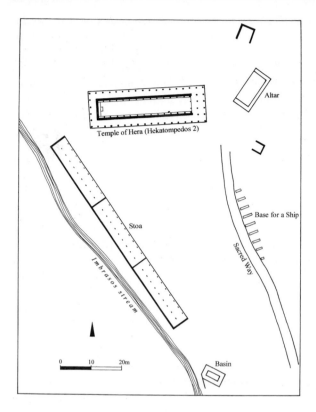

Figure 11.9 The second Temple of Hera and the Samian Sanctuary of Hera (Heraion), seventh century BC

versions, with rooms at the rear, would become a distinctive form in Greek architecture, and was often used in sanctuaries and in agoras, or city centers, to mark the edge of the space. In this shelter from intense summer sun or winter rains, a variety of activities took place, from business and law courts to social encounters. The stoa at Samos is among the earliest known examples of the type.

The sanctuary survived in this form until the second quarter of the sixth century BC, when a major remodelling was done in conjunction with the erection of a new temple to Hera, a colossal temple in the Ionic order.

VOTIVE OFFERINGS, FOREIGN CONTACTS, WRITING, AND COINAGE

Worshippers routinely left offerings on the grounds of a sanctuary, either modest gifts such as clay statuettes, or rich presents, which in later times might include statue groups of life-size bronze or marble figures. A striking early example of such a votive gift is a bronze statuette from Thebes, dedicated to Apollo ca. 700 BC by a man named Mantiklos (Figure 11.10). The statuette shows well how the Geometric style lived in sculpture as well as in two-dimensional paintings on pottery. The body parts seem separate, stuck together, the triangular face on the tall neck, the triangular torso, and the cylindrical thighs that flare out from the tiny waist. Transitions between them are abrupt. And yet, despite what we would call the unreality of the portrayal, this little man has charm.

Figure 11.10 Mantiklos's dedication to Apollo, bronze figurine, from Thebes (Boeotia), Greece

Near Eastern borrowings: the alphabet

The identity of the dedicator is known from the inscription written on the thighs. The words are written *boustrophedon* (lines of words written in alternating directions, an accepted practice in Greek writing from the eighth into the fifth centuries BC): "Mantiklos offers me as a tithe to Apollo of the silver bow; do you, Phoibos, give some pleasing favor in return" (Boardman 1978: fig. 10, p. 30). This is an early Greek inscription, indeed the earliest known dedicatory inscription. The Greeks adopted an alphabet from the Phoenicians in the mid eighth century BC, thus ending some four centuries of illiteracy after Linear B fell out of use. This alphabet is still used by the Greeks today. Who thought to invent this alphabet and why and where are still unknown, but, because contacts with Phoenicians were largely commercial, a commercial context seems most likely.

The Greeks added four new letters at the end and allotted vowels a particular prominence not seen in Phoenician. At first, as we see on Mantiklos's statuette and elsewhere, the script was written in both directions, and upside down, and with letters sometimes on their sides. Only with time did the left-to-right direction become standard. Different cities and regions of Greece had variants in letter forms in the pre-Classical period. The Euboeans, early colonizers, carried their script to Italy, where it passed to the Etruscans and thence to the Romans and later Europeans.

Among the many beneficiaries of the resurgence of writing was literature. The *Iliad* and the *Odyssey*, epic poems about the Trojan War and Odysseus's long journey home, were compiled and codified in the later Iron Age. For later Greeks, the author was Homer. Homer may have been simply the first to write down the poems, developed through centuries of telling and retelling. History too could emerge from the shadowy realm of legend. Indeed, the Greeks used as their benchmark of time the first Olympic Games, said to have been held in 776 BC (by our reckoning). These games were held every four years. Later events would be dated according to the closest Olympiad: such and such happened two years after the thirtieth Olympiad, for example.

Writing also nicely documents the contacts between Greeks and foreigners. In the mid seventh century BC, Herodotus tells us, Ionian and Carian pirates were hired by the Egyptian king Psamtik I (Psammetichos, in Greek) to fight in his struggle to capture the throne of Egypt from the Assyrians. After he succeeded, he granted land in the Nile Delta to the soldiers, the first important Greek presence in Egypt. Perhaps their descendants formed part of a contingent of mercenaries who fought the Nubians with Psamtik II in the early sixth century BC. These soldiers travelled far up the Nile. At Abu Simbel, on the shin of one of the colossal seated statues of Ramses II, they carved their names and exploits, touristic graffiti one can still see today.

Near Eastern borrowings: coinage

Coinage, another key borrowing from the Near East, enters our story here; it will become of enormous importance for cities of the Mediterranean and the Near East. The use of coins began in the late seventh century BC in Lydia, a non-Greek kingdom in West Anatolia, whose capital, Sardis, was blessed with a stream that carried electrum flecks down from the mountains. Electrum, a natural alloy of gold and silver, was the material of the first coins. A crude device was stamped on one side, a deep punch mark on the other. Coins evidently satisfied the need to regulate the measures of electrum used for payment. The ratio of gold to silver in the electrum varied, however, which proved a cause for dissension. By the mid sixth century BC, the Sardians had learned how to separate gold from silver. Croesus (ruled 559–546 BC), the last king of independent Lydia, was the first to issue separate coinages in gold and silver, but still coins of large denominations (Figure 11.11a). Later, in the late fifth century BC, bronze coins, worth much less, were instituted. The invention of coinage took the Greek world by storm. From the early sixth century BC, many Greek cities issued coinage, always marked with a distinctive motif, such as the head of Athena and an owl for Athens, or the head of Pan and a griffin for the northern Black Sea city of Panticapaeum (Figure 11.11b and 11.11c). Sometimes the name of the city was inscribed, in whole or in part.

Contacts with the Near East and Egypt were indeed crucial in the development of Greek culture. Not only the alphabet and coinage, but also art motifs (the Orientalizing movement of the late eighth and seventh centuries BC) and some cultic ceremonies came from the Near East, while Egypt contributed its vast experience of working stone for architecture and sculpture. The effects of this last, the Egyptian tradition of stone working, would change profoundly the appearance of the Greek city and landscape. It is thus to architecture and sculpture that we shall now turn.

Figure 11.11 (opposite) Lydian and Greek coins in the Numismatic Museum, Athens. Not drawn to the same scale. (a) Lydian silver coin, sixth century BC, with lion and bull, and simple punch mark. (b) Athenian silver tetradrachm, fifth century BC, with Athena and owl. (c) Gold stater from Panticapaeum, mid fourth century BC, with Pan and a griffin

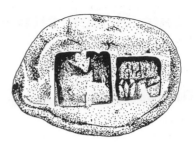

a

b

c

CHAPTER 12

Archaic Greek cities, I

The Doric and Ionic orders of Greek architecture, and East Greek cities to the Ionian revolt

The built environment of the Greek city underwent important changes in the later seventh and sixth centuries BC. The conventions of Greek architecture, or *orders*, that developed at that time remained in place with little change through the Hellenistic period. The influence of these designs has been huge. The Romans would absorb these conventions into their own rich architectural repertoire, and pass them on to the medieval European and Islamic worlds. The effects are still with us today. We shall now look in detail at the elements of the architectural orders. So important is an understanding of these conventions for an appreciation of the appearance of Greek and Roman public buildings that, however tedious the effort may seem, this will be time well spent. We shall then examine the cities of the eastern Aegean, flourishing centers of Greek civilization in the sixth century BC, before moving in the next chapter to two prominent cities of the Greek peninsula, Sparta and Athens.

THE DORIC AND IONIC ORDERS

As we have seen in the succession of temples at the Samian Heraion, by the late seventh and early sixth centuries BC Greek architecture had evolved considerably from the simple structures represented by the models from Perachora and the Argive Heraion. The changes took place especially in religious architecture. Greek society reserved its finest materials, its best workmanship, for the homes of the gods and the accompanying buildings in their sanctuaries. In contrast, the homes of mortals remained modest through the Classical period. Later, when the conquests of Alexander the Great brought Near Eastern and Egyptian grandeur into the habits of the Hellenistic kings, the palace would become a prominent element in the plans at least of the capital cities.

Temple architecture in the early Archaic period developed from changes on two fronts: first, the materials used; and second, the ground plan, elevation, and decoration. Stone gradually replaced mud brick and wood, a development surely guided by Greek appreciation of huge Egyptian temples of stone. Details of form and decoration, carefully deployed in a fairly narrow range of proportional relationships, gradually coalesced into two main systems of design, the Doric and Ionic orders. Changes came slowly but steadily. As seems true particularly in religious architecture, builders hesitated to tamper with tradition. Each new temple stood solidly with the past, decked with features already tested elsewhere, but always there was some new detail that expanded ever so slightly the possibilities of the style.

The Doric order was the design system developed on the Greek mainland in the late seventh century BC. The Ionic order emerged a quarter century later, in East Greece. The Doric order would flourish through the Hellenistic period, afterwards appearing rarely, whereas the Ionic and its variant, the Corinthian, would have a longer life, enjoying great popularity during the Roman Empire.

Both Doric and Ionic temples followed the same basic principles for foundations and for the ground plan. Rectangular in shape, temples were usually oriented east–west, with the entrance on the east. Whatever the irregularities of the ground, they were masked by a levelling course, the *euthynteria* (Figure 12.1). On top of this were placed three steps, of which the uppermost was called the *stylobate*. The upper surface of the stylobate marked the floor level of the temple. The temple proper consisted of cult rooms aligned on the main axis of the temple, surrounded by a colonnade, placed on the edge of the stylobate. The norm in the Doric order was six columns on the short sides, 13 (twice the short side plus one) on the long. A gabled roof covered both cult rooms and the colonnade. The rooms were normally three in number, an entrance porch, or *pronaos*; then the *naos* or *cella*, the large room that housed the image of the deity; and behind, with access only from the west, not from the cella, a rear porch or *opisthodomos*, providing the ground plan a symmetrical counterpart for the pronaos (Figure 12.2).

Through the centuries, the Greeks would preserve in the elevation of both orders the traditional scheme of the horizontal member (the lintel) resting on the vertical (the post, or column), even though the true arch was known from the fifth century BC. It is in details of the elevation, however, that the differences between the Doric and Ionic orders become marked. Although both orders use columns, the forms are quite distinct. The Doric column stands directly on the stylobate, whereas the Ionic column shaft rests on a round base. The concave grooves of Doric fluting end in a sharp line, or *arris*, whereas a thin flat band separates the grooves

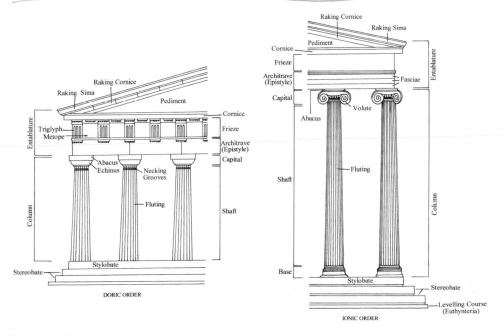

Figure 12.1 Elevations of the Doric and Ionic orders: key elements

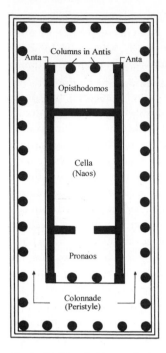

Figure 12.2 Typical ground plan of a Greek temple

of Ionic fluting. The contrast in capitals is perhaps what the eye searches out first. The Doric capital consists of two parts, the round *echinus*, which resembles a flattened mushroom cap or, as the ancient name indicates, a sea urchin, and above it, the square *abacus*. The Ionic capital, in contrast, is marked by a *volute*, an upside-down scroll, with a thin, square abacus above. The capitals form the transition from the column shaft to the *entablature*, the upper section of the temple. The notion of a capital was not an invention of the Greeks. The Egyptians used them, as did the Minoans and Mycenaeans. The forms of their capitals seem ancestral only to the Doric capital, however. The Ionic volute appears to be a variant of a scrolled palm leaf capital, the Aeolic capital, used in East Greece and the Levant during the earlier Iron Age.

The entablature consists of three main parts. The lower two portions are two horizontal zones. The *architrave* or *epistyle*, the lower of the two, rests on the columns, and is usually left plain in the Doric style, but carved in three progressively projecting horizontal bands, called *fasciae*, in the Ionic. Above this lies the frieze, in which, as with the column capitals, the differences between the Doric and Ionic orders are particularly distinct. In the Doric frieze, *triglyphs*, or vertically grooved pieces that project from the surface, alternate with *metopes*, plain spaces. The Ionic frieze is plain, with perhaps at the top, in later times, a row of dentils, teethlike projections. When money was plentiful, metopes and the Ionic frieze might be decorated with relief sculpture.

The top element of the entablature is the *cornice* (or *geison*) which forms the eaves along the sides of the building and, at the short ends, the base for the gable. The gable, the broad triangular space formed by the sloping roof, is called the *pediment*. The pediment is bordered on the bottom by a horizontal course (the *cornice*, which we have met already), and by two sloping courses, the inner plain *raking cornice* and the higher, projecting *raking sima* with a distinctive undulating profile. Here too free-standing sculpture might be placed, finances permitting. The roof itself was built of a timber framework, on which terracotta or even marble roof tiles were placed, broad pan tiles with upturned edges and curved cover tiles which covered the spaces between the pan tiles. To keep out the rain, tiles overlapped each other.

Certain details were highlighted with brightly colored paint: the triglyphs and associated peg-like elements (*guttae*, *mutules*, and *regulae*), parts of the column capitals, some moldings, and the backgrounds of metopes, friezes, and pediments when sculpture was placed in them.

The origins of the details of Greek architectural decoration are obscure. Some details may represent the translation into stone of features of earlier wooden construction. The triglyph, for example, was explained by Vitruvius, the Roman architect and writer, as a plaque covering the ends of beams; the little peg-like protrusions below the cornice and the triglyphs would be the fastenings. It is a mark of their conservatism that the Greeks would preserve these tiny features long after the practical function had ceased. But this attractive theory is difficult to prove. The wooden superstructures of early temples have not survived, but as far as we can tell they were not nearly as complicated as the monumental stone versions of later times.

EARLY DORIC TEMPLES AT THERMON, OLYMPIA, AND KERKYRA (CORFU)

Experimentation leading to the crystalization of the Doric order seems to have begun in the early seventh century BC in Corinth and its environs. By the later century, the Corinthian fever had spread to other parts of Greece. Although fragmentary preservation has made it impossible to track the process with precision, we can note the appearance of characteristic Doric features at various temples of the early Archaic period.

The Temple of Apollo at Thermon, of ca. 630 BC, shows early evidence for the installation of a Doric entablature. This temple had stone foundations, but its walls and columns were made of mud brick and wood, now vanished. The entablature was evidently also of wood, since stone parts have not been found. The use of the Doric order in the entablature is conjectured from a series of terracotta metope plaques that have survived, painted with such mythological scenes as Perseus and the Gorgon. A few, it is important to note, are wider than the majority; this differentiation suggests that the builders of this temple had worked out a solution to the Doric corner problem.

Symmetrical though the Doric order may seem, it does have one unresolved difficulty: how should the corner triglyphs align with the column below? Normally every other triglyph is centered above a column. But if this principle is followed at the corner, the column capital will protrude. On the other hand, if the column is pulled back beneath the architrave, triglyph and column will no longer be aligned. At Thermon, a compromise was reached. The metopes at the ends of the frieze were made wider than the others, thus pushing the corner triglyph out to sit over the edge of the column.

The Temple of Hera at Olympia, ca. 600 BC, offered another solution to the Doric corner problem. As at Thermon, this temple was built of mud brick and wood on stone foundations. In contrast with the temple at Thermon, here the placement of the columns is known, and in this lay the answer. The corner columns were contracted, that is, brought in slightly from the proper corner position, set in closer to the next column instead of repeating the normal spacing between columns. As a result, the end metopes could remain the same length as the others, but the outer edge of the corner triglyph would align with the outer edge of the column below. Over the centuries the wooden columns of this temple were replaced with stone versions, each with its capital in the appropriately up-to-date style. The result must have been something of a mishmash; even today one can see capitals of different sizes and styles. One wooden column still stood in the second century AD when the Greek doctor and travel writer Pausanias visited Olympia.

The temple was decorated as well with two large terracotta disks placed at the apex of the roof. *Acroteria*, as such roof decorations were called, would become highly popular. They could include human figures as well as abstract or floral motifs.

In contrast with the above temples, the superstructure of the Temple of Artemis at Kerkyra (Corfu), ca. 600 BC, survives in ample fragments, demonstrating that the building was made of stone. In addition to being the earliest stone temple, it was one of the largest, 49m × 23.46m. Like the Temple of Hera at Olympia, this temple was laid out with the three standard rooms, pronaos, cella, and opisthodomos (Figure 12.3). A double row of columns inside the cella assisted in supporting the roof. The colonnade, 8 × 17 columns, was set well apart from the cella, allowing for a second, inner colonnade which was never added. Since a double colonnade is known as a *dipteral* arrangement, this version at Kerkyra, without the inner row, is called *pseudo-dipteral*. The pseudo-dipteral plan allows for the extra size a dipteral plan offers, but saves money because the inner columns are not built. Kerkyra displays the earliest example of this plan.

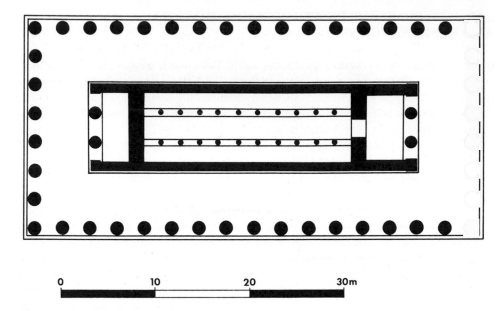

Figure 12.3 Plan, Temple of Artemis, Kerkyra

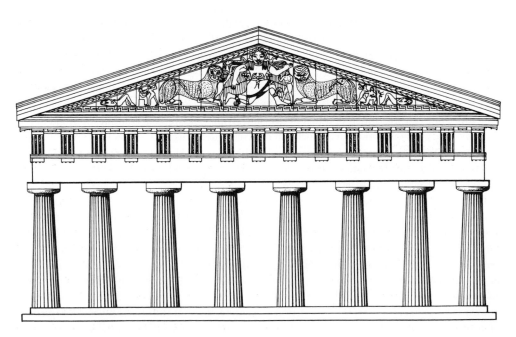

Figure 12.4 Restored elevation, Temple of Artemis, Kerkyra

Sculptural decoration on the exterior of temples will become a hallmark of Greek cities and sanctuaries, with the reliefs generally illustrating myths of local interest or of grand cosmological concern. With the well-preserved sculptures from its west pediment, the temple at Kerkyra gives us an early and striking example of this type of decoration (Figure 12.4). The huge figure of the Gorgon Medusa, 2.79m in height, dominates the scene. The snake-haired Medusa had the unfortunate gift of turning to stone anyone who looked at her. She was beheaded by the hero Perseus, specially equipped by Athena and Hermes with a mirror to look indirectly at Medusa, a sickle, a bag, Hades's cap of darkness for invisibility, and winged shoes for a quick escape. Medusa had a revenge of sorts: she would be esteemed by Greeks and Romans for her power to ward off evil. Her face, an apotropaic talisman, was a prominent protecting image on their armor. Indeed, her ability to frighten away danger may explain why this myth was chosen to decorate the pediment.

In the Kerkyra pediment Medusa is shown with a round, mask-like face with a grotesque grin, typical of her depiction in Archaic art. She is down on one knee in a pose that symbolizes running. Flanking her are two tiny, upright figures, her children, the human Chrysaor and the winged horse Pegasus, and beyond them, two panthers who, like Medusa, snarl at those who approach the temple. So far the figures have fit fairly well into the triangular space, but beyond the panthers the rapidly descending ceiling creates problems for the artist. In scenes unrelated to Medusa and on a far smaller scale, standing men spear kneeling and seated figures, and in the corner, two men, fallen victims, lie on their backs, their knees drawn up to scrape the raking cornice. More experimentation would be needed before sculptors could fill this awkward space with a scene unified in scale and theme.

EARLY IONIC TEMPLES AT SAMOS AND EPHESUS

While the Doric order became standard on the Greek mainland and in West Greece, the Ionic style was preferred in East Greece. Eventually the two merged in the later fifth century BC on the Athenian Acropolis, as we shall see. The earliest temples clearly in the Ionic style date from the second quarter of the sixth century BC. In addition, they are colossal, ca. 100m × 50m. None survives well, unfortunately (with the exception of the later Temple of Apollo at Didyma), since they served as convenient sources of cut stone for medieval and later building projects.

At the Samian Heraion, architects Rhoikos and Theodoros constructed the third major Temple to Hera above the seventh-century BC temple. The huge plan, 102m × 51m, included a double colonnade with eight columns on the front, ten on the back, and 21 on the sides. The interior rooms consisted of a pronaos and cella only, each with two rows of columns. Accompanying the temple was a new altar, the first in the Ionic style. Since the Ionic order permitted taller, slenderer proportions than the Doric, the columns could rise high. This multitude of tall columns arranged like a forest must have produced an overpowering effect on the viewer. This temple and the contemporary Temple of Artemis at nearby Ephesus were built on low ground, both originally by the sea, undramatic settings that perhaps promoted the development of such majestic designs.

The third temple of Hera was burned ca. 530 BC. A fourth and final version was begun by the tyrant Polykrates in the 520s. Work continued into the Roman period, but the temple was never finished. The Polykratean temple was slightly larger than its predecessor, with three rows of eight columns on the east end, three rows of nine on the west, and two rows of 24 on the long sides (Figure 12.5).

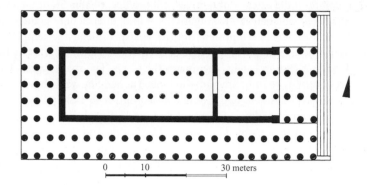

0   10   30 meters

Figure 12.5 The fourth Temple of Hera, Samian Heraion

At Ephesus on the Anatolian mainland an enormous Temple to Artemis was begun ca. 560 BC. This too replaced earlier, smaller temples. The temple was designed by Chersiphron of Knossos and his son Metagenes. Like Theodoros of Samos, they wrote a treatise about their project. Now lost, these books were perhaps known to Vitruvius, the Roman architect of the first century BC whose own book on Greek and Roman architecture has survived to the present day.

The temple measured ca. 115m × 51m, and according to tradition was built on foundations of alternating layers of charcoal and fleece in order to counteract the effects of the marshy ground. Its entrance lay on the west instead of the usual east; the western entrance is seen elsewhere in West Anatolian temples, however, probably a survival from earlier worship of the Anatolian mother goddess with whom the Greek Artemis was combined. Like its contemporary on Samos, this temple was dipteral. On the front, it had three rows of eight columns; in the rear, two rows of nine. Certain columns displayed an unusual feature: their lower drums were sculpted with figures. This distinctive gift was the offering of Croesus, king of Lydia, renowned for his wealth and for his love of Greek culture. The temple was burned in 356 BC, on the night of the birth of Alexander the Great, so it was said, by one Herostratus, an arsonist whose sole, and successful, aim was to make his name immortal. In the Hellenistic period the temple was rebuilt on a similarly grand scale.

Today one can appreciate only the dimensions of the Artemision, marked by scattered marble ruins and one re-erected column (often selected by a stork as an ideal nesting spot), in marshy ground on the outskirts of the modern town of Selçuk. Behind the waterlogged ruins lies a remarkable story of archaeological discovery. Although Hellenistic critics included this famous temple among their Seven Wonders of the World, it had completely disappeared by modern times. Earthquakes and reuse of its fine ashlar masonry for medieval building projects destroyed the temple; layers of silt carried down from the hills by the Cayster River buried the site. In the nineteenth century an Englishman, John Turtle Wood, set out to find the temple. The location of the Roman city was known, but the temple lay hidden somewhere outside its walls, somewhere in the marshy fields in what had become quite an isolated region. Wood searched in vain from 1863 to 1874. Eventually, a fragmentary stone inscription found in the Roman theater provided the key. According to the inscription, sacred images were to be brought from the Temple of Artemis to the theater, to be present during performances or assemblies. The route from the temple was specified: along the Sacred Way that led to the Magnesian Gate. Wood then located the Magnesian Gate and followed the marble paved street, buried well below the surface, from the city to the temple.

EAST GREEK CITIES IN THE ARCHAIC PERIOD: SAMOS, MILETUS, AND THE IONIAN REVOLT

A good example of an East Greek city in the Archaic period is Samos, the capital of the island of the same name. This city lay 6.5km east of the Heraion, on the site of the modern port of Pithagorio (Tigani). During the rule of the tyrant Polykrates (538–522 BC), the city was a regional power, economically strong and endowed with an effective fleet. Prosperity came not only from the Heraion, a major pilgrimage site, but also from the fertile land, with its wine enjoying considerable fame. The city itself underwent much new building. Although most has disappeared, the visitor can still appreciate the general layout (Figure 12.6). The harbor was the focus, although its piers, serving both commercial and military needs, have gone. Also gone is Polykrates's palace from its commanding position on the acropolis. Remains of the city's fortification wall survive, however, 6.7km long, still with gates and towers. And one can even walk through most of the Tunnel of Eupalinos, the most famous of the Polykratean building projects. The 1km-long tunnel, one section of an aqueduct that brought water to the city from an inland spring, was bored through the mountain behind the town. The tunneling began simultaneously at each end, with the two sections eventually joining with a small degree of error, 2m horizontally and 3m vertically. This feat of engineering, unparalleled in its time, was overseen by Eupalinos of Megara. The fortifications, the protected water supply, and the fleet marked the efforts of Polykrates to protect Samos from an attack by the Persians. But these precautions were ultimately unsuccessful: in 519 BC, after the death of Polykrates, the Persians captured the city.

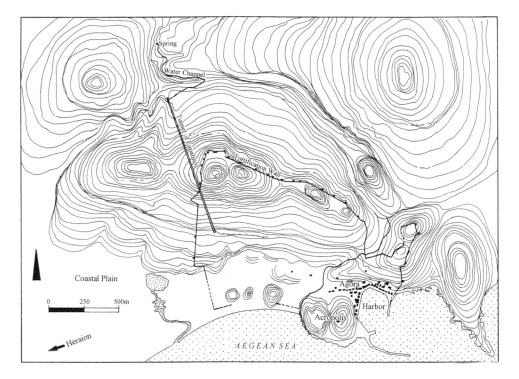

Figure 12.6 City plan, ancient Samos

The physical remains of other towns from Archaic East Greece are not so well known. According to ancient Greek literary sources, however, this region distinguished itself for its commercial and intellectual achievements. The city of Miletus to the south of Ephesus was particularly prominent. Located on a small glove-shaped peninsula jutting into the Aegean and on nearby hills, Miletus grew prosperous from maritime trade. It was one of the great colonizing cities, with some 90 foundations to its name, especially in the Hellespont, Sea of Marmara, and Black Sea regions. Among its citizens were Thales, Anaximenes, and Anaximander, important pioneers in philosophy and science. This brilliant epoch came to an end in 494 BC, with the collapse of the Ionian Revolt against Persian control.

Under Cyrus the Great, the Achaemenid Persians had expanded westwards into Anatolia in the middle of the sixth century BC. In 546 BC, they defeated the Lydians, the major power of West Anatolia, capturing Sardis, their capital, and Croesus, their king. The Greek city-states of the coast, incapable of uniting against the threat, quickly fell to Cyrus. But Persian control proved loose, and, apart from paying tribute, the Greek cities were given considerable autonomy to govern themselves. In 499 BC this compromise arrangement was wrecked when Aristagoras, the tyrant of Miletus, led an uprising against the Persians and, with the help of the Athenians, burned the provincial capital of the Persians at Sardis. The Ionian cities could not capitalize on this act of defiance, however, and were no match for the sharp Persian reaction. In 494 BC, the revolt ended with a Persian naval victory off the island of Lade and the capture and sack of Miletus. Most Milesian men were killed, the women and children taken into slavery. This event was considered such a catastrophe for the Greek world that, when a tragedy about the fall of Miletus was produced in Athens, the audience burst into tears and the author was fined for provoking undue emotional distress.

The Ionian Revolt had major consequences for the rest of Greece as well. Athens had participated in the raid on Sardis, but so far had escaped punishment. "Master, remember the Athenians!" a servant of the Persian king Darius was commanded to whisper daily into the royal ear. In 490 BC, the Persians set out to extract revenge.

CHAPTER 13

Archaic Greek cities, II

Sparta and Athens

During the Archaic period, ca. 600–479 BC, a general prosperity among city-states created a balance of strength and influence between regions. By the second quarter of the fifth century BC, power had concentrated in the hands of two, Sparta and Athens. At the end of the century they would fight each other in the Peloponnesian War, a protracted, draining conflict that finished with the defeat of Athens. The character of Spartan society differed dramatically from that of Athens. Indeed, that Greek culture produced two such contrasting city-states has fascinated observers from antiquity to the present day. Although *Sparta* has contributed only modestly to the archaeological evidence for ancient Greece, its historical importance calls for a brief look at the nature of its society. We shall then turn to *Athens*, to its pre-Classical political development and to its important art and architectural remains.

SPARTA

Sparta was unique. Located in a fertile plain in the south-east Peloponnesus, by the early seventh century BC Sparta had conquered not only Laconia, its home region, but also the south-west province of Messenia, thereby amassing an unusually large territory for a Greek city-state. Full citizenship was restricted to Spartans proper, although they formed only a small percentage of the total population. The subject peoples included the *perioikoi*, in effect citizens with lesser rights, autonomous in their villages but with little say in the state government, yet eligible to serve in the army, and the *helots*, tenant farmers or serfs without any rights. While these last worked the farms owned by the citizens, the male citizens devoted their energies to training for warfare. In maintaining their military readiness, the Spartans' first goal may have been to keep their own subjects in line, the second to ward off enemies. In both they were successful: for several centuries until their stunning defeat at Leuctra in 371 BC the Spartans fielded the finest infantry in the Greek world.

During the Archaic and Classical periods, writers had no place in this society, so all reports about Sparta were written by outsiders, men from other city-states. As a result, sorting through the biases and finding the reality of Spartan society has been a distinct challenge for generations of historians. It seems clear, however, that during the sixth century BC Spartan daily life became notoriously austere. Men lived in barracks until age 30, even when married, and thereafter ate together in mess halls. Women also trained physically, to ensure the birth of strong children. Group solidarity was all important. Individuality was discouraged, products of creativity such as fine arts restricted. Even money was regarded as corrupting. Coinage was not issued; iron bars served as the medium of exchange, when required. The world outside Sparta was regarded with deep suspicion.

The system of government remained essentially an oligarchy, continuing with little change from the later Iron Age through the Classical period. Although there was an assembly of citizens, important decisions were taken by smaller bodies, five *ephors* and a council of elders, including two hereditary kings, relics from the past, who had authority in times of war.

The city itself has left few ruins. In one of the famous object lessons an ancient writer has left modern archaeologists, Thucydides, the historian of the Peloponnesian War, remarked that buildings alone do not indicate a city's greatness. No one would ever guess that dull Sparta was the equal of Athens with its magnificent architecture. One must wonder what mistakes we have made in the interpretation of prehistoric cultures, simply by ranking settlements according to size.

ATHENS IN THE ARCHAIC PERIOD

In contrast, Athenian writers flourished, leaving detailed accounts of their city's society and history. Athens followed a line of development different from that of Sparta, one that led toward a democracy in which its male citizens had an equal voice. By the late seventh century, the city-state of Athens controlled the entire region of Attica. Class conflicts raged. Solon, a famous wise man elected *archon*, or magistrate acting as head of state, for the year 594 BC, attempted to solve them with a revision of the constitution and law code in which the debt-laden peasant farmers were championed against the rich. The farmers' crippling debts were cancelled, but to soothe the other side the privilege to hold high office was still reserved for wealthy landholders.

These reforms did not eradicate class tension. In subsequent years resentment increased between the people of the interior and the coast dwellers, with the former supporting Peisistratos in his attempts to seize the polis. Eventually successful, Peisistratos, a benevolent tyrant, ruled from ca. 560 to 527 BC. His sons proved less congenial. One, Hipparchos, was murdered in 514 BC, the other, Hippias, overthrown in 510 BC. A new leader came to the fore, Kleisthenes, who organized the citizenry into ten artificial tribes, each with city, coastal, and interior contingents. Each tribe sent 50 men to a "Council of 500." A *prytany*, or portion of the council, took care of daily affairs for a period of 36 days. In addition, the Popular Assembly continued, open to all citizens, as did the Areopagus, the open-air jury court. These developments of the late Archaic period marked the maturing of Athenian democracy and would continue in force for almost 200 years, until the Macedonians took control of the city in the later fourth century BC.

In developments in architecture and art Athens played a seminal role, again in striking contrast with Sparta. Although Athens is best known for its fifth-century BC buildings, much remains from the Archaic period (Figure 13.1). The center of the city is dominated by two hills. On the Pnyx, the smaller of the two, the Popular Assembly held its meetings. The larger hill immediately to the east, the Acropolis, or "high city," had been the fortified center of the city since the Bronze Age. By the sixth century BC, the Acropolis was turning into a religious sanctuary, the home of Athena, the patron goddess of the city, and a host of other deities. Sixth-century BC temples include two predecessors to the famous fifth-century BC Parthenon (one in the mid sixth century, then a replacement in the 480s); a Temple to Athena Polias (Athena worshipped specifically as the goddess of the city), built by the tyrant Peisistratos; and a series of treasuries (storehouses for precious religious offerings) of which only striking but fragmentary sculptural decoration survives. The outdoor spaces of this hilltop sanctuary would have contained many free-standing life-size sculptures, votive offerings to the goddess (see below).

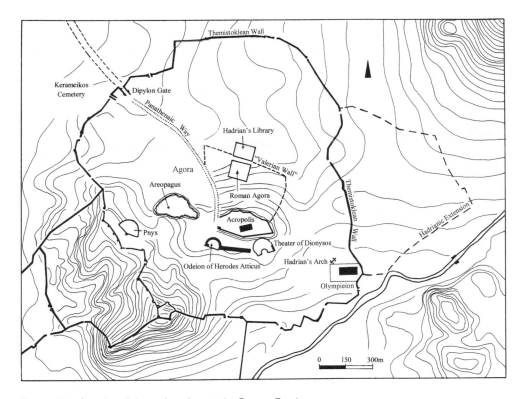

Figure 13.1 City plan, Athens, Iron Age to the Roman Empire

An additional cult center of importance was planned for a site to the south-east of the Acropolis. Here Peisistratos laid foundations for a monumental Temple to the Olympian Zeus, but he never finished it. Resumption of construction had to wait until the second century BC, with the temple eventually completed by the Roman emperor Hadrian in the second century AD.

The city's civic center, the Agora, situated on low ground north of the Acropolis, took on this secular role during the early Archaic period; previously this land had served variously for housing and for burials (Figure 13.2). Its territory had precise borders, which ca. 500 BC were officially marked by boundary stones inscribed with the phrase "I am the boundary of the Agora." Although not a sanctuary, the Agora was endowed nonetheless with a certain sanctity. Basins for holy water, *perirrhanteria*, were placed at its entrances, reminders that the public functions taking place in the Agora often had a religious cast. For those who might sully the dignity of the precinct, entry was forbidden. The fourth-century BC orator Aeschines could thus remark: "So the lawmaker keeps outside the perirrhanteria of the Agora the man who avoids military service, or plays the coward or deserts, and does not allow him to be crowned nor to enter public shrines"; and his contemporary, Demosthenes: "Surely those who are traitors to the commonwealth, those who mistreat their parents, and those who do not have clean hands, do wrong by entering the Agora" (Camp 1986: 51).

A variety of functions took place in the Agora, some connected with buildings, some not. With a brief tour of the area we can get an idea of the institutions of Athenian city life during the Archaic period. By the end of the sixth century BC, important civic buildings lined the foot of

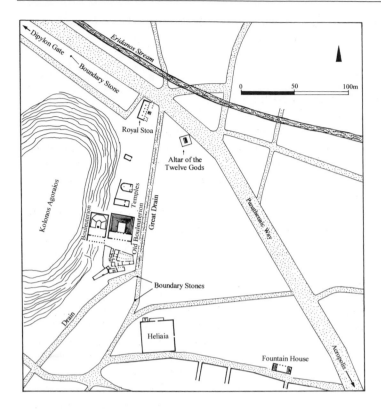

Figure 13.2 Plan, Agora, Athens, ca. 500 BC

the low hill on the west, the Kolonos Agoraios, thereby giving architectural definition to the western edge of the Agora. Among the most significant were the small Royal Stoa and the Old Bouleuterion. In the former, a structure originally of the late sixth century BC, the *basileus*, the second highest official of the city and the overseer of religious observances, had his base. At a later date, ca. 400 BC, the law codes of the city, inscribed on stone slabs, would be set up on the walls for the public to inspect. The Old Bouleuterion, a square building with seating on three sides, dated to ca. 500 BC, housed the Council of 500 set up by the reforms of Kleisthenes.

The south edge of the Agora was defined by the Heliaia (mid sixth century BC), an open-air law court, the largest in Athens, and the Southeast Fountain House, whose large basins of water were supplied from sources north-east of the city by means of clay pipes.

The north and east sides of the Agora were not yet defined by buildings. The central space was used at this time for gatherings of various sorts, including theatrical performances and athletic contests, both occurring under the umbrella of religion, and for market stalls. The most important monument here was the Altar of the Twelve Gods, identified by an inscribed statue base. Dedicated in 522 BC under the Peisistratids, this altar marked the center of the city from which distances were measured, and served as a recognized haven for those seeking refuge. Close by the Altar of the Twelve Gods the Panathenaic Way crossed the Agora on the diagonal. This route from the Dipylon Gate was used for the great procession up to the Acropolis during the Panathenaia, the annual festival to Athena.

The most important civic buildings would be in place in the Agora by ca. 400 BC. The area continued as the civic center through the Roman Empire, with many changes made to its architecture and monuments. During the Middle Ages buildings fell into ruin and were gradually covered over; eventually the area became a residential neighborhood. In 1931 an American team received permission to buy the land, clear the houses, and begin exploration of the ancient remains below. Excavations have continued ever since.

ARCHAIC ART: POTTERY AND SCULPTURE

Of all the objects made by the ancient Greeks, none has affected our understanding of their world as much as their pottery and sculpture. The figural imagery painted on pots and carved in sculpture, both free-standing and relief, has given us a multitude of pictures of ancient Greek people and animals, real, legendary, and divine, and the world, natural and built, within which they lived, and of their actions and behavior. In addition, with the widespread exports of their pottery, from western Europe to the Black Sea region, the Greeks transmitted their culture to a variety of non-Greek neighbors. Here we shall have a look at the production of pottery and sculpture during the Archaic period.

Attic black-figure and red-figure pottery

The painters esteemed in antiquity, however, were not pot painters but those artists who painted great narrative panels hung on the walls of public buildings. We know the subject matter and something about the techniques used, thanks to the comments of ancient authors, but the actual paintings have disappeared. The ancient writers ignored decorated pottery; the manufacture of pottery was considered a craft in ancient Greece, so its makers had little social status. But pottery has survived well, in contrast to the panel paintings. The habit of the Etruscans, a non-Greek people of central Italy, of including imported Attic (= Athenian) vases among their grave offerings has guaranteed a good supply of complete examples (for the Etruscans, see Chapter 18). Indeed, the museums of Italy, Western Europe, and North America are filled with complete pots excavated, or looted, from Etruscan burials. When we think of Greek painting, it is this decorated pottery that springs to mind.

The leading producer of decorated pottery in the Archaic and Classical periods was Athens, replacing Corinth, the city whose ceramic industry dominated in the Orientalizing period. Athenian potters and painters used two main techniques, black-figure and red-figure. To these a third would be added in the fifth century BC, white-ground (painting on a white background). Black-figure developed smoothly from Protoattic, the seventh-century style in Athens. Figures and decorations were painted in black onto a background of unpainted orange-red, the distinctive natural color of the clay of Athens (see Figure 13.3). Details were incised before firing, fine lines cut through the black to expose the orange-red color below. The black itself was not actually a paint, but was a refined solution of clay; with its finer particles, this paste was more compact than the clay used for the pot and reacted differently during the firing process. When applied by the artist, this "paint" would have an orange-red color similar to that of the background. Only later during the firing, thanks to careful manipulation of the chemical reactions of the ferric oxide in the clay and the paste, would the distinctive contrast between red and black be achieved.

The normal sequence of firing consisted of three stages: (1) *oxidation*: oxygen is let into the kiln; the clay and the "paint" stay red; (2) *reducing*: the air vent is closed, cutting the oxygen supply; the fire heating the kiln takes oxygen from the ferric oxide in the clay; the ferric oxide (Fe_2O_3) turns into black-colored iron oxides (either FeO or Fe_3O_4); and (3) *partial reoxidation*:

Figure 13.3 The Nessos Amphora.
Protoattic vase, ca. 615 BC, found in Athens

oxygen is let in again; the black pot returns to the original red; the more compact "paint" will do the same, but more slowly. The firing process needs to be stopped in the middle of this change, after the pot has turned red but while the "paint" is still black. Getting this right took skill; many pieces show failure.

Red-figure was simply the reverse: the background was covered with black, whereas the figures and decorations were left in the natural clay color, orange-red (see Figure 13.4). Details were added into the figures with the concentrated clay solution, which would turn black in the firing; incision of lines was not used on red-figure vases. Red-figure was developed ca. 530 BC as an alternative to black-figure, perhaps by the anonymous pot painter known today as the "Andokides Painter." Both techniques continued to be used through the Late Classical period (fourth century BC) until the winds of inspiration finally died out and the public demanded something new.

Mythological subjects were always popular with vase painters. The Nessos Amphora is an example of late Protoattic, almost early Attic black-figure pottery that illustrates mythological themes (Figure 13.3). On the neck, the hero Herakles kills Nessos, a centaur. Both figures are labeled. Below, large gorgons, with wings and monstrous heads, chase Perseus, the killer of their sister, Medusa.

By the later sixth century BC, genre (daily life) subjects became increasingly popular. At the same time a major development in style took place, indeed one of the great turning points in the history of western art. Twisting poses were now depicted in both vase painting and relief sculpture, giving the illusion of depth, of the third dimension. This interest in optical reality represents a major break with the profile-oriented two-dimensional depictions of figures standard in the art traditions of the Near East, Egypt, and Mediterranean basin. This change came about through experiments in drawing in the newly developed red-figure technique. Why this happened is not clear, but the broadened range of popular subjects, favoring daily life as well as mythological or sacred scenes, may be a factor.

A red-figure amphora decorated by Euthymides shows nicely these changes in both subject and drawing technique (Figure 13.4). The amphora, made ca. 510 BC, was found in an Etruscan tomb at Vulci, in central Italy. Three naked men, mature (as their beards indicate), are carousing in the street after a drinking party. One holds a drinking cup while another teases him with a staff. What is noteworthy is the attempt of the painter Euthymides to show these men – their bodies anyway – twisting or in three-quarter view. The diagonal line down the back of the central reveler conveys this, as does the foreshortened drawing of the chest of the man on the left, in which the right side of his chest is broader than the more distant left side. But this man's right arm is too thin, so the perspective drawing seems distorted, inaccurate. These important experiments in foreshortening taking place in the workshops of Athens gave rise to rivalries between painters, as evidenced by the boast Euthymides painted on this vase: "as never Euphronios [could do]."

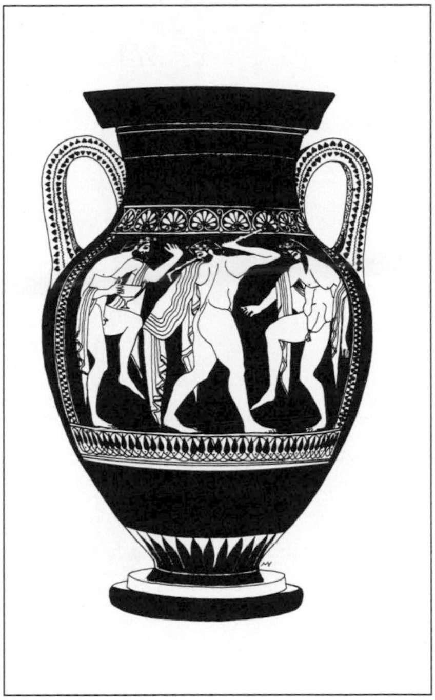

Sculpture

Life-sized, and indeed over-life-sized, sculpture in stone developed in the later seventh century BC. Although Egyptian craftsmen did not work in Greece, the influence of Egyptian sculpture on Greek artists was of crucial importance. The earliest sculptors may well have been the stoneworkers already familiar with quarrying and dressing stone for architecture, now adding a specialization as carvers of figures. The forms used in Greek sculpture derived from smaller-scale examples in such materials as ivory, wood, and bronze – such as Mantiklos's dedication (Figure 11.10) – with some reinforcement from the standard poses of Egyptian statuary. From the beginning Greek sculpture featured free-standing male and female statues, types known as the *kouros* (pl. *kouroi*) and *kore* (pl. *korai*), from Greek words meaning youth and young woman. Many cities produced them, with Athens leaving us a particularly fine set. The earliest included some colossal kouroi, their size inspired by Egyptian examples, but the appeal of this hugeness was short-lived. The Heraion at Samos has yielded an especially well-preserved example from 580 BC, created shortly before the first monumental temple to Hera was completed (Figure 13.5). From an inscription on his thigh we learn that Isches the Rhesian dedicated the statue ("Rhesian" may refer to a tribe or district on the island). Made of local Samian black-veined marble and measuring 4.73m in height, this colossal kouros stood on the Sacred Way, a marker of the prestige of its dedicator and his family. Stone and metal statues of any size were costly; only the wealthy could afford such offerings. As for poorer people, their gifts to the gods included small terracotta figurines, mass produced in molds.

The representations of men and women such as the kouroi and korai are generic, rather than specific portraits, and hence they could fill a variety of functions. Kouroi and korai served as votive offerings left at sanctuaries, as we have just seen at Samos, as tomb markers, and perhaps, in the case of certain kouroi, as cult statues. When a precise identification was desired, names could be carved on the base or on the statue itself. For example, a pair of just over life-size (1.97m) kouroi found at Delphi (Figure 13.6) have usually been identified as Kleobis and Biton, two brothers whose edifying story is told by Herodotus (Book 1.31). These men heroically pulled their mother, a priestess of Hera at the Argive Heraion, to the temple in a cart in place of the usual oxen. After their mother prayed to the goddess to reward them for this admirable deed, her sons entered the temple, fell asleep, and never woke up. For the ancient Greeks, a people particularly wary of the sudden shifts in fortune that life bestows, the gift of death at the height of one's physical powers was an appealing concept.

Figure 13.4 Three revelers, on an Attic red-figure amphora painted by Euthymides, from Vulci. Antikensammlungen, Munich

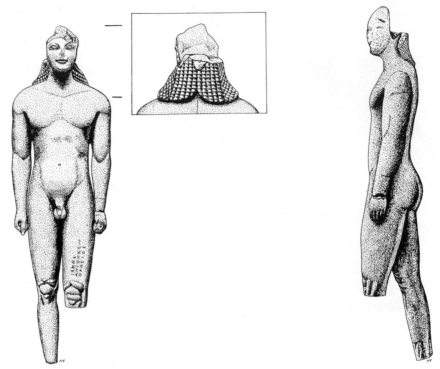

Figure 13.5 Colossal kouros, Heraion, Samos: (a) front; (b) back of head; and (c) side. Archaeological Museum, Samos

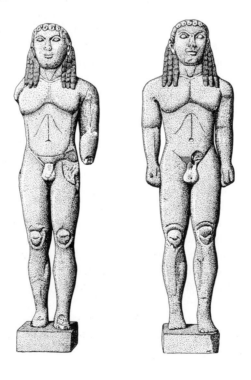

Figure 13.6 Kleobis and Biton. Archaic kouroi found in Delphi. Archaeological Museum, Delphi

Figure 13.7 Kore no. 682, from the Athenian Acropolis. Acropolis Museum, Athens

A sculptor from Argos, Polymedes (but the inscription is damaged here), made the pair ca. 580 BC. Like all kouroi, Kleobis and Biton are for all intents and purposes nude (these two wear boots); they are muscular, conveying the Greek ideal of the male body; they stand in an Egyptian pose with one foot slightly advanced and fists clenched at their side, with weight equally distributed over both legs; their body parts are indicated with lines and grooves, forming independent patterns; and their faces seem cheerfully bland, with the characteristic Archaic smile, large almond-shaped eyes, scroll-like ears, and beaded hair that falls in regular rows. During the following decades, sculptors will smooth the transitions between body parts in an increasingly lifelike way. By the Classical period, this evolution will result in a more naturalistic depiction of the human body, one which would be esteemed by the Romans as well as the Greeks, by the Italian Renaissance and indeed by us today.

Male nudity was accepted in Greek culture, in sharp contrast with the Ancient Near East and Egypt. The reason for this is unclear, although religious practices developed during the later Iron Age must have been a factor: athletic contests such as the Olympic Games, always celebrated as religious festivals, required that the athletes participate nude. Women were regarded differently; apart from Spartan girls, who exercised naked as did boys, the respectable Greek woman did not indulge in public nudity. Consequently, the kore, although showing the same benign facial features and the same frontality as the kouros, is always dressed. The challenge for the sculptor lay in the depiction of the clothing, and eventually in the accurate portrayal of the body beneath the drapery.

One common form of dress popular in the later Archaic period is worn by "Kore no. 682" from the Athenian Acropolis, ca. 530–520 BC (Figure 13.7). She wears a *himation* (shawl) over a *chiton*, a cylindrical piece of cloth with openings for the head and arms, with loose sleeves buttoned over the shoulders, and worn with a belt. This costume generates many folds, an appreciated source of decoration for sculptors and painters. Indeed, our kore, like many others, pulls the chiton out from her thigh, thus creating folds in a highly decorative fan-like pattern.

The "Kore no. 682" originally held an offering in her outstretched right hand, but the forearm and hand, made in a separate piece of marble, have disappeared. By the mid to late sixth century BC, life-sized statues could be hollow cast in bronze, thus permitting in a single piece a variety of poses. Most bronze statues have disappeared, however, melted down by later generations for weapons. Shipwrecks and accidental caches are the best sources for those that have survived.

Because many traces of paint have survived on it, the "Kore no. 682" illustrates another notable feature about ancient sculpture. All Greek statues were painted in bright colors. This fact comes as a shock, since we are so accustomed to Classical statuary being the natural color of stone. But they were not made that way. The paint has simply worn off.

Free-standing individuals were by no means the only form of sculpture produced during the Archaic period. Relief sculpture decorated gravestones and votive plaques as well as the outsides of buildings. We have already examined the early Archaic pedimental sculpture from the Temple of Artemis at Kerkyra; in the next chapter we will look at another famous example of architectural sculpture, the reliefs from the Siphnian Treasury at Delphi.

THE PERSIAN WARS

In 490 and again in 480–479 BC the Persians attacked the city-states of mainland Greece as punishment for their part in the Ionian Revolt. These wars, one of the key events in Greek history, mark the transition from the Archaic to the Classical period. The fifth-century BC historian Herodotus wrote a gripping account of these battles and their background, and we are most fortunate that this text has survived. The three major battles ended in Greek victories: Marathon, on the north coast of Attica (490 BC); the naval battle off the island of Salamis, just offshore from Athens (480 BC); and the land battle at Plataea, inland, by the north-west frontier of Attica (479 BC). The unexpected victories against the vast Persian Empire exhilarated the Greeks, giving them new confidence. At the same time, the wars had brought tragedy. Ionia was crushed, and Athens itself was sacked. When the Persian army approached the city in 480 BC, the Athenians abandoned their capital, seeking refuge by their ships. Although faith in their ships proved justified at the Battle of Salamis, the Athenians could not prevent the Persians from occupying Athens and destroying it. This destruction has proved a boon to archaeologists, however. Upon their return, the Athenians dug large pits on the Acropolis, shoveled in the ruined votive and architectural sculpture and covered them, thereby purifying their great sanctuary. Thus was preserved the magnificent series of Archaic sculpture now on display in the Acropolis Museum. The destruction also gave rise to the great urban renewal projects of the mid to late fifth century BC, which we shall examine below, in Chapter 15.

CHAPTER 14

Greek sanctuaries

Delphi and Olympia

We have already visited one popular Greek religious center (or sanctuary), the Samian Heraion. However, because of their importance for Greek culture and because of the great variety in settings, buildings and other material remains, and ceremonial, sanctuaries deserve further attention. In this chapter and the next we shall examine three major cult centers: the sanctuaries of Apollo at *Delphi*; Zeus at *Olympia*; and Athena, on the Acropolis at *Athens*. Only the last lay within a city; the first two, in contrast, were located in the countryside. Nonetheless, Delphi and Olympia were pilgrimage sites renowed throughout the Greek world, with activities and monuments intimately linked with all Greek cities, near and far.

DELPHI: THE SANCTUARY OF APOLLO

The dramatic setting of Delphi never fails to leave a lasting impression. Located 166km to the north-west of Athens in the region of Phocis, the ancient holy place lies on steeply sloping ground at the foot of two south-facing cliffs, the Phaedriades, or the Shining Ones, part of the larger Mount Parnassos. The ground drops to a gorge below, then rises on the south toward another hill crest. The Gulf of Corinth is visible in the far distance to the west.

The site contains two sanctuaries, the larger and best-known dedicated to Apollo, the smaller to Athena Pronaia (not examined here). Other buildings lie outside the boundaries of the temenoi. A village existed to run the sanctuaries and cater to pilgrims and tourists, just as one does again today, but neither it nor any other town in the region ever played an important role in the political life of ancient Greece. Although Delphi continued as a religious center throughout Classical antiquity, its heyday was from the eighth to the late fourth century BC.

The Temple of Apollo and the oracle

The Sanctuary of Apollo, a large rectangle crammed with buildings and monuments, is dominated by the Temple of Apollo and the Sacred Way that zigzags up to it (Figure 14.1). The Greeks were much given to consulting oracles for advice about the future, and here, in this temple, the most famous oracular god in the Greek world had his seat. The vehicle for prophecy was a middle-aged woman, the Pythia, through whom Apollo was believed to speak.

Three certain versions of the temple have been discovered. The earliest, perhaps from the mid seventh century BC, burned down in an accidental fire in 548 BC. It was replaced by a large Doric temple, completed in 506 BC, financed by the Alkmaionid family of whom the Athenian reformer Kleisthenes was a member. After this second temple was destroyed by an earthquake in 373 BC, a third version was erected on the same plan; its restored dimensions are 58.18m × 21.64m. The colonnade of the temple had six columns on the short sides, fronting the usual

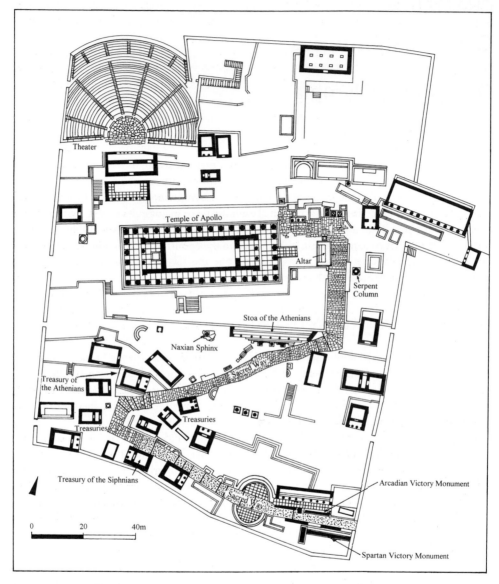

Figure 14.1 Plan, Sanctuary of Apollo, Delphi

pronaos and opisthodomos, but 15 columns on the long sides instead of the typical 13. Because of special cultic needs, the building was lengthened by the addition of an *adyton*, or inner sanctuary, sited behind the usual cella but at a slightly lower level, over a cleft in the bedrock. The adyton is said to have contained the tomb of the god Dionysos, ruler in Delphi during the three winter months when Apollo went on vacation to the northern land of the Hyperboreans; perhaps the stone omphalos, or navel, which marked for the ancient Greeks the center of the earth; a gold statue of Apollo; and a laurel tree. The cleft in the rock in itself was an opening to the powerful and mysterious forces of the earth. And here, amidst these sacred objects and associations, the Pythia sat on a tripod, Apollo's sacred seat, in order to receive the divine inspiration. Today little is left to see, this major center of paganism having been thoroughly destroyed by Christians.

In the early years of the sanctuary, the oracle took place only once per year, on Apollo's birthday in late February. Eventually, formal consultations were granted once each month, for the nine months of Apollo's residence at Delphi. On other days during these nine months, quick answers could be obtained through the drawing of black or white beans, meaning "yes" or "no," or beans with answers written on them. Such consultations were cheaper as well as being simpler.

The nine grand sessions were invested with great ceremony. The Pythia, and there might be two or three of them, working in shifts to handle all the inquiries, would purify herself with water at the Castalian Spring and with the smoke of laurel leaves and barley meal. Then a goat had to be sacrificed, to make sure the day was auspicious. The goat had to shiver, with the help of the sprinkling of cold water if need be, since the Pythia shivered when she uttered Apollo's prophesies. If this was successful, the Pythia went into the temple, drank special water, chewed laurel leaves, and took her seat on the tripod. In addition to the suggestive power of the situation, it may well be that gases rising from the cleft in the rock beneath the adyton put the Pythia into a trance. She was now ready for the god to inhabit her body and answer questions.

The inquirers purified themselves with holy water and drew lots to determine their places in line. Some, including those consulting on behalf of certain city-states, had the privilege of jumping to the head of the line. All had to purchase and offer on the altar an expensive sacred cake, with states paying much higher prices than did individuals. The sacrifice of a sheep or goat was then expected, with much of the meat going to the local townspeople. What happened next has been the subject of controversy. According to the traditional view, the inquirer put his question to a priest, who relayed it to the Pythia. She gave her answer, crying or shouting, with the priest rendering the utterance into poetic meter intelligible for the inquirer. The reality probably was much less romantic: the Pythia answered the inquirer directly, delivering her divinely inspired message in simple-to-understand prose.

The Pythia answered specific questions; she did not predict the future in general. Some of her answers were recorded by ancient authors, but we have to be careful, for not all are trustworthy: answers for the early years especially, ca. 750–450 BC, seem to have been inventions after the fact, predictions that suited the reputation created by the Greeks themselves about the oracle. Because governments were among the inquirers, the famous early responses, even if legendary, have much to say about the political role of the oracle. Her answers reveal that she stayed politically alert, avoiding controversy. Advice and blessings, for example, were routinely bestowed upon groups of early colonists before they set off, thereby ensuring her key role in the founding of new cities. Her most famously clever response, reported by Herodotus, was given to the Lydian king Croesus, one of Delphi's most generous benefactors. When threatened by the advancing Persians under Cyrus the Great, he inquired whether he should attack. If he did, the oracle replied, he would destroy a mighty empire. Not seeing the ambiguity in the advice, Croesus confidently marched forward, only to discover that the mighty empire to be destroyed was his own.

The final utterance (perhaps apocryphal) attributed to the oracle is a sad one, recounting its demise in a message delivered to the fourth-century AD Roman emperor Julian the Apostate, who attempted in vain to revive pagan cults in a world turning to Christianity: "Tell the king, the fairwrought hall has fallen to the ground. No longer has Phoebus [Apollo] a hut, nor a prophetic laurel, nor a spring that speaks. The water of speech even is quenched" (Fontenrose 1978: 353).

The Siphnian Treasury

Although the Temple of Apollo and its oracle were the centerpieces, the sanctuary had much more to offer. On the climb up the Sacred Way, the pilgrim passed countless monuments and small buildings, the tightly packed accumulation of centuries. Treasuries would stand out, small buildings simple in plan with a single room and a porch, built by individual cities to safeguard the valuable offerings made by their citizens. Some bearing lavish sculptural decoration resembled ornate boxes. The most famous is the Siphnian Treasury, built ca. 530–525 BC by the inhabitants of the small Cycladic island of Siphnos wealthy from gold and silver mines.

Today only the foundations remain *in situ*, but the original appearance of the treasury can be reconstructed from surviving material (Figure 14.2). Built in the Ionic style using Naxian and Siphnian marble, with Parian marble for its sculpture, the treasury was decorated with a sculpted frieze on all four sides, sculptures in the two pediments, and intricately carved mouldings. The usual two columns *in antis* holding up the porch were here carved in the shape of women: *caryatids*, a rare but striking feature in Greek architecture. Used earlier at Delphi, caryatids will make their most famous appearance on the fifth-century BC Athenian Acropolis, on the South Porch of the Erechtheion.

The sculpture that filled the east pediment is well preserved. Its subject, drawn from mythology as was typical, must have been of particular interest to ancient pilgrims because it connected with Delphi. Angry because the Pythia refused to prophesy for him, Herakles stole the sacred tripod. Apollo has grabbed hold of it, and the two struggle to pull it out of the hands of the other. Between them stands the arbitrator, Zeus, the tallest, most imposing figure in the scene, placed in the center of the pedimental triangle.

Figure 14.2 Siphnian Treasury (reconstruction), Delphi

The frieze is best preserved on the east (the back) and north (alongside the Sacred Way). The sculptures are attributed to two artists: possibly Endoios or Aristion of Paros was responsible for the east and north sides, and another, of unknown name, for the west (the front) and south. Again, mythological themes have been picked. Episodes from the Trojan War appear on the east and west, the judgment of Paris (west) and the assembled gods who watch as Thetis implores Zeus to support her son, Achilles, unappreciated by his fellow Achaean warriors (east). To their right (still on the east), a battle takes place, with such warriors as Menelaos and Hector.

The north frieze depicts the battle of the gods against the giants (Figure 14.3), a favorite allegory for the ancient Greeks, with the gods representing the forces of order and civilization, the giants chaos and barbarism. The fighters were well arranged for easy identification by the pilgrims who viewed this from the Sacred Way: the gods advance toward the right, the giants toward the left. In addition, labels were used. The deities included Kybele, an Anatolian goddess, in her lion-drawn chariot. The lion is taking a vicious bite out of a giant, whose expression of pain and shock we can easily imagine, even though his helmet hides his face. An illusion of depth is given by overlapping shields and figures, but since the more distant figures are not smaller than those in the foreground, as we would expect in our own conventions of painting, that illusion is ineffective for us. The scene remains resolutely two-dimensional. Traces of paint remind us that the frieze would have been colorfully painted.

Figure 14.3 Gods vs. Giants, North Frieze (detail), Siphnian Treasury, Delphi. Archaeological Museum, Delphi

Commemorative monuments

A sanctuary contained not only buildings but also objects offered in thanks for a great range of successful outcomes. Donors included individuals, as we have already seen, but also governments. At prestigious Delphi, a ceremonial center revered by the entire Greek world, the monuments erected by city-states included commemorations of some of their greatest triumphs.

The city-states rarely acted in concert; the major exception was the struggle to repel the Persian invaders in the early fifth century BC. In remembrance of those Greek victories, a series of important trophies were displayed or erected at Delphi. Spoils seized from the Persians at the Battle of Marathon in 490 BC were set out for public view at the Treasury of the Athenians (a building of the late sixth century BC), probably in the triangular space along its south side. Further up the Sacred Way, the Stoa of the Athenians (usually dated to 478 BC) sheltered another prize captured by the Athenians, prows from the boats that formed a pontoon bridge erected across the Dardanelles (Hellespont) by the Persian King Xerxes, and cables that lashed them together. Like the spoils from Marathon these items have long vanished, but an inscription in large letters that survives on the front of the top step of the stoa gives the vital information (Figure 14.4).

Another monument celebrating a victory in the Persian Wars stood just to the east of the altar of the Temple of Apollo: the Serpent Column, honoring the victory at Plataea in 479 BC. Three intertwined serpents of bronze rose straight up, their heads flaring out to create a base for a gold tripod. The lower coils were inscribed with the names of the city-states who joined together to defeat the Persians. At Delphi, only the circular, stepped base of stone on which the column stood can be seen. Miraculously, much of the column has survived, not in Delphi, though, but in Istanbul. The Serpent Column was one of many items brought by Constantine from different parts of the Roman Empire to Constantinople in the early fourth century AD to decorate and give prestige to his new capital city. Prominently displayed on the *spina*, the central division of the *hippodrome*, the huge stadium for chariot races, the ruined bronze column can still be seen today. The serpent heads have been knocked off, but one was recovered in the nineteenth century and is now exhibited in the Istanbul Archaeological Museum.

The monuments celebrating the triumphs over the Persians were exceptional. More typical were monuments that commemorated victories of one Greek city-state over another, evidence that the religious sanctuary served as a wide-open forum for publicity of all sorts. Close to the lower entrance of the sanctuary, for example, the Spartans erected a grand monument to celebrate their decisive naval victory over the Athenians at Aigospotamoi in 404 BC: two rows of bronze statues of the admiral, the ship captains, and gods, perhaps 39 figures total. Opposite, as if to tweak Spartan noses, the Arcadians later put up a monument in 369 BC to their recent victory over the Spartans: nine bronze statues, showing Apollo, Nike (Victory), and seven Arcadian heroes. It is amusing to note that one of the four sculptors engaged by the Arcadians had earlier worked on the Spartan monument.

A different type of commemoration, the last to be mentioned here, is the honoring of athletic victors. Celebrations of Apollo included the Pythian Games, competitions in athletics and –

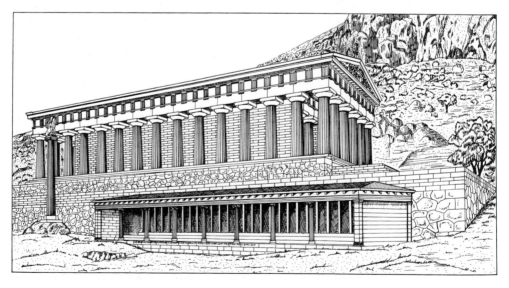

Figure 14.4 Stoa of the Athenians and Temple of Apollo (reconstruction), Delphi

Figure 14.5 Charioteer of Delphi, bronze statue, Delphi. Archaeological Museum, Delphi

because Apollo was considered an accomplished lyre player – music. In contrast with the three other major games at Olympia, Isthmia, and Nemea, the Pythian Games were held every two years, not every four. Events took place in the stadium uphill, just outside the temenos.

Victors in games habitually presented thank-offerings to the gods. At Delphi, the best-known of such votives is a life-size bronze statue, the Charioteer of Delphi (Figure 14.5), the one figure to survive complete from a larger sculptural group consisting of a chariot drawn by four horses with a groom in attendance, placed in the sanctuary to the north-west of the Temple of Apollo. The group was dedicated by Polyzalos, tyrant of Gela, a Greek city in Sicily, to commemorate his victory in a chariot race in either 478 or 474 BC. Polyzalos was not the actual racer. In chariot races, in contrast with other events, the sponsor of the winning team counted as the winner, not the actual driver – a situation that resembles modern horse racing, in which the owner receives the trophy with horse and jockey looking on. The Charioteer, a young man, wears the costume of his profession, a high-belted tunic, with sleeves fastened down to avoid flapping during the race.

This statue was made by the lost-wax casting process, a technique developed in the Iron Age for making small bronze figurines. The casting of life-size bronze statues began in the later sixth century BC. The liberating effects on Greek sculpture were enormous. Life-size sculpture based on Egyptian models had been stiff and symmetrical. This technique of lost-wax casting allowed artists to express in bronze statuary a variety of movements heretofore never attempted in stone. Eventually the hugely expanded repertoire of motions achieved in bronze would be created in stone sculpture as well.

Typically, life-size statues such as the Charioteer consisted of several pieces first cast separately, later joined together. In this process, the image desired is created in a thin layer of beeswax applied over a clay core. A clay mold is then placed over the beeswax, and fixed in place by iron or bronze pins (chaplets) stuck across the mold and the beeswax into the clay core. The entire construct – mold, beeswax image, and clay core – is then heated at high temperature. The wax melts and runs out, leaving a thin hollow space; the clay elements are baked hard. Finally, the molten bronze is poured into the empty space previously occupied by the beeswax. When cooled, the clay elements are removed, leaving the cast bronze item, to be joined to other cast pieces and given finishing touches.

As was usual for bronze statues, the Charioteer's eyes were made of white paste and, for the iris and pupils, shiny dark stone, to make the face seem alive – a convention we have encountered already in the Ancient Near East and Egypt. Whatever the impact of his shining eyes, his expression remains pleasant yet impassive, a personality type that attracted artists of the Early Classical period.

OLYMPIA: THE SANCTUARY OF ZEUS

The Sanctuary of Zeus at Olympia (also known as the Altis) offers a distinct contrast from Delphi, in its setting and buildings and indeed in its personality. Like Delphi, however, Olympia lies in an area outside the mainstream of Greek power politics. It too became a Panhellenic sanctuary, with the appeal of its athletic games, held every four years, reaching every corner of the Greek world.

Olympia lies in a flat, fertile, wooded plain in the north-west Peloponnesus some 12km from the sea; the Arcadian mountains rise not far to the east. This attractive spot is marked by distinctive landscape features, the conical Hill of Kronos on the north, and two rivers, the Kladeos and the Alpheios, which join to the south-west of the sanctuary.

Olympia became prominent during the eighth century BC, as the numerous dedications of expensive large bronze cauldrons on tripods attest. Indeed, the ancient Greeks believed the Olympic Games began in 776 BC, a date that became the starting point for their recorded history. In later centuries, Olympia was embellished with numerous buildings, including its two famous temples, to Hera and to Zeus (Figure 14.6). Thanks to Roman interest the prosperity of Olympia continued to the end of antiquity, when the Christian emperor Theodosius the Great ended the games in AD 393 as part of a general clamp-down on pagan cults. But major earthquakes had already seriously damaged the site in the fourth century AD; later flooding of the Alpheios and Kladeos in the Middle Ages would leave the ruins buried under several meters of silt. Rediscovered in 1766 by the English antiquarian Richard Chandler, Olympia has been revealed to the modern world largely through the excavations of the German Archaeological Institute from 1875 to the present.

As was typical, the sacred precinct was marked off by a low wall. Ritual focused on two places: the tomb of Pelops, a legendary king of Olympia, and the main altar, made not of stone but of ash from burnt offerings, as if to emphasize the remote, primeval origins of the cult. On either

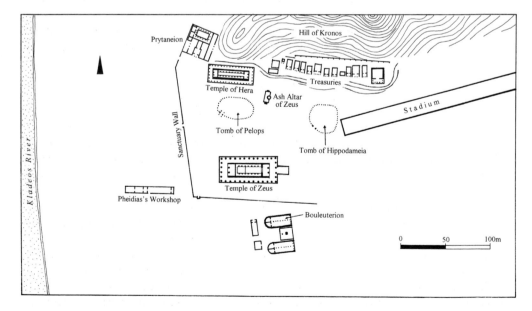

Figure 14.6 Plan, Sanctuary of Zeus, ca. 400 BC, Olympia

side stood the temples, to the north at the base of the Hill of Kronos the early Archaic Temple of Hera, and to the south, raised up on an artificial platform, the larger Temple of Zeus, one of the major buildings of Classical Greece (Figure 14.9). In addition to the two major temples and the great altar, the temenos also included a series of treasuries, neatly aligned at the foot of Mount Kronos. Most were built by city-states of Greek Sicily and South Italy. None has survived well, and none had the elaborate sculptural decoration seen on the Siphnian Treasury at Delphi.

The Early Classical style in Greek sculpture

The sculptures of the Temple of Zeus plunge us into the different style of the Early Classical period. To understand the transition from Archaic to Early Classical in art, let us turn briefly to the sculpted pediments from the Temple of Aphaia on the island of Aegina. Aegina, located close to Athens in the Saronic Gulf, prospered during the Archaic period as a commercial center; its coinage, distinctively stamped with the image of a turtle, is well known. The Temple to Aphaia, a local goddess, was built ca. 490 BC in the remote north-east part of the island. Although the sculptures of the west pediment stayed in place, the originals from the east pediment were somehow damaged, then replaced some 10–15 years later by a new group. Both pediments show scenes of combat, apparently Greeks vs. Trojans, with Athena presiding in the center. The different dates of carving, although not far apart, in this case do mark a distinct change in mood and decoration, with the west pediment still very firmly in the Archaic style, and the east pediment in the new Early Classical style.

The contrast can best be seen by comparing the figure of a wounded warrior placed in the corner of each pediment. The west warrior (Figure 14.7), pulling out a spear or arrow from his chest (the spear, now missing, would have been made of bronze or wood) while holding his legs and torso in a stiff, strenuous position, manages to smile the typical Archaic smile. Death seems remote. The somber portrayal of the east warrior (Figure 14.8) is much more credible, at least for us today. Although the way he balances his weight on the upright shield can hardly be called realistic, the downward turn of his mature, bearded face conveys the seriousness of his wound, the depth of his pain. This new expression of mood and pose and also costume (for clothed figures) will be developed in the sculptures from the Temple of Zeus at Olympia.

The Temple of Zeus: architecture and sculpture

The Temple of Zeus was built ca. 470–457 BC, during the Early Classical period, by the architect Libon from the nearby town of Elis (Figure 14.9). Measuring 64m × 28m, the temple was in its time the largest on mainland Greece. The purely Doric design has the standard ground plan, colonnade (six columns on the ends, 13 on the long sides), and Doric triglyph and metope frieze. Building materials included a local limestone conglomerate, covered with stucco, with the sculpture and certain architectural details of Parian marble.

Impressive though the architecture is, the building is badly ruined. The special reputation of this temple in modern times rests on its well-preserved sculptural decoration: the pedimental sculpture; and twelve sculpted metopes, placed just inside the colonnade, six each above the entrances to the pronaos and the opisthodomos. In contrast, the sculpture that earned the temple great fame in antiquity no longer exists: the colossal gold-and-ivory cult statue of Zeus.

The two pedimental sculpture groups rank among the most fascinating monuments of ancient Greek art because of the great emotional and intellectual resonance of the stories they illustrate. Each side conveys a message important to the Greeks after their triumph over the Persians:

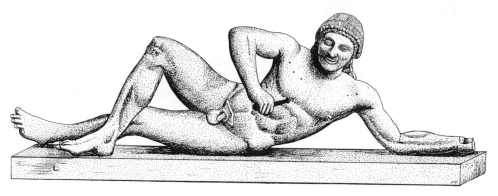

Figure 14.7 Fallen Warrior, west pediment, Temple of Aphaia, Aegina. Glyptothek, Munich

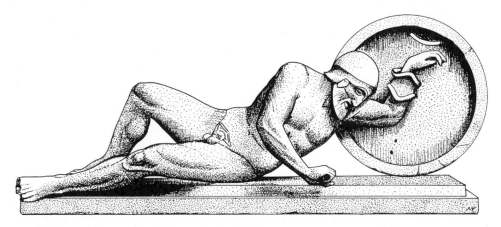

Figure 14.8 Fallen Warrior, east pediment, Temple of Aphaia, Aegina. Glyptothek, Munich

Figure 14.9 Temple of Zeus and Ash Altar (reconstruction), Olympia

confidence in the victory of justice (west pediment), but anxiety about unknown menaces lurking in the future (east pediment).

The east pediment, over the entrance to the temple, displayed a scene from the mythical history of Olympia. The scene appears quiet, but behind lies a dark story that invests the figures with tragic grandeur. Knowing the story is in fact crucial for an appreciation of this pediment. Oinomaos, king of Olympia, is about to race the latest suitor for the hand of his daughter, Hippodameia. With his magic horses and weapons, he is confident he will win again and kill the suitor. Pelops, the challenger, believes he will win, for he has bribed the king's charioteer to substitute wax linchpins in place of the metal pins. The charioteer is himself in love with Hippodameia – a further complication. In the pediment, we see the two contestants before the race begins. They stand on either side of Zeus, in front of whom they have offered sacrifices and sworn the oath of fair play. Oinomaos's wife, Sterope, and his daughter, Hippodomeia, accompany the king and Pelops; beyond, the chariots and attendants await the race. In the corners of the pediment the viewer receives a foreshadowing of the tragedy that lies ahead. An old man seated on the right, shown with sagging chest and balding head, looks on with anxiety, his right hand clenched alongside his face. In the far corners, reclining male figures personifying the two rivers of Olympia, the Alpheos and the Kladeos, watch with detached interest.

The old man, sometimes identified as a seer, is right to feel horror. During the chariot race the wax linchpins melt, the chariot collapses, and Oinomaos dies. When the betraying charioteer makes a pass at Hippodameia, Pelops hurls him into the sea. Before the man drowns, he pronounces a curse on Pelops and his descendants: the curse that runs through the house of Atreus and animates a vast cycle of Greek tragedy.

The west pediment, in contrast, shows its subject at the high point of the action (Figure 14.10). In another mythological scene, this one taking place in Thessaly (northern Greece), the

Figure 14.10 Apollo, Lapiths, and Centaurs, west pediment (detail), Temple of Zeus, Olympia. Archaeological Museum, Olympia

centaurs, creatures who are half man, half horse, have been invited to the wedding feast of Perithoos, the king of the Lapiths, early human inhabitants of Thessaly. The centaurs drink too much, then attack the Lapith women. Outraged, the Lapith men fight back, led by Perithoos and his friend, Theseus. The pediment shows the brawl in full tilt, with centaurs, Lapiths, and Lapith women biting, pulling, struggling against each other. Whereas the contorted faces of the centaurs clearly express the passion and effort of the fight, the faces of the Lapiths remain unnaturally calm. But the Lapiths and centaurs represented a larger issue. Like the gods and the giants of the Siphnian Treasury, the Lapiths and centaurs were favorite allegorical figures, stand-ins for the struggle of the forces of order against chaos and barbarism.

Swift resolution seems likely. Apollo stands in the center of the pediment and stretches out his right arm, ordering a halt to the fighting. Reason, law, and civilization, Apollo's causes, will triumph. Such is the reassuring message of this west pediment.

In the metopes, the other set of architectural sculpture that decorates the exterior of the temple, attention is shifted to the hero Herakles. The twelve metopes show Herakles performing the twelve labors demanded by king Eurystheus of Argos. Restricted by the metope shape and by the subject matter, the sculptor has skillfully varied the composition and emotional expression. There is no repetition here. Herakles is first young, later mature, with a beard. Some scenes show the action in progress, some show Herakles resting, the labor completed. Athena sometimes appears, an encourager or a comforter, but in some plaques she is absent.

The cult statue depicted Zeus seated on his throne, the whole made of gold and ivory (= *chryselephantine*) over a wooden framework, a statue so big that the god's head reached the top of the roof. It is easy to imagine ancient pilgrims overwhelmed by this looming presence in the semi-darkness of the cella. The statue was the work of the Athenian sculptor Pheidias in the 430s, well after the temple was completed; indeed, his workshop at Olympia has been discovered. By this time Pheidias had finished the chryselephantine cult statue of Athena Parthenos for the great temple on the Athenian Acropolis (see Chapter 15). But he had left Athens under a cloud, disgraced by charges that he had embezzled some of the gold destined for the statue of the goddess. The statue of Zeus, named during the Hellenistic period as one of the Seven Wonders of the World, ended its days in Constantinople, another prize brought by Constantine to give luster to his new capital. It was destroyed in AD 476 when the building in which it was housed, the Lauseion, caught fire.

The Olympic Games and Greek athletics

Just outside the borders of the temenos one finds the buildings used for athletic training and competition. The modern visitor is often surprised at how modest they were. The grandiose facilities of the modern Olympic Games (established in 1896) lead one to expect something comparable in antiquity.

The stadium one sees today was built ca. 350 BC and lies outside the sanctuary. The earlier track, or the simple terrain where races took place, had been located in part inside the sacred precinct. The change may reflect the diminishing importance of the religious tie, as some have said, or simply the need to find a larger space. The stadium measures 192.27m long, or 600 Olympic feet, a distance originally fixed by Herakles, according to legend. The rectangular clay track covered with sand has stone starting lines with grooves for toe holds at each end. All races were run back and forth on the straight, but ending, whatever the length, at the west, closest to the sacred precinct. A stone channel for water encircled the track, furnished at intervals with basins for the refreshment of those dehydrating in the late summer heat in this shadeless place.

Sloping earth embankments built up around the track provided good views for some 40,000 spectators, who would sit or stand on the ground. Later stadia would have stone seating, supported either by the natural hillside or on vaulted chambers built on flat ground, this last a specialty of Roman architecture.

Most events were held in the stadium, but the chariot races were run in a separate field, the hippodrome, described by Pausanias as lying well outside the sanctuary to the south of the stadium. Flooding of the Alpheios River has unfortunately washed away all traces.

Athletic training took place in the gymnasium and the palaestra, and Greek cities normally had at least one of each. These buildings were also places for socializing and, for boys, for schooling. The word "gymnasium" is derived from *gymnos*, "naked," reminding us of the Greek custom of exercising naked, whereas "palaestra" is related to the Greek word for wrestling. Both gymnasium and palaestra feature an open-air space in the center, enclosed by colonnaded porticoes and sometimes additional rooms. The gymnasium was a public complex, often outfitted with special facilities for running, but otherwise distinctions between gymnasium and palaestra were often blurred. Olympia has an example of each, adjacent to each other just outside the temenos. They are both from the Hellenistic period. The gymnasium, of the second century BC, included an all-weather covered running track on its east side, the same length as the track in the stadium. The palaestra, much smaller, dates from the third century BC, and consists of a courtyard surrounded by a Doric colonnade, with rooms behind on three sides. Ionic and Corinthian columns were used as well, for the inner row of the south colonnade (Ionic) and the entrance porch (Corinthian).

Gymnasia and palaestras might provide rudimentary bathing facilities. Athletes covered their skin with olive oil before exercising, and afterwards scraped off the oil and collected dirt with a special curved bronze tool known as a *strigil*. The Greeks washed simply with cold water, grudgingly admitting the use of hot water in the Classical period, but the Romans, as we shall see, unabashedly enjoyed hot water and counted public baths among their major civic institutions.

Athletic contests originated as sacred festivals and always were held at religious centers. Four sanctuaries were renowned for their games, making up the prestigious *periodos*, or circuit: Olympia, Delphi, Isthmia, and Nemea. Other sanctuaries might hold contests with a more local appeal. At Olympia and Nemea, Zeus presided, with the athletes offering him their prayers. Apollo ruled at Delphi, Poseidon at Isthmia. Although prizes for victory were simple, a crown from branches of a sacred olive tree being presented at Olympia, the prestige was great. The home city would bestow additional honors and money. The Athenians rewarded a victor at any of the four games with a lifetime of free meals. It is no wonder that the Altis itself was filled with the dedications of grateful victors. The most amusing is perhaps a large stone weighing 143.5kg, on display in the Olympia Museum, inscribed as follows: "Bibon, the son of Pholos, threw me over his head with one hand." Stone throwing was not an official event at Olympia; nonetheless Bibon's achievement must have caused a sensation.

The Olympic Games were held every four years in late summer, their central day falling on the second or third full moon after the summer solstice. Heralds from Elis, the nearby city that controlled Olympia, traveled throughout the Greek world, announcing the dates of the festival, inviting participants, and proclaiming the special Olympic truce. For a period of one month, later extended to three, city-states sending contestants agreed to lay down their arms and suspend their disputes. In the long history of the Olympic Games, only rarely did political disputes flare up enough to jeopardize the contest, a remarkable achievement. The Nemean Games, in contrast, suffered a fair amount from the rivalries of nearby states.

Before the Olympic Games began, the competitors were required to train for one month in Elis. Just before the festival, officials, athletes, and their retinues walked to Olympia, the journey of 58km taking two days. Spectators, meanwhile, and those who supplied them with food, lodging, votive offerings, and souvenirs had been flocking to Olympia from all over.

The program of events varied throughout the long history of the Games. The first day, however, was always devoted to prayers and sacrifices, and to the oath of fair play, sworn by competitors, male relatives, and trainers in front of the statue of Zeus Horkeios (Zeus of the Oaths) in the Bouleuterion, or Council House. The competition lasted three to five days, followed by the closing ceremonies, the awarding of the prize wreaths. Events included foot races of various lengths; a foot race in which the contestants wore armor; boxing; wrestling; the pankration, a no-holds-barred combination of wrestling and boxing; the pentathlon, a combination of five events – the discus throw, long jump, javelin throw, running, and wrestling; and chariot racing, with teams of both two and four horses. Although many of the sports are familiar today, the equipment used and style of execution might seem strange. Long jumpers, for instance, swung themselves forward with the help of weights gripped in each hand, and boxers protected their hands only with leather strips, with slightly padded gloves appearing in the Hellenistic period. Another curious feature for us today was the nudity of the competitors, a practice established in the later eighth century BC, according to one charming but hardly satisfying ancient explanation, when a runner so impressed the public by winning his race even though his shorts had fallen off.

Contestants were male citizens of Greek city-states. Thus excluded were women, foreigners, and slaves. A woman could, however, win from afar, as the sponsor of a chariot team. Kyniska, a Spartan woman, did so, and set up two monuments at Olympia to honor her success. The inscription on the larger monument read:

> Sparta's kings were fathers and brothers of mine,
> But since with my chariot and storming horses I, Kyniska,
> Have won the prize, I place my effigy here
> And proudly proclaim
> That of all Grecian women I first bore the crown.

(Swaddling 1984: 42)

Only certain women were permitted as spectators: the priestess of Demeter Chamyne, the goddess of the harvest, whose presence was required, and virgins; and eventually, single women who were not virgins, including 'women of dubious character' according to Dio Chrysostom. Married women were rigorously barred. These arcane regulations may reflect some early link between the games and fertility rituals. A separate athletic festival for women was held at Olympia every four years, the Heraia, to honor the goddess Hera. The foot race was the only event, contested by three age groups of girls.

Already by the Late Classical period (fourth century BC), the religious authority of the games was diminishing. At Olympia, this trend is marked by the construction inside the sacred precinct of a political monument: the Philippeion, a lavish circular building of the 330s BC housing gold and ivory statues of Philip II of Macedonia, the conqueror of Greece, and his family. Professionalism of athletes was on the rise too, with athletes during the Roman period following a circuit of a multitude of crowd-pleasing festivals in order to make their living. But for the Christians, such contests were tainted by their association with the pagan gods, and thus had to be prohibited. In AD 393, on orders of the emperor Theodosius I, all pagan festivals were abolished, including the Olympic Games.

CHAPTER 15

Athens in the fifth century BC

Early Classical period: ca. 480–450 BC

High Classical period: ca. 450–400 BC

The fifth century BC marked the high point of Athens, with extraordinary achievements in literature, architecture, and visual arts matched by political power and wealth. Its only rival for leadership of the Greek world was Sparta, always militarily strong. This dominance would be brief. Although Athens continued as an intellectual center in the fourth century BC and indeed beyond, defeat at the hands of the Spartans in 404 BC and the dissolution of its empire at the end of the long Peloponnesian War ended both Athens's power and the profits reaped from the states once subject to it. In this chapter we shall examine the major material remains of fifth-century BC Athens – the building program on the Acropolis and the Classical Agora – and explore how the Acropolis monuments, in particular, served to enhance the prestige of the city in this its century of glory.

HISTORICAL INTRODUCTION

When the Persians retreated after their defeats at Salamis and Plataea, the Athenians returned to rebuild their city, sacked in 480 BC. Although the Persians had been defeated, no one knew whether they would regroup and attempt conquest once again. In this climate of uncertainty, the Athenians decided a strong set of fortification walls was needed. The leading statesman of the time was Themistokles, whose far-sighted promotion of shipbuilding in the 480s (paid with silver mined at Laurion, in south-east Attica) had saved Athens from annihilation at the Battle of Salamis. Under his guidance new walls were quickly erected around Athens and its port of Peiraeus. Any available stone was used for the lower portions of the walls, including pieces from destroyed buildings and even sculpted funerary stelai; the upper reaches were made of mud brick. During the following decades town and port were linked by the Long Walls, a corridor of parallel walls, with a third wall reaching eastwards to protect the secondary harbor at Phaleron (Figure 15.1).

Precautions against a Persian return were also undertaken on a larger stage. The Delian League, formed in 478 BC, was a coalition of states under the leadership of Athens that maintained a large navy, with states contributing either ships or money. The member states tended to be the coastal and island cities of the Aegean and the Sea of Marmara. The sacred island of Delos, centrally located, was selected as the site of the League's treasury. Periodic battles with the Persians did take place, notably along the south coast of Turkey and in Egypt, but the Persians never seriously threatened the mainland of Greece or the Aegean islands. Indeed, a formal peace may have been concluded with the Persians in the middle of the century.

Figure 15.1 Attica

Nevertheless, Athens tightened its grip over the member states, gradually transforming the League into an Athenian empire. The Persian menace may have receded, but Sparta and its allies presented new challenges. Member states no longer had the option of furnishing ships. Only money was accepted: a tribute, not a contribution. Pretences of equality were further stripped when, in 454 BC, the treasury of the League was moved from Delos to Athens.

According to tradition, before the Battle of Plataea, the Greek city-states had taken an oath never to rebuild the temples destroyed by the Persians in 480 BC: "Of the shrines burnt and overthrown by the barbarians I will rebuild none, but I will allow them to remain as a memorial to those who come after of the impiety of the barbarians" (Wycherley 1978: 106, from Lycurgus, *Against Leokrates* 80–1). Conspicuous among these ruins were the sacred buildings on the

Athenian Acropolis, the cult center of Athens. By the middle of the fifth century, however, the Athenians decided to rebuild. The sentiment sworn in the Oath of Plataea seemed irrelevant: the Persian threat had diminished, and more significantly, Athens had become a major power. Under the leadership of Perikles, the leading statesman from ca. 461 to 429 BC, the Athenians expressed their city's greatness in a major reconstruction of the sanctuary to Athena on the Acropolis.

Athenian ambitions did not go unchallenged. Opponents in central and southern Greece, including such economic centers as Corinth, persuaded Sparta to lead their cause. War broke out in 431 BC: the Peloponnesian War. This confrontation between Athens and Sparta and their allies lasted until 404 BC, ending with a Spartan victory and occupation of Athens and the pulling down of the Athenian walls. But the war had exhausted Sparta as well; it was unable to capitalize on its success. In 394 BC, Athens, now freed of Spartan tutelage, rebuilt its walls under the leadership of Konon and regained a measure of its former importance.

THE ATHENIAN ACROPOLIS

Settlements were usually located with an eye for defense, as we have seen. Coastal towns might take advantage of peninsulas surrounded by the sea. For cities both coastal and inland, a hill or mountain top, easily fortified, was desirable; indeed the term "acropolis," or "high city" in Greek, was commonly used throughout the Greek world to designate such a feature. The Acropolis at Athens is thus by no means unique among naturally protected locations in the Greek world, but it is the best known.

The Athenian Acropolis is a natural broad-topped hill rising 90m above the city below. In the distance, the plain in which the city lies is enclosed by mountains, sacred elements in the landscape – Mount Hymettus with its double horned peak (south-east), Mount Pentelikos (north-east), Mount Parnes (north-west), and the Aigaleos ridge (west) – and the Aegean Sea (south). The earliest known use of the hilltop dates to the Bronze Age. Features of the Mycenaean citadel can still be seen, including a stretch of Cyclopean masonry belonging to the fortification wall. Only in the Archaic period did the primary function change from fortress to religious sanctuary, with the worship of Athena predominating. During medieval and early modern times, the Acropolis became a fortified village, the ancient buildings adapted for new needs. Drawings by western European travellers show us the Acropolis clustered with houses. With the naming of Athens as the capital of modern Greece in 1833, an intense interest arose in rediscovering the appearance of the city in Classical times: the newly created country wished to identify itself with ancient glory. The Acropolis was soon stripped of its medieval and Ottoman accretions; the four buildings that dominate the Acropolis today – the Parthenon, the Propylaia, the Temple of Athena Nike, and the Erechtheion – are all products of the Periklean building program of the second half of the fifth century BC (Figures 15.2 and 15.3). Major excavations followed in the later nineteenth and early twentieth centuries, with Greek and German archaeologists exploring down to bedrock in order to clarify the architectural history of the site. Reconstruction and conservation of the ancient buildings continue to the present day, tasks all the more urgent with the increasingly destructive air pollution and acid rain of modern industrialized Athens.

The Parthenon: architecture

The Parthenon, or Temple to Athena Parthenos, Athena in her aspect as warrior maiden, is the earliest and most important building of the Periklean refurbishing of the Acropolis (Figure 15.4). Although a Doric temple, the Parthenon incorporates several Ionic features, a fusion suitable for

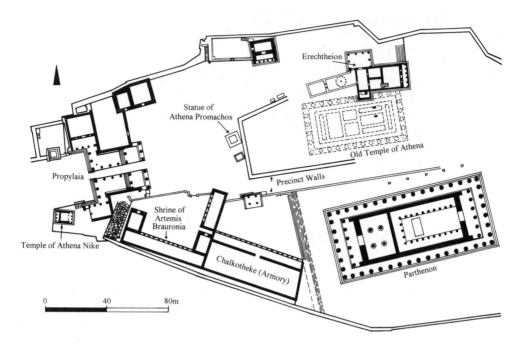

Figure 15.2 Plan, the Acropolis, Athens, fifth century BC

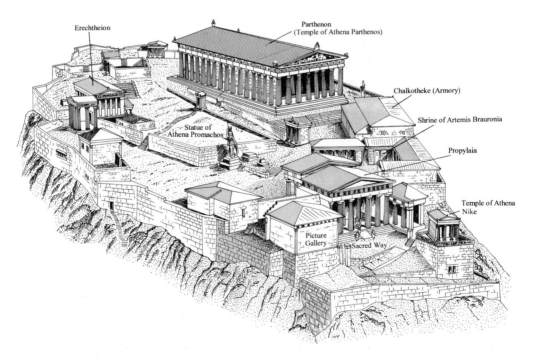

Figure 15.3 The Acropolis (reconstruction), Athens, fifth century BC

Figure 15.4 The Parthenon, seen from the west. This photo, taken in 2001, shows scaffolding used in recent restoration activity

an empire that now reached across the Aegean to East Greece, the heartland of Ionic architecture. Its architects were Iktinos and Kallikrates, but its complex sculptural decoration was the work of Pheidias, who also served as overseer of the entire Acropolis building program. Built between 447 and 438 BC, the Parthenon was the third temple on the site, replacing a smaller temple from the mid sixth century BC and a second, larger building, under construction when the Persians sacked the Acropolis in 480 BC. Preservation of the Parthenon long after the end of pagan religion was ensured by the conversion of the temple first into a Christian church, later into a Muslim mosque. In 1687, however, its center was destroyed in an explosion, when an artillery shell from attacking Venetians hit gunpowder stored there by the Ottomans. Much of the surviving sculptural decoration was removed to Britain in the early nineteenth century by Lord Elgin; purchased by the government, the sculpture entered the collections of the British Museum. The Parthenon itself has undergone various restorations in modern times, most recently from the 1980s to the present.

The builders of the Parthenon took advantage of the preparatory work done for the late Archaic temple destroyed by the Persians. In particular, they reused much of the foundation platform. Because the new temple was somewhat larger than its predecessor, adjustments had to be made. The temple lies over the sharp southward slope of the Acropolis bedrock, so on the south, especially, the foundations had to be built up in many courses in order to provide a level surface for the temple.

The ground plan of the Parthenon departs from the typical in a few important respects (see Figure 15.2). The colonnade consists of eight columns on the short sides and 17 on the long sides, an expansion of the usual Doric column count that imparts rather the feeling of a massive Ionic temple. Following the standard Greek procedure of building temples from the outside in, the colonnade would have been the first portion of the temple erected. From the east, one passed through a truncated porch (*prostyle hexastyle*, or six columns, with the end two being placed in front of the wall ends) into the cella, home of the gold and ivory cult statue made by Pheidias. A two-storeyed Doric colonnade, supporting a gallery on the upper floor, framed the statue behind as well as on the sides in a U-shaped formation. Recent research of Manolis Korres has revealed that the east wall of the cella contained windows on either side of the doorway; the cella and the cult statue were hence better lit than previously thought. A second room lay adjacent to the cella on the west. This room, entered from the truncated porch on the west, was called the Parthenon, the chamber of the virgin, but apparently served as a treasury rather than as the home of a cult statue. Two, or perhaps four, Ionic columns held up the roof. Since the proportions of Ionic columns could be taller and slenderer than Doric, there was no need for a second tier in order to reach the roof beams.

The elevation of the temple follows the arrangement expected for the Doric order. Since no expense was spared, the temple was decorated with sculpted metopes on all four sides, and sculpted pediments. Unusual, however, is the addition of a sculpted frieze, an Ionic feature, high inside the colonnade, on the top of the exterior walls of the cella, the Parthenon, and the two truncated porches.

Also unusual are the deviations from strict vertical and horizontal lines and proportional arrangement, the so-called "refinements." The stylobate, for example, is not flat, but curves slightly from the center down to the four corners, as if four people held a sheet by its corners, billowed it up into the air, then pulled it down slowly. The centers of the long sides are some 10cm higher than the corners. Other "refinements" include the thickening of the corner column one-fortieth more than the normal column diameter; corner contraction, that is, the setting in from the corner, in this case a distance of ca 0.60m, of the corner columns; the slight tilt inward of the columns; the upward tapering of the columns; the leaning inward of the long walls of the cella; and the slight outward tilt of the entablature and pediments. All of these variants are measurable and sometimes can be verified with the naked eye. Many have been observed on earlier and later temples, in particular Doric rather than Ionic, but nowhere else have they all been combined as here. The precise carving of the appropriate blocks must have required much additional time. Why the bother?

The purpose of these deviations has been much debated. Vitruvius, the Roman architect, who had consulted a book about the Parthenon by Iktinos and Karpion, proposed that the architects compensated for anticipated optical illusions. Since a long horizontal line seems to sag, it should look perfectly horizontal if its middle is raised. Modern commentators have made other suggestions. Perhaps the curve of the stylobate is actually perceived as more pronounced, a deliberate exaggeration that makes the stylobate appear larger than it really is. A third interpretation, which correlates well with intellectual trends in Classical Athens, favors the tension created between expectations and appearances: one expects straight lines, but sees (or senses) curves and tilts. The lines of the building thus never quite explain themselves. The building remains a mystery that the viewer cannot stop contemplating. The correct answer or answers may be impossible to find, but in any case, the abundant use of refinements is a mark of the sophistication of the design of this great temple.

The Parthenon: sculptural decoration and the cult statue

The sculptural decoration of the Parthenon was not simply famously beautiful; it had important messages to impart. As typical for ancient Greek temples, the exterior carried the figural decoration. The interior was reserved for the cult statue, without additional imagery. The sculpture illustrated themes that concerned both the city, its patron goddess, Athena, and its religious practices, and the continuing need for the forces of order and civilization to fight for victory. Absent are any pictures of the rulers or prominent citizens of Athens. This last feature, a characteristic of Classical Greek art, contrasts strongly with, for example, the art of the Ancient Near East and Egypt, in which the divinity and the monarch are habitually shown in beneficial partnership.

This lavish and complex program of sculpture took some time to complete. The *metopes* were the first component of the sculptural decoration to be carved, from ca. 447 to 442 BC, followed by the *frieze* and the *cult statue* (both finished by 438 BC, along with the building itself), and finally, the *pedimental sculptures* (by 432 BC). This, and other details of the construction of the Parthenon, we know from building accounts, inscriptions carved on stone which recorded for public appreciation sources of money and exactly how it was spent.

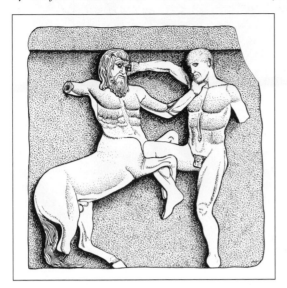

Figure 15.5 Parthenon, South Metope no. xxxi

The metopes

All 92 metopes contained sculpture. Many were destroyed or damaged in the explosion of 1687, but enough have survived to give a good idea of subject matter and style. The metopes illustrated the combats of Lapiths vs. Centaurs, Gods vs. Giants, Greeks vs. Amazons, and probably Greeks vs. Trojans, all allegories for the battle of Order vs. Chaos, Civilization vs. Barbarism – which for fifth-century BC Greeks specifically meant their conflict with the Persians. The styles vary, indicating that the design and execution of the metopes was done by several artists, but all display the optically realistic treatment of the human body developed first in late Archaic sculpture and vase painting (Figure 15.5).

The frieze

The frieze, far better preserved than the other sculpture, records the procession during the Panathenaic Festival that led through the city up to the Acropolis, with the aim of presenting a newly woven, brightly colored *peplos* to dress the venerable cult statue of Athena Polias, Athena as patron goddess of the city. The Panathenaia, the most important religious festival of Athens, was held every year in mid-August (in our calendar) to celebrate the birthday of Athena. Every fourth year a grander version took place, the Great Panathenaia. The centerpiece of this quadrennial procession was a monumental peplos displayed like a sail on a ship pulled on a wheeled cart. At the base of the Acropolis the giant peplos was then taken down from the ship and carried up to be hung in a temple as a backdrop until replaced in the next Great Panathenaia. In the time of Pausanias at least, the ship was parked nearby until the next festival, on view for tourists.

The frieze measures 160m in total length, ca. 1m in height. It shows only portions of the procession; the ship, for example, is lacking. The scenes are clear enough, even if the exact understanding of who is doing what, and when, has been much debated. Horses and riders, all young men, gather on the west side, then advance, picking up speed, along both long sides, the north and the south (Figure 15.6). At the east end of the long sides, other participants in the procession appear, men carrying hydriae, or water jars; officials; women; and sheep and cows for

Figure 15.6 Parthenon, West Frieze, Slab II, nos 2–3

sacrifice. On the east side, in the presence of seated gods the peplos is displayed, a folded cloth (although perhaps originally painted with gods battling giants, the subject always woven into the peplos).

This frieze would have been difficult to see, placed high up in the shadows of the narrow colonnade. Nevertheless the sculptors took no short cuts. Some aids were granted the viewer: the frieze was thicker at the top than at the bottom, and the figures would have been painted bright colors. Otherwise, the artists worked to please Athena. Details of bodies and clothes are precisely carved. The composition is sophisticated and varied; participants in the procession are shown in a great variety of poses, with overlapping in particular of horses and riders. How different from the stately, repetitious procession of tribute bearers at Persian Persepolis!

The pediments

With this lively scene from the Panathenaia, the frieze offered worshippers a connection with the actual religious life of the city. In the pediments, the sculptors returned to mythology, the favorite source of subject matter. Unlike the metopes, with their allegorical treatment of recent Greek history, the pediments show episodes from the distant mythical past of Athens. In depicting regional legend, they resemble the east pediment of the Temple of Zeus at Olympia, with the fateful chariot race about to begin. All pedimental figures were completed on the invisible back side as well as the front, another testimony to the reverential attitude of the artists toward work done for this temple.

Only a small number of the pedimental figures were decently preserved when Lord Elgin stripped the Parthenon of sculpture. Because these pieces are so few, the original appearance of the pediments eludes us. Pausanias noted only the basic subjects, not the complete cast of characters or their arrangement in the triangular space. Furthermore, the explosion of 1687 seriously damaged the sculpture. Drawings made earlier, in 1674, by French painter Jacques Carrey help, but they are not as precise as we might wish; in any case by Carrey's time some portions, notably the center of the east side, had already disappeared.

In the important position over the main entrance to the temple, the east pediment depicted the distinctive birth of Athena: she emerged fully armed from the head of her father, Zeus, when he was knocked on the head by Hephaistos. Zeus and Athena must have been shown in the now vanished center. The miraculous event, so important for the city of Athens, was witnessed by divinities arrayed on either side of Zeus and Athena, standing, sitting, or even reclining to fit the height of the pedimental space diminishing into the corners. These deities represented the other cults of Athens welcoming Athena within their midst.

The west pediment showed Athena's victory in her contest with Poseidon for the position of patron deity of the city (Figure 15.7). A miracle was required of each. When Poseidon struck the ground with his trident, water had bubbled forth – salt water, appropriate for the god of the sea. Athena then created an olive tree on the barren Acropolis, a feat that was life-sustaining for humans at least, in contrast with the salt water spring. The miraculous olive tree may have occupied the center of the pediment, with an excited Athena and Poseidon stepping back on either side, the event witnessed by gods, goddesses, horses and chariots, and perhaps families prominent in the legendary origins of the city.

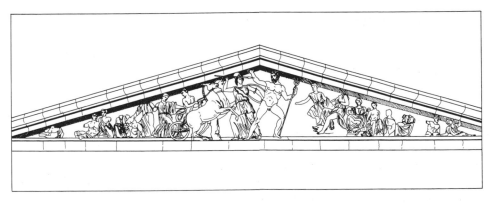

Figure 15.7 Parthenon, west pediment (reconstruction), after the drawings of Carrey (1674) and Quatremère de Quincy (1825)

The cult statue

The final piece of sculptural adornment was the cult statue itself, a work of Pheidias. This colossal chryselephantine statue of Athena disappeared in late antiquity, but the detailed description left by Pausanias, statuettes that roughly copy it (Figure 15.8), and depictions on coins provide evidence for a reconstruction. With its complex array of victory imagery, the statue, as indeed the entire temple, was a reminder that Athena led the Greeks to triumph against the Persians. The goddess stood ca. 12m high. She wore a peplos and her armor: a breastplate and a triple-crested helmet, and with her left hand she held a spear and shield. A snake lay curled by her left foot, just inside the shield. In her outstretched right palm, supported on a column, she held a statue of Nike, winged victory, her offering to the city. The colossal Athena was a vehicle for

Figure 15.8 The Varvakeion Athena, a marble statuette; a Roman copy of the Athena Parthenos. National Archaeological Museum, Athens

display of allegorical myths appropriate for Greek victory: the Greeks fought Amazons on the outside of the shield; gods pitted against giants, possibly painted, on the inside; and Lapiths vs. centaurs on the thick edge of her sandals. An unusual scene, in contrast, appeared on the statue's base: the birth of Pandora, attended by gods. After Prometheus had stolen fire for humans against the will of the gods, Zeus in anger had Pandora created and sent to earth, carrying with her a box filled with all possible miseries. The box once opened, the evils escaped, becoming an ineradicable part of human existence. Here in the Parthenon, the appearance of Pandora seems intended as a caution to the Athenians in their hour of triumph.

Like the later Zeus of Olympia, the statue was made of a skin of ivory and costume of thin sheets of gold fitted onto a wooden framework. The gold, weighing 44 talents (= approx. 1,120kg), belonged to the city, was inventoried every four years by the state treasury, and could be removed for safe-keeping. Pheidias was accused of stealing some of this precious material. Whether this was true or simply slander, he left Athens for Olympia, where he made the statue of Zeus. Where he ended his days is unknown. Whatever the truth of his complex life, his sculpture – votives for the Acropolis, the complex program conceived for the Parthenon, and the cult statue for Olympia – has stood as a benchmark for Classical Greek art in its grandeur, nobility of expression, and precision of execution.

The Propylaia

When the construction of the Parthenon was coming to an end, attention turned to the entrance to the Acropolis. Here, on the west end of the rock, a new monumental gateway was built, the Propylaia (Figure 15.9). Mnesikles, the architect, worked on the building from 437 to 432 BC on the eve of the Peloponnesian War, at which point work stopped even though the finishing touches had not yet been applied.

In ground plan, the Propylaia consists of a main hall on the west–east axis, which gives access to the Acropolis, and flanking chambers on the north-west and south-west. The main hall is built on two main levels, reflected in the original two-part roofing, with the east section somewhat higher than the west. A cross-wall marks the point where the east section begins; it is pierced by five passageways, with the central one, a ramp, being the widest. On the west and east exteriors,

Figure 15.9 Propylaia, south-west wing, as restored, and Temple of Athena Nike with bastion, from north-west

the Propylaia displays the Doric order, with a wider spacing for the central ramp, but three pairs of Ionic columns, tall and slender, line the west portion of the central passageway. One can still see some of the ceiling coffers, the marble blocks carved with squares, one inside the other, that were placed over the cross-beams as ceiling decoration.

The side chambers of the Propylaia differ, the north from the south, creating an asymmetrical plan. A small room on the north-east, provided with benches and wall paintings, served as a rest stop for pilgrims. Although the façade is identical on the south-west, no corresponding room lies behind it. Space on this south-west rock spur was apparently at a premium. The plan of the Propylaia was truncated, the resulting space granted to the small Temple of Athena Nike. Larger halls projected for the north-west and the south-east were never built.

The south exterior wall of the Propylaia, visible when one has passed through the building onto the Acropolis, shows the lifting bosses still in place, the best sign that the building was never finished. These bosses were grips for the pulley ropes used to lift the blocks. In the finishing of a building, these would be lopped off, and the surface polished.

The view of a fifth-century BC pilgrim onto the Acropolis from the east side of the Propylaia differed considerably from what a tourist sees today, because the whole area has now been cleared; the low walls and subsidiary buildings that once blocked direct views and the many votive offerings no longer exist. The Parthenon was largely screened off by a low wall running from its north side to the south-east corner of the Propylaia. Behind the wall lay two complexes, now completely ruined, a shrine to Artemis Brauronia and the Chalkotheke, a storage for bronze objects such as armor and cauldrons. Immediately facing the pilgrim was a colossal bronze statue, made by Pheidias, of Athena Promachos, Athena as warrior goddess, one of the countless votives that packed the Acropolis. This imposing statue stood in front of another walled sector, the center of the Acropolis. The pilgrim could thus proceed either to the left, toward the Erechtheion, or to the right, down the narrow corridor that led to the main entrance of the Parthenon. At last, at the east end of the Acropolis, he or she would have a magnificent, unobstructed view of the Parthenon.

The Temple of Athena Nike

Just south of the Propylaia, high above the steps leading up to the sanctuary, the Temple of Athena Nike (winged victory) occupies the prominent south-west bastion of the Acropolis (Figure 15.9). It was built later than the Parthenon and the Propylaia, in the 420s, during the Peloponnesian War. The small one-room temple is Ionic, but has columns on two sides only because of space restrictions on the bastion. The capitals of the corner columns are striking. The corner volutes turn out onto the diagonal, thus offering a solution to the problem of how a two-dimensional Ionic volute capital might gracefully fit in the corner position, appearing the same whether seen from the front or the side. Although logically satisfying, the solution did not win adherents and is not seen in later buildings.

The temple bore rich sculptural decoration, unfortunately badly damaged: a frieze showing battle scenes, and pediments. The best-known sculpture decorated the outside of the barrier, ca. 1m high, that enclosed the small compound on the north, west, and south. This frieze, ca. 42m in length, shows Nikai, or Victories, erecting trophies or bringing sacrificial animals in the presence of a seated Athena (who is shown once on each side). One even stops to adjust her sandal. The lively effects of costume are heightened here as the sculptors give the feel of the Nikai striding through the wind, their chitons billowing and twisting every which way.

The Erechtheion

The last of the four great buildings of the Periklean program is the most unusual: the Erechtheion, an Ionic temple on the north edge of the Acropolis, built between 421 and 405 BC (Figure 15.10). Its name honors Erechtheus, a legendary king of Athens, and the temple itself may stand on the site of the Mycenaean palace, known as the "House of Erechtheus." The Erechtheion sheltered a variety of cults, which fact, combined with the irregular ground levels, accounts for its eccentric design. Most prominent of these was the shrine of Athena Polias, Athena as the patroness of the city of Athens, the oldest, most venerable cult of the goddess. It was to this particular Athena that the peplos carried to the Acropolis in the Panathenaic procession and depicted on the Parthenon frieze was presented.

Like the Parthenon, the Erechtheion was elegantly built of Pentelic marble on limestone foundations, but

Figure 15.10 Erechtheion, west façade

with some details in dark limestone from Eleusis. Column capitals and other architectural decoration, including a poorly preserved frieze, were elaborately carved. In ground plan, the Erechtheion consists of a main building, oriented east–west, to which two porches have been attached, a north porch with six Ionic columns, and a smaller south porch, with its six famous caryatid columns. The east façade is traditional. On the west, however, one can clearly see the different floor levels, with the stylobate of the north porch much lower than the floor of the main building and the caryatid porch (Figure 15.10).

Many shrines and holy places were scattered both inside and in the immediately surrounding ground. They represent an impressive concentration of sacred, ancient relics of the city. Although Pausanias described them, his details do not allow us to pinpoint their locations. The interior arrangement of the temple is controversial, for example, since remodelings through the centuries have stripped most traces of the ancient rooms. The shrine of Athena Polias, outfitted with an oil lamp made of gold, always lit, a bronze palm tree above it that contained a chimney to the roof, and some spoils from the Persian Wars, was housed somewhere in the main building. Other holy spots both inside and out included altars to Erechtheus, the hero Bootes, and Hephaistos; the olive tree and the salt water spring created by Athena and Poseidon in their contest for supremacy over the city; marks of Zeus's thunderbolt in a square hole in the floor of the north porch, with a corresponding opening in the roof above; the tombs of Kekrops, traditionally the first king of Athens; a shrine to Pandrosos, one of his daughters, who with her sisters leapt from the Acropolis when struck with madness after opening against orders the chest concealing the child god Erichthonios in the form of a snake; and a crypt for snakes, where Erichthonios dwelled as the guardian of the Acropolis.

THE THEATER OF DIONYSOS AND CHOREGIC MONUMENTS

The slopes of the Acropolis are crowded with the remains of miscellaneous monuments and shrines from many periods. The south slope is dominated by two theaters. The best preserved lies on the west, the Odeion of Herodes Atticus, built during the Roman Empire in the mid second century AD. Of greater significance is the Theater of Dionysos, to the east. Although the structure itself dates from the fourth century BC with many later remodelings, it was on this site that the Athenian tradition of theatrical representations first began, with a great flowering in the fifth century BC.

Like athletics, theater developed as a religious celebration, but always in honor of the god Dionysos. Performances included dances and processions, music and chanting, all taking place on a low flat ground, the *orchestra*, with spectators seated on higher ground, the *theatron*. Behind the orchestra might be a flimsy backdrop, the *skene*, a word which originally meant "tent" or "hut." Such simple arrangements evidently sufficed for the fifth century BC, the golden age of Athenian drama. In the following centuries all these components would be built in permanent materials and laid out in certain proportions, with the Romans in due course adapting this Greek architectural form to their needs. The Greek theater will be examined more closely in the next chapter, when we visit the well-preserved theaters at Epidauros and Priene.

Theatrical performances were presented in competition, with well-to-do citizens, or *choregoi*, financing the productions. The winners received tripods, and habitually erected monuments to display their trophies around the Theater of Dionysos and along a street that ran to the east, the Street of the Tripods. One of these choregic monuments is virtually intact, the elaborate Monument of Lysikrates, erected in 335–334 BC (Figure 15.11). In addition to its fine

Figure 15.11 Lysikrates Monument, Athens

preservation, this small building holds a special place in the development of Greek architecture because it marks the earliest use of Corinthian capitals on the exterior of a building (the fifth-century BC Temple of Apollo at Bassae had at least one on the interior).

The Lysikrates Monument consists of a cylindrical structure standing on a square base. It is decorated with columns with Corinthian capitals; screen walls of stone connecting the columns, thereby closing the colonnade; an Ionic frieze that shows Dionysos chased by pirates, who turn into dolphins when they are thrown into the sea; and, on its rooftop, a base for the victory tripod (the tripod no longer exists). Corinthian capitals are carved in the form of acanthus leaves arranged around vestigial volutes. Round in shape, they have the advantage over the rectangular Ionic capital of looking the same from all sides. Corinthian capitals did not bring a new order of architecture to rival Doric and Ionic, but instead were grafted onto the Ionic order as an alternative to the standard Ionic volute capital. Immensely popular, they would become a staple of Hellenistic Greek and Roman architecture.

THE LOWER TOWN: HOUSES AND THE AGORA

Apart from such major sectors of excavation as the Agora and the Kerameikos cemetery, the city that spread out from the Acropolis to the Themistoklean walls is known from bits and pieces only, revelations gained when, for example, a building site is obligatorily but hastily explored before a new structure goes up. Ruins are duly recorded onto the overall urban plan, another tiny fragment added to the larger jigsaw puzzle. Under a thriving modern capital where property means big money, this is how knowledge of earlier habitation is gained, morsel by morsel.

Urban plan and houses

Athens in the fifth century BC was the largest of the Greek city-states, with a population estimated at 150,000 to 200,000 people. Even though the Persian destruction offered Athenians an occasion for change, long-established traditions of urban organization held firm: the layout of streets continued to be haphazard, with narrow, twisting streets of hard earth and gravel. This contrasts with the tidy orthogonal grid plans favored for newly founded towns including, close by, the Peiraeus, the port of Athens, laid out by Hippodamos of Miletus, the pioneer city planner in the mid fifth century BC, at the urging of Themistokles and his successors.

We can imagine that much of the space inside the walls of Athens was given over to houses. The typical city house, as attested especially by excavated examples nestled in the hills to the west of the Acropolis and to the south of the Agora, was modest: irregular in outline and simple in plan, small rooms without distinctive character arranged around a central court. Lighting was poor: windows did not exist, so light entered via the doorways from the court, or was provided by oil lamps, small terracotta holders for olive oil and a wick. Doorways were blocked by curtains, not door flaps. Some houses had an upper storey (Figure 15.12). Country houses could be larger and, freed from the constraints of cramped city building sites, regular in contour.

Building materials were far more modest than those used for temples. Walls consisted of mud bricks on stone foundations, the whole protected with a coating of stucco and a roofing of clay tiles on a timber framework. Flooring was normally of beaten earth and clay, or, exceptionally, of pebble designs laid in cement. Furniture was simple, shifted from room to room as needed, including portable braziers that provided heating. For interior wall decoration a simple application of color would typically suffice. Water was not piped to private homes. Instead, people relied on wells, sometimes supplemented with cisterns for the collection of rainwater. For sanitation, people made do with stone-lined pits serving as cesspools; in many towns waste was simply tossed into the street.

Figure 15.12 Houses (reconstructed), fifth century BC Athens

The main hydraulic engineering project of Classical Athens was the Great Drain, established in the early fifth century BC, which still runs north–south along the west side of the Agora, collecting run-off in its stone-lined channel and carrying it northwards to the Eridanos River. In addition, water was piped in from outlying springs to a scattering of public fountains, such as in the Agora as we have seen, but in general aqueducts were rare before the Romans.

The Agora

During the fifth century BC, building activity in the Agora, the city center, alternated with efforts on the Acropolis. From 479 BC to mid-century, a period when the Acropolis lay fallow because of the Oath of Plataea, construction was lively in the Agora. The Persians had destroyed the Agora as well as the Acropolis, but because most of its buildings served secular purposes, they could be rebuilt without violating the Oath. After a slowdown during the Periklean period, when resources were directed toward rebuilding the shrines of the city on the Acropolis and elsewhere, several new buildings were erected during the Peloponnesian War. By the end of the fifth century BC, the existing buildings sufficed for the main civic activities; little was added in the following century, the Late Classical period (Figure 15.13).

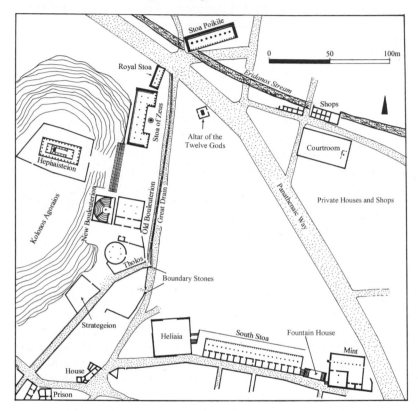

Figure 15.13
Plan, Agora,
Athens,
ca. 400 BC

Early Classical buildings included the Painted Stoa, or Stoa Poikile, discovered in 1981 on the north end of the Agora. This building contained famous paintings on large wooden panels, highly praised by ancient authors; the best-known scene depicted the Athenian victory at Marathon. None has survived. The Tholos, a round structure also Early Classical in date, served as the headquarters, dining hall, and dormitory of the Prytany, the 50 men from the larger Boule, or Council of 500, that handled the daily business of the city for a period of 35–6 days. At this time too Kimon dedicated three large herms to mark his victory over the Persians at Eion in 476 BC. A *herm* was a plain rectangular shaft with a portrait head of the bearded god Hermes on top and male genitalia half-way down. The prestige conferred by Kimon's dedication assured the popularity of the herm, and from then on they were commonly set up at entrances of houses and shrines and at public crossroads to bring good luck, success, and protection. So many stood near the north-west entrance to the Agora that they gave their name to the neighborhood: "The Herms."

During the early Periklean period, work began on an impressive temple dedicated to Hephaistos, god of the forge, and to Athena, here goddess of arts and crafts, patrons for the many craftsmen who worked in the vicinity. Excellently preserved, thanks in large part to its reuse as a Christian church, the Hephaisteion still dominates the area from its commanding location on the western hill, the Kolonos Agoraios (Figure 15.14). Indeed, this temple was situated in order to be seen from the front, from the Agora; a focus on the front view was unusual for Greek temples, but would become a hallmark of Roman temples.

Figure 15.14 Hephaisteion, Athens. View from the south-west

Begun ca. 450 BC but not completed until ca. 420 BC, the Hephaisteion did not replace an earlier shrine, but was a new conception. This temple is traditionally Doric in plan and elevation. As was true for its contemporary, the Parthenon, its sculptural decoration was abundant and costly. With some emphasis on the short east side facing the Agora, the sculpture consisted of the east and west pediments, poorly preserved; 18 metopes depicting deeds of Herakles and of the great Athenian hero Theseus, placed on the east side and in the four spaces immediately adjacent on the north and south; and friezes of battle scenes, one placed above the east pronaos and extending north and south across the space covered by the colonnade to the very edges of the temple, the second, showing Lapiths vs. Centaurs, above the west opisthodomos only, not the adjoining colonnade. The bronze cult statue of the two gods, made by Alkamenes, has not survived.

Excavations have revealed that the Hephaisteion was surrounded by formal plantings. Discoveries of planting pits with large terracotta flowerpots indicate that two rows of bushes lined the temple on the long north and south sides, three rows on the west. This find emphasizes an overlooked aspect of ancient topography, the importance of setting. Texts make clear that trees, plants, and water were important components of sanctuaries; archaeological excavations, by stripping away vegetation, give a false picture of the landscape.

Other mid-fifth-century BC buildings in the Agora include the state prison, a curious structure situated beyond the south-west corner of the Agora. Its unusual plan features a central corridor flanked by small rooms, leading to a courtyard at the rear. In this prison the philosopher Socrates met his end in 399 BC, forced to kill himself with a drink of poisonous hemlock.

In the later fifth century, several new civic buildings were added to the Agora. On the west side, a New Bouleuterion rose adjacent to the still existing Old, also to serve the 500-member Council. Military activities were centered in the Strategeion, a meeting hall for generals (*strategoi*)

tentatively identified with a poorly preserved structure just south of the Tholos. New stoas included the Stoa of Zeus in the north-west: a Doric building with two projecting wings, serving the cult of Zeus Eleutherios (Freedom), but also, like all stoas, offering shelter for anyone who wished.

On the south side of the Agora the South Stoa I contained administrative offices and rooms where officials could dine, reclining on couches as was the Greek custom. The many coins discovered in this building indicate its role in the commercial life of the city. Nearby lay a good source of the bronze coins, the Mint. Bronze coins, popular from the fourth century BC on, form the great majority of coins found during the Agora excavations. They served for ordinary purchases, in contrast with the valuable silver and gold coins.

"Agora" in a larger sense denotes the central market area of a city. Outside the formally marked sacred political and religious precinct, Athenians found all the services they might wish. Evidence for them comes from literature as well as from excavations. Such businesses included: shoe-makers, barbers, metalworkers, sellers of wine, perfume, fish, vegetables, nuts, horses, clothes, and even stolen goods. "Everything will be for sale together in the same place at Athens, figs, summoners, bunches of grapes, turnips, pears, apples, witnesses, roses, medlars, haggis, honeycombs, chickpeas, lawsuits, beestings-pudding, beesting cures, myrtle berries, allotment machines, irises, lambs, water clocks, laws, indictments." So quotes Athenaios, an Alexandrian writing ca. AD 200, from a much earlier Athenian comedy, *Olbia*, by the fourth-century BC playwright Euboulos (Wycherley 1978: 91). The comic juxtaposition of food and legal matters, all available in the agora, makes clear the happy chaos that must have reigned in the Athenian Agora.

CHAPTER 16

Greek cities and sanctuaries in the Late Classical period

Late Classical period: ca. 400–323 BC

The Late Classical period, from the end of the Peloponnesian War to the conquest of central and southern Greece by Philip II of Macedonia in 338 BC, seems an anti-climax after the domination of Athens and Sparta in the previous century, a pause before the dramatic conquests of Alexander the Great and the spread of Greek culture throughout West Asia and Egypt. Nonetheless, cities continue, and indeed the fourth century BC (stretching into the Hellenistic period) has left important evidence for certain aspects of urban life and rural religious practices that would have been familiar to city dwellers. In this chapter, we shall explore the *Sanctuary of Asklepios* and the theater at Epidauros; city plans and houses at *Priene* and *Olynthos*; and royal burials at *Vergina* and *Halikarnassos* (see Figure 11.1).

HISTORICAL SUMMARY

The Peloponnesian War ended with the Spartan capture of Athens in 404 BC. The Spartans ordered the dismantling of the city walls and installed a compliant government. But the Spartan triumph was short-lived; the Athenians soon retook control of their city. Spartan leaders proved incapable of governing in the outside world, and particularly susceptible to the lure of money and bribes. In addition, losses of soldiers during the war had severely reduced the already small Spartan citizenry. In 371 BC, a Spartan army was defeated at the Battle of Leuctra by a federated state led by Thebes. Sparta, invincible no longer, never recovered from this blow.

Thebes and later the Arcadian League held sway briefly, but neither dominated mainland Greece in a sustained way as had Athens and Sparta in the fifth century BC. While the city-states continued to quarrel, a new force was rising on the northern edge of the Greek world that would soon sweep them away. Philip II came to power in Macedonia in 359 BC. Although speaking a dialect of Greek, the Macedonians lay on the fringes of Greek culture and had contributed little to Greek political, socio-economic, and artistic life. Philip II was of a different mettle from his predecessors. Strengthening Macedonia through military reforms, he eventually challenged the city-states to the south, including Athens, and defeated them at the Battle of Chaeronea in 338 BC. Two years later, while preparing to lead the combined Macedonian and Greek forces eastwards against the Persian Empire, he was assassinated.

Philip's ambitions were fulfilled by his son, Alexander III, better known as Alexander the Great. Only 20 years old when he succeeded his father, Alexander soon led his conquering army into Asia and defeated the Persians in three key battles, Granicus (in north-west Turkey), Issos (in south Turkey), and Gaugamela (in northern Iraq). After sacking Persepolis, he marched as

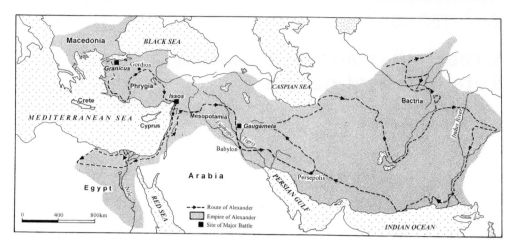

Figure 16.1 The conquests of Alexander the Great

far east as the Indus River (Figure 16.1). His soldiers refused to go further, so he turned back; he died soon after of a fever in Babylon, in 323 BC. He was 33 years of age. With Alexander's conquests, West Asia and Egypt were brought into the fold of Greek culture. The newly formed Greek kingdoms of the Hellenistic period would be much influenced, however, by the Near Eastern and Egyptian cultures they were now controlling.

THE SANCTUARY OF ASKLEPIOS AT EPIDAUROS: A NEW DIRECTION IN RELIGIOUS PRACTICE

Epidauros was renowned as the center of the cult of the healing god Asklepios. Attaining popularity in the fourth century BC, worship of Asklepios illustrates an important development in Greco-Roman religious life: the desire to complement increasingly sterile official cults with divinities who responded directly to personal appeals.

According to a common legend, Asklepios was the son of Apollo and a mortal woman, Koronis; the centaur Chiron raised him and taught him the art of healing. Asklepios was generally depicted as a mature bearded man, with a staff around which a snake was coiled. The main public festival at Epidauros took place in late April to early May. Included were an initial purification by washing, sacrifices, a formal banquet, and athletic and music competitions – features standard in the worship of any god, as we have seen. Peculiar to Asklepios were the devotions, performed throughout the year, of individuals seeking to have their illnesses cured. The suppliant would first cleanse himself or herself by bathing, then spend the night in the *abaton*, a long stoa inside the sanctuary (Figure 16.2). Asklepios, or one of his sacred snakes, appeared in a dream and revealed the appropriate treatment. If cured, the patient might present as a thank-offering a stele on which the medical problem, the treatment, and the successful outcome were reported. Such inscriptions vividly recreate ancient Greek medical practices. Some reports are wonderfully improbable, such as the woman pregnant for five years who prayed to the god for relief, then gave birth to a five-year-old boy. Others, more credible, record special diets, exercise, and therapeutic baths.

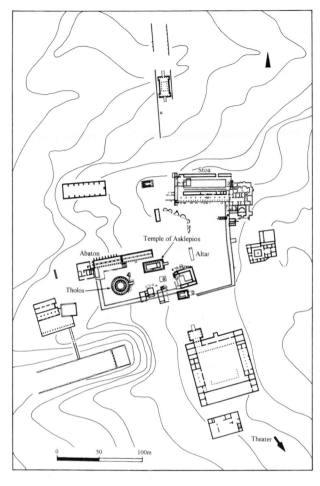

Figure 16.2 Plan, the Sanctuary of Asklepios, Epidauros

The sanctuary is peacefully situated on flat ground amidst trees, with ruggedly profiled hills in the distance. Excavations were conducted here beginning in 1881 by Greek archaeologists P. Kavvadias and V. Stais. The principal structures inside the sacred precinct, dating from the fourth century BC, are the Temple of Asklepios, the *tholos* or round building (here known as the Thymele), and the abaton. The buildings have been largely destroyed, leaving only foundations. With one exception, they do not impart as lively a picture of the activities that went on here as do the inscriptions and literary texts. The exception is the tholos, with its mysterious, intriguing foundations: six concentric rings of tufa (a volcanic stone) with doors in the inner rings, creating a maze in the inner three passages. Cuttings in the stone suggest wooden steps led from the main floor down into this crypt. The purpose of this unique maze, indeed of the entire building, remains uncertain. The tholos was certainly prestigious: surviving architectural pieces show a high quality of work. According to the building accounts, inscribed on stone, construction lasted over 30 years, payment being dependent on a steady trickle of donations. But faith was kept, the building completed. One popular view interprets the crypt as a home of the god's sacred snakes, but a leading specialist on Epidauros, R. A. Tomlinson, prefers to identify the tholos as a funerary monument for Asklepios as a mortal (in contrast to the temple, which honored Asklepios as a god).

The theater

The best-preserved structure at Epidauros lies not inside the sanctuary, but nearby: the theater, designed by Polykleitos (not to be confused with the fifth-century BC sculptor of the same name) and erected in the later fourth century BC (Figures 16.3 and 16.4). Theatrical performances were religious rituals for the Greeks, so it is not surprising that this sacred center should have one. The theater accommodated ca. 14,000 people, a testimony to the broad regional appeal of these festivals. The curved seating, or *cavea*, was built against a hillside and occupied more than a half circle. Stone seating gave the form regularity, the site permanence. Several passages allowed spectators access to seats. The horizontal *diazoma* divides the cavea into upper and lower halves, with the upper half steeper than the lower. Vertical stairways are found throughout, with twice as many in the upper half. At the base of the cavea lies the circular *orchestra*; here the chorus performed, chanting and dancing. Beyond lay the stage building, or *skene*, a platform for the solo actors (the *proskene*) with a backdrop. In the Greek theater, the skene is not attached to the cavea, but is separated by passageways on either side, *parodoi*, marked here at Epidauros by post and lintel doorframes. The Romans would later attach the skene to the cavea, now reduced to a half circle, thereby creating a unified architectural structure. Through time, with solo actors dominant in Greek and Roman theater, the stage building with its vertical backdrop became increasingly elaborate. Because the skene at Epidauros has survived only in foundations, the stage building is better appreciated elsewhere, such as at Priene (for the Classical-Hellenistic type) and Aspendos (the Roman type).

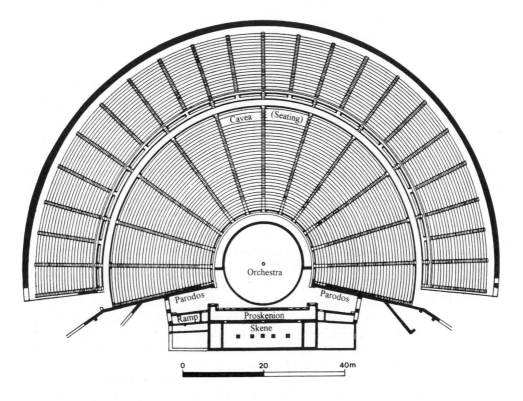

Figure 16.3 Plan, Theater, Epidauros

Figure 16.4 Theater, Epidauros. The stage building is modern

PRIENE: A SMALL GREEK CITY

The city of Priene, located in south-west Turkey near the Aegean Sea, is justly famous as an unusually well-preserved example of a Late Classical-Hellenistic city plan. It was never an important town, however, and its population was small, perhaps only 4,000. Despite its size, the city managed to equip itself with the public buildings characteristic of Greek city-states, including those necessary for democratic government. In the late Hellenistic period, its prosperity faded and, to the great fortune of archaeologists, the buildings were never replaced. As a result of this modest destiny, Priene shows us an ancient Greek city in a comprehensive way that richer, much rebuilt centers such as Athens cannot (Figure 16.5).

The building history of Priene is striking, for the city occupied two different sites in the Meander River valley. Although the existence of the early town, founded by Greek emigrants in the Iron Age, is attested from literary sources and coins, the exact location has never been identified; it must lie buried deep in accumulated silt. Indeed, as the river carried eroded earth down from the hills, the shoreline was continually shifting westward, and the town found itself more and more inland. In the middle of the fourth century BC, the citizens of Priene decided to move closer to the seacoast. Magnificently situated on a bluff overlooking the Meander River and, in the distance, the Aegean Sea, with a protecting mountain looming behind, this second Priene makes a dramatic impression on visitors.

With the river actively continuing to bear silt, even in their second location the people of Priene found themselves farther and farther from the sea, their economic prospects fading. A widespread destruction deposit indicates a damaging blow in the late second to early first century

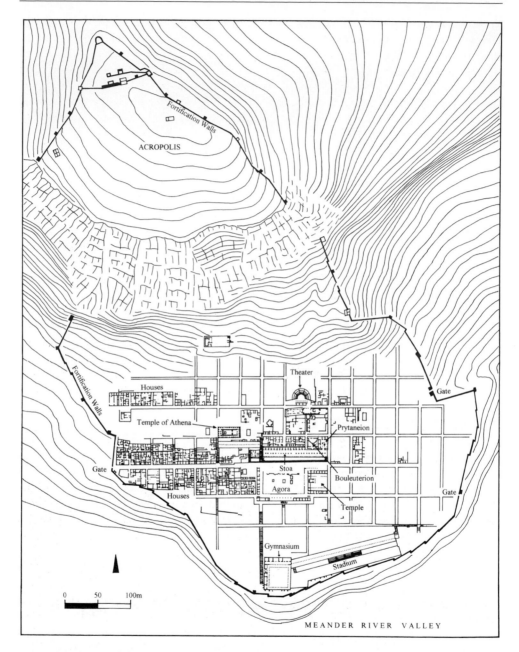

Figure 16.5 City plan, Priene

BC, possibly connected with the violent revolt of Mithridates VI, king of Pontus, against the Romans in 88–85 BC. Habitation dwindled, and the town would never recover.

The plan of the city refounded in the fourth century BC can be understood clearly both in overall scope and in details, thanks to excavations conducted by the German Archaeological Institute notably in 1895–8. The fortifications mark the perimeter, walls of neatly cut ashlar blocks that can still be followed for most of their length, tracing the curve of the bluff on which the city is located. In addition, the defense system incorporated the mountain behind. The layout of the town within the walls features streets at right angles in accordance with the principles of planning associated with the fifth-century BC urbanist, Hippodamos of Miletus. As in most planned Greek cities, the Hippodamian rules are not scrupulously followed. The agora, for example, does not straddle precisely the axis of the main east–west street, and the stadium, carved into a restricted space on the lower hillside, could fit only on the diagonal. In addition, the city proper lies on sloping ground; this too necessitated adjustments. The east–west streets, more-or-less level, permitted wheeled vehicles, but the north–south paths were too steep; steps were often added. As in many Aegean villages before the advent of the motor car, foot traffic, animal and human, must have predominated.

The open-air rectangle of the agora or city center is neatly defined by stoas on all four sides. The precise geometric form of this planned public space, characteristic of newly founded cities in Greco-Roman antiquity, contrasts with the irregular, ever-changing urban centers that developed gradually over the centuries, such as the Athenian Agora. The stoas themselves are simple structures, but inside their sheltered colonnades a great variety of activities took place: legal affairs, government offices, shops, perhaps shrines, and simply meeting and chatting; and they always offered good shelter during a cold winter rain or on a hot summer day.

Stoas also served as architectural screens hiding diverse buildings behind; with their uniform line of columns, they preserved the harmonious appearance of the public square. Here at Priene, the eastern stoa masks a small temple, probably dedicated to Zeus; and behind the western stoa lay a meat and fish market. Nestled against the hill behind the impressive north or Sacred stoa stands one of Priene's best-preserved buildings, the Bouleuterion or Council Chamber (Figures 16.6 and 16.7). The bouleuterion looks like a small indoor theater. Almost square in outline, it

Figure 16.6 Bouleuterion, Priene

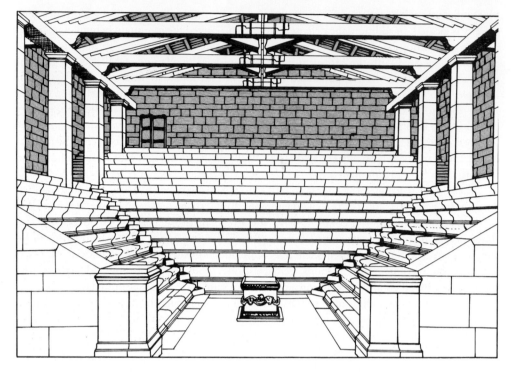

Figure 16.7 Bouleuterion, interior (reconstruction), Priene

has steeply rising rows of stone benches on three sides, seating for an estimated 640 people, and on the fourth side, between two doorways, a recess lined with stone benches for the presiding officials. In the center of the room stood a small altar used for the sacrifices performed at the beginning of each meeting. The wooden roof has not survived. Because of the width of the building, 14.3m, the roof needed the additional support of pillars set inside the room.

Below the agora on the side opposite the Bouleuterion lie the gymnasium and the stadium, cut into the south slope of the bluff in the second century BC. Because of the steep terrain, the stadium has a truncated plan, with seating on the north (city) side only. Fragments of the stone starting line, an addition of the Roman period, still exist, with cuttings that once held an elaborate starting mechanism, a rig of posts and cords that assured a simultaneous start for all eight runners. The gymnasium is noteworthy for unusual features preserved in the rooms on the north side of the court. The central hall served as a schoolroom for boys, many of whom carved their names on the walls. Over 700 names can still be read: for example, "The place of Epikouros son of Pausanias." Next to the lecture hall was a washroom. Stone basins placed on either side of the doorway served for rinsing feet, a row of basins along the rear walls of the room for hands and faces.

Up the hill from the Bouleuterion one reaches the theater. Built early in the city's existence, it preserves its Hellenistic Greek character despite some modifications in the Roman period (Figure 16.8). In Greek fashion as seen at Epidauros, the cavea is larger than a semicircle, although the rear section is truncated at the sides, and is separated from the skene by parodoi. But some features in this theater differ from Epidauros. Five stone armchairs, perhaps reserved for priests, line the orchestra. The stage building consists of two parts, a high raised platform in

Figure 16.8 Theater (reconstruction), Priene

front, the proskene (proscenium), and an even taller portion behind. The façade below the proskene is decorated with twelve columns that mark off a series of doors and panels, an effective backdrop for Classical plays performed in the orchestra by the chorus and solo actors. In the post-Classical theatrical tradition, the chorus lost much of its importance. The prominence of the solo actors was emphasized by placing them on top, not in front, of the proskene. For all spectators except the dignitaries in the front-row armchairs, the view would have been immeasurably improved.

To the west of the theater lie the remains of the Temple of Athena, the most important shrine of the city. Its terrace above the north-west corner of the agora dominates Priene, but only the foundations and five re-erected columns survive to indicate the temple's original dimensions. The temple is Ionic, not surprising considering that the architect, Pytheos, denounced the Doric order with its intractable corner triglyph problem as incurably defective. The ground plan is standard, provided with the standard pronaos, cella, and opisthodomos; in contrast, the surrounding colonnade differs from the expected, consisting of only eleven columns on each of the long sides instead of the normal thirteen. The proportions of the temple were much admired, and indeed Pytheos wrote a book about them (it hasn't survived). The temple is also of note for its distinguished patron. Alexander the Great, when he passed through in 334 BC, offered to finance the construction in return for the privilege of making the dedication. The Prienians gratefully accepted.

Below the temple, the main street continues westward from the agora to the main residential area of the town. The paved street, which slopes gently downward, has a good-sized drain running down its center. Off it on either side lie the foundations of numerous houses.

These discoveries, together with the Athenian houses (above, Chapter 15) and the roughly contemporaneous examples from Olynthos and Delos, give us a good picture of the home life of the solid citizen in ancient Greece.

As in other Greek cities, at Priene the houses consisted of a central courtyard lined by colonnaded porches and rooms behind (Figures 16.9 and 16.10). But here the rooms at the rear end of the court are emphasized: the roof line is higher, and consequently the columns of the porch are taller, more prominent. This architectural unit of a porch plus main room (*oikos*) recalls the megaron of Bronze Age Trojan and Mycenaean architecture.

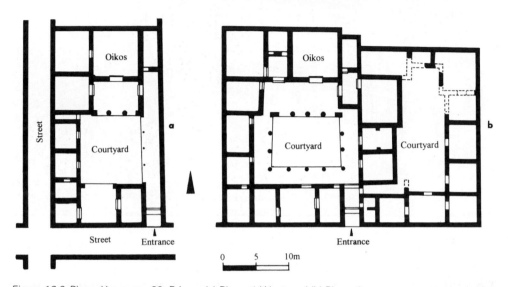

Figure 16.9 Plans, House no. 33, Priene: (a) Phase 1-West; and (b) Phase 2

OLYNTHOS: HOUSES

Additional information about Greek houses has come from Olynthos in northern Greece; with over 100 houses excavated, this constitutes the biggest sample yet known. Olynthos flourished from 432 BC until its destruction by Philip II in 348 BC; final abandonment occurred in 316 BC. Excavations were conducted in four seasons from 1928 to 1938 by David Robinson of Johns Hopkins University. With building foundations nicely preserved, the city layout emerges clearly, as do the plans of individual homes. The well-exposed urban plan makes us think of Priene, and indeed the population of the two towns was roughly the same. In contrast with Priene, however, religious buildings are lacking and public buildings are few; no doubt the excavators did not explore the appropriate places.

Certain aspects of the housing recall Priene. Blocks of adjacent houses sharing walls are neatly arranged along straight streets, laid out in parallel lines. Houses are similarly hidden from the street by an enclosure wall, and, inside, the courtyard is the focus. But there are differences. The normal shape of the Olynthian house is square, not rectangular (Figure 16.11). Moreover, behind the court lies a portico, the *pastas*, an intermediate space between the court and the small rooms behind. Also distinctive is the *andron*, or men's dining room. This, the most elaborate

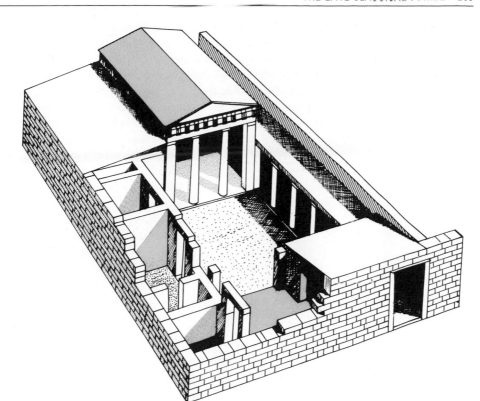

Figure 16.10 House no. 33, Phase 1-West (reconstruction), Priene

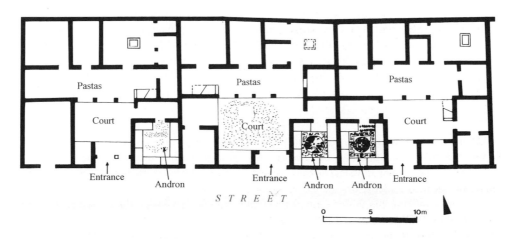

Figure 16.11 House plans, Olynthos

room of the house, frequently decorated with a floor mosaic, was set apart from the other rooms, with entrance often through a smaller anteroom. Here the man of the household received his guests; together they ate while reclining on benches set alongside the walls. Ancient Greek society permitted considerable freedom for men, but respectable women were restricted to the house and family, for whose maintenance and well-being they were responsible. Wives would not join these dinner parties. The only women present might be musicians and other entertainers.

As for the food, ancient Greek meals might well strike us as dull, simple, and lacking in variety. For one thing, tomatoes, peppers, and potatoes, mainstays of modern Mediterranean cooking, had not been introduced. New World plants, they were brought to Europe by Spanish explorers of the sixteenth century. Meals included bread, eggs, cheese, soup, cooked cereals, fish (especially dried and salted fish) but rarely meat; garlic, onions, beans and lentils, nuts and olives; olive oil (also used for frying); for dessert, figs and other fruits, and cakes, sweetened with honey (neither sugar cane nor the sugar beet was available). Wine, a staple drink, was routinely diluted with water, five parts water to two parts wine, with the water politely poured first into the krater, or mixing bowl; sometimes other, to us incredible, substances were added, such as sea water and even chalk or powdered marble. As today, certain places were famous for their specialties. The wine of the east Aegean was especially praised, from Rhodes, Knidos, Samos, Chios, and Lesbos. These islands and cities, and Thasos in the north Aegean, exported wine in large plain clay transport amphoras of distinctive shape (Figure 16.12). Often their handles were stamped while the clay was still wet. These stamps, which are widely found in east Mediterranean archaeological sites, give valuable information about manufacturers, public officials, and dates.

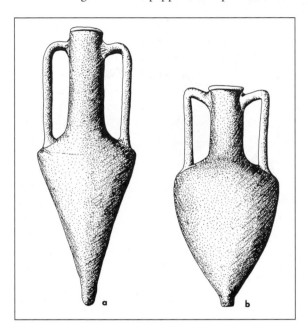

Figure 16.12 Transport amphoras from the Athenian Agora: (a) Chian, fourth century BC; and (b) Rhodian, third century BC

Floor mosaics

Floor mosaics were a characteristic feature of later Greek and then Roman cities, both in private houses and in public buildings. The floor mosaics from Olynthos are among the earliest from the Greek world. Floor mosaics, designs created by, first, colored pebbles and, later, cut pieces of stone set into cement, originated in the late fifth century BC at Olynthos and Corinth, becoming popular in the fourth century BC. Earlier mosaics have been discovered at such Iron Age towns as Ziyaret Tepe (south-east Turkey) and Gordion, but these Neo-Assyrian and Phrygian examples did not have direct descendants. Why the fashion arose in Greece in the later Classical period is not clear.

Mosaics fall into two groups according to the type of material used, *pebbles* and *tesserae*. For pebble mosaics, the earlier of the two types, naturally shaped and colored pebbles were used to make the picture, sometimes with baked clay or lead strips added as outlines. By careful juxtaposition of the colors, images could be shaded. In this the craftsmen making mosaics were following the artistic conventions already developed for prestigious mural painting in which volume and depth of space were indicated by shading, that is, by contrasts of light and dark achieved by the manipulation of different tones of color. Although the pebble mosaics of Olynthos are important, the finest known series comes from Pella, the capital of ancient Macedonia.

During the early Hellenistic period, pebbles were replaced by tesserae, cut pieces of stone, glass, or terracotta of various colors. By the second century BC, craftsmen could even cut pieces 1mm square; the mosaic technique that utilized such tiny pieces was called *opus vermiculatum*. With tesserae, shading could be controlled with greater precision. Tessellated mosaics were costly, however, because the laying of a mosaic floor demanded considerable time. Nevertheless, mosaics continued in popularity as floor decorations for the houses of the wealthy and certain public spaces (such as walkways under porticoes) through the Roman Empire – and in late antique and Byzantine times, notably in churches, for wall and ceiling decoration, and, in some regions such as Jordan, for floors.

The Alexander Mosaic from Pompeii is the best-known example of an early tessellated mosaic (Figure 16.13). Found in the *exedra*, a reception room of the House of the Faun, this large floor, 5.1m × 2.7m (without its perspective border), made ca. 100 BC, is believed to copy a lost wall painting of the late fourth century BC. In the panel, Alexander the Great faces off against Darius III, the Persian king, in the crucial Battle of Issos. In the lower half of the scene, soldiers, weapons, and horses collide and intertwine. The upper half is spare, with a dead tree indicating the landscape and upraised spears punctuating the otherwise empty space. In this void Darius, in the higher, focal point of the picture, makes eye contact with Alexander on our left; the confrontation of the two men rising above the mayhem distills the clash of powerful armies. Observed in a photograph or on the wall, as the mosaic is now displayed in the Archaeological Museum in Naples, the scene can be appreciated in its entirety. The ancient viewer, in contrast,

Figure 16.13 The Alexander Mosaic, House of the Faun, Pompeii. Archaeological Museum, Naples

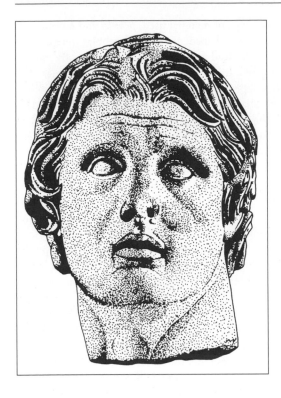

standing on the floor, had to be content with a close look at a few details or a distorted raking view.

Many other images of Alexander the Great have survived, made both during his lifetime and after, when a recollection of the great conqueror could serve as an inspiration (Figure 16.14). The portraits seen in sculpture and on coins may not be strictly faithful likenesses, but thanks to certain conventions – always a young man with distinctive wind-swept hair – his was an easily recognizable image. For imparting the message, recognition was all-important.

Figure 16.14 Alexander the Great, sculpture from Pergamon. Archaeological Museum, Istanbul

VERGINA AND HALIKARNASSOS: ROYAL BURIALS

With Alexander the Great, his father, Philip II, and Alexander's Macedonian generals who divided up their empire, kingship becomes an important element in the Greek world – a development of interest for us, because rulers, as we have seen so often, make significant contributions to the artistic and architectural environments of cities. Late Classical and Hellenistic monarchs are no exception. Priene, in contrast, has little to contribute here, being democratically governed, and without spectacular conquests or other achievements that merited expensive public commemorative monuments. (Priene did, however, receive gifts from outsiders; as noted earlier, Alexander the Great financed the completion of the Temple of Athena.) We shall now turn elsewhere, to tombs at Vergina and Halikarnassos – indeed both outside the heartland of Greek culture – to find striking examples of royal initiatives in material culture in the fourth century BC.

The importance of burials as expressions of wealth and power has been another theme characterizing many cultures of the Ancient Near East, Egypt, and the Bronze Age Aegean. Greece has differed from this pattern. After the early Iron Age with the spectacular burial at Lefkandi and the great funerary vases at the Dipylon cemetery in Athens, burials become relatively modest. When pressure did increase for public display, reaction set in: at Athens in 317 BC anti-luxury laws were passed in order to curb lavish spending on burial monuments. Excavations at Priene, so informative about other aspects of its urban plan, report little about the disposal of the dead, which took place outside the city walls. With the renaissance of kingship, the Greek world once again saw important attention devoted to burials.

Vergina

Among the many discoveries made by Manolis Andronikos of the University of Thessaloniki at Vergina, ancient Aegai, an early capital of Macedonia, the most spectacular were three royal tombs dated to 350–300 BC. Two of them, Tombs II and III, were found intact. Andronikos assigned Tomb II to Philip II. Evidence for this attribution is strong. Greaves (metal shin guards) of different lengths recall Philip's lameness. A tiny ivory portrait shows a man with only one good eye, which was the case for Philip; this distinctive characteristic is, moreover, a feature of the skull found in the tomb, as a forensic reconstruction of the skull has revealed. Tomb III may well belong to Alexander IV, the posthumous son of Alexander the Great, but the occupant of the other tomb is unknown.

The tombs were built of masonry and then hidden, buried beneath a broad low tumulus. In plan they are simple: Tomb I has one small room only, without a doorway; Tombs II and III consist of an antechamber and main room behind, both rooms barrel vaulted. Tomb II, the largest of these tombs, measures 4.46m wide by 9.50m deep. Its façade resembles the short end of a Doric order temple, with two half-columns, an architrave, a triglyph and metope frieze, and, above, a horizontal frieze panel painted with a hunting scene.

Tomb I, discovered robbed, was nonetheless decorated with a wall painting quickly hailed as one of the most important finds of Greek art in modern times. On the north wall in a space measuring 3.5m × 1.0m, Hades has seized Persephone and is carrying her off in his chariot. The colors are white, yellow, and purple. The drama of the composition, the quick, impressionistic brushwork, and the use of light and shadow to create volume make for a picture much more nuanced and expressive than the relatively stiff drawings on Attic black and red-figure pottery. This wall painting fulfills all expectations we have about the quality of monumental Greek painting, an art highly esteemed by the ancients, but which has almost entirely disappeared.

Halikarnassos

At the time of Priene's refoundation ca. 350 BC, not far to the south, in the city of Halikarnassos, the most celebrated of all funerary monuments in the Greek world was being erected: the Mausoleum. In contrast with the tombs at Vergina, the Mausoleum was visible, an expensive public display of royal prestige. Halikarnassos (modern Bodrum) was a small port founded by Dorian Greeks during the Iron Age migrations to the east Aegean; later it joined the Ionian confederation. Its most famous son was the historian Herodotus. During the fourth century BC, this region, known as Caria, was administered for the Persians by the Hecatomnids, a non-Greek Carian family based in inland Mylasa (modern Milas). Soon after he inherited the throne in 377 BC, Mausolus moved his capital from Mylasa to the seacoast, to Halikarnassos, embellishing it with new fortifications, a protected harbor, temples, and a palace. Upon his death, Artemisia, his widow and sister (a royal marriage in the Egyptian tradition), oversaw the completion of his magnificent tomb designed by Pytheos of Priene and Satyros of Paros and decorated in the Greek style. So splendid were its design, materials, and decoration that its name, Mausoleum, entered common parlance to denote any elaborate above-ground funerary monument.

The Mausoleum survived into the Middle Ages, when its final demolition took place at the hands of the Knights of St John, crusaders who used its cut stone in the building of their castle in the harbor. But its appearance can be reconstructed from descriptions of Pliny the Elder and Vitruvius, and from British (1857 and 1865) and Danish (1966–77) archaeological investigations at the site (Figure 16.15).

Figure 16.15 Mausoleum (reconstruction), Halikarnassos

The Mausoleum stood on the slope a short way above the harbor, in the north-east part of a large terrace, ca. 105m × 242m. Measuring ca. 30m × 36m × 42m, the building rose in four stages above the burial chamber. The subterranean tomb chamber was approached by a broad descending staircase, at the bottom of which were found horses, killed as a sacrifice. A massive stone plug blocked further entrance, but thieves broke in nonetheless, perhaps in the Middle Ages.

Of the building proper, the lowest stage was a tall base rising in three tiers. The second stage consisted of a temple-like colonnade of 36 Ionic columns surrounding a "cella." Above this, the third stage, a roof of 24 steps, rises like a pyramid to a small platform on which stood the fourth and final element, a statue of Mausolus and Artemisia in a quadriga, a chariot drawn by four horses.

The structure was lavishly decorated with sculpture. Pliny reports that the four best-known sculptors of Greece were commissioned to do a side each, Scopas (east), Bryaxis (north), Timotheus (south), and Leochares (west), but attempts to distinguish different hands in the best-preserved part of the sculpture, the reliefs from the top of the base that show the battle between Greeks and Amazons, have been futile. The other sculpture is highly fragmentary, and its placement on the monument remains hypothetical.

The Mausoleum illustrates the cultural mix that characterized the city of Halikarnassos. Erected by a non-Greek ruling family in the sway of Greek culture, the monument combines both native Anatolian and Greek elements. Although architectural details and sculptural style are Greek, the concept of the monument – a temple-like building on a high base – is very much at home in non-Greek West Anatolia. Distinguished predecessors include the Nereid Monument from Xanthos, ca. 380 BC, and, for the roof, the mid-sixth-century BC Pyramid Tomb at Sardis. Much of the pictorial imagery comes from the standard tradition of Greek architectural sculpture, and does not follow the lead of the Nereid Monument with its scenes of historical narration. Since this iconography in part recalled the victorious struggle of the Greeks against the Persians, we may be surprised that it was reproduced here by non-Greek rulers nominally subject to the Persian king. The allure and prestige of Greek art must have been so considerable as to outweigh the political references. Or, quite simply, the allegories embedded in the sculpture may have been invisible for Mausolus, Artemisia, and their Carian subjects.

CHAPTER 17

HELLENISTIC CITIES

Death of Alexander the Great: 323 BC

Attalos III bequeathes Pergamon to Rome: 133 BC

Battle of Actium: 31 BC

The nature of Greek civilization was considerably changed by the conquests of Alexander the Great. With the spread of Greek rule throughout western Asia and Egypt, the Greeks confronted and intermingled with neighboring cultures in a way never before imagined. This chapter explores four themes that dominate the Hellenistic period, with impact on the nature of cities: the continuing development of Greek art and architectural forms and styles; the effects of kingship on the urban experience; the Greek confrontation with non-Greek cultures; and the city as multi-cultural commercial center. Examples that illustrate these themes will be one rural temple, the Temple of Apollo at *Didyma*, and three cities, *Pergamon, Alexandria*, and *Delos*.

HISTORICAL INTRODUCTION

The conquests of Alexander the Great placed the Near East and Egypt in the hands of the Greeks. After Alexander's untimely death, a power struggle was inevitable: such tremendous spoils would not go uncontested. Alexander's young widow and son were no match for his battle-hardened Macedonian generals and soon disappeared. The generals divided the vast territory among themselves, and, in the Macedonian pattern, established new states which they and their descendants would rule as kings during the following three centuries (Figure 17.1). Prominent among them were Ptolemy, who took Egypt, establishing his capital at the newly founded Alexandria on the Mediterranean coast; Seleukos, ruling the Levant, Syria, and south-east Anatolia, with capitals at Seleucia (Seleukeia) on the Tigris and later also at Antioch; and Lysimachos, controlling Greece and western Asia Minor. In this age of kingdoms, the old Greek city-state continued in name only, a quaint tradition without effective power. The democracy of Athens was replaced by a governmental system indeed much older – and one that would lead smoothly to the Roman and later medieval empires.

The term 'Hellenistic' refers to these centuries of Greek ascendancy in the eastern Mediterranean and the Near East, even when (as in Mesopotamia and farther east) Macedonian kingdoms soon gave way to non-Greek local rule. The period witnessed important advances in knowledge, thanks to scientists, philosophers, and compilers, and to such institutions as the state-sponsored libraries at Alexandria and Pergamon, in which learning was carefully organized and preserved. In the arts, sculpture, painting, coinage, and mosaics elaborated the Greek tradition. But Greek culture, although spread over the surface of this vast territory, filtered down to the

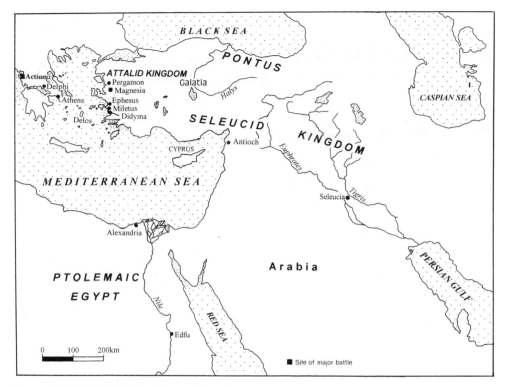

Figure 17.1 Major Hellenistic cities and kingdoms

non-Greek subject peoples in varying degrees. In Asia Minor, Hellenization penetrated all levels of society, but in Egypt and the Levant, the pre-Greek cultures held sway among the masses. The Greek rulers themselves were not entirely immune to oriental cultures: the Egyptian concept of divine kingship, for example, had an irresistible appeal.

The period also saw the increasing military and commercial involvement of the Romans in the eastern Mediterranean, with accompanying territorial gains. Strictly a regional Italian power in the fourth century BC, by the end of the Hellenistic period Rome controlled the entire Mediterranean. The culmination in the east came with a naval victory at the Battle of Actium in 31 BC. By routing Cleopatra, queen of Egypt, and her ally Mark Antony, Octavian (later Augustus Caesar) completed the Roman takeover of Greece, Asia Minor, Cyprus, the Levant, and Egypt.

DIDYMA: THE TEMPLE OF APOLLO

Greek temple architecture was notable for its conservatism, and this attitude continued in the Hellenistic period. But the new era also valued the dramatic, the startling. No building exemplifies better this typically Hellenistic combination of the traditional with the innovative than the Temple of Apollo at Didyma (Figure 17.2). Moreover, ruined though it is, the Temple of Apollo is the best surviving example of the colossal Ionic temples of East Greece. From it we get some idea of the dimensions, the grandeur of the Temples of Hera at Samos, of Artemis at Ephesus.

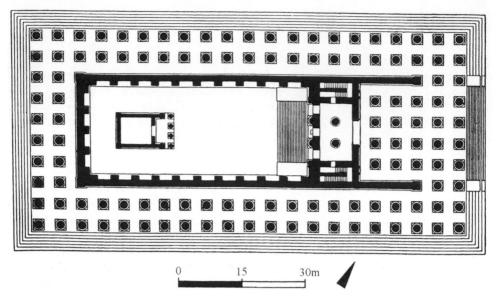

Figure 17.2 Plan, Temple of Apollo, Didyma

The temple is the principal building at Didyma, a religious center that contained, in addition to the major sanctuary of Apollo, a smaller sanctuary to Artemis, and numerous public buildings that catered to the welfare of pilgrims, such as stoas, shops, and baths. Immediately south of the temple was a stadium, the site of athletic events held every four years during the major festival, the Great Didymeia. The steps of the temple were used as seats; still visible are the many names carved on them by spectators.

Didyma belonged to the city of Miletus. Located some 20km to the south, Didyma was connected to Miletus by a processional route, a Sacred Way. Like Delphi, Didyma's Apollo sanctuary featured an oracle, but here a sacred spring served as the stimulus. The first major temple, built in the Archaic period, was burned in 494 BC by the Persians when they sacked Miletus and suppressed the Ionian revolt.

During the following 150 years the temple lay in ruins and the oracle did not operate. When Alexander the Great passed through, or so the story has it, the oracle and the sacred spring came back to life, and soon a new temple was begun, the temple one visits today. Designed by the architects Paionios of Ephesus and Daphnis of Miletus under the patronage of Seleukos, work continued throughout Classical antiquity, a period of 600 years. The temple was never finished. Traces of incomplete work can be seen on the exterior south walls of the temple: mason's marks (here, large letters), rough-picked surfaces, and bosses for securing lifting ropes – all of which were normally removed in the final finishing of a wall. The oracle was permanently shut down in the late fourth century AD during the reign of Theodosius I, as were all pagan cults. The building itself suffered severely in subsequent earthquakes. The visible remains of the temple were brought to the attention of western Europe by travellers beginning in the mid eighteenth century. Partial excavation followed during the nineteenth century, but the full clearing of the temple was not completed until 1906–13, under the direction of Theodor Wiegand for the Royal Prussian Museum in Berlin. After a long hiatus, the German Archaeological Institute resumed exploration in 1962, with a focus on areas outside the temple.

Didyma is located on a flat plain not far from the sea. A sacred grove of trees surrounded the temple on its west, north-west, and south west sides; and indeed the temple, with its many tall, slender columns, must have given the impression of a majestic forest. On the large stylobate, ca. 109m × 51m, a dipteral (double) colonnade around the cella was planned, ten columns wide on the short ends, 21 on the long, for a total of 108 columns, plus an additional twelve inside the pronaos. Three columns, nearly 2m in diameter, still stand to a height of 19.7m, giving an idea of the imposing vertical dimension of the temple. The normal order of construction was here reversed, with the colonnade coming after the cella. The variety of bases of the porch columns and their decorations demonstrates that columns were set up and completed in different periods, with many columns in fact never erected at all.

If the outside of the temple follows the traditions of Ionic architecture, the interior breaks from the typical, offering one surprise after another. At the back of the pronaos comes the first surprise: the expected entrance to the cella through the pronaos is blocked by an impossibly high threshold without steps. Above is a room, the east chamber, entered from inside the temple (see below); from here priests may have announced the oracular messages.

To proceed further into the temple, one must follow one of the two barrel-vaulted passages that descend from the far corners of the pronaos. One emerges from the dark, cave-like tunnels into daylight and another surprise: the cella of this temple has been replaced by an unpaved open-air court (ca. 53.5m × 21.5m) at a level much lower than that of the stylobate. At the far end of this *adyton*, or sacred area, stood a mini Ionic temple, the *naiskos*, which sheltered the bronze statue of the god, with either inside or just outside the sacred spring and laurel tree that inspired the oracle. The north walls of the adyton are carved with architectural plans, blueprints of a sort, to ensure uniformity in measurement and form: a network of finely incised lines, straight and curved, up to 20m long, that show design details of the columns and other architectural elements of the temple, their capitals and bases. These diagrams were incised ca. 250 BC when the adyton walls were built, well after the deaths of the initial architects, Paionios and Daphnis. Similar drawings have been found at Priene (Temple of Athena) and Sardis (Temple of Artemis) and in Egypt and in certain Gothic churches in western Europe (Chartres and Reims, for example).

From the west side of the adyton a broad flight of steps leads up to the east chamber, the room of the oracular messages. Staircases at each end give access to the roof. Some sculptural decoration was provided for the temple, notably pilaster capitals and frieze for the upper edge of the inner adyton walls, showing griffins. In Roman imperial times a frieze was carved for the exterior entablature. The head of Medusa appeared here as she had for centuries, protecting the temple against evil, but unlike the fierce gorgon of the early Archaic temple at Kerkyra, the Roman Medusa at Didyma is fleshy, petulantly frowning, and thoroughly tamed.

PERGAMON: A CITY IN THE ATHENIAN TRADITION

If the Hellenistic sense of the dramatic emerges clearly in the Temple of Apollo at Didyma, its finest urban expression comes in the layout of Pergamon, one of the leading cities of western Asia Minor during Hellenistic and Roman times. The siting of the city was spectacular, on a hilltop that rises at the back of a small coastal plain. The fortified summit, or acropolis, contained the palace and certain key public and religious buildings. The city continued down the gentler south slope (the other sides are steep), eventually spreading by Roman times onto the plain, now occupied by the modern town, Bergama (Figure 17.3). In its very layout, with palaces and temples raised high, Pergamon reminds us that this was the capital of a kingdom, not a

Figure 17.3 City plan, Pergamon

democracy – in striking contrast with Priene, where the agora and bouleuterion lie in the center of the city, with the Temple of Athena benevolently looking down from one corner. The correspondence at Pergamon between the natural topography and hierarchical society cannot be said to characterize Hellenistic cities – Alexandria, for example, lies on flat ground – but must be considered nonetheless a fortuitous and instructive coincidence.

Although inhabited from prehistoric times, this hilltop location was developed as a major city only from ca. 300 BC. Lysimachos, one of the generals succeeding Alexander the Great, entrusted a large part of his fortune to his officer Philetairos to guard at Pergamon. In 281 BC Lysimachos was killed in battle. When no one contested the treasure, Philetairos used this money, 9,000 talents (estimated by George Bean in 1966 as the equivalent of £10,000,000), to entrench himself on Pergamon's hilltop. By adopting his nephew Eumenes as his son, he founded a dynasty that would last until 133 BC. The Attalid kingdom soon expanded; at its height, after the territorial gains that followed its victory (with the Romans) over Antiochus III at Magnesia in 190 BC, it controlled most of western Asia Minor – roughly the equivalent of the Lydian kingdom of the sixth century BC. The Pergamenian kings viewed their capital as the cultural center of the Greek world, the Athens of its day; following the Athenian model, Pergamon became a major center for the visual arts. During the Roman period, the city continued in importance, its population swelling to ca. 150,000 in the second century AD.

The Acropolis

As the administrative, religious, and cultural heart of the ancient city, the acropolis has been the focus for archaeologists and tourists in modern times. The German Archaeological Institute, excavating at Pergamon from 1878 to the present, devoted its earliest campaigns to the acropolis. In recent years, project director Wolfgang Radt and colleagues have returned here to reconstruct portions of the Trajaneum, a major post-Hellenistic temple dedicated to the deified Roman emperor Trajan, the building that now dominates the skyline.

Fortifications, palaces, and the water supply

The hilltop forms a north–south arc, bowing out toward the east. Buildings are arranged in three sectors, north, east, and west, with protection secured on the north; royal palaces on the east; and a major shrine and the state library on the west. The vertiginous theater is nestled in the western curve of the hill. The northernmost tip of the acropolis is naturally protected, with the land dropping sharply. Here stood an arsenal or military storehouse of the third to second centuries BC, and next to it a barracks. The outer wall of the barracks, part of the north-east Hellenistic fortification wall, is particularly well preserved, with 32 courses of ashlar masonry still in place, and, with its seemingly sheer drop, shows how well protected this citadel once was.

To the south of the barracks, along the east edge of the citadel, first Philetairos, then his successors, built palaces, four complexes in all, loosely connected. These palaces, preserved only in ground plan, were large peristyle houses of the sort already standard in Greek domestic architecture: rooms arranged around porticoed open-air courts; decoration included mosaic floors. Cisterns, used for water storage, formed part of the sophisticated water supply system, developed probably in the second century BC. Water was brought to the city in a triple pipeline of terracotta pipes from a mountain source ca. 45km to the north. For the final ascent to the citadel, pipes possibly of bronze or lead were used, buried underground, their ends held fast by stone blocks cut with appropriately sized holes. Forced upwards under pressure, the water reached a central reservoir on the citadel; from here it flowed to the palaces and then down the hill to houses and public fountains and through the sewers. This water supply system was an early example of the sort of hydraulic engineering project that the Romans would extensively develop.

The Temple of Athena and commemorative sculpture

On the west curve of the acropolis lies the city's earliest and most important temple. The Temple of Athena, a Doric order temple of the fourth century BC, offers some surprises: it is rather small (stylobate: 21.77m × 12.27m), and it is oriented north–south, although parallel to the dominant contour, the west edge of the acropolis. But Pergamon envisaged itself as a cultural heir of Athens, so the choice of both Athena as patron goddess and the Doric order that defined her main temple in Athens can be understood as appropriate homage. A formal, permanent boundary to the space was created in the second century BC with the construction of stoas on three sides, the temple and the edge of the hill forming an oblique fourth side. The stoas had two storeys, with the Doric order used in the lower, the Ionic in the upper.

Figure 17.4 Gaul killing his wife and himself, Roman copy in marble, after a Hellenistic bronze original. Museo Nazionale Romano delle Terme, Rome

Beginning in the later third century BC, the kingdom won important victories. Chief among the vanquished enemies were the Gauls, central and east Europeans who raided Greece and Asia Minor in the third to second centuries BC, terrorizing the region, then extracting money in exchange for peace. Attalos I, king of Pergamon 241–197 BC, resisted their exorbitant demands, and in the ensuing battles ca. 230 BC defeated them. The Gauls retreated to central Anatolia, "Galatia," establishing themselves there. For Pergamon, these victories boosted the power and prestige of the city: these were triumphs that recalled the Greek defeat of the Persians in the early fifth century BC. The patron goddess of the city deserved thanks. The court in front of her main temple was judged the best place for display of appropriate commemorative monuments, notably a series of bronze statues of defeated Gallic warriors. The bronze originals have disappeared, but inscribed statue bases and later Roman copies in stone of certain statues have survived. The most dramatic shows a warrior who, having killed his wife, now thrusts his sword into his own chest (Figure 17.4). The statues are of interest not only for the extreme emotion they convey and the poignant, dignified treatment of the humbled enemy (so different from the degrading depictions of the enemy in Egyptian and Ancient Near Eastern art), but also for the ethnographic information about a non-Greek people: the mud-caked hair, the mustache, the torque worn around the neck.

The stoas too served as vehicles for the message of Pergamenian triumph, with relief sculptures of captured weapons decorating the front of their upper storey. And lest such achievements go unnoticed outside Asia Minor, the victories were also commemorated with sculpture on the Athenian acropolis (the so-called Lesser Attalid Dedication) and at the major international sanctuaries at Delphi and Delos.

The library

To the north of the Athena Sanctuary lay one of Hellenistic Pergamon's greatest cultural institutions, the library. Built by Eumenes II (ruled 197–159 BC), the library consisted of four small rooms plus an entrance, with additional storage elsewhere to accommodate 200,000 scrolls. Manuscripts were stored on shelves that lined the walls. Avid collectors, the kings of Pergamon were notorious for their aggressive methods of acquisition. In one case, the owners of Aristotle's library hid it rather than let it be impounded; as a result, the manuscripts rotted. Eventually, in 41 BC, the Pergamenian library was presented by Mark Antony to Cleopatra VII of Egypt, the last of the Ptolemies, after a fire burned the Alexandrian library. This collection would in turn be destroyed in AD 642 by the Arab conquerors of Byzantine Egypt.

The main writing material in Greek and Roman antiquity was papyrus, made from a reed-like plant (*cyperus papyrus*) grown especially in the Nile delta. During a shortage in the second century BC, the Pergamenians promoted an alternative writing material, heretofore little used: parchment (the word in fact derives from the name "Pergamon") or vellum, made out of treated and scraped calf or lamb skins. Too thick to be rolled into scrolls, these skins were cut into sheets and bound together as pages; thus originated the *codex*, or paged book, the format we still use today. The eventual triumph in late antiquity of parchment over papyrus is due to Christian practice; from the second century AD on, the more durable parchment and the codex had become the preferred material and format for biblical texts.

The theater

The Temple of Athena overlooks the most dramatic structure of Pergamon, the theater (Figure 17.5). Built against an unusually steep hillside, this theater is confined to a narrow wedge of seating. Nevertheless, a crowd of 10,000 could sit here. The long narrow reinforced terrace was judged too unstable for a permanent stage building, so a skene made of wood would be set up for festivals, then taken down afterwards. Holes still visible in the terrace served for the inserting of the supports. The terrace was dominated at its north end by a Temple of Dionysos, the god in whose honor theatrical performances were given. Originally of the second century BC, remodelled in the early third century AD, the Ionic prostyle temple was placed at the top of a long flight of steps with the focus on its front, a design standard in Roman temples of the Tuscan (native Italian) tradition.

Figure 17.5 Theater, Pergamon

The Great Altar

Immediately to the south of the Athena sanctuary, the palaces, and the gateway to the acropolis, downhill on a slightly lower level, stood three more important public and religious buildings (Figure 17.6). The first is the Upper Agora, an open court lined with Doric stoas on three sides;

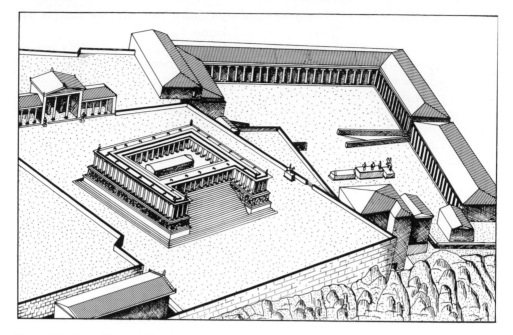

Figure 17.6 Great Altar and Upper Agora (reconstruction), Pergamon

the upper city's main street crossed this market area. The second building consisted of a *heroon*, devoted to the cult of the rulers of Pergamon, venerated as heroes after their deaths – not as gods, it should be noted, in contrast with the Hellenistic rulers of Egypt. The third and most famous is the Great Altar, dedicated to Zeus and Athena, built by Eumenes II some time after 190 BC to commemorate military victories. The building stood by itself, not as an appendage to a temple. It was, however, placed in orientation to the Temple of Athena above: its west side aligned with the temple's long west side.

Although it faced west, the altar (measuring ca. 36m × 34m) was set within a large walled compound entered from the east. The visitor, coming in at the back, had to walk halfway around the altar in order to ascend it, a programmed route that allowed a proper sequential inspection of the relief sculptures decorating the platform on which the altar stood. Indeed, the sculptures were placed at the bottom of the building so they could be inspected, in contrast with architectural sculpture from earlier times (Figure 17.7). By climbing the steps on the west one reached the altar proper, a table inside an open-air porticoed court.

Today only the foundations can be seen, a large grid. The famous relief sculptures that decorated the building are now displayed in Berlin, where they were taken during the first excavation campaigns (1878–86). The sculptures on the exterior show a subject long familiar in Greek art, the battle of gods vs. giants: an allegory for the struggles of Greeks against the forces of chaos, of which the Pergamenian triumphs over their rivals, some non-Greek but many Greek, might be considered the latest chapter. Unusual, however, was the deliberate arrangement of the gods to suit the route followed by the visitor – an organization of the subjects that conformed to the Hellenistic love of compiling and classifying. On the east, for example, upon entering the court the viewer would see the main Olympian gods, such as Zeus and Athena, Apollo, Artemis, and Leto. On the north-west wing, facing the distant sea, were sea gods, such as Okeanos and

Figure 17.7 Great Altar (detail), Pergamon. Pergamon Museum, Berlin

Triton. To ensure proper understanding, the names of the gods were inscribed above the frieze, the names of the giants below. Sculptors carved their names below those of the giants; fragments of 15 names of a total of perhaps 40 have survived, but little is otherwise known about these artists. The style of the reliefs, sometimes called Baroque after the resemblance to seventeenth-century European art styles, emphasizes strong emotions, violent gestures caught in mid action, and, with deep drilling, the dramatic contrasts of light and shadow. These sculptures, a high point of Hellenistic art, would exert much influence on later Greek and Roman sculpture.

A second, smaller frieze decorating the interior walls of the altar court illustrated the life of Telephos, son of Herakles and legendary ancestor of the kings of Pergamon. This sculptural program makes a political statement: by linking the Pergamenian monarchs with the great heroes of the legendary past, this allegory aimed to legitimize their right to rule. Like the gigantomachy, this relief also had lasting artistic consequences. Carved in the mid second century BC, shortly after the gigantomachy, this frieze is the earliest known example of continuous narration, that is, an episodic story that unfolds in panel after panel – as we shall see, a type of pictorial presentation that the later Romans would greatly enjoy.

Down the hill: the Sanctuary of Demeter and the Gymnasium

The south slope was always an integral part of the city. Philetairos included the upper half in his fortified city, his walls passing above the already existing Demeter Sanctuary. Eumenes II enlarged the fortified area with a new set of walls, over 4km in length, that extended down to the base of the south slope where one entered through a monumental gateway. His city was over four times larger than that of Philetairos. During the Roman Empire the city expanded onto the plain. In each of these three major stages, the city was laid out according to a different grid plan. Under Philetairos, the grid was not strictly followed. Indeed, the topography of the hillside did not favor a strict Hippodamian grid plan, and certain streets gently curved. With Eumenes II, the new grid followed a new orientation. The Romans, ca. AD 100, changed the grid and orientation once again; strictly applying the grid, they integrated new buildings on the acropolis (such as the Temple of Trajan) with construction on the plain.

Buildings uncovered on the south slope include those appropriate to a residential area, such as houses, shops, baths, and market areas (such as the Lower Agora). But in the middle lie two major religious and public complexes, the Sanctuary of Demeter and the Gymnasium, both explored in the early twentieth century.

The Sanctuary of Demeter, the goddess of agricultural plenty, existed in pre-Hellenistic times. A mystery cult, the rites of Demeter were conducted in secret, for initiates only (as was the case at Eleusis, just outside Athens, the center of the worship of Demeter), and the layout of the sanctuary reflects this. The Ionic temple and accompanying altar lie in a long rectangular court, enclosed on three sides by stairs and on the fourth by the entrance gateway (propylon). The east half of the long north side is occupied not by a stoa but by benches cut out of the rock, seats for the participants in the mysteries. This important fertility cult had great appeal to women. Reflections of this can be seen in the dedication of the temple and altar by Philetairos and his brother Eumenes to their mother, Boa, and also in the patronage of Apollonis, queen and wife of Attalos I, thanks to which the construction of the sanctuary was completed.

The huge gymnasium complex lies just to the east. As noted earlier, not only sports training but also a wide range of social, intellectual, and religious activities took place in a Greco-Roman gymnasium. Built on three levels well adapted to the sloping ground, the gymnasium at Pergamon ranks among the most spectacular examples of the type. The upper level, much remodelled in Roman imperial times, consisted of a court lined with porticoes; rooms off the portico include a small theater, originally roofed, used for lectures and concerts, and a hall with an apse on either end, devoted to the cult of the deified Roman emperors. Beyond the east portico a bath complex was added in Roman times.

The south portico fronts on an extremely long stoa that extends far beyond the borders of the courtyard. Below it lies an extra track, roofed – an unusual feature that allowed exercise in inclement weather. Originally the track was lit by windows in the south wall, but in the late Hellenistic period the windows were blocked in order to strengthen the walls.

The middle court immediately downhill from the underground track features a long rectangular exercise area, itself lined on the north by a stoa. At one end of this court is an altar and small temple, dedicated, inscriptions tell us, to Hermes and Herakles. The temple walls were inscribed with the names of young men victorious in athletic contests held here. From this middle level one descends to the lowest court, a roughly triangular area reserved as a playground for boys, via a staircase with a rare type of Hellenistic ceiling consisting of two barrel vaults that meet at right angles. The impressive fortification towers seen today on top of this wall were added by the Byzantines in the twelfth century, when these walls marked the limits of a smaller town much contracted from its Roman heyday.

The Asklepeion

The cult of Asklepios was brought to Pergamon in the fourth century BC and thrived throughout Hellenistic and Roman antiquity. The sanctuary lies at the edge of the town, 2km to the south-west of the gate of Eumenes II, approached by a street lined with porticoes. Continuously remodelled and improved through antiquity, the remains visible today stem largely from an important refurbishing during the reign of the Roman emperor Hadrian (ruled 117–38). The physician Galen, along with Hippokrates (of Kos) one of the best known doctors of Greco-Roman antiquity, practiced here in the later second to early third centuries AD.

Pergamon, Athens, and Rome

Pergamon cultivated its role as the cultural successor of Athens, with sculpture and architecture visually reinforcing this theme. As noted earlier, the Pergamenian kings promoted their military triumphs with art and architecture in the great pan-Hellenic centers of Delphi and Delos, and also in Athens itself. In addition to the Lesser Attalid Dedication on the Athenian acropolis, the kings of Pergamon presented Athens with two elaborate stoas. The better preserved, a majestic two-storeyed stoa, a donation of Attalos II (159–138 BC), was erected on the east side of the Athenian agora. Reconstructed in the 1950s, the building now houses the Agora Museum and the offices of the Agora excavations.

The Attalid dynasty came to a rapid end with Attalos III (ruled 138–133 BC), a bizarre, cruel man with an interest in poisons. His strangest act was his last: in his will, he left his kingdom to Rome. Although involved for decades in the squabbles of the Hellenistic kings, drawn in to help first one side, then another, the Romans had resisted establishing a permanent presence in the eastern Mediterranean. But the bequest of Attalos III could hardly be refused. Rome took possession of western Asia Minor, reorganized it as the province of Asia, and during the next 100 years gradually assumed control of the entire east Mediterranean region.

ALEXANDRIA: CAPITAL OF A BICULTURAL KINGDOM

Alexandria, the capital of Egypt under the Ptolemaic dynasty and the major Hellenistic and Roman city of the eastern Mediterranean, offers a striking contrast with Pergamon. Most significantly, few remains of the ancient city have come to light. A large modern city lies on top, always an impediment for archaeological knowledge, but much had already been destroyed even before Alexandria was revived in the nineteenth century as a seaport to connect modern Egypt with rich Europe. Our knowledge of ancient Alexandria comes principally not from archae-ological remains but from written sources, especially from the detailed description of Strabo, the geographer and traveller from Asia Minor who visited Egypt in 25 BC at the beginning of Roman rule. The topography offers a second contrast: Alexandria lies on flat ground. Lastly, while Greek Pergamon grew within the Hellenized world of western Asia Minor, the Ptolemies controlled a land with its own distinct and deeply rooted civilization. While not blending particularly well – rather like mixing oil with water – at least Greeks and Egyptians cohabited without too much friction.

Alexandria was founded by Alexander the Great, the first of many cities he created along his route of conquest. Alexander laid out the basic plan of the city, but the Macedonian architect Deinokrates is credited with arranging the details (Figure 17.8). For this newly founded settlement on flat land, a grid plan seemed appropriate and practical. But the many parks and gardens and the use of broader streets helped soften the severity of the traditional grid plan and make it more appealing. Two main streets crossed at the center of the plan. In addition, a causeway was built, the *heptastadion*, to connect the small island of Pharos with the mainland;

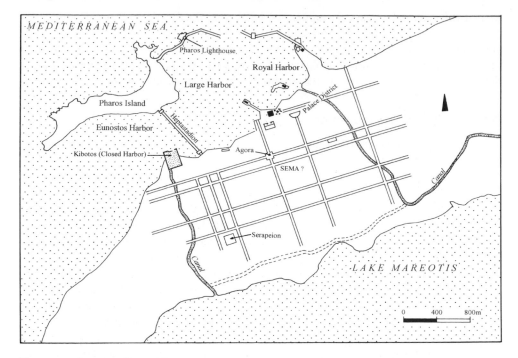

Figure 17.8 City plan, Alexandria

harbors thus lay on either side. The city was linked with the Nile via Lake Mareotis to the south, and canals. Notable Hellenistic buildings included the palaces and gardens of the Ptolemies; the Mouseion, a research center in the palace complex that included the great Library; the Sema, which sheltered the tombs of Alexander the Great and the Ptolemies; the Pharos, the monumental lighthouse that took its name from the island on which it stood; the Serapeion, a temple to Serapis (see below) with accompanying shrines to the Egyptian goddess Isis, among others; and the cemeteries. Except for the cemeteries and fragmentary remains of the Serapeion and the Pharos, all the above have disappeared.

The Pharos

The Pharos, or lighthouse, ranked among the Seven Wonders of the World, a list made during the Hellenistic period that apparently considered only monuments from the region controlled by Alexander the Great and his successors. Although largely destroyed, the Pharos stood into the Middle Ages and can be reconstructed with a good amount of certainty from ancient descriptions, depictions on coins, and medieval Arabic descriptions, as well as from its surviving base, incorporated into the late fifteenth-century Mamluk Fort of Qait Bey. In recent years, underwater exploration in the harbor, directed by French archaeologist Jean-Yves Empereur, has revealed additional traces of the building. Designed by Sostratos of Knidos during the reign of Ptolemy II (ruled 285–246 BC), the Pharos consisted of three sections, each one inset from the one below: square on the bottom; octagonal in the center; and circular on the top with, inside, the beacon, a fire whose light was projected far out to sea by reflectors. The original height of the Pharos is estimated at ca. 120m.

Greeks and Egyptians: separate but equal?

The Ptolemies remained resolutely Greek, with, for example, only the last of its rulers, Cleopatra VII, learning the Egyptian language. Nonetheless, attempts were made to connect the two cultures. The Ptolemies married their siblings, royal marriages that recalled the traditional Egyptian style. Further, the Ptolemies were careful to respect Egyptian religious traditions, allowing Egyptian temples to continue as always and supporting them with generous donations. Indeed, ancient Egyptian temples – their layout, decoration, symbolism, and function – are best understood by examining Ptolemaic examples. In newly built temples in the traditional style, such as the Temple of Horus at Edfu (in Upper Egypt), the Ptolemies had themselves depicted in the time-honored way, piously venerating the gods. The style of these reliefs carved on temple columns and walls was always pure Egyptian. Only their names indicate that the rulers shown were not Egyptian but Greek.

Figure 17.9 Serapis, basalt statue, Roman copy of an early Hellenistic original. Villa Albani, Rome

The creation of the Hellenistic god Serapis shows how a mixture of Greek and Egyptian could work (Figure 17.9). A combination of the Egyptian Apis bull and Greek divinities, notably Hades, the Greek god of the underworld, this god, shown in realistic Greek style as a mature man with a beard, was promoted in order to unite the inhabitants of Egypt, both Greeks and Egyptians, in religious practice. The Egyptians did not take to Serapis, perhaps because he did not look at all Egyptian, but the Greeks and later Romans worshipped him with enthusiasm. Here was a deity who powerfully combined the Greek underworld with Egyptian mystic beliefs, an association that became increasingly appealing as cults offering the promise of life after death gained ground in the Classical world.

Painted decoration in the cemeteries of Alexandria tried blends of Greek and Egyptian motifs and styles, but the results were awkward, never quite gelling. How different this situation is from the Archaic period, when Greek art smoothly absorbed and digested Egyptian practices in sculpture and architecture! Now, in the Hellenistic period, like Egyptian art, Greek art was set in its aims and conventions. Neither had much to say to the other.

DELOS: A COMMERCIAL CENTER

In contrast with Pergamon and Alexandria, grand capitals of kingdoms, the tiny island of Delos in the central Aegean prospered in the mid Hellenistic period as a commercial port, specializing in the slave trade (Figure 17.10). Under the nominal control of Athens with the Romans keeping

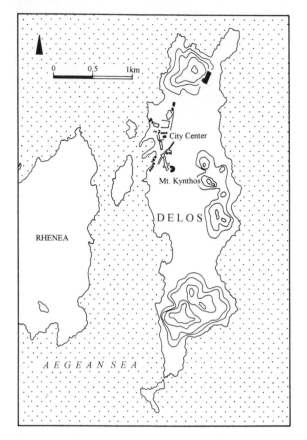

Figure 17.10 Overall plan, Delos

a close watch, Delos was effectively run by and for the merchants who had settled there from all parts of the Mediterranean. The Italian contingent was especially important; indeed Delos gives us the earliest remains of a Roman trading community anywhere in the Mediterranean.

Delos had long been venerated as the place where Leto gave birth to her twins, Apollo and Artemis. From the Iron Age on, the sanctuaries to the twin gods attracted pilgrims from the entire Greek world. Holding special importance for Ionian Greeks, including Athens as well as the islanders and cities of Ionia proper in the east Aegean, Delos was the site of the Delian League and its treasury in the fifth century BC, then continued in the following centuries as a small but independent city-state.

The status of Delos changed dramatically in 166 BC. Rome awarded the island to Athens, who established the island as a free port: goods could be brought in, sold, and exported without taxes on the transactions. For the next century, until it was sacked by troops of Mithridates VI, king of Pontus, in 88 BC during his revolt against Rome, and again by pirates in 69 BC, Delos was a highly prosperous commercial center, the Singapore or Hong Kong of the eastern Mediterranean. After the first century BC destructions, its commercial and religious importance declined drastically. In addition, with trading patterns changed during the Roman Empire, there was no need to resurrect Delos. Only a small number of inhabitants continued until final abandonment in the seventh century AD.

Excavations conducted on Delos since 1873 by the French School of Archaeology at Athens have uncovered much of the ancient city (Figure 17.11). The sheltered harbor on the west coast

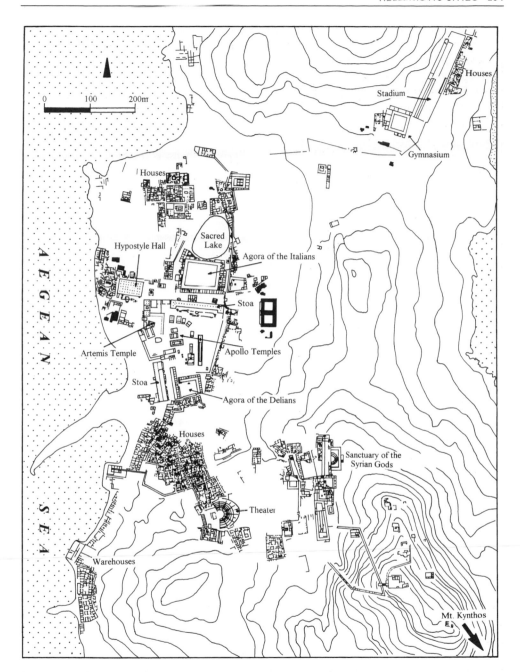

Figure 17.11 Plan, city center, Delos

served as the focus for settlement. The sanctuaries, established early, lie close by. To the north and to the south spread the residential and commercial districts, with newer shrines among them. Certain houses of the Hellenistic period are particularly magnificent, with peristyle courts decorated with fine mosaics. But life here was fragile: on this waterless island survival depended on careful collection of rainwater in cisterns underneath the courtyards.

The commercial buildings consisted notably of warehouses and agoras. As large spaces both covered and uncovered, such architecture rarely gives clues as to the precise actitivities that went on inside them. At Delos we are much helped by inscriptions, which mention (often in fragmentary form) who was doing what, but even they infrequently answer the questions we might like to ask. For example, where were the thousands of slaves bought and sold? We don't know, for any of a number of spaces might have served the purpose. Warehouses lining the shore south of the harbor are good candidates, for they are separated from the residential neighborhood behind by a wide street, a possible division between the transient commerce coming and going by sea and the permanent housing behind. Less likely, perhaps, is the Stoa of Poseidon or Hypostyle Hall (modern name) of the late third century BC (Figures 17.12 and 17.13). Its architecture is unusual and puzzling: its precise function is unknown, although it has been classified as a commercial building. A large covered hall, it measures 65.45m × 34.30m. Solid

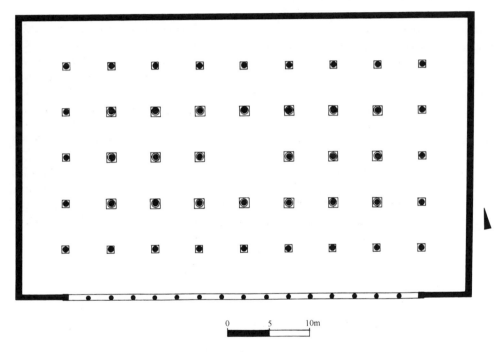

Figure 17.12 Plan, Hypostyle Hall, Delos

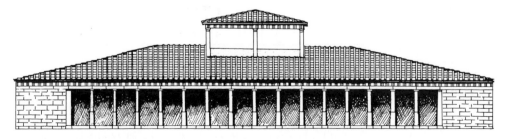

Figure 17.13 Hypostyle Hall (reconstruction), Delos

walls form three sides and turn into the fourth, where a line of 15 Doric columns form a broad entrance. Inside, the hipped roof is held up by 44 columns, arranged nine columns in five rows, with no column in the center. The outer 24 are Doric, the taller, inner 20 Ionic; the eight central columns, forming a square, held up a lantern with a *clerestory*, for illumination. A clerestory is a section of a building that rises above adjacent parts; the higher walls carry windows, bringing light into the interior. We met the clerestory in Egyptian houses and the Hypostyle Hall at Karnak, and we will see it again in the basilicas of Roman architecture and of Early Christian church architecture.

The agoras, open-air squares, have often been cited as places where slaves were traded. But this is only a possibility, not proven. Clearly commercial centers, the agoras tend to be filled with religious items, such as altars and shrines, but this reminds us of the religious atmosphere in which business was conducted in Hellenistic Delos. In the absence of a strong governmental authority, the gods were invoked as witnesses; transactions were always sealed with oaths sworn to the gods.

The largest agora of Delos, the Agora of the Italians, lacking the religious features seen in other agoras, must have served a different purpose. Built in the late second century BC, this agora consists of an irregular rectangle, roughly 70m × 50m, lined with a portico of 112 Doric columns (Figure 17.14). Beyond the portico lay alcoves. Shops were entered from the outside, thus separated from the functions of the interior of the agora. Could this be a center for the slave trade? Evidence is not forthcoming. Instead, equipped with a palaestra and bath for sports, a space usable for the gladiatorial combats Romans enjoyed watching, and possibly a banquet hall, this agora may have been a clubhouse and recreational facility for the Italian community on Delos. With an entry through a single propylon, the walled space looks defensible too, a consideration that may have interested a minority community far from home. If so, the agora may well have been put to the test in 88 BC, when the soldiers of Mithridates VI attacked, massacring the Italians in the eastern Aegean. After the defeat of Mithridates and the reassertion of Roman power, the agora was repaired, but then was finally abandoned in 60–50 BC as Delos fell into decline.

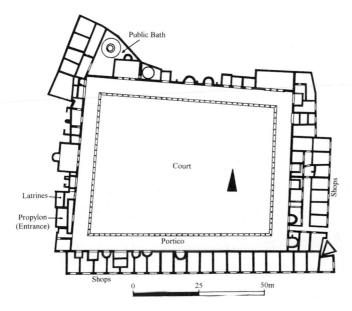

Figure 17.14 Plan, Agora of the Italians, Delos

PART THREE

CITIES OF ANCIENT ITALY AND THE ROMAN EMPIRE

CHAPTER 18

Greek and Etruscan cities in Italy

Greek settlements in South Italy and Sicily: eighth to third centuries BC

    Syracuse captured by the Romans: 212 BC

The Etruscans: flourished from the eighth to second centuries BC

In the later first millennium BC, the center of power in the Mediterranean basin shifted westward to the city of Rome. Rome was established as a permanent settlement during the early Iron Age, but several centuries passed before this village grew to regional and international prominence. As it developed, the Roman state borrowed from, then conquered, two urban cultures well established on the Italian peninsula beginning in the early Iron Age: the Greek (in south Italy and on Sicily) and the Etruscan (centered in Etruria, largely modern Tuscany, north of Rome). Other cultures encountered and absorbed would exert less tangible influence: Phoenician settlements in western Sicily, Sardinia, coastal Spain, and North Africa, of which the greatest was the city of Carthage near modern Tunis; and several rural, regional cultures in Italy and Sicily. Before we turn to Rome itself, let us examine the urban achievements of the first mentioned, the Western Greeks and the Etruscans, keeping in mind their place in the culture history of the Mediterranean basin and their legacy to the Romans (Figure 18.1).

GREEK CITIES IN SOUTH ITALY AND SICILY: PAESTUM AND SYRACUSE

Greek colonization of the Italian peninsula and Sicily began in the mid eighth century BC, according to the assertions of such later Greek historians as Thucydides (later fifth century BC) and to discoveries of Greek pottery of the geometric style on urban sites in Italy. The Greeks did not step into the unknown; instead, these towns represented a new chapter in ongoing trans-Mediterranean trade relations, developed notably by the Phoenicians. The earliest such settlement was established by Euboean Greeks at Pithekoussai on the island of Ischia near modern Naples. Other foundations quickly followed, with Kyme (Cumae) on the Italian mainland opposite Pithekoussai and Naxos on the east coast of Sicily among the earliest; the latest colonies were established in the fifth century BC. The Greeks stayed on the coastal plains, thus minimizing confrontations with local peoples. A rural area for agriculture, precisely delimited, surrounded the town; the countryside contained important religious sanctuaries as well as farmhouses. As for the broad limits of their territory, the Greeks did not seize land north of Naples, no doubt because it fell within the hegemony of the powerful Etruscans (see below), nor did they settle in western Sicily and Sardinia, areas already claimed by the Phoenicians.

Figure 18.1 Italy and the central Mediterranean

Important colonizers included the island of Euboea and the cities of Corinth, Megara, and Miletus; Athens and Sparta surprisingly founded only a few. Reasons for this great wave of emigration to south Italy, Sicily, and elsewhere (notably the Black Sea region) include over-population and consequent food shortage in the homeland; an escape for political dissidents in societies in ferment; and a sense that Greek life could be effectively conducted, even thrive, on distant soil. Institutions were similar, with West Greek cities organized as *poleis*, self-governing city-states. In contrast, tyrannies dominated, democracy never gaining a solid foothold. Relationships with the founding, or mother, cities were normally strong, but it is important to note that the new towns were not satellites of the founding cities but instead enjoyed complete independence. Prospering especially from agriculture but also from trade, the Greek cities of south Italy and Sicily made their mark in the Mediterranean and were accepted as full-fledged members of the Hellenic world. Indeed, we have already encountered an important sculpture group dedicated by a Sicilian Greek at the panhellenic sanctuary at Delphi: the "Charioteer of Delphi," the gift of Polyzalos, tyrant of the city of Gela, after his victory in the chariot races in the Pythian Games at Delphi in either 478 BC or 474 BC (Figure 14.5).

The history of the Western Greeks differed somewhat from that of Greeks to the east. They did not have to face the threat of Persian invasion; but Carthage was a perpetual menace, and the region, lying between Carthage and Rome, suffered during the ongoing conflict between these two cities, the Punic Wars (264–146 BC). The Greek cities gradually fell to the expanding Roman Republic, the takeover completed with the Roman capture of Syracuse in 212 BC. At least on Sicily, however, Greek language and culture continued until the Arab invasion of the island in the ninth century AD.

Paestum (Poseidonia)

Poseidonia, generally called by its later Roman name of Paestum, is the best known of the Greek cities on the Italian peninsula, thanks to four well-preserved monuments: three temples of the sixth and fifth centuries BC and the figural paintings from the Tomb of the Diver. Serious exploration of the site began in the eighteenth century, with excavations conducted throughout the twentieth century primarily by Italian archaeologists.

Founded ca. 600 BC by migrants from the south Italian Greek colony of Sybaris, Poseidonia was located on a low ridge just inland from the modern coastline in an area with scant traces of previously existing inhabitants. The attraction was fresh water and good farm land. In the absence of a natural anchorage, ships were simply hauled up onto the beach. For two centuries the city remained Greek; democracy developed here, as a bouleuterion discovered in the agora attests. In 400 BC, the Lucanians, an Italic people based in the interior, captured the city. The Romans absorbed the town in 273 BC, establishing a Latin colony and changing its name to Paestum. Decline soon set in. A major north–south road built in 133 BC, the Via Popilia, bypassed Paestum, and cities in the Bay of Naples (60km to the north) became the prosperous centers for maritime trade. The silting up of local streams caused flooding and created malarial swamps. During the later empire population declined, and by the seventh to ninth centuries AD settlement had shifted completely to the healthier hills inland.

Aerial photos have shown that in the Roman period, at least, the city was laid out according to Hippodamian principles, with parallel streets crossed by others at right angles (Figure 18.2). A 4.8km-long fortification wall, originally Greek, enclosed the city, with four main gates roughly aligned with the compass points. Although the sixth-century BC plan of Poseidonia is not known, it has been assumed that the early city was similarly organized in a grid. Such a plan is known from surveys conducted at sixth-century BC Metapontum, another Greek colony in south Italy, and seems characteristic of layouts of cities newly founded on flat ground. The orientation of Greek Poseidonia's plan must have differed from the Roman, however, for the north and south city gates and the three great pre-Roman temples form a line that deviates from the Roman grid.

The three Archaic and Classical temples, built in the Doric order favored in West Greece, are among the best preserved anywhere in the Greek world (Figure 18.3). Despite general conformity to the standard principles of Greek architecture, all show certain features of construction and design that can be classified as regional West Greek practice. Some details, such

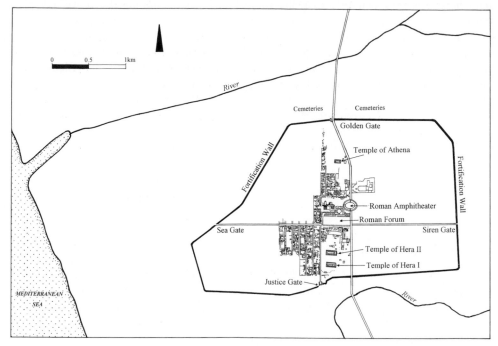

Figure 18.2 City plan, Paestum

as those that anticipated solutions used in Periklean buildings on the Athenian acropolis, indicate that West Greece was no architectural backwater, but instead a center of innovation.

The temples stand in a north–south line in the middle of the city, each oriented toward the east. They are built of local stones, travertine (a local limestone) and sandstone, for, unlike in Aegean Greece, marble was lacking in this region. The oldest is the Temple of Hera I, dated to the mid sixth century BC. Some of its features diverge from the expected. Measuring ca. 54.3m × 24.5m, thus broader than usual, its colonnade has nine columns on the short sides, 18 on the long. In addition, the cella, whose floor is higher than that of the porch, a Western Greek feature, has a central row of columns, recalling – perhaps deliberately, perhaps accidentally – the earlier temple of Hera on Samos. This row may have served to divide the sacred space into two, perhaps for two cults, with one side for Hera, the other for Zeus. Columns feature a favorite Greek architectural refinement: *entasis*, a convex swelling, here almost a bulging out, of the vertical line. The *echinus*, the lower half of the column capital, resembles a flattened mushroom with its especially low, broad profile.

The second great temple, built ca. 500 BC, was dedicated to Athena, according to finds of votive figurines recognizable as Athena (Figure 18.4). This temple, ca. 33m × 14.5m, has a colonnade with the normal six columns on the short sides, 13 on the long, a front porch (pronaos) but no opisthodomos. Above the colonnade lies an unusual entablature: from bottom to top, (a) an architrave of the usual sort, (b) an extra course of sandstone; (c) a triglyph and metope frieze, not sculpted; and (d) a pedimental space without a horizontal cornice on the bottom, but with, at the top, pronounced projecting raking cornices.

When we enter the temple, we see that the deep porch, set well behind the outer colonnade, is framed by eight Ionic columns: four on the façade and two on each side (the second of which

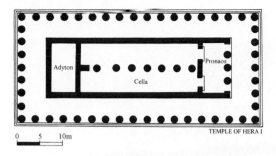

TEMPLE OF HERA I

0   5   10m

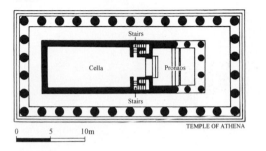

TEMPLE OF ATHENA

0   5   10m

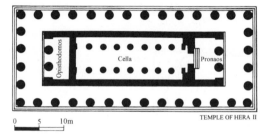

TEMPLE OF HERA II

0   5   10m

Figure 18.3 Plans, Archaic and Classical temples from Paestum: Temple of Hera I, Temple of Athena, and Temple of Hera II

is engaged in the anta). This use of Doric and Ionic columns in the same building marks the first appearance of a combination so strikingly developed 50 years later on the Athenian acropolis. The porch columns and cella walls are not aligned with the columns of the outer colonnade – another feature common in West Greece. The cella has no interior columns, in contrast with the Temple of Hera I, but two elaborate stairwells flank its doorway, providing access perhaps to an upper room over-looking the cella and the cult statue.

The last, largest, and best preserved of the three is the Temple of Hera II, built ca. 470–460 BC next to the earlier Temple of Hera I. Again, the votive materials indicate the dedicatee. It measures ca. 60m × 24.25m. Its exterior columns, arranged six on the short sides, 14 on the long, were originally covered with stucco, in order to hide irregularities in the stone and imitate marble – another Western Greek feature. Both porch and opisthodomos are present, each with two columns *in antis*. The cella has two rows of internal columns, thereby creating a nave and two aisles; the columns directly supported the ceiling and roof, but not, apparently, a gallery above the aisles. The exterior elevation is standard Doric. Neither metopes nor pediments were sculpted. Architectural refinements include curvature of the stylobate, the slight tilting in of columns, and entasis; except for the latter all rare in West Greece – but all will be present in the Parthenon.

The cemeteries lay outside the city, as was typical in the Greek world. Particularly striking is the Tomb of the Diver of ca. 480 BC, discovered by Mario Napoli in 1968 during explorations 1.5km to the south of the city. This simple burial of a man with few grave goods would hardly merit our attention were it not for its well-preserved figural paintings, important survivals of panel paintings from the Early Classical period. The tomb was constructed of five travertine slabs, four sides and a lid, all painted, inserted into a rectangular cutting in the rock, fitting around an unpainted floor (Figure 18.5). The underside of the lid illustrates a young man diving from a platform into a pool, the scene that gives its name to the tomb. The four sides show men at a banquet, reclining on benches, with two per bench as was typical, and attendant servants and musicians. Two pairs are romantically occupied, while others watch them or else play *kottabos* (a game in which one flings wine dregs from a cup at a target), or play the flute and the lyre. The scenes seem straightforward depictions of daily life, although because of the funerary context, we

Figure 18.4 Temple of Athena, Paestum

Figure 18.5 Tomb of the Diver (reconstruction), Paestum

should keep open the possibility of other meanings, such as funerary celebrations or activities projected for the afterlife (see below, concerning Etruscan tomb art). In terms of composition and technique, the painting consists of figures and objects placed on a ground line with no attempt at depth of space, and solid colors (without shading or added internal details) within outlines – features that we would expect of Archaic Greek art.

Syracuse

The island of Sicily, centrally located in the Mediterranean just 3km from the Italian peninsula and 160km from Africa, has always been a crossroads of cultures. In Greco-Roman antiquity, Syracuse was its most important city. Founded by Corinthians in the second half of the eighth century BC, the town expanded from the small but defensible island of Ortygia ("the Partridge") with harbors on either side to the mainland beyond. In the mid sixth century BC island and mainland were linked by an artificial causeway (Figure 18.6). The city became one of the largest in the Greek world: its population during the Classical period may have reached 250,000, comparable only to Athens.

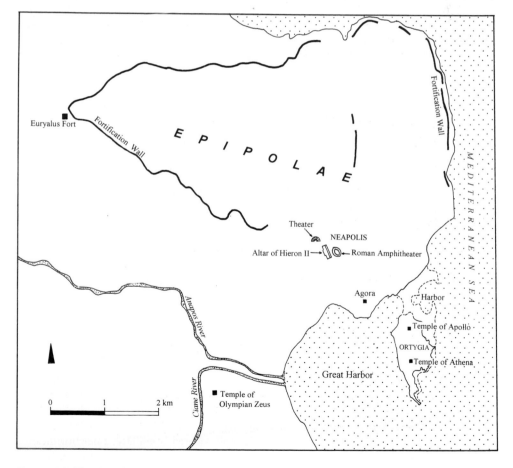

Figure 18.6 City plan, Syracuse

Syracusan prosperity derived from agriculture, limestone quarries, and the harbors. But the city's political history was turbulent. As was typical in Sicily, tyranny rather than democracy remained the dominant form of government. As elsewhere, the ruler had an important role in creating works of art and architecture. However, in a brief evaluation of three tyrants, we shall see that not all Syracusan rulers saw the need to promote themselves through art and architecture.

In 480 BC, the deposed tyrant of Himera (north Sicily) requested help from the Carthaginians. In response, Gelon, tyrant of Gela and Syracuse, marched forth at the head of a coalition force and won a great victory. The triumph at Himera over the non-Greek Carthaginians became the western equivalent of the Battle of Salamis, the Greek victory over the Persians; indeed, Herodotus recorded them taking place on the very same day. According to Diodorus Siculus, the Carthaginians were able to secure light armistice terms; grateful to Damarete, Gelon's wife, for her helpful intervention, they presented her with a gold crown weighing 100 talents. In commemoration of the victory she had a *decadrachm* struck from this gold, a coin worth ten Attic drachmas, an unusually large denomination: the "Damareteion" it was called, named after her. The coin has not survived. But its commemorative purpose may be reflected in a beautiful silver decadrachm that has come down to us. Depicted on the coin are, on the obverse (front),

Figure 18.7 Silver decadrachm with Arethusa, Syracuse. British Museum, London

a horseman in a quadriga, and on the reverse, the profile head of Arethusa, the local water nymph who served as the symbol of the city, surrounded by dolphins (Figure 18.7). After long believing that it celebrated the victory at Himera, numismatists now prefer to date this coin later, with some specialists connecting it with the expulsion of the tyrants in 466 BC.

Gelon himself celebrated his victory by commissioning two major Doric temples, one at Himera, the other at Syracuse, on Ortygia. The latter, dedicated to Athena, measures 52m × 22m, with six columns on the short end, 14 on the long. Local limestone was used for its construction, with marble for details. Rich touches (now disappeared) included doors of gold and ivory; in addition, the statue of Athena placed outside on the summit of a pediment was supplied with a golden shield, its reflection visible far out to sea. In the seventh century AD the temple was converted into a Christian church, with many elements, notably columns, incorporated into the design.

In 415–413 BC, the Athenians attempted to capture Syracuse, then an ally of Sparta. A dismal failure, this expedition opened the way to the Spartan triumph over Athens at the end of the Peloponnesian War. Soon after, the Carthaginians invaded Sicily, also unsuccessfully. By 405 BC the important tyrant Dionysios I had come to power. Ruthless at home, aggressive abroad, fighting against Carthage, the Etruscans, and other Greek cities, he ruled until 367 BC, controlling at one point over half the island. In contrast with many other rulers examined in this book, he did not choose to advance himself through visual imagery, sculpted or painted, or create great religious monuments. Instead, he patronized poets and writers; he himself composed tragedies. The architectural project for which he is remembered is military: a new fortification system protecting Syracuse. Ortygia was reinforced, and a new wall reached out to enclose the Epipolae plateau, an area eight times that previously fortified. At the far corner lay the Euryalus

Hill, crucial for defense. Little is known of the fort built here by Dionysios, but later reinforcement of the fourth and third centuries BC is well preserved. It includes a sophisticated complex of towers, dry moats or ditches cut from the bedrock, and underground passages allowing soldiers quick access to the different parts of the walls and to the dry moats, in order to clear them of debris thrown in by the enemy.

The third century BC was dominated by the tyrant Hieron II (ruled ca. 271–216 BC). He showed himself a true ruler of the Hellenistic age: influenced by the monarchs of the Hellenistic east, he and his wife Philistis were the first rulers of Syracuse to have themselves depicted on the city's coinage. His building projects consist of big public monuments, exactly what we expect from a successful ruler, the remodeling of a theater and a monumental altar. The theater illustrates the transition from Greek design to Roman. Enlarged to hold 15,000 people, the theater, cut out of a hillside, consisted of a half-circle of seating with a closely placed stage building with an elaborate architectural backdrop. Unified seating and stage building would become the hallmark of the Roman theater, with the Romans surpassing the Greeks by their ability to construct on flat ground (with vaults) as well as on hillsides. Near the theater Hieron II had a monumental altar built for the annual sacrifice of 450 oxen at the feast of Zeus Eleutherios. Not associated with a temple but free-standing – recalling in this feature, at least, the later Altar of Zeus at Pergamon – this altar is notable for its huge size (198m × 22.8m).

Hieron II had developed a close and friendly connection with Rome. After his death, the relationship soon turned sour, and in 212 BC the Romans captured and sacked the city after a bitter siege lasting two years. Among the victims was Archimedes, a brilliant mathematician and inventor. With this victory the Romans completed their takeover of South Italy and Sicily, and focused their attention on their long-standing rival in the central Mediterranean, Carthage.

CARTHAGE

Although Carthage lies outside the scope of this chapter, its historical importance justifies this brief homage. Founded by Phoenicians from Tyre in the late ninth century BC, Carthage, located just north of modern Tunis, became the greatest of the many Phoenician colonies in the central and west Mediterranean. Supported by a rich agricultural hinterland and good harbors and well placed for trade, the city expanded its sphere of influence throughout the western Mediterranean. Eventually it came into conflict with Rome, also expanding, The two clashed in three series of wars, the Punic Wars (264–146 BC), which included such dramatic exploits as a march over the Alps into Italy by the Carthaginian army, complete with elephants, under the leadership of the general Hannibal. In the end the Romans defeated the Carthaginians and destroyed the city in 146 BC. Recolonized by the Romans in the later first century BC, Carthage became a major urban center during the Roman empire and late antiquity. Excavations conducted since the late nineteenth century, and intensively since the 1970s, have revealed much of the city's Punic and especially Roman past.

THE ETRUSCANS

We now turn to the Etruscans, a people occupying the Italian peninsula north of Rome during much of the first millennium BC. Distinct from the Greeks, heavily influential on the Romans who eventually absorbed them, the Etruscans had a singular culture that is still imperfectly understood. Before examining their cities, with a focus on architecture and tombs, a short survey of key aspects of Etruscan history and culture is in order.

Etruscan history and culture

We follow the Romans in naming the Etruscans: "Etrusci," not the Greek "Tyrrhenoi," or their own names, "Rasenna" or "Rasna." Like the Greeks and the Latins (Romans), they were an urban culture with important international connections. Much was absorbed from the Western Greeks with whom they traded, such as the alphabet, the Archaic style in sculpture and painting, and the monumentality of temples, yet close inspection reveals that the Etruscans had their own customs, divinities, and beliefs, which often seem, when judged by a Greco-Roman yardstick, full of quirks.

With their homeland close to Rome, the Etruscans were the first great rival of the Romans, and indeed ruled that city during the sixth century BC. They had a lasting influence on Roman culture. The extent of their contribution is debated, but seems to include the Tuscan temple type, the atrium house, realism in sculpture, the toga, the alphabet, so-called "Roman" numerals, rituals for laying out a city and divining the will of the gods, and a taste for bloodthirsty games.

Their language, written in a form of the Euboean Greek alphabet (which they transmitted to the Romans), first attested ca. 700 BC, nevertheless differs from Greek, Latin, or the other languages of ancient Italy. Indeed, it is not a member of the Indo-European language group, and has no known relatives. Because surviving texts are short, the language is imperfectly understood. Promise of a breakthrough was held out by the discovery in 1964 at Pyrgi, the harbor of Caere (Cerveteri), of three gold plaques, dated to ca. 500 BC, with the longest-known dedicatory inscriptions, all from Thefarie Velianas, a king of Caere, to the goddess Uni (Roman Juno) (= the Phoenician goddess Astarte). Two were written in Etruscan, and a third in Punic (Phoenician/Carthaginian). Unfortunately, the Punic and Etruscan texts are not exact translations of each other, so the value for decipherment was limited.

For Etruscan history, we rely particularly on Roman literature. The other main sources of knowledge about the Etruscans are their tombs, the impressive rock-cut chambers with painted or carved walls, in their most elegant manifestations, and, when untouched by tomb robbers, wonderful repositories of objects both local and foreign. Their cities, in contrast, have been poorly preserved, often beneath later towns, and have traditionally been of little interest for archaeologists accustomed to the handsome rewards of the tombs. Recent excavations of cities are aiming to rectify this gap.

The heartland of the Etruscans was Etruria, a triangular area marked by the Arno River on the north, the Tiber River and the Apennine Mountains on the east, and, as a north-west–south-east hypotenuse, the Tyrrhenian Sea on the west. This well-watered land of hills and plains is favorable for agriculture and the raising of animals. In addition, the region has mineral resources, iron (notably on the island of Elba), copper, and silver, in particular. International commerce developed in these resources, to judge especially from the Greek pottery found in Etruria, although major cities were never located directly on the seacoast, a response to the menace of piracy, an activity in which the Etruscans themselves earned notoriety.

The origins of the Etruscans have been a subject of controversy ever since Classical antiquity. In the eighth and seventh centuries BC, Etruscan culture attained a degree of sophistication unmatched by the other cultures of the peninsula. This unusual and rapid rise has piqued the curiosity of generations of scholars. What is the explanation? Were the Etruscans one of the many peoples already in place on the Italian peninsula in the early first millennium BC, or did they immigrate to Italy from elsewhere?

According to one theory circulating in ancient times, Etruscan culture was brought to Italy by invaders. Herodotus tells us they came from western Asia Minor, Lydian refugees from a famine. Other Greek writers identified them with Pelasgians, a shadowy Aegean people of the pre-literate period. Indeed, there are some surprising parallels in Anatolia: the tumulus burials (shared with the Lydians and Phrygians of Anatolia), and the inscription, in a language that resembles Etruscan, on a late sixth-century BC funerary stele from the north-east Aegean island of Lemnos.

In an opposing opinion, Dionysios of Halikarnassos (first century BC) concluded that the Etruscans were not immigrants into Etruria, but had always lived there. Indeed, archaeological evidence indicates a continuous evolution from the early Iron Age Villanovan Culture of northern and central Italy to the Etruscan. But the striking parallels with features from the Aegean, Anatolia, and even Europe to the north suggest that foreign influences penetrated Etruria in the formative stage of Etruscan culture. Thus, both sides in the ancient argument were to some extent correct.

The Etruscans did not have a unified government, but instead, like the Greeks, were organized in city-states, grouped in a league traditionally consisting of twelve members. Kings and aristocrats ruled the cities. During the eighth and seventh centuries, the Etruscans extended their influence northwards to the Po River valley, and to the south, to Latium and Campania. Etruscan kings ruled in Rome itself from ca. 600 to 509 BC. The Etruscans then suffered an extended series of blows. Defeated in a naval battle by Syracuse in 474 BC, Etruscan sea power declined. Gauls raided into Italy from the north in the fifth and fourth centuries BC, and Umbro-Sabellian tribes took the Etruscan cities of Campania in the course of their migrations westward across the peninsula. A long struggle with Rome ensued, ending finally in the early first century BC in complete Roman victory. Etruscans received Roman citizenship in 90 BC, and indeed Etruscan civilization was by this point completely absorbed into the Roman world.

Cities and their architecture

As stated above, the cities have not survived well in the archaeological record. City sites were long inhabited, even up to the present day in such interior towns as Perugia and Orvieto, causing the altering or obliterating of early remains. In addition, only the foundations of houses were made of stone, the superstructure consisting of perishable materials such as wood and sun-dried mud bricks. The same mix of materials, stone foundation and mud brick superstructure, seems favored in city walls, likewise often poorly preserved. But the attention of archaeologists is increasingly turning to the remains of cities to answer questions about Etruscan society that the better-explored tombs cannot.

In southern Etruria, the distinctive topography determined the siting of cities. River valleys have cut through the tufa, a soft volcanic stone that predominates here, leaving prominent hills with steep sides. Such bluffs offered fine defensive advantages, and the Etruscans habitually selected them for their

Figure 18.8 Villanovan hut-urn. Museo Nazionale Preistorico, Rome

town sites right from the early Iron Age or Villanovan period (from the tenth century BC). Homes then were simple, one-room huts with wattle-and-daub walls and thatched roofs. Design, construction details, and decoration of such houses are best known from small terracotta hut-urns, one popular type of container for the ash and bone remains of a cremated body (Figure 18.8). Such house models recall those from Iron Age Greece, indicating similar house design even if the Greek models served a different function: votives, not ash urns.

Town layout in the Etruscan heartland was apparently determined by the topographic demands of individual sites. Streets had to conform to the irregular contours of the hilltop locations. But the Etruscans were renowned for an orthogonal town plan, dominated by two main streets that crossed at right angles in the center of the town. The Romans favored this feature, and called the two streets the *cardo* (running north–south) and the *decumanus* (east–west). Orthogonal layouts are known especially from colonies on more hospitable level terrain; see below for a well-known example, Marzabotto. Within Etruria, the necropolis at Orvieto shows an orthogonal plan, with streets oriented according to the compass. In part of the contemporary cemetery at Cerveteri, efforts were made to create a regular plan.

Roman authors record the Etruscan ritual for laying out a new city. The Romans themselves borrowed the rite at an early date. The founder of a city yoked a bull and a cow to a plough and dug the perimeter line of the town. At the places where gates were intended, the founder lifted the plough out of the ground and carried it across the space. The gateways were thus breaks in the sacred circle, places through which mortals, animals, and their unclean possessions could pass. According to Servius (fourth century AD), the ideal Etruscan town had three gates, three main streets, and three main temples to the supreme divinities Jupiter, Juno, and Minerva. No Etruscan town has as yet displayed these features. They can be seen, however, at Cosa, a Roman colony planted in Etruria in 273 BC (see Chapter 19).

Marzabotto and Acquarossa

In the late sixth century BC, the Etruscans established a colony at the site of Marzabotto, near Bologna in the Po Valley, across the Apennines from Florence. Its ancient name is unknown. The settlement had a relatively short life. Gauls raiding from the north destroyed the town in the fourth century BC as they pushed the Etruscans back into their Etrurian heartland. Well-studied, Marzabotto is the classic example of early Etruscan orthogonal town planning.

As a new foundation, the town could be neatly planned. Indeed it was, with wide streets running north–south and east–west, and narrower streets in between (Figure 18.9). Although a single north–south artery is known, three broad east–west streets were discovered. One of the east–west streets can be identified as the decumanus, because there is a surveyor's mark at the intersection of the north–south street and only one of the east–west streets. All streets were lined with one or two drainage canals; stepping stones laid in the center of some streets protected pedestrians in case of overflowing rain, mud, and sewage. Temples and altars stood on a terrace to the north-west of the town proper, with three of the temples sharing the same orientation as the town grid. In contrast with Greek cities, an agora or city center with public buildings seems absent.

Both temples and houses consisted of wood and mud-brick superstructures erected on stone foundations. The houses were organized around a large central court bordered by a low wall and provided with a basin and, below, a cistern for the collecting of drinking water (Figure 18.10b). A covered drain ran out to the street. At the rear of the court, a large room opened in its entire width onto the court. This room was flanked on either side by a smaller room. This layout recalls

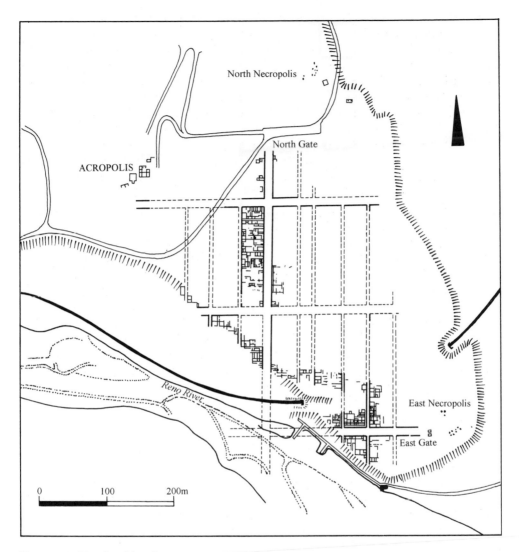

Figure 18.9 City plan, Marzabotto

the later Roman atrium house, thus suggesting an Etruscan ancestry for the distinctive Roman house form.

A Swedish expedition conducted from the 1960s at Acquarossa, near Viterbo, has discovered important remains of Etruscan houses dating to the seventh and sixth centuries BC. The lower courses were built of tufa blocks, the superstructure of the usual mud bricks reinforced with timber vertical and horizontal members. In addition, twigs were interwoven between the vertical and horizontal beams, then covered with plaster. This type of wall construction, wattle-and-daub, was described by Vitruvius, the important Roman architect and writer. Elements of the roof construction were found as well: roof tiles, both pans and covers, and, for the ridge pole, larger curved ridge tiles. The pan tile is the flat tile with its edges turned up, whereas the cover tile, as its name suggests, is a u- or v-shaped tile placed upside down over the edges of joining

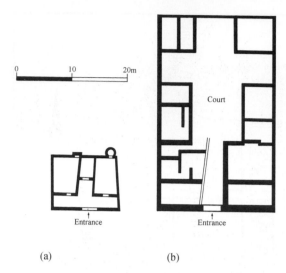

0   10   20m

Court

Entrance

Entrance

(a)   (b)

Figure 18.10 House plans, from
(a) Acquarossa and (b) Marzabotto

pan tiles in order to prevent rain from entering between the tiles. One pan tile even had one large hole and a small hole next to it, a small skylight or smoke hole.

The plans of the houses do not focus on a central court (Figure 18.10a). Instead, a porch leads into two rooms, or a small paved entrance hall gives access from the street to rooms to the right, left, and rear.

Veii and the "Tuscan Temple"

Veii, the Etruscan city closest to Rome, was important and powerful until Rome conquered it in 396 BC. Situated on a hill, the inhabited area of Veii displays an irregular layout (determined by the topography) with occasional sections in a grid. But investigations in this area have been sporadic. Of greater interest for us is the temple in the Portonaccio sanctuary outside the city walls. Although the sanctuary site is poorly preserved and details of the reconstruction are debated, this temple serves as a typical example of the Tuscan temple, an Etruscan form that would take its place in the forefront of Roman religious architecture.

The Tuscan temple was discussed at length by the Roman architect Vitruvius in his treatise *de Architectura*. The only book by an ancient artist or architect that has survived to modern times, this work has had enormous influence on the understanding and appreciation of Greco-Roman architecture. The Tuscan temple differs in key ways from the Greek temple (Figure 18.11). It sits raised on a podium, and, as Vitruvius tells us (Book IV. 7, 1–5), it should be nearly square, six parts in length, five parts in width, and further, it is divided into two equal parts, a deep porch in the front, and a cella (or cellas) in the rear half. One enters from the front only, where a special flight of steps leads up to the porch. The columns had smooth shafts, but sat on bases. The capitals of this so-called "Tuscan order" are similar to the Greek Doric. Overall the Tuscan temple offered an aesthetic impression quite different from the Greek: sitting high on a podium and with emphasis on the front, in contrast with the visual unity of the Greek temple provided by the surrounding steps and colonnade.

The temple at Veii consisted of a columned pronaos (porch) and a triple cella. The principal divinity worshipped here was Menrva, the later Roman Minerva. The reconstruction shows the

Figure 18.11 Reconstruction of an Etruscan temple, such as the Portonaccio Temple, Veii

Figure 18.12 Apollo, terracotta statue from Veii. Museo Nazionale di Villa Giulia, Rome

wide eaves, designed to protect the mud-brick walls from the elements, which give the building its distinctive top-heavy appearance.

The temple is dated to ca. 500 BC on the basis of its painted terracotta decorations. These terracottas consist of plaques that covered the wooden structure of the roof; *antefixes*, the decorations along the bottom of the roof tiles on the two long sides, some with spouts for the evacuation of rainwater; and *acroteria*, here a group of statues that stood one after another in a line on the ridgepole of the roof. Acroteria, both stone and terracotta, commonly decorated the roof lines of Greek temples. The Etruscans, who absorbed this Greek habit, became particularly fond of them. The best-known Etruscan acroterion comes from Veii, the lifesized "Apollo," a terracotta work whose style recalls that of Archaic Greek sculpture (Figure 18.12). This statue and its companions from the Portonaccio temple were hollow, and fired in a kiln; their bases were specially shaped to fit the curved tiles that protected the ridgepole. The examples from Veii were discovered broken, but carefully buried, a sign of the reverence in which they were held.

Tombs

The most striking monuments of the Etruscans are their tombs. Constructed in permanent material (frequently carved out of the bedrock, volcanic tufa), and often containing lively wall paintings, sarcophagi with sculpted decoration, and abundant grave goods, Etruscan tombs recall Egyptian burials and indicate a similar devotion to preparations for the afterlife. Surviving in vast numbers, these tombs and their contents are the major source of information about Etruscan culture. In addition, the tombs have been important repositories for Greek vases. The Etruscans appreciated Attic pottery, imported it, and placed it in their graves. Like Egyptian graves, Etruscan tombs have fascinated travellers, beginning in the Renaissance. George Dennis, a British traveller, published in 1848 a famous account of his explorations, widely consulted still today: *The Cities and Cemeteries of Etruria.* In addition to travellers, the tombs have also attracted looters, from antiquity to the present. With unscrupulous collectors ready to pay big money for ancient objects, tomb robbers are in steady supply. Because of these illegal excavations for which no records are kept, valuable information about the Etruscans has been lost for ever.

The Etruscans buried their dead in various ways. In the early centuries, cremation was the norm. In northern Etruria, cremation remained popular until the end of Etruscan civilization. By the fifth and fourth centuries, inhumation had become the prevailing rite in the south. In inhumation, the body was wrapped in linen cloths, and set on a funeral couch or stone-carved equivalent, or else placed inside a sarcophagus of wood or terracotta, or a stone imitation of a wooden chest. After cremation, the ashes were placed in an urn, either metal or ceramic (such as Figure 18.8), itself placed in a tomb. A terracotta sarcophagus (probably a large ash urn) of ca. 525 BC from Caere (modern Cerveteri) shows a man and wife, lifesize, reclining on a banquet couch (Figure 18.13). Unlike the Greeks and early Romans, Etruscan women dined with their husbands, one mark of the greater mixing of the sexes in private and public life. The couple smiles in the Archaic manner borrowed from the Greeks, but within a few centuries Etruscan urns and sarcophagi will show distinct portraits of individuals, not generic types (Figure 18.14). It is possible that the Roman predilection for realistic portraiture derived from Etruscan practices.

The tombs themselves were either carved out of the tufa or built underground with blocks of tufa. Sometimes a cluster of tombs was covered with a tumulus. In other cases, the tombs were not signalled above ground. The interiors of the tombs resembled the inside of a house, with rooms with pitched roofs, and, as such, complement knowledge about houses gleaned from the surviving foundations and debris discovered at habitation sites.

At Tarquinia, the vast cemeteries extend over the hills that ring the city. The Tomb of the Augurs, ca. 530 BC, is a good example of an early chamber tomb with well-preserved wall paintings (Figure 18.15). The tomb itself is small, a single chamber. The painted decorations display the arrangement popular from the sixth century onwards. In earlier tombs, painting was concentrated around a real or false doorway; depictions of animals or monsters, the guardians of the gateway, were frequent. In the Middle Archaic Tomb of the Augurs, the entire wall space of the chamber is covered. This decoration is divided into four horizontal zones: from bottom to top, (1) a dado, or base, painted black; above this, (2) a tall zone with human figures walking on a red base line; then (3) stripes, in place of the entablature; finally (4) a pedimental space. The rear wall has a false door painted on it, a door with a solid lintel resting on posts that slope inward, door leaves strengthened with broad studs, the symbolic gateway to the world of the dead. Male mourners stand on either side. Their costumes are forerunners of the Roman toga.

The rest of the room shows activities honoring the dead, funeral games and the attendant festivities. The Romans relished the violent spectacle of gladiator combats; these too began as

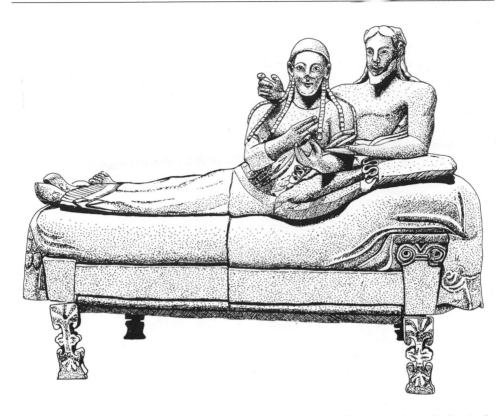

Figure 18.13 Terracotta sarcophagus of a married couple, from Caere (Cerveteri). Museo Nazionale di Villa Giulia, Rome

funeral games, and it is tempting to search for their origin in Etruscan practice. On the long side, two nude men whose names were painted above them wrestle over a stack of metal basins, prizes for victory. Their contest recalls Greek practice. But other figures painted on the walls of this tomb depart from the Greek world. To the left of the wrestlers, a robed man holds a curved staff. This official has been interpreted as an Etruscan version of the Roman *augur*, or soothsayer; hence the name of the tomb. To the right, a man wearing a demon mask holds by leash a dog and a man, blindfolded by a sack over his head, whose thigh the dog is ferociously biting. Blood is drawn; the shedding of blood, often depicted, was done for ritual or symbolic reasons. Blood gave vitality to dead souls, for example. Elsewhere, a similarly masked man is taunting a runner. These masked men are labelled *phersu* (= Latin *persona*), and seem to represent figures from the underworld. In the pedimental spaces, lions attack a deer or gazelle.

Other scenes popular in tomb decoration include daily life, as in the scene of fishermen on their boat, surrounded by birds, depicted on the rear wall of the interior chamber in the Tomb of Hunting and Fishing, Tarquinia, ca. 510–500 BC. In the period just after 480 BC, paintings of banqueters stretched out on couches and the dancers who entertained them became popular (see Figure 18.13 for an earlier sculptural representation). It is not known whether the depictions of banquets recalled the earthly life of the deceased, the funerary banquet held in his or her honor, or the delights of life in the hereafter. The Tomb of the Leopards, ca. 480–470 BC, also from Tarquinia, contains a good example of this subject.

Figure 18.14 Terracotta funerary urn, from Volterra. Deceased man (lid); battle with Gauls (front). Worcester (Massachusetts) Art Museum

Paintings in tombs of later centuries become gloomier, as if to reflect the pessimism of a society aware of its irreversible decline. Quality of execution is no less good, however. The Tomb of Orcus, at Tarquinia, shows new tendencies. The tomb consists of two chambers originally dug separately, but later joined by a corridor for unknown reasons. The first chamber was decorated ca. 350 BC, the second in the early third century BC. A banquet scene, damaged, decorated the walls of the first chamber. A demon, Charun, now is present at this oft-shown meal, thereby making clear that the event is taking place in the underworld. In Greek mythology, Charon was the man who ferried the deceased across the River Styx, one element in the descent to the underworld. The Etruscan Charun derives from the Greek Charon, but does not have a boat or the oar that are the attributes of the Greek figure. Instead he wields a hammer and is depicted in far more hideous form than Charon. He has companions such as the death angel Vanth and Tuchulcha, a monster who hovers by Theseus in the underworld scene in the second chamber of the Tomb of Orcus. In the painting from the first chamber of the Tomb of Orcus, Charun, himself painted in a macabre greenish-blue, the coloring of a decomposing body, is magnified by the presence of dark clouds that hover behind the banqueters.

A different type of Etruscan tomb was favored at Caere (Cerveteri). Here tumuli, sometimes up to 33m in diameter, have been piled above clusters of underground rock-cut tombs. Between

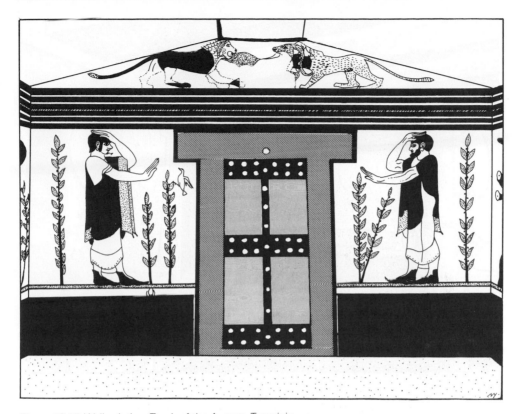

Figure 18.15 Wall painting, Tomb of the Augurs, Tarquinia

tumuli ran streets, with ruts cut for ancient hearses still visible. Sometimes tombs follow the same orientation, suggesting a family group; they would be reused for new burials. The tumulus, added on top, gave a touch of monumentality to a family plot.

In early tombs, rooms were strung out in a line, on an axis. The interiors were modeled on contemporary house types. We see a steep gabled roof line and a ridgepole in the Tomb of the Thatched Roof, early seventh century BC. Later tomb types are more compact in the arrangement of rooms. In the "Complex Etruscan Tomb Plan," rooms were placed next to each other, with their entrances off the main axis. Architectural features in this rock-cut construction included corbeled vaulting in the entrance area, doorframes, windows cut through to rear chambers, ceiling beams, columns with capitals, and an adaptation of a porch.

One of the largest tombs at Caere is the Tomb of the Painted Reliefs, early third century BC. In a layout popular in the Etruscan Hellenistic period, the tomb consists no longer of small chambers but of a single large space, its low ceiling held up by square pillars. The room is provided with ledges and niches for up to approximately thirty burials. There are no wall paintings. Instead, the walls and pillar faces display objects of daily life, such as cups, tools, kitchen tools, and armor, all carved from the rock or formed in stucco; this relief sculpture was then painted. Cerberus, the three-headed dog, guards the underworld, but humans are not shown. These relief sculptures count as an unusual decoration for an Etruscan tomb, and among the most striking. A simpler, earlier tomb with relief motifs is illustrated here, the Tomb of the Shields and Chairs, ca. 600–550 BC, also from Caere (Figure 18.16).

Figure 18.16 Tomb of the Shields and Chairs, Caere (Cerveteri)

Just as the Etruscans believed a person had a fixed number of years to live, so they believed their cities and indeed their nation had a finite existence. Their nation was destined to last ten *saecula*, a saeculum "corresponding to the longest lifetime of any person born at the moment the saeculum commenced" (E. Richardson 1976: 249). And indeed, if we reckon 10 × 80 years and begin at 800 BC, we reach the time of Augustus, by which time Etruscan culture had been absorbed into the Roman. The Etruscans were astonishingly prescient about the duration of their civilization.

CHAPTER 19

Rome from its origins to the end of the Republic

Traditional foundation: 21 April, 753 BC

Etruscan rule: ca. 600–509 BC

The Roman Republic: 509–27 BC

Julius Caesar: prominent from 60 BC until his assassination in 44 BC.

   His heir: Octavian

Battle of Actium: 31 BC

Octavian proclaimed Augustus in 27 BC

We now turn to the Romans, whose great civilization was the last to dominate the Mediterranean region in ancient times. From modest beginnings at a fording point on the Tiber River in central Italy, the city of Rome eventually controlled a huge territory stretching from Britain to North Arabia, from the Danube River to Morocco. Admiring and assimilating Greek and Etruscan culture in particular, the Romans created their own social and artistic synthesis, an outlook that would profoundly influence the Mediterranean world and Europe well after the demise of pagan antiquity, through the Middle Ages to the present day.

Roman history is divided into two main periods. After the initial settlement and a century of rule by Etruscan kings, the Romans organized themselves as a republic. The Roman Republic, the formative age of Roman civilization, lasted for nearly 500 years, from 509 to 27 BC. After decades of disruptive civil war, Octavian, later called Augustus, brought peace to the waning republic, then transformed the state into a newly harmonious unity, the empire. Prosperous and powerful for two centuries, the empire began to fracture in the third century AD. The Roman Empire would nonetheless last into the Middle Ages, until AD 476 in its western half, according to conventional periodizations, and until AD 1453 in its eastern, Byzantine half. This book will trace the Romans to the fourth century AD only, to the end of pagan antiquity, when the character of the empire was profoundly transformed by the change of the state religion to Christianity.

We begin with the origins of Rome and its subsequent development during the Republic. Because evidence from the city is fragmentary, Republican Rome having been heavily remodeled and rebuilt in imperial and medieval times, we shall complement our examination of Rome with visits to other, better preserved towns for a fuller understanding of the period: in particular Cosa, but also (in Chapter 21) two cities originating in the Republic that continued during the Empire – Pompeii and Ostia.

GEOGRAPHY

The city of Rome straddles the Tiber River at a point some 24km inland from the Mediterranean Sea, at a ford (using the little island in the Tiber) on the north–south route leading northward to Etruscan territory, and on the east–west route important in the transport of salt from the sea to the Sabine herders and other peoples in the interior. This trade is reflected in an ancient street name still used today, the "Via Salaria," the "Salt Road." The Tiber marks the boundary between Etruria (the Etruscan heartland) to the north, and Latium, a region dominated by Rome. Latium consists primarily of a plain, but also includes the Alban Hills and their lakes, created by volcanic activity; these hills are a good source of tufa, the soft brown volcanic stone that Roman builders favored. Rome itself encompasses seven main hills, projections of plateaus extending like fingers westward toward the Tiber. Originally streams ran in the valleys in between the hills. Three of the hills are close by the river, the Capitoline, the Palatine, and the Aventine, while the other four lay behind, the Quirinal, the Viminal, the Esquiline (a cluster of smaller hills), and the Caelian (Figure 19.1). As was true in Etruscan cities (and Veii is very close, only 20km to the north-east), early occupation took places on the hills.

EARLY HISTORY AND SETTLEMENT, CA. 753–509 BC

The early history of Rome, such as it can be reconstructed from the legends recounted notably by Livy, a historian of the Augustan period, divides into two periods, the first under the rule of four Latin kings (ca. 753–600 BC), the second under the rule of three Etruscan kings (ca. 600–509 BC). According to legend, Rome was founded either by Aeneas, a Trojan prince fleeing the destruction of his home, or by Romulus and his twin brother Remus on 21 April, 753 BC. As happened to such other leaders as Moses and Telephos (the mythical founder of Pergamon), Romulus and Remus, grandsons of a deposed king of Alba Longa and potential threats to the usurper, were set adrift in a basket into the river. Instead of overturning and drowning, the babies were rescued and reared to a glorious destiny. In this case, the rescuer was a she-wolf, who nursed the boys at her own breasts until a herdsman and his wife took the children under their care. From the early third century BC the Romans maintained a statue of a she-wolf to commemorate the miraculous event, and indeed kept wolves in cages on the Capitoline Hill. In adulthood, Romulus and Remus restored their grandfather to his throne, then founded a new city nearby: Rome (Roma, in Latin). Romulus killed his brother in an argument, but went on to rule. In the fabrication of the legend, the names of the city and its founder have mingled; which came first, Roma or Romulus, is not known.

Archaeology contributes an architectural and topographical reality to this mythological picture of early Rome. The earliest known settlement was on the Palatine Hill. Foundations of huts have been discovered, with holes to support the posts of the simple houses cut into the rock. Houses were simple: one room, with walls of wattle-and-daub and vertical poles supporting a thatched roof. They recall the houses of Iron Age Greece, and fit well with our picture of other Iron Age villages in central Italy. Further evidence for the appearance of these houses comes from hut-urns, small pots in the shape of huts that held the ashes of a cremated body (such as Figure 18.8). The steeply sloped roofs of these urns include a hole for the evacuation of smoke, and suggest that the roofing material was straw or thatch. Such a hut stood on the slope of the Palatine in later centuries. Carefully maintained until the fourth century AD, often restored, the Casa Romuli (House of Romulus) provided a conscious reminder of the humble origins of the city.

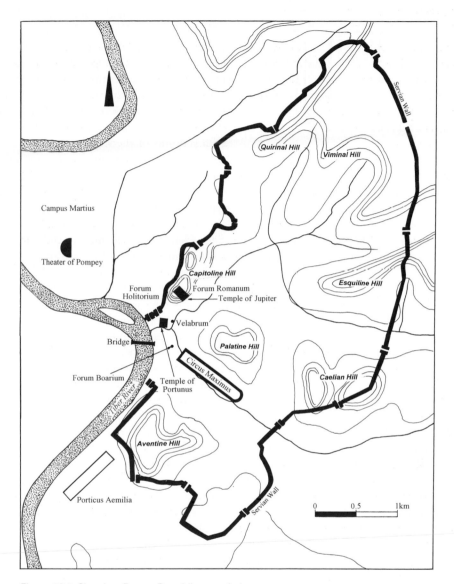

Figure 19.1 City plan, Rome, Republican period

The area at the foot of the north slope of the Palatine Hill was destined to be the site of the Roman Forum. In earliest times, however, this low-lying, swampy terrain served as a burial ground. In the eighth century BC, cremation was practiced. The ashes of the deceased were placed inside hut urns or small pots; these were in turn put in a larger pot, itself set inside a circular pit dug from the ground.

Changes in the town's material culture occurred in the sixth century BC, the century of Etruscan rule. The Etruscans, noted for their skills at regulating water, drained the swamps and channelled the streams that fed them, especially in the area that would become the center of the town, the Forum Romanum. Above, on the Capitoline Hill that lies adjacent to the Palatine,

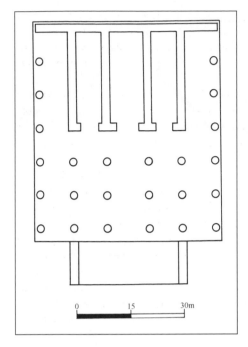

0   15   30m

Figure 19.2 Plan (reconstruction), Temple of Jupiter Optimus Maximus, Rome

they built their citadel and their principal temple, dedicated to the god Jupiter. The possible remains of this early Temple of Jupiter Capitolinus, or Jupiter Optimus Maximus, have been discovered under the Renaissance Palazzo dei Conservatori and the adjacent Palazzo Caffarelli on the south side of the Campidoglio, the square designed by Michelangelo for the twin summits of the Capitoline Hill. Because the ruins are scanty, the appearance of the temple cannot be reconstructed with certainty (Figure 19.2). We do know it had three cellas in typical Etruscan fashion, with Jupiter housed in the center, Juno and Minerva on either side. These three became the chief divinities of the Roman state. An Etruscan artist, Vulca of Veii, was commissioned during the reign of Tarquin the Proud (530–509 BC) to make a terracotta cult statue of a standing Jupiter, painted red, wielding a thunderbolt. This cult statue has vanished, but the terracotta figures from the Portonaccio Sanctuary at Veii (see Figures 18.11 and 18.12), roughly contemporaneous, give some idea of its appearance. The temple would later burn twice, in 83 BC and AD 80, to be rebuilt magnificently each time, with the original layout piously preserved.

THE ROMAN REPUBLIC: CIVIC INSTITUTIONS

For nearly 500 years after securing independence from the Etruscan kings in the late sixth century BC, Rome, the city itself and the territories it took over, was organized as a republic. The word "republic" comes from the Latin *res publica*, "the public thing," the Roman term for their state – a loose, vague title for a strong, life-shaping notion of a social entity with clearly defined obligations and rewards for its members. As in the Greek "democracy" ("power of the people"), participation in running the republic was restricted. Male citizens took charge, thereby excluding a large part of the population: women, slaves, and freedmen, and conquered peoples. Within the male citizenry, power was weighted in favor of aristocratic families, especially if wealthy: the patricians, as opposed to the common people, the plebeians. The central institution of this oligarchy was the Senate, a council of, in the second century BC, 300 wealthy, influential citizens, largely ex-magistrates, who were appointed for life. The Senate advised the magistrates, who in turn brought their proposals to the citizenry at large for ratification (see below). Indeed, the Latin formula *Senatus populusque romanus* (abbreviated SPQR), "the Senate and the Roman People," by whose authority laws were issued, indicates the prestige and power of the Senate. As the republic grew, the increasingly powerful plebeians forced concessions from the patricians, thereby gaining greater access to the ruling groups – a development that recalls the social and political evolution of Archaic and Classical Athens.

In addition to the Senate, certain decisions were taken by various assemblies to which all citizens, patricians and plebeians, were assigned either by birth or by level of wealth. The assemblies were run by magistrates, generally aristocrats, of whom the consuls were the most important. The magistrates controlled the proceedings, presenting their agenda of legislative proposals, but the assembly voted the final decisions.

Serving as a method of organizing the Roman people, the assemblies (*comitia* in Latin) were four in number: (1) The Curiate Assembly (*Comitia curiata*) was divided into 30 *curiae*, possibly originating in kinship groups or regional families. Duties of this assembly included the confirming of appointments of magistrates and priests. (2) The Centuriate Assembly (*Comitia centuriata*) was based on military organization, for its basic unit, the *centuria*, was, in the army, a group of 100 men, the smallest unit of a legion (one legion = 60 centuriae). However, by the fourth century BC the direct link between the military and this assembly was lost; the centuria became simply a voting unit. This assembly consisted of 193 *centuriae*, arranged in five ranks according to property ownership. The greater one's wealth, the greater one's influence. Poorer men filled the lower ranks; although far outnumbering the higher, their greater numbers gave them no advantage in voting power. This assembly voted laws and declared war and peace. (3) In the Plebeian Tribal Assembly (*Comitia plebis tributa*) and the related (4) People's Tribal Assembly (*Comitia populi tributa*), this last open to patricians as well as plebeians, the citizens were grouped according to 35 tribes, 4 urban (the city of Rome) and 31 rural (in Italy). Election of certain officials, enactment of certain laws, and the holding of minor trials constituted their role in government.

Conceived when the Roman Republic consisted of the city of Rome and, by the late third century BC, the Italian peninsula, the system eventually broke down, overwhelmed by the expansion throughout the Mediterranean that took place in the second century BC. The rapid inclusion of great numbers of people, territory, and wealth disrupted the equilibrium of the social contract between groups, leading to abuses and social unrest, and in the first century BC, dictatorship and civil war.

THE EXPANSION OF ROME

The dramatic expansion of Rome originated in the early fourth century BC with the conquest of Veii, the Etruscan city closest to Rome. Then in 390 BC came a setback: raiding Gauls sacked Rome. In response, the Romans built their first fortification wall, ca. 380 BC. Called the Servian Wall after Servius Tullius, a sixth-century BC king incorrectly believed to be its builder, this wall, 11km long, enclosed an area of 400ha on the east bank of the Tiber; included were the famous seven hills. The city later developed well beyond the confines of this wall, although the area inside continued to be defined as the city proper. A longer successor, enclosing a much larger area, the Aurelian Wall, the second and final fortification of the ancient city, would come only much later, in AD 271, its construction prompted by the unsettled conditions of the later empire.

In the Samnite Wars of the late fourth and early third centuries BC, the Romans confronted and defeated their neighbors in central Italy, notably the Samnites, the Etruscans, and the Gauls. Soon conflicts spread to the south, to a war with the Greek city of Tarentum (ending in 272 BC), and then to a dispute with Carthage for control of the island of Sicily (the First Punic War, 264–241 BC). By the later third century BC, Rome controlled all peninsular Italy, plus the islands of Sicily, Corsica, and Sardinia. The absorption in particular of the Etruscan and Greek regions with their rich cultural traditions had a tremendous impact on Roman society.

Continuing conflict with Carthage (Second Punic War, 218–201 BC, and Third Punic War, 149–146 BC) led to a decisive Roman victory and to Roman control over the west and central Mediterranean.

To celebrate these ongoing victories, the *triumph* became an institution: a parade in Rome, paid for by the victor from the spoils. From the early second century BC, these triumphs were commemorated by large free-standing arches (see the Arch of Titus and the Arch of Constantine, in Chapters 22 and 24 below).

From ca. 200 BC, the Romans were increasingly drawn into the conflicts between Hellenistic monarchs in the eastern Mediterranean, with territorial gains often the reward for their military assistance. In 146 BC, Greece fell under *de facto* Roman control. Shortly thereafter, with the Pergamene inheritance of 133 BC, the province of Asia was established in western Anatolia. The Romans expanded westward too. In 58–51 BC, Julius Caesar marched into north-west Europe, conquering the area of modern France, Belgium, Germany west of the Rhine, and part of Switzerland. Caesar was assassinated in 44 BC, a victim of the civil unrest that marked this turbulent final century of the Roman Republic. Peace came only in 31 BC, when Caesar's adopted son and successor, Octavian, defeated his rival Mark Antony and the Egyptian queen Cleopatra VII at the Battle of Actium off the north-west coast of Greece, thereby securing for Rome possession of the entire eastern Mediterranean. In 27 BC Octavian adopted the title Augustus. The Republic and the period of Roman expansion had come to an end; the Roman Empire had begun.

ROADS, CAMPS, AND COLONIES

The integration of these far-flung territories into the Roman state demanded an effective infrastructure. Three key components of this infrastructure were *roads*, the establishment of *army camps*, and the foundation of new towns, or *colonies*.

Roads

By the first century AD, a vast network of roads would cover the empire. An early example was the Via Appia, or the Appian Way, from Rome to Campania (the area around Naples), paved at the beginning of the Samnite Wars in the late fourth century BC. Other famous roads included the Via Flaminia, leading north from Rome to the Adriatic city of Ariminum (modern Rimini), and the Via Egnatia, from Albania's Adriatic coast to Thessaloniki and Byzantium (later Constantinople). Roman roads, at least the great intercity routes built by the state as opposed to local or private sources, were remarkable in that they were not simply dirt tracks for wheeled vehicles, but were stone-paved, suitable for all weather, and well-maintained. In addition, security was constantly monitored. These qualities were deemed essential for facilitating rapid communications and deployment of troops across long distances.

Methods of construction varied. In the north-eastern empire (Thrace, Asia Minor, and Syria), the standard components of roads were three: (1) the edges were marked by large stones laid flat; (2) a central line of smaller stones, set vertically on edge, divided the road into two; and (3) small stones filled the two lanes. Elsewhere a trench might be dug, a foundation laid with edges curbed to hold in the road and help drainage, and finally a surface added in a different material, such as gravel or sand. Many roads would be suitable for both foot travellers and vehicles; others, in steep areas, would have steps, and so use would be restricted to foot traffic.

Roads were marked at an interval of one Roman mile (= 1.485km) by stone milestones of varying shapes and sizes, inscribed with distances and perhaps dates of construction or repair and the names of the reigning emperor, local officials, and military units. For the traveller, road maps and itineraries existed, although they were diagrams, not to scale, or lists of places on a single route, with distances marked. The traveller could count on roadside establishments at periodic intervals, for room and board, mail service, stables and other transportation services.

Army camps

Army camps (Latin *castrum*, pl. *castra*) were established throughout Roman territory, but especially in frontier zones. The layout of these camps utilized a standard plan, a square with straight streets crossing at right angles, with the commander's tent placed in the center, soldiers' barracks and other facilities neatly arranged along the streets (Figure 19.3). These camps closely resembled plans for newly founded towns. Indeed, Greco-Roman city plans featuring the Hippodamian grid must have influenced camp layout – and camp layout in turn influenced town plans. The camps themselves often developed into permanent towns, such as Eboracum (modern York, England), Colonia Agrippina (Cologne, Germany), and Augusta Praetoria (Aosta, Italy).

Castra could be either "marching camps" for overnight stays, or permanent forts. Polybius, the Greek historian of the second century BC, has left a clear description of how a marching camp was set up. First, the standard was planted to mark the site of the commander's tent. Around this the rest of the camp was then laid out in regular fashion, with a margin of empty space left by

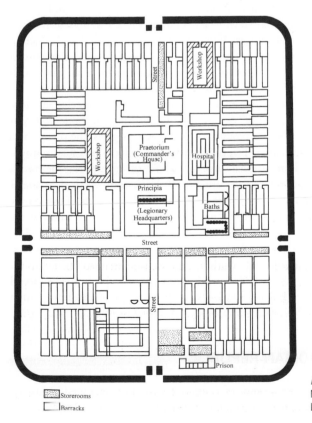

Figure 19.3 Diagram, legionary fort, Novaesium, on the Rhine frontier in Lower Germany

the outer walls, space for mustering soldiers, for drills, for assembling cattle and booty, and to serve as extra space that enemy fire would have to cross.

Colonies: early Ostia

The Roman *colonia* differed from the Greek colony in that it was not a regular settlement autonomous from the mother city that founded it, but a town initially established in order to assure military control or political domination of a region, both on land and (in coastal locations) on sea. Ostia, later developed as the port of Rome, was one of the earliest such colonies, founded in the mid fourth century BC at the mouth of the Tiber to control maritime and river traffic and to protect Rome against incursions by sea. Laid out as a military camp, although rectangular (measuring 194m × 125m), not the usual square, Ostia had the standard features of two bisecting main streets, the cardo (north–south) and the decumanus (east–west), with a forum where they crossed. In later centuries, as the Romans consolidated their control in Italy, the need for fortified camps in the Italian peninsula diminished. A town might then safely expand beyond the original confines of the camp, as indeed happened at Ostia by the first century BC (for the later development of Ostia, see Chapter 21).

In the later Republic and during the Empire, colonies were established to relieve population pressure in large cities, and to reward veterans with gifts of free land, sometimes confiscated from previous owners. The size of colonies varied in population, from a few hundred families to several thousand, and in territory as well, including both the urban center and farmland.

Their government imitating the institutions of Rome itself, colonies were controlled by a council (or senate) and officials (magistrates). Likewise civic buildings recalled those seen in the capital, such as the temple to the three gods Jupiter, Juno, and Minerva; and the *curia* (meeting place of the Senate), the *comitium* (meeting place of the Assemblies), and the *basilica* (law courts; miscellaneous business matters). Deliberately placed in frontier zones or in conquered lands, such cities extended the patterns of Roman urban life to the diverse peoples of the empire.

The *colonia* was officially established according to a fixed routine. First came religious rites, attributed by the Romans to Etruscan practice. A ritual boundary line, the *pomerium*, was ploughed by a bull and cow yoked to a bronze plough. At the streets or gates, the plough was lifted up and replaced on the other side. After this, the land for the colonia was surveyed in a process called centuriation by a team of professional surveyors who used in particular the *groma*, an instrument with two bars crossing at right angles and plumb lines, with which right angles and their straight extensions could be determined. The land was divided into quadrants by the cardo and the decumanus, and then into long narrow units. The basic measure of land was the *century* (*centuria*, in Latin), ca. 50ha, itself consisting of 100 *heredia*. One *heredium*, ca. 0.50ha, the usual plot assigned to one particular farmer or family, was considered the amount of land necessary for a family to support itself. Marble fragments of a map of AD 77 recording individual *centuriae*, numbered and with the owners and tax rates listed, have survived from the city of Arausio (modern Orange) in southern France. Typically, a bronze copy of this information would be displayed in the local town hall, with a linen copy forwarded to Rome.

COSA, A TOWN OF THE ROMAN REPUBLIC

Despite the interest of Ostia and the importance of Rome itself, well documented in literary sources, later construction in these long-lived cities has destroyed or damaged the remains from the Republican centuries. The fragments from Rome are too important to ignore, however, and we shall examine them shortly. But first let us visit a Republican town that can be appreciated in its entirety: Cosa, a colonia founded in 273 BC, implanted in territory conquered from the Etruscan city of Vulci, strategically placed to block Etruscan access to the sea. Like Priene (above, Chapter 16), this town owes its importance in modern archaeology to its modest destiny in antiquity. Cosa was sacked in 70–60 BC, perhaps by pirates; subsequent occupation was modest. Medieval and modern times passed it by. Because the town is mentioned only briefly in ancient literary sources, our knowledge of Cosa depends on the excavations conducted in 1948–54 and 1965–72 under the direction of Frank Brown of the American Academy in Rome.

The town occupied an area of 13.25ha on a hill by a good harbor 140km north of Rome. The surrounding farmland was fertile, and in fact most Cosans (90 percent of the citizens) lived outside the walled town. A lagoon behind the harbor gave rise to a prosperous local industry, a fishery with a specialty in eels and mullets, and perhaps production of *garum*, a fish sauce much loved by the Romans.

The citadel, known as the Arx, occupied the town's highest point. The Romans planned the rest of the town from sitings taken here. The city walls were erected first, an irregular perimeter just under 2km in length, with three gates, one postern, and 18 towers. Measuring 2m in thickness, of irregularly shaped blocks of hard limestone, these sturdy walls are still well preserved to a height of 9–10m. Despite the varying contours of the site, the space inside was laid out in a regular grid (Figure 19.4), a determined imposing of order on unruly nature that recalls urban planning at Priene.

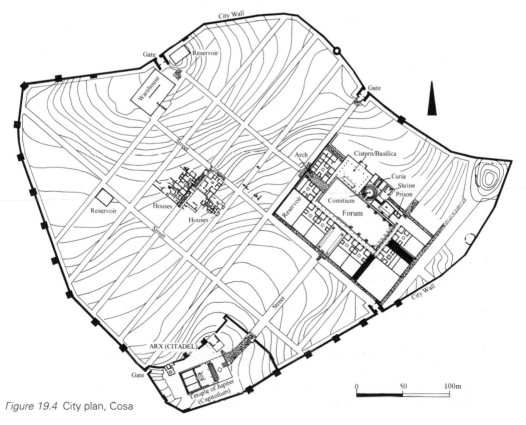

Figure 19.4 City plan, Cosa

The Arx, protected with its own set of fortification walls, contained the principal shrine of the town, the Temple of Jupiter with, in front, a cistern and a court with an altar. As at Rome, the area sacred to Jupiter lay on high ground. The temple stood on a high podium; in plan, the temple contained a front porch, with four columns, and the usual triple cella. The superstructure has been reconstructed on the basis of terracotta fragments of architectural decorations, with help from comments of Vitruvius (Figure 19.5). The temple was originally built after 241 BC, then rebuilt ca. 150 BC, with the varying styles of its terracotta decorations suggesting a lengthy period of refurbishing and repair.

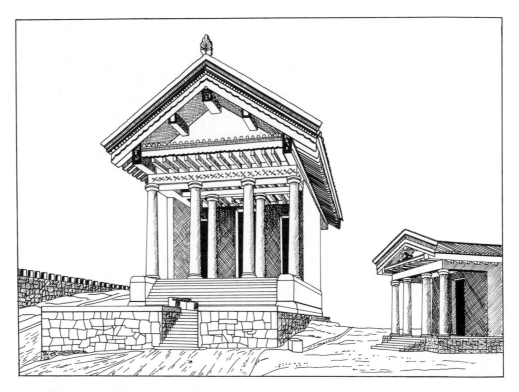

Figure 19.5 Arx temples: Capitolium and Mater Matuta (reconstruction), from Cosa

A major street led directly from the Arx downhill to the other important sector of the town, the *forum*, or city center, a rectangular space lined with buildings devoted to civic functions (Figure 19.6). By the later third century BC, such buildings included the comitium, the meeting place of the assembly of the people, here a circular open-air area with steps, and behind it, the curia, a covered rectangular hall, the home of the local senate, or council of elders. A shrine and a prison flanked the comitium on one side, a cistern on the other. In the second century BC, additions included a commemorative triple arch at the north-west entrance to the forum and a basilica erected over the cistern. Archive and office buildings lined the rest of the forum.

The *basilica* is a building type that became common in the Roman world from the second century BC. In the fourth century AD, the basilica plan was adapted as the standard design for Christian churches. Not a religious building in Roman times, the basilica provided space for lawyers, judges, and other officials involved in city and legal affairs. It was always located

Figure 19.6 Forum, sixth phase (reconstruction), Cosa

alongside a forum or a similar open space, with one of its sides penetrated by doors. The basilica typically consists of a central rectangle, roofed, surrounded by a peristyle and walkways, also covered, on all four sides. The central roof rises higher than that over the side halls. This raised roofline allowed for a line of windows, an architectural arrangement known as a clerestory (used in the Hypostyle Hall, Delos: Chapter 17).

Arches, vaults, concrete, and concrete facing

In the north-west entrance into the forum lie the ruins of a triple archway, one of the earliest Roman examples of the *voussoir arch*, or *true arch*. Perhaps invented in the Near East, used rarely in fourth-century BC Greek and Etruscan architecture, the true arch would become a hallmark of Roman architecture. The true arch is made of voussoirs, wedge-shaped stones that direct the pressure from the weight of the stones to the side as well as directly down (see Figure 2.18a).

The arch is a two-dimensional form. When continued in three dimensions, it becomes a *barrel* (or *tunnel*) *vault* (Figure 2.18b). Other types of vaults were also used in Roman architecture, notably the groin vault, the result of the intersection of barrel vaults (Figure 2.18c).

In Cosa's triple archway, mortared rubble is one element used in its construction, an early use of *concrete*. Concrete is a mixture of lime, sand, and water, a combination that makes a sort of glue with the property of hardening well. By the time of Augustus, the Romans habitually included as well volcanic dust from Etruria–Latium–Campania, a dust called "pozzolana" after the town of Pozzuoli (ancient Puteoli) on the Bay of Naples. This compound produced a particularly strong concrete which had the added virtue of being hydraulic: it could set underwater, and so could be used for harbor foundations and as an impervious lining for aqueducts and cisterns. Concrete would also be mixed with an aggregate, such as rubble – small irregular stones – to make the core of a wall. Like the true arch, concrete would become a characteristic feature of Roman architecture: a miracle substance that would permit during the imperial period an astonishing array of architectural forms that departed radically from traditional Greek and even Italic practice.

A concrete core of a structure would normally be faced with cut stones or brick, to give a regular appearance to the exterior (Figure 19.7). Well-known patterns of facings include (1) *opus incertum*, small stones of irregular shape; (2) *opus reticulatum*, small stones cut with a square face, placed in a diamond pattern; and (3) *opus testaceum*, a facing of bricks or tiles. The first was popular in the second and early first centuries BC, the second especially in the first century BC and the first century AD, and the third from the mid first century AD on. An elegant facing could be provided by marble revetments, thin slabs of marble. Marble was expensive, however, because it had to be imported from distant sources in northern Italy or the Aegean region.

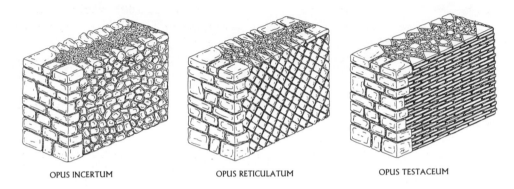

OPUS INCERTUM   OPUS RETICULATUM   OPUS TESTACEUM

Figure 19.7 Three types of Roman wall facing: *opus incertum, opus reticulatum*, and o*pus testaceum*

ROME DURING THE REPUBLIC

The excavations of Cosa give a picture of the overall aspect of a town of the Republican period, with walls, a grid plan, citadel, forum, and even private houses, and information on its economy (its port and lagoon, and farmlands). But to what extent does this reflect the situation of Rome itself?

The 500 years of the Republic witnessed a tremendous development in the capital city. Assessing the growth of Rome in these centuries is difficult, because architectural remains tend to be fragmentary, damaged or destroyed by construction activity in later imperial times. Literary sources, however, provide indispensable help for understanding the appearance and functioning of the city. What seems clear is that during the later Republic the city of Rome assumed its characteristic form, with most standard building types introduced then. Many stood in the Roman Forum; our survey of the Republican capital will thus be concentrating on that central place of the city. We shall see that the buildings at Cosa represent a distillation of the civic architecture of Rome. The orderly layout of Cosa is not, however, copying a precedent from the capital city, which grew organically over many centuries, but instead derives from its foundation at a precise moment in time.

The Roman Forum (Forum Romanum)

The low ground to the north of the Palatine Hill and to the east of the Capitoline Hill served from early times as the civic center of the city of Rome (Figure 19.8). Because of centuries of use and modifications, the building history of the area is extremely complicated. Until early modern times, the area was covered with houses and served as an integral part of the city. Antiquarian interest intensified in the early nineteenth century, with systematic excavation beginning in 1870. Further stimulus for exploration came during the dictatorship of Benito Mussolini, 1922–43, in his drive to link Fascist Italy with the glories of ancient Rome. Work continues today, with attention to problems of preservation in the heart of a large congested city.

This land was originally marshy, crossed by streams. To render the area useful, the streams needed to be chanelled. And indeed, the Etruscan kings did just that, according to Livy. A sewer, the *cloaca maxima*, was built across the area for the evacuation into the Tiber River of stream and rainwater and liquid wastes; eventually it was lined with stone and vaulted with concrete, an impressive construction that measured ca. 2.0m–4.5m wide, 2.7m–4.2m high.

During Republican times, the forum consisted of an irregular rectangle, with its corners at the Curia, the site of the later Temple of Antoninus, the Temple of Castor, and the Temple of Saturn (see Figure 19.8). Leading into the forum was the Sacred Way, an old street whose existence indicates the intertwining of religious and civic here at Rome as already seen in Athens and the Ancient Near East. Like the Athenian Agora, the Roman Forum developed over many centuries, with buildings placed here and there, as the need arose, not in an ordered arrangement. This haphazard development contrasts with that of the forum at Cosa and with the later Imperial Fora of Rome itself.

Religious buildings

Religious buildings in the forum included three major temples to the deities Vesta, Saturn, and Castor, and an important shrine, the Lacus Iuturnae. Vesta was the goddess of the hearth. Her temple contained not a cult statue but instead the sacred hearth fire of the state; the hearth and its fire were symbols central to Roman religion. The temple itself was round. Originally it resembled an Iron Age Italic hut with a thatched roof. But the building was repeatedly destroyed, damaged by fires, and rebuilt many times; its final version, erected by Julia Domna, the wife of Septimius Severus, in the late second century AD, was an elegant marble tholos surrounded by 20 columns with Corinthian capitals.

The original Temple of Saturn dated from the early Republic, but the extant remains are from a rebuilding in 42 BC and later refurbishing (after a fourth-century AD fire). The temple stands on a high podium, in typical Italic style. The temple contained the state treasury. Saturn himself was a god of agricultural fertility and indeed of civilized life. His cult statue, made largely of ivory, was filled with vegetal oil, a fruit of his magnanimity.

The last of these deities, the divine twins Castor and Pollux, were honored twice in the forum. According to legend, Castor and Pollux helped the Romans defeat the Latins at the Battle of Lake Regillus in 496 BC. After the battle they were seen watering their horses at the Juturna Spring (*Lacus Iuturnae*). These divine protectors received early tributes in the Roman Forum. At the spring, a stone fountain building was erected in their honor. Nearby, a Temple to Castor (and perhaps Pollux) was built. The visible ruins come especially from the rebuilding in the Augustan period: the temple stood on a high podium, but otherwise was largely Greek in feel, with a peristyle of Corinthian columns around all four sides.

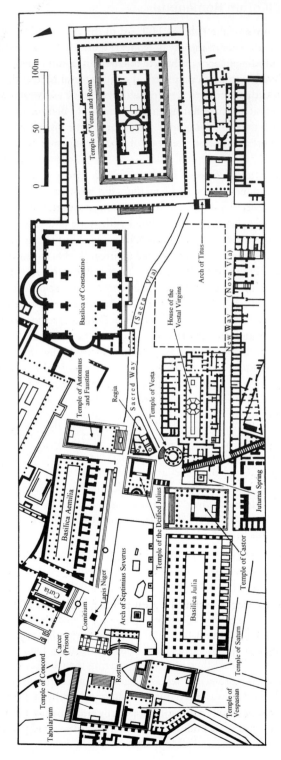

Figure 19.8 Plan, Forum Romanum, Rome

Civic buildings

The forum contained many structures that served governmental and other civic functions. The Regia, a small building, was the headquarters of the *pontifex maximus*, the head of the state religion. The Senate met in the Curia; this meeting hall underwent various reconstructions, the present building having been erected by Diocletian after a fire of AD 283, but based on the version begun by Julius Caesar in 44 BC. The Comitium, an officially consecrated open area, served as the meeting area for the Comitia curiata. Originally without architectural form, it eventually was given a fan shape, with steps. The rostra, the platform for speakers, originally stood here, but later Augustus had a new set built at the north-west end of the forum. *Rostra*, a plural word, means ships' beaked prows. From the third century BC, the bronze battering rams of defeated warships were displayed here. The Lapis Niger (black stone) is an area paved with black marble (in the time of Caesar or Augustus) that covered earlier shrines, including, according to legend, the tomb of Romulus. But no tombs have been discovered here, despite many artifacts from the early periods of the city's occupation.

Two covered halls lined the north and south sides of the forum, the Basilica Aemilia (or Basilica Paulli) and the Basilica Julia. The Basilica Aemilia of 179 BC was the first in Rome, but it was essentially rebuilt in 54–34 BC by L. Aemilius Paullius and his son, then restored by Augustus after a fire of 13 BC, and again in AD 22. A row of shops gave onto the forum; passages led between the shops into the basilica proper. Its central nave measured 82m × 16m, its two side aisles 7.5m in width each. For Pliny the Elder, a prominent writer of the first century AD, this was one of the most beautiful buildings in the city, thanks especially to its high-quality Phrygian marble. The Basilica Julia, begun by Julius Caesar in 54 BC from the spoils from his Gallic wars, finished by Augustus, and refurbished after later fires, was built between the Temples of Castor and Saturn, opposite the Basilica Aemilia. This basilica was used especially for banking.

The Tabularium, on the west side of the Forum on the side of the Capitoline hill, is the best-preserved building from Republican Rome. Here the state archives were housed. An inscription gives its date of construction, 78 BC, and records its patron, the consul Q. Lutatius Catulus, and its architect, Lucius Cornelius. The plan is irregular and somewhat uncertain; it did have at least two storeys, the upper one being an arcade framed with Doric pilasters from which one had a good view over the forum. During the Renaissance, modifications were made, the most important being Michelangelo's replacing of the ruined upper sections with the Palazzo del Senatore.

The Capitoline and Palatine Hills

The Roman Forum was bordered on the west and south by the Capitoline and Palatine Hills, respectively. On the Capitoline stood the most important shrine of the city, the Temple of Jupiter, while on the Palatine Hill upper-class Romans had their city mansions. Also on the Palatine was the Temple to Magna Mater, the great mother, built after 203 BC (consecrated in 191 BC), but later burned and rebuilt. This shrine housed the sacred black stone of the Anatolian mother goddess brought to Rome from Pessinus in central Anatolia, an early and famous example of the syncretistic in-gathering of cults from the many peoples conquered by the Romans.

Outside the Roman Forum

Much is known about areas outside the Forum Romanum during the Republican period. In the remainder of this chapter we shall visit markets, theaters, the circus, bridges, and aqueducts (see Figure 19.1).

Figure 19.9 Temple of Portunus, Rome

Markets

The main market area was located near the river. Important markets include the Forum Holitorium, a fruit and vegetable market; the Forum Boarium, the "cattle market," a commercial area crammed with shops and warehouses; and the nearby Velabrum, a huge general market. These market areas also contained temples. Two are particularly well preserved, one round, one rectangular. The rectangular temple, the Temple of Portunus, the god of the ford in this place where in earliest times the Tiber was crossed, is particularly well preserved thanks to its transformation into a church (Figure 19.9). Built in the first century BC, it is a good example of a Tuscan-type temple with strong Greek influence. Tuscan elements include the high podium (2.3m high) on which it sits; and its frontality, marked by a broad flight of steps on the front side and a deep front porch with only attached columns around the sides and rear of the cella. Greek influence includes the Ionic capitals and the shallow pediment. The "Portunium," the district around this temple, was a center for flower and garland dealers.

An additional market hall stood somewhat to the south alongside the Tiber: the Porticus Aemilia, built by two officials, the aediles M. Aemilius Lepidus and L. Aemilius Paullus, in 193 BC, with restoration in 174 BC. This long hall (487m × 60m) was one of a series of market halls that served as distribution points for goods shipped on the river. In design it consisted of parallel rows of linked barrel vaults, with arched openings in their long sides creating a large interior space. The Porticus Aemilia was built of concrete, whereas others were wooden.

Bridges

Permanent bridges eventually spanned the Tiber; two are of particular interest for us. The Aemilian Bridge (Pons Aemilius) was the first stone bridge, complementing wooden and pontoon bridges; its piers, erected in 179 BC, were connected by arches in 142 BC. The bridge was partially destroyed by floods in 1557 and 1598; in 1887 two of the three remaining arches were taken down, leaving only one arch still surviving; the bridge is thus known today as the Ponte Rotto, the Broken Bridge. To the north of the city lies the Milvian Bridge (Pons Mulvius); the important road leading to the north, the Via Flaminia, crossed the Tiber here. The Via

Figure 19.10 Pont du Gard, France

Flaminia was built in 220 BC, but the stone version of the bridge arrived a century later in 109 BC. It was here in AD 312 that Constantine defeated his rival Maxentius, thereby securing his rule over the western half of the Roman Empire.

Aqueducts

Aqueducts (Latin *aqua*, pl. *aquae*) were the channels by which water was brought to towns and cities. Water flowed downwards, by gravity, from distant sources. Channels were normally underground, but if necessary, could be carried on arches. Rome would eventually be serviced by many aqueducts. The oldest was the Aqua Appia, built in 312 BC by the censors Appius Claudius Caecus (the paver of the Via Appia) and C. Plautius Venox. Most of its length (16km) from an as yet unidentified spring lay underground. The Aqua Appia served low-lying areas, notably the Forum Boarium. The longest of the city's aqueducts was the Aqua Marcia, 91km in length, of which 80km lay underground. It carried 187,000m³ of water per day, a capacity exceeded only by the Anio Novus aqueduct (190,000m³ per day).

For a spectacular example of an aqueduct surviving from the immediately post-Republican era, we turn to southern France, to the Pont du Gard of AD 14 (Figure 19.10). This bridge was but one segment of an aqueduct that brought water from Uzès to the Roman town of Nemausus (modern Nîmes). The level of the water channel slowly fell 18m over its length of 48km. Three storeys and 54m high, the bridge carried the water channel, lined with hydraulic cement, at its top, and thereby ensured that the carefully maintained level of the water channel would not be interrupted by the river valley. Each storey contained typical round Roman arches, the uppermost level (with the water channel on top), the smallest, marked by the smallest arches.

The Theater of Pompey and the Circus Maximus

Republican Rome also saw the building of theaters, under Greek influence, and formal structures for amusements, notably the Circus Maximus. The early Theater of Pompey (55 BC) would remain the city's most important. The general Pompey, after winning victories in the eastern

Mediterranean, celebrated by building Rome's first stone theater and an enclosed peristyle garden behind. Although the theater was often rebuilt in antiquity, being much favored by emperors, only the substructure of the cavea still remains; in addition, its contours are preserved in the modern street plan of Rome. More details are known thanks to mentions in literary sources and to its appearance in the surviving fragments of the Forma Urbis, a marble plan of the city carved in the Severan period between AD 203 and 211.

The theater is based on Greek models, since theater originated as a Greek practice. Theaters of both wood and stone had already been in use in Italy, especially in southern areas under more direct Greek influence. Although theatrical performances had originated in Greek religious practice, evidently by the first century BC that association had diminished. Pompey renewed this religious connection by having a Temple to Venus Victrix constructed at the top of the cavea, facing the stage, and three, perhaps four, additional shrines. Subsequent Roman theaters did not include such temples. Greek theaters were built on hillsides; this one was not, but instead, profiting from Roman technological advances, was erected on vaults of concrete faced in part with opus reticulatum. The plan departs from the typical Greek theater in having a semicircular cavea. Seating is estimated at 11,000. But it still has open parodoi and a low wide stage, probably made of wood but decorated with portrait sculpture. During the empire Roman theaters would be much elaborated. The cavea and stage building were connected in a single unified structure. Multi-storey stage buildings, decorated with marble revetments, featured complex architectural frameworks of architraves and columns, creating niches for the display of full-size statues.

The Circus Maximus, Rome's oldest and largest track for horse racing events, was laid out south of the Palatine Hill in the early republic. The first starting gates, probably wooden but painted in bright colors, are dated to 329 BC. The long narrow track was divided lengthwise down the middle by the *spina*, at first only a natural stream that happened to run through this area, but later elaborated with bridges and structures holding sculpture and such other monuments as an obelisk of the Egyptian king Ramses II. Enlargement to its final size, 621m × 118m, took place in the late Republic. Seating in permanent materials was eventually provided in the lowest of the three cavea zones, first wooden seats, later stone. According to Pliny, maximum capacity was 250,000, a number that indicates the huge popularity of the favorite event, races of chariots drawn by four horses. Teams, or factions, were like modern professional sports teams, with directors and patrons and full support staff as well as the racers themselves, and of course followed by avid fan groups. A race normally consisted of seven laps around the spina; a full day consisted of 24 races.

Republican Rome: summary

Despite the fragmentary nature of the surviving evidence, we can nonetheless obtain a picture of Republican Rome, especially in the second and first centuries BC, as a prosperous city with developed religious, governmental, commercial, and leisure activities, with an infrastructure of roads, bridges, sewerage, and water circulation. The imperial period will continue the lines established during the Republic, adding notably palaces, huge municipal bath complexes, and public commemorations in sculpture – all the result of the change in government and patronage of art and architecture from oligarchy to monarchy. Important, too, will be the enlarging of the repertoire of architectural forms, developments linked to the use of concrete. We turn first to the city of Rome at the time of Augustus, the transition from Republic to Empire.

CHAPTER 20

Rome in the age of Augustus

Augustus (born 63 BC; ruled 31 BC–AD 14)

The city of Rome was transformed during the reign of Augustus, the first of the Roman emperors. Augustus understood uncannily well the impact that images, buildings, and materials could have on the prestige of a city. He set a new standard for the physical world of the Roman city that would continue for several centuries. Before we examine some of his building projects in Rome, let us first look briefly at his life and at one famous image of him, with a view to identifying elements that he considered important in the creation of the urban environment.

AUGUSTUS, THE FIRST OF THE ROMAN EMPERORS

Octavian, the grandnephew and adopted son of Julius Caesar, assumed complete control of the Roman state after defeating Mark Antony and Cleopatra at the Battle of Actium in 31 BC. Four years later, the Senate granted him the title Augustus, and it is under that name that we know him best. Until his death in AD 14 he ruled the Roman Empire with enormous vision and competence, bringing enduring peace and prosperity after decades of civil war. Interestingly, this great ruler who understood so well the value of grandeur in the public arena cultivated a personal life style of moderation, of deliberation, of self-control. Two sayings attributed to him by the late first- to early second-century biographer Suetonius show clearly his outlook on life: a favorite Greek proverb, "Make haste slowly" (reflecting his energy combined with deliberation) and, at the end of his life, the remarkable words: "How does it look? Have I performed the comedy of life properly?"

The Augustus of Primaporta

The majestic statue of Augustus from Primaporta brings to the fore his understanding of the power of images (Figure 20.1). The work combines Greek and Roman features, idealized and specific, a calculated blend that served as an official image of the emperor. The head portrays Augustus as a young man. Following the realistic tradition of Etruscan and Roman portraiture, the features appear specific, such as the broad skull and the narrow chin, and confirm Suetonius's description of Augustus as extremely handsome. This attractive, idealized face had become a standard image, one that Augustus used until the end of his long life, in accordance with the Greek view that portraits should function as types, not as optically faithful records.

With the body, however, the image departs from reality, for Suetonius described Augustus as rather short, even if well-proportioned. The body reproduces the stance and the heavy musculature of the "Doryphoros" of Polykleitos, a Greek work of the fifth century BC much

Figure 20.1 Augustus of Primaporta, marble statue from Rome. Vatican Museums

copied by the Romans, and so connects Augustus with the idealized heroic image that Greeks projected in statues of nude athletes. But Augustus is clothed, even if the cuirass is revealingly form-fitting. His military garb specifically identifies him as a soldier and recalls his personal heroism on behalf of the Roman state. Further, the armor serves as a vehicle for details about Augustus's military achievements. Relief sculpture on the cuirass includes the depiction of a Parthian returning captured standards to a Roman, a symbol of peace brought to the uneasy eastern frontier of the Roman empire.

The statue may be a marble copy of a bronze original made after the Romans retrieved their standards in 20 BC. It was found in 1863 at Primaporta outside Rome in a villa perhaps belonging to Livia, Augustus's wife; it may have stood outdoors as a garden decoration, as stone statuary often did in Roman times.

AUGUSTUS AND THE ARCHITECTURE OF ROME

We return to the city of Rome itself with another declaration that Suetonius attributed to Augustus, that he found the city made of brick and left it made of marble. Augustus realized the importance of making the capital Rome into an architectural showcase for the world. As with the other arts, his grand design featured the integration of Greek forms and materials with traditional Italic features. Marble, a favorite Greek material heretofore imported into Rome, now became familiar, thanks to the opening of an Italian source, the Carrara quarries of north-west Italy.

Among Augustus's many architectural contributions, three buildings in particular illustrate his approach to symbols, architecture, and the image of his own personality: the House of Augustus, the Forum of Augustus, and the Ara Pacis (Altar of Peace). Let us begin with the simplest, the House of Augustus.

The House of Augustus

For a ruler of such wealth and power, the house Augustus chose to live in was surprisingly modest. It would not have been simple: a building of at least two storeys, its rooms fairly small but certainly well appointed. Wall paintings were of high quality, often showing architectural scenes. But this was not the lavish palace preferred by many of his successors. For Augustus, this moderation was important. Also significant was the symbolic value of its location. The house stood on the Palatine Hill in a sector where modern archaeology has revealed remains of Iron Age houses of earliest Rome. Indeed, one would have seen nearby a model of the House of Romulus. The proximity allowed Augustus to connect symbolically with the legendary founder of the city. Also adjacent to the house was the Temple of Apollo Palatinus; Apollo was credited with giving Augustus key support in his victory at Actium. The house, already burned and rebuilt in Augustus's lifetime, seems to have been abandoned after his death and seriously damaged during the great fire during the reign of Nero, in AD 64.

Imperial fora: the Forum of Julius and the Forum of Augustus

The greatest architectural complex in the city of Rome during this period was the Forum of Augustus. In order to understand it, we must first backtrack to the Forum of Julius (Figure 20.2).

Julius Caesar, the dominant military and political leader from ca. 60 BC until his assassination in 44 BC, was, like Augustus after him, active in improving the architecture and services of the capital. In 54 BC he commissioned a monumental public square to serve as an expansion of the crowded Roman Forum. Because of its desirable downtown location, the land, purchased from

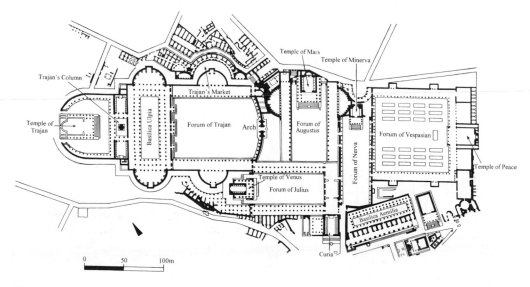

Figure 20.2 Plan, imperial fora, Rome

private owners, was extremely expensive. The resulting Forum of Julius consisted of an open-air space lined with colonnades. A Temple of Venus Genetrix dominated the square. Julius considered himself a descendant of Venus, the goddess of love. As the mother of Aeneas, the Trojan hero associated with the origin of Rome, Venus was additionally venerated as a special ancestress of the Roman state. Although a temple in a colonnaded court was a Greek concept, the Greekness further emphasized by the use of marble as an elegant building material, an Italic flavor was achieved by placing the temple on a high podium at one end of the space. The temple was dedicated by Julius Caesar in 46 BC, but completed by Augustus. The Forum of Julius was the first of a series of imperial fora, regular self-contained architectural units each planned separately, all so different from the Roman Forum which had developed gradually and irregularly over many centuries.

The Forum of Augustus builds on the concept of the Forum of Julius: a centrally located civic complex that is monumental; civilized with its Hellenic decoration; connected with the gods (by including a temple); and rich with symbolism important for the state. After his victory over the assassins of Julius Caesar at the Battle of Philippi in northern Greece in 42 BC, Octavian (later Augustus) vowed to build a temple to Mars the Avenger (Mars Ultor). The Forum of Augustus would be the frame for the new temple. Work on the forum probably had begun by 24 BC; the temple was eventually dedicated in 2 BC, although not quite finished. Like the Forum of Julius, this forum consisted of a rectangular space (measuring ca. 125m × 90m) lined by two colonnaded porticoes. New, however, were the semicircular spaces (hemicycles) beyond the colonnaded portico, possibly unroofed spaces that brought light through the colonnades. The columns were made of different colored stone, with the fine Corinthian capitals of white marble. Like the Temple of Venus Genetrix in the Forum of Julius, the Temple of Mars Ultor, placed against the rear wall of the forum, was the focus of the broad rectangular space (Figure 20.3). Its Corinthian order establishing the Greek tone, the temple also showed traditional Italic features such as the high platform on which it stood and its frontality, with a broad flight of steps leading up to the porch.

Figure 20.3 Forum of Augustus with Temple of Mars Ultor (reconstruction), Rome

Dio Cassius, a senator and historian of the late second to early third centuries AD, gave a detailed list of the activities that took place in this forum. Noted especially as the center for administration of the provinces, the Forum of Augustus was also the place where boys formally put on the toga, symbol of manhood; commanders sent abroad began their missions; and the Senate voted triumphs to victorious generals, and where those same victors paid homage to Mars, god of war, by dedicating to him their crown and scepter of victory and captured military standards.

This forum was appropriately decorated with allusions, in sculpture, to the illustrious past of the Roman state. Subjects were carefully chosen for their symbolic value in this space so important for functions of the state. In the prominent large niche in each of the hemicycles stood statues that combined references to the founders of the Latin nation and of Rome itself: on the west, Aeneas carrying his father and leading his son out of burning Troy, and on the east, Romulus, bearing on his shoulders the trophy from the first Roman victory in the 750s BC. Other niches were filled with statues of important people, such as members of the Julian family, and perhaps a colossal statue of Augustus. Only a few fragments of these statues survive.

Inside the temple, the cult statues were apparently three: Mars, of course, fully armed as the Avenger, but with him Venus with Cupid (on his right) and the divine Julius Caesar (to his left). The pediment displayed similar figures.

Above the Corinthian colonnade 62 caryatids supported a second storey, smaller-scale copies of the caryatids from the Erechtheion on the Athenian acropolis. For the Romans these caryatids were not merely decorative. According to Vitruvius, they represented defeated peoples, subjected in order to bring about peace. Between the caryatids were shields decorated with the heads of gods. Horned Jupiter heads, perhaps Jupiter Ammon, an important syncretistic deity of Egypt, may refer to the Roman capture of Egypt.

Ara Pacis

The last of the great architectural monuments from the city of Rome during the reign of Augustus is the Ara Pacis Augustae, the Altar of Augustan Peace, a modest-sized (ca. 10m²) free-standing altar designed for sacrifices to the goddess Pax, or Peace (Figure 20.4). Voted by the Senate in 13 BC, then built on the Campus Martius along a main thoroughfare, the Via Flaminia, the altar was officially dedicated in 9 BC. The monument did not survive intact into modern times. Sculptural pieces have turned up under the privately owned Palazzo Fiano since the sixteenth century, with excavations carried out in 1903 and 1937–8. The altar was then re-constructed with the surviving fragments, although not on its original location or orientation.

The altar proper lay inside an open-air space bounded by an enclosure wall, with entrances on the west (main entrance) and the east. Relief sculpture decorated the entire monument, with the figural scenes on the upper half of the outside of the precinct wall attracting most attention. The monument commemorates the peace brought to the Roman state by Augustus, and discreetly honors Augustus as a new founder of the city and state, a worthy successor of Romulus and Aeneas. As we have seen, these themes, the bringing of peace and the linking of the Augustan present with the legendary origins of the state, play an important role in the public arts of Augustan Rome. The style of the sculpture is very much in the naturalistic tradition of Greek art, a fact that reminds us that, however Italic or Roman the subjects, a Greek manner of presentation still mattered enormously.

The east and west doorways were flanked by large relief panels with allegorical scenes emphasizing the divine and heroic underpinnings of the Roman state. On the north-east side a

Figure 20.4 Ara Pacis, Rome

personification of the goddess Roma sits on a pile of armor. The message is clear: peace through conquest, with Roma defeating her enemies in order to bring peace. On the left side is a well-preserved (and partly restored) panel showing "Fruits of Peace." A female personification of plenty, variously identified as Mother Earth (Tellus), Venus, Italia, or Peace, holding two babies, sits on a rock, surrounded by animals, plants, and fruits. On either side, nymph-like creatures framed by billowing cloaks attest to peace on both land and sea. They ride animals: one woman is on swan back, above an overturned jug, which represents the beginning of a spring, whereas on the other side we see a nymph on a rather frightening sea creature.

Beside the west entrance, the main entry to the altar, the fragmentary north-west panel shows the she-wolf suckling Romulus and Remus. Mars, the boys' father, and the shepherd who later raised the children, look on. On the better-preserved south-west panel, Aeneas, just landed in Latium, pours a libation of thanks onto an altar. Two boys bring fruit and a sow for sacrifice.

The south and north exteriors, again the upper half (the lower half being carved throughout in elegant floral patterns), are decorated with a different kind of scene altogether. Here we see men, women, and children in procession, coming to celebrate the laying of the foundation stone of the altar on 4 July 13 BC (Figure 20.5). Augustus walks among them, in the center of the south side, but he is inconspicuous, as befitted the public persona he liked to project. Also processing are officials, priests, and members of Augustus's family, including women and children, each person illustrated with a slightly different stance, movement, or expression. The scene is tranquil, calm, dignified. The style recalls that of the Parthenon frieze, with idealized naturalistic

Figure 20.5 Procession frieze (detail), Ara Pacis, Rome

representations of people, but differs from that frieze, also a religious procession, with its different cast of characters: horseback riders, animals brought for sacrifice, and gods in attendance, but not the political leadership. The reliefs of Achaemenid Persepolis (above, Chapter 10) match the calm of the Ara Pacis. But at Persepolis the processors bear tribute; the king awaits, seated, at the end. The smooth functioning of the empire is emphasized, but so too is the distinction between ruler and ruled. Augustus, in contrast, hides his rulership, instead taking his place among the many functionaries who together embody the Roman state.

The message imparted by the Ara Pacis procession is the orderly, beneficial rule of Augustus and his family. With such other pictorial vehicles for ideology as the mythological panels on the east and west sides of the Ara Pacis and the sculpture of the Forum of Augustus, and the lesson proclaimed by his discreet house carefully located on the Palatine Hill, Augustus could feel confident that public art and architecture in the capital city contributed fully to the new chapter in Roman history: the end of decades of civil war and the renewal of the Roman state. Legitimacy stressed by connections with the key gods and heroes of the Roman people; his own achievements made clear, never for his own glory, but always, really, for the stability and prosperity of the

Roman state – these themes Augustus made basic to his concept of rule. There is something very Greek about this – fifth-century BC Athenian, that is. Augustus's successors, as we shall see, will continue to adorn the city with great monuments. But in a Hellenistic rather than Periklean manner they will offer themselves the grandeur, private as well as public, that they considered appropriate to their imperial status.

CHAPTER 21

Italy outside the capital

Pompeii and Ostia

Let us leave Rome for the moment and visit two cities where archaeological excavations have given valuable information about ancient Roman town life that complements what we have learned from the capital city. Pompeii was a modest-sized farming city located near Naples. Developed during the Republic, it was destroyed in the early Empire by the eruption of the volcano Vesuvius. Ostia, Rome's port city, prospered from the Republic into the late Empire. Because of the extensive preservation of their ruins, these two towns count among the richest archaeological sites of Roman Italy.

POMPEII

Pompeii occupies a special place in Roman archaeology, for this city and its neighbors, notably Herculaneum, were remarkably well preserved under the volcanic debris that rained down from Mount Vesuvius in AD 79. The ruins give an unequalled glimpse of the daily life of town dwellers during the late Republic and early Empire. In contrast, in Rome itself, because of continuing rebuilding throughout the Empire, remains from these periods are only sporadically preserved. Explorations began at Herculaneum in 1732, and at Pompeii in 1748 under government patronage of the Kingdom of the Two Sicilies, the first major archaeological excavations on a Classical site. At first, methods were primitive; only in the 1860s, under the direction of Giuseppe Fiorelli, did investigations take on a systematic form. Excavations have continued ever since, with most of Pompeii now uncovered.

Historical introduction

Pompeii is located on the Bay of Naples south of the city of Naples (Figure 21.1). The town lay well sited close to the sea at a crossroads point where an important route to the interior branched off from the coast road. The larger region of Campania and the Bay of Naples had already seen much development by the time Pompeii was first settled in the sixth century BC. Greeks had established themselves at the north end of the bay two centuries earlier, first at Pithekoussai on the island of Ischia, then at Kyme (later Cumae) on the mainland opposite. A late sixth-century BC Doric temple in the Triangular Forum records their influence in early Pompeii. Etruscans expanded into Campania in the sixth century BC, only to be expelled by the Greeks in 474 BC; finds of Etruscan pottery in deep soundings excavated below Pompeii's main forum attest to their contacts with the town. By the fifth century BC, Pompeii was the preserve of the Samnites, a local people related to the Latins. But the Romans were expanding, and in 290 BC they defeated the Samnites and took control of Campania. Pompeii remained ethnically Samnite, however. In the 80s BC, Pompeii joined other Campanian cities in the "Social War," an unsuccessful

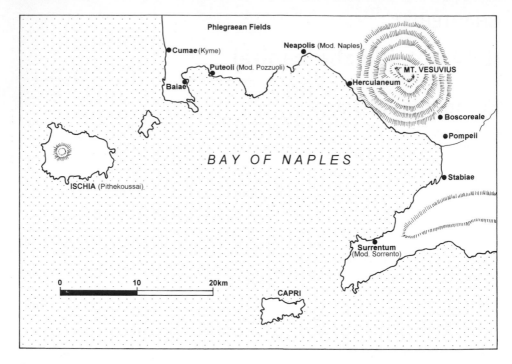

Figure 21.1 Bay of Naples

uprising against Roman domination. In the aftermath of his victory, the Roman general Sulla established a veterans' colony in Pompeii, with his veterans displacing local Samnite notables. The Romanization of the city was now complete.

During the first century AD Pompeii prospered as a commercial and farming center, with a population of 10,000–20,000. Its chief commodities included wool, flowers and perfume, and *garum*, a highly prized fish sauce made of fermented sardine entrails. In AD 62 Nature struck a first blow with a damaging earthquake. Then in the year 79, on 24 August, Vesuvius erupted without warning, spewing forth pumice, stone, poisonous gases, ash, and mud. Most people escaped, but some were trapped; the forms of their bodies would be preserved in the volcanic matrix long after flesh and bone had disintegrated. A letter written some 30 years later by Pliny the Younger to the historian Tacitus describes the catastrophe, recounting how Pliny's uncle, Pliny the Elder, met his death. Pompeii and Herculaneum were largely covered, Pompeii by 4m of pumice and ash, Herculaneum by up to 16m of volcanic mud. Salvage and looting went on, and possibly even sporadic occupation at Pompeii, but full-scale reconstruction must have seemed an impossible task. The ruined towns soon fell into oblivion.

Town plan

The early city lay in the south-west, a small area with irregular streets (Figure 21.2). The forum lies within this sector. By the fourth century BC the town expanded north of the forum, now following a grid plan. City blocks in the north area contain some of Pompeii's oldest surviving houses. A circuit wall ca. 1200m × 720m was erected some time in the third century BC, enclosing fields and gardens. Around 200 BC a further expansion took place toward the east.

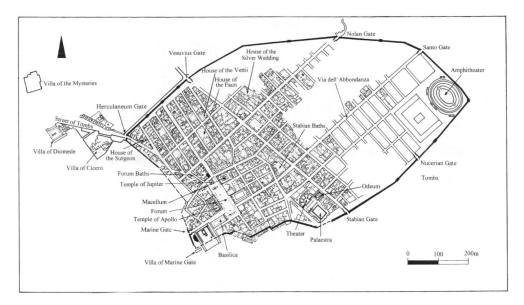

Figure 21.2 City plan, Pompeii

During the second century BC, the last Samnite period, the town had two major north–south and east–west streets; much building took place, including the theater, baths, and the portico that framed the forum. The arrival of Sulla's veterans stimulated a new building boom, with such structures as the amphitheater and odeum erected in the first century BC.

The forum

The forum and its surrounding area contain the city's most important group of public buildings (Figure 21.3). The forum itself is a long (142m) and unusually narrow rectangular space. Originally colonnades lined the area, porticoes or covered walkways that hid most buildings behind in the typical Hellenistic fashion already seen at Cosa. Prominently visible at the north, short end of the forum, however, was the Temple of Jupiter. The temple was built in the second century BC in the Italic style, on a high podium with steps in front, but with Corinthian columns. When Pompeii became Roman in the first century BC, the interior space of the temple was modified so that Juno and Minerva could take their place alongside Jupiter. With the revered Roman triad now installed, this central temple mirrored the venerable Capitolium of Rome itself – an important connection with the capital city. The formality of the forum was further marked by the display of statues of prominent citizens and by a prohibition on wheeled vehicles.

Behind the screen of the colonnades stood buildings that served a variety of religious, civic, and commercial purposes. Connected with the forum were at least two temples in addition to the Capitolium. A Temple of Apollo lies parallel to the forum, standing on a podium inside its own colonnaded precinct. The temple uses Corinthian capitals, whereas the precinct features Ionic. The cult of Apollo began as early as the sixth century BC, as inscribed Etruscan vases attest, but the temple was built later, in the second century BC.

Across the forum, another temple honored the deified emperor Vespasian. Vespasian had contributed to repairs after the earthquake of 62, and so was awarded this prominent place on the east side of the forum. Emperors were routinely worshipped as divinities; the cult of the

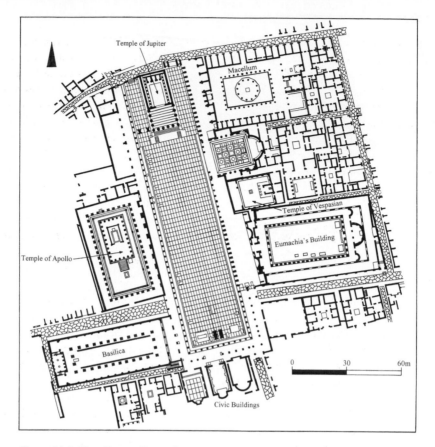

Figure 21.3 Plan, Forum, Pompeii

deified emperor served to link towns throughout the huge empire not only with the distant
capital, but also with each other.

Civic buildings occupied the south end of the forum. The Comitium met here. So too did the
duoviri, the chief magistrates of the town; the *aediles*, who policed the city; and the town council,
whose members were called the *decuriones*. On the south-west lies the *basilica*, placed at a right
angle to the forum. Built ca. 125 BC, this is the earliest preserved example of the type anywhere,
a large roofed hall (ca. 60m × 26m) with the higher-ceilinged central part allowing for a
clerestory. Its columns were made of baked brick, an unusual choice of material for the late
Republic, but covered with stucco in order to imitate more expensive stone. Ionic capitals were
used on the lower level, Corinthian above. This building housed many functions, such as law
courts and business activities.

Commerce was the purpose of the remaining major buildings that lined the east side of the
forum. The largest is Eumachia's building (AD 14–37), a guild hall for the wool processors of
Pompeii. Eumachia, a wealthy woman, dedicated the building in the names of herself and her
son. Not being citizens, women could not participate directly in the political process, but their
public-minded gifts were always welcome. In the extreme north-east lies the *macellum*, a complex
containing the meat and fish markets and a small chapel to the imperial cult.

Street life

Leaving the forum for other sectors of the town, the visitor has a wide choice of streets to follow. The most impressive is today called the Via dell'Abbondanza. Like many other streets, it is paved with lava blocks, has sidewalks and kerbs and large stepping stones at intersections to get safely over any mud or sewage. Shops were frequent. They include *thermopolia*, wine shops or snack bars, with big clay storage jars embedded in the counter for easy serving of the beverages. Hot wine was a great favorite. We can also see a mill and bakery, with stone mills for grinding flour and an oven for baking bread. Street walls display advertisements for carpenters, politicians, and gladiatorial shows, among others. Representations of phalloi are widespread, and have helped identify brothels. Graffiti are everywhere. "Vote for Lucius Popidius Sabinus – his grandmother worked hard for his last election and is pleased with the results," reads one election appeal – or humorous put-down. Sex and love are popular topics. "Fortunatus, you sweet little darling, you great fornicator, this is written by someone who knows you!" reads one. Another, more serious: "Noete, light of my life, goodbye, goodbye, for ever goodbye!" (Grant 1971: 208 and 210).

Theaters and the amphitheater

Like all Roman towns of any size, Pompeii had its own theaters. The theater district lay in the south part of the city. A large horseshoe-shaped theater was built in the Greek manner against a natural slope; its date, late third or first half of the second centuries BC, places it earlier than any surviving theater in Rome. The final remodeling took place in the Augustan period. In Roman fashion, the stage building was connected with the seating, and the stage itself was placed low so that important spectators sitting in the front rows could see well.

Next to the large theater is the *odeum*, a small roofed theater seating 1000–1500 people. It was built ca. 80–75 BC, well after the large theater. The odeum (= Greek *odeion*) became a favorite building type in the Roman world, a small hall for concerts and recitals, always covered, a useful complement to the large open-air theater adapted from the ancient Greeks.

Behind the large theater lies a large square surrounded by a Doric colonnade, intended as a shelter for spectators in case of rain and as a backstage area for the theater. By the time of the city's destruction this portico served as a barracks for gladiators, according to the striking finds: helmets, armor, weapons, and related equipment, as well as graffiti referring to teams of gladiators. On the east side of the colonnade, in excavations of 1767–68 skeletons of at least 52 people were discovered, including children, and much jewelry. These people surely gathered here intending to flee through the nearby Stabian Gate to the harbor, but died before they could escape.

Gladiators were the combatants in the brutal spectacles enjoyed by the Romans. Fights to the death by armed men had distant origins in funeral rites of Etruscans and Campanians. By the third and second centuries BC, such combats, detached from funerary contexts, became a standard part of public celebrations, often sponsored by a wealthy person. The popularity of such entertainment continued unabated through the imperial period. Often originating as prisoners of war, gladiators became true professionals, well-trained and well-equipped, because the rewards for success could be enormous. The repertoire of combats expanded ever creatively. Gladiators might face exotic wild animals imported from afar or unarmed criminals, already sentenced to death. On the grand scale, mock battles were presented, even naval battles when an arena could be filled with water.

The structure developed to present these spectacles was the *amphitheater*. The word means "double theater," and indeed the Roman amphitheater was completely round or oval. The amphitheater at Pompeii, built ca. 80 BC in the east sector of the town, is one of the oldest surviving examples. Originally it was called not an amphitheater but "arena and spectacula." *Arena* meant the space, or sand, where the events took place, while *spectacula* meant the viewing area where spectators sat. Pompeii's amphitheater was unusual in being excavated into the ground, its floor thus lying below ground level, its seating partially supported by earth yet also rising above ground. Although the shows in amphitheaters were normally free, seating was regulated according to social status, with important people in the best seats at the bottom, the middle classes in the middle zones, and the poor – and perhaps most women – at the top.

The amphitheater seated 20,000, with spectators coming both from the city and from the surrounding region. Indeed, the Roman historian Tacitus recorded a riot that erupted in the amphitheater in AD 59 between Pompeiians and fans from nearby Nuceria. The event is confirmed in a Pompeiian wall painting that shows both amphitheater and fighting men. Because there were deaths, the Roman Senate banned Pompeii from staging such spectacles for ten years.

Baths

By the time of the eruption, Pompeii had four large public bath complexes and many smaller ones. Public baths were an important institution of the Roman world. Although some wealthy houses had their own washing facilities, most people went to the public baths. The baths were not simply for cleaning oneself, but were social centers where one exercised, relaxed, ate, attended cultural events, and met friends and business associates. They generally opened at noon and closed at sunset. Men and women had separate areas or, in small complexes, separate hours or days. The grandest bath buildings were those of the capital city during the later empire. As one would expect, the Pompeiian examples were more modest.

The origins of Roman bath complexes are disputed. Since many of the technical terms for components of baths were Greek, the Romans may have taken much from the Hellenistic Greeks. But local practices, such as taking advantage of the natural hot springs in Baiae, in Campania, surely contributed to the tradition.

The Stabian Baths, the earliest at Pompeii, were built originally in the second century BC, later remodeled after 80 BC. The plan is irregular (Figure 21.4), but does include the key rooms of the typical bath complex. One entered from the street into the changing room (*apodyterium*), continued into a warm room (*tepidarium*), possibly a small sweat room (*laconicum*), and a hot room (*caldarium*), then ended with a dip into a cold pool (*frigidarium*). The Stabian Baths also have a large open-air swimming pool (*natatio*), a court (*palaestra*) for exercise, smaller rooms, and a latrine.

Heating originally came from portable braziers, following Greek practice, but eventually the warm and hot rooms were heated from below the floor. In this *hypocaust* system, the floors of these rooms were raised on piles of bricks so that hot air from central furnaces could circulate freely in the space below. Some bath complexes also contained walls fitted with flues for hot air, a type of supplemental heating popular especially in the northern, colder areas of the empire, in Germany, Gaul, and Britain.

Seneca, who lived above a bath establishment in first-century AD Rome, gives colorful testimony about the crowded, lively, vibrant world of the baths. Rich men made grand entrances accompanied by their servants; bath personnel circulated, offering equipment such as bath oil, food such as cakes and sausages, and services such as plucking hair and giving massages; and slaves operated the furnaces and kept the premises clean.

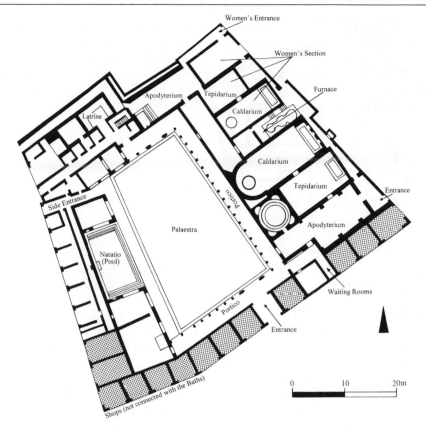

Figure 21.4 Plan, Stabian Baths, Pompeii

The Roman bath culture depended on the aqueducts bringing large quantities of water; maintaining the aqueducts necessitated in turn economic and political stability. With the disruptions of the Middle Ages, the system fell apart. In western Europe, the bath culture came to an end by the ninth century. In the politically stable east, in contrast, baths have continued without break through Byzantine, Arab, and Ottoman Turkish cultures to the present day.

Houses

The many well-preserved private houses rank high among the important finds at Pompeii and Herculaneum. Built at different times during the Republic and the early Empire, the houses document developing architectural and decorative styles with a completeness unparalleled in the Roman world.

The traditional Italic house of the well-to-do features an *atrium* (pl. *atria*), probably a legacy of the Etruscans. Atrium houses are prominent at Pompeii and Herculaneum, as town houses, not apartments and not free-standing villas surrounded by gardens. They extend right to the street, with shops lining the street side of many, and they share walls with adjacent houses. Construction is of rubble and stone faced with concrete, plastered and, on interior surfaces, often decorated.

The Roman architect Vitruvius described five different types of atrium houses. Two types dominate, the Tuscan (the most popular) and the *tetrastyle*. The House of the Surgeon, originally

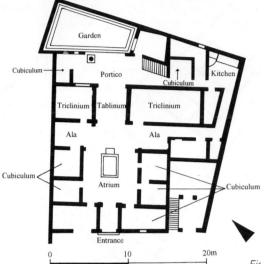

Figure 21.5 Plan, House of the Surgeon, Pompeii

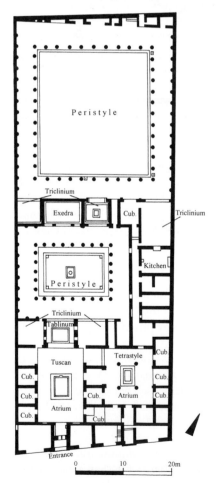

of the fourth century BC, one of the earliest surviving houses from Pompeii, has a Tuscan atrium at its core (Figure 21.5). From the street one passes through an entrance vestibule (*fauces*) into the atrium. The room opens to the sky through the *compluvium*; rain can then fall into a basin (*impluvium*) and water tank below. The specifically Tuscan feature of this atrium is the absence of columns around the basin; the ceiling is supported instead by strong rafters. The compluvium provides another important service: it lets in light, which otherwise enters only through small slit windows and the portico at the back, supplemented by oil lamps and tallow candles. This main room must have been pleasant in warmer weather, but impossibly chilly in colder seasons. The family would then retreat with their portable braziers to smaller enclosed rooms.

Off the atrium lie those smaller rooms, symmetrically arranged for the most part. Furniture tended to be simple and portable, so the purpose of any particular room could be quickly changed. The main functions are as follows: small rooms (*cubiculum*, pl. *cubicula*) usable as bedrooms; two wings (*alae*) in which bust portraits of ancestors were kept; and, at the rear, the most important rooms, the dining room (*triclinium*) and the main reception room (*tablinum*).

Figure 21.6 Plan, House of the Faun, Pompeii

Here, in the tablinum, the owner and his family formally greeted guests. A wealthy man would have many "clients," people who looked to him for advice, money, and support, and he received them here.

The House of the Surgeon has a portico and a garden at the back. The unusual trapezoidal shape of the garden reflects the odd shape of the property. Likewise the kitchen occupies a curiously shaped corner; in such houses, kitchens were small and squeezed in wherever possible.

Hellenistic Greek influence combines with traditional Italic in the House of the Faun, built in 185–175 BC but later modified (Figure 21.6). The largest house in Pompeii, occupying an entire city block, the House of the Faun consists of three parts: public and private quarters, and peristyle gardens. The public section is the Tuscan atrium, entered from the street and laid out as in the House of the Surgeon. The private area centers on a *tetrastyle atrium*, Vitruvius's second type, an atrium in which four columns surround the impluvium and hold up the ceiling.

Behind these public and private atria lie the peristyles, gardens surrounded by a colonnade. Colonnaded courts enjoyed popularity in the Greek world, but they did not contain gardens. On Delos, for example, the best Hellenistic houses have colonnaded courts with mosaic floors in the center. But Delos has no natural water supply, and rainwater had to be collected and used sparingly. In any case Romans valued and enjoyed gardens. Explorations of the cavities left by plant roots have allowed researchers to reconstruct the kinds of plants cultivated, and to replant some gardens as the ancients might have done.

The first peristyle at the House of the Faun was added in ca. 125 BC; a second, larger peristyle was added in the first century BC. Between them lies a room of a type borrowed from the Greeks, an *exedra*, a retreat. The floor of this exedra was decorated with the famous "Alexander Mosaic" (see Chapter 16).

A variant layout occurs in the House of the Vettii, a house remodeled in the late period by two newly rich freedmen and wine merchants, Aulus Vettius Restitutus and Aulus Vettius Conviva,

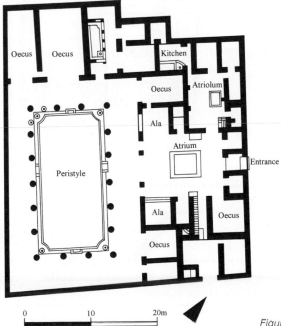

0   10   20m

Figure 21.7 Plan, House of the Vettii, Pompeii

and restored in modern times. The plan of the house is compact, but complex (Figure 21.7). The entrance leads into the main atrium, large with a deep impluvium (Figure 21.8). The atrium lacks a tablinum; instead, one passes directly to the peristyle garden. To the side of the large atrium lies a small, private atrium supplied with a *lararium*, a shrine to the *lares*, the deities who protected house and family. From here one has access to the kitchen and to the servants' quarters. The house has *oecae* (sing. *oecus*), dining rooms in the Greek style, large rooms opening onto the peristyle. These rooms are decorated with the complex architectural scenes characteristic of the fourth and last style of Pompeian wall painting.

Figure 21.8 Atrium, House of the Vettii, Pompeii

Wall paintings and the Villa of the Mysteries

The eruption of Vesuvius preserved hundreds of wall paintings in Pompeii and the surrounding region – the important core of surviving Roman wall paintings. They date of course to the late Republic and early Empire only; to continue the story of Roman painting after AD 79, one needs to look elsewhere.

The wall paintings of Pompeii and neighboring towns and indeed of other contemporary towns (notably Rome) were classified into four groups by the German scholar August Mau in 1882. The types overlap, both chronologically and even in style, but nonetheless remain a useful way to understand different approaches to the art of decorating walls. The first two styles, at least, originate in the wall painting tradition of the Greek East, in such places as Delos (First Style) and Alexandria (Second Style).

The First Style is the easiest to pick out, because it solely depicts well-cut stone masonry. Figures are absent. This style appears early, beginning in the early second century BC. The Second Style, from ca. 90 BC, introduces architecture and the illusion of three-dimensional space. Theatrical scenery and the architectural backdrops of stages influenced the development of this style. But in a famous variant at the Villa of the Mysteries outside Pompeii, human figures enact a dramatic cult ceremony in front of only a minimal architectural backdrop.

Villas, in the parlance of Classical archaeology, were large independent houses that stood in the countryside. Generally the centers of large estates, they combined living quarters with rooms devoted to farm activities. The Villa of the Mysteries has a complicated building history, unravelled in Italian excavations of 1909–10 and 1929–30. Construction began ca. 200 BC, with a *cryptoporticus* (a high platform with plain arches framing a walkway) and, on top, an atrium. Additions in the late second century BC included the main peristyle, a small tetrastyle atrium, and baths. A semicircular exedra was built on the podium terrace some time in the first century AD. Rooms now totaled over 60. In the final years of Pompeii, agricultural installations were added right in the middle, as if the villa had become strictly a business center. Finds of a winepress, a heap of onions in the main bedroom, and farm tools (pruning hooks, hammers, picks, hoes, and shovels) have helped define the character of this villa in its final years.

The important paintings of Dionysiac Mysteries after which the building is named decorate the walls of a modestly sized room (7m × 5m) in the heart of the villa (Figure 21.9). They date to ca. 50 BC. The paintings are 3.3m high, with the figures 1.5m high. In front of a Second Style background of dark red panels divided by columns, a young woman of unknown identity undergoes an initiation rite into the Mysteries of the god Dionysos. The scenes unfold in a continuous narrative, like a comic strip, with figures realistically depicted in the finest Hellenistic–Roman manner. The story combines the real with the imaginary, for our initiate confronts a variety of personages, some of whom – satyrs, a winged female brandishing a whip, and Dionysos (Bacchus) and his consort Ariadne – step directly from Greco-Roman mythology. None of the figures is labelled, and surviving texts say nothing about these scenes. As a result, the precise meaning of the images and their presence in this country villa remain unexplained.

The Third Style of wall painting, the "ornamental" style, downplays architecture and instead emphasizes two-dimensional framed spaces, sometimes with small panels inserted in the large fields as if they were paintings hung separately on the walls. The frames themselves can be highly decorative. This style appears in Rome during the reign of Augustus and continued in use at Pompeii until the earthquake of 62. In the final years of the city, the Fourth Style held sway. This style combines characteristics of the two previous styles, by featuring large paintings

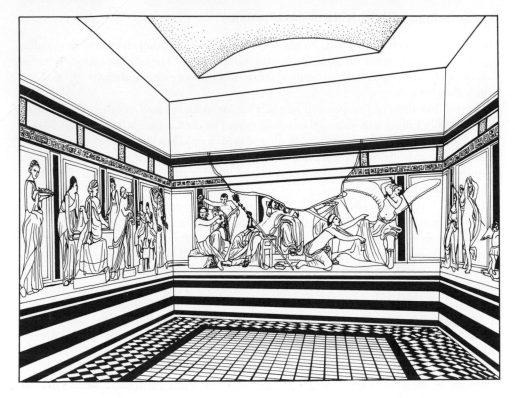

Figure 21.9 Mysteries wall paintings, Villa of the Mysteries, Pompeii

of three-dimensional architecture and figures set inside complex frames. It is this style that has a prominent place in the House of the Vettii.

OSTIA

While the ruins of Pompeii give us an unparalleled look at a medium-sized Roman town dependent on agriculture, the remains of Ostia, the port of Rome, located at the mouth of the Tiber River, document a city of commercial importance. Like Pompeii, Ostia gives information about Roman urbanism that is unavailable from Rome itself. Unlike Rome, Ostia faded after antiquity. The neglected harbors became swampy and malarial; habitation dwindled. Sand dunes covered the Roman ruins, an excellent protecting blanket.

Ostia began ca. 350 BC as a fort (*castrum*), guarding access to the Tiber River and to Rome (above, Chapter 19). Its thick walls enclosed a rectangular area of just over 2ha (Figure 21.10). With two main streets crossing at right angles and leading to four city gates, this fortified settlement was an early example of the grid plan in Italy. During the Punic Wars, it was used as a military port.

During the second and first centuries BC, Ostia expanded beyond the walls of the original colony. To feed the large population of Rome, imported food supplies were crucial. Ostia's harbor became a key port of entry for grain, notably from Sicily (late Republic) and Egypt

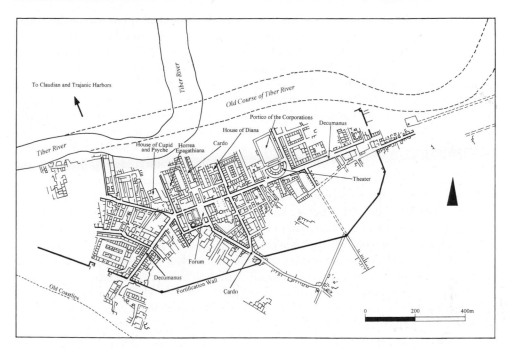

Figure 21.10 City plan, Ostia

(during the Empire); the grain was stored in large warehouses (*horrea*) in both Ostia and Rome. As a measure of the town's growth, new walls were built ca. 80 BC, enclosing an area of 64ha. The old castrum became the forum of the enlarged town, at the crossing of the two principal roads, the cardo (north–south) and the decumanus (east–west).

The commercial importance of Ostia continued to grow, thanks especially to the intervention of the emperors Claudius and Nero. In the early Empire, the mouth of the Tiber proved too small to accommodate the city's maritime traffic. Moreover, the river and the port kept filling with silt. As a result, an artificial harbor was built 2–3 km north of the Tiber mouth, begun during the reign of Claudius ca. AD 42 and finished under Nero. It measured ca. 1,000m across and had a lighthouse, but was not adequately protected from winds. A canal linked the port to the Tiber; modern Rome's airport, Fiumicino, built on the site of the ancient harbor, took its name from this ancient canal. Under Trajan, ca. AD 112, a hexagonal harbor was added next to Claudius's port. An urban center developed by these harbors. Eventually, in the late Empire, the settlement, now walled, was granted status as a town separate from Ostia, with the name of Portus. But through the second century, the harbor area remained under the control of Ostia, fueling Ostia's growing prosperity and expanding population: 50,000–60,000, according to one estimate (Meiggs 1973), but only 22,000, according to another (Storey 1997).

Commercial buildings

Ostia has yielded much evidence for commercial complexes, warehouses, and shops. The Portico of the Corporations (Piazzale delle Corporazioni), located behind the small theater, exemplifies the Ostian business center. The portico as well as the theater originated in the Augustan age, but were remodeled in the late second or early third century AD. The business complex consisted of a rectangular area, ca. 125m × 80m, framed by a double colonnaded portico; in the center lay a garden with a small temple dedicated perhaps to Mercury. Behind the portico, 61 small rooms served as branch offices for businesses dealing with shipping in the Mediterranean. Many offices advertised their specialty in the mosaic pavement in front of their door. The image of an elephant with the legend *Stat(io) Sabratensium*, for example, signaled traders from Sabratha in Tripolitania (modern Libya) who dealt in ivory, and who may even have arranged the transport of African elephants for the Colosseum. Like the variety of religious cults attested in Ostia, this business portico speaks eloquently for the cosmopolitan character of the city.

Ostian warehouses include the Horrea Epagathiana et Epaphroditiana, built by two freedmen, Epagathus and Epaphroditus, during the reign of Antoninus Pius (138–61). Brick was the construction material. Indeed, at Ostia, instead of rubble facing on a cement core (as at Pompeii), regular courses of bricks were preferred. The exterior of the warehouse contained shops open to the street. Over 800 shops (tabernae) are known from Ostia. They normally consist of a single tall, deep, barrel-vaulted room, often equipped with a loft for storage or sleeping. A small window over the door would provide lighting when the front door panels were closed.

A grand entry lined with brick columns and pediment marked the passage from the street to the interior court of the warehouse. A double gate with iron bolts provided security. The inner court was paved with mosaics and surrounded by arched porticoes. The building had 16 rooms on the ground floor. Stairs with separate entrances led to the upper storeys, to offices and possibly apartments for the owners.

Some warehouses contained traces of the products traded. In one example north-east of the forum, 100 *dolia* (huge pottery vats) were discovered sunk in the ground – a capacity of more than 84,000 liters of oil or wine.

Residential buildings: insulae

The term *insula* (pl. *insulae*), literally "island," denoted a city block and also a multi-storeyed apartment building, an essential component of urban housing during the Roman Empire. With population increasing, urban residents often resorted to such housing. In Rome itself, some 90 percent of the population lived in them. But ancient apartment buildings have survived poorly from the capital; at Ostia preservation is much better.

The widespread construction of concrete insulae is partly attributable to the Great Fire in Rome in AD 64, during the reign of Nero. Building materials for ordinary dwellings had been wood and mud brick – cheap, but also highly combustible. After the fire rebuilding was regulated. Flame-resistant materials predominated; the use of wood diminished. Street widths were specified. Building height was restricted to 4–5 storeys maximum, ca. 24m under Nero, 20m under Trajan. Apartment buildings sprang up, structures that satisfied the new building codes. As in many cities, however, we can imagine that regulations were not always followed, that architectural quality and maintenance could be poor, side streets dark, noisy, and filthy.

In appearance insulae resembled warehouses (Figure 21.11). They were large with sturdy walls of concrete with brick facing, the brick normally exposed, not plastered over. The exterior might well include shops. Multiple entrances gave access into the building and to individual apartments – a help if fires needed combatting. Central courts, if present, provided air and light, supplementing windows on the exterior.

The typical apartment was relatively spacious. A wide corridor hall with small rooms off it dominated the plan. At either end lay the larger reception and dining rooms. Mosaics in geometric patterns often covered floors; in poorer dwellings, patterns in the brick flooring

Figure 21.11 Apartment house (reconstruction), Ostia

sufficed. Walls were painted simply. Utility rooms might include a kitchen, but no chimney. Toilets were a luxury; normally one used common toilets on the ground floor. Other facilities available on the ground floor might be running water and, in the court, an oven for baking. Easier access to these features may explain why apartments on the lowest floors were the costliest, the most desirable. A good example of an Ostian insula is the House of Diana of ca. AD 130–40, named after an object found there, a terracotta relief plaque showing the goddess Diana.

In the late empire, from the third century AD, as Ostia's population declined, luxurious free-standing houses of the sort seen at Pompeii made a comeback. Despite the general commercial decline, evidently Ostia had value as a place of retreat for wealthy Romans. The House of Cupid and Psyche of the fourth century AD exemplifies this trend. In contrast with Pompeiian houses, the luxury of this house is displayed not in wall paintings, but in the decoration of polychrome marble on the floor and the walls – a characteristic of the centuries to come, in grand public buildings and churches as well as in the houses of the well-to-do.

CHAPTER 22

Rome from Nero to Hadrian

Imperial patronage and architectural revolution

Emperors of the first to early third centuries AD:

Julio-Claudians (AD 14–69)

Tiberius	ruled 14–37
Gaius (Caligula)	37–41
Claudius	41–54
Nero	54–68

Three short reigns in Galba, Otho, and Vitellius	68–69

Flavians (69–96)

Vespasian	69–79
Titus	79–81
Domitian	81–96

High Empire (96–193)

Nerva	96–98
Trajan	98–117
Hadrian	117–138
Antoninus Pius	138–161
Marcus Aurelius	161–180
Commodus	180–192
Pertinax	192–193

Severans (193–235)

Septimius Severus	193–211
Caracalla	211–217
Elagabalus	218–222
Severus Alexander	222–235

Rome, the capital city, continued as the nucleus of the empire until well into the fourth century AD. We have traced the development of Rome from its origins through the reign of Augustus, noting the many changes brought about in its appearance by the absorption of Etruscan and Greek artistic and architectural forms, and by the changing requirements of civic life. This chapter and Chapter 24 will follow the city through the imperial centuries.

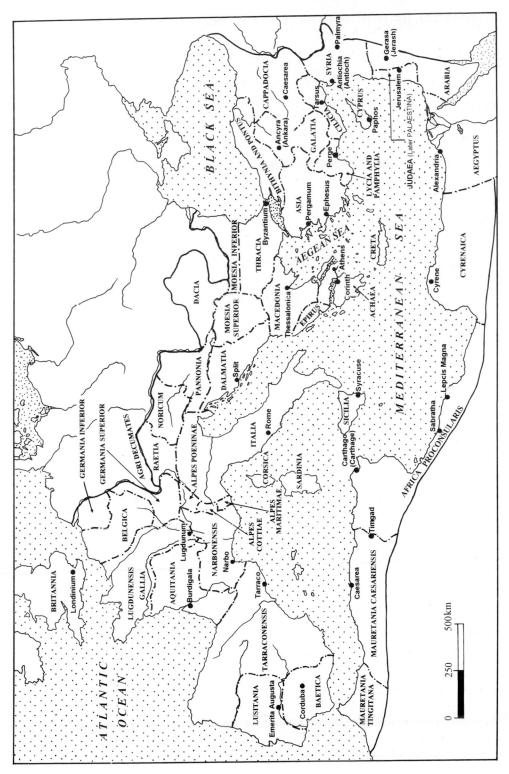

Figure 22.1 The Roman Empire during the reign of Hadrian: the provinces, with selected provincial capitals and other major cities

HISTORICAL INTRODUCTION: THE EMPIRE

The two centuries following the death of Augustus marked the great period of prosperity and power for the Roman Empire (Figure 22.1). The enormous territory, consolidated by Augustus with the takeover of Egypt (30 BC) and the final conquest of Spain and Europe west of the Rhine and south of the Danube, further enlarged with the conquests of Britain (43 AD) and Dacia (roughly modern Romania) (101–6 AD), was held successfully against both external and internal challenges. During this era of the *Pax Romana* (Roman Peace), agriculture, industry, and trade thrived, bringing a stable and prosperous life to a large number of ethnically, religiously, and linguistically diverse peoples.

This diverse population contained important social differences, with citizens, free non-citizens, and slaves as distinct groups. Citizenship, although restricted at first, was eventually granted to all free people in the third century. Slaves, always numerous, provided cheap labor. Despite the social boundaries, throughout the first and second centuries it was possible to change status, for a slave to become free, for a free non-citizen to become a citizen. In the later Empire, even among the citizenry socio-economic class distinctions would become more rigid, impeding social mobility.

An important agent for stability, for peace and prosperity throughout the huge empire was the army. Well organized and trained, the army consisted at first of citizens performing their civic duty, later of professional soldiers. During the first two centuries AD, the army was primarily stationed not in the heart of the empire but along the 10,000km frontier. Never numerous, with a maximum of 400,000 men, the army could maintain the frontier as long as attacks from outside were not simultaneous; troops redeployed as needed to a zone of crisis. Only one neighboring power could match Roman strength: the Parthians, ruling in Persia and Mesopotamia from 210 BC to 225 AD. In later centuries, attacks would come simultaneously at different points along the frontier, thus straining the Roman defenses.

The army helped spread Roman institutions to the provinces. As we have seen, the army camp, or *castrum*, often developed into a town, with merchants and other providers of services to the camp settling close by. Farmers worked to supply the army and the towns as well as their own needs. In addition, new towns (*coloniae*) were created for retired army veterans, with the principles of camp layout – two principal streets, the *cardo* and the *decumanus*, crossing at right angles, with a forum at the crossing – followed in planning the settlement. The essential shrines and institutions of the Roman state occupied places of honor, even if the local government controlled its immediate affairs: the temple to Jupiter, Juno, and Minerva; a shrine to the cult of the defied emperor; the forum and its civic buildings. Other factors sustaining Roman social and economic cohesion included the legal system developed in the Republic; a stable monetary system, with coinage in gold, silver, and bronze, including small denominations for ordinary transactions; and the well-maintained network of communications. Shared by countryside and city alike, by the distant provinces and Italy, by Latin speakers and others, these features were recognized by all as signs of membership in this far-flung community, the Roman Empire.

ROME: THE IMPERIAL CAPITAL

The major difference from Republican Rome is the rule and patronage of emperors. Augustus, the first emperor, or *princeps* as he styled himself, appreciated that his rule marked a transition from the Republic to something new. To ensure stability, he stressed continuity with what

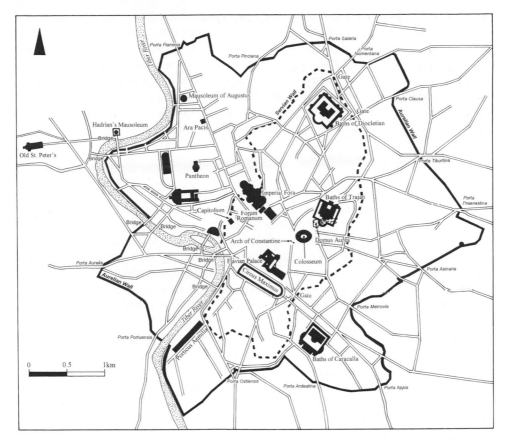

Figure 22.2 City plan, Rome, imperial period

had come before. His avoidance of personal ostentation, for example, counted as one way he paid homage to ancient Republican ideals. His successors gradually abandoned Augustus's low profile, adopting instead the opulent trappings of kingship popular in the Hellenistic world. This changing concept of kingship was mirrored in the appearance of Rome, in the grandiose palaces, temples, commemorative monuments, and civic buildings commissioned by the emperors (Figure 22.2). Embedded in this architecture is a revolution in forms, made possible by the use of concrete, a breaking away from the traditional post-and-lintel system enshrined in the conservatism of Greek architecture. The essentials took place within a short time, from the reigns of Nero to Hadrian. The effects would continue to resound ever after in European and Mediterranean architecture.

PALACES

The population of Rome swelled to over one half million, possibly up to a million by the first century AD, huge for an ancient city, but befitting the capital of such an enormous state. Most people lived in squalor, in ramshackle multi-storey apartment buildings along narrow streets unlit at night. Disaster was endemic, with collapsing buildings and fires, the most famous of which was that of 64 during the reign of Nero. The wealthy, served and protected by retainers, were spared such hardships and could enjoy the stimulations of this great city. Their luxurious dwellings have largely disappeared, but we can imagine their houses as grand versions of those examined at Pompeii. In contrast, the residences of the emperors have survived to a certain extent. Three palaces give a perspective on the royal expectations in the post-Augustan centuries: the *Domus Aurea* (Golden House) of Nero; the *Flavian Palace* on the Palatine Hill; and *Hadrian's Villa* at Tivoli, outside Rome. All were far more sumptuous than Augustus's house. In addition, all three display architectural innovations that distinguished this period.

The Domus Aurea

Nero became emperor in 54 at the age of 17, and soon gained a reputation for capriciousness and cruelty. He was also given to grandeur, best expressed in his ambitious projects for a new palace. Unsatisfied with Tiberius's Domus Tiberiana on the Palatine Hill, he began a new residence, the Domus Transitoria, which extended from the Palatine across low ground to the Esquiline Hill to the north. This palace was destroyed in the great fire of 64, which started in the Circus Maximus and spread northward with devastating results. Burned completely was half the center of the city: three of the city's 14 administrative regions, with an additional seven regions damaged. Nero quickly set out to build a replacement, with the help of Severus, an architect, and Celer, an engineer. Thanks to annexation of additional land, the new palace, known as the Domus Aurea, the Golden House, occupied an even larger tract of land in the heart of the city than did its predecessor, ca. 50ha. A combination of parks, lakes, and buildings, the Domus Aurea was a country villa placed in a downtown urban setting. In its large entrance court stood a colossal bronze statue of Nero by the sculptor Zenodorus. According to the late first-century writer Suetonius, the statue measured 120 Roman feet (= 35.48m) in height.

An artificial lake was created in the low-lying land beyond (the site of the later Colosseum). The palace proper, the residential wing, stood on the south slope of the Esquiline Hill (Figure 22.3). The whole complex – lake, gardens, and residence – was built over after Nero's death, probably as a way of reviling his memory (*damnatio memoriae*). The descriptions of Suetonius and Pliny the Elder, however, together with the remains of architecture and wall paintings

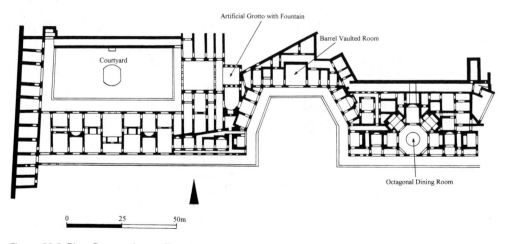

Figure 22.3 Plan, Domus Aurea, Rome

discovered in modern times make clear the lavishness of the building. Of prime importance was the central dining room, an original and influential piece of architectural design (Figures 22.4 and 22.5). Octagonal in plan, the room had a complicated but regular arrangement of recessed niches alternating with the straight walls. Most unusually, a revolving ceiling (perhaps some sort of canopy?) representing the heavens covered the room; above it was a dome. The ceiling is long gone, but the dome survives: a segmented dome, that is, not a continuous half sphere, but a series of eight curving panels, made of concrete. Round or octagonal spaces had heretofore been roofed with straight-sided conical roofs, like the traditional Chinese laborer's hat. The dome, which curves out as it descends, represents a new concept of roofing. The spherical dome, which we shall see shortly in the Pantheon, is simply the arch form turned in a full circle. Since the Romans had already made the arch a preeminent feature of their architecture, their developing of the dome should not surprise us. The Domus Aurea illustrates as well the Roman interest in curvilinear forms and interior space, both antithetical to Greek architectural design, in which the rectilinear post-and-lintel structure and the exterior view dominated.

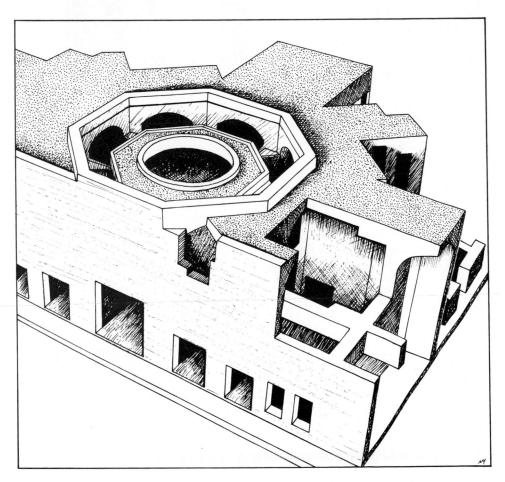

Figure 22.4 Octagonal dining room from the outside (reconstruction), Domus Aurea, Rome

Figure 22.5 Octagonal dining room, Domus Aurea, Rome

The Flavian Palace (Domus Augustiana)

The Palatine Hill, the site of Augustus's home, the House of Livia, and the wattle-and-daub hut attributed to Romulus, continued through the imperial centuries as the location of the royal residence. Indeed, the name of the hill often denoted the residence: the Palatium, or, in English, the palace.

Tiberius, Augustus's successor, replaced the modest House of Livia with a grander residence on the north side of the hill overlooking the Forum Romanum. This, the Domus Tiberiana, was refurbished in the late first century by the Flavian emperor Domitian and supplemented by a much larger palace on the south half of the hill, the Domus Augustiana (or Augustana), multi-storeyed, full of dramatic views and architectural surprises, the design of the architect Rabirius.

The Flavian Palace, as we might call the new building, consisted of two sections, one public or official, the other private (Figure 22.6). Entry into the official part came from the north, through a modest off-center doorway into a plain but large vaulted room. From there one entered the north side, with three state rooms. The *basilica*, a rectangular hall with an apse at the south end, was roofed with a barrel vault, unusual for the period. The center room served as the royal audience hall, with the imperial throne placed in the apse at the south. The smallest of the three rooms was the *lararium*, the shrine for the household gods. To the south of this block lay a peristyle court, flanked by small rooms with curvilinear plans; beyond the court one reached the

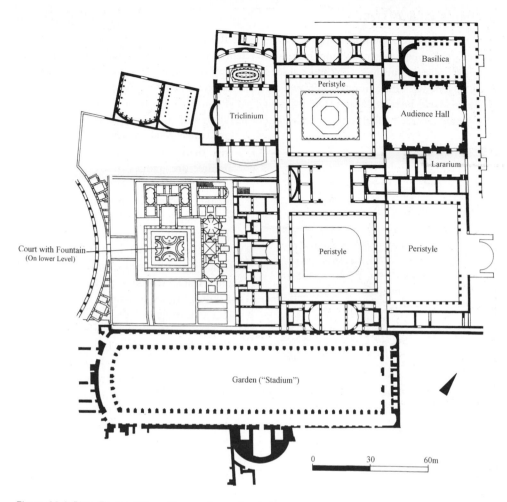

Figure 22.6 Plan, Flavian Palace (Domus Augustiana), Rome

triclinium, the large formal banquet hall. Doors opened from the long sides of this room onto gardens with oval fountains.

By passing from the peristyle court into an adjacent peristyle garden, one entered the private sector of the palace. From this point the hill sloped down toward the Circus; in compensation, the palace became multi-storyed. In fact, a formal entrance existed on the lowest level, through a curving portico on the south; one then proceeded into a court with a fountain. North of the court lay octagonal rooms with domed roofs, successors of the octagonal dining room of the Domus Aurea. The influence of the Domus Aurea is seen as well in the frequent use of curvilinear spaces, made possible by the use of concrete.

To the east of this private block was a large garden in the shape of a stadium, 160m × 50m, lined on three sides by a two-storeyed portico. From its south end the imperial box overlooked the Circus Maximus. Direct access from palace to viewing stand is a design feature that will be repeated in the fourth-century capital, Constantinople.

Hadrian's Villa at Tivoli

One emperor who chose not to live in the center of Rome on the Palatine Hill was Hadrian. Hadrian stood out in other ways too. He traveled relentlessly throughout the empire, for peaceful as well as military purposes. The most ardent champion of Greek culture since Augustus and Nero, he renewed official interest in Greek art and architecture in the capital city.

The residence he built 25km east of Rome at Tivoli is known as Hadrian's Villa (Figure 22.7). This sprawling (ca. 120ha), eclectic collection of pavilions and courts, water features, gardens, and substantial buildings has survived well, thanks to its suburban location. The architecture ranges from the standard to the surprising. Examples of the latter include reminiscences of places Hadrian visited on his travels. The "Island Pavilion" (traditionally but misleadingly called the "Maritime Theater"), a building constructed on a circular island, recalls Herod the Great's Herodium palace (23–15 BC), 12km south of Jerusalem. Egypt is represented throughout the villa by sculpture in pharaonic styles. A traditional identification of a grotto-like banquet hall at the end of a long narrow pool as an Egyptianizing complex designed to recall the Nile has recently been dismissed, however; MacDonald and Pinto have newly labeled these two features, long known as the "Canopus" after the Egyptian town famous for its Temple to Serapis, as the "Scenic Triclinium" and the "Scenic Canal" (Figure 22.8).

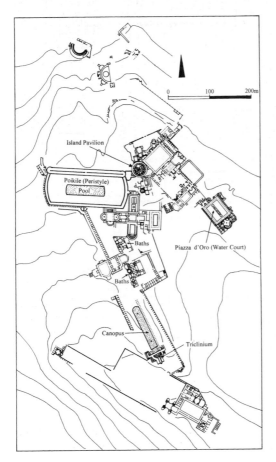

Figure 22.7 Plan, Hadrian's Villa, Tivoli

Like the Domus Aurea, Hadrian's Villa includes innovative architectural design; Hadrian took an active interest in architecture, and may have designed certain features himself. The half dome of the Canopus/Scenic Triclinium is a segmented dome, but with segments that curved horizontally as well as vertically – possibly the "pumpkin" dome scorned by the prominent architect Apollodorus of Damascus. Atop the colonnade re-erected at the north end of the Canopus/Scenic Canal, one sees a Roman variant on the standard Greek entablature. Horizontal members alternate with arches, the arches thereby breaking the traditional horizontal trabeation of Greek architecture. This alternation became standard in later imperial architecture.

Another striking complex is the Piazza d'Oro (renamed by MacDonald and Pinto as the "Water Court"), a large building (ca. 59m × 88m) consisting of an octagonal vestibule, a large porticoed court with a water canal in the center, and, opposite the entry, a nymphaeum

Figure 22.8 Canopus (Scenic Canal), Hadrian's Villa, Tivoli

(fountain) chamber. This room must have been astonishing, with a fountain in the center, a fountain in each of the four corners, and a sixth broad curving fountain at the rear, opposite the courtyard. Also astonishing is its curvilinear ground plan, reproduced at the level of architrave, held up by slender columns. What sort of roof this chamber had, if any, is unknown. Although pointing to trends in later Roman architecture, the oval and curvilinear forms recall Baroque design in Rome 1,500 years later, especially the architecture of Borromini.

TEMPLES

Religious architecture, ever conservative, still relied heavily on the Greek and Tuscan traditions, although the spirit of innovation burst forth even here. Striking use of the traditional and the new can be seen in the two major temples built under Hadrian, the *Pantheon* and the *Temple of Venus and Roma.*

The Pantheon

Hadrian was responsible for rebuilding the Pantheon, a temple dedicated to all gods (Figures 22.9, 22.10, and 22.11). The Pantheon was originally built in 27 BC by Marcus Agrippa, a confidant of Augustus. Damaged in a fire of AD 80, the temple was restored by Domitian. Hadrian's version was a complete rebuilding; the architect of this unique design is unknown, but Hadrian himself surely took a great interest in it. All traces of the earlier plan were obliterated, although Agrippa's dedicatory inscription was kept, curiously enough. Turned into a Christian church

Figure 22.9 Pantheon, Rome

with few modifications of the Hadrianic structure, the building has been extremely well preserved.

The construction of Hadrian's Pantheon began in ca. 117 and was finished by 126–8, according to its brick-stamps. Brick-stamps represent a distinctive component of the archaeological record of imperial Rome. Baked bricks were used as building materials from the time of Augustus, with great popularity from Nero to Hadrian. The bricks made in and around Rome were stamped with different types of information from the reign of Augustus through Caracalla, then again from the reign of Diocletian (284–306). This information could include: the type of product; the source of the clay or the name of the brickyard; the owner of the clay source; the brick maker; or the consuls in office when the brick was made. This last is especially useful for dating purposes from AD 110 to 164, the period when consuls might be named in stamps, because consuls, well known from literary sources, served for one-year terms.

The unusual design of the Pantheon combined traditional Etruscan (Tuscan) and Greek architectural features with innovations. The temple consists of two parts, a Tuscan–Greek porch approached from a large colonnaded court, and, behind, a circular cella covered by a hemispherical dome. The two join awkwardly by means of an intermediate zone with niches. The porch, deep with a broad flight of steps on the front only and raised on a podium, all in the Tuscan manner, is covered with a pediment and gabled roof held up by monolithic columns of Egyptian granite with Corinthian capitals. Marble, widely used, gives an elegant effect. The cella, in contrast, is made largely of concrete, with brick and stone elements. Here the builders

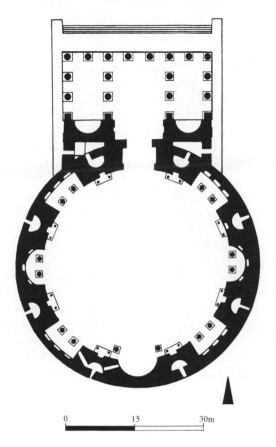

0   15   30m

Figure 22.10 Plan, Pantheon

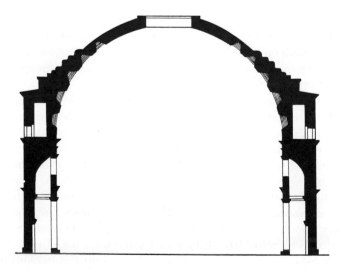

Figure 22.11 Cross-section, Cella, Pantheon

developed innovative construction techniques, although much is hidden from the visitor's eye. The walls are not solid, but are composed of vaulted spaces, one on top of the other. The vaults of bricks redirect the downward pressure toward the eight massive piers in the circle and give variety and resilience to the structure. The dome itself is made of concrete that was poured over a huge wooden frame, the weight of the concrete lightened with inclusions of pumice instead of the heavier aggregate used in the lower walls.

Although the hemispherical dome springs from the internal wall at a height equal to the radius of the dome, the exterior wall rises well above this starting point, permitting the extra support of buttressing against the lower part of the dome. Because of this compensation, from the outside one cannot discern the complete shape of this dome. Instead, the dome appears shallow, only slightly curved.

The inside reveals unimpeded the full hemisphere. The dome is decorated with coffers, or squares one inside the other. At the top is an oculus, an opening to the sky. The worshipper can look up into the heavens; sunlight and even rain and snow penetrate the temple. The sun as it crosses the sky illuminates a different spot with each passing minute. Drain holes in the floor carry off water.

The dome of the Pantheon had great influence on post-antique architecture. In religious architecture the embodiment of the divine, the celestial, as in the Byzantine Haghia Sophia or the Islamic Dome of the Rock, in a secular building such as the Capitol in Washington, D.C., the dome represents the triumph of human thought and rationalism, the symbol of a certain idea of Roman civic order. No need to be surprised, then, by the first three lines of an inscription installed in 1632 by Pope Urban VIII at the rear of the Pantheon's porch: "The Pantheon, the most celebrated edifice in the whole world" (MacDonald 1976: 94).

The Temple of Venus and Roma

The Temple of Venus and Roma, magnificently constructed with lavish materials, survives only in ground plan (see Figure 19.8). Begun after the Pantheon, in 121, and dedicated probably in 135, it was completed in the region of Antoninus Pius. To erect it, Hadrian had the colossal statue of Sol (the Sun, formerly Nero) transferred to the north-west of the Flavian amphitheater (the Colosseum). The large temple (136m × 66m) sits raised on a high stylobate of seven steps, standing free in the center of a large platform (145m × 100m) at the east end of the Forum Romanum. The platform is bordered by a colonnade of Egyptian gray granite columns on the long sides only; the formal entrance to the precinct lies on the south, through a propylon in the middle of the colonnade.

The temple itself looked Greek from the exterior, being a rectangle surrounded by a typical Greek peristyle, ten Corinthian columns on the short ends, 20 on the long. Inside, there were two cellas, the western, facing the Roman Forum, for the goddess Roma (Rome), the eastern for Venus. The temple was made of concrete faced with brick, then covered with marble imported from Greece. Technical details of the architectural decorations indicate that the workmen too came from the Aegean region. The use of foreign materials and workmen, a shift in the habits of the previous century, reflects the wide-ranging tastes of the well-traveled Hadrian, but also indicates the increasing prominence of cities and regions outside the capital and Italy. Apollodorus, Trajan's chief architect, criticized the building as lying too low; if placed on a higher platform, its unusual width would have had greater visual impact. Such frank comments were not appreciated by Hadrian, especially since they followed earlier expressions of contempt. Eventually Hadrian had Apollodorus put to death.

COMMEMORATIVE MONUMENTS

Before we continue with important civic buildings of the capital, further donations of emperors, let us turn to two commemorative monuments whose sculptural decorations were important visual reminders of the military successes of their imperial donors. The *Arch of Titus* and the *Column of Trajan* carry on the tradition of historical relief sculptures made for public exhibition, a distinctive tradition in Roman art seen first in the Ara Pacis that will continue into the late Empire even after the capital shifted to Constantinople.

Figure 22.12 Arch of Titus, Rome. View from the south-east

The Arch of Titus

When a general won a great victory, he was entitled to a parade in Rome. The general rode in splendor, accompanied by his soldiers. Captives were forced to march, and captured booty was carried for all to see. The victory parade, or *triumph*, was often commemorated afterwards by a monumental arch. The first of these was built in 196 BC, but no longer survives. Of those that do remain, two are of particular interest for us: the Arch of Titus and the Arch of Constantine (see below, Chapter 24).

The Arch of Titus is a monumental free-standing single arch made of stone, the curved arch framed inside a rectilinear shape (Figure 22.12). Built after 81 by Domitian to honor his deceased brother Titus, the Arch commemorated the earlier suppression, in 70, of a Jewish revolt in Palestine by Vespasian and Titus, his son. Notable among the decorations are the two panels of relief sculptures placed just above eye level on the inside of the arched passageway. These two scenes illustrate not the war, but two moments in the triumphal procession held in Rome after the victory had been secured.

In both scenes the figures march westward toward the Temple of Jupiter on the Capitoline, the revered center of Roman religion. On one side we see the high point of the parade, the victorious general in his chariot pulled by four horses, with spear-holding soldiers around (Figure 22.13). In this fictitious recreation the divine joins in with the mortal, for Titus's chariot is guided by Roma, the female personification of the city of Rome, while the winged goddess Victory crowns Titus with a wreath. The figures are in motion, all different, even those standing or barely walking. The upper part of the panel is largely empty except for the spears, whose lines create striking patterns. The visual force of the scene is emphasized by the deep cutting of the relief, which allows for strong shadows.

The panel on the opposite side of the walkway shows another moment in the procession, the carrying of important spoils from the Temple of Jerusalem, sacked and destroyed: the menorah, or huge seven-branched candlestick; the gold table with ritual objects; and the long thin ceremonial horns (Figure 22.14). In two synecdochic scenes, then, we get the essence of the imperial triumph and the crushing defeat of one of the many subject peoples.

Figure 22.13 Emperor in Triumphal Procession, relief sculpture, Arch of Titus

Figure 22.14 Triumphal Procession with Menorah, relief sculpture, Arch of Titus

Trajan's Column

In contrast, Trajan's Column offers a long continuous spiral of pictures in order to convey a similar message (Figure 22.15). The first of several columns carved with narrative bands that were erected in Rome and Constantinople, this column commemorates the emperor Trajan not only with the sculpted images of his victorious campaigns in Dacia (modern Romania), but also with a bronze statue of him on top; in addition, his ashes were kept in a golden urn in the base. The column, made of Luna marble from the Carrara quarries, measures 29.78m in height, 3.83m in diameter at its base, 3.66m at the top; it sits on a rectangular block 5.37m high. Its 17 drums contained an internal staircase of 185 steps, in rectilinear flights in the base but spiral inside the column proper. Forty-three window slits cut into the column provide air and light to the stairs. Today, other elements of the Forum of Trajan (see below) – the flanking libraries, the adjacent Basilica Ulpia, and the nearby Temple to the divine Trajan – survive only in foundations, and the statue of Trajan was replaced in 1588 by one of St. Peter, but the sculpted scenes, one of the major monuments of Roman art, are still in place.

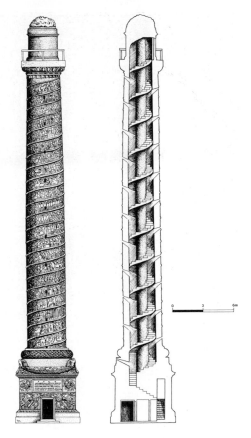

Figure 22.15 Trajan's Column, Rome

The sculpture shows Trajan's two Dacian campaigns of 101–2 and 105–6. The narrative is arranged on a continuous band that begins at the bottom and winds in a spiral to the top of the column, for a total length of 200m. Battles, preparations, marching, transporting, the rivers and hills, the camps – with over 2,500 figures in 155 scenes, the sculpture gives us a pictorial record of a military campaign unparalleled in ancient art (Figure 22.16). The source may have been paintings done by artists on the campaigns, both on panels and on scrolls, as attested by ancient authors. Although some concession was made for viewing the sculptures – the bands become taller as the column gets higher: 0.89m at the bottom vs. 1.25m at the top – these pictures would have been difficult to see even for the viewer with perfect eyesight willing to climb up in both libraries. The monument must have commanded respect more for its artistic concept than for its ability to impart information to the passer-by.

CIVIC BUILDINGS

Civic buildings in Rome were also vehicles for imperial largesse, important elements of propaganda for the emperors. The best known from our period of architectural innovation are the *Colosseum*, *Trajan's Forum* (in which the Column stood) and *Market*, and the *Baths of Trajan*.

Figure 22.16 Relief sculpture (detail), Trajan's Column

Colosseum (Flavian amphitheater)

The most famous amphitheater in Rome was built under the Flavian emperors, begun by Vespasian and dedicated by him in 79, finished by Titus and rededicated in 80 (Figure 22.17). Formally known as the Flavian amphitheater, the building became better known from AD 1000 as the Colosseum, thanks to the colossal statue of Sol (the Sun) that stood nearby during the later Empire.

As noted at Pompeii (above, Chapter 21), the amphitheater, or double theater, is an architectural type prominent in towns of Italy and the central and western parts of the empire, but rarely seen in the eastern half. The Colosseum, a large oval (arena: 86m × 54m; overall building: 188m × 156m), was built on the site of the artificial lake of Nero's Domus Aurea; the Flavians thus reclaimed part of the city center for the people. The building was used for gladiatorial games and for shows with wild animals (*venatio*, pl. *venationes*), including hunting. The last gladiatorial combats took place in 404, but the venationes continued well into the sixth century. The destruction of the building began in the ninth century, excavation and restoration in the nineteenth century.

The Colosseum was built of concrete, with occasional brick facing, and with a façade of high-quality travertine quarried near Tivoli. The seating was covered with marble. The exterior

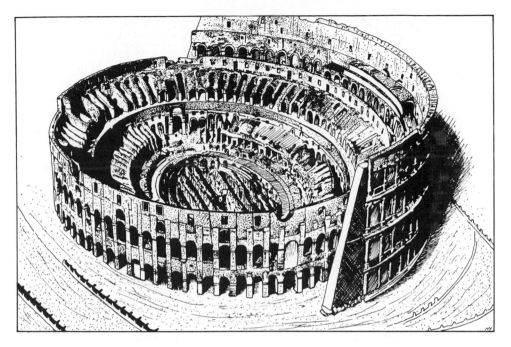

Figure 22.17 Colosseum (Flavian amphitheater), Rome

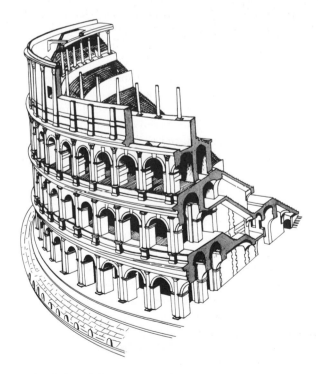

Figure 22.18 Cross-sectional view, Colosseum

consisted of four storeys (Figure 22.18). The first three featured arches flanked by attached columns, a Roman decorative combination. The lower storey had columns in the Tuscan order; the second storey Ionic; the third, Corinthian. The top storey was a solid wall with Corinthian pilasters, with a rectangular window between every other pair. The total height of the exterior was 48.5m. Statues may have been intended to fill the arches of the second and third storeys; although they are shown on coins, they may not have existed, for no statue bases were found.

The cavea, or seating, held ca. 45,000 people. Placed above five annular passages, the seating rose at differing slopes. The outer two passages were vaulted, carrying additional vaults above. Stairs led to the seats. Spectators had tickets, or tokens, for their reserved seat, marked with the number of their *vomitorium* (entrance way), *gradus* (row), and *locus* (seat). Some seats would be protected from the sun by awnings attached at the top of the arena. A narrow passage, probably for patrolling armed guards, and a fence separated the spectators from the arena. The emperor's box was on the south, opposite a box for magistrates; both were reached by separate ceremonial entrances.

The arena was surfaced with wood. Below it lay a complex warren of four parallel rows of cells surrounded by three annular passages, an area provided with drainage. At one end machinery lifted wild animals up to the arena.

Trajan's Forum

Trajan's Forum was the last, largest, and most complex of the imperial fora, a group of five formal public spaces adjacent to the Forum Romanum and the Capitoline Hill. Begun by Julius Caesar and Augustus, the fora were augmented by (a) Vespasian's Forum Pacis (Forum of Peace) of 75, Vespasian's commemoration of his bringing peace after the chaos that followed Nero's death; then by the (b) Forum Transitorium, or Forum of Nerva, a narrow space with a Temple of Minerva on a high podium at one end, begun by Vespasian, finished by Domitian, but dedicated by Nerva; and finally by (c) Trajan's Forum (see Figure 20.2).

The Forum of Trajan was designed by Trajan's favorite architect and engineer, Apollodorus of Damascus, and dedicated in 113. The Forum served as a location for affairs of government, notably certain law courts and archives. It consists of several parts: a porticoed square with exedrae on the north and south – a deliberate echo of the Forum of Augustus; a basilica; two libraries with Trajan's Column in between; and a temple to the deified Trajan at the rear. The Market of Trajan lies to the north, built, like part of the forum, after a partial levelling of the Quirinal Hill.

One entered the square through a gate with three openings that resembled a triumphal arch, originally decorated on top with a statue group showing the emperor, fresh from his triumphant campaigns in Dacia riding in a chariot pulled by six horses. In the center of the square stood an equestrian statue of Trajan. Beyond the square lay the Basilica Ulpia, placed transversely, so that its entrances were on the long sides, not the short, in contrast with the typical basilican plan. Inside, this basilica had the expected nave and two side aisles. Unusual, however, was the use of apses at both of the short ends. A statue of Liberty stood in the north apse; here slaves were set free. The south apse may have been devoted to the imperial cult.

Two libraries lay beyond, one devoted to Latin works, the other to Greek. Between them stood the remarkable Column of Trajan, and beyond, the Temple to the Divine Trajan.

Trajan's Market (Mercati Traiani)

According to the inscription on its base, the height of Trajan's Column equalled the depth of earth removed from the Quirinal Hill in the preparation of the Forum and adjacent Market of Trajan. This large commercial complex, at least six storeys high, is nestled in the deepest part of the cut, just north of – and physically separate from – the northern exedra of the forum's square (Figure 22.19). Its more than 170 rooms and halls have traditionally been identified as shops and offices, devoted to the trade in food and to governmental activities. Food sold included such spices as pepper (hence the name of the street, the Via Biberatica, that winds through the third level) and fish (fish tanks have been discovered).

The large basilical hall off the Via Biberatica ranks as an important creation in the Roman architectural revolution. Made of concrete, it consists of a tall nave with a clerestory crossed by seven intersecting vaults (groin vaults) supported on piers – a feature that would recur in the huge bath buildings of the later Empire. Two storeys of shops lay to either side of the nave. The market hall, indeed the whole complex, with its complicated asymmetrical multi-storeyed plan, contrasts with the contemporary but conservative Augustan design of the Forum of Trajan. Both approaches had their value in the imperial architecture of the capital city.

Figure 22.19 Trajan's Market (reconstruction), Rome

Baths of Trajan

Public baths were an essential feature of a Roman town, as we have seen already at Pompeii. In the capital city with its large population, baths were numerous; thanks to the properties of concrete, they could also be large, with huge spaces covered by vaults. Emperors of the later empire, eager to demonstrate their generosity, often chose the bath complex as an appropriate way both to provide a public service and to express imperial grandeur.

The Baths of Trajan represent an important step in the monumentalization of the bath complex (Figure 22.20). The principles of public bathing had been established already in the republic, with rooms of varying degrees of heat, and a cold water pool. Although following the design of earlier baths in the imperial capital, notably those of Titus, Trajan's bath building measured three times the size of Titus's, containing not only bathing facilities but also rooms for a variety of social and recreational purposes, such as lecture rooms, libraries, meeting rooms, and gardens. The layout would set the model for bath complexes of the next several centuries, such as the much better preserved baths of Caracalla (211–16) (Figure 22.21) and Diocletian (ca. 298–306).

Erected on the Oppius Hill (the south slope of the Esquiline), on a terrace atop the ruins of the Domus Aurea, the baths were the work of Apollodorus of Damascus. The bath building lies in the middle of a large platform, 250m × 210m. The east and west sides of the platform are

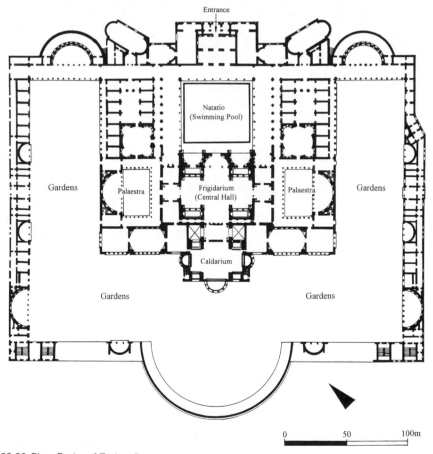

Figure 22.20 Plan, Baths of Trajan, Rome

Figure 22.21 Air view, Baths of Caracalla, Rome

lined with small rooms; in between, surrounding the main building on three sides, were gardens. The main rooms, entered from the north, lay on a north–south axis, with subsidiary rooms arranged symmetrically on either side. After entering, one reached first the swimming pool, surrounded by colonnades on three sides, with exedra on the south. To either side of the pool lay small rooms, uniform in size, and two rotundas with niches, possible frigidaria. Continuing beyond the pool, one came to a central hall (with, to the east and west, palaestras, or rectangular courtyards for exercising, with hemicycles attached), then bathing rooms and finally, in the southernmost position to catch the sun, the caldarium, with three vaulted bays supplied with rectangular niches and semicircular apses.

ROYAL TOMBS

Tombs, as we have seen, often served as vehicles for the prestige of the occupant or his surviving successors. Indeed, the monumentality of the pyramids at Giza and the lavish sculptural decoration of the Mausoleum at Halikarnassos immortalized the names of those buried within. But tombs need not be grandiose. Even kings might prefer their burials hidden, as in New Kingdom Egypt. In the Roman Empire, both styles prevailed, the simple and the grand. We shall look at a few examples of the grand: the mausolea of Augustus and Hadrian, and, briefly in Chapter 24, those of Diocletian and Constantine.

The prototype for the imperial mausoleum is the Mausoleum of Augustus, the tomb of Augustus, his family, and most of his Julio-Claudian successors. He built it early in his reign, ca. 28–23 BC, a period when he must have considered monumentality a necessary reinforcement of his rule. The mausoleum was centrally located near the Tiber and the Via Flaminia in a park open to all. Ordinary people, in contrast, were buried outside the city. The tomb consisted of a circular mound 87m in diameter, 44m in height, formed by concentric concrete walls and vaulted passages covered by earth and decorated with trees and, on top, a bronze statue of Augustus. This circular tomb recalled traditional Etruscan and Italic tumuli – another careful choice of image on the part of Augustus.

Augustus was cremated, as was the fashion from ca. 400 BC into the second century AD. Trajan too was cremated, his ashes placed in the base of his commemorative column. During the second century, inhumation gradually replaced cremation throughout the empire, with carved stone sarcophagi becoming popular. Burial rites of the emperors varied, when known at all. The treatment of Hadrian's body, for example, is uncertain. Hadrian did, however, begin a new imperial tomb, which would be used by emperors and their families from Hadrian through Caracalla, a mausoleum whose external appearance followed the Augustan precedent. From the outside, the tomb resembled the Augustan mound: a circular building 64m in diameter placed inside a low square platform, rising toward the center, with trees and a statue of Hadrian in a quadriga. Inside, the plan differed from that of Augustus's mausoleum. A spiral ramp led to three square burial chambers placed one on top of the other, with access by stairs from one to the other. Strategically located along the west bank of the Tiber, the mausoleum became part of the city's fortifications in the sixth century. Renamed the Castel Sant'Angelo after the reerection of a statue of the archangel Michael, the mausoleum would serve the papacy as a fortress into modern times. Lovers of Italian opera know it well, for it is from its parapet that Floria Tosca leaps to her death.

This colorful post-antique career of Hadrian's Mausoleum reminds us that the stories of these buildings and monuments do not end with the fourth century AD, the end of pagan antiquity and the end of this book, but continue on through the Middle Ages and the modern era. They were variously ruined quickly or slowly; built over or left exposed; pillaged for building materials; reconverted and reused; or survived virtually intact – and were then slowly brought back to the consciousness of the public from the Renaissance on, through the interests and efforts of artists, architects, historians, and archaeologists (amateur and professional), popes and politicians, and indeed the public at large.

CHAPTER 23

Roman provincial cities

The Eastern Empire

"Hunting, bathing, having fun, laughing – That is living!" (Finley 1977: 73). This phrase (in Latin) was discovered scratched onto the paving of the forum of Thamugadi, a Roman city in Algeria, and for many Romans of the prosperous and peaceful first through early third centuries it must indeed have expressed their view of the ideal life. We have already examined Roman cities in the Italian peninsula, the heartland of the Roman Empire: Cosa, Ostia, Pompeii, and Rome itself. Let us now travel outside Italy to see how provincial cities resemble or differ from those in the heartland. The candidates for a visit are many. How to choose? It seems most instructive to stay in the eastern Mediterranean, a region whose urban history we have been tracking since the beginning of this book. Moreover, the evidence from the eastern half of the Empire is particularly rich. Shifts in habitation in this region led to the abandonment of many major Roman cities – and hence to their preservation.

We shall examine seven examples from the eastern Mediterranean, beginning with *Athens*, and then moving in a clockwise direction to *Ephesus* and *Pergamon*, *Perge*, *Palmyra*, *Jerash*, and *Lepcis Magna* (see Figure 22.1). These cities raise questions about Roman cities that we should keep in mind as we explore our examples. Seven themes seem of particular interest. First, the blend of Roman culture with pre-existing cultures, and how this mix was expressed in the urban landscape will be key in this region with its several thousand years of urban experience. Athens was a cultural heirloom for the Romans, a seat of revered Greek culture, but nonetheless the Romans introduced their favorite building types. Second, religious syncretisms, or the multiplicity of cults, result in variations of temple and tomb structures. In Ephesus and Pergamon, Egyptian cults mingled with Greek and Roman religions, whereas in Syrian Palmyra the Classical mixes with the native Near Eastern. Third, the varying economic bases of towns, dependent on the geographic location of cities, may affect the appearance of cities, and the experiences of their inhabitants. Fourth, city layouts may vary, with newly founded cities having different types of plans from older, established cities. In addition, local topographies can affect city plans. Fifth, building types and plans, the elements of the physical world of the city: to what degree are they uniform throughout this region, to what degree do they differ? Sixth, the traditions of construction: to what degree were these techniques local, to what degree brought from Italy? Seventh and last, we are also interested in benefactors, imperial and local: who were they, and what did they hope to gain from their gifts to their city? In sum, what constitutes a Roman city? Can we indeed recognize a Roman city, no matter where we might be in the Empire?

ATHENS

"Greece, the captive, took her savage victor captive, and brought the arts into rustic Latium" (Alcock 1993: 1). So wrote Horace about the lasting power of Greek culture for the Romans despite the latter's military conquest of the Greek world. For the Romans, no city better symbolized the achievements of Greek culture than Athens. Although not the major commercial and administrative city of the Greek peninsula under Roman rule, now organized as the province of Achaia – that was Corinth, destroyed by the Romans in 146 BC, then resettled as a colony in 44 BC – Athens retained its special aura. The city maintained its reputation as an intellectual center for many centuries, even after the crippling attack in 267 of the Herulians, a Germanic tribe from eastern Europe. The end of its long tradition finally came in 529, when the Byzantine emperor Justinian closed its famous philosophical schools.

When a Roman emperor wished to emphasize his philhellenism, he would donate a magnificent new monument to Athens, thereby paying homage to this city and to the intellectual and artistic life that it had nurtured for centuries. The two emperors who drew most upon Greek models for urban architecture were Augustus and Hadrian. Indeed, they both made gifts to Athens (see the map of Athens, Figure 13.1). Augustan monuments include the Temple of Roma, a small circular temple placed east of the Parthenon, its Ionic order copying that of the recently refurbished Erechtheion; and the Roman Agora, a porticoed rectangular market square built to the east of the older, established agora. The most important building of this period was the large Odeion of Agrippa, a covered theater built in 15 BC in the older agora, a donation of Augustus's son-in-law.

Hadrian visited Athens in 133; in honor of his trip, he built a monumental gate (Figure 23.1). The gateway combines Roman and Greek forms: a Roman arch below, but Greek post-and-lintel

Figure 23.1 Hadrian's Arch, Athens

forms in the upper tier. It marks the boundary between the established earlier Greek city and the sector newly developed by the Romans, enclosed in an extension of the city wall. This function was noted by the inscriptions carved on its lower friezes: "This is Athens, the ancient city of Theseus" (on the west) and "This is the city of Hadrian, not of Theseus" (on the east). Other building projects of Hadrian included a library, built next to the earlier Roman Agora, and the completion of the Olympieion, the huge temple to Zeus begun in the late sixth century BC and much advanced, but not finished, in 175–164 BC. The Olympieion, at least, lies just to the east of Hadrian's arch, thus inside Hadrian's city.

Imperial patrons were not alone in making gifts to the city. Local philanthropy existed too. Herodes Atticus, a wealthy Athenian of the mid second century, donated the large odeion built into the south-west slope of the Acropolis as a memorial to his wife, Regilla.

After the Herulian attack of 267, a new defensive wall was built, the "Valerian Wall." The area enclosed was much smaller than that of the Themistoklean Wall with its Hadrianic extension, and shows clearly how dramatically the city had shrunk. However great its lingering prestige, Athens had now become an economic backwater, a minor town important only for its region. This situation continued through the Middle Ages and the Ottoman period. In 1834, the fortunes of the city once again changed sharply, with its selection as the capital of the recently independent Kingdom of Greece.

EPHESUS AND PERGAMON

The vital centers of the Greek areas of the Roman empire lay not on the Greek peninsula, but further east: on the east Aegean coast in the province of Asia (Ephesus and Pergamon), in the province of Syria (Antioch, today the Turkish city of Antakya), and Egypt (Alexandria) – all well-established in the earlier Hellenistic period. Ancient remains of the last two cities are difficult of access, being overlain by silting (Antioch) and later occupation (both). Ephesus, however, and much of Pergamon have been the objects of rewarding archaeological excavations, thanks to shifts in settlement location from ancient to medieval and modern times that have made the ancient remains easier to reach.

Pergamon in Roman times we have already touched upon in Chapter 17. The Trajaneum, or Temple of the Divine Trajan, of the early second century was the main building of this period on the Acropolis. It set the orientation for the grid plan that determined orientations of new construction even down on the plain below. We also noted the Asklepeion, the sanctuary just out of the city, with its important construction of the second century.

Ephesus was the capital of the Roman province of Asia, with a large population estimated at 250,000. Occupied since the Bronze Age, it was an important Greek and then Roman city, internationally famous for its Temple of Artemis and blessed with good harbor facilities. In late Roman times, its commercial and political prominence came to an end, as silting from the Cayster River filled the harbor. Today the Roman ruins lie several kilometers from the Aegean coastline (Figure 23.2). By Justinian's time (sixth century) the site of the Roman city was given up in favor of a defensible inland location, around the tomb and basilica church of St. John, the apostle and evangelist.

The Roman city has been brought to light by Austrian excavations conducted since 1897. A walk through the extensive ruins gives a good impression of the grandeur of this major Roman city (Figure 23.3). The topography has much affected the city's layout, for the city lies between two hills. A central street (Curetes Street), dominating the plan, runs downhill from the west

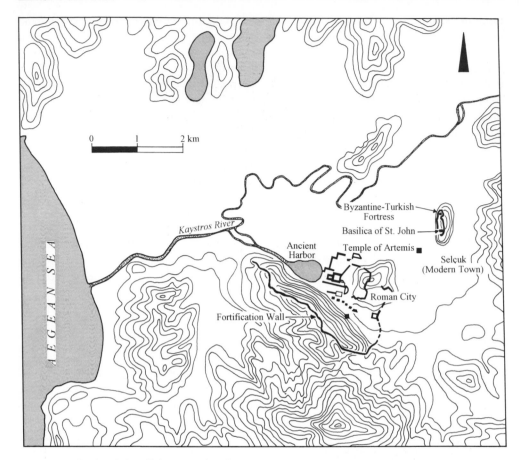

Figure 23.2 Regional plan, Ephesus and environs

through the saddle between the two hills. On the south hillside, at least, excavations have revealed well-preserved houses of the wealthy, arranged on terraces. The main street continues down to the Library of Celsus, then turns north toward the Greco-Roman theater (where St. Paul was denounced as a troublemaker to the assembled multitude by a maker of statues of Artemis), then west again going straight to the harbor. This last leg is a fourth- or fifth-century reworking, complete with the then still unusual addition of street lights.

Excavation projects at large Greco-Roman sites in Turkey have been encouraged by the government to restore selected buildings. The Austrian excavators at Ephesus are now focusing on the hillside houses mentioned above. Earlier, they restored the façade of the Library of Celsus (Figure 23.4). This library was built in 110 by Gaulius Julius Aquila in honor of his father, Gaius Julius Celsus Polemaenus, proconsul of Asia in 106–7. Its beautiful façade is decorated with projections and niches that recall the stage buildings of Roman theaters. Statues personifying qualities of Celsus, such as Wisdom and Virtue, fill the niches on either side of the central doorway. Behind the façade, the building is simpler and smaller. A single interior room originally was equipped with three storeys of galleries for the storage of manuscripts. Celsus himself was buried in a basement chamber, in a lead coffin placed inside a marble sarcophagus, found *in situ* but not opened. It was rare for an individual to be buried inside the city limits, and is a mark of Celsus's distinction.

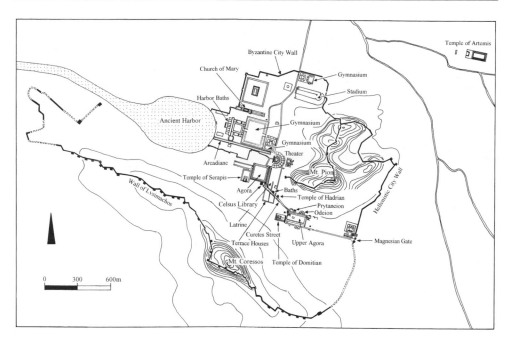

Figure 23.3 City plan, Ephesus

Figure 23.4 Library of Celsus and South Gate of the Agora, Ephesus

In the eastern Mediterranean, local building traditions were hardly changed by the arrival of the Romans. Cut stone was still favored, whereas the concrete and brick constructions typical in Italy and the central and western Mediterranean were unusual. A striking contrast of the two types of construction can be seen in two temples traditionally (although not without controversy) attributed to Serapis, one at Ephesus, the other at Pergamon. Serapis was the Ptolemaic hybrid of the Egyptian Apis with the Greek Hades (see above, Chapter 17); his cult remained popular both in Egypt and in regions with commercial contacts with Egypt during the imperial centuries. At Ephesus, the Temple of Serapis of the early second century looks like a standard Greco-Roman temple. Its post-and-lintel structure comes from the Greek tradition, as does its decoration, Corinthian columns on the porch, and carved architectural decorative motifs such as bead-and-reel and egg-and-dart. Roman in concept is its imposing frontality, with steps leading up to the entry. Indeed the front view is all there is, for the temple is nestled against the hillside, built on a terrace cut out of the bedrock. One cannot walk around it. The cella is a single room, modest in size; cuttings for water channels indicate the importance of water in the cult. To the Egyptian tradition belongs the massive scale of the temple, especially its front porch. The columns are monoliths 14–15m high, and the door frame is constructed of colossal blocks. The wheels that held the ends of the gigantic door flaps rolled along large arcs cut into the floor blocks.

The Temple of Serapis, or the Temple of the Egyptian Gods, at Pergamon is quite different. Known today as the Red Hall (Kızıl Avlu, in Turkish), this building complex lies at the base of the acropolis hill, on flat ground. The Red Hall is made of baked bricks and concrete, an unusual choice in Roman Asia Minor. Massive, the building rose two storeys high. Marble veneer would have covered the walls, but that has been stripped away. A Christian church was later constructed inside (also the fate of the Serapeion at Ephesus), thereby altering and even destroying some of the pre-Christian architectural features.

The identification of the Red Hall as a temple for Egyptian gods is not certain. However, several striking features make this likely. The complex is extremely large. The main building measures 60m × 26m. It is flanked by round towers with a smaller court in front of each. In front of this three-part structure lies a huge court (ca. 200m × 100m) today mostly covered by modern buildings. Under this court the Selinus (modern Bergama) River still flows today; it has been proposed that this river was symbolic of the Nile. In addition, caryatid columns used in the smaller courts that flank the main building have been carved on two sides with men and women, both in realistic Greco-Roman style, but some wearing Egyptian pharaonic headgear. The Red Hall contained a colossal statue, perhaps of Serapis. This statue was hollow, and a priest could climb into it and speak out, as if he were the god speaking. The hole in the statue base can still be seen.

A current project of the German Archaeological Institute in Istanbul to document and analyze afresh this building may provide new answers about its identification and function. Whatever the results, the Red Hall remains unique in Asia Minor, a monumental complex constructed in brick, a construction technique brought from afar. Clearly the effect sought from its scale, layout, and materials was very special indeed.

PERGE

Royal patronage has proved an important factor in the embellishment of towns, likewise the interest of wealthy benefactors, such as Herodes Atticus. Almost always these patrons were men. Unusual, then, is the city of Perge in Pamphylia, on the south coast of Asia Minor, where the most famous benefactor was a woman, Plancia Magna. Of distinguished family, Plancia Magna was nonetheless no mere appendage to male glory; inscriptions of dedications and commemorations found in the Turkish excavations at Perge have revealed that in the early second century she was the leading force of her family.

Perge lies a few kilometers inland from the port town of Attaleia (today's Antalya) focusing on a low flat hill, the sort of formation much appreciated in this area. For much of Perge's history, the flat hill became the defended acropolis. Here, excavations have recovered finds dating as far back as the Early Bronze Age; a possible Hittite city is still unattested, however. Probably in the Hellenistic period settlement expanded down the slope of the hill, then, in late Hellenistic and Roman times, to the south of the hill on slightly sloping, almost flat ground. A wall surrounded the town, built by the Seleucids in the third century BC, supplemented by an enlargement in the fourth century AD. Outside the walled town lay a theater, built up against a nearby hill, and a well-preserved stadium. Also outside was a Temple to Artemis, which according to literary sources was the most famous building of Perge. Despite much prospecting in the region, it has not yet been found.

The city is divided by crossing streets into four unequal areas (Figure 23.5), with city blocks of different sizes. The main north–south street, porticoed on both sides and with a stone-lined watercourse down the middle, runs from an elaborate nymphaeum (fountain building) at the base of the acropolis southward to the entrance gates. The Hellenistic gate is marked by a round tower at either side (Figure 23.6). According to inscriptions, Plancia Magna renovated the gate, adding its horseshoe-shaped court and a monumental triple archway at the north end of the court. The interior walls of the court were lined with two levels of niches, seven above and below on each side, each filled with a statue of a founder or prominent citizen of the city (Figure

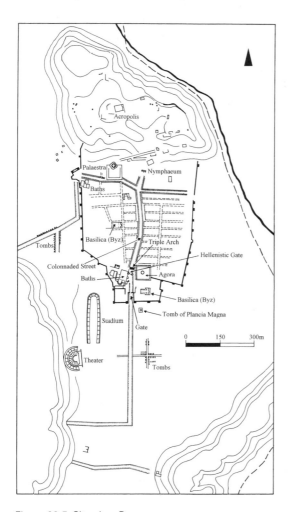

Figure 23.5 City plan, Perge

Figure 23.6 South Gate, Perge

Figure 23.7 Court inside South
Gate, Perge

23.7). Indeed, much sculpture has been found at Perge, now on display in the Antalya Museum. Its local production was substantial, although not rivalling that of Aphrodisias in the Maeander River valley to the north-west, whose nearby marble quarries were exploited for an industry with a lively export trade.

PALMYRA

Palmyra, the "place of palms," the Roman version of Tadmor, the old Semitic name, is located at an oasis in the Syrian desert. Although occupied since prehistoric times, its early settlements are poorly known. The city's great prosperity and most surviving architecture date from the late Hellenistic period to the late third century AD. Especially in the second and third centuries, Palmyra grew rich from long-distance caravan trade, from its central position on an east–west trade route between the Mediterranean coast and the Euphrates River and Mesopotamia. Political conditions in the Near East made this route important at this time. To the south, the Nabataeans, who earlier dominated trade from their capital city of Petra (in modern Jordan), were annexed by the Romans in the early second century and lost their commercial ascendancy. In addition, Palmyra was well placed between long-standing rivals, the Romans and, to the east, the Parthians, the rulers of Mesopotamia and Iran. Although the city belonged to the Romans, the Palmyrenes were Semitic. Their culture was thus a blend of local Syrian with an admixture of Mediterranean Greco-Roman elements.

The Romans took control of Palmyra some time in the first century. Hadrian visited in 129 with great celebration. The most dramatic episode in the city's history occurred in the later third century. After the Sassanian Persians (the successors of the Parthians) defeated and captured the Roman emperor Valerian at Edessa in 260, Roman rule in Syria seemed to crumble. A Palmyrene tribal leader, Odainat (Odaenathus, in Latin), stepped into the gap to protect his city's interests. He declared himself king of Palmyra, although remaining nominally a vassal of Rome. Acting as Rome's regional ally, he consolidated his position with victories over the Sassanians. His success was short-lived: in 267 he was assassinated. His widow, Bat Zabbai (better known as Zenobia), took charge as regent for her infant son, and quickly put into motion an ambitious program of conquest. Her armies captured Egypt and marched into Asia Minor. Then she proclaimed her son Augustus, that is, a ruler independent of Rome. At this the Romans finally reacted. In 272, the emperor Aurelian attacked and captured Palmyra, but spared the city. Zenobia, by most accounts, was taken to Rome and displayed to the crowd in Aurelian's triumphal procession; she spent the rest of her life in comfortable detention in Tivoli, outside Rome. Soon after Aurelian's victory, the Palmyrenes massacred the occupying garrison; in revenge, the Romans sacked the city. The city never recovered from this blow.

Palmyra is an extremely evocative site. The warm colored, intricately carved classical architecture of this abandoned oasis city spreads out in the desert sands at the foot of a bare mountain (Figure 23.8). From the seventeenth century, western travellers began to visit and write about the ruins. Systematic exploration began in the late nineteenth century with a Russian team; German, French, Swiss, Polish, and Syrian researchers have followed.

The architecture of Palmyra is, in general, Greco-Roman, but modifications were made by this Semitic people with their own gods and their own customs. The main colonnaded street,

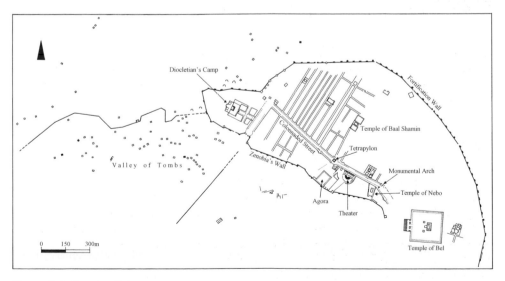

Figure 23.8 City plan, Palmyra

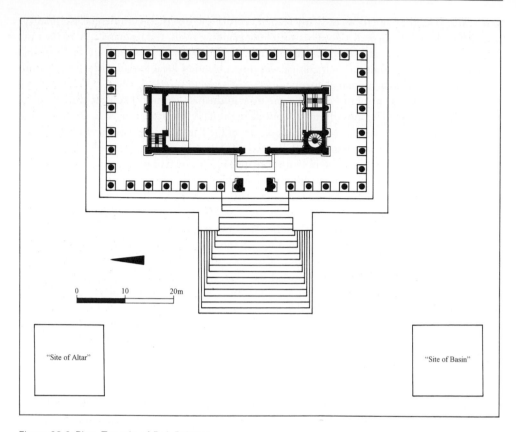

"Site of Altar"

"Site of Basin"

Figure 23.9 Plan, Temple of Bel, Palmyra

with its monumental arched gateway and tetrapylon, is firmly Roman; so too is the theater. Colonnaded streets, gateways and theaters are architectural forms fulfilling functions found throughout the Roman world, so the Roman architectural style comes as no surprise. Different in style, in contrast, are temples and tombs, building types that reflect local religious practices.

The major temple at Palmyra was consecrated to the Semitic god Bel. The cult on this site must antedate the temple of the Roman period, for the orientation of the precinct and temple differs from that of the central colonnaded street and the rough grid plan of the city proper. Built in the first half of the first century, dedicated in 32, the Temple of Bel shows a remarkable synthesis of Near Eastern and Greco-Roman forms (Figures 23.9). From the outside, the temple follows the Classical tradition. The temple lies inside a large precinct lined by porticoes. The temple is rectangular, oriented north–south, and surrounded by a colonnade of the typical Roman sort. Inside the colonnade, the exterior north and south walls of the cella are decorated with attached Ionic columns (Figure 23.10).

Other features of the temple, especially its interior plan, differ significantly from standard Greek and Roman practice. Stone beams connecting the top of the cella walls with the outer colonnade, the supports for the roofing, were decorated with relief sculpture; subjects include local gods with worshippers, and a procession of priests and veiled women with a camel carrying a small shrine. From a flight of steps on the west, on the long side, one enters the temple by stepping into a central hall, lit by two pairs of windows cut high in the two long walls. To the

Figure 23.10 Temple of Bel, Palmyra. View from the south-east

north and the south lie two small rooms reachable by broad steps, the shrines of Bel and other local gods. In three corners of the building, stairwells led up to rooftop terraces, another feature not seen in the standard Roman temple.

Burials were made in towers solidly built of stone masonry and located in the desert west of the city. The tower tombs, of which more than 150 are known, were ten storeys high, with long rectangular niches projecting lengthwise back from the central room in which the body would be placed. The opening would be blocked by a stone plaque with a sculpted bust of the deceased, his or her name carved in the local Aramaic language. Many of these sculpted plaques have survived. Their style is stiff, hieratic; they display the local conventions favored by this city on the fringes of the empire, not the classic realism of standard Roman portraits.

JERASH (GERASA)

Gerasa, better known as Jerash, the name of the modern town on the site, is of great interest for the good preservation of its Roman buildings, and especially for its city plan. The city plan follows for the most part a standard grid, but includes fascinating eccentricities, the result, it seems, of survivals from pre-Roman settlement and from topographic irregularities. Jerash lies 48km north of Amman (ancient Philadelphia), the capital of Jordan. The ancient city was established in the Hellenistic period, possibly by the Seulecid king Antiochos IV Epiphanes (175–164 BC), as a town named Antioch on the Chrysorhoas (the Golden River). Briefly a possession of the Jewish Hasmonean kingdom, in 63 BC the town passed to the Romans, and was assigned by Pompey to the Decapolis, a group of ten cities in the Jordan River valley

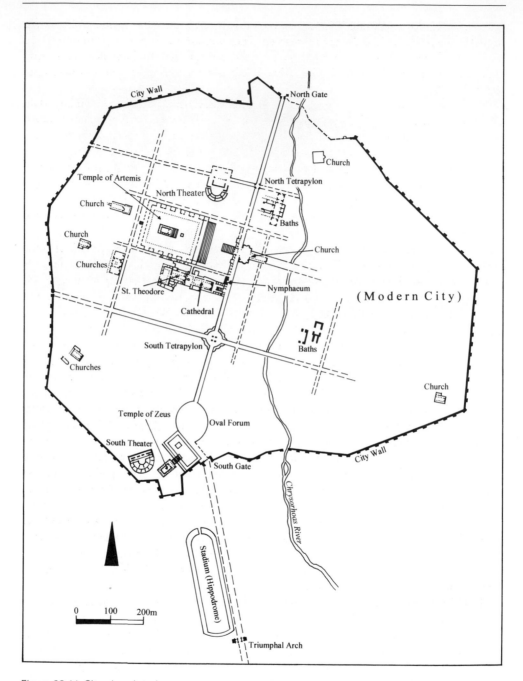

Figure 23.11 City plan, Jerash

and vicinity. Hadrian visited in 130. The city was medium sized, ca. 100ha enclosed within walls erected in the second half of the first century AD. The Chrysorhoas River runs north–south in a valley right through the middle of the city; ancient Jerash was built on both sides, on ground sloping down toward the river. By the early second century, the population may have been 10,000–15,000.

From the mid third to the late fourth centuries the city declined. It later became an important Christian center, and prospered from agriculture, mining, and caravan trade until it was captured by Sassanian Persians (614) and Arabs (635) and then abandoned. A modern village was established on the eastern half of the ancient city in 1878 by Circassian refugees. The ancient city came to the attention of western Europe from the early nineteenth century, thanks to travellers; surface exploration intensifed in the later nineteenth century, with soundings and clearing of ruins in the twentieth century. Yale University, in collaboration first with the British School of Archaeology in Jerusalem, then with the American School in Jerusalem, conducted excavations here from 1928 to 1934.

Because of the absence until modern times of nearby settlement with an appetite for reusing ancient building materials, the architecture of Jerash has survived relatively well. The architecture is a rich, successful blend of Hellenistic and Roman imperial styles. Also grand is the urban layout, with its breathraking irregular oval plaza and the magnificent cardo, the north–south street lined with colonnades (Figure 23.11). The visible remains are primarily Roman, mostly streets and public buildings. Few private or domestic remains have been excavated.

The city was heralded on the south by a large triumphal arch probably built to commemorate Hadrian's visit in 128–9. It is 37.5m wide, and has three arched passageways with an additional arch design at either side. The stadium or hippodrome lies just to the north. One then reaches the main south gate and the city walls. The main gates were at the north and the south, leading to the main intercity road from Petra north to Bosra and Damascus. They don't quite align. From the south gate one proceeds obliquely to the Oval Forum (Figure 23.12). This plaza, irregular in shape and slightly sloping toward the south, measures ca. 66m × 99m. Its stone paving is arranged in concentric rows. It is framed by Ionic colonnades on two sides. The third of its three curving sides, the south-west, is occupied by a hill with, on a high podium, a Temple of Zeus, from the early first century but finished in the 160s. This temple is Romano-Syrian in type, with emphasis on the front and the imposing staircase that led up to it. The single high-ceilinged cella was surrounded by a peristyle of unfluted columns, 8 × 12. Its cella wall has scalloped niches on the exterior, broad pilasters on the interior. Below the temple lies a broad terrace with a large altar; the terrace is supported by a series of vaulted chambers. Adjacent to the temple, indeed sharing the same hillside, is the South Theater, originally from the first century, with an elaborate stage building, or *scaenae frons*.

The Oval Forum is one of those brilliant created spaces that overwhelms and disorients, like Bernini's baroque St. Peter's Square in the Vatican City. The plaza serves as a point of juncture, for the cardo then changes direction slightly and heads straight toward the north gate. From this point on the city is laid out in an orthogonal grid plan, apparently early imperial in date. It is believed that the contrasting orientation between the south gate and the oval plaza reflects an earlier urban plan. At two major street intersections the cardo is marked by a tetrapylon, the southernmost set in a circular space, with tabernae round about. This marking of the cardo is unusual and dramatic, and gives visual emphasis to one's walk through the city.

The major Roman building in the center of the city is the Temple of Artemis, built in the second century. The richly decorated temple, 6 × 11 columns, is in the Corinthian order and measures 52.5m long. It sits toward the rear of a porticoed platform 121m × 161m, dramatically

Figure 23.12 Oval Forum, Jerash

positioned at the top of a broad flight of steps rising up the west slope of the city's hill from the cardo. The entrance porch of the temple is deep, an element that emphasizes the front, a design feature in the classic Tuscan-Roman manner.

Two bath complexes lie east of the cardo. The northernmost has a large, well-preserved room roofed by a true pendentive dome made of stone. Across the cardo to the west lies the north theater, with a rectangular plaza to its north side. A third, smaller theater lies to the north outside the city wall.

The final curiosity in the city plan of Jerash occurs in the north gate, built in 115: the gate is wedge-shaped in ground plan. The road from the northern city of Pella does not meet the cardo of Jerash on axis; instead, it comes in at an angle of 18° on the north-west. With its wedge shape, the north gate is able to face squarely both the Pella road (on the north) and the city's cardo (on the south). Buildings with this function of masking a change in direction are seen elsewhere in the Roman east. An elaborate example is the Monumental Arch at Palmyra, which marks a change of 30° in the orientation of the central Colonnaded Street.

LEPCIS MAGNA

Roman Africa included the entire north coast, and was divided into three sections, according to the pre-Roman heritage of each: Egypt to the east; a Greek sector focused on Cyrene (north-east Libya); and a Phoenician sector centered on Carthage. We shall look at only one city from this region, Lepcis Magna. Two themes will be of particular interest here: the effects of an enthusiastic

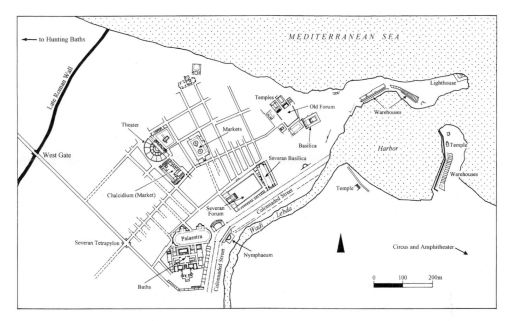

Figure 23.13 City plan, Lepcis Magna

imperial patron on the appearance of the city, and the development of the city plan, from pre-Roman to Roman imperial times.

Lepcis (sometimes written Leptis) Magna lies 120km east of Tripoli, the capital of modern Libya. It was originally a Punic settlement of before 500 BC, located at a small natural harbor on the Mediterranean coast, where a *wadi* (a river) empties into the sea. Brought under Roman control in the mid first century BC, Lepcis was the easternmost of the three cities that formed and gave their name to the province of Tripolitania, and the city was favored by the emperors Augustus and especially Septimius Severus, a native son. It became prosperous from its trans-Saharan trade for such items as ivory, wild beasts for the arenas, gold dust, carbuncle (a fiery-red stone), precious wood such as ebony, and ostrich feathers. Its prosperity was rocked by the Vandal conquest in 455, and settlement came to an end with the Arab attack in 643. Buried in sand dunes, the city was well preserved until the twentieth century when Italian archaeologists began excavations in the 1920s, during the Italian occupation of Libya.

Two pre-Roman roads shaped the Roman growth of the city (Figure 23.13), the (roughly) north–south road to the interior, the Via Trionfale, which became the cardo, and the main east–west coastal road, which became the town's decumanus. The early Punic settlement lay in the north, by the seacoast and the harbor. Early Roman imperial buildings constructed in this area include the Old Forum (Forum Vetus), of the first century BC and first century AD, with six temples, a basilica, and a curia; a porticoed market building (originally late first century BC); and a theater (early first century) on the site of a Punic cemetery.

Outlying areas were soon developed. During the reign of Hadrian, following the construction of an aqueduct, a huge bath complex was erected on the south edge of the city. A palaestra was attached a few decades later. To the east, well beyond the Wadi Lebda, an amphitheater was built in 56, with a large circus added in the following century. To the far west lay the Hunting Baths, a late second-century concrete vaulted building with paintings and mosaics. Hunters, wild beasts, and Nilotic landscapes appear in the wall paintings and mosaics. The hunters are even named: Nuber, Iuginus, Ibentius, and Bictor. To the south, up the Wadi Lebda, were two large cisterns and a massive dam intended to prevent flooding of the city.

With the lavish benefactions of Septimius Severus (ruled 193–211), Lepcis took on a new luster. Indeed, Lepcis is the best example in this chapter, at least, of how imperial favor could make a major difference in the appearance of a good-sized city. We shall look at the four major building projects of this period: the colonnaded street; the tetrapylon that marks the crossing point of the cardo and the decumanus; the forum and basilica; and the remodelling of the harbor. All buildings have counterparts elsewhere in the empire. What is distinctive is the ambition and richness of the program: so many major projects achieved in a space of 20 years, and the abundant use of imported marble and granite. The expense was tremendous.

The colonnaded street led from the harbor south along the Wadi Lebda, 366m long, 21m wide. The flanking porticoes had columns of green Karystos marble, carrying arches instead of the usual architraves. Because of the already existing bath and palaestra complex, the road needed to make a bend. This point was marked not with a wedge-shaped arch that crossed the street (as we have seen at Palmyra), but on the side by a large nymphaeum (fountain building).

The tetrapylon (built in 203) was a multiple arch with crossing passageways opening onto all four directions. Its decoration included four large relief panels on the attic, sculpture designed to honor Septimius Severus and his family. One panel shows Septimius Severus in a chariot, accompanied by his two sons, escorting a line of prisoners and followed by his cavalry. Elsewhere he is shown more as a god. In a scene of sacrifice, he and his wife, Julia Domna, together with divinities, are sacrificing a bull; this is the first time that the wife of an emperor is shown taking part in official activities. On an arch, the family is shown in concord, holding sacred objects, surrounded by divinities. This family peace would prove illusory: Septimius Severus's son Caracalla would have his brother murdered in the presence of their mother, and that was only the start of the violence that wracked this dynasty. The inner face of the arch contained eight figured panels. All carving was done by sculptors from Aphrodisias in Asia Minor.

The third of the major Severan projects consisted of a forum with an adjacent basilica. The Forum was a huge open space nearly 60m wide, with tall arcaded porticoes on three sides. The columns were of green and white striped cipollino marble from Euboea, with capitals of Pentelic marble (the type of marble used for the Parthenon). It was paved with Proconnesian marble (from quarries on the island of Prokonnesos in the Sea of Marmara). On the fourth side stood a large temple on a high podium, possibly dedicated to Bacchus (or Liber Pater; that is, Dionysos) and Hercules (Herakles), the patron deities of the city. The pedestal sculptures (capitals and bases) were of Pentelic marble; the 112 columns of the temple and of the adjacent basilica were of red Aswan granite (from Egypt).

The Basilica, built next to the Forum, was a large rectangular hall, ca. 30.5m in height, with side aisles and galleries. A large, concrete-vaulted apse with a pair of engaged columns was placed at either end of the nave. Beside them stood a pair of pilasters with sculpted scenes referring to Bacchus and Hercules.

Before Severus, the harbor consisted of quays and warehouses along the sheltered natural anchorage of the wadi mouth, especially on the west bank. The remodelled harbor was a basin of 21ha, with a narrow entrance between two projecting artificial moles. Along the west mole stood warehouses and, at the tip, a lighthouse; along the east mole, a signal tower, a small temple, and a row of warehouses fronted by a portico. Further along, a Temple of Jupiter stood on a high stepped podium and faced the harbor. Arrangements for securing the ships, with steps down and mooring rings, are well preserved.

CONCLUSIONS

This brief examination of eastern provincial cities has emphasized selected themes, as noted at the beginning of the chapter. To our final question, what constitutes a Roman city, we can give an answer. There was a certain uniformity of public building types, such as the colonnaded street, the forum, temples, baths, a theater. Moreover, they were built in the Greco-Roman architectural style, although with regional variations. In these eastern cities, cut stone is the preferred building material, not brick and concrete; this results from the construction techniques established well before the arrival of the Romans. In addition, and importantly, these cities display a predilection for a firm framework in their layout, with a cardo and decumanus that cross, major streets that form the main axes of the town plan. Often an orthogonal grid was added on top of that. Irregularities were frequent, resulting from such factors as the exigencies of the local topography or from pre-Roman plans. But the desire for a city-wide structure, greater than any individual concern, was always present. This concept of urban planning owes much to the organization of the Roman *castrum*. We have also seen the importance of imperial patronage, as well as the contributions of wealthy men and occasionally women. The material well-being of one's town was important to support and protect in the first through third centuries AD. So yes, we can indeed recognize a Roman city, its physical appearance and the activities that went on in it, despite the regional differences of geography, climate, religious practices, and ethnicity.

CHAPTER 24

Late antique transformations

Rome, Jerusalem, and Constantinople in the age of Constantine

Selected Roman Emperors from the Severans to Constantine I

Fifteen emperors (period of anarchy): 235–270

Aurelian: 270–275

Six emperors: 275–284

Diocletian: 284–305

    Beginning of the Tetrarchy: 293

Constantine I (the Great): 306–337

    Battle of Milvian Bridge: 312

    Edict of Milan: 313

    Foundation of Constantinople: 324

The age of Constantine the Great marks the end of antiquity and the beginning of the Middle Ages, a new chapter in the history of the Mediterranean and Near East. Fascinating though they are, the Middle Ages lie outside the scope of this book. This chapter presents some elements that characterize this transformation, in particular features that have an impact on the changing appearance and functions of cities in the Mediterranean basin. We will end our journey in Constantinople, for here, in this new capital city of the Roman Empire, both an ending and a new beginning are most strongly felt (for places mentioned in this chapter, see Figure 22.1).

HISTORICAL SUMMARY

After the Severan dynasty, the Roman Empire entered a turbulent period, with great instability at the top in the office of emperor. At the same time, threats from outside were increasing, primarily from the Sassanian Persians on the east, and from Goths and other Germanic tribes of northern Europe. In response to this, Aurelian had a defensive wall built around the capital (see Figure 22.2). The Aurelian Wall, begun in 271, was Rome's second fortification wall, following the Servian Wall of the fourth century BC. The new wall was 19km long, with 381 towers and 18 gates, and was made of concrete faced with brick, almost all reused, but with gates of stone. The wall enclosed a much larger area than that enclosed by the Servian Wall; this reflects the growth of the city in later Republican and imperial times. It was still in use in 1870, when the city was captured from the papacy during the campaign to unify Italy. Much of it still survives.

Internal and external disintegration was staved off by Diocletian, who reigned from 284 to 305. He instituted important reforms, which included new laws, and a power-sharing scheme known as the tetrarchy, whereby the two halves of the empire, the Latin-speaking west and the Greek-speaking east, would each be governed by an emperor (the *augustus*) with an assistant (the *caesar*). The two augusti would retire after 20 years, to be replaced by the caesars, who would in turn select new assistants. Diocletian and his colleague Constantius I duly retired in 305, but then the system collapsed because of the conflicting ambitions of their successors. War broke out among the rivals. Primacy in the west was settled in 312 with the victory of Constantine I (son of Constantius) over Maxentius at the Battle of the Milvian Bridge on the northern outskirts of Rome. After his defeat of Licinius in 324 at Chalcedon (opposite Byzantium), Constantine I was left as the sole ruler of the entire Roman Empire, both halves now integrated once again. But the unity was short-lived. The split between east and west continued to deepen. Constantine himself moved the imperial capital eastward, from Rome to Byzantium, renamed Constantinople. After his death, the threats from the north continued; in the fifth century, the western half of the empire was overrun by the Germanic invaders. Goths sacked Rome in 410, the Vandals took North Africa in 439, the Visigoths captured Spain and Portugal, and the Ostrogoths seized parts of Italy and the Balkans. In 476 the last Roman emperor in the west resigned; even the fiction of a Roman rule was finished. In the east, however, the Roman Empire continued until 1453. In modern times this state has been commonly known as the Byzantine Empire.

In addition to the move of the capital, the reign of Constantine was notable for the entry of Christianity into the public arena. At the Battle of the Milvian Bridge, Constantine allegedly saw a vision of a cross, and heard a voice saying, "In this sign you will conquer." Although his own personal attitude toward Christianity is not known, some claiming he converted on his death-bed, with the Edict of Milan of 313 he at least allowed Christianity the status of a legal religion. By the late fourth century, during the reign of Theodosius I, Christianity would be proclaimed the only legal religion. This change of religion is one symptom, although a major one, of numerous changes in Roman society that took place in the fourth and fifth centuries.

PALACES: PIAZZA ARMERINA AND THE PALACE OF DIOCLETIAN

A good place to start to see the changes of this period is to contrast two palaces of the late third through early fourth centuries. The *Piazza Armerina* in inland Sicily is a sprawling country villa that recalls Hadrian's Villa at Tivoli, whereas the *Palace of Diocletian* at Split (on Croatia's Adriatic coast) is a rigidly planned complex that recalls the Roman military camp, but with features that will be taken up in future architecture.

The Piazza Armerina was built in the early fourth century by an unknown person of distinction and wealth. This palace consists of a series of pavilions, placed in a tighter arrangement than Hadrian's Villa (Figure 24.1). It is famous for its many floor mosaics, covering approximately 3,000m². Illustrated here is a comic chariot race, in which the chariots are pulled by flamingoes and pigeons and ridden by boys (Figure 24.2). The style is late antique, and is an excellent example of art of this period. Such floor mosaics will continue to be laid elsewhere, with a notable sixth-century example in the Great Palace at Constantinople.

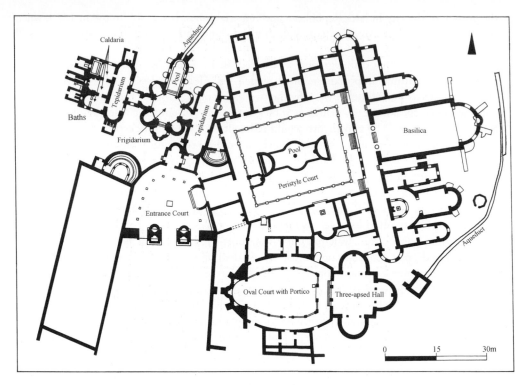

Figure 24.1 Plan, Piazza Armerina

Figure 24.2 Mosaic from Piazza Armerina (detail): Comic Chariot Race

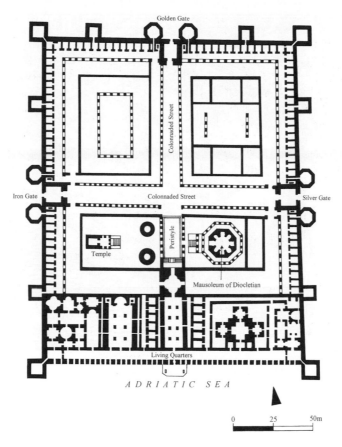

Figure 24.3 Plan, Diocletian's Palace, Split

The Palace of Diocletian at Split offers a different synthesis of past and future (Figures 24.3 and 24.4). It was laid out in a near square, 175m and 181m × 216m, with fortified walls with square and octagonal towers; inside, two main streets cross, like a cardo and decumanus. The feeling is definitely that of a fortified military camp, a result perhaps of the uncertainty of the times, and so Diocletian, who indeed included military leadership among his duties, honored a Roman principle of planning developed many centuries before. Inside, however, certain features are characteristic of the late third to early fourth centuries, not earlier. First, in one centrally placed peristyle court, the porticoes are arcaded, with, at the rear, a Greek-type pediment combined with a Roman arch, a favorite design of late Roman architecture (Figure 24.5). And second, the emperor's mausoleum is a building of the type known as the martyrium, a free-standing round or, as here, octagonal building which would become the standard form for marking the burial of an important or saintly person or, in Christian times, the site of a major religious event (such as the Nativity of Jesus).

Also included in this palace complex is a Golden Gate (Porta Aurea) on the north; Constantinople will later have its own celebrated Golden Gate. A Temple of Jupiter with a barrel vault lies symmetrically opposite the mausoleum, on the other side of the peristyle court. And on the south side, a big rectangular hall with two additional halls to the west are among the

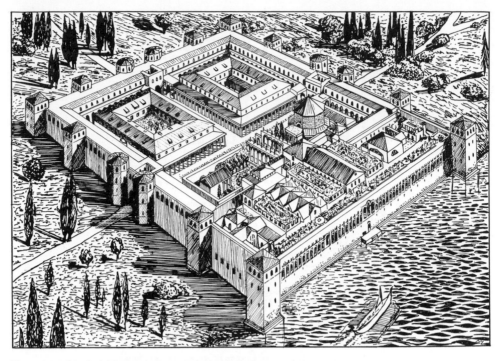

Figure 24.4 Diocletian's Palace (reconstruction), Split

Figure 24.5 Peristyle Court, Diocletian's Palace

reception rooms opening onto a seaside gallery running the full length of the building (here labelled "Living Quarter"). The rest of the palace is not well known, because of the alterations caused by later rebuilding.

ROME

By the later third century, Rome was packed with buildings. What was still needed? How indeed could an emperor make an architectural mark on the city as had, say, Augustus or Hadrian? Solutions were found. Diocletian contributed a major bath complex, the largest yet built in Rome, a development of the type seen in the Baths of Trajan. Constantine himself added a Basilica, or rather completed a basilica begun by his rival, Maxentius, in the Forum Romanum. In addition, Constantine constructed a triumphal arch adjacent to the Colosseum. This arch is of importance for its sculptural decoration, a mixture of old and new. These three types – baths, basilica, and triumphal arch – are all familiar from earlier Roman tradition, however. A new direction comes in this period with the construction of the first public churches. Old St. Peter's will serve as a good example of this particular change.

The Basilica of Maxentius and Constantine

This massive basilica, also called the New Basilica (Basilica Nova), was begun by Maxentius in 306–10 and finished by Constantine after 313 (Figure 24.6). It was erected in the Forum

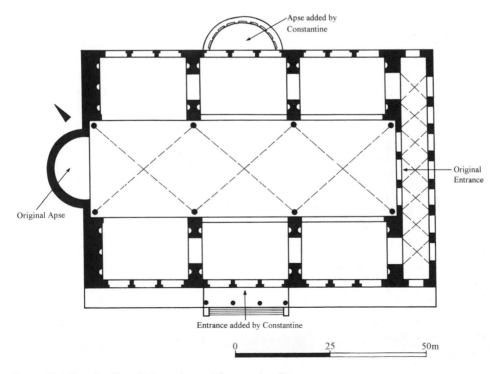

Figure 24.6 Plan, Basilica of Maxentius and Constantine, Rome

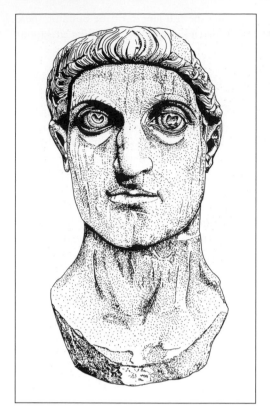

Figure 24.7 Constantine the Great, colossal marble sculpture. Capitoline Museums, Rome

Romanum, on the north side (Figure 19.8). The building stands on a concrete platform 100m × 65m. The nave is 80m long, 25m wide; its greatest height is 38m. Three bays on the north survive. The nave has arcaded windows at the top, a sort of clerestory; concrete groin vaults in the ceiling; and interior walls faced with red brick. The exterior of the basilica was covered with white stucco, imitating masonry. Originally oriented east–west, Constantine changed this plan by placing an apse on the north and stairs to the forum on the south.

On a huge base in a west apse of the basilica stood a colossal seated statue of Constantine, made in 324–30. Fragments were found in 1486. In a tradition going back to Near Eastern practice, the statue was composed of different materials: a brick core; the body of wood covered by bronze; and the head and limbs made of Pentelic marble. The head is 2.6m high, and weighs 8–9 tons (Figure 24.7). It was joined with plaster to the neck. The emperor's eyes are slightly upturned; although the head is clearly from the Greco-Roman style, the fixed gaze and upward turn of the eyes projects us into the Middle Ages, when the Christian emperor, considered an intermediary between ordinary people and God, was depicted in an optically non-realistic manner.

The Arch of Constantine

The Arch of Constantine has been called the "Gateway to the Middle Ages" by modern art historians because of its frieze, among the earliest examples of the medieval style on a prominent imperial monument. Built in 312–15 to commemorate Constantine's victory over Maxentius, and to celebrate his co-rule with Licinius, the arch has three arched passages, the central being the largest (Figure 24.8). The arch is noteworthy for its eclectic mix of sculptural decoration. Panels were taken from monuments of the second century, roundels from the Hadrianic period, rectangular plaques from the period of Marcus Aurelius, and stuck on in the attic of the arch. Contemporary, however, are the friezes just above the side arches. The frieze, in six panels on all four sides of the monument, recounts the campaign of Constantine, from his departure from Milan to the Siege of Verona (Figure 24.9), the Battle of the Milvian Bridge, and his addressing the Roman people in the Forum Romanum and distributing money. While the second-century sculpture is pure classical in style, with optically realistic views of the human body in action, the frieze is rigid, formally laid out with the emperor in the center. In addition, squat body proportions are used, and people are not shown as individuals, but as types. For observers since

Figure 24.8 Arch of Constantine (north side), Rome

Figure 24.9 Siege of Verona, relief sculpture, south-west frieze, Arch of Constantine

the Renaissance, it has been surprising that an emperor would choose to reject the classical style (esteemed by western Europe since the Renaissance) in favor of what was judged an inferior medieval style. For medieval is in fact what this style is, and there is no doubt that it was sanctioned from on high. Why? The breakdown of the classical style and the adoption of the medieval style is a great moment in the history of European art. Its explanation is not evident, but must be due to many factors at work throughout the vast empire. The change was not abrupt, and indeed Greco-Roman art continued to exert influence, to varying extents, throughout the Middle Ages. Apparently art was changing in order to reflect a new hierarchical concept of society, with the emperor firmly on top, others fixed in their particular ranks and professions.

These friezes fulfill the mission of visually explaining the status of societal groups; optical realism was no longer sought.

CHURCHES

Directly following the Edict of Milan in 313, Christian churches began to be built in the open. The first major church in Rome was St. John Lateran (later much rebuilt), located on the edge of the capital, thus well away from the heart of the city and its important shrines such as the Capitolium and the Pantheon. Another shrine had already developed on the west bank of the Tiber at the tomb of St. Peter. In the early fourth century, a major church was erected on this site. This was the Old St. Peter's; it would stand for over 1,000 years until replaced by an even more magnificent church, the Renaissance–Baroque St. Peter's cathedral still in use today.

Rome: Old St. Peter's

Old St. Peter's makes clear a key development in early church architecture: an already existing architectural type, the basilica, a civic building, was adapted for use as a religious building (Figures 24.10 and 24.11). In contrast with standard Greco-Roman religion, where ceremonies were held at an exterior altar, Christianity preferred to hold its ceremony, the eucharist or recreation of the last meal held between Jesus and his twelve apostles, at an indoor altar. The basilica form proved convenient. This plan would become standard for church design, and has continued so to the present day.

Like the standard Roman basilica, Old St. Peter's was divided into a central nave (with clerestory) and side aisles, but its columns did not run around all four sides, but along the long sides only. Entry was through the short side. At the opposite end was an apse. This church had two side arms; at the crossing of nave and side arms was the main altar, the focus of the ceremony. The tomb of St. Peter lay below the altar. The nave and the side aisles provided space for the participants and observers. The nave was decorated with figural mosaics. In front of the building was a courtyard, called an atrium (not to be confused with the atrium of a Roman house, as at

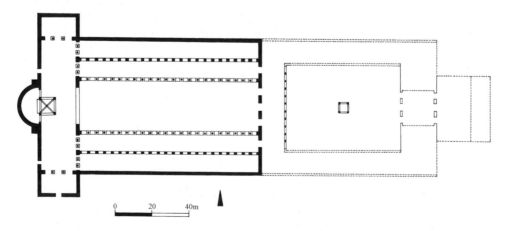

Figure 24.10 Plan (reconstruction), Old St. Peter's Basilica, Rome

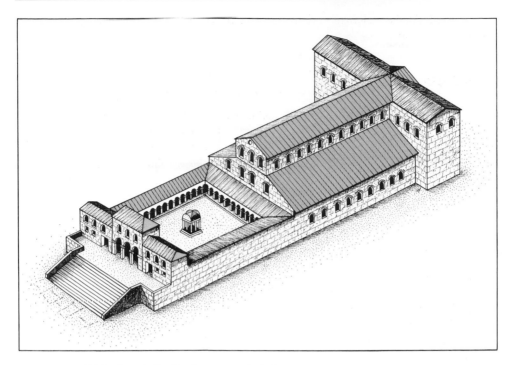

Figure 24.11 Old St. Peter's Basilica (reconstruction), Rome

Pompeii) surrounded by porticoes. Eventually this church would become popular as a burial site, for it was desirable to be buried near a great saint.

JERUSALEM

The layout of Jerusalem was altered by Constantine to reflect its new status as a place of importance and pilgrimage for Christians. But first, some background: let us quickly summarize the history of Jerusalem during the Roman Empire. At the time of Jesus's birth, the city was controlled by Herod the Great, a local ruler subservient to the Romans. A Jewish uprising against the Romans in 66–73 was crushed by Titus; during this, the Second Temple, which Herod had rebuilt, was destroyed. This event is referred to in the relief sculpture on the Arch of Titus in Rome, as we have seen (Figures 22.13 and 22.14). A subsequent revolt led by Bar Kochba in 132–5 during the reign of Hadrian gave rise to another harsh Roman response. This time, the city was renamed Aelia Capitolina, and laid out with a cardo and a decumanus and, at their crossing point, the main forum (Figure 24.12; compare with Figure 10.10).

Church of the Holy Sepulchre

Under Constantine, the prestige of the city was directed toward Christian matters. A cathedral with a baptistery was constructed on the north edge of the main forum. Thus the old Roman pattern was repeated, of the forum (civic center) with the principal temple to the main gods, Jupiter, Juno, and Minerva, but now this prestigious combination was given Christian content.

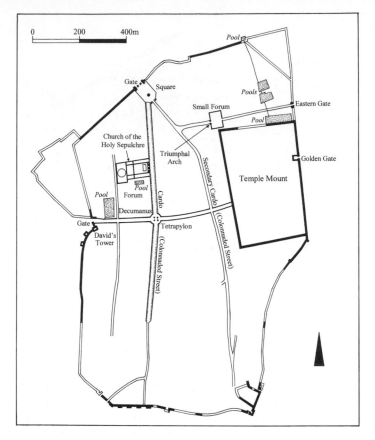

Figure 24.12 City plan,
Jerusalem, fourth century
AD

Likewise, existing Roman traditions would also be adapted in other spheres. Church architecture, as we have seen, saw the Roman basilica transformed for religious use by Christians. In pictorial art, many Greco-Roman motifs were reinterpreted for a Christian audience, and the style was simply that of the prevalent Roman art of the day.

During the construction of this church, a rock-cut tomb was discovered: not a surprise in itself, for this area had served as a Jewish burial ground in earlier times. But identified as the tomb of Jesus and thus the site of the Resurrection, the central event in Christianity, this tomb was soon sheltered by a round martyrium, known as the Rotunda of the Anastasis (Resurrection). With the church soon to house relics of the True Cross (the wooden cross on which Jesus died), the four-part complex of atrium court, basilica church, second courtyard, and rotunda became a major destination for Christian pilgrims (Figure 24.13).

The Constantinian rotunda and church were destroyed in 1009 by al-Hakim, a Fatimid ruler, then rebuilt in 1048 with the sponsorship of the Byzantine emperor Constantine IX Monomachos. The Crusaders made many modifications after they captured Jerusalem in 1099. The church today is thus quite different from the fourth-century original.

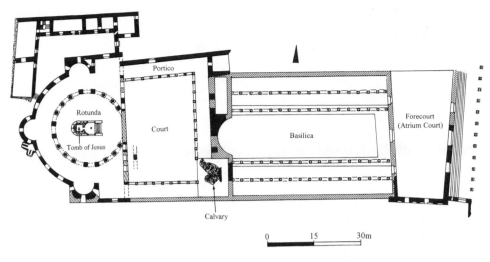

Figure 24.13 Plan (reconstruction), Church of the Holy Sepulchre, Jerusalem, fourth century AD

CONSTANTINOPLE, THE "NEW ROME"

Although always supporting Rome, and now adding new buildings to the religious centers of Jerusalem and Antioch, Constantine turned his eyes to the north-east, to the city of Byzantium. Recognizing the greater richness of the eastern half of the empire, and the practical benefits of having a headquarters closer to the eastern and Danube frontiers, Constantine decided to move the imperial capital from Rome to Byzantium. The dedication ceremony took place in the hippodrome on 11 May, 330. Byzantium, occupied since the Bronze Age, and refounded as a Greek city during the Iron Age, had played a modest role in Greek and Roman history. In the late second century, because it had supported an unsuccessful rival of Septimius Severus, Severus captured and sacked the city, but then he rebuilt its walls (they no longer survive). The city's location on a peninsula at the southern end of straits (the Bosporus) leading from the Sea of Marmara to the Black Sea was now considered of strategic and commercial value. This remarkable position as a crossroads, both maritime and land (between Europe and Asia), earned the city its role as an imperial capital for 1,600 years, first Byzantine, then Ottoman.

Few traces of Constantine's new capital survive, because Constantinople was much rebuilt in subsequent centuries. However, from literary sources in particular we can get some idea of what he did, how he redesigned the city to make it worthy of its new role as imperial capital (Figure 24.14). Of importance were the new city walls, defining the limits of the capital; these walls, however, no longer exist. The main street, or Mese, led from the tip of the peninsula down its spine, forking at the later Forum of Theodosios before continuing toward the land walls. The street soon passed through the Forum of Constantine, an oval plaza with a commemorative porphyry column in the center, with a bronze statue of Constantine as Helios, the sun god, on top (this statue survived until toppled in a storm in 1106). The column shaft was not decorated with sculpture. However, during the dedication of the new capital, prestigious items from the Greco-Roman past and from the Christian present were placed inside the base, such as the Palladium, a venerable statue of Athena thought to come originally from Troy. This forum was the site of civic buildings of the new city. Although the ground level of Constantine's oval forum

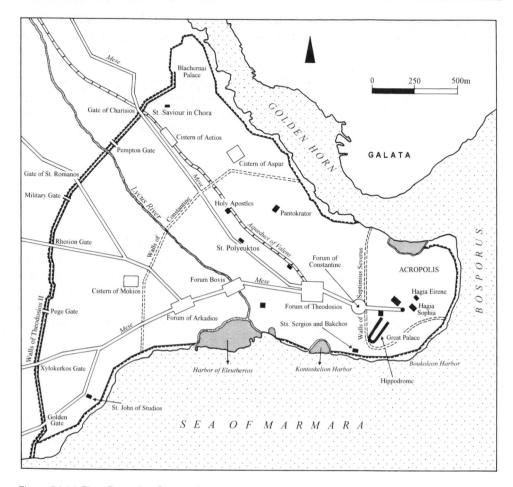

Figure 24.14 Plan, Byzantine Constantinople (Istanbul), to 1453

now lies 3m below today's streets, the column still stands, although damaged and without the statue on top, as a series of column drums held in place by metal bands.

The other great institution was the Hippodrome, a stadium for chariot races, built by Septimius Severus ca. 200, later rebuilt by Constantine. Adjacent to the royal palace (which would be developed in succeeding centuries), the Hippodrome was a long narrow circus, 480m × 117.5m, a track with one straight end, for the start and finish, and a curved end, which was supported by a huge construction of vaulting on the south end, the *sphendone*, which extended the flat land where the hill sloped down toward the Sea of Marmara. As the main public gathering place of the city, the Hippodrome was decorated with prestigious items taken from different parts of the empire. Today all that remains from the Constantinian period is the fragmentary bronze Serpent Column from Delphi (see Chapter 14), which served as a marker along the spina, the central divider of the hippodrome track. The Serpent Column celebrated the Greek victory over the Persians at Plataea in 479 BC. By bringing this commemorative monument to his new capital and by setting it up in such a prominent position, Constantine made clear that his state, his city was not something entirely new, but had deep roots in the past achievements of the region.

Likewise Theodosios I, an emperor of the later fourth century, would erect on this very same spina an Egyptian obelisk carved in the time of Thutmose III (sixteenth century BC): an even deeper reach into the past.

Constantine was buried in Constantinople in a round mausoleum, a martyrium. This building served as a chapel or church right from the start, it seems, supplied with an altar. At some point, either in 336 or 356–7, relics of the apostles Timothy, Luke, and Andrew were housed here until an adjacent cruciform church was completed and dedicated in 370. This Church of the Holy Apostles became the burial site of Byzantine royalty for several hundred years. Rebuilt during the reign of Justinian (ruled 527–565), the church was already in ruins by the time of the Latin sack of the city in 1204. Neither tomb nor church has survived.

IN CONCLUSION

What legacy has pre-Christian antiquity left for the cities of this new world order? Good fortifications, important streets, a hippodrome for the much-loved chariot races, an exalted placed for the emperor's residence in the layout of the city, and, thanks to the Romans, the dome, the symbol of heaven, the appropriate roof for the place of worship. What dies away? Features are never abruptly cancelled. More often than not a city with all its qualities slowly fades away, bypassed now by the trade routes, its harbor filled in by a silt-bearing river, its back broken by invaders or an earthquake or the growth of swamps hospitable to malarial mosquitoes. Newly important cities try to remember: when it remains useful, the past survives. But they must innovate, too. Urban life is always recreating.

Further Reading

Preface

African cities: Connah 1987; S. McIntosh and R. McIntosh 1993; and other papers in T. Shaw, Sinclair, Andah, and Okpoko 1993.
Chinese cities: Chang 1986; Wheatley 1971.
Mesoamerican cities: Sabloff 1989; Sanders and Webster 1988.
Reference: Hawkes 1974.

Introduction

Cities: Childe 1950; Kostof 1991 and 1992; Lynch 1984; Mumford 1938 and 1961; Sinclair, Shaw, and Andah 1993; Sjoberg 1960; Stein 1998; Wheatley 1972; Wirth 1938; Zenner 1996.
Archaeological aims and methods, including dating methods: Fagan 1996; Hayden 1993; Heizer 1959; Joukowsky 1980; Wenke 1999; Willey and Sabloff 1993.
Ethnoarchaeology: David and Kramer 2001.
Geography and history of the Mediterranean: Braudel 1973.
Calendars and chronology: Bickerman 1980; Biers 1992; Ehrich 1992; Richards 1998.
Tell formation: Rosen 1986; Schiffer 1987.

Neolithic towns

General: Childe 1953; Meyers 1997; Nissen 1988 and 1995; Redman 1978; Roaf 1990; Sasson 1995; Ucko, Tringham, and Dimbleby 1972; Wenke 1999.
Agriculture: Bar-Yosef and Meadow 1995.
Ain Ghazal figurines: Schmandt-Besserat 1998.
Anatolia: M. Özdoğan 1995; M. Özdoğan and N. Başgelen 1999; Sey 1996; Yakar 1991.
Çatal Höyük: Mellaart 1967; Todd 1976.
Çayönü: Çambel and Braidwood 1980; M. Özdoğan and A. Özdoğan 1989; A. Özdoğan 1995.
Jericho: Bar-Yosef 1986; Kenyon 1957.
Ubaid period: Henrickson and Thuesen 1989.

Mesopotamian cities

Reference: Meyers 1997; Sasson 1995.
General: J. Curtis 1982; Kuhrt 1995 (history); Lloyd 1984; Meyers 1997; Roaf 1990; Roux 1980; Weiss 1985.

Geography and environment: Buringh 1957; Butzer 1995.

History of exploration: Larsen 1996; Lloyd 1980.

Cities and city planning: Adams 1966; Aufrecht, Mirau, and Gauley 1997; Frankfort 1950; Kubba 1987; Lampl 1968; Lapidus 1969 and 1986; Oppenheim 1969; Pollock 1999; Stone 1995; Van De Mieroop 1997.

Daily life: Nemet-Nejat 1998.

Population: C. Kramer 1980; Postgate 1994.

Protoliterate (Uruk) period: Adams 1966 and 1981; Adams and Nissen 1972; Algaze 1993; Nissen 1988; Pollock 1999.

Sumerians: Crawford 1991; S. Kramer 1963; Pollock 1999; Postgate 1992.

Art and architecture: Collon 1995; Cooper 1990; Frankfort 1996; Gunter 1990; Lloyd 1984; I. Winter 1985.

Cylinder seals: Collon 1987.

Food: Wilkins, Harvey, and Dobson 1995.

Materials and industries: Moorey 1994.

Religion: Jacobsen 1976; Black and Green 1992.

Royal rituals: Kuhrt 1987.

Writing: Michalowski 1990; Pollock 1999; Schmandt-Besserat 1996; C. B. F. Walker, in Hooker *et al.* 1996.

Specific cities

Babylon: Oates 1979.

Habuba Kabira: Strommenger 1985.

Khafajeh: Delougaz 1940.

Mari: Gates 1984.

Nimrud: Mallowan 1966.

Nineveh: Stronach and Lumsden 1992.

Persepolis: Schmidt 1953; Wilber 1969.

Ur: Canby 2001; Moorey 1977; Pollock 1991; Woolley 1934 and 1982.

Uruk: Adams and Nissen 1972; Nissen 1988 and 1995.

Indus Valley Civilization

General: Allchin and Allchin 1968 and 1982; Chakrabarti 1997; Kenoyer 1998; Possehl 1994; Wheeler 1968.

Urbanism: Possehl 1990.

Harappa: Meadow 1991.

Lothal: Rao 1979 and 1985.

Mohenjo-Daro: Mackay 1938; Marshall 1931.

Writing: Parpola 1994.

Egypt

General: Baines and Malek 1984; James 1979 and 1982; Kemp 1989; Sasson 1995; Shaw and Nicholson 1995.

Urbanism: Fairman 1949; Hassan 1993; Kemp 1977a and 1977b; D. O'Connor 1993; Redford 1997.

History: Trigger, Kemp, O'Connor, and Lloyd 1983.
Kingship: O'Connor and Silverman 1995.
Art and architecture: Arnold 1991; Robins 1997; W. S. Smith 1998.
Pyramids: Edwards 1993; Lehner 1997.
Temples: Wilkinson 2000.
Archaic period: Spencer 1993.
Saqqara: Lauer 1976.
Akhenaten: Redford 1984.
Valley of the Kings: Reeves and Wilkinson 1996.
Tutankhamun: Reeves 1990.
Daily life: Strouhal 1992.
Mummification: Ikram and Dodson 1998.
Writing: W. V. Davies, in Hooker *et al.* 1996.
Rescue excavations at Abu Simbel, Buhen, etc.: Säve-Söderbergh 1987.

The Aegean Bronze Age

General: Dickinson 1994; Rutter 1997.
Art and architecture: Graham 1987; Hood 1978.
Chronology: Manning 1999; Warren and Hankey 1989.
Knossos: Palmer 1969; Soles 1995.
Mycenae: Iakovidis 1979; Mylonas 1966.
Pylos and Messenia: Davis 1998.
Thera: Doumas 1983 and 1992.
Writing: J. Chadwick, in Hooker *et al.* 1996.

Anatolia, Cyprus, and the Levant

General: Sasson 1995; Sey 1996.
Hattusha/Boğazköy: Neve 1992 (in German); Seeher 1999.
Troy: Blegen 1963; Wood 1985. For results from the current excavations, see the periodical
    Studia Troica, vol. 1 (1992 – present).
Cyprus: Karageorghis 1982; and S. Swiny, Hohlfelder, and H. Swiny 1997.
    Enkomi: Courtois, J. Lagarce, and E. Lagarce 1986 (in French).
    Kition: Karageorghis 1976.
    Late Bronze Age Cyprus: Knapp 1997.
Ugarit: A. Curtis 1985; Klengel 1992; Saadé 1979 (in French); Yon 1992; Yon 1997 (in French).
Sea Peoples: Sandars 1985.
Cape Gelidonya and Uluburun Shipwrecks: Bass *et al.* 1967; Bass 1987 and 1991; Pulak 1997
    and 1998.

Greek cities and civilization

General reference: Bickerman 1980; Biers 1992; de Grummond 1996; Fagan 1996; Finley
    1977; Grant and Kitzinger 1988; Hornblower and Spawforth 1996; Stillwell 1976; Talbert
    2000.
Greek history: Bury and Meiggs 1975; Ehrenberg 1969; Hammond 1967; Osborne 1996.

Art and archaeology of Greece, general: Biers 1996; Boardman 1993; Kostof 1995; Robertson 1975; Roebuck 1969; Snodgrass 1987; Whitley 2001.

Iron Age Greece: Boardman 1999; Coldstream 1977; Descoeudres 1990; Osborne 1996; Polignac 1995; Snodgrass 1971; Thomas and Conant 1999.

Iron Age sites

Lefkandi: Catling and Lemos 1990; Popham, Calligas, and Sackett 1993; Popham, Touloupa, and Sackett 1982.

Archaic Greece: Osborne 1996; Snodgrass 1980.

Art and architecture of the Classical period: Pollitt 1972.

Greek architecture: Coulton 1977; Dinsmoor 1950; Korres 1995; Kostof 1995; Lawrence 1996; Scully 1979.

Greek cities and houses in Anatolia: Sey 1996.

Greek fortifications: Winter 1971.

Greek cities: Bean 1979; Martin 1974 (in French); Murray and Price 1990; Owens 1991; Tomlinson 1992; Ward-Perkins 1974; Wycherley 1967.

Greek sculpture: Boardman 1978, 1985, and 1995; Leipen 1971; Mattusch 1988 and 1996; Spivey 1996; Stewart 1990, 1993, and 1996.

Greek pottery: Cook 1997; Grace 1961.

Greek coinage: Kraay 1966; Carradice and Price 1988.

Maps: Dilke 1985.

Technology: Landels 1978; Roebuck 1969; White 1984.

Writing: B. Cook, in Hooker *et al.* 1996.

Food: Dalby 1996; Wilkins, Harvey, and Dobson 1995.

Athletics and sports: Miller 1991; Morgan 1990; Raschke 1988; Romano 1993.

Sanctuaries and religion: Marinatos and Hägg 1993; Parke 1967; Tomlinson 1976.

Athens: Neils *et al.* 1992; Parke 1977; Simon 1983.

Delphi: Bommelaer 1991 (in French); Fontenrose 1978; Walker 1977.

Didyma: Bean 1979; Fontenrose 1988; Tuchelt 1992 (in German).

Ephesus: Bean 1979; Wood 1877.

Epidauros: Tomlinson 1983.

Olympia: Morgan 1990; Raschke 1988.

Samos: City: Tölle 1969 (in German). Heraion: Kyrieleis 1981 and 1993. Colossal kouros: Kyrieleis 1996 (in German).

Theater: Bieber 1961; Green 1994.

Athens: Camp 2002; Wycherley 1978.

Agora: Camp 1986; Thompson 1971.

Acropolis: Bowie and Thimme 1971; Hurwit 1999; Korres 1995; Leipen 1971; Neils *et al.* 1992; Pollitt 1972; Rhodes 1995; and Tournikiotis 1996.

Miletus: Greaves 2002.

Sardis: Hanfmann *et al.* 1983.

Late Classical sites

Mausoleum: Jeppesen n.d.

Olynthos: Cahill 1991.

Priene: Bean 1979; Rumscheid 1998; Schede 1964 (in German).

Vergina: Andronicos 1984.

Hellenistic art and architecture: Nielsen 1994; Pollitt 1986; R. Smith 1991; Stewart 1993.

Mosaics: Dunbabin 1999.

The Alexander Mosaic: Cohen 1997.
Hellenistic cities
  Alexandria: Bowman 1986; Fraser 1972; Hölbl 2001.
  Delos: Bruneau and Ducat 1983 (in French); Rauh 1993.
  Pergamon: Bean 1979; Radt 1984 and 1999 (this last in German).

Italy and the Roman Empire: cities and civilizations

General reference: Bickerman 1980; Biers 1992; de Grummond 1996; Fagan 1996; Finley 1977; Hornblower and Spawforth 1996; Stillwell 1976; Talbert 2000.
Etruscan civilization: Bonfante 1986; E. Richardson 1976.
Etruscan writing: Bonfante, in Hooker *et al.* 1996.
Etruscan art and architecture: Boethius 1978; Brendel 1995.
Roman civilization (general): Cornell and Matthews 1982; Grant and Kitzinger 1988; Scarre 1995; Wacher 1987.
Roman art: Boardman 1993; Elsner 1998; Ling 1991; Ramage and Ramage 2000.
Roman history: Scullard 1980 and 1982.
Roman Italy: Potter 1987.
Western Greeks: Pugliese Carratelli 1996; Ridgway 1992.
Paestum: Pedley 1990.
Sicily: Finley 1979; Holloway 1991.
  Syracuse: Wescoat 1989.
Carthage: Hurst 1987; Lancel 1995.
North Africa: MacKendrick 1980; Mattingly 1995; Raven 1993.
Roman cities: Fentress 2000; Grimal 1983; MacDonald 1986; Owens 1991; Stambaugh 1988; Ward-Perkins 1974.
Rome (city): Anderson 1997; Nash 1968; L. Richardson 1992.
Urban population: Storey 1997.
Early and Republican Rome: Bremmer 1987; Dupont 1992; Potter 1987.
Augustan Rome: Favro 1996.
Cosa: Brown 1980; McCann *et al.* 1987.
Ostia: Meiggs 1973.
Pompeii and Herculaneum: Grant 1971; Laurence 1994; Ling 1987; Parslow 1995; L. Richardson 1988; Wallace-Hadrill 1994; Zanker 1998.
Aqueducts: Aicher 1995; Hodge 1992.
Roman architecture (general): Adam 1999; Anderson 1997; Boethius 1978; Kostof 1995; MacDonald 1982 and 1986; Sear 1989; Ward-Perkins 1981.
  Baths: Yegül 1992.
  Bridges: C. O'Connor 1993.
  Circuses: J. H. Humphrey 1986.
  Diocletian's Palace, Split: Wilkes 1993.
  Forum of Trajan, Rome: Packer 1997.
  Hadrian's Villa: MacDonald and Pinto 1995.
  Pantheon: MacDonald 1976.
  Piazza Armerina: Wilson 1983.
  Theaters: Bieber 1961.
  Tombs: Toynbee 1971.

Economy: Greene 1986.

Gardens: Jashemski 1979–93.

Roman sculpture: Kleiner 1992; Mattusch 1996.

Mosaics: Dunbabin 1999; Ling 1998.

Roman daily life: Dupont 1992; Paoli 1963.

Burial practices: Toynbee 1971.

Food: Wilkins, Harvey, and Dobson 1995.

Maps and roads: Dilke 1985; French 1996.

Crafts and technology: Adam 1999; Landels 1978; Roebuck 1969; Strong and Brown 1976; White 1984.

Cities of the Roman Empire:

    Anatolia (Asia Minor): Sey 1996.

    Egypt: Bowman 1986.

    Ephesus: Scherrer 2000.

    Greece: Alcock 1993; Tobin 1997.

    Jerash: Browning 1982; Wharton 1995.

    Jerusalem: Wharton 1995.

    Near East: Ball 2000; Levick 1987.

    Lepcis Magna and North Africa: MacKendrick 1980; Mattingly 1995; Raven 1993; Ward-Perkins 1993.

    Palmyra: Browning 1979.

    Pergamon: Bean 1979; Radt 1984 and 1999 (this last in German).

    Perge: Boatwright 1993.

    Western Empire: Drinkwater 1987; Grimal 1983.

Architecture in the age of Constantine the Great: Krautheimer 1986.

Bibliography

Adam, J.-P. (1999) *Roman Building: Materials and Techniques*, trans. A. Mathews, London: Routledge.

Adams, R. McC. (1966) *The Evolution of Urban Society*, Chicago: Aldine.

—— (1981) *The Heartland of Cities: Surveys of Ancient Settlement and Land Use on the Central Floodplain of the Euphrates*, Chicago: University of Chicago Press.

Adams, R. McC. and Nissen, H. J. (1972) *The Uruk Countryside*, Chicago: University of Chicago Press.

Aicher, P. (1995) *Guide to the Aqueducts of Ancient Rome*, Wauconda, IL: Bolchazy-Carducci.

Alcock, S. (1993) *Graecia Capta: The Landscapes of Roman Greece*, Cambridge: Cambridge University Press.

Algaze, G. (1993) *The Uruk World System: The Dynamics of Expansion of Early Mesopotamian Civilization*, Chicago and London: University of Chicago Press.

Allchin, B. and Allchin, F. R. (1968) *The Birth of Indian Civilization*, Harmondsworth: Penguin Books.

—— (1982) *The Rise of Civilization in India and Pakistan*, Cambridge: Cambridge University Press.

Anderson, J. (1997) *Roman Architecture and Society*, Baltimore and London: Johns Hopkins University Press.

Andronicos, M. (1984) *Vergina: The Royal Tombs and the Ancient City*, Athens: Ekdotike Athenon.

Arnold, D. (1991) *Building in Egypt: Pharaonic Stone Masonry*, Oxford and New York: Oxford University Press.

Aufrecht, W. E., Mirau, N. A., and Gauley, S. W. (eds) (1997) *Urbanism in Antiquity: From Mesopotamia to Crete*, Sheffield: Sheffield Academic Press.

Baines, J. and Malek, J. (1984) *Atlas of Ancient Egypt*, Oxford: Phaidon.

Ball, W. (2000) *Rome in the East: The Transformation of an Empire*, London and New York: Routledge.

Bar-Yosef, O. (1986) "The Walls of Jericho: An Alternative Interpretation," *Current Anthropology* 27: 157–62.

Bar-Yosef, O. and Meadow, R. (1995) "The Origins of Agriculture in the Near East," in Price and Gebauer 1995: 39–94.

Barrelet, M.-Th. (ed.) (1980) *L'archéologie de l'Iraq du début de l'époque néolithique à 333 avant notre ère*, Paris: Centre National de la Recherche Scientifique.

Bass, G. (1987) "Oldest Known Shipwreck Reveals Splendors of the Bronze Age," *National Geographic* 172 (December): 692–733.

—— (1991) "Evidence of Trade from Bronze Age Shipwrecks," in Gale 1991: 69–82.

Bass, G. *et al.* (1967) *Cape Gelidonya: A Bronze Age Shipwreck*, Philadelphia: American Philosophical Society.

Bean, G. (1979) *Aegean Turkey*, 2nd edn, London: Murray.

Bickerman, E. (1980) *Chronology of the Ancient World*, rev. edn, London: Thames and Hudson.

Bieber, M. (1961) *The History of the Greek and Roman Theater*, Princeton: Princeton University Press.

Biers, W. (1992) *Art, Artefacts, and Chronology in Classical Archaeology*, London: Routledge.

—— (1996) *The Archaeology of Greece*, 2nd edn, Ithaca and London: Cornell University Press.

Black, J. and Green, A. (1992) *Gods, Demons and Symbols of Ancient Mesopotamia: An Illustrated Dictionary*, London: British Museum Press.

Blegen, C. (1963) *Troy and the Trojans*, London and New York: Thames and Hudson.

Boardman, J. (1978) *Greek Sculpture: The Archaic Period. A Handbook*, London: Thames and Hudson.

—— (1985) *Greek Sculpture: The Classical Period. A Handbook*, London: Thames and Hudson.

—— (ed.) (1993) *The Oxford History of Classical Art*, Oxford: Oxford University Press.

—— (1995) *Greek Sculpture: The Late Classical Period and Sculpture in Colonies and Overseas. A Handbook*, London: Thames and Hudson.

—— (1999) *The Greeks Overseas*, 4th edn, London: Thames and Hudson.

Boatwright, M. T. (1993) "The City Gate of Plancia Magna in Perge," in D'Ambra 1993: 189–207.

Boethius, A. (1978) *Etruscan and Early Roman Architecture*, Harmondsworth: Penguin.

Bommelaer, J.-F. (1991) *Guide de Delphes: le site et le musée*, Paris: de Boccard.

Bonfante, L. (ed.) (1986) *Etruscan Life and Afterlife*, Warminster: Aris & Phillips.

Bowie, T. and Thimme, D. (eds) (1971) *The Carrey Drawings of the Parthenon Sculptures*, Bloomington and London: Indiana University Press.

Bowman, A. (1986) *Egypt after the Pharaohs 332 BC–AD 642: from Alexander to the Arab Conquest*, Berkeley: University of California Press.

Braudel, F. (1973) *The Mediterranean and the Mediterranean World in the Age of Philip II*, 2 vols, 2nd rev. edn, trans. S. Reynolds, New York: Harper and Row.

—— (1980) *On History*, trans. S. Matthews, Chicago: University of Chicago Press.

—— (1993) *A History of Civilizations*, trans. R. Mayne, New York: Penguin Books.

Bremmer, J. (1987) "Romulus, Remus and the Foundation of Rome," in Bremmer and Horsfal 1987: 25–48.

Bremmer, J. and Horsfal, N. (eds) (1987) *Roman Myth and Mythography. Bulletin Supplement* 52, London: University of London, Institute of Classical Studies.

Brendel, O. (1995) *Etruscan Art*, 2nd edn, New Haven and London: Yale University Press.

Brown, F. (1980) *Cosa: The Making of a Roman Town*, Ann Arbor: University of Michigan Press.

Browning, I. (1979) *Palmyra*, Park Ridge, NJ: Noyes Press.

—— (1982) *Jerash and the Decapolis*, London: Chatto and Windus.

Bruneau, P. and Ducat, J. (1983) *Guide de Délos*, 3rd edn, Paris: École Française d'Athènes.

Buringh, P. (1957) "Living Conditions in the Lower Mesopotamian Plain in Ancient Times," *Sumer* 13: 30–57.

Bury, J. and Meiggs, R. (1975) *A History of Greece to the Death of Alexander the Great*, 4th edn, London: Macmillan Press.

Butzer, K. (1995) "Environmental Change in the Near East and Human Impact on the Land," in Sasson 1995: 123–51.

Cahill, N. (1991) *Olynthus: Social and Spatial Planning in a Greek City*, Ph.D. dissertation, University of California at Berkeley, Ann Arbor, MI: University Microfilms.

Çambel, H. and Braidwood, R. J. (eds) (1980) *Prehistoric Research in Southeastern Anatolia*, Istanbul: Edebiyat Fakültesi.

Camp, J. (1986) *The Athenian Agora: Excavations in the Heart of Classical Athens*, London: Thames and Hudson.

—— (2002) *The Archaeology of Athens*, New Haven and London: Yale University Press.

Canby, J. V. (2001) *The "Ur-Nammu" Stela*, University Museum Monograph 110, Philadelphia: University of Pennsylvania Museum of Archaeology and Anthropology.

Cannadine, D. and Price, S. (eds) (1987) *Rituals of Royalty: Power and Ceremonial in Traditional Societies*, Cambridge: Cambridge University Press.

Carradice, I. and Price, M. (1988) *Coinage in the Greek World*, London: Seaby.

Catling, R. and Lemos, I. (1990) *Lefkandi II: The Protogeometric Building at Toumba. Part I: The Pottery*, London: British School of Archaeology at Athens.

Chakrabarti, D. (1997) *The Archaeology of Ancient Indian Cities*, Delhi: Oxford University Press.

Chang, K. C. (1986) *The Archaeology of Ancient China*, 4th edn, New Haven and London: Yale University Press.

Childe, V. G. (1950) "The Urban Revolution," *Town Planning Review* 21: 3–17.

—— (1953) *New Light on the Most Ancient East*, 4th edn, New York: W. W. Norton.

Cohen, A. (1997) *The Alexander Mosaic. Stories of Victory and Defeat*, Cambridge: Cambridge University Press.

Coldstream, J. (1977) *Geometric Greece*, London: Methuen.

Collon, D. (1987) *First Impressions: Cylinder Seals in the Ancient Near East*, London: British Museum Press.

—— (1995) *Ancient Near Eastern Art*, London: British Museum Press.

Connah, G. (1987) *African Civilizations: Precolonial Cities and States in Tropical Africa. An Archaeological Perspective*, Cambridge: Cambridge University Press.

Cook, R. (1997) *Greek Painted Pottery*, 3rd edn, London and New York: Routledge.

Cornell, T. and Matthews, J. (1982) *Atlas of the Roman World*, Oxford: Phaidon.

Cooper, J. (1990) "Mesopotamian Historical Consciousness and the Production of Monumental Art in the Third Millennium B.C.," in Gunter 1990: 39–51.

Coulton, J. (1977) *Greek Architects at Work: Problems of Structure and Design*, London: Paul Elek.

Courtois, J.-C., Lagarce, J., and Lagarce, E. 1986. *Enkomi et le bronze récent à Chypre*, Nicosia: A. G. Leventis Foundation.

Crawford, H. (1991) *Sumer and the Sumerians*, Cambridge: Cambridge University Press.

Cunliffe, B. (ed.) (1987) *Origins: The Roots of European Civilisation*, London: BBC Books.

Curtis, A. (1985) *Ugarit (Ras Shamra)*, Cambridge: Lutterworth Press.

Curtis, J. (ed.) (1982) *Fifty Years of Mesopotamian Discovery: The Work of the British School of Archaeology in Iraq, 1932–1982*, London: British School of Archaeology in Iraq.

Dalby, A. (1996) *Siren Feasts: A History of Food and Gastronomy in Greece*, London and New York: Routledge.

D'Ambra, E. (ed.) (1993) *Roman Art in Context: An Anthology*, Englewood Cliffs: Prentice Hall.

David, N. and Kramer, C. (2001) *Ethnoarchaeology in Action*, Cambridge: Cambridge University Press.

Davis, J. L. (ed.) (1998) *Sandy Pylos: An Archaeological History from Nestor to Navarino*, Austin: University of Texas Press.

de Grummond, N. (ed.) (1996) *An Encyclopedia of the History of Classical Archaeology*, 2 vols, London and Chicago: Fitzroy Dearborn.

Delougaz, P. (1940) *The Temple Oval at Khafajah*, Chicago: University of Chicago Press.

Descoeudres, J.-P. (ed.) (1990) *Greek Colonists and Native Populations*, Oxford: Clarendon Press.

Dickinson, O. (1994) *The Aegean Bronze Age*, Cambridge: Cambridge University Press.

Dilke, O. (1985) *Greek and Roman Maps*, London: Thames and Hudson.

Dinsmoor, W. (1950) *The Architecture of Ancient Greece: An Account of its Historic Development*, 3rd edn, revised, London: B. T. Batsford.

Doumas, C. (1983) *Thera, Pompeii of the Ancient Aegean: Excavations at Akrotiri 1967–79*, London: Thames and Hudson.

—— (1992) *The Wall-paintings of Thera*, Athens: The Thera Foundation – Petros M. Nomikos.

Drinkwater, J. F. (1987) "Urbanization in Italy and the Western Empire," in Wacher 1987: 345–87.

Dunbabin, K. M. D. (1999) *Mosaics of the Greek and Roman World*, Cambridge: Cambridge University Press.

Dupont, F. (1992) *Daily Life in Ancient Rome*, trans. C. Woodall, Oxford and Cambridge, MA: Blackwell.

Edwards, I. E. S. (1993) *The Pyramids of Egypt*, rev. edn, London: Penguin Books.

Ehrenberg, V. (1969) *The Greek State*, 2nd edn, London: Methuen.

Ehrich, R. (ed.) (1992) *Chronologies in Old World Archaeology*, 2 vols, 3rd edn, Chicago and London: University of Chicago Press.

Elsner, J. (1998) *Imperial Rome and Christian Triumph*, Oxford: Oxford University Press.

Fagan, B. (ed.) (1996) *The Oxford Companion to Archaeology*, Oxford and New York: Oxford University Press.

Fairman, H. (1949) "Town Planning in Pharaonic Egypt," *Town Planning Review* 20: 32–51.

Favro, D. (1996) *The Urban Image of Augustan Rome*, Cambridge: Cambridge University Press.

Fentress, E. (ed.) (2000) *Romanization and the City: Creation, Transformations, and Failures*, Portsmouth, RI: Journal of Roman Archaeology.

Finley, M. (ed.) (1977) *Atlas of Classical Archaeology*, London: Chatto and Windus.

—— (1979) *Ancient Sicily*, rev. edn, London: Chatto and Windus.

Fontenrose, J. (1978) *The Delphic Oracle. Its Responses and Operations with a Catalogue of Responses*, Berkeley, Los Angeles, and London: University of California Press.

—— (1988) *Didyma. Apollo's Oracle, Cult, and Companions*, Berkeley, Los Angeles, and London: University of California Press.

Frankfort, H. (1950) "Town Planning in Ancient Mesopotamia," *Town Planning Review* 21: 98–115.

—— (1996) *The Art and Architecture of the Ancient Orient*, 5th edn, New Haven and London: Yale University Press.

Fraser, P. (1972) *Ptolemaic Alexandria*, Oxford: Clarendon Press.

French, D. (1996) "Roman Roads," in Fagan 1996: 612–14.

Gale, N. H. (ed.) (1991) *Bronze Age Trade in the Mediterranean*, Jonsered: Paul Åströms Förlag.

Gates, M.-H. (1984) "The Palace of Zimri-Lim at Mari," *Biblical Archaeologist* 47: 70–87.

Grace, V. (1961) *Amphoras and the Ancient Wine Trade*. Excavations of the Athenian Agora, Picture Book No. 6, Princeton: American School of Classical Studies at Athens.

Graham, J. W. (1987) *The Palaces of Crete*, rev. edn, Princeton: Princeton University Press.

Grant, M. (1971) *Cities of Vesuvius, Pompeii and Herculaneum*, New York: Macmillan.

Grant, M. and Kitzinger, R. (eds) (1988) *Civilization of the Ancient Mediterranean: Greece and Rome*, 3 vols, New York: Charles Scribner's Sons.

Greaves, A. (2002) *Miletos: A History*, London and New York: Routledge.

Green, J. (1994) *Theatre in Ancient Greek Society*, London and New York: Routledge.

Greene, K. (1986) *The Archaeology of the Roman Economy*, London: B. T. Batsford.

Grimal, P. (1983) *Roman Cities*, translated and edited by G. Michael Woloch, Madison: University of Wisconsin Press.

Gunter, A. (ed.) (1990) *Investigating Artistic Environments in the Ancient Near East*, Washington, D.C.: Smithsonian Institution Press.

Hammond, N. (1967) *A History of Greece*, 2nd edn, Oxford: Oxford University Press.

Hanfmann, G. (1975) *Roman Art*, New York: W. W. Norton.

Hanfmann, G. *et al.* (1983) *Sardis from Prehistoric to Roman Times: Results of the Archaeological Exploration of Sardis 1958–1975*, Cambridge, MA, and London: Harvard University Press.

Hassan, F. A. (1993) "Town and Village in Ancient Egypt: Ecology, Society and Urbanization," in T. Shaw *et al.* 1993: 551–69.

Hawkes, J. (ed.) (1974) *Atlas of Ancient Archaeology*, New York: McGraw-Hill.

Hayden, B. (1993) *Archaeology: The Science of Once and Future Things*, New York: W. H. Freeman.

Heizer, R. F. (ed.) (1959) *The Archaeologist at Work*, New York: Harper and Row.

Henrickson, E. and Thuesen, I. (eds) (1989) *Upon this Foundation: The 'Ubaid Reconsidered*, Copenhagen: Carsten Niebuhr Institute of Ancient Near Eastern Studies, University of Copenhagen, and Museum Tusculanum Press.

Hodge, A. (1992) *Roman Aqueducts and Water Supply*, London: Duckworth.

Hölbl, G. (2001) *A History of the Ptolemaic World*, trans. T. Saavedra, London: Routledge.

Holloway, R. (1991) *The Archaeology of Ancient Sicily*, London and New York: Routledge.

Hood, S. (1978) *The Arts in Prehistoric Greece*, Harmondsworth: Penguin.

Hooker, J. *et al.* (1996) *Reading the Past: Ancient Writing from Cuneiform to the Alphabet*, London: British Museum Press.

Hornblower, S. and Spawforth, A. (eds) (1996) *The Oxford Classical Dictionary*, 3rd edn, Oxford and New York: Oxford University Press.

Humphrey, J. H. (1986) *Roman Circuses: Arenas for Chariot Racing*. London: B. T. Batsford.

Hurst, H. (1987) "Carthage: the Punic City," in Cunliffe 1987: 135–47.

Hurwit, J. M. (1999) *The Athenian Acropolis*, Cambridge: Cambridge University Press.

Iakovidis, S. E. (1979) *Mycenae-Epidaurus*, Athens: Ekdotike Athenon.

Ikram, S. and Dodson, A. (1998) *The Mummy in Ancient Egypt*, London: Thames and Hudson.

Jacobsen, T. (1976) *The Treasures of Darkness: A History of Mesopotamian Religion*, New Haven: Yale University Press.

James, T. G. H. (1979) *An Introduction to Ancient Egypt*, London: The Trustees of the British Museum.

—— (ed.) (1982) *Excavating in Egypt: The Egypt Exploration Society 1882–1982*, Chicago: University of Chicago Press.

Jashemski, W. (1979–93) *The Gardens of Pompeii, Herculaneum and the Villas Destroyed by Vesuvius*, 2 vols, New Rochelle, NY: Caratzas Brothers, 1979, vol. 1; Aristide D. Caratzas, 1993, vol. 2.

Jeppesen, K. (n.d.) *The Maussolleion at Ancient Halicarnassus*, Ankara: Dönmez Yayınları.

Joukowsky, M. (1980) *A Complete Manual of Field Archaeology*, Englewood Cliffs: Prentice-Hall.

Karageorghis, V. (1976) *Kition*, London: Thames and Hudson.

—— (1982) *Cyprus, From the Stone Age to the Romans*, London: Thames and Hudson.

Kemp, B. (1977a) "The City of el-Amarna as a Source for the Study of Urban Society in Ancient Egypt," *World Archaeology* 9: 123–39.

—— (1977b) "The Early Development of Towns in Egypt," *Antiquity* 51: 185–200.

—— (1989) *Ancient Egypt: Anatomy of a Civilization*, London and New York: Routledge.

Kenoyer, J. M. (1998) *Ancient Cities of the Indus Valley Civilization*, Karachi and Oxford: Oxford University Press.

Kenyon, K. (1957) *Digging Up Jericho*, London: E. Benn.

Kessler, H. and Simpson, M. (eds) (1985) *Pictorial Narrative in Antiquity and the Middle Ages*, Washington, D.C.: National Gallery of Art.

Kleiner, D. (1992) *Roman Sculpture*, New Haven and London: Yale University Press.

Klengel, H. (1992) *Syria, 3000–300 B.C.*, Berlin: Akademie Verlag.

Knapp, A. B. (1997) *The Archaeology of Late Bronze Age Cypriot Society: The Study of Settlement, Survey and Landscape*, Glasgow: University of Glasgow, Department of Archaeology.

Korres, M. (1995) *From Pentelicon to the Parthenon*, Athens: Melissa.

Kostof, S. (1991) *The City Shaped: Urban Patterns and Meanings through History*, London: Thames and Hudson.

—— (1992) *The City Assembled: The Elements of Urban Form through History*, London: Thames and Hudson.

—— (1995) *A History of Architecture, Settings and Rituals*, 2nd edn, Oxford and New York: Oxford University Press.

Kraay, C. (1966) *Greek Coins*, London: Thames and Hudson.

Kraeling, C. H. and Adams, R. McC. (eds) (1960) *City Invincible*, Chicago: University of Chicago Press.

Kramer, C. (1980) "Estimating Prehistoric Populations: An Ethnoarchaeological Approach," in Barrelet 1980: 315–34.

Kramer, S. N. (1963) *The Sumerians: Their History, Culture, and Character*, Chicago and London: University of Chicago Press.

Krautheimer, R. (1986) *Early Christian and Byzantine Architecture*, 4th edn, rev. with S. Ćurčić, New Haven and London: Yale University Press.

Kubba, S. A. A. (1987) *Mesopotamian Architecture and Town Planning from the Mesolithic to the End of the Proto-historic Period c. 10,000–3,500 B.C.*, Oxford: BAR International Series.

Kuhrt, A. (1987) "Usurpation, Conquest and Ceremonial: From Babylon to Persia," in Cannadine and Price 1987: 20–55.

—— (1995) *The Ancient Near East, c. 3000–330 BC*, 2 vols, London and New York: Routledge.

Kyrieleis, H. (1981) *Führer durch das Heraion von Samos*, Athens: Deutsches Archäologisches Institut Athen.

—— (1993) "The Heraion at Samos," in Marinatos and Hägg 1993: 125–33.

—— (1996) *Der grosse Kuros von Samos (Samos vol. X)*, Bonn: Rudolf Habelt.

Lampl, P. (1968) *Cities and Planning in the Ancient Near East*, New York: George Braziller.

Lancel, S. (1995) *Carthage: A History*, trans. A. Nevill, Oxford and Cambridge, MA: Blackwell.

Landels, J. (1978) *Engineering in the Ancient World*, London: Chatto and Windus.

Lapidus, I. M. (ed.) (1969) *Middle Eastern Cities: A Symposium on Ancient, Islamic, and Contemporary Middle Eastern Urbanism*, Berkeley: University of California Press.

—— (1986) "Cities and Societies: A Comparative Study of the Emergence of Urban Civilization in Mesopotamia and Greece," *Journal of Urban History* 12: 257–92.

Larsen, M. T. (1996) *The Conquest of Assyria: Excavations in an Antique Land, 1840–1860*, London: Routledge.

Lauer, J.-P. (1976) *Saqqara: The Royal Cemetery of Memphis, Excavations and Discoveries since 1850*, London: Thames and Hudson.

Laurence, R. (1994) *Roman Pompeii: Space and Society*, London and New York: Routledge.

Lawrence, A. (1996) *Greek Architecture*, 5th edn revised by R. Tomlinson, New Haven and London: Yale University Press.

Lehner, M. (1997) *The Complete Pyramids*, London: Thames and Hudson.

Leipen, N. (1971) *Athena Parthenos: A Reconstruction*, Toronto: Royal Ontario Museum.

Levick, B. (1987) "Urbanization in the Eastern Empire," in Wacher 1987: 328–44.

Levinson, D. and Ember, M. (eds) (1996) *Encyclopedia of Cultural Anthropology*, 4 vols, New York: Henry Holt.

Ling, R. (1987) "A New Look at Pompeii," in Cunliffe 1987: 148–60.

—— (1991) *Roman Painting*, Cambridge: Cambridge University Press.

—— (1998) *Ancient Mosaics*. London: British Museum Press.

Lloyd, S. (1980) *Foundations in the Dust: A Story of Mesopotamian Exploration*, rev. and enlarged edn, New York: Thames and Hudson.

—— (1984) *The Archaeology of Mesopotamia*, rev. edn, London: Thames and Hudson.

Luff, R. and Rowley-Conwy, P. (eds) (1994) *Whither Environmental Archaeology?* Oxford: Oxbow Books.

Lynch, K. (1984) *Good City Form*, Cambridge, MA: MIT Press.

McCann, A. *et al.* (1987) *The Roman Port and Fishery of Cosa*, Princeton: Princeton University Press.

MacDonald, W. L. (1976) *The Pantheon: Design, Meaning, and Progeny*, London: Allen Lane.

—— (1982) *The Architecture of the Roman Empire. I: An Introductory Study*, rev. edn, New Haven and London: Yale University Press.

—— (1986) *The Architecture of the Roman Empire. II: An Urban Appraisal*, New Haven and London: Yale University Press.

MacDonald, W. L. and Pinto, J. (1995) *Hadrian's Villa and Its Legacy*, New Haven and London: Yale University Press.

McIntosh, S. K. and McIntosh, R. J. (1993) "Cities without Citadels: Understanding Urban Origins along the Middle Niger," in T. Shaw *et al.* 1993: 622–41.

Mackay, E. J. H. (1938) *Further Excavations at Mohenjodaro*, New Delhi: Government of India.

MacKendrick, P. (1980) *The North African Stones Speak*, Chapel Hill: University of North Carolina Press.

Mallowan, M. (1966) *Nimrud and its Remains*, 3 vols, London: Collins.

Manning, S. W. (1999) *A Test of Time. The Volcano of Thera and the Chronology and History of the Aegean and East Mediterranean in the Mid Second Millennium BC*, Oxford: Oxbow Books.

Marinatos, N. and Hägg, R. (eds) (1993) *Greek Sanctuaries: New Approaches*, London and New York: Routledge.

Marshall, J. (1931) *Mohenjo-daro and the Indus Civilization*, London: Probsthain.

Martin, R. (1974) *L'urbanisme dans la Grèce antique*, Paris: A. & J. Picard.

Matthews, W. and Postgate, J. N. (1994) "The Imprint of Living in an Early Mesopotamian City: Questions and Answers," in Luff and Rowley-Conwy 1994: 171–212.

Mattingly, D. J. (1995) *Tripolitania*, London: B. J. Batsford.

Mattusch, C. (1988) *Greek Bronze Statuary: From the Beginnings through the Fifth Century B.C.*, Ithaca: Cornell University Press.

—— (1996) *Classical Bronzes: The Art and Craft of Greek and Roman Statuary*, Ithaca: Cornell University Press.

Meadow, R. (ed.) (1991) *Harappa Excavations 1986–1990: A Multidisciplinary Approach to Third Millennium Urbanism*, Madison: Prehistory Press.

Meiggs, R. (1973) *Roman Ostia*, 2nd edn, Oxford: Clarendon Press.

Mellaart, J. (1967) *Çatal Hüyük, A Neolithic Town in Anatolia*, London: Thames and Hudson.

Meyers, E. (ed.) (1997) *The Oxford Encyclopedia of Archaeology in the Near East*, 5 vols, Oxford and New York: Oxford University Press.

Michalowski, P. (1990) "Early Mesopotamian Communicative Systems: Art, Literature, and Writing," in Gunter 1990: 53–69.

Miller, S. (1991) *Arete: Greek Sports from Ancient Sources*, 2nd expanded edn, Berkeley, Los Angeles, and Oxford: University of California Press.

Moorey, P. R. S. (1977) "What Do We Know About the People Buried in the Royal Cemetery?" *Expedition* 20: 24–40.

—— (1994) *Ancient Mesopotamian Materials and Industries: The Archaeological Evidence*, Oxford: Clarendon Press.

Morgan, C. (1990) *Athletes and Oracles: The Transformation of Olympia and Delphi in the Eighth Century B.C.*, Cambridge: Cambridge University Press.

Mumford, L. (1938) *The Culture of Cities*, New York: Harcourt, Brace.

—— (1961) *The City in History*, New York: Harcourt, Brace & World.

Murray, O. and Price, S. (eds) (1990) *The Greek City: From Homer to Alexander*, Oxford: Clarendon Press.

Mylonas, G. (1966) *Mycenae and the Mycenaean Age*, Princeton: Princeton University Press.

Nash, E. (1968) *Pictorial Dictionary of Ancient Rome*, 2 vols, rev. edn, London: Thames and Hudson.

National Geographic Society (U.S.), Special Publications Division (1981) *Splendors of the Past: Lost Cities of the Ancient World*, Washington, D.C.: National Geographic Society.

Neils, J. *et al.* (1992) *Goddess and Polis: The Panathenaic Festival in Ancient Athens*, Hanover, NH: Hood Museum of Art; and Princeton: Princeton University Press.

Nemet-Nejat, K. R. (1998) *Daily Life in Ancient Mesopotamia*, Westport: Greenwood Press.

Neve, P. (1992) *Hattusa: Stadt der Götter und Tempel*, Mainz am Rhein: Philipp von Zabern.

Nielsen, I. (1994) *Hellenistic Palaces*, Aarhus: Aarhus University Press.

Nissen, H. J. (1988) *The Early History of the Ancient Near East, 9000–2000 B.C.*, trans. E. Lutzeier with K. J. Northcott, Chicago: University of Chicago Press.

—— (1995) "Ancient Western Asia Before the Age of Empires," in Sasson 1995: 791–806.

Oates, J. (1979) *Babylon*, London: Thames and Hudson.

O'Connor, C. (1993) *Roman Bridges*, Cambridge: Cambridge University Press.

O'Connor, D. (1993) "Urbanism in Bronze Age Egypt and Northeast Africa," in T. Shaw *et al.* 1993: 570–86.

O'Connor, D. and Silverman, D. (eds) (1995) *Ancient Egyptian Kingship*, Leiden: E. J. Brill.

Oppenheim, A. L. (1969) "Mesopotamia – Land of Many Cities," in Lapidus 1969: 3–18.

Osborne, R. (1996) *Greece in the Making, 1200–479 BC*, London and New York: Routledge.

Owens, E. (1991) *The City in the Greek and Roman World*, London: Routledge.

Özdoğan, A. (1995) "Life at Çayönü During the Pre-Pottery Neolithic Period," in Prehistory Department, Istanbul University 1995: 79–100.

Özdoğan, M. (1995) "Neolithic in Turkey: The Status of Research," in Prehistory Department, Istanbul University 1995: 41–59.

Özdoğan, M. and Başgelen, N. (eds) (1999) *Neolithic in Turkey, the Cradle of Civilization: New Discoveries*, Istanbul: Arkeoloji ve Sanat Yayınları.

Özdoğan, M. and Özdoğan, A. (1989) "Çayönü: A Conspectus of Recent Work," *Paléorient* 15: 65–74.

Packer, J. (1997) *The Forum of Trajan in Rome*, Berkeley and Los Angeles: University of California Press.

Palmer, L. (1969) *A New Guide to the Palace of Knossos*, New York: Praeger.

Paoli, U. (1963) *Rome: Its People, Life, and Customs*, trans. R. Macnaghten, London: Longman.

Parke, H. (1967) *Greek Oracles*, London: Hutchinson.

—— (1977) *Festivals of the Athenians*, London: Thames and Hudson.

Parpola, A. (1994) *Deciphering the Indus Script*, Cambridge: Cambridge University Press.

Parslow, C. (1995) *Rediscovering Antiquity: Karl Weber and the Excavation of Herculaneum, Pompeii, and Stabiae*, Cambridge: Cambridge University Press.

Pedley, J. (1990) *Paestum. Greeks and Romans in Southern Italy*, London: Thames and Hudson.

Polignac, F. de (1995) *Cults, Territory, and the Origins of the Greek City-State*, trans. J. Lloyd, Chicago: University of Chicago Press.

Pollitt, J. (1972) *Art and Experience in Classical Greece*, Cambridge: Cambridge University Press.

—— (1986) *Art in the Hellenistic Age*, Cambridge: Cambridge University Press.

Pollock, S. (1991) "Of Priestesses, Princes, and Poor Relations: The Dead in the Royal Cemetery of Ur," *Cambridge Archaeological Journal* 1: 171–89.

—— (1999) *Ancient Mesopotamia: The Eden that Never Was*, Cambridge: Cambridge University Press.

Popham, M., Calligas, P., and Sackett, L. (eds) (1993) *Lefkandi II: The Protogeometric Building at Toumba. Part 2: The Excavation, Architecture and Finds*, Oxford: The British School of Archaeology at Athens.

Popham, M., Touloupa, E., and Sackett, L. (1982) "The Hero of Lefkandi," *Antiquity* 56: 169–74.

Possehl, G. (1990) "Revolution in the Urban Revolution: The Emergence of Indus Urbanism," *Annual Review of Anthropology* 19: 261–82.

—— (1994) *Harappan Civilization: a Recent Perspective*, 2nd rev. edn, New Delhi: American Institute of Indian Studies.

Postgate, J. N. (1992) *Early Mesopotamia: Society and Economy at the Dawn of History*, London and New York: Routledge.

—— (1994) "How Many Sumerians Per Hectare? Probing the Anatomy of an Early City," *Cambridge Archaeological Journal* 4: 47–65.

Potter, T. (1987) *Roman Italy*, London: British Museum Publications.

Prehistory Department, Istanbul University (1995) *Readings in Prehistory: Studies Presented to Halet Çambel*, Istanbul: Graphis.

Price, T. D. and Gebauer, A. B. (eds) (1995) *Last Hunters – First Farmers*, Santa Fe: School of American Research Press.

Pugliese Carratelli, G. (ed.) (1996) *The Western Greeks: Classical Civilization in the Western Mediterranean*, London: Thames and Hudson.

Pulak, C. (1997) "The Uluburun Shipwreck," in S. Swiny, Hohlfelder, and H. W. Swiny 1997: 233–62.

—— (1998) "The Uluburun Shipwreck: An Overview," *International Journal of Nautical Archaeology* 27: 188–224.

Radt, W. (1984) *Pergamon. Archaeological Guide*, 3rd edn, trans. D. Boyd, J. Carpenter, and M. Schneeweiss, Istanbul: Türkiye Turing ve Otomobil Kurumu.

—— (1999) *Pergamon: Geschichte und Bauten einer Antiken Metropole*, Darmstadt: Primus.

Ramage, N. H. and Ramage, A. (2000) *Roman Art*, 3rd edn, London: Laurence King.

Rao, S. R. (1979) *Lothal: A Harappan Port Town (1955–62)*, vol. 1, New Delhi: Archaeological Survey of India.

—— (1985) *Lothal: A Harappan Port Town (1955–62)*, vol. 2, New Delhi: Archaeological Survey of India.

Raschke, W. (ed.) (1988) *The Archaeology of the Olympics: The Olympics and Other Festivals in Antiquity*, Madison: University of Wisconsin Press.

Rauh, N. (1993) *The Sacred Bonds of Commerce: Religion, Economy, and Trade Society at Hellenistic Roman Delos, 166–87 B.C.*, Amsterdam: J. C. Gieben.

Raven, S. (1993) *Rome in Africa*, 3rd edn, London and New York: Routledge.

Redford, D. (1984) *Akhenaten: The Heretic King*, Princeton: Princeton University Press.

—— (1997) "The Ancient Egyptian 'City': Figment or Reality?" in Aufrecht, Mirau, and Gauley 1997: 210–20.

Redman, C. (1978) *The Rise of Civilization: From Early Farmers to Urban Society in the Ancient Near East*, San Francisco: W. H. Freeman.

Reeves, N. (1990) *The Complete Tutankhamun*, London: Thames and Hudson.

Reeves, N. and Wilkinson, R. H. (1996) *The Complete Valley of the Kings*, London: Thames and Hudson.

Rhodes, R. (1995) *Architecture and Meaning in the Athenian Acropolis*, Cambridge: Cambridge University Press.

Richards, E. G. (1998) *Mapping Time: The Calendar and its History*, Oxford: Oxford University Press.

Richardson, E. (1976) *The Etruscans: Their Art and Civilization*, Chicago: University of Chicago Press.

Richardson, L. (1988) *Pompeii: An Architectural History*, Baltimore and London: Johns Hopkins University Press.

—— (1992) *A New Topographical Dictionary of Ancient Rome*, Baltimore and London: Johns Hopkins University Press.

Ridgway, D. (1992) *The First Western Greeks*, Cambridge: Cambridge University Press.

Robertson, M. (1975) *A History of Greek Art*, 2 vols, Cambridge: Cambridge University Press.

Robins, G. (1997) *The Art of Ancient Egypt*, London: Trustees of the British Museum.

Roaf, M. (1990) *Cultural Atlas of Mesopotamia and the Ancient Near East*, Oxford and New York: Facts On File.

Roebuck, C. (ed.) (1969) *The Muses at Work: Arts, Crafts, and Professions in Ancient Greece and Rome*, Cambridge, MA, and London: MIT Press.

Romano, D. (1993) *Athletics and Mathematics in Archaic Corinth: The Origins of the Greek Stadion*, Philadelphia: American Philosophical Society.

Rosen, A. M. (1986) *Cities of Clay: The Geoarcheology of Tells*, Chicago and London: University of Chicago Press.

Roux, G. (1980) *Ancient Iraq*, 2nd edn, Harmondsworth: Penguin Books.

Rumscheid, F. (1998) *Priene: A Guide to the 'Pompeii of Asia Minor'*, Istanbul: Ege Yayınları.

Rutter, J. (1997) *The Prehistoric Archaeology of the Aegean* (http://devlab.dartmouth.edu/history/bronze_age/)

Saadé, G. (1979) *Ougarit, Métropole Canaéenne*, Beirut: Imprimerie Catholique.

Sabloff, J. (1989) *The Cities of Ancient Mexico*, London and New York: Thames and Hudson.

Sandars, N. K. (1985) *The Sea Peoples: Warriors of the Ancient Mediterranean, 1250–1150 BC*, rev. edn, London: Thames and Hudson.

Sanders, W. and Webster, D. (1988) "The Mesoamerican Urban Tradition," *American Anthropologist* 90: 521–46.

Sasson, J. (ed.) (1995) *Civilizations of the Ancient Near East*, 4 vols, New York: Charles Scribner's Sons.

Säve-Söderbergh, T. (ed.) (1987) *Temples and Tombs of Ancient Nubia: The International Rescue Campaign at Abu Simbel, Philae and Other Sites*, New York and London: UNESCO and Thames and Hudson.

Scarre, C. (1995) *The Penguin Historical Atlas of Ancient Rome*, London: Penguin Books.

Schede, M. (1964) *Die Ruinen von Priene*, 2nd edn, Berlin: Walter de Gruyter.

Scherrer, P. (ed.) (2000) *Ephesus: The New Guide*, trans. L. Bier and G. Luxon, Istanbul: Ege Yayınları.

Schiffer, M. B. (1987) *Formation Processes of the Archaeological Record*, Albuquerque: University of New Mexico Press.

Schmandt-Besserat, D. (1996) *How Writing Came About*, Austin: University of Texas Press.

—— (1998) "'Ain Ghazal 'Monumental' Figurines," *BASOR* 310: 1–17.

Schmidt, E. (1953) *Persepolis I*, Chicago: University of Chicago Press.

Scullard, H. (1980) *A History of the Roman World, 753–146 BC*, 4th edn, London and New York: Methuen.

—— (1982) *From the Gracchi to Nero: A History of Rome from 133 B.C. to A.D. 68*, 5th edn, London: Methuen.

Scully, V. (1979) *The Earth, the Temple, and the Gods*, rev. edn, New Haven and London: Yale University Press.

Sear, F. (1989) *Roman Architecture*, rev. edn, London: Batsford Academic and Educational.

Seeher, J. (1999) *Hattusha-Guide: A Day in the Hittite Capital*, Istanbul: Ege Yayınları.

Seton-Williams, V. and Stocks, P. (1993) *Blue Guide: Egypt*, 3rd edn, New York: W. W. Norton.

Sey, Y. (ed.) (1996) *Housing and Settlement in Anatolia: A Historical Perspective*, Istanbul: Türkiye

Ekonomik ve Toplumsal Tarih Vakfı Yayınları/Turkish Economic and Social History Foundation Publications.

Shaw, I. and Nicholson, P. (1995) *British Museum Dictionary of Ancient Egypt*, London: Trustees of the British Museum.

Shaw, T., Sinclair, P., Andah, B., and Okpoko, A. (eds) (1993) *The Archaeology of Africa: Food, Metals and Towns*, London and New York: Routledge.

Simon, E. (1983) *Festivals of Attica: An Archaeological Commentary*, Madison: University of Wisconsin Press.

Sinclair, P. J. J., Shaw, T., and Andah, B. (1993) "Introduction," in T. Shaw *et al.* 1993: 1–31.

Sjoberg, G. (1960) *The Preindustrial City, Past and Present*, Glencoe: Free Press.

Smith, R. R. R. (1991) *Hellenistic Sculpture: A Handbook*, London: Thames and Hudson.

Smith, W. S. (1998) *The Art and Architecture of Ancient Egypt*, 3rd edn, revised with additions by W. K. Simpson, New Haven: Yale University Press.

Snodgrass, A. (1971) *The Dark Age of Greece: An Archaeological Survey of the Eleventh to the Eighth Centuries B.C.*, Edinburgh: Edinburgh University Press.

—— (1980) *Archaic Greece: The Age of Experiment*, London: Dent; and Berkeley: University of California Press.

—— (1987) *An Archaeology of Greece: The Present State and Future Scope of a Discipline*, Berkeley, Los Angeles, and London: University of California Press.

Soles, J. S. (1995) "The Functions of a Cosmological Center: Knossos in Palatial Crete," *Aegeaum* 12: 405–14.

Spencer, A. J. (1993) *Early Egypt: The Rise of Civilisation in the Nile Valley*, London: Trustees of the British Museum.

Spivey, N. (1996) *Understanding Greek Sculpture: Ancient Meanings, Modern Readings*, London: Thames and Hudson.

Stambaugh, J. (1988) *The Ancient Roman City*, Baltimore and London: Johns Hopkins University Press.

Stein, G. J. (1998) "Heterogeneity, Power, and Political Economy: Some Current Research Issues in the Archaeology of Old World Complex Societies," *Journal of Archaeological Research* 6: 1–44.

Stewart, A. (1990) *Greek Sculpture: An Exploration*, New Haven and London: Yale University Press.

—— (1993) *Faces of Power: Alexander's Image and Hellenistic Politics*, Berkeley and Los Angeles: University of California Press.

—— (1996) *Art, Desire and the Body in Ancient Greece*, Cambridge: Cambridge University Press.

Stillwell, R. (ed.) (1976) *The Princeton Encyclopedia of Classical Sites*, Princeton: Princeton University Press.

Stone, E. C. (1995) "The Development of Cities in Ancient Mesopotamia," in Sasson 1995: 235–48.

Storey, G. (1997) "The Population of Ancient Rome," *Antiquity* 71: 966–78.

Strommenger, E. (1964) *5000 Years of the Art of Mesopotamia*, photos by M. Hirmer; translated by C. Haglund, New York: Harry N. Abrams.

—— (1985) "Habuba Kabira South/Tell Qannas and Jebel Aruda," in Weiss 1985: 83–6.

Stronach, D. and Lumsden, S. (1992) "UC Berkeley's Excavations at Nineveh," *Biblical Archaeologist* 55: 227–33.

Strong, D. and Brown, D. (eds) (1976) *Roman Crafts*, London: Duckworth.

Strouhal, E. (1992) *Life in Ancient Egypt*, Cambridge: Cambridge University Press.

Swaddling, J. (1984) *The Ancient Olympic Games*, reprint of the 1980 edn, London: The Trustees of the British Museum.

Swiny, S., Hohlfelder, R., and Swiny, H. (eds) (1997) *Res Maritimae: Cyprus and the Eastern Mediterranean from Prehistory to Late Antiquity*, Atlanta: Scholars Press.

Talbert, R. J. A. (ed.) (2000) *Barrington Atlas of the Greek and Roman World*, Princeton: Princeton University Press.

Thomas, C. and Conant, C. (1999) *Citadel to City-State: The Transformation of Greece, 1200–700 B.C.E.*, Bloomington: Indiana University Press.

Thompson, D. (1971) *The Athenian Agora: An Ancient Shopping Center*. Excavations of the Athenian Agora, Picture Book No. 12, Princeton: American School of Classical Studies at Athens.

Tobin, J. (1997) *Herodes Attikos and the City of Athens: Patronage and Conflict under the Antonines*, Amsterdam: J. C. Gieben.

Todd, I. (1976) *Çatal Hüyük in Perspective*, Menlo Park, CA: Cummings.

Tölle, R. (1969) *Die Antike Stadt Samos*, Mainz am Rhein: Philipp von Zabern.

Tomlinson, R. (1976) *Greek Sanctuaries*, London: Paul Elek.

—— (1983) *Epidauros*, London: Granada.

—— (1992) *From Mycenae to Constantinople: The Evolution of the Ancient City*, London: Routledge.

Tournikiotis, P. (1996) *The Parthenon and its Impact in Modern Times*, Athens: Melissa; and New York: Harry N. Abrams.

Toynbee, J. (1971) *Death and Burial in the Roman World*, Ithaca: Cornell University Press.

Trigger, B., Kemp, B., O'Connor, D., and Lloyd, A. (1983) *Ancient Egypt: A Social History*, Cambridge: Cambridge University Press.

Tuchelt, K. (1992) *Branchidai – Didyma: Geschichte und Ausgrabung eines antiken Heiligtums*, Mainz am Rhein: Philipp von Zabern.

Ucko, P., Tringham, R., and Dimbleby, G. W. (eds) (1972) *Man, Settlement and Urbanism*, London: Duckworth.

Van De Mieroop, M. (1997) *The Ancient Mesopotamian City*, Oxford: Clarendon Press.

Wacher, J. (ed.) (1987) *The Roman World*, 2 vols, London and New York: Routledge and Kegan Paul.

Walker, A. (1977) *Delphi*, Athens: Lycabettus Press.

Wallace-Hadrill, A. (1994) *Houses and Society in Pompeii and Herculaneum*, Princeton: Princeton University Press.

Ward-Perkins, J. (1974) *Cities of Ancient Greece and Italy: Planning in Classical Antiquity*, London: Sidgwick & Jackson.

—— (1981) *Roman Imperial Architecture*, Harmondsworth: Penguin Books.

—— (1993) *The Severan Buildings of Lepcis Magna: An Architectural Survey*, ed. by P. Kenrick, London: Society for Libyan Studies.

Warren, P. and Hankey, V. (1989) *Aegean Bronze Age Chronology*, Bristol: Bristol Classical Press.

Weiss, H. (ed.) (1985) *Ebla to Damascus: Art and Archaeology of Ancient Syria*, Washington, D.C.: Smithsonian Institution.

Wenke, R. (1999) *Patterns in Prehistory*, 4th edn, Oxford and New York: Oxford University Press.

Wescoat, B. (ed.) (1989) *Syracuse, the Fairest Greek City*, Rome: De Luca.

Wharton, A. (1995) *Refiguring the Post Classical City: Dura Europos, Jerash, Jerusalem, and Ravenna*, Cambridge: Cambridge University Press.

Wheatley, P. (1971) *The Pivot of the Four Quarters: A Preliminary Enquiry into the Origins and Character of the Ancient Chinese City*, Chicago: Aldine.

—— (1972) "The Concept of Urbanism," in Ucko, Tringham, and Dimbleby 1972: 601–37.

Wheeler, R. E. M. (1968) *The Indus Civilization*, 3rd edn, Cambridge: Cambridge University Press.

White, K. (1984) *Greek and Roman Technology*, London: Thames and Hudson.

Whitley, J. (2001) *The Archaeology of Ancient Greece*, Cambridge: Cambridge University Press.

Wilber, D. (1969) *Persepolis, the Archaeology of Parsa, Seat of the Persian Kings*, London: Cassell.

Wilkes, J. J. (1993) *Diocletian's Palace, Split: Residence of a Retired Roman Emperor*, Sheffield: The Department of Ancient History and Classical Archaeology, University of Sheffield.

Wilkins, J., Harvey, D., and Dobson, M. (eds) (1995) *Food in Antiquity*, Exeter: University of Exeter Press.

Wilkinson, R. H. (2000) *The Complete Temples of Ancient Egypt*, New York: Thames and Hudson.

Willey, G. W. and Sabloff, J. A. (1993) *A History of American Archaeology*, 3rd edn, New York: W. H. Freeman.

Wilson, R. J. A. (1983) *Piazza Armerina*, London: Granada.

Winter, F. (1971) *Greek Fortifications*, London: Routledge and Kegan Paul.

Winter, I. (1985) "After the Battle is Over: The Stele of the Vultures and the Beginning of Historical Narrative in the Art of the Ancient Near East," in Kessler and Simpson 1985: 11–32.

Wirth, L. (1938) "Urbanism as a Way of Life," *American Journal of Sociology* 44: 1–24.

Wood, J. (1877) *Discoveries at Ephesus: Including the Site and Remains of the Great Temple of Diana*, London: Longmans, Green, and Co.

Wood, M. (1985) *In Search of the Trojan War*, London: BBC.

Woolley, C. L. (1934) *Ur Excavations, Vol. 2: The Royal Cemetery*, London and Philadelphia: British Museum and University Museum.

—— (1982) *Ur of the Chaldees*, rev. and updated by P. R. S. Moorey, London: Herbert Press.

Wycherley, R. (1967) *How the Greeks Built Cities*, 2nd edn, London: Macmillan.

—— (1978) *The Stones of Athens*, Princeton: Princeton University Press.

Yakar, J. (1991) *Prehistoric Anatolia: The Neolithic Transformation and the Early Chalcolithic Period*, Tel Aviv: Institute of Archaeology, University of Tel Aviv.

Yegül, F. (1992) *Baths and Bathing in Classical Antiquity*, New York: The Architectural History Foundation; and Cambridge, MA, and London: MIT Press.

Yon, M. (1992) "Ugarit: The Urban Habitat – The Present State of the Archaeological Picture," *BASOR* 286: 19–34.

—— (1997) *La cité d'Ougarit sur le tell de Ras Shamra*, Paris: Éditions Recherche sur les Civilisations.

Zanker, P. (1998) *Pompeii: Public and Private Life*, trans. D. L. Schneider, Cambridge, MA: Harvard University Press.

Zenner, W. P. (1996) "Cities," in Levinson and Ember 1996, vol. 1: 202–6.

Illustration sources

All maps, plans, and line drawings have been drawn by Neslihan Yılmaz, unless otherwise noted.

Chapter 1

1.2　after Bar-Yosef and Meadow 1995: 74, fig. 3.5.
1.3　Photograph by Peter Dorrell, University College London; courtesy of Stuart Laidlaw, Institute of Archaeology, UCL. Reproduced with permission.
1.6　after A. Özdoğan 1995: pl. 2.
1.7　after Mellaart 1967: 62, fig. 12.
1.8　after Mellaart 1967: 128, figs. 41–2.
1.9　after Mellaart 1967: pl. 59.

Chapter 2

2.2　after Roaf 1990: 60.
2.3　after Frankfort 1996: 21, fig. 4.
2.4　after Nissen 1988: 101, fig. 40.
2.5　after Roaf 1990: 63.
2.7　Neslihan Yılmaz and Margaret Reid.
2.9　after National Geographic Society 1981: 40.
22.10　after Nissen 1988: 120–1, fig. 50.
2.11a and b)　after drawing by Elizabeth Simpson, in I. Winter 1985: 13, fig 3 (obverse); and 16, fig. 18 (reverse); with permission from Irene Winter.
2.12　after the reconstruction by Hamilton D. Darby (as in Frankfort 1996: 43, fig. 36).
2.14　Photo: Courtesy of The Oriental Institute of The University of Chicago. Reproduced with permission.
2.15　after Hawkes 1974: 173.
2.16　Photo: Courtesy of The University Museum, University of Pennsylvania. Reproduced with permission.
2.19　after Lloyd 1984: 168, fig. 115.

Chapter 3

3.2　Margaret Reid and Neslihan Yılmaz.
3.4　after Hawkes 1974: 173; and Roaf 1990: 101.
3.5　after A. Eggebrecht, W. Konrad, and E. Pusch, eds (1978) *Sumer, Assur, Babylon: 7000 Jahre Kunst und Kultur zwischen Euphrat und Tigris* (Hildesheim: Roemer- und Pelizaeus-Museum): 16, fig. 9.
3.6　after Canby 2001: pl. 10.

3.7   after Frankfort 1996: 109, fig. 117.
3.8   after a drawing by A. S. Whitburn: in, for example, C. L. Woolley, *The Sumerians* (New York: W. W. Norton, 1965), 157, fig. 27.
3.10   after M.-H. Gates 1984: 73.
3.11   after M.-H. Gates 1984: 76–7; and Lloyd 1984: 166, fig. 113.
3.13   after M.-H. Gates 1984: 83.

Chapter 4

4.2   after Wheeler 1968: 39, fig. 7.
4.3   Photo: Copyright J. M. Kenoyer. Reproduced with permission.
4.4   after Chakrabarti 1997: pl. 8, and comments from G. Possehl (personal communication).

Chapter 5

5.3   after Spencer 1993: 82, fig. 61.
5.4   after C. Hobson, *Exploring the World of the Pharaohs* (London: Thames and Hudson, 1987): 59.
5.5   after Lehner 1997: 76.
5.6   after Spencer 1993: 76; and Lehner 1997: 75.
5.7   after Lehner 1997: 77.
5.8   after C. Aldred *et al.*, *Le temps des Pyramides* (Paris: Gallimard, 1978): 305, fig. 362.
5.9   after C. Aldred *et al.*, *Le temps des Pyramides* (Paris: Gallimard, 1978): 305, fig. 361.
5.11   Photo: Charles Gates.
5.12   after Lehner 1997: 64–5.
5.13   after C. Aldred *et al.*, *Le temps des Pyramides* (Paris: Gallimard, 1978): 309, figs 376 and 383–4.
5.15   Photo: Courtesy, Museum of Fine Arts, Boston. Reproduced with permission. ©2002 Museum of Fine Arts, Boston. All Rights Reserved.
5.16   after C. Aldred *et al.*, *Le temps des Pyramides* (Paris: Gallimard, 1978): 316, fig. 417.

Chapter 6

6.1   after Kemp 1989: 150, fig. 53.
6.2   after W. B. Emery, H. S. Smith, and A. Millard, *The Fortress of Buhen* (London: Egypt Exploration Society, 1979): pl. 3.
6.4   after J. Ruffle, *The Egyptians* (Ithaca, NY: Cornell University Press, 1977): 65.
6.5   after C. Aldred *et al.*, *L'Empire des Conquérants* (Paris: Gallimard, 1979): 310, fig. 393.
6.6   Photo: Charles Gates.
6.7   after C. Aldred *et al.*, *L'Empire des Conquérants* (Paris: Gallimard, 1979): 308, fig. 390.
6.8   after C. Aldred *et al.*, *L'Empire des Conquérants* (Paris: Gallimard, 1979): 301, fig. 377; and C. Hobson, *Exploring the World of the Pharaohs* (London: Thames and Hudson, 1987): 137.
6.9   Photo: Charles Gates.
6.11   after C. Hobson, *Exploring the World of the Pharaohs* (London: Thames and Hudson, 1987): 107.
6.12   after C. Hobson, *Exploring the World of the Pharaohs* (London: Thames and Hudson, 1987): 108.
6.13   after Fairman 1949: 38, fig 3.
6.14   after W. S. Smith 1998: 182, fig. 304.
6.15   after Reeves and Wilkinson 1996: 99, 122, and 164.
6.17   Photo: Charles Gates.

Chapter 7

7.2　after G. Cadogan, *Palaces of Minoan Crete* (London and New York: Methuen, 1976): 56–57, fig. 6.

7.6　Drawing by Juliana Bianco, from Graham, J. W., *The Palaces of Crete*, fig. 58. Copyright © 1987 by Princeton University Press. Reprinted by permission of Princeton University Press.

7.7　after Graham 1987: fig. 8.

7.10　Photo: Marie-Henriette Gates.

7.12　after S. Iakovidis, *Mycenae-Epidaurus* (Athens: Ekdotike Athenon, 1979): 48.

7.14　Margaret Reid and Neslihan Yılmaz

7.15　Photo: Charles Gates.

7.16　Photo: Alison Frantz Collection, American School of Classical Studies at Athens.

7.17　after D. Preziosi and L. Hitchcock, *Aegean Art and Architecture* (Oxford: Oxford University Press, 1999): 157, fig. 97.

Chapter 8

8.2　after M. Korfmann *et al.*, *A Guide to Troia* (Istanbul: Ege Yayınları, 1997): 28 and 75, fold-out plan.

8.3　after Seeher 1999: final fold-out plan.

8.4　Photo: Charles Gates.

8.5　after Seeher 1999: 121, fig. 125.

Chapter 9

9.1　after Karageorghis 1982: 104; and Sandars 1985: 42 and 101.

9.3　after Courtois and J. and E. Lagarce 1986: 3; and V. Karageorghis, *Les anciens Chypriotes: Entre Orient et Occident* (Paris: Armand Colin, 1991): 90.

9.4　after C. F. A. Schaeffer, *Enkomi-Alasia: Nouvelles Missions en Chypre 1946–1950* (Paris: Klincksieck, 1952): 244, fig. 90.

9.5　after A. Curtis 1985: 50, fig. 3; Yon 1992: 22, fig. 2; and Yon 1997: 6, fig. 1.

9.6　after Saadé 1979: 10, fig. 11; and Yon 1997: 47, fig. 20.

9.7　after Yon 1992: 28, fig. 6a; and Yon 1997: 89, fig. 44.

9.8　after Saadé 1979: 133, fig. 38; and A. Curtis 1985: 87, fig. 5.

Chapter 10

10.2　after Strommenger 1964: 438, fig. 50.

10.5　after Strommenger 1964: 445, fig. 52.

10.6　after Strommenger 1964: 446, figs. 53 and 55.

10.7　after Stone 1995: 246.

10.11　after Lloyd 1984: 224, fig. 167.

10.12　after Oates 1979: 148, fig. 100; and D. J. Wiseman, *Nebuchadrezzar and Babylon* (Oxford: The British Academy and Oxford University Press, 1985): 46, fig. 3.

10.13　after Kuhrt 1987: 34, fig. 3.

10.15　after Frankfort 1996: 352, fig. 414.

10.16　Photo: Courtesy of The Oriental Institute of the University of Chicago. Reproduced with permission.

10.17　Photo: Courtesy of The Oriental Institute of The University of Chicago. Reproduced with permission.

Chapter 11

11.2   after a watercolor by Andrew Fletcher.
11.3   after Finley 1977: 145.
11.5   after Popham, Calligas, and Sackett 1993: pl. 5.
11.6   Photo: Alison Frantz Collection, American School of Classical Studies at Athens.
11.8   after Kyrieleis 1981: 80, fig. 56 top.
11.9   after Kyrieleis 1981: 80, fig. 56 bottom; and fold-out plan at the end.
11.10 Photo: Courtesy, Museum of Fine Arts, Boston. Reproduced with permission. ©2002 Museum of Fine Arts, Boston. All Rights Reserved.

Chapter 12

12.3   after Coulton 1977: 42, fig. 10a.
12.4   after Coulton 1977: 42, fig. 10b.
12.5   after Lawrence 1996: 93, fig. 130.
12.6   after Tölle 1969: fold-out plan after p. 40.

Chapter 13

13.1   after Finley 1977: 148.
13.2   after Camp 1986: 37, fig. 21; and Finley 1977: 150.
13.3   Photo: Alison Frantz Collection, American School of Classical Studies at Athens.
13.7   Photo: Alison Frantz Collection, American School of Classical Studies at Athens.

Chapter 14

14.1   after P. Amandry, *Delphi and its History* (Athens: "Greece – an Archaeological Guide" Editions, 1984): 34–5.
14.4   after P. Amandry, *Delphi and its History* (Athens: "Greece – an Archaeological Guide" Editions, 1984): 8–9.
14.6   after B. Ashmole, *Architect and Sculptor in Classical Greece* (New York: New York University Press, 1972): 5.
14.9   after E. Melas, ed., *Temples and Sanctuaries of Ancient Greece*, London: Thames and Hudson, 1970, p. 114 (itself after an 1894 reconstruction by F. Adler).
14.10 Photo: Alison Frantz Collection, American School of Classical Studies at Athens.

Chapter 15

15.1   after Finley 1977: 147.
15.2   after Lawrence 1996: 108, fig. 159.
15.3   after A. Powell, *Ancient Greece: Cultural Atlas for Young People* (New York and Oxford: Facts on File, 1989): 76–7.
15.4   Photo: Charles Gates.
15.7   after Bowie and Thimme 1971: 40–1 and 90.
15.9   Photo: Alison Frantz Collection, American School of Classical Studies at Athens.
15.10 Photo: Charles Gates.
15.11 Photo: Charles Gates.
15.12 Two drawings from R. E. Wycherley, *The Stones of Athens*, p. 242, fig. 68: 3 and 5. Copyright © 1978 by Princeton University Press. Reprinted by permission of Princeton University Press.
15.13 after Camp 1986: 89, fig. 66.

Chapter 16

16.2   after Tomlinson 1983: 42, fig. 5.
16.4   Photo: Charles Gates.
16.5   after Finley 1977: 208.
16.6   Photo: Charles Gates.
16.7   after Wycherley 1967: 131, fig. 37.
16.8   after Rumscheid 1998: 163, fig. 147.
16.9   after Rumscheid 1998: 146, figs 128 and 129.
16.10 after Rumscheid 1998: 147, fig. 130.
16.11 after R. A. Tomlinson, *Greek and Roman Architecture* (London: The Trustees of the British Museum, 1995): 38, fig. 20.
16.13 after Cohen 1997: 9–12 and 88.
16.15 after Jeppesen n.d., back cover.

Chapter 17

17.2   after Dinsmoor 1950: 230, fig. 83.
17.3   after Radt 1984: 74, fig. 38; and W. Radt, *Pergamon* (Cologne: DuMont, 1988): 78, fig. 8.
17.5   Photo: Charles Gates.
17.6   after Radt 1984: 39, fig. 3.
17.8   after Hölbl 2001: Map 3.
17.11 after Finley 1977: 170; and P. Zaphiropoulou, *Delos, Monuments and Museum* (Athens: Krene Editions, 1983): fold-out plan at the end.
17.12 after Bruneau and Ducat 1983: 162, fig. 37.
17.13 after Bruneau and Ducat 1983: 162, fig. 38.
17.14 after Bruneau and Ducat 1983: 169, fig. 42.

Chapter 18

18.2   after Pedley 1990: 13, fig. 3; and 31, fig. 8; and Finley 1977: 130.
18.3   after Pedley 1990: 42, fig. 18; 56, fig. 27; and 82, fig. 49.
18.4   Photo: Charles Gates.
18.5   after Pedley 1990: 90, fig. 54.
18.6   after Finley 1977: 82; and Wescoat 1989: 11, figs 2a–b.
18.9   after Boethius 1978: 72, fig. 62; and R. Bianchi Bandinelli, *Les Etrusques et l'Italie avant Rome* (Paris: Gallimard, 1973): 364, fig. 418.
18.10 after Bonfante 1986: 192, fig V-32, nos 6 and 10.
18.11 after a model reconstruction based on descriptions by Vitruvius, in the University of Rome, Istituto di Etruscologia ed Antichità Italiche (illustrated, for example, in M. Stokstad, *Art History*, 2nd edn (Upper Saddle River, NJ, and New York: Prentice Hall and Harry N. Abrams, 2002): 226, figs 6–3.

Chapter 19

19.1   after Finley 1977: 105–6; Paoli 1963: 17, and fold-out plan at the back; and Scarre 1995: 21.
19.2   after Boethius 1978: 46, fig. 34.
19.3   after Scarre 1995: 63.
19.4   after Brown 1980: fold-out plan at back.

19.5 Drawing of Brown 1980: fig. 68. [F. E. Brown, *Cosa: The Making of a Roman Town*. Ann Arbor: University of Michigan Press. Copyright © by the University of Michigan 1980. Reprinted with permission of the University of Michigan Press.]

19.6 Drawing of Brown 1980, fig. 73. [F. E. Brown, *Cosa: The Making of a Roman Town*. Ann Arbor: University of Michigan Press. Copyright © by the University of Michigan 1980. Reprinted with permission of the University of Michigan Press.]

19.7 after Sear 1989: 74, fig. 40.

19.8 after Hanfmann 1975: 130–1, fig. 2; and Finley 1977: 108.

19.9 Photo: A. F. Kersting. Reproduced with permission.

19.10 Photo: The Conway Library, Courtauld Institute of Art. Reproduced with permission.

Chapter 20

20.2 after Finley 1977: 108.

20.3 after Ward-Perkins 1981: 31, fig. 8.

20.4 Photo: Fototeca Unione at the American Academy, Rome. Reproduced with permission.

Chapter 21

21.1 after Grant 1971: 25, fig. 2.

21.2 after Finley 1977: 127.

21.3 after E. La Rocca, M. and A. de Vos, and F. Coarelli, *Guida archeologica di Pompeii* (Milan: Arnoldo Mondadori, 1976): 105.

21.4 after Sear 1989: 40, fig. 19; and Paoli 1963: 222, fig. 30.

21.5 after Paoli 1963: 55, fig. 12.

21.6 after E. La Rocca, M. and A. de Vos, and F. Coarelli, *Guida archeologica di Pompeii* (Milan: Arnoldo Mondadori, 1976): 269.

21.7 after Grant 1971: 124.

21.10 after Finley 1977: 113.

Chapter 22

22.1 after Cornell and Matthews 1982: 107; and Scarre 1995: 63.

22.2 after Cornell and Matthews 1982: 90 and 206.

22.3 after Sear 1989: 98, fig. 53.

22.4 after a model in the Museo della Civiltà Romana; photo in MacDonald 1982: pl. 32.

22.6 after Sear 1982: 150, fig. 87.

22.7 after Sear 1982: 173, fig. 100; 175, fig. 102; 177, fig. 103; and 180, fig. 106.

22.8 Photo: Charles Gates.

22.9 Photo: Fototeca Unione, at the American Academy, Rome. Reproduced with permission.

22.10 after Sear 1982: 167, fig. 96.

22.11 after MacDonald 1982: pl. 105.

22.12 Photo: The Conway Library, Courtauld Institute of Art. Reproduced with permission.

22.15 after an engraving by Enea Vico (1523–67), reproduced in R. Bianchi Bandinelli, *Rome: The Center of Power, 500 B.C. to A.D. 200*. Transl. by P. Green (New York: George Braziller, 1970): 239, fig. 264. The engraving showed the spiral incorrectly, the inscription correctly; the drawing here has been reversed, to show at least the spiral in the correct direction.

22.18 after Ward-Perkins 1981: 69, fig. 31.

22.19 after MacDonald 1982: pl. 75.

20.20 after MacDonald 1982: pl. 73; and Sear 1982: 156, fig. 90.

22.21 Photo: Fototeca Unione, at the American Academy, Rome. Reproduced with permission.

Chapter 23

23.1   Photo: Charles Gates.
23.2   after Finley 1977: 212.
23.3   after Scherrer 2000: fold-out plan at back; and Finley 1977: 212.
23.5   after Finley 1977: 215; and M. E. Özgür, *Perge*, 2nd edn (Istanbul: NET Turistik Yayınlar, 1989): 4.
23.6   Photo: © 1998 John Kunstadter, Jr. Reproduced with permission.
23.7   Photo: © 1998 John Kunstadter, Jr. Reproduced with permission.
23.8   after Finley 1977: 235; and Browning 1979: 46–7 and 82–3.
23.9   after Ward-Perkins 1981: 357, fig. 232b; and Browning 1979: 100, fig. 41.
23.10   Photo: Charles Gates.
23.11   after Finley 1977: 224; and Browning 1982: 83, Map 3.
23.12   Photo: A. J. Kersting. Reproduced with permission.
23.13   after Finley 1977: 76.

Chapter 24

24.1   after Wilson 1983: 12, fig. 1.
24.3   after Finley 1977: 137.
24.4   after the reconstruction of Ernest Hébrard, often reproduced (e.g. M. Wheeler, *Roman Art and Architecture*, Oxford and New York: Oxford University Press, 1964: 145, fig. 127).
24.6   after after M. Stokstad, *Art History*, 2nd edn (Upper Saddle River, NJ, and New York: Prentice Hall and Harry N. Abrams, 2002): 284.
24.10   after Krautheimer 1986: 55, fig. 22.
24.11   after M. Stokstad, *Art History*, 2nd edn (Upper Saddle River, NJ, and New York: Prentice Hall and Harry N. Abrams, 2002): 297.
24.13   after R. Ousterhout, "The Church of the Holy Sepulchre (in Bologna, Italy)," *Biblical Archaeology Review* 26:6 (2000): 24.
24.14   after C. Mango, "Constantinople," in A. Kazhdan *et al.*, eds, *Oxford Dictionary of Byzantium* (Oxford: Oxford University Press, 1991): 509.

Index